1500 E. MEDICAL CENTER DRIVE
ROOM 2G332, BOX 0054
ANN ARBOR, MICHIGAN 48109-0054

LABORATORY QUALITY ASSURANCE

LABORATORY QUALITY ASSURANCE

Peter J. Howanitz, M.D.

Associate Director, Clinical Laboratories and
Associate Professor of Pathology
University of California, Los Angeles
Center for Health Sciences
Los Angeles, California

Joan H. Howanitz, M.D.

Chief, Clinical Pathology
West Los Angeles VA Medical Center
Los Angeles, California

McGRAW-HILL BOOK COMPANY

New York St. Louis San Francisco Auckland Bogotá Hamburg Johannesburg Lisbon
London Madrid Mexico Milan Montreal New Delhi Panama Paris San Juan
São Paulo Singapore Sydney Tokyo Toronto

Notice

Medicine is an ever-changing science. As new research and clinical experience broaden our knowledge, changes in treatment and drug therapy are required. The editors and the publisher of this work have checked with sources believed to be reliable in their efforts to provide drug dosage schedules that are complete and in accord with the standards accepted at the time of publication. However, readers are advised to check the product information sheet included in the package of each drug they plan to administer to be certain that the information contained in these schedules is accurate and that changes have not been made in the recommended dose or in the contraindications for administration. This recommendation is of particular importance in connection with new or infrequently used drugs.

DEDICATED TO OUR DAUGHTER JOAN,
FOR HER PATIENCE WITH ALL OUR
PREOCCUPATIONS

LABORATORY QUALITY ASSURANCE

Copyright © 1987 by McGraw-Hill, Inc. All rights reserved. Printed in the United States of America. Except as permitted under the United States Copyright Act of 1976, no part of this publication may be reproduced or distributed in any form or by any means, or stored in a data base or retrieval system, without the prior written permission of the publisher.

1234567890HALHAL89876

ISBN 0-07-029672-3

This book was set in Times Roman by Compset, Inc. The editor was Beth Kaufman Barry; the production supervisor was Avé McCracken; the cover was designed by Edward R. Schultheis. Project supervision was done by Editing, Design & Production, Inc. Halliday Lithograph Corporation was printer and binder.

Library of Congress Catalog in Publication Data

Laboratory quality assurance.

Includes bibliographies and index.
1. Diagnosis, Laboratory—Quality control.
I. Howanitz, Peter J.   II. Howanitz, Joan H.
[DNLM: 1. Chemistry, Clinical—trends. 2. Diagnosis, Laboratory—standards. 3. Laboratories—standards.
4. Quality Assurance, Health Care. 5. Quality Control.
QY 23 L1226]
RB37.L2754   1987   616.07′5   86-10363
ISBN 0-07-029672-3

CONTENTS

	CONTRIBUTORS	vii
	PREFACE	ix
1	Introduction to Quality Assurance—Joan H. Howanitz, M.D., and Peter J. Howanitz, M.D.	1
2	The Statistics of Quality Control—Irwin M. Weisbrot, M.D.	20
3	General Principles of Patient Preparation and Specimen Handling—Edward P. Fody, M.D.	55
4	General Aspects of Laboratory Quality Assurance—Steven J. Steindel, Ph.D.	80
5	Manufacture of Quality Control Materials—Richard S. Thuma, Joseph L. Giegel, Ph.D., and Alan H. Posner, Ph.D.	101
6	Performance Characteristics and Analytic Goals—John W. Ross, M.D., and Noel S. Lawson, M.D.	124
7	Components of Biologic and Analytic Variation—Per Winkel, M.D., Doc. Med. Sci., and Adam Uldall, Ph.D.	166
8	Assessment of Analytic Variability in Clinical Chemistry—John A. Lott, Ph.D., and Suman T. Patel, Ph.D.	185
9	Quality Assurance in Hematology—Paul Bachner, M.D.	214
10	Quality Assurance in Microbiology—Ron B. Schifman, M.D.	244
11	Quality Control in the Blood Center and Transfusion Service: Current Practices—Herbert F. Polesky, M.D.	270
12	Qualitative and Semiquantitative Tests: Clinical Microscopy, Physician's Office, Bedside, and Self-Performed—Carl E. Speicher, M.D., and Thomas D. Stevenson, M.D.	287
13	Quality Assurance in Anatomic Pathology—Donald W. Penner, M.D.	296
14	Proficiency Testing—John H. Rippey, M.D.	317
15	Laboratory Licensure and Accreditation—John K. Duckworth, M.D.	334

16	Quality Assurance and Laboratory Information Flow—David Chou, M.D., Donald P. Connelly, M.D., Ph.D., and James S. Fine, M.D.	354
17	Future Trends in Laboratory Quality Assurance—Peter J. Howanitz, M.D. and Joan H. Howanitz, M.D.	371

INDEX 391

LIST OF CONTRIBUTORS

PAUL BACHNER, M.D.
Chairman, Department of Pathology
United Hospital
Port Chester, New York

DAVID CHOU, M.D.
Staff, Department of Biochemistry
Director, Laboratory Computer Systems
 and Primary Laboratory Center
The Cleveland Clinic Foundation
Cleveland, Ohio

DONALD P. CONNELLY, M.D., Ph.D.
Associate Professor, Department of
 Laboratory Medicine and Pathology
and
Director, Laboratory Data Division
University of Minnesota
Minneapolis, Minnesota

JOHN K. DUCKWORTH, M.D.
Chairman, Department of Pathology
Methodist Hospitals of Memphis
Memphis, Tennessee

JAMES S. FINE, M.D.
Assistant Professor
and
Head, Information and Specimen
 Processing
Department of Laboratory Medicine
University of Washington
Seattle, Washington

EDWARD P. FODY, M.D.
Chief, Laboratory Service
John L. McClellan Memorial Veterans
 Hospital
and
Associate Professor of Pathology
 Pharmacology
University of Arkansas for Medical
 Sciences
Little Rock, Arkansas

JOSEPH GIEGEL, Ph.D.
Formerly with American Dade
Miami, Florida

NOEL S. LAWSON, M.D.
Associate Pathologist
St. John Hospital
and
Clinical Associate Professor, Department
 of Pathology
Wayne State University School of
 Medicine
Detroit, Michigan

JOHN A. LOTT, Ph.D.
Professor, Department of Pathology
Ohio State University
Columbus, Ohio

SUMAN T. PATEL, Ph.D.
Chemicals Division
Eastman Kodak
Rochester, New York

DONALD W. PENNER, M.D.
Pathologist, Health Sciences Centre
and
Professor of Pathology, Faculty of
  Medicine
University of Manitoba
Winnipeg, Manitoba, Canada

HERBERT F. POLESKY, M.D.
Director, Memorial Blood Center of
  Minneapolis
and
Professor, Department of Laboratory
  Medicine and Pathology
University of Minnesota
Minneapolis, Minnesota

ALAN POSNER, Ph.D.
American Dade
Miami, Florida

JOHN H. RIPPEY, M.D.
Pathology Department
St. Luke's Hospital Laboratory
Kansas City, Missouri

JOHN W. ROSS, M.D.
Director, Laboratories
Kennestone Hospital
Marietta, Georgia

RON B. SCHIFMAN, M.D.
Assistant Professor of Pathology
University of Arizona College of Medicine
and
Tucson Veterans Administration Medical
  Center
Tucson, Arizona

CARL E. SPEICHER, M.D.
Professor and Director, Clinical
  Laboratories
The Ohio State University
University Hospitals
Columbus, Ohio

STEVEN J. STEINDEL, Ph.D.
President, Prism Associates
Atlanta, Georgia

THOMAS STEVENSON, M.D.
Professor of Pathology, College of
  Medicine
Ohio State University
Columbus, Ohio

RICHARD S. THUMA
Director, Research Operations
American Dade
Miami, Florida

ADAM ULDALL, Ph.D.
Department of Clinical Chemistry
Herlev Hospital
Herlev, Denmark

IRWIN M. WEISBROT, M.D.
Pathology Department
Norwalk Hospital
Norwalk, Connecticut

PER WINKEL, M.D.
Department of Clinical Chemistry
University Hospital
Copenhagen, Denmark

PREFACE

Laboratory quality assurance practices are changing in response to new technologies, cost pressures, and the increased awareness of their ultimate affect on patient care. The goal of this book is to summarize current practices, to identify where further changes are likely to occur, and to indicate where changes are needed. The first seven chapters review the basic aspects of quality assurance applicable to the entire clinical laboratory in general. Chapter 1 is an overview of quality assurance. This is followed by fundamental chapters on statistics, patient preparation, general factors which influence laboratory quality, control materials, analytic goals, and biologic and analytic variation. Chapters 8 through 12 cover specific subspecialty areas of the clinical laboratory: chemistry, hematology, microbiology transfusion services, and clinical microscopy. Chapter 12 also addresses some of the problems related to quality control of physician's office, bedside, and self-performed testing, while Chapter 13 addresses quality assurance in anatomical pathology. Chapters 14 and 15 review proficiency testing and laboratory accreditation. The book concludes with a chapter on quality assurance of laboratory information systems (Chapter 16) and speculates on future trends in laboratory quality assurance (Chapter 17).

Rapid advances in laboratory quality assurance procedures have led to many changes in our daily practices. The influence of these advances extends to each section within the clinical laboratory and ultimately to virtually every patient who has laboratory work performed. With the help of our expert contributors, we are optimistic that this work will provide insight into past quality assurance experiences, current practices, and the form quality assurance may take in the future.

CHAPTER 1

INTRODUCTION TO QUALITY ASSURANCE

Joan H. Howanitz, M.D.
Peter J. Howanitz, M.D.

What is quality? Often quality is considered the goodness of an object or activity, with dictionary definitions such as degree of excellence coming to mind. Quality, however, has two aspects, an objective reality that is constant and measureable as well as a subjective aspect that is closely tied to utility or value. Because there is no universally accepted measure of value, quantitative physical measurements are the usual standards by which quality is judged. Quality, therefore, can be defined as conformance to requirements.[1]

In the clinical laboratory, unfortunately, quality assurance often is thought of as simply the inclusion of control samples that mimic patient specimens into each analytic run. However, quality assurance includes all actions necessary to provide adequate confidence that test results satisfy given requirements or standards. Laboratory quality assurance thus should be thought of in much broader terms, as a system to prevent and control errors that occur from the time a test is ordered until the time it is interpreted, or, as some might say, any error in the "brain-to-brain" transmission (Fig. 1-1). The term *quality assurance* is used for the total system designed to ensure the quality of results, whereas the term *quality control* is more restrictive, referring only to those procedures that must be completed before a particular batch of results is reported.[2] Surveillance of laboratory procedures should be systematic, periodic, and documented, but quality assurance is an expensive, time-consuming task that must be balanced with prompt, efficient service. Laboratory quality control procedures generate 30 percent or more of a laboratory's costs.

Laboratory quality control has its roots in industry, even though this origin has been likened to claiming that "modern head and neck surgery had its beginnings in the Tower of London."[3] In manufacturing, product requirements are precisely defined,

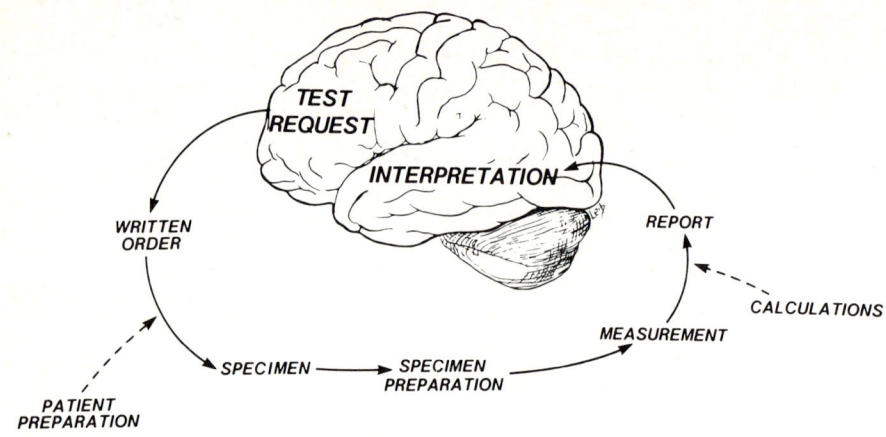

FIGURE 1-1
Outline of steps from time test is requested until the result is interpreted.

and concepts such as "zero defects" in making a quality product are inherently clear to employees. Because the laboratory's "product" is a result that varies with the individual patient, performance standards cannot be easily defined even for patient populations. Instead, quality control samples that simulate patient specimens are used to set performance standards. To reflect performance adequately, however, controls must mimic clinical specimens in chemical and physical composition and must be treated in the analysis like a clinical specimen. The control must not be identical to the standard or calibrator used in the assay, because the control is intended to provide an independent check on the assay's reliability. Use of controls forms the basis of a laboratory's internal quality control program. Laboratory quality assurance also includes external quality control (survey) programs to ensure accuracy of results as well as accreditation programs aimed at defining standards for personnel, methods, equipment, maintenance, and report generation.

INTERNAL QUALITY CONTROL

Background

Internal quality control consists of those procedures used by the laboratory staff for the continual assessment of laboratory work in order to decide if the results are reliable. The main objectives are to ensure day-to-day consistency of measurements and to quantify random variation.

In the clinical laboratory of 50 years ago, determinations were performed manually, with most measurements taking several hours. Two milliliters of serum was considered a "micro" sample, and in the average laboratory no more than 12 analytes could be

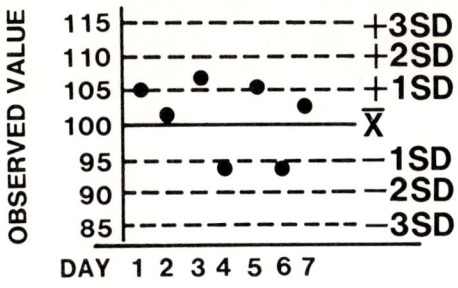

FIGURE 1-2
Levey-Jennings (Shewhart chart). Control values are plotted by day.

determined. During this time, quality control procedures were rudimentary or nonexistent, although controls were used for serologic procedures, which at that time consisted mainly of complement fixation methods for syphilis.[4] By the 1950s, Levey and Jennings[5] had determined acceptable day-to-day performance limits with daily duplicate values obtained using frozen plasma pools.

For interpretation, these workers plotted results on quality control charts, thereby introducing the clinical laboratory to what are known today as Levey-Jennings charts (Fig. 1-2). These also are known as Shewhart charts, after the control procedure described in 1931 by Shewhart for manufactured products.[6] Shortly after the introduction of control charts by Levey and Jennings, Henry and Segalove[7] choose ± 3 standard deviations (SD) from the mean ($\bar{x}$) as the action limits, that is, the limits beyond which an analytic run is rejected. These workers realized there are "two dangers when using control charts: (1) looking for trouble that does not exist, and (2) not looking for trouble when it does exist." They therefore recommended 3 SD limits if the precision is adequate, but 2 SD if these limits are too broad compared with the required precision. Subsequently, use of frozen, pooled quality control materials and plotting of results on Levey-Jennings charts spread rapidly, but in most laboratories action limits of $\bar{x} \pm 2$ SD were adopted.

As the number of determinations performed increased, especially with the introduction of automated chemistry equipment in the 1960s, the demand for control material increased. Eventually, commercially available pools became available and, at least until recently, the pools used for clinical chemistry in the United States usually have been in the form of lyophilized material based on a matrix of human serum. The problems associated with both nonhuman- (bovine, equine) and human-based materials have been reviewed by Fraser and Peake.[8] Because of the stability and large size of pools, laboratories can use batches of material for a year or more. Improvements in quality control materials include freedom from hepatitis by third-generation testing and availability of analytes at several levels. Data reduction and comparisons with other laboratories using aliquots of the same pool often now are provided by the control manufacturer. When comparison data are reported for groups using the same types of instruments and reagents, they become a valuable tool in troubleshooting assay problems. Although these comparisons are a type of external quality control (see below), they also have been referred to as expanded internal quality control.

Control Materials

Problems with lyophilized material include instability of some analytes and biases compared with patient specimens. Over the past few years nonhuman, often bovine-based, material has been introduced into the United States market, and recently liquid quality control material with increased stability for a number of analytes has become available. Differences between methods are observed with use of both lyophilized and liquid control material. The magnitude of these biases depends on the analyte, the level of the analyte, and the method.[9] The biases seen with control material do not necessarily reflect differences in patient results (see Chapter 6). Biases presumably are due to matrix effects and can be positive or negative, negligible or large. For certain analytes, biases may be caused by factors other than matrix effects; for example, extracts of animal tissues are often used to obtain elevated enzyme levels, and thus the isoenzymes present may have different properties from those of human origin. Commercial quality control materials are now readily available for most commonly measured chemistry analytes, many serological tests, and a number of routine hematology procedures. Stability of the hematology control materials remains a problem (see Chapter 9). For a discussion of manufacture of control materials, see Chapter 5.

Control Use

Precision is the closeness with which replicate analyses can be made, whereas accuracy is the closeness to true value (Fig. 1-3). Internal quality control systems are used to quantify and minimize imprecision. When comparison data are available, internal quality control programs provide information on accuracy, although traditionally external quality control programs are used for this purpose.

Variability in assay results or imprecision is quantitated using the control sample results. Statistical evaluation of results also comes from industry, where William S. Gossett, alias "Student," working at the Guinness brewery, developed methods to accommodate small sample sizes.[10] The distribution of variation of control values is assumed to be Gaussian and is expressed as standard deviation (SD) or percent coefficient of variation (%CV) (see Chapter 2). Analytic imprecision sometimes is called *random error* or *random variation*. Because imprecision is predictable and unavoidable, random variation is a better term than random error. Random variation potentially can be made smaller but it cannot be eliminated, therefore it is not an error in the same sense as a mistake such as mislabeling a specimen. Data from internal quality control systems are used to determine necessity of systems correction and whether or not patient results should be reported.

Originally a set of standards and controls was analyzed with each assay or analytical run. As automation has been introduced, the analytical run and its length have been redefined. For quality control purposes, an analytical run is an interval within which the accuracy and precision of the measuring system is expected to be stable.[11] The length of the run is specific for a given analytical system and application and often is defined in terms of time such as an 8-hour shift. Control material, usually at more than one level, is used at least once during the "run." For each analyte measured, the

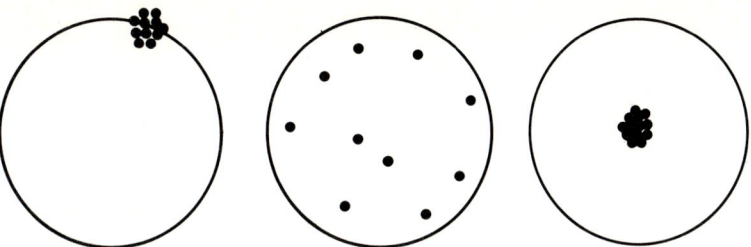

FIGURE 1-3
The true value is represented by the circle and estimates of the value by the dots. From left to right the diagrams represent precision but inaccuracy; accuracy but imprecision; accuracy and precision.

Health Care Financing Agency (HCFA) and the Centers for Disease Control (CDC) require inclusion of one standard at the upper limit of reportable range and one control in the "normal" range each 24 hours. The College of American Pathologists (CAP) and the Joint Commission on Accreditation of Hospitals have similar requirements.[12]

Ideally, controls are placed randomly in the analytical run, but this may lead to practical difficulties. In addition, because certain analytical systems are subject to imprecision such as system drift, it may be desirable to use controls at fixed intervals throughout the analytical run. Of course, insofar as possible, control material should have a stable analyte level and mimic unknowns to prevent problems arising from differences in matrix. Two concentrations of analyte are recommended, and three control levels are appropriate for a number of analytes. The use of controls at various analyte levels allows for improved interpretation of analytical errors that occur. The analyte levels should be in clinically important ranges.

For most routine analysis, unassayed controls, that is, controls that have not been assigned values for any given analyte, are used. A lot of control material large enough to last a year or more is purchased; after the first 20 to 30 days of use, the mean and SD of the analytes are determined in the laboratory in which the controls are used. Thus once a year or so the laboratory is burdened with running two set of controls, the "old" controls with established mean and SD values as well as the "new" controls. For low-volume determinations, especially those assays that are performed infrequently, the mean and standard deviation for controls are problematic to establish. Often assayed controls, that is, controls with values assigned by the manufacturer, are used for these purposes. Here, too, the National Committee for Clinical Laboratory Standards (NCCLS) recommends that the individual laboratory establish control limits; but in the case of assayed controls, provisional target values can be set up by obtaining the 20 results needed for calculations on fewer than 20 runs.[11]

Other approaches to quality control have been used, especially for unstable analytes; for example, patient data are used to calculate "average of normals." The uncertainty regarding stability of the patient population and the difficulty in calculation have discouraged use of this technique for all but a few specific uses.[13] For hematology (see Chapter 9), however, patient indices have several advantages over commercial

TABLE 1-1
CAP MODIFIED RULES

Run rejected when:
1 *One control in use:*
  a One observation $> \bar{x} \pm 3$ SD
  b Two consecutive observations $> \bar{x} \pm 2$ SD
  c Or whenever patient results appear unlikely
2 *Two controls in use:*
  a One observation $> \bar{x} \pm 3$ SD
  b Two observations $> \bar{x} \pm 2$ SD
     (same control, two consecutive runs, or both controls, same run)
  c Or whenever patient results appear unlikely

Source: Haven GT, Lawson NS, Ross JW: QAS notes. *Pathologist* 1980, 34:619.

whole blood controls, including economy and the ability to monitor analytical performance frequently.[14]

Evaluation of Control Results

Quality control rules are usually based on the mean of the individual control values collected over time, with the limits customarily based on multiples of the standard deviation. Quality control rules are designed to detect excess imprecision and shift or drift in the analysis that may reflect on the quality of patient data. The rules are used to determine whether or not patient data from an analytical run can be reported. However, warning signals may be ignored in some cases after taking into account such considerations as biological variation, medical usefulness of the determination (see below), and the type and magnitude of the rule violation. Quality control rules must detect both random variation and systematic error. Random variation or imprecision is dispersion of results around the expected value, whereas systematic error is a fixed bias that may be positive or negative, constant or proportional to concentration. Imprecision and systematic errors can be distinguished by using samples with known multiples of analyte concentrations and plotting operational lines (see Chapter 8).

Ideally, the quality control rules chosen provide a high rate of error detection with a low rate of false rejection. Most laboratories use rejection limits as the mean $\bar{x} \pm 2$ SD. Limits of $\bar{x} \pm 2$ SD are very sensitive to true error but lead to a high rate of false rejection especially when more than one control is used. This occurs because false rejection rates are additive: with one control the rate is 4.5 percent, with two 9 percent, etc. In practice, usually control values greater than $\bar{x} \pm 2$ limits SD are repeated which reduces the false rejection rate, but at the expense of sensitivity to true error.[15]

Because of the high incidence of false run rejections for procedures with more than one control, use of other rules has become popular. The so-called multirules, such as CAP modified rules (Table 1-1) and the Shewhart procedure, also called the Westgard multirule technique (Table 1-2), can be applied both within and between assay runs.

TABLE 1-2
SHEWHART RULES

Warning rule (if exceeded, then data require further inspection):

1_{2S} One observation $> \bar{x} \pm 2$ SD

Rejection rules (used if warning rule exceeded; run rejected if any of the rules are violated):

1_{3S} One observation $> \bar{x} \pm 3$ SD
2_{2S} Two observations $>$ same limit; that is, $\bar{x} + 2$ SD or $\bar{x} - 2$ SD (same control, two consecutive runs, or two different controls, same run)
R_{4S} Difference between two observations within run > 4 SD (two different controls, one $> \bar{x} + 2$ SD and the other $> \bar{x} - 2$ SD)
4_{1S} Four consecutive observations $>$ same limit; that is, $\bar{x} + 1$ SD or $\bar{x} - 1$ SD (same control, four consecutive runs, or two different controls, two consecutive runs)
10_x Ten consecutive observations on same side of mean (same control, ten consecutive runs, or two different controls, five consecutive runs)

Source: Westgard JO, Groth T, Burnett RW, et al: A multi-rule Shewhart chart for quality control in clinical chemistry. *Clin Chem* 1981, 27:493.

The Shewhart rules are abbreviated in the form A_L, where A is the number of observations and L is the control limit derived from Gaussian statistics. Rules for ranges are used in the form R_L, where R is the absolute difference between two control results in the same run and L is the limit.

Assuming no between-run variation, two controls per run yield a false rejection rate of 1 in 200 runs using the 1_{3S} rule alone and 1 in 1,000 runs using the 2_{2S} rule alone. These two rules used together produce a false rejection rate of 1 in 160 runs.[18] The multirule system appears to allow improved error detection with low probability of false rejection. With the multirule procedure, control values outside $\bar{x} \pm 2$ SD give a warning that requires further inspection of the control data to determine whether or not the run should be rejected (Fig. 1-4).

Rules should be selected that avoid high false positive rejection rates but that are responsive to increases in systematic as well as random error.[17] As the number of controls per run increases, the rules used should be modified as indicated in Table 1-3. Generally, random error is detected by using the 1_{3S} and R_{4S} rules, whereas systematic error is detected with 2_{2S}, 4_{1S}, or 10_x rules.[17]

The performance characteristics of the multirule procedures have been estimated from "power functions" that are computer-generated plots of the probability of rejection versus the size of the analytical errors that are to be detected. Because these models do not take into account the between-run component, the actual error level may be greater than predicted and the number of control observations too small.[19]

Cusum (cumulative summation) techniques have been advocated as a sensitive detector of systematic error. The procedure involves subtracting a constant value from the observed values and accumulating the differences (Table 1-4), which are plotted as a cusum graph (Fig. 1-5). Criteria for deciding when the error is too large to be

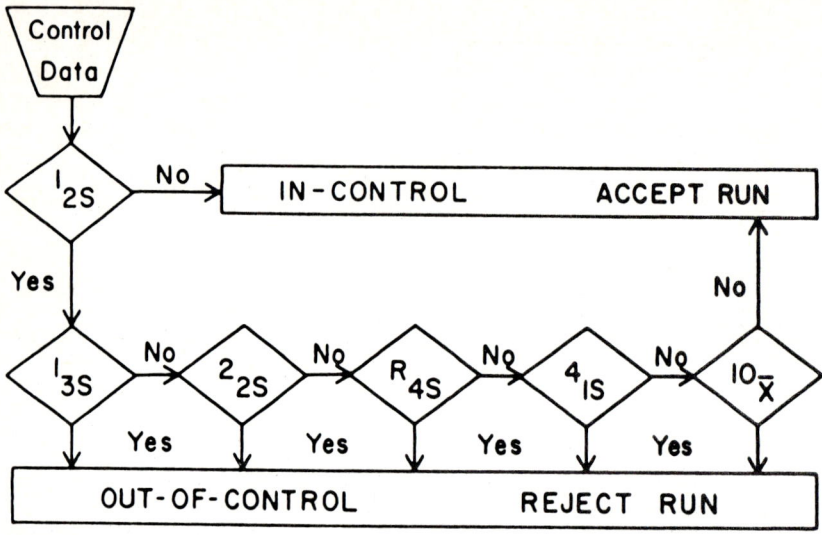

FIGURE 1-4
Quality control rule diagram. The 1_{2s} rule is used as a screen. (From Westgard, 1981 (17) with permission from Clinical Chemistry.)

acceptable are qualitative. With systematic error, cusum values increase steadily, with the larger the error, the steeper the slope. Care must be used in choosing the constant value: the closer the value is to the overall mean, the easier it is to detect slope changes.[20] Recently, Schoen et al.[21] have advocated use of a quality log in which cusum techniques are used along with clinically useful limits criteria (see below). Inconvenience in calculation and plotting results as well as difficulty of interpretation have adversely affected the popularity of the cusum technique.

A minority of laboratories currently use other types of criteria to determine run rejection on a routine basis. Criteria that have been used include those based on reference ranges, biologic variation, and "medical usefulness criteria."[22] Whatever the criteria used, once an assay run has been determined to be out of control, the patient results should not be reported, and solving of the identified problem should begin. Efforts should be made to resolve the underlying problem. For example, if a procedure is found to be out of calibration, the question "why" should be asked. Did someone fail to follow the correct procedure? Was the recommended calibration frequency correct? Was there adherence to calibrator expiration dates? These and the myriad of other questions that could be asked about even this one problem make it clear why standards for skills and knowledge of laboratory personnel are a critical factor in laboratory quality assurance.

EXTERNAL QUALITY CONTROL

External quality control or survey programs refer to a system of retrospectively comparing results from different laboratories by means of an external agency. The major

TABLE 1-3
CONTROL RULES DEPENDING ON NUMBER OF CONTROLS USED PER RUN

Number of observations	Within run	Consecutive runs
1	1_{2S}	4_{1S}
2	$1_{3S}, 2_{2S}, R_{4S}$	$4_{1S}, 10\bar{x}$
3	1_{3S}, (2 of 3)$_{2S}, R_{4S}$	$9\bar{x}$
4	$1_{3S}, 2_{2S}, R_{4S}, 4_{1S}$	$8\bar{x}$

Source: Modified from Westgard JO, Groth T, Burnett RW, et al: A multi-rule Shewhart chart for quality control in clinical chemistry. *Clin Chem* 1981, 27:493.

TABLE 1-4
CUSUM CALCULATION

Day	Observed (O)	(O − C)*	Cusum†
1	42	+2	+ 2
2	41	+1	+ 3
3	43	+3	+ 6
4	38	−2	+ 4
5	41	+1	+ 5
6	42	+2	+ 7
7	42	+2	+ 9
8	39	−1	+ 8
9	41	+1	+ 9
10	38	−2	+ 7
11	43	+3	+10
12	40	0	+11
13	42	+2	+12
14	39	−1	+11
15	43	+3	+14

*C = constant (= 40).
†Accumulated difference: $(O_1 - C), (O_1 - C) + (O_2 - C)$, etc.

purpose of these programs is to establish analytical goals and to assist in their achievement. Accuracy—that is, the extent to which a result conforms to the true value—is assessed by using these systems. Because it is frequently impossible to define the true value, accuracy comes to mean conformance to an assumed value, which is determined by the "state of the art" in measuring the true value. Marked method differences occur, making agreement between the estimate of a quantity and its true value difficult to determine. For example, in the Federal Republic of Germany, where accuracy controls with assigned values determined by reference laboratories are used, the assigned values for a creatinine control have been shown to vary from 1.2 to 1.8 mg/dl depending on

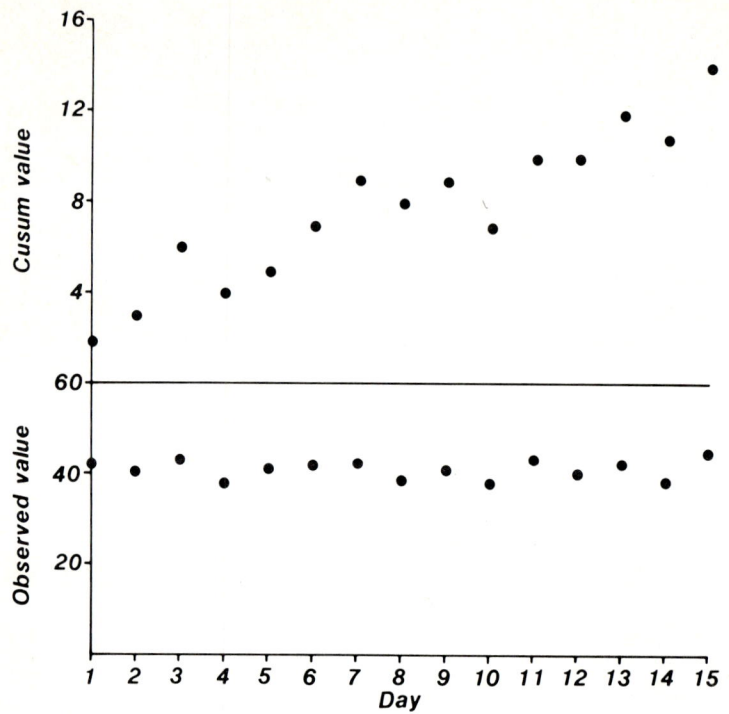

FIGURE 1-5
Data from Table 4 plotted on cusum (top) and Levey-Jennings (bottom) charts.

which modification of the Jaffe reaction is used.[27] Thus, attaining the "correct value," defined as the best estimate of a quantity of a material as measured with a particular analytical technique, becomes the goal. Often the "correct" value is assigned by the consensus of laboratories performing a measurement, and although legally it is equivalent to truth, the "correct" or consensus value may in fact be inaccurate (see below).

For practical purposes, we measure inaccuracy or bias between laboratories by assessing mean values obtained with control samples and comparing these to mean values obtained by other laboratories, usually through comparison data provided by survey control data from societies such as the American Association for Clinical Chemistry (AACC) or the College of American Pathologists (CAP). Comparisons also can be obtained by using daily quality control results, so-called expended internal quality control. A major advantage of using internal quality control results is the number of challenges per year, in contrast to the roughly four to six per analyte per year for most surveys. Surveys, however, at least at present, have a larger number of laboratories contributing to their data base as well as several other advantages that complement expanded internal programs (see Chapter 17). The main objective of survey programs is to establish between-laboratory comparisons and, where they exist, agreement to standards (see Chapter 4).

External quality assessment started when laboratorians sent fresh or frozen specimens to each other and compared results. A pilot survey of clinical laboratories in 1949[18] showed interlaboratory coefficients of variation of 16 percent for glucose, 28 percent for calcium, and 64 percent for urea nitrogen; by 1985, the percent CV for these three analytes was 3.3, 2.3, and 2.9, respectively.[28]

Currently surveys are carried out by sending essentially identical samples to participating laboratories, with the results then reported and compared. For a given analyte, often there is no agreed-upon standard material or method and, therefore, the "correct" or target result often is determined by consensus. Because survey results commonly are evaluated by a democratic rather than a scientific process, if the majority are using analytical methods that are subject to error or bias, the "correct" value may be inaccurate. That is, inaccuracy of survey results depends on the popularity of inaccurate methods. Because generally peer groups are used for comparison, there is a tendency to maintain the status quo and downgrade innovation.[23] (For further information on target values, see Chapters 6 and 14.)

Other biases may occur with survey results. To the extent that the quality control sample receives special handling, the value in estimating the precision and accuracy of patient results is potentially lost. Thus, ideally, in each participating laboratory the survey quality control samples are treated in exactly the same manner as a patient specimen. In spite of these limitations, target values determined from survey participant results have been shown to have excellent correlation with National Bureau of Standards (NBS) definitive results, at least for a number of chemistry analytes.[29]

Data from various surveys are presented as calculations or graphs to facilitate interpretation (see Chapter 14). Calculations commonly used include the Z score (Chapter 2) and the SDI (see below), and graphic representations used include frequency distribution and two-way (Youden) plots.[30] Generally, for CAP surveys, two data passes are made to eliminate outliers; then the mean and SD are calculated (for additional information, see Chapter 14). If a method is used by at least 20 laboratories, the results also are expressed as the standard deviation index (SDI) (Table 1-5).[31] For most CAP surveys, criteria used to define results as unacceptable are ± 2 SD from the mean for the peer group. A result determined by a precise method may be close to the mean but designated as unacceptable because of a small peer group CV.[32] In contrast, a result obtained with a less precise method may be relatively far from the mean but within 2-SDI limits because of a larger peer group CV. Thus, for very precise methods, fixed criteria (Table 1-6) for evaluation of results are more appropriate.[32]

RELIABILITY OF RESULTS

In defining the state of the art for any analytical method, we must not lose perspective. No quality control system, however sophisticated, can make up for the deficiencies of an unsound analytical method. Reliability or correctness of a laboratory result depends not only on precision and accuracy, but on method sensitivity and specificity as well as the appropriateness of the reference interval. Two references of importance regarding these points are the International Federation of Clinical Chemistry's recommen-

TABLE 1-5
STANDARD DEVIATION INDEX

$$\text{SDI} = \frac{\text{laboratory's value} - \text{mean for method}}{\text{standard deviation for method}}$$

Example: A laboratory's result and method for glucose are

    Result: 94 mg/dl

    Method: name = orthotoluidine
                  group mean = 92.4 mg/dl
                  standard deviation (SD) for method = 4.9
                  calculation:

$$\frac{94 - 92.4}{4.9} = 0.3 \text{ SDI}$$

Ratings: Values within 1 SDI = good, between 1 and 2 SDIs = acceptable, > 2 SDI = unacceptable.

Source: 1985 Manual CAP Surveys: Interlaboratory Comparison Program. Skokie, IL, College of American Pathologists, 1984.

TABLE 1-6
FIXED CRITERIA FOR CAP SURVEYS

Sodium	± 4 mmol/L
Potassium	± 0.5 mmol/L
pH	± 0.04
pCO_2	± 3 mmHg or ± 10%, whichever is greater
pO_2	± 6 mmHg or ± 10%, whichever is greater

Source: Chemistry Resource Committee: Fixed criteria in blood gas survey. College of American Pathologists. *Summing Up* 1984, 14:5.

dations for the assessment of analytical methods for routine use[33] and an editorial by Sunderman on reference values.[34] The laboratorian, in addition, plays a vital role in controlling preanalytical variation and interferences (see Chapters 3 and 4), participating in test selection, and controlling timeliness of reporting. To ensure optimal patient care, quality assurance procedures must provide for adequately trained personnel, specific and sensitive methods, proper instrument maintenance, as well as appropriate and stable standards.

Specificity is the ability of a method to measure the component that it is supposed to measure. To a large degree, specificity is controlled by the appropriate choice of analytical methods. For example, lack of specific analytical methods has led to disastrous effects as exemplified by the case of vitamin B_{12}. Introduction of nonspecific radioassays that inadvertently measured true cobalamin as well as cobalamin analogs led to misdiagnosis of as many as 20 percent of patients with true vitamin B_{12} deficiency.[35] The knowledge, expertise, and vigilance of laboratorians in method evaluation are critically important in preventing this type of error. Sensitivity is the minimum amount of analyte that a method can detect; assessment of sensitivity obviously is an important aspect of method evaluation.

An instrument quality control program should consist of (1) performance verification, (2) function verification, and (3) instrument maintenance.[36] Performance verification consists of those activities used to test and ensure that an instrument is properly calibrated and working correctly. Function verification includes activities designed to check mechanical and electronic functions, whereas instrument maintenance refers to activities that prolong instrument life and that minimize breakdowns or malfunctions. In addition, testing should be performed to verify that the equipment is in compliance with safety requirements.

The frequency with which these functions are performed depends on usage, although unfortunately many manufacturers' recommendations are based on time periods. Each step must be documented and, where possible, specific criteria and limits set (i.e., temperature limits such as 37 ± 1°C). In addition to the manufacturers' manuals for specific instruments, the following publications are helpful in establishing instrument quality control procedures:

1 *Medical Equipment Management in Hospitals*. American Society for Hospital Engineering of the American Hospital Association. Chicago, IL, American Hospital Publishing, 1982.

2 Alexander LR, Barnhart ER: *Photometric Quality Assurance Instrument Check Procedures*. Atlanta, GA, U.S. Department of Health and Human Services, 1980.

3 *reparation of Manuals for Installation, Operation and Repair of Laboratory Instruments*, ed 2. Villanova, PA, National Committee for Clinical Laboratory Standards, 1978.

4 *Guidelines for Service of Clinical Laboratory Instruments*. Villanova, PA, National Committee for Clinical Laboratory Standards, 1978.

5 Koenig AS, Day JC, Sodeman TM, et al: *Laboratory Instrumentation Verification and Maintenance Manual*, ed 3. Skokie, IL, College of American Pathologists, 1982.

ANALYTICAL GOALS

In each laboratory, the mean and standard deviation of control results are calculated and a set of control rules to follow are chosen. In doing so, a system is put into place to detect deterioration in quality, but the quality may not have been good enough in the first place. Unless control limits are adequate to ensure reasonably good quality of results, the internal quality control program is useless and misleading.[23]

Setting analytical goals for a given test affects its cost, reliability, and ultimately its usefulness. What should the analytical goals be? For a given analyte, establishment of acceptable allowable limits of error depends on the medical needs as well as to some extent on the state of the art (see Chapter 6 for details). Problems encountered in setting standards include differences among physicians in the criteria they use in medical decisions.[24] The allowable analytical error for a given determination also depends on the biological variation of the analyte and the medical application for the test, that is, whether the test is used for population surveys, for an individual in determining whether or not the result is abnormal, or for detecting trends. The question "Are the values significantly different?" is important for the clinician in following a patient during the course of a disease and determining if treatment is effective. Because overall precision of an assay influences comparison of two or more observations, imprecision needs to be minimized when results are compared over time.[25] If two results differ by at least 2.8 SD, where SD is the between-run SD of the method used, a significant difference exists with about 95 percent certainty.[26]

Identifying and Preventing Mistakes

Inaccuracy of a result can be due to a wide variety of problems including systematic error and mistakes or blunders. Mistakes such as mixed-up specimens or errors in calculation are often difficult to control, because by their nature they occur in a unpredictable manner. Because specimen mix-ups are among the most serious and frequent laboratory errors, there is interest in developing effective techniques to detect this type of error. To avoid mistakes such as decimal-point errors, laboratory data also should be checked for absurd values, that is, results that are impossible or very unlikely to occur, and for unlikely combinations of values. Many improvements are being made in this area as report generation is computerized (see Chapter 16). With computer reporting of results, calculation and transcription errors have been markedly reduced, and programs to eliminate absurd values and delta checks (see below) have become readily available.

Delta Check

The *delta check* (also called previous value check), a system based on detection of changes in an individual's test results, is used for detection of nonanalytical errors.[37] Cumulative reports kept by the laboratory are used to compare test results for specimens obtained at different times from the same patient. Delta checks are used to identify factors that do not necessarily affect analytical error as monitored by internal and external quality control procedures but that result in laboratory errors. Examples of errors detected by this system include specimen misidentification, calculation, and transcription errors. Delta check methods vary in the limits set for the difference between the patient's results (delta) and the number of analytes checked simultaneously. If the limits set are too narrow, a large number of false positive signals will occur. At a 5 percent false positive rate, delta check methods detect only about 50 percent of mislabeled specimens. In addition, if the actual mislabeling rate is 1 percent, only about 10 percent of the specimens flagged by the delta check will actually have been mislabeled.[38] A multivariate delta check that monitors absolute values is reported to give an improved true positive rate.[39]

Blind Controls

Blind quality control samples, that is, samples that are not known to the analyst as quality control samples, also are used to detect nonanalytical error. Use of blind control samples overcomes the problem of special handling of quality control samples that handicaps many quality control programs. Problems that can be detected with use of blind quality control samples include problems with specimen handling, failure to perform all tests requested, incorrect reporting of results, and unnecessarily long turnaround times.[40]

ACCREDITATION

Accreditation programs, a further development to improve laboratory performance, generally include encouragement of use of internal quality control programs, support of external quality control programs, and other means of promoting quality assurance such as educational and inspection programs.

Accreditation programs are an important part of laboratory quality assurance because of their educational role in maintaining laboratory standards. Programs such as that of the College of American Pathologists (CAP) and the Joint Commission on Accreditation of Hospitals (JCAH) provide guidelines for controlling aspects of quality assurance such as specimen collection and reports. The CAP accreditation program, which began in the early 1960s, was established as an educational, peer review laboratory improvement program designed for the benefit of the patient.[41] The voluntary program of inspection and accreditation provides for on-site inspection every 2 years and an interim-year self-inspection by checklist. The checklists used in the CAP inspections provide a large list of specific standards for each laboratory section (for details on laboratory accreditation and licensure, see Chapter 15).

The checklist items cover various aspects of specimen collection, personnel, equipment, reagents, laboratory procedures, and reports. When considering these checklists items, it is helpful to remember the following ground rules as enumerated by Diamond:

    a If it isn't written, it didn't happen.
    b Any recorded datum has significance only if limits of tolerance are stated.
    c Limits of tolerance have significance only if there are written instructions on how to proceed if the limits are exceeded.
    d Corrective actions have significance only if recorded.[42]

In 1979, the Board of Commission on Accreditation of Hospitals (JCAH) announced acceptance of satisfactory accreditation by the College of American Pathologists (CAP) as compliance with JCAH laboratory standards. Current JCAH Standards for Pathology and Medical Laboratory Services include many items that are similar to CAP requirements. In addition, as part of the hospital's quality assurance program, quality and appropriateness of patient care provided must be monitored and evaluated and identified problems resolved. Using objective criteria, all major clinical functions including laboratory services must be monitored by routine collection of information about the services provided and the periodic assessment of this information.

The goal is to find problems through use of monitors or screens and resolve any important problems that are found. Monitors include those that are continuous, such as the laboratory's internal and external quality control programs, as well as reports of patient injuries, utilization review activities, and problem-focused studies. For example, the hospital transfusion committee, required by the JCAH, is intended to improve transfusion practices through utilization review and developing guidelines for safety, efficacy, and efficiency of blood transfusion.[43] After standards are set, audit criteria are then developed and patient charts are screened. If the required elements are not present, the chart undergoes a further review. If, for example, the committee sets an audit criterion that specifies that a patient receiving platelet transfusion must have a platelet count below 20,000/µl, the chart of a patient with a pretransfusion platelet count of 100,000/µl would be flagged for review. If the platelet transfusion was valid—that is, if the patient had documented platelet dysfunction—no further action need be taken, but if no valid reason can be found, further action must be taken. When assessment of data collected by the various monitoring or screening techniques indicates that important problems exist, mechanisms must be in place to resolve the problem and to evaluate the effectiveness of the action taken. The goal is to identify trends so that problems can be identified early and corrected promptly, because the majority of serious patient injuries are preceded by clearly identifiable trends.[44]

THE LABORATORIAN'S ROLE IN QUALITY ASSURANCE

Laboratory precision has been improving for a number of analytes, and in some cases analytic precision exceeds medically useful limits.[28] But precision is only one measure of quality, and as precision goals are reached, resources need to be directed elsewhere in order to improve quality. The goal of quality assurance procedures should be to eliminate all errors. Is this realistic? When told that everyone makes mistakes, Gambino answers, "How many dropped babies would you accept in the hospital nursery? One in 1000? One in 10,000? No one ever gives a number because the goal is always zero dropped babies."[45]

In order to attain the goal of error-free work, it is essential to create a quality assurance program aimed at preventing problems.[1] Problems are prevented by creating the proper attitudes in the laboratory staff and monitoring a variety of critical parameters.

In addition to their roles in providing prompt, accurate laboratory results and participating in hospital quality assurance progams, laboratorians also play an important part in educating users in cost-effective test strategies, monitoring laboratory usage, and interpreting laboratory results. For example, the pattern of tests made available to clinicians by the laboratory influences usage.[46] In addition, laboratorians play an important role in monitoring laboratory usage. Clinicians do not always adhere to the older tradition of "before ordering a test, decide what you will do if it is (a) positive, or (b) negative, and if both answers are the same don't do the test."[47] The laboratorian's input into interpretation of results also is an important part of a complete laboratory quality assurance program. Added to the monies wasted, each unnecessary diagnostic test puts the patient in jeopardy of incurring the "Ulysses syndrome," in which a previously healthy person has a false positive result and thus makes a long journey through various diagnostic procedures, and before returning to the point of outset, experiences a number of perilous but pointless adventures.[48] In contrast, significant data may not be appreciated and may not be acted upon appropriately.[49]

Setting of appropriate standards, developing effective monitors to ensure that standards are met, and solving the problems identified by these systems requires dedicated laboratorians who possess a broad knowledge of clinical laboratory medicine and a wide range of skills in laboratory management. In areas such as the study of preanalytical variation, development of sensitive and specific tests, refinements in determining reference intervals, and contributions to understanding appropriate test selection and data utilization, laboratorians have an exceptional opportunity to contribute to improvements in patient care.

REFERENCES

1. Crosby PB: *Quality Is Free.* New York, Mentor, 1979.
2. How to ensure quality, editorial. Lancet 1982, 2:196.
3. Batsakis JG: Analytical goals and the College of American Pathologists. *Am J Clin Pathol* 1982, 78(suppl):678.
4. Diamond I: The hospital laboratory 50 years ago. *Pathologist* 1985, 39:41.
5. Levey S, Jennings ER: The use of control charts in the clinical laboratory. *Am J Clin Pathol* 1950, 20:1059.
6. Shewhart WA: *Economic Control of Quality of Manufactured Product.* Princeton, NJ, D. Van Nostrand, 1931.
7. Henry RJ, Segalove M: The running of standards in clinical chemistry and the use of the control chart. *J Clin Pathol* 1952, 5:305.
8. Fraser CG, Peake MJ: Problems associated with clinical chemistry quality control materials. *CRC Crit Rev Clin Lab Sci* 1980, 12:59.
9. Howanitz PJ, Howanitz JH, Lamberson HV, et al: Analytical biases with liquid quality control material. *Am J Clin Pathol* 1983, 80(suppl):643.
10. Gosset WS: Errors of routine analysis. *Biometrika* 1927, 19:151.
11. *Internal Quality Control Testing: Principles and Definitions.* Proposed Guidelines NCCLS C24-P 5(8):171, 1985.
12. Diamond I (ed): Are controls becoming uncontrollable? *CAP Laboratory Accreditation Newsletter.* 1985, 12:4.
13. Cembrowski GS, Chandler EP, Westgard JO: Assessment of "average of normals," quality control procedures and guidelines for implementation. *Am J Clin Pathol* 1984, 81:492.
14. Cembrowski GS, Westgard JO: Quality control of multichannel hematology analyzers: Evaluation of Bull's algorithm. *Am J Clin Pathol* 1985, 83:337.
15. Blum AS: Computer evaluation of statistical procedures, and a new quality-control statistical procedure. *Clin Chem* 1985, 31:206.
16. Haven GT, Lawson NS, Ross JW: QAS notes. *Pathologist* 1980, 34:619.
17. Westgard JO, Groth T, Burnett RW, et al: A multi-rule Shewhart chart for quality control in clinical chemistry. *Clin Chem* 1981, 27:493.
18. Haven GT, Lawson NS, Ross JW: Quality control in the 1980's, in Homberger H and Batsakis J (eds): *Clinical Laboratory Manual: 1982.* East Norwalk, CT, Appleton-Century-Crofts, 1982.

19 Westgard JO, Groth T: Power function for statistical control rules. *Clin Chem* 1979, 25:863.
20 Whitehead TP: *Quality Control in Clinical Chemistry.* New York, John Wiley & Sons, 1977.
21 Schoen I, Custer E, Graham G, et al: Quality control log with CUSUM and clinically useful limits criteria. *Arch Pathol Lab Med* 1985, 109:333.
22 Fraser CG: Use of appropriate analytic goals. *Am J Clin Pathol* 1983, 79:759.
23 Tonks DB: Some faults with external and internal quality control programs, editorial. *Clin Biochem* 1982, 15:67.
24 Elion-Gerritzen WE: Analytic precision in clinical chemistry and medical decisions. *Am J Clin Pathol* 1980, 73:183.
25 Ross JW, Fraser MD: The authors' reply. *Am J Clin Pathol* 1983, 79:760.
26 Reed AH, Henry RJ: Accuracy, precision, quality control, and miscellaneous statistics, in Henry RJ, Cannon DC, Winkelman JW (eds): *Clinical Chemistry: Principles and Technics.* Hagerstown, MD, Harper & Row, 1974.
27 Stamm D: A new concept of quality control of clinical laboratory investigations in the light of clinical requirements and based on reference method values. *J Clin Chem Clin Biochem* 1982, 20:817.
28 Skendzel LP, Barnett RN, Platt R: Medically useful criteria for analytic performance of laboratory tests. *Am J Clin Pathol* 1985, 83:200.
29 Hartmann AE, Naito HK, Burnett RW, et al: Accuracy of participant results utilized as target values in the CAP Chemistry Survey Program. *Arch Pathol Lab Med* 1985, 109:894.
30 Youden WI: The sample, the procedure and the laboratory. *Anal Chem* 1960, 32:23A.
31 *1985 Manual CAP Surveys: Interlaboratory Comparison Program.* Skokie, IL, College of American Pathologists. 1984.
32 Chemistry Resource Committee: Fixed criteria in blood gas survey. College of American Pathologists. *Summing Up* 1984, 14:5.
33 Buttner J, Borth R, Boutwell JH, et al: Quality control in clinical chemistry: Part 2. Assessment of analytical methods for routine use. *Clin Chim Acta* 1975, 63:F1.
34 Sunderman FW: Current concepts of "normal values," "reference values," and "discrimination values" in clinical chemistry. *Clin Chem* 1975, 21:1873.
35 Kolhouse JF, Kondo H, Allen NC, et al: Cobalamin analogues are present in human plasma and can mask cobalamin deficiency because current radioisotope dilution assays are not specific for true cobalamin. *N Engl J Med* 1978, 299:785.
36 Koenig AS, Day JC, Sodeman TM, et al: *Laboratory Instrumentation Verification and Maintenance Manual,* ed 3. Skokie, IL, College of American Pathologists, 1982.
37 Nosanchuk JS, Gottmanm AW: CUMS and delta checks. *Am J Clin Pathol* 1974, 62:707.
38 Sheiner LB, Wheeler LA, Moore JK: The performance of delta check methods. *Clin Chem* 1979, 25:2034.
39 Iizuka Y, Kume H, Kitamura M: Multivariate delta check method for detecting specimen mix-up. *Clin Chem* 1982, 28:2244.
40 Glenn GC, Hathaway TK: Quality control by blind sample analysis. *Am J Clin Pathol* 1979, 72:156.
41 Duckworth JK, Gregg DP: How and when the accreditation program began, and where it is today. *Pathologist* 1974, 28:23.
42 Diamond I: Quality control revisited. *Pathologist* 1980, 34:333.
43 Grindon AJ, Tomasulo PS, Bergin JJ, et al: The hospital transfusion committee: Guidelines for improving practice. *JAMA* 1985, 253:540.
44 Craddick, JW: The medical management analysis system: A professional liability warning mechanism. *QRB* 1979, 5:2.

45 Gambino, SR: Quality control: Can we achieve error free work? *MLO,* March 1985.
46 Wong ET, Steffes MW: A fundamental approach to the diagnosis of diseases of the thyroid gland. *Clin Lab Med* 1984, 4:655.
47 Cochrane, AL: *Effectiveness and Efficiency: Random Reflections on Health Services.* London, Burgess and Son, 1972.
48 Benson ES: Initiatives toward effective decision making and laboratory use. *Hum Pathol* 1980, 11:440.
49 Link K, Centor R, Buchsbaum D, et al: Why physicians don't pursue abnormal laboratory tests: An investigation of hypercalcemia and the follow-up of abnormal test results. *Hum Pathol* 1984, 15:75.

CHAPTER 2

THE STATISTICS OF QUALITY CONTROL

Irwin M. Weisbrot, M.D.

Some understanding of basic statistics is necessary before quality control (QC) procedures can be implemented and comprehended. However, statistics remains but a tool, not the end. No compilation of means, standard deviations, and deltas by itself ever saved a single laboratorian from embarrassment. Unless the data are examined, compared to previous experience, related to the clinical or analytical problem at hand, and acted upon, they are merely expensive and useless.

Simple inspection of simple data, even without any statistical reduction, by an experienced and dedicated analyst is more useful than masses of means and deviations produced by a "QC statistical package" and dumped forthwith into the lap of the disinterested. The value of statistics lies with organizing and simplifying data, and with them permitting some objective estimate of the probability that a change of a given magnitude has indeed occurred.

BASIC STATISTICS

The statistics of QC are generally simple and reflect intuitive insights set to limited mathematical ground rules to keep us honest. Means and standard deviations are the mainstay, with some use of t-tests, F-tests, and other derivatives of the Gaussian (normal) distribution. Linear regression and other distributions such as the binomial, the Poisson, and chi square are useful. Distribution-free statistics (nonparametric) are seldom used.

Definitions

Population   A population comprises the whole universe of values—for example, all the fasting glucose values of hospital patients on a given day or month.

Sample   A sample is a portion of a population—for example, a set of 25 fasting glucose values on male patients over 90 years of age on a given day.

Parameter   A parameter is a numerical value that characterizes a population—for example, mu (μ) represents the mean and sigma (σ) the standard deviation of a population.

Statistic   A statistic is a numerical value that characterizes a sample—for example, $\bar{x}$ represents the mean and s the standard deviation of a sample. A statistic is often the only estimate of a parameter available to the analyst.

Central Limit Theorem   The central limit theorem is a concept, both intuitive and mathematical, that the means of many small samples will eventually have a normal or Gaussian distribution and will reflect the center of the population being sampled.

Error   The word "error" is related to the word "errant," meaning "wandering." Error implies departure from or wandering away from the center.

Analytic error may be described as

1 Random or unpredictable between replicate determinations, quantified as standard deviation
2 Systematic or regularly and predictably different from the true value, quantified as mean difference, the difference between the true value and the mean of replicate determinations
3 Constant, or unrelated to concentration
4 Proportional, or related to concentration

Accuracy   Accuracy implies freedom from all error. An accurate determination produces the truth or a true quantitative value. In practice, accuracy is relative to the state of the analytic art or to an arbitrary convention.

Bias   Departures from accuracy are caused by bias, which has more than one meaning:

1 A quantitative estimate of the departure of a determination from the truth calculated as the difference between the true value and the mean of several replicates (mean difference).
2 Failure of a sample to reflect the target population yields a biased sample.

Precision   Precision defines that component of analytical accuracy revealed by the closeness with which repeated determinations agree. Random events over which the analyst has no control are presumed to be the cause of this variation. Studies of precision may be (1) short term—within run; (2) intermediate—day to day; (3) long term—months or years.

Imprecision Interval Quantitative estimates of lack of precision are usually calculated as the standard deviation of replicate or repeated determinations. The data are generally assumed to be Gaussian or normally distributed.

Random A data distribution in which all values are equally likely to occur is termed *random*. In the everyday world of experience, random means unpredictable. No formula or algorithm can predict the next event. In a table of logarithms or square roots, it is possible to calculate the next number. Not so for a table of random numbers. Such tables are useful for minimizing bias in experimental situations and in such practical matters as the placement of quality control pools on analytical trays.

Confidence Interval (CI) The interval or spread of values within which the true population parameter probably falls, when the parameter is estimated from a sample, is the confidence interval. Intuitively, we expect a small difference in the mean value for fasting glucose of humans to vary somewhat with each small group we sample. By appropriate calculations (see below), the probability that the true population mean lies between certain limits can be stated. In general, the larger the sample or the more small samples we pool, the smaller is the confidence interval; that is, the narrower is the range of uncertainty within which the true population parameter lies. (Compare with the central limit theorem.)

Degrees of Freedom (df) This term indicates the number of values used in a statistical calculation that can have impact on the conclusion. For instance, if nine values and the mean of a sample of ten are known, then the tenth value is fixed; it has no freedom. A practical example from proficiency surveys on differential leukocyte counting will further illustrate the concept. If, in distinguishing neutrophils from nonneutrophils, a single mistake is made, this will appear as two errors, one for neutrophils and one for nonneutrophils; in reality, the system has only one degree of freedom.

Probability (p) Probability refers to the relative frequency of an event. Common p values in everyday statistics are $p < .05$ and $p < .01$, which are arbitrary levels at which judgment is accepted or rejected. However, inherent in this use is a measure of subjectivity depending on the risk of making a mistake. In assessing the clinical value of an expensive method, we may wish less than a 1 percent ($p < .01$) chance of erroneously concluding that it is more accurate and precise than cheaper methods. However, if a commercial airline had a 50:50 chance of having more accidents than its competitors, we would not worry too much if our use of another airline were based on an erroneous conclusion.

Significance In statistical hypothesis testing, significance refers to a judgment as to whether two or more data groups are to be considered different. A difference is termed significant if $p < .05$ that chance or a random event caused it. If $p < .01$, a difference is termed highly significant. This does not mean important, valuable, or even believable. It merely indicates that under the conditions of the experiment, with the information at hand, and the statistical test used, the data appear different.

Null Hypothesis The null hypothesis states: There is no difference (between the means, standard deviations, etc.) that cannot be explained by chance alone. This is the rigorous way of stating the problem, and the only entity for which the statistics (which will be demonstrated below) actually test. Accepting the null hypothesis (which is generally done when p exceeds .05) means rejecting the idea that a difference really exists. Rejecting the null hypothesis does not prove that a difference does exist; it merely indicates that chance alone seems insufficient to explain the observed difference. In statistical shorthand, the null hypothesis is symbolized as

$$H_0 : \mu_1 = \mu_0 \text{ or } (\mu_1 - \mu_0) = 0$$

There is no difference between the means.

Rejecting H_0 implies that the alternate hypothesis, H_1, is true:

$$H_1 : \mu_1 \, (\mu_0 = \text{ the alternate hypothesis })$$

There is a difference between the means.

Basic Calculations

Rounding Off and Significant Figures To simplify calculations and to conserve paper, numbers must be rounded off. For the sake of analytical truth, the number reported should not have more significant numbers (alleged accuracy) than the method can yield. Derived numbers, such as means and standard deviations, theoretically have an infinite length. In practice, they are reported to one or two numbers beyond analytical certainty.

The following convention for rounding numbers produces minimal bias.[1] If the last number is 4 or less, retain the preceding number; if it is 6 or more, increase the preceding number by 1. If the last number is 5, the preceding number is made even.

Examples:

$$\text{pH} = 7.424 \text{ rounds to } 7.42$$
$$\text{pH} = 7.426 \text{ rounds to } 7.43$$
$$\text{pH} = 7.425 \text{ rounds to } 7.42$$
$$\text{pH} = 7.435 \text{ rounds to } 7.44$$

When doing statistics with electronic calculators, it is advisable to retain as many decimal places as possible, rounding off at the end.

TABLE 2-1
HEMOGLOBIN DETERMINATIONS, g/dl

	Technologist A	Technologist B	Technologist C
	9.1	9.0	8.5
	9.1	9.1	8.6
	9.2	9.1	9.0
	9.3	9.3	9.3
	9.4	9.5	9.5
	9.5	9.5	9.7
	9.5	9.6	9.8
	9.5	9.6	9.8
	9.5	9.7	
	9.6	9.8	
$\bar{x}$	9.37	9.42	9.28
s	0.18	0.28	0.52

Measures of Central Tendency The mean, median, and mode are common measures of central tendency. The mean or average is the most useful estimate of the central tendency of a set of numbers. Consider the results obtained by Technologist A running 10 replicate hemoglobin determinations, Table 2-1. The *mean* is 9.37 g/dl, calculated by

$$\bar{x} = \frac{1}{n} \sum_{n}^{i=1} x_i$$

or sum (Σ) the n individual values (x_i) [the numbers are not grouped into intervals ($i = 1$)], then divide by n. The median refers to the value at the 50th percentile. Half are above and half are below. This value occurs between 9.4 and 9.5 in the example. The *mode* refers to the most frequent value, in this example, 9.5.

Measures of Dispersion or Variability The range, a central portion of the range, and the average deviation from the mean are all estimates of the dispersion of values around the central tendency. Although descriptively useful, they are of limited use in making inferences. The average deviation from the mean by Technologist A is 0.16 g/dl (Table 2-2).

Standard deviation is the most common and most useful description of dispersion. It is defined operationally as

$$s = \sqrt{\frac{\Sigma(x_i - \bar{x})^2}{n - 1}}$$

or take the difference of each value from the mean, square it, sum, divide by $n - 1$ degrees of freedom, and then take the square root (Table 2-2). Squaring removes the

TABLE 2-2
CALCULATION OF STANDARD DEVIATION
Technologist A

	x_i	$d = (x_i - \bar{x})$	d^2
	9.1	−0.27	0.0729
	9.1	−0.27	0.0729
	9.2	−0.17	0.0289
	9.3	−0.07	0.0049
	9.4	+0.03	0.0009
	9.5	+0.13	0.0169
	9.5	+0.13	0.0169
	9.5	+0.13	0.0169
	9.5	+0.13	0.0169
	9.6	+0.23	0.0529
	93.7		0.3091
$\bar{x}$	9.37	0.16	
v			0.0343
s			0.18

negative signs, a source of serious confusion in calculating average deviation. Another term for standard deviation is *standard error*.

Variance (v) Variance is the square of the standard deviation and is manipulated in a statistical procedure known as analysis of variance (ANOVA), which quantifies the portion of total variance that each variable component contributes. For mathematical reasons, standard deviations cannot be averaged, but the weighted mean or pooled variance may be used to summate dispersion. Calculate the overall standard deviation of Technologists A, B, and C in Table 2-1 as follows:

$$s = \sqrt{\frac{(n_A - 1) s_A^2 + (n_B - 1) s_B^2 + (n_C - 1) s_C^2}{n_A + n_B + n_C - 3}}$$

$$s = \sqrt{\frac{9(0.0324) + 9(0.0784) + 7(0.2704)}{25}}$$

$$= 0.34$$

To calculate standard deviation without first determining the mean, use the formula

$$s = \sqrt{\frac{\Sigma x^2 - (\Sigma x)^2/n}{n - 1}}$$

where Σx^2 indicates that each x_i is squared, then added. $(\Sigma x)^2$ indicates that the sum of all the x_i is squared. This formula is used in calculators and computers.

The Confidence Interval of Sigma Experience and intuition suggest that the estimate of sigma (σ) provided by the calculation of standard deviation from a small sample, as in Table 2-2, may not be perfect. We expect subsequent trials of 10 to produce somewhat different results. Appendix 2-1 permits determination of the limits between which the true population will most likely be, given a legitimate sample.

For example, if $s = 0.18$ for 9 df, then:

$$\text{Upper limit} = 0.18 \times 1.746 = 0.31$$
$$\text{Lower limit} = 0.18 \times 0.6657 = 0.12$$

In other words, there is a 95 percent chance that the true population standard deviation lies between 0.31 g/dl and 0.12 g/dl. Note that as df increases, the interval decreases.

This simple calculation has considerable implications for routine quality control techniques. Presume that a daily Ca^{2+} analysis on a new QC pool yields $s = 0.2$ mg/dl after 31 days. Appendix 2-1 indicates that sigma lies between 0.16 and 0.26. Subsequent conclusions as to whether the method is in control may be erroneous if 0.2 is considered sacrosanct. Continued observation of how the pool varies in day-to-day use, experience with the technical method, clinical correlation, and external testing are necessary.

Coefficient of Variation (CV) The ratio $s/\bar{x}$ is known as the coefficient of variation when expressed as a percentage, or the relative standard deviation when expressed as a decimal. The CV is a convenient statistic relating variation to concentration. In Table 2-1, the CVs for the analyses of hemoglobin by Technologists A, B, and C are 1.9 percent, 3.0 percent, and 5.6 percent, respectively.

Standard Error of the Mean (SEm) Just as repeated data sets may be expected to yield differing standard deviations, so we expect the means of repeated small samples to differ somewhat. The magnitude of that variation is estimated as the standard error of the mean, where

$$\text{SEm} = \frac{s}{\sqrt{n}}$$

This statistic is important to the understanding of the t-test (see below), which tests for the significance of differences between means. For the means attained by each technologist in Appendix 2-1, the SEm are 0.057, 0.088, and 0.18.

Standard error is another word for standard deviation. If the technologists performed the same experiment many times, without changing technique, the standard deviation of those means should be very close to the SEm. It should be clear, then, that the SEm provides a way of estimating the confidence interval within which the underlying population mean probably lies. Thus SEm relates to the central limit theorem.

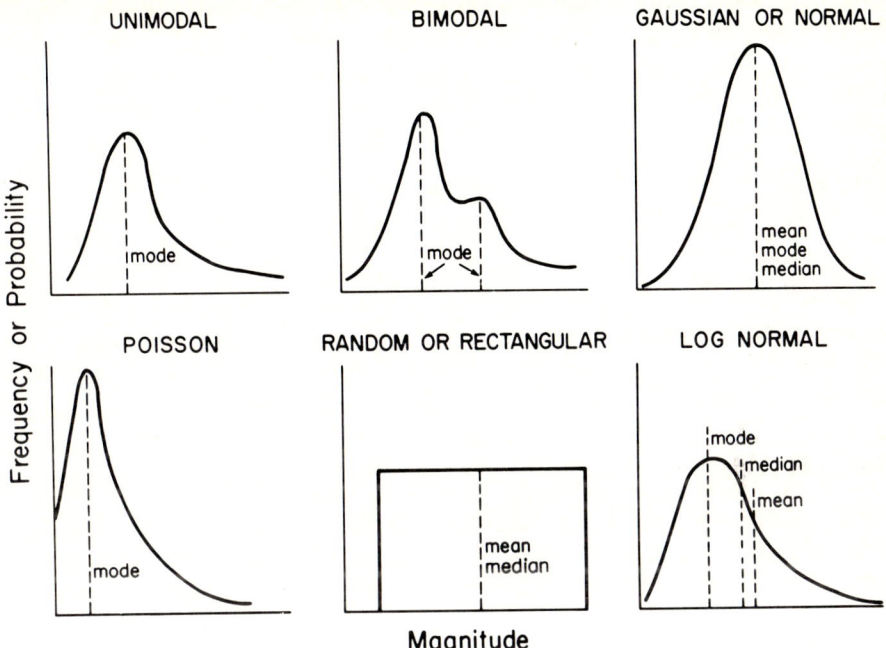

FIGURE 2-1
Examples of data distributions.

Data Distributions

When magnitude is plotted against frequency or probability, the data's distribution pattern becomes evident. These distributions frequently confer unique mathematical properties on the data, allowing extensive descriptive analysis and permitting inferences concerning the data. Figure 2-1 illustrates some data distributions.

Normal or Gaussian Distribution The properties of the normal or Gaussian distribution were originally discovered during the study of replicate measurements. The tendency for central clustering with symmetrical tails containing the less frequent values is evident. The mean, mode, and median are identical. The Gaussian distribution is the basis for most common parametric statistics. Figure 2-2 illustrates the relationship of standard deviation (sigma) to the normal distribution: 68.2 percent of the values fall within one standard deviation above or below the mean. Two standard deviations included 95.4 percent, and three standard deviations above and below the mean include 99.6 percent of all the values.

The formula for Z calculates how many sigmas from the mean a given value lies. The area under a portion of the curve gives the probability of an event occurring. Appendix 2-2 is a simplified table of areas under the tails of the Gaussian curve.

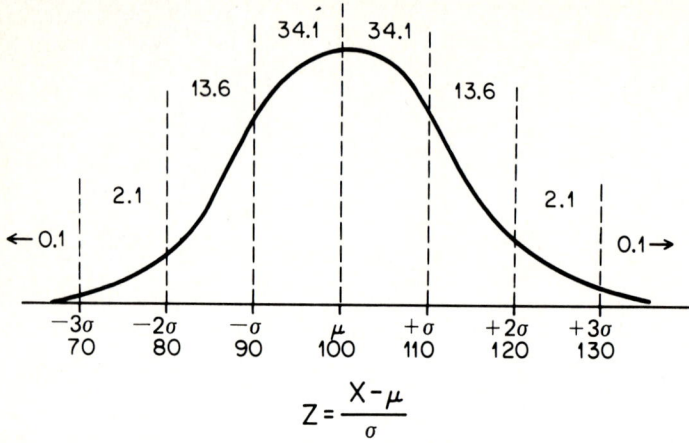

FIGURE 2-2
The normal (Gaussian) distribution. The mean (μ) = 100. The standard deviation (σ) = 10. The percent of all values included in each standard deviation above or below the mean is shown.

Example 1

Referring to the data in Fig. 2-2, what is the probability of glucose values exceeding 112 g/dl?

$$Z = \frac{112 - 100}{10} = 1.2$$

Consulting the table, the one-tailed equivalent area for $Z = 1.2$ is 0.115; therefore $p = .115$, or 11.5 percent of the values are 112 or greater.

Example 2

What range of values includes the central 77 percent of all the data? We wish to exclude 23 percent, half from each tail; we find under the two-tailed table that $Z = 1.2$. Then:

$$\pm 1.2 = \frac{x - 100}{10}$$

Rearranging,

$$x = (\pm 1.2 \times 10) + 100$$

Thus the required central range is 88 to 112. Noting from Fig. 2-1 that the central 68 percent extends from 90 to 110, our answer seems reasonable.

Example 3

What percentage of glucose values lies between 85 and 105? Using the one-tailed table to find the excluded values from each side of the mean:

$$Z = 85 - 100/10 = 1.5$$

For $Z = -1.5$, the excluded area is 0.067, to the left of the mean:

$$Z = 105 - 100/10 = 0.5$$

The equivalent area is 0.309 to the right of the mean. Subtracting each area from unity, we have

$$1 - 0.067 - 0.039 = 0.624 \text{ or } 62.4\%$$

An important feature, apparent from Fig. 2-2, is that values far from the mean constitute a very small fraction of the total. In the small-number statistics commonly used in the laboratory, when values lie two or three standard deviations from the mean, they are often suspect. Although they may be legitimate members of the target population, they very likely may be from another population. Hence the emphasis on 95 percent and 99 percent limits of acceptability.

The standard deviation interval (SDI) is similar to Z, but represents the calculation performed on $\bar{x}$ and s rather than on mu and sigma. In many proficiency surveys, the SDI of the individual participant value is given as a measure of the departure from the mean value of the entire method cohort.

Example: The reported value for hemoglobin = 18.6 by the manual cyanmethemoglobin method. Two hundred participants produced a mean of 17.23 with a standard deviation of 0.38.

$$SDI = 18.6 - 17.23/0.38 = +3.6$$

Your reported value is 3.6 SDI above the mean. Because well over 99.9 percent of the participants attained a lower value, you are very likely wrong, for some reason.

When the numbers are fairly large, the percentages shown in Fig. 2-2 and the values listed for Z in Appendix 2-2 will aid in estimating the significance of SDI. When SDI = +1.0, then 50 percent + 34.1 percent or 84.1 percent of participants reported lower values and 15.9 percent higher. When SDI = −0.6, then 50 percent + 27.4 percent or 77.4 percent were higher. Generally, an SDI of ±2.0 or greater represents an unacceptable result; 95 percent of the values were closer to the participant mean, the value in question lying in the 2.5 percent lower or upper tail.

The use of SDI as a grading tool presumes that the data have a Gaussian distribution.

Poisson Distribution The Poisson distribution, contrary to the Gaussian distribution, describes rare events. The peak value occurs close to zero, with a long tail toward infinity (Fig. 2-1). Cells suspended in diluent for counting, emissions from unstable atoms, and leukocytes distributed over a blood film are examples of laboratory phenomena that follow the Poisson distribution.

The standard deviation of the Poisson distribution is the square root of the mean,

$$s = \sqrt{m}$$

It is apparent, then, that the confidence interval of an enumeration is a function of the average number of particles counted. For the typical leukocyte count of 10,000/µl, 200 cells would be counted using a counting chamber. The standard deviation = $\sqrt{200}$ = 14; thus the 2s, or the 95 percent confidence interval, of the count is approximately 172 to 228. Multiplying by the usual dilution factor of 50 yields 8,600 to 11,400. In addition, the random variation of cells distributing themselves in a counting chamber could lead to considerable departure from the mean. When filling and pipetting errors are introduced, further degradation of the method occurs.[2]

By contrast, a simple electronic cell counter, using a 1:500 suspension, and processing 500 µl, will enumerate 10,000 cells (20 cells/µl × 500 µl); the $s = \sqrt{10,000}$ or 100. Apart from technical problems, theoretical CVs of 1 percent are possible, the expected 95 percent interval of the count now being 9,800 to 10,200.

The ratio $s/\sqrt{m}$ provides a rational procedure for evaluating the random behavior of systems that may be influenced by unconscious equalization or instrumental failure. For instance, in chamber counting, if the cells are truly randomly distributed in the chamber, and the boxes are counted objectively, then the ratio $s/\sqrt{m} = 1$. Assuming that $\bar{x}$ estimates $\bar{m}$, ratios of the actual s and $\bar{x}$ less than unity imply departure from expected randomness. Similarly, for atomic emissions in radioimmunoassay, replicate counts should produce a $s/\sqrt{m}$ ratio of unity.

The probability of a given event in the Poisson distribution is given by the formula

$$P_x = e^{-\lambda} \cdot \lambda^x / x!$$

where P_x = probability of an occurrence
e = the natural number 2.7183+
λ = the mean of the distribution
! = factorial multiplication

Example: The true myeloblast count on a properly prepared peripheral blood smear is 1 percent. What is the probability of encountering three myeloblasts on a 100-cell differential count? Appendix 2-3 simplifies the calculation:

$$P_3 = \frac{(2.7183)^{-1} \cdot 1^3}{3 \times 2 \times 1} = .061$$

or about 6 percent.

The probability reduces considerably if more cells are enumerated. For a 200-cell differential count, if the true count is 2/200, the probability of encountering 6/200 is

$$P_6 = \frac{(2.7183)^{-2} \cdot 2^6}{6!} = .012$$

The Poisson distribution has been used to estimate the probability of discovering parasitic ova in stool specimens.[3] Correction for coincident passage of two or more particles in electronic particle counters is based on this distribution.

Binomial Distribution and the Binomial Expansion The statistics of data categorized as *either/or* are based on the mathematics of the binomial expansion:

$$(p + q)^n$$

where p = the probability of the event occurring (success)
$q = 1 - p$, the probability of the event not occurring (failure)
n = the number of trials
$p + q = 1.0$

A simple case occurs when $p = .5$. The probability of six consecutive quality control values above the mean is $.5^6 = .016$. The binomial expansion for five trials is $(p + q)^5$, yielding

$$p^5 + 5p^4q + 10p^3q^2 + 10p^2q^3 + 5pq^4 + q^5 = 1$$

A practical example may make clear that each term expresses a probability of an event. Presume that a test is 70 percent sensitive, so that $p = .7$, that patient will have a positive test and $1 - p = .3$. Then the expansion yields:

$$0.16807 + 0.36017 + 0.3087 + 0.1323 + 0.02835 + 0.00243 = 1$$

The probability that five of five patients could have a positive test is given by $p^5 = .16807$ or only about 17 percent. The probability that two of five would be positive and three of five negative is given by $10p^2q^3$ or $p = .1323$ or about 13 percent; the probability of three or more patients being positive is given by the additive probability of the first three terms, or .83692. The formula for the binomial expansion simplifies these calculations:

$$P_{(x)} = \frac{n!}{x!(n-x)!} \cdot p^x q^{n-x}$$

where $P_{(x)}$ = probability of x occurrence
n = number of tries
p = probability of success (sensitivity) = .7
$q = 1 - p$ = probability of failure = .3
$!$ = factorial = chain multiplication

The standard error (SE) of the binomial distribution is useful in evaluating the performance of differential leukocyte counts:

$$SE = \sqrt{p \cdot q/n}$$

Example: What is the confidence interval of a 100-cell differential count that yields 60 percent neutrophils and 40 percent nonneutrophils?

$$SE = \sqrt{.60 \times .40/100} = .049$$

Taking ± 2 SE as an estimate of the 95 percent limits, the percent neutrophils could be as low as 50 percent or as high as 70 percent and still be samples of the same cell population.[4] Of course, the techniques of preparing and scanning the smear are additional variables.

The Chi-Square Distribution Chi square (χ^2) compares observed versus expected occurrences and has many applications in the clinical laboratory. The basic algorithm is

$$\chi^2 = \Sigma \frac{(\text{observed} - \text{expected})^2}{\text{expected}}$$

where observed (O) and expected (E) refer to the number of observations. Based on the null hypothesis that there is no difference between the data samples except that caused by chance, E is the weighted average of each category.

An example from differential leukocyte counting will elucidate the χ^2 test. Table 2-3 compares the results of a 100-cell differential with that of a 200-cell differential on the same smear. Are the observed distributions significantly different? The final tabulation yields $\chi^2 = 7.297$. Referring to Appendix 2-4, critical χ^2 for 3 df is 7.81. As we have not exceeded that value, we conclude that the distribution of cells in the two counts differs only by chance; that is, they are not proven to be different. Three degrees of freedom are used because df is one less than the number of categories. With only one degree of freedom, the Yates correction for continuity may be applied to a borderline test. Subtract .5 from each ($O - E$) and proceed.

Chi square may be used as general test for the agreement of data distributions such as a test for linearity (see linear regression) and as a test to decide if data have a Gaussian distribution.[5]

Random Distribution Data for which no algorithm or formula can predict the next event are called random. All values are equally probable. The distribution is rectangular (Fig. 2-1). Whenever possible, random number tables such as Appendix 2-5 should be used to assign the position of controls in analytical trays to expose the controls to the conditions experienced by patient specimens during the analysis.

Assume a tray of 30 positions with the first position a standard, leaving positions

TABLE 2-3
COMPARISON OF TWO DIFFERENTIAL COUNTS BY CHI SQUARE

Category	Observed	Expected	O − E	(O − E)²	(O − E)²/E
		Count #1: 100 cells			
Neutrophil	45	$\frac{115}{300} \times 100 = 38.3$	6.7	44.89	1.172
Lymphocyte	30	$\frac{80}{300} \times 100 = 26.7$	3.3	10.89	0.408
Monocyte	15	$\frac{55}{300} \times 100 = 18.3$	−3.3	10.89	0.595
Eosinophil	10	$\frac{50}{300} \times 100 = 16.7$	−6.7	44.89	2.688
		Count #2: 200 cells			
Neutrophil	70	$\frac{115}{300} \times 200 = 76.7$	−6.7	44.89	0.585
Lymphocyte	50	$\frac{80}{300} \times 200 = 53.3$	−3.3	10.89	0.204
Monocyte	40	$\frac{55}{300} \times 200 = 36.7$	3.3	10.89	0.297
Eosinophil	40	$\frac{50}{300} \times 200 = 33.3$	6.7	44.89	1.348
					Σ 7.297

2–30 for specimens. Assume that the low control is selected from the vertical columns and the high control from the horizontal. The placement of the controls would be as follows:

Day	Low	High
1	9	5
2	29	3
3	11	7
4	25	19
5	27	18
6	2	9
7	7	6

Many computers will generate suitable random numbers, and large tables of random numbers are to be found in statistical handbooks.

Linear Regression Bivariate data (x, y points) that can be represented and analyzed by the mathematics of the straight line are said to be *linear*. Linear analysis is used extensively in method comparison experiments, calibration, predicting future val-

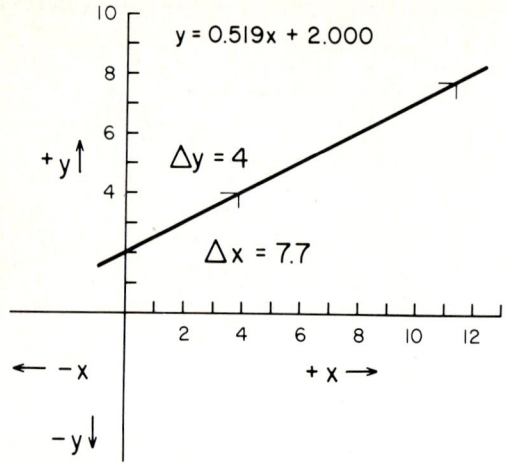

FIGURE 2-3
The basic features of the straight line; positive coordinates. (*Source:* Weisbrot IM: *Statistics for the Clinical Laboratory.* Philadelphia, JB Lippincott, 1985, p 32.)

ues, and, of course, in testing new methods for linearity. Often simple calibration points can be plotted on graph paper and drawn mechanically. But most such data require more arithmetic manipulation.

Data are said to be linear when they can be represented as the equation of a line:

$$y = mx + b$$

where y = dependent variable values
x = independent variable values
m = slope = proportionality constant = regression coefficient = $\Delta y/\Delta x$
b = y intercept, when $x = 0$

Figure 2-3 illustrates these features. Slopes and intercepts may be positive or negative.

Least squares analysis is the usual technique for linear regression. The matrix for calculation is shown in Table 2-4. Slope for n (x, y) points is calculated as

$$m = \frac{n \sum xy - (\sum x)(\sum y)}{n \sum x^2 - (\sum x)^2}$$

The y-intercept is calculated as

$$b = \bar{y} - m\bar{x}$$

TABLE 2-4
LEAST SQUARES LINEAR REGRESSION
(BUN Automated versus Manual)

x	y	x²	y²	xy	y_c	$(y_c - y)$	$(y_c - y)^2$
10	8	100	64	80	10.724	2.724	7.420
13	12	169	144	156	13.532	1.532	2.347
15	16	225	256	240	15.404	−0.596	0.355
18	20	324	400	360	18.212	−1.788	3.197
20	24	400	576	480	20.084	−3.916	15.335
25	22	625	484	550	24.764	2.764	7.640
28	26	784	676	728	27.572	1.572	2.471
35	39	1225	1521	1365	34.124	−4.876	23.775
44	42	1936	1764	1848	42.548	0.548	0.300
52	48	2704	2304	2496	50.036	2.036	4.145
Σ 260	257	8492	8189	8303		0.000	66.985
x̄ 26.0	25.7						
s 13.9	13.3						

$$(S_{y \cdot x})^2 = \frac{66.985}{n - 2}; \quad S_{y \cdot x} = \sqrt{\frac{66.985}{8}} = 2.89$$

Source: Weisbrot IM: *Statistics for the Clinical Laboratory.* Philadelphia, JB Lippincott, 1985, p 34.

From the data of Table 2-4,

$$m = \frac{10(8{,}303) - (260 \times 257)}{10(8{,}492) - (260)^2} = \frac{16{,}210}{17{,}320} = 0.936$$

$$b = 25.7 - (0.936)26.0 = 1.364$$

The regression of y on x is

$$y = 0.936x - 1.364$$

As an **average** relationship, y increases proportionately only 93.6 percent as much as each x, with each y-value having a fixed or systematic bias requiring the addition of 1.364 to bring x and y into agreement.

The least squares mathematics fits a line through the data points such that the sum of the squares of the vertical distance of each y-value from the line is a minimum.

The deviation of points around the line is expressed as $S_{y \cdot x}$. Also called the standard error of the estimate, "S sub y on x" is the standard deviation of the data points around the mean as represented by the line. It is determined from the differences between calculated and actual y-values ($y_c - y$) using 2 df (see Table 2-4). It is an estimate of intermethod imprecision.

Approximately ±2 $S_{y \cdot x}$ represents the 95 percent confidence interval of a future single value of y given x. The 95 percent CI of an **average** y given x is

$$\frac{\pm 2S_{y \cdot x}}{\sqrt{n \text{ data pairs}}}$$

More precise estimates require more complex arithmetic. Other derived statistics, such as the variance of the estimate of the slope and of the y-intercept, are best programmed into a computer, for which excellent formats are available.[6] **The major pitfall of least squares is the requirement that x values be known exactly.** Theoretically, only variance in y is permitted. Within limits, however, no serious error is introduced.[7] For those situations with considerable variance in x, the regression method of Deming is suggested.[8]

Chi-Square Test for Linearity The last column of Table 2-4 represents $(O - E)^2$ for the y-values. Divide each by y_c (the expected value) and sum; $\chi^2 = 3.090$. Degrees of freedom are determined as $n - 1$, minus each parameter estimated from the data, of which there are two, m and b; then df = 7. From Appendix 2-4, the critical value is 14.02. We have no reason to infer that the data are not linear.

Correlation Coefficient (r) Linear correlation or Pearson's product moment is a simple agreement statistic that relates two independent measurements on each member of a sample group. The correlation coefficient has no dimension; it can vary between $+1$ and -1. An r of zero implies no correlation at all, $+1$ perfect agreement, and -1 perfect inverse agreement.

Formulas for r: A number of formulas are available; the simplest is

$$r = m(Sx/Sy)$$

where m = slope
Sx = standard deviation of x-values
Sy = standard deviation of y-values

From the data of Table 2-4, the correlation between BUN methods is $r = 0.978$.

Coefficient of Determination (r^2) The amount of variance contributed by the spread of data points from low to high is given by r^2. From the relationship

$$S_{y \cdot x} \sim S_{\text{population}} \sqrt{1 - r^2}$$

$$\frac{S_{y \cdot x}^2}{S_{\text{population}}^2} \sim 1 - r^2$$

the proportion of variance contributed by variation around the line (intermethod imprecision) is estimated. Thus, for $r = 0.9$, $r^2 = 0.81$, leaving 0.19 for 19 percent as the contribution of intermethod imprecision to the total variance, perhaps less clinically advantageous than advertised.

Pitfalls of r Using automated methods, data that are functionally related, such as different methods for sodium, should have high r values of at least around 0.97. In general, the correlation coefficient, like linear regression, is influenced strongly by range of data and outliers. Merely increasing the range can improve the apparent r, without any improvement in the analytical method whatsoever. Certain nonparametric calculations of r are less range dependent.[9] Remember, r refers to linear correlation: Data fitting other functions may yield an r of zero, even though x and y are very predictably related.

Outliers or "Exotic" Values   An outlying value is so far from the central tendency of the sample that it is presumed to belong to a different data set. Such a decision, however, presumes that the underlying data distribution is known. However, what is an outlier for the Gaussian distribution may be perfectly expected in the Poisson distribution. In the random distribution, no value is an outlier.

Common outlier procedures involve excluding data more than $3s$ or $3.5s$ from the mean and recalculating. A suggested outlier procedure based on range excludes a value if the next closest value is more than one third the data range.[10]

A useful statistical technique, which is applicable to the small numbers used in calibrating a QC pool, allows removal of outliers and symmetrical trimming, with good estimates of the standard deviation.[11] However, no outlier rule is perfect, and what may at first appear to be an outlier may be a legitimate value as experience and n increase.[12]

Cumulative Sums (Cusums)   Deviations from the target value of a QC material are added, preserving their positive or negative signs. If the data are plotted, trends toward a loss of control can be seen. Often a V-mask is constructed, and when the plot crosses the boundaries, control is considered lost.[13] Exceeding a predetermined standard deviation interval is a simpler process.[14]

F-Test and t-Test

The F-test for the difference between standard deviations and the t-test for the difference between the means are the most important tests based on Gaussian distribution theory, designed to function with small samples of around 30 or so. Conceptually, these tests function by determining whether the confidence intervals of the estimates of the parameters in question overlap sufficiently that they may be considered as samples from the same population; or they overlap so little that they may well be from different underlying populations.

F-Test on the Variance   If the ratios of the variances, corrected for df, exceed critical values (F-table, Appendix 2-6), then they are very likely different.

$$F_{ratio} = \frac{\text{variance } A_{(n-1\ df)}}{\text{variance } B_{(n-1\ df)}}$$

To determine whether the precision of Technologist C is different from Technologist B (Table 2-1), we have

$$F = \frac{0.2704}{0.0784} = 3.449$$

From Appendix 2-6 for 7 df numerator and 9 df denominator, critical $F = 3.29$. Because it is a 95 percent table (alpha $= 0.05$), we are 95 percent certain that chance alone did not cause the difference (reject the null hypothesis), and conclude that a real difference may exist.

t-Test on the Means If the absolute difference between two means is such that they are separated by a multiple of standard errors of the mean, the means well may be from samples of different populations. The basic formula is

$$t = \frac{\bar{x} - \mu_0}{s/\sqrt{n}}$$

The t-distribution is similar to the Z-distribution, but it has large tails and is dependent on df. As df increases, Z- and t-distributions become identical. Many variations of the t-test are available[15]; the Student's and the paired are most often used.

Student's t-Test (t-Independent) The difference between the means of two samples (bias) is divided by the pooled SEm. Note that the pooled SEm is derived from the pooled variances (see p. 25).

$$t = \frac{|\bar{x}_1 - \bar{x}_2|}{\sqrt{\text{pooled variance}\left[\frac{1}{n_1} + \frac{1}{n_2}\right]}} \quad \text{or} \quad \frac{\bar{x}_1 - \bar{x}_2}{\sqrt{\frac{(n_1 - 1)s_1^2 + (n_2 - 1)s_1^2}{n_1 + n_2 - 2} \cdot \left[\frac{1}{n_1} + \frac{1}{n_2}\right]}}$$

From Table 2-1, are the means of Technologists B and C different?

$$t = \frac{|9.42 - 9.28|}{\sqrt{\frac{9(0.0784) + 7(0.2704)}{16} \cdot (0.1 + 0.125)}} = 0.732 \text{ NS}$$

Critical t (16 df) $= 2.120$ two-tailed. We accept the null hypothesis. Chance alone could account for the observed difference at least 95 percent of the time.

The pooled SEm is used because it is the best estimate available from the presumed single underlying population declared by the null hypothesis. Because SEm is so large, the small difference between the means disappears in the imprecision interval. Further, in strict usage, the positive F-test on the variances of B and C precludes using this form of the t-test.

The Paired t-Test (t-Dependent) A more rigorous form of the test germane to the clinical laboratory is the paired t-test, which compares the results of two different methods on the specimen. Are the means of two different glucose methods different (Table 2-5)? In this test, the mean difference (bias) is subtracted from the difference

TABLE 2-5
PAIRED t-TEST
(Glucose Levels, Fasting Men, Each by Two Methods)

	o-Toluidine	Glucose-oxidase	d	d-Bias	(d-Bias)²
1	61	59	2	−0.3	0.09
2	68	68	0	−2.3	5.29
3	71	70	1	−1.3	1.69
4	75	76	−1	−3.3	10.89
5	78	74	4	1.7	2.89
6	84	80	4	1.7	2.89
7	90	81	9	6.7	44.89
8	93	90	3	0.7	0.49
9	98	99	−1	−3.3	10.89
10	105	103	2	−0.3	0.09
$\bar{x}$	82.3	80.0	2.3		Σ80.10
s	14.1	13.9			

Mean difference (bias) = 2.3

$$s_d = \sqrt{\frac{80.1}{n-1}} = 2.98$$

$$t = \frac{\text{bias}}{s_d/\sqrt{n}} = \frac{|\text{bias}| \cdot \sqrt{n}}{s_d} = \frac{2.3 \times 3.16}{2.98} = 2.439$$

Critical $t_{0.95}$ for 9 df = 2.262

Source: Weisbrot IM: *Statistics for the Clinical Laboratory.* Philadelphia, JB Lippincott, 1985, p 26.

between each pair, and the standard deviation of differences (s_d) is used in the calculation:

$$t = \frac{|\text{bias}|}{s_d/\sqrt{n}} \quad \text{or} \quad t = \frac{|\text{bias}| \cdot \sqrt{n}}{s_d}$$

In the example, $t = 2.439$ and exceeds critical t for 9 df in the two-tailed table. The null hypothesis is rejected; that is, a significant difference exists. A Student's test on this data would be nonsignificant: The variance due to the spread of values outweighs the small intermethod imprecision estimated by s_d.

Pitfalls of the t-Test A statistically significant t-test may not always imply a real-world difference, or vice versa. The equation for t indicates that as n increases, t increases; a large s_d (poor agreement between each pair) may yield a small t-value.

One-Tailed versus Two-Tailed Tests A one-tailed test concerns a single direction: Is one mean greater or smaller? A two-tailed test is concerned only with the magnitude: Is the difference, regardless of direction, significant? By convention, two-tailed tests are used. In effect, a large difference must be found before a significant difference can be declared. However, if repeated studies always show the same direction of difference, it may be real.

FIGURE 2-4
Alpha error. A biased sample of a population leads to the conclusion that there are two separate populations. The null hypothesis is falsely rejected. In the .95 statistical tables used in this chapter, alpha = .05.

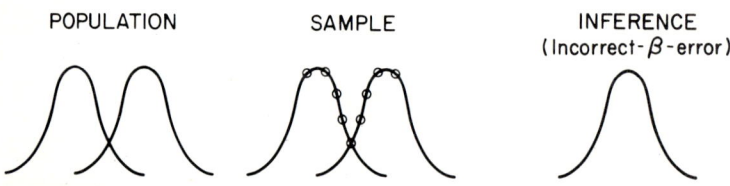

FIGURE 2-5
Beta error. A biased sample of two populations leads to the conclusion that only a single underlying population exists. The null hypothesis is falsely accepted.

Errors of Inference A statistical test can state only the probability of an event, not the fact of the event. Two types of statistical errors of inference may occur.

Alpha Error (Type 1 Error) Because of a biased sample, we declare a difference to exist when it really does not. We falsely reject the null hypothesis. This is implied in the significance level of the table, for example .95, $p < .05$ or 0.99, $p < .01$. There is only less than 5 percent or 1 percent probability that chance alone caused the difference (Fig. 2-4).

Beta Error (Type 2 Error) Because of a biased sample, we declare no difference to exist when it really does (Fig. 2-5). We falsely accept the error. This type of error is frequently overlooked. Graphs for easily estimating beta error are available.[15] The power of a test to yield the correct information is $1 - \beta$.

APPLICATION OF STATISTICS TO QUALITY CONTROL

Quality control procedures are grouped for convenience into two broad categories: (1) internal, or those performed on station, which are concerned largely with control of precision; and (2) external, based largely on proficiency surveys, which provide a guide to accuracy, depending on the criteria established for the correct result.

There is overlap, of course. The meticulous use of analytical balances, reference-quality spectrophotometers, and National Bureau of Standards reference materials can assure accuracy. The standard deviations yielded by the participants of the survey can indicate the state-of-the-art limits, which an individual laboratory should not exceed.

Internal and external quality control both use large pools with multiple constituents and not entirely predictable stability and reactivity with all methods.[16]

Internal Quality Control

Standard Deviation Following the determination of the standard deviation by a daily analysis over 20 to 30 days, a QC chart is prepared to represent the subsequent control observations graphically (Fig. 2-6). Centered on the mean, the $\pm 2s$ and $\pm 3s$ intervals are indicated on the y-axis and the day on the x-axis. In addition to plotting the daily values, some evidence of action to deal with out-of-control values should be documented.

Whatever the theoretical and practical difficulties of using pools and this statistic,[16] pool concentrations are selected for medically significant levels. For many determinations, two pools are used, either at medically significant levels or near the limits of the dynamic range.

The following control rules (decision criteria) may be applied[17]:

1_{2s} One control value exceeds $2s$ from the mean; a warning to examine for other evidence of poor control.

FIGURE 2-6
Levey-Jennings or Shewhart QC chart. (*Source:* Weisbrot IM: *Statistics for the Clinical Laboratory.* Philadelphia, JB Lippincott, 1985, p 64.)

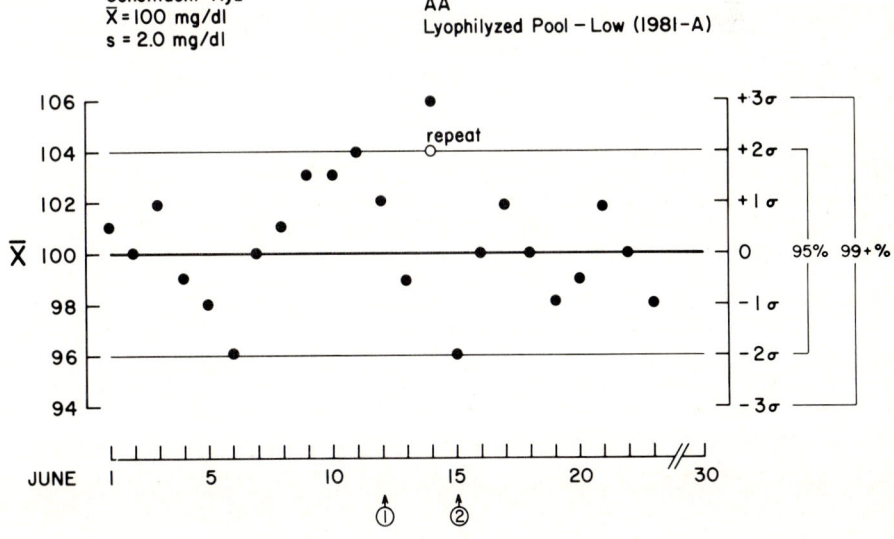

1_{3s} One control value exceeds $3s$ from the mean; the run of patient values should be rejected and the cause determined.

2_{2s} Two consecutive control observations exceed either $+2s$ or $-2s$ from the mean; reject the patient run.

R_{4s} When two pools at different concentrations are used, reject the sum of a $4s$ range between them; that is, one $+2s$ and the other $-2s$ from their respective means.

4_{1s} When four consecutive control results exceed $+1s$ or $-1s$.

Binomial Distribution

$7\bar{x}$, $10\bar{x}$ When 7 to 10 consecutive control results are on the same side of the mean value, reject the run. If the probability of occurrence on each side of the mean is .5, then $p = (.5)^7 = .008$ that a shift has not occurred. Even four such values, as in the 4_{1s} rule, have a probability of only .06.

The fallacy of repeating an out-of-control observation (day 14, Fig. 2-6) is also clear. If the probability of a $3s$ observation being within the expected distribution is less than 0.01, then requiring a successive determination to be so extreme before declaring an out-of-control situation would require an event with a probability $<.0001$.

Although not very rigorous, these considerations may serve as simple guides when inspecting QC charts.

Cusums Although no longer frequently used, cusums may be simplified so that exceeding $2.7s$ from the mean signals loss of control.[14]

Use of Internal QC Control Rules The rules listed above are all discernible by inspection of the QC chart, without additional arithmetic. One could computerize the entire scheme and have an alarm announce loss of control. Regular inspection by an intelligent person is probably less expensive and more flexible.

Loss of Precision and Accuracy The first three control rules (1_{2s}, 1_{3s}, 2_{2s}) indicate primarily diminished precision. The last four (R_{4s}, 4_{1s}, $10\bar{x}$, cusums) suggest a systematic error, perhaps loss of accuracy. These interpretations, of course, are predicated on the accurate calibration and continued stability of the QC pool itself. This is particularly true for the short-lived multipart hematology QC whole blood suspensions. For these, consider the manufacturer's labeled value as a zero point and plot departures up or down. This will overcome the problems of differing assay values. A large, systematic departure from the manufacturer's mean can be evaluated by reference methods.

The true standard deviation of a new pool may take longer than 20 to 30 days to establish and should be recalculated as experience continues.[18] Remove outliers cautiously as recommended.[11] Underestimating the standard deviation leads to frequent alarms and disinclination to act; overestimation leads to longer periods of peace and quiet than one ought to expect in the clinical laboratory.

Power of the Internal QC Rules to Detect Error Extensive computer simulation of the rules has been accomplished; typical curves are illustrated in Fig. 2.7. As the

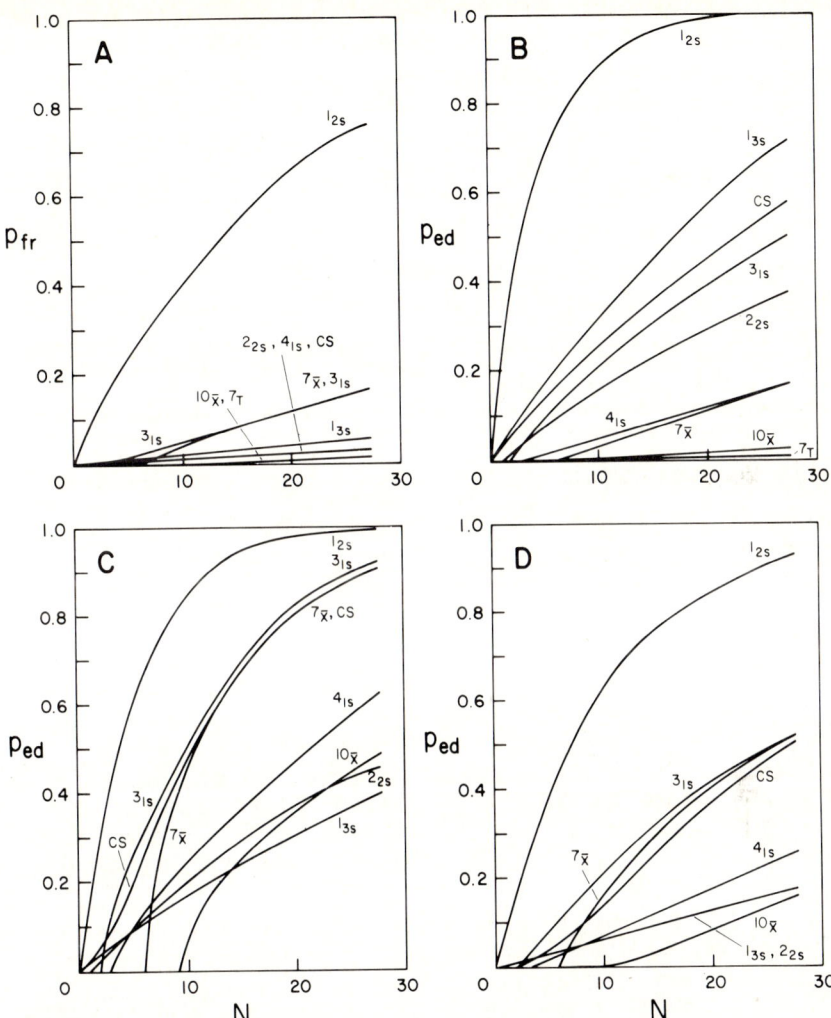

FIGURE 2-7
Responses of QC rules as the number (N) of QC observations increases. A, probability of false rejection of a run as N increases. B, probability of correctly detecting a 50 percent increase in random errors. C, probability of correctly detecting a systematic shift equivalent to one standard deviation in magnitude. D, probability of correctly detecting systematic drift during a run equal to one standard deviation. (*Source:* Modified from Westgard JO, Groth T, Aronsson T, et al: Performance characteristics of rules for internal quality control. *Clin Chem* 1977, 23:1857.)

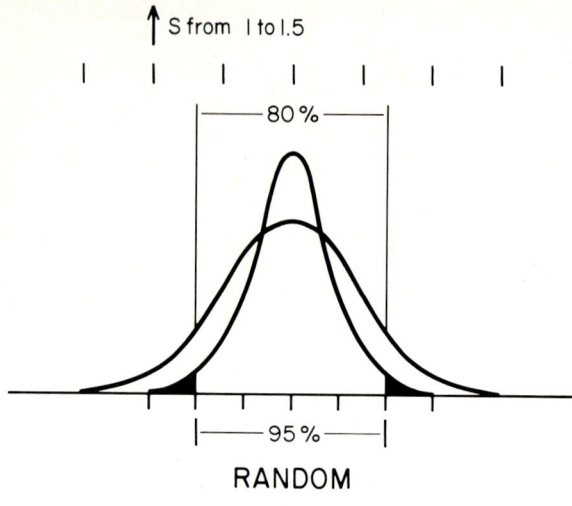

FIGURE 2-8a
The standard deviation of the analytic method has increased by 50 percent. The central 4s (95 percent) interval of the control chart is now equivalent to about the central 2.7s of the actual behavior of the method, or about the central 80 percent of values. Thus only 20 percent of the QC values will give an out-of-control signal.

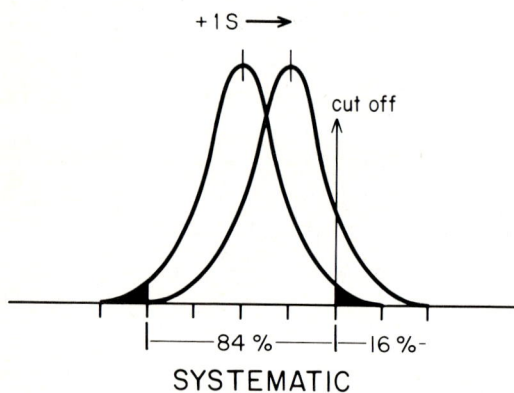

FIGURE 2-8b
The mean of the analytic method has shifted upward the equivalent of 1s (without a change in precision). Thus the central 4s (95 percent interval) of the control chart is no longer truly central with respect to the method. It corresponds to 3s below and 1s above the new shifted mean; this is equivalent to 84 percent of the QC values appearing "in control" and only 16 percent giving an out-of-control signal.

number of QC determinations increases, the likelihood of error detection increases $(1 - \beta)$, but the probability of a false out-of-control signal (β) also rises. Observe that the probability of false error detection is low (about .05 for 1_{2s}), but that the probability of error detection with one or two QC observations is also relatively low, seldom greater than 0.2.

The sensitivity (or lack of sensitivity) of the 1_{2s} rule in detecting increases in random or in systematic error may be appreciated from Figures 2-8a and b. In a single QC determination, a 50 percent increase in standard deviation of the analytic method will be detected only about 20 percent of the time; 80 percent of the time the result will fall in the expected 95 percent interval. Similarly, Figure 2-8b illustrates the effect of a one-standard-deviation upward systematic shift of the analytic method. Eighty-four percent of the time, a single QC determination will fall within the previously determined limits and indicate good control.

The F-Test When standard deviation of a well-established pool appears to have increased, use the F-test with appropriate df for the numerator and infinite df for the denominator (σ is presumed to be known).

The t-Test When a gradual drift trend is observed in a QC pool, regress the observed values (y) against the day of the month (x, $1 - 30$). If there is no drift, the slope of the line should be zero. Do a t-test; is the slope different from zero?

$$t = \frac{\text{slope}}{\sqrt{\frac{(S_{y \cdot x})^2}{\Sigma(x - \bar{x})^2}}} \qquad df = n - 2 (x, y \text{ pairs})$$

Internal QC—Chi Square and Binomial Theorom Applied to Hematology
Comparisons of a three-part, automated differential leukocyte count against the percentage distribution of 100-cell counts gave many positive tests, indicating poor agreement. We pooled the results of twelve 100-cell counts by 12 technologists. These 1200 cell counts now gave good agreement of the **percentage** cell distribution by chi square, but we noted a systematic tendency of higher monocyte counts at the expense of granulocytes by the automated count. Grouping the data into lymphocytes and nonlymphocytes and calculating the standard error of the binomial distribution, we found that the overall standard error of technologists was about 4.6 percent, whereas about ± 1.1 percent was expected in theory from a count of 1200. This indicated that problems of cell distribution on the smears and perhaps lack of consistent diagnostic criteria were present. But, as a 100-cell count, the technologists functioned as predicted. The standard deviation of lymphocytes versus nonlymphocytes on 20 replicate automated counts was about ± 0.6 percent. From this, it was estimated that the instrument sorts about 5000 cells.

Multiple QC Samples Often, more than one tray of samples, each with its own QC pool, are run. A QC chart using the SEm can be devised. If three trays are always run, the mean of the three QC observations can be plotted with $\pm 2s/\sqrt{3}$ and $\pm 3s/\sqrt{3}$ limits indicated, as an additional chart.

Use of Patient Data Pools and preserved cell suspensions are not exposed to the insults that patient specimens receive during collection, transport, and processing. Method-sample interactions may be different for patient specimens. Data from actual patient specimens can be examined. Inspecting results for unexplained large changes from previous values, called delta checks, has been useful,[19] as have the expected numerical relations among such data as the electrolyte series.[20] These are best accomplished routinely with on-line computer assistance. Individually they may be applied during investigation of specific problems and during spot checks of patients' charts.

Patient Data: Application of the Central Tendency To discover systematic error or loss of calibrational accuracy, statistical maneuvers with routine patient data are useful. These maneuvers function best for those tests performed routinely, so that many individuals who have values within the reference interval are tested.

Average of Normals (AON) Groups of patient values within the reference interval are averaged. A control chart is prepared assuming the reference interval to be $+2s$ and $-2s$ around the mean. If sets of 16 are used and the reference interval is 100 ± 20, the 95 percent limits on the chart are $100 \pm 20 \sqrt{16}$. The SEm has a Gaussian distribution even if the underlying population does not. Many years ago our AON chart for glucose rose sharply. Standards and controls were correct. It turned out that a new dietician was offering coffee with sugar to patients whose breakfasts had to be delayed for their blood tests.

Extensive computer simulation indicates that the method works best when the standard deviation of the population is relatively small compared with the standard deviation of the method and the number of patient values is relatively large.[21]

Bull's moving average has been applied extensively in hematology and is particularly useful when applied to erythrocyte indices—MCV, MCH, MCHC—but has been used for other determinations as well.[22] The differences of groups of patients (usually 20) from the mean population value for the constituent are subjected to a complex algorithm. Essentially, departures from the central tendency are minimized by taking the square root of the difference of each value from the population mean, preserving its + or − sign, dividing by N, and adding to the population mean. The resultant series of control values are plotted. Reports have been favorable,[23] and we have detected faulty reagents that affected patient samples but not stabilized cell suspensions (see also Chapter 9).

External Quality Control

Proficiency Surveys Proficiency surveys, although too often regarded as a police function rather than a professional QC tool, have led to great analytical advances. Except for new and exotic tests by difficult techniques, referees now serve only to assure that the analytes have survived manufacture and distribution, and that expected target levels have been attained.

For most constituents the mean of the participants serves as the target or "correct" value; often, each method cohort will have its own mean target (and also standard deviation). Extensive studies, enlisting the National Bureau of Standards to perform analyses by definitive methods, have substantiated this approach.[24] Other approaches also are taken (see Chapters 6 and 14).

The paired *t*-test applied to the annual series of participant values against the target value for the particular method will indicate the statistically significant systematic error. Often survey data will also be available for a well-accepted method, a well-documented method, or a method of well-understood bias.

The standard deviation of a particular method represents the data after combing for obvious errors in transcription and obvious exotic values. Initial calculation of the standard deviation may be followed by the exclusion of values beyond $3s$, and then a final calculation. Some surveys provide standard deviation interval (see above) as the basis for grading. Participant values beyond $2s$ may be regarded as signs of poor proficiency. Obviously, then, about 5 percent or more of participants are at risk for failure.

The F-test may be used to decide if a failing participant value is associated with wide QC pool limits. Select the QC pool with the concentration closest to the target value. Perform the F-test with $(n - 1)$ df for the calibrational variance as the numerator over infinite df for the survey variance.

Even simpler, one can place the offending value on the appropriate QC chart. If it is within control limits, the standard deviation of the pool may be too lenient, and the method may not be in adequate control for the state of the art.

Nonquantitative Data

Nonquantitative or qualitative data usually involve subjective decisions that are not easily managed by usual QC statistics.

Nominal Data Many diagnostic tests report the presence or absence of a disease or abnormality. These range from tissue and cytological diagnosis to tests for occult blood. Not only do these tests suffer from interobserver error, but repeat observations by the same person may disagree.

Receiver-operator curves (ROC) that plot true positives against false positives may define the usefulness of nominal decisions.[25] However, construction of these curves requires knowledge of the final outcome, the opinion of "Olympian" experts, or a consensus of referees or participants, usually 80 percent.

Ordinal Data Results may be graded as to intensity or seriousness of the observation, such as mild, moderate, and severe dysplasia; 1+ to 4+ intensity of color change; negative, weakly reactive, reactive syphilis serology.[26] In the scale, it is possible to assign a weighted value penalizing the direction of the most serious error. Thus, confusing a weakly reactive with a reactive serology carries less penalty than confusing negative with reactive.[27] This allows a quantitative estimate of performance.

Chance Agreement Observed agreement may not, by itself, be a reliable guide to proficiency. Agreement may occur by chance. Two observers may both categorize 60 percent of cells as benign and 40 percent as malignant; the binomial theorem indicates agreement in 52 percent of cases by chance alone ($0.60^2 + 0.40^2 = 0.52$).[26]

Titers Test results reported as titers have always exhibited great variability within and between laboratories. Converting the data to logarithms allows the determination of geometric means and geometric standard deviation, which permits more precise quality control than the usual one-tube dilution allowance.[28]

REFERENCES

1 Williams GM, Schork MA: Some statistical implications of rounding in College of American Pathologists Survey. *Am J Clin Pathol* 1976, 66:162.
2 Weisbrot IM, Ewing NS: An evaluation of the Haema-Count MK-4 S platelet counting system. *Am J Clin Pathol* 1974, 62:693.
3 Greenberg ER, Beck JR: The effects of sample size on reticulocyte counting and stool examination. *Arch Pathol Lab Med* 1984, 108:396.
4 Rumke CL: The statistically expected variability in differential leukocyte counting, in Koepke JA (ed): *Differential Leukocyte Counting.* Chicago, College of American Pathologists, 1977, pp 39–45.
5 Weisbrot IM: *Statistics for the Clinical Laboratory.* Philadelphia, JB Lippincott, 1985, pp 156–158.
6 Natrella MG: *Experimental Statistics.* National Bureau of Standards Handbook 91. Government Printing Office, 1963, chap. 5.
7 Cornbleet PJ, Gochman N: Incorrect least-squares regression coefficients in method comparison analysis. *Clin Chem* 1979, 25:432.
8 Hathaway NN: Some comments on linear regression analysis by the method of WE Deming, letter to the editor. *Clin Chem* 1980, 26:1511.
9 Feinstein AR, Kramer MS: Clinical biostatistics LII, A primer on quantitative indexes of association. *Clin Pharmacol* 1980, 28:130.
10 Reed AH, Henry RJ, Mason WB: Influence of the statistical method used on the resulting estimate of normal range. *Clin Chem* 1971, 17:275.
11 Healy MRJ: Outliers in clinical chemistry quality control schemes. *Clin Chem* 1979, 25:675.
12 Martin HF, Gudzinowicz BJ, Fanger H: *Normal Values in Clinical Chemistry.* New York, Marcel Dekker, 1975, p 452.
13 Thiers RE, Gaw TW, Reed AH, Oliver LK: Sample stability: A suggested definition and method of determination. *Clin Chem* 1976, 22:176.
14 Westgard JO, Groth T, Aronsson T, deVerdier CH: Combined Shewhart-cusum control chart for improved quality control in clinical chemistry. *Clin Chem* 1977, 23:1881.
15 Natrella MG: *Experimental Statistics.* National Bureau of Standards Handbook 91. Government Printing Office, 1963, chap. 3.
16 Bretaudiere, J-P, Dumont G, Rej R, Bailly M: Suitability of control materials: General principles and methods of investigation. *Clin Chem* 1981, 27:798.
17 Westgard JO, Groth T: A multi-rule Shewhart chart for quality control in clinical chemistry. *Clin Chem* 1981, 27:493.
18 Martin HF, Gudzinowicz BJ, Fanger H; *Normal Values in Clinical Chemistry.* New York, Marcel Dekker, 1975, pp 451–453.
19 Nosanchuk JS, Gottman AW: CUMS and delta checks: A systematic approach to quality control. *Am J Clin Pathol* 1974, 62:707.
20 Cembrowski G, Westgard JO: Performance characteristics of quality control procedures employing patient data algorithms, abstracted. *Am J Clin Pathol* 1982, 78:265.
21 Cembrowski GS, Chandler EP, Westgard JO: Assessment of "average of normals" quality control procedures and guielines for implementation. *Am J Clin Pathol* 1984, 81:492.
22 Bull BS: A statistical approach to quality control, in Lewis SM, Coster JF (eds): *Quality Control in Haematology.* New York, Academic Press, 1975, chap. 9.
23 Koepke JA, Protextor TJ: Quality assurance for multichannel hematology instruments. *Am J Clin Pathol* 1981, 75:28.
24 Gilbert RK: Accuracy of clinical laboratories by comparison with definitive methods. *Am J Clin Pathol* 1978, 70:450.

25 Robertson EA, Zweig MH, Van Steirteghem AC: Evaluating the clinical efficacy of laboratory tests. *Am J Clin Pathol* 1983, 79:78.
26 Cicchetti DV: Assessing observer and method variability in medicine. *Conn Med* 1978, 42:253.
27 Cicchetti DV, Keitges P, Barnett RN: How many is enough? A statistical study of proficiency testing of syphilis serology. *Health Lab Sci* 1974, 11:299.
28 Singer JM, Edberg SC, Selinger M, Amram M: Quality control of the latex-fixation test. *Am J Clin Pathol* 1979, 72:591.

APPENDIX 2-1

ABBREVIATED TABLE FOR CONFIDENCE LIMITS FOR SIGMA: CENTRAL 95% INTERVAL (TWO-SIDED)

Degrees of freedom	Upper limit	Lower limit	Degrees of freedom	Upper limit	Lower limit
5	2.248	0.5899	30	1.321	0.7909
6	2.052	0.6143	35	1.291	0.8039
7	1.918	0.6344	40	1.268	0.8146
8	1.820	0.6513	50	1.234	0.8314
9	1.746	0.6657	60	1.210	0.8443
10	1.686	0.6784	70	1.192	0.8544
15	1.509	0.7240	80	1.178	0.8627
20	1.417	0.7535	90	1.166	0.8697
25	1.360	0.7747	100	1.157	0.8757

Source: Adapted from Lindley DV et al: Tables for making inferences about the variance of a normal distribution. *Biometrika* 1960, 47:433–438.

APPENDIX 2-2

SIMPLIFIED TABLE OF AREAS UNDER THE TAILS OF A NORMAL CURVE

z	One-tailed	Two-tailed
0.0	0.500	1.000
0.1	0.460	0.920
0.2	0.421	0.841
0.3	0.382	0.764
0.4	0.345	0.689
0.5	0.309	0.617
0.6	0.274	0.549
0.7	0.242	0.484
0.8	0.212	0.424
0.9	0.184	0.368
1.0	0.159	0.317
1.1	0.136	0.271
1.2	0.115	0.230
1.3	0.097	0.194
1.4	0.081	0.162

APPENDIX 2-2 (continued)

SIMPLIFIED TABLE OF AREAS UNDER THE TAILS OF A NORMAL CURVE

Z	One-tailed	Two-tailed
1.5	0.067	0.134
1.6	0.055	0.110
1.7	0.045	0.089
1.8	0.036	0.072
1.9	0.029	0.057
2.0	0.023	0.046
2.1	0.018	0.036
2.2	0.014	0.028
2.3	0.011	0.021
2.4	0.008	0.016
2.5	0.006	0.012
2.6	0.005	0.009
2.7	0.003	0.007
2.8	0.003	0.005
2.9	0.002	0.004
3.0	0.001	0.003

APPENDIX 2-3

EXPONENTS OF e AND FACTORIALS

Negative exponents of e	Factorials
$e^{-0} = 1.0$	$0! = 1.00000000$
$e^{-1} = 0.367879$	$1! = 1.00000000$
$e^{-2} = 0.13533528$	$2! = 2.00000000$
$e^{-3} = 0.04978706$	$3! = 6.00000000$
$e^{-4} = 0.01831563$	$4! = 24.0000000$
$e^{-5} = 0.00673794$	$5! = 120.000000$
$e^{-6} = 0.00247875$	$6! = 720.0$
$e^{-7} = 0.00091188$	$7! = 5,040$
$e^{-8} = 0.00033546$	$8! = 43,320$
$e^{-9} = 0.00012340$	$9! = 362,880$
$e^{-10} = 0.00004539$	$10! = 3,628,900$
$e^{-11} = 0.00001670$	$11! = 39,916,800$
$e^{-12} = 0.00000614$	$12! = 479,001,600$
$e^{-13} = 0.00000226$	$13! = 6,227,020,800$
$e^{-14} = 0.00000083$	$14! = 8.71783 \times 10^{10}$
$e^{-15} = 0.00000030$	$15! = 1.30767 \times 10^{12}$
$e^{-16} = 0.00000011$	$16! = 2.09228 \times 10^{13}$
$e^{-17} = 0.00000004$	$17! = 3.55687 \times 10^{14}$
	$18! = 6.40237 \times 10^{15}$
	$19! = 1.21645 \times 10^{17}$
	$20! = 2.43290 \times 10^{18}$

Source: Weisbrot IM: *Statistics for the Clinical Laboratory.* Philadelphia, JB Lippincott, 1985, p 184.

APPENDIX 2-4

SIGNIFICANT χ^2, 95%

Degrees of freedom	1	2	3	4	5	6	7	8	9	10
χ^2	3.84	5.99	7.81	9.49	11.07	12.09	14.07	15.51	16.92	18.31

APPENDIX 2-5

RANDOM NUMBERS

79	50	05	53	07	19	70	18	09	46	00	13	65
29	79	71	90	28	28	69	42	75	99	98	26	06
11	96	65	49	40	73	90	81	47	03	08	20	66
64	85	21	36	58	22	66	35	80	27	91	68	69
42	35	26	37	42	90	61	06	07	40	93	16	45
25	77	63	39	93	32	84	26	52	55	27	69	88
27	78	66	88	45	75	16	57	52	52	69	30	48
62	42	44	81	17	29	55	05	02	45	62	40	99
77	32	50	35	36	34	62	30	57	15	63	88	21
69	64	76	20	27	82	89	70	04	63	22	82	63
01	74	45	12	91	88	03	84	12	29	81	69	61
84	55	68	02	95	92	28	06	51	84	43	56	42
65	58	27	24	40	60	10	25	80	00	33	60	54
76	32	72	62	55	33	78	78	53	43	85	76	53
27	22	34	31	46	84	91	81	30	21	28	32	20
37	25	79	46	34	40	94	05	06	40	62	29	72
42	76	65	06	74	18	08	47	01	84	35	11	04
62	20	56	86	85	16	03	85	68	02	33	14	91
28	41	32	35	67	96	75	42	46	33	69	62	44
34	81	80	00	23	31	51	87	88	44	08	92	42
97	85	98	77	78	74	44	29	53	13	58	28	05
05	29	94	82	60	16	04	83	89	14	94	61	33
39	31	00	62	21	44	20	46	09	93	78	56	29
94	73	44	85	60	37	66	31	01	38	70	54	28
78	24	28	74	80	60	96	83	54	92	06	48	05
86	26	62	89	63	43	63	51	00	46	49	26	99

Source: Weisbrot IM: *Statistics for the Clinical Laboratory.* Philadelphia, JB Lippincott, 1985, p 186.

APPENDIX 2-6

F-RATIO (F 0.95)

	\multicolumn{10}{c}{Degrees of freedom for numerator}
	1	2	3	4	5	6	7	8	9	10
1	161	200	216	225	230	234	237	239	241	242
2	18.5	19.0	19.2	19.2	19.3	19.3	19.4	19.4	19.4	19.4
3	10.1	9.55	9.28	9.12	9.01	8.94	8.89	8.85	8.81	8.79
4	7.71	6.94	6.59	6.39	6.26	6.16	6.09	6.04	6.00	5.96
5	6.61	5.79	5.41	5.19	5.05	4.95	4.88	4.82	4.77	4.74
6	5.99	5.14	4.76	4.53	4.39	4.28	4.21	4.15	4.10	4.06
7	5.59	4.74	4.35	4.12	3.97	3.87	3.79	3.73	3.68	3.64
8	5.32	4.46	4.07	3.84	3.69	3.58	3.50	3.44	3.39	3.35
9	5.12	4.26	3.86	3.63	3.48	3.37	3.29	3.23	3.18	3.14
10	4.96	4.10	3.71	3.48	3.33	3.22	3.14	3.07	3.02	2.98
11	4.84	3.98	3.59	3.36	3.20	3.09	3.01	2.95	2.90	2.85
12	4.75	3.89	3.49	3.26	3.11	3.00	2.91	2.85	2.80	2.75
13	4.67	3.81	3.41	3.18	3.03	2.92	2.83	2.77	2.71	2.67
14	4.60	3.74	3.34	3.11	2.96	2.85	2.76	2.70	2.65	2.60
15	4.54	3.68	3.29	3.06	2.90	2.79	2.71	2.64	2.59	2.54
16	4.49	3.63	3.24	3.01	2.85	2.74	2.66	2.59	2.54	2.49
17	4.45	3.59	3.20	2.96	2.81	2.70	2.61	2.55	2.49	2.45
18	4.41	3.55	3.16	2.93	2.77	2.66	2.58	2.51	2.46	2.41
19	4.38	3.52	3.13	2.90	2.74	2.63	2.54	2.48	2.42	2.38
20	4.35	3.49	3.10	2.87	2.71	2.60	2.51	2.45	2.39	2.35
21	4.32	3.47	3.07	2.84	2.68	2.57	2.49	2.42	2.37	2.32
22	4.30	3.44	3.05	2.82	2.66	2.55	2.46	2.40	2.34	2.30
23	4.28	3.42	3.03	2.80	2.64	2.53	2.44	2.37	2.32	2.27
24	4.26	3.40	3.01	2.78	2.62	2.51	2.42	2.36	2.30	2.25
25	4.24	3.39	2.99	2.76	2.60	2.49	2.40	2.34	2.28	2.24
30	4.17	3.32	2.92	2.69	2.53	2.42	2.33	2.27	2.21	2.16
40	4.08	3.23	2.84	2.61	2.45	2.34	2.25	2.18	2.12	2.08
60	4.00	3.15	2.76	2.53	2.37	2.25	2.17	2.10	2.04	1.99
120	3.92	3.07	2.68	2.45	2.29	2.18	2.09	2.02	1.96	1.91
∞	3.84	3.00	2.60	2.37	2.21	2.10	2.01	1.94	1.88	1.83

(Row labels = Degrees of freedom for denominator)

Source: Merrington M, Thompson CM: Tables of percentage points of the inverted beta (F) distribution. *Biometrika* 1943, 33:73, by permission.

Degrees of freedom for numerator								
12	15	20	24	30	40	60	120	∞
244	246	248	249	250	251	252	253	254
19.4	19.4	19.4	19.5	19.5	19.5	19.5	19.5	19.5
8.74	8.70	8.66	8.64	8.62	8.59	8.57	8.55	8.53
5.91	5.86	5.80	5.77	5.75	5.72	5.69	5.66	5.63
4.68	4.62	4.56	4.53	4.50	4.46	4.43	4.40	4.37
4.00	3.94	3.87	3.84	3.81	3.77	3.74	3.70	3.67
3.57	3.51	3.44	3.41	3.38	3.34	3.30	3.27	3.23
3.28	3.22	3.15	3.12	3.08	3.04	3.01	2.97	2.93
3.07	3.01	2.94	2.90	2.86	2.83	2.79	2.75	2.71
2.91	2.85	2.77	2.74	2.70	2.66	2.62	2.58	2.54
2.79	2.72	2.65	2.61	2.57	2.53	2.49	2.45	2.40
2.69	2.62	2.54	2.51	2.47	2.43	2.38	2.34	2.30
2.60	2.53	2.46	2.42	2.38	2.34	2.30	2.25	2.21
2.53	2.46	2.39	2.35	2.31	2.27	2.22	2.18	2.13
2.48	2.40	2.33	2.29	2.25	2.20	2.16	2.11	2.07
2.42	2.35	2.28	2.24	2.19	2.15	2.11	2.06	2.01
2.38	2.31	2.23	2.19	2.15	2.10	2.06	2.01	1.96
2.34	2.27	2.19	2.15	2.11	2.06	2.02	1.97	1.92
2.31	2.23	2.16	2.11	2.07	2.03	1.98	1.93	1.88
2.28	2.20	2.12	2.08	2.04	1.99	1.95	1.90	1.84
2.25	2.18	2.10	2.05	2.01	1.96	1.92	1.87	1.81
2.23	2.15	2.07	2.03	1.98	1.94	1.89	1.84	1.78
2.20	2.13	2.05	2.01	1.96	1.91	1.86	1.81	1.76
2.18	2.11	2.03	1.98	1.94	1.89	1.84	1.79	1.73
2.16	2.09	2.01	1.96	1.92	1.87	1.82	1.77	1.71
2.09	2.01	1.93	1.89	1.84	1.79	1.74	1.68	1.62
2.00	1.92	1.84	1.79	1.74	1.69	1.64	1.58	1.51
1.92	1.84	1.75	1.70	1.65	1.59	1.53	1.47	1.39
1.83	1.75	1.66	1.61	1.55	1.50	1.43	1.35	1.25
1.75	1.67	1.57	1.52	1.46	1.39	1.32	1.22	1.00

APPENDIX 2-7

t-TEST (CRITICAL VALUES OF $t_{0.95}$)

Degrees of freedom	One-tailed	Two-tailed
5	2.015	2.571
6	1.943	2.447
7	1.895	2.365
8	1.860	2.306
9	1.833	2.262
10	1.812	2.228
11	1.796	2.201
12	1.782	2.179
13	1.771	2.160
14	1.761	2.145
15	1.753	2.131
16	1.746	2.120
17	1.740	2.110
18	1.734	2.101
19	1.729	2.093
20	1.725	2.086
25	1.708	2.080
30	1.697	2.042
40	1.684	2.021
60	1.671	2.000
120	1.658	1.980
∞	1.645	1.960

To determine the CI of the mean for small n, use the t-table instead of the Z-table. Multiply the SEm by the t-value for the appropriate df, two-tailed for the usual centered CI or one-tailed for an upper or lower limit (95%).

CHAPTER 3

GENERAL PRINCIPLES OF PATIENT PREPARATION AND SPECIMEN HANDLING

Edward P. Fody, M.D.

All laboratory testing can be divided into three phases: preanalytical, analytical, and postanalytical. By far, most attention is given to the analytical phase, with millions of dollars being spent on prodigious instrumentation designed to produce results quickly and cost effectively. The postanalytical phase also has received a great deal of attention recently, as laboratory computers assume more of the burden of reporting results in a rapid and accurate fashion.

By contrast, the preanalytical phase of laboratory testing, which is the interval from when the clinician orders a laboratory procedure until the specimen is analyzed, has not received a great deal of study. This lack of study is unfortunate because errors in the preanalytical phase have great potential for producing erroneous results. Figure 3-1 illustrates the cycle for ordering and reporting laboratory tests. Any break in the cycle will result in the clinician failing to receive the report, and the laboratory will be blamed even though it controls only half the cycle.

The preanalytical phase of laboratory testing can be subdivided into two parts, patient preparation and specimen handling. Patient preparation concerns any nonintrinsic patient factor, other than disease, that might alter laboratory results. These factors include fasting, posture, preparation of collection site, diurnal variation, physical activity, and medication. Specimen handling deals with the container into which the specimen is placed and subsequent manipulations prior to analysis.

PATIENT PREPARATION

Prior to collection of a blood specimen, a patient should be fasting, preferably at least 12 hours, for two major reasons. Lipemia, as occurs after a fatty meal, causes direct interference with the optical determinations used in many laboratory measurements

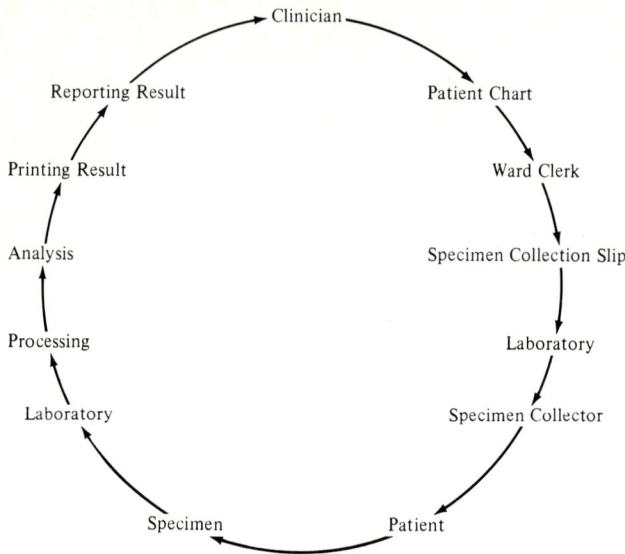

FIGURE 3-1
Ordering and reporting cycle for laboratory tests.

(see p. 65 and Chapter 4). Also, recent meals directly alter certain analytes, making sequential comparison difficult if the variable of food ingestion is not controlled.

Effects of Meals

Recent food ingestion primarily affects blood analytes, whereas urine values show only small changes. Triglycerides may rise more than 10-fold after a fatty meal and require 12 hours to return to basal values.[1] Cholesterol levels generally reflect long-term dietary trends and are little affected by recent meals; however, this is not true for all patients.[2] A meal high in protein tends to increase urea nitrogen concentration, but has only a modest effect on glucose. In contrast, a carbohydrate load elevates blood glucose rapidly, with levels returning to baseline in about 3 hours. Table 3-1 summarizes the effect of meals on some selected analytes.[3]

Prolonged fasting may also affect laboratory results. In this condition, decreases in levels of C_3, albumin, prealbumin, and transferrin have been documented, and glucose levels tend to decline. In starvation, serum bilirubin increases owing to decreases in bilirubin clearance.[4-6]

Diurnal Variation

Diurnal variation exists for many analytes, making results uninterpretable if specimen collection time is unknown. These diurnal variations may be intrinsic (usually dependent on patterns of sleep and wakefulness) or may be secondary to meals, exercise, or other activities that tend to occur at certain times of the day.

TABLE 3-1
EFFECT OF RECENT MEALS ON SELECTED BLOOD ANALYTES

Analyte	Change
Glucose*	Increase
Alkaline phosphatase†	Increase
Triglycerides†	Increase
β-Lipoprotein	Increase
Urea nitrogen‡	Increase
Uric acid‡	Increase
Phosphate*	Decrease
Cholesterol	Little change
pH	Slight decrease
Amino acids‡	Increase
Insulin*	Increase
Bilirubin	Increase
Lactate	Increase
Pyruvate	Increase
Sodium	Increase

*Effect most pronounced following meal high in carbohydrates.
†Effect most pronounced following meal high in fat.
‡Effect most pronounced following meal high in protein.
Source: Young, DS: Blood variability, in Brown SS, Mitchell FL, Young DS (eds): *Chemical Diagnosis of Disease.* New York, Elsevier North Holland, 1979.

Corticosteroids were among the first analytes for which circadian variation was described. In healthy individuals, corticotropin (ACTH) and cortisol secretion peak early in the morning and decline gradually during the day.[7] Growth hormone follows an inverse pattern, peaking shortly after the onset of sleep, at which time cortisol levels are low.[7] Prolactin is secreted maximally during sleep.[8] Although of lesser magnitude, a diurnal pattern similar to that for growth hormone and prolactin occurs with thyrotropin; however, serum thyroxine levels do not reflect this change.[9–11] Posture and sodium intake play important roles in regulating renin-angiotensin-aldosterone secretion, but a diurnal variation exists as well, with the nadir occurring in midafternoon.[3]

Serum protein and albumin concentrations tend to fall during the night, probably due to postural effects.[12] Serum iron is subject to marked variations, but iron-binding capacity tends to remain constant. Some studies indicate that serum iron has a diurnal pattern with peaks in the afternoon.[13] Calcium shows a mild nadir in the afternoon, whereas zinc decreases slightly around midday. Most other metals show little variability.[3] Bilirubin concentration is highest in the morning, probably due to overnight fasting. Electrolytes show only a small diurnal variation in plasma, but urinary changes are greater.[14,15] Serum enzymes do not have a significant variability. Urine tends to be maximally concentrated during the night, at which time urinary creatinine clearance values are lowest.[3] Urinary excretion of enzymes is also high at this time.[16]

The menstrual cycle has profound effect on many analytes. Of course, plasma and urine levels of gonadotropins, prolactin, estrogens, androgens, and progesterone are tied directly to the menstrual phase. Cholesterol is highest just prior to the onset of menstruation and falls at the time of ovulation. Protein, albumin, and globulins are decreased at the time of ovulation, whereas fibrinogen increases at the onset of menstruation. Creatinine, magnesium, uric acid, sodium, and chloride are highest around the time of menstruation, in contrast to phosphate and iron, which tend to be low.[3] The premenstrual syndrome is associated with hyperprolactinemia.[17]

In addition to short-term variability, several analytes show long-term cyclical changes as well, although these are not usually very important. For example, warm weather causes increases in blood and plasma volumes, gamma-globulins, and lactate dehydrogenase, which then decrease with the onset of colder weather.

Posture

Assuming the standing position has a number of important physiologic consequences, including decreases in blood volume, blood pressure, and heart rate. In contrast, reciprocal changes occur when a subject assumes a supine position. Postural changes may be exaggerated in hypertensives[18] and in patients with hypoproteinemia.[19,20]

Statland et al. studied the effect of postural changes on 17 analytes in a group of healthy volunteers.[21] Upon assuming the standing position, increases of 5 percent or more were noted for total protein, albumin, iron, total lipids, cholesterol, alanine aminotransferase, acid phosphatase, and alkaline phosphatase. Increases of less than 5 percent were noted for sodium, potassium, calcium, chloride, phosphate, urea, and creatine.

Substances with significant protein binding show a positive increment upon assuming the erect posture. The amount of increase is roughly proportional to the extent of protein binding. For example, calcium, which is only about 50 percent protein bound, shows a lesser increment than cholesterol, which is mainly bound.[3,22,23] This change should be borne in mind when measuring substances with extensive protein binding, such as thyroxine or phenytoin. Nonprotein-bound components, such as free thyroxine or ionized calcium, are unaffected by changes in posture. Enzymes increase when the patient assumes a standing posture.

Unlike the physiologic changes noted above, very dramatic alterations occur in certain endocrine substances. As the patient changes from the supine to the upright posture, catecholamines, angiotensin, renin, aldosterone, and antidiuretic hormone may increase severalfold, with such changes complete in 15 to 30 min.[24]

Tourniquet Application Time

Although undesirable, it is standard practice to apply a tourniquet for collection of venous blood specimens. Use of a tourniquet causes venous dilation, stasis, and fluid leakage across capillary walls below the point of application. After a short time, hypoxemia and acidosis supervene.

Statland et al. made an extensive study of the effects of tourniquet application on blood analytes.[25] After 1 min of tourniquet application, a 6 percent increase in albumin and a 3 percent increase in calcium occur. After 3 min, increases of 5 percent or more were found in bilirubin, alkaline phosphatase, aspartate aminotransferase, cholesterol, and iron. Generally, the concentration of proteins and protein-bound constituents increases following tourniquet application, whereas filterable substances remain unaltered. Important determinants are the degree and the duration of occlusion.[3]

Potassium and lactate may be elevated by fist flexion during venipuncture.[26] Growth hormone, cortisol, and catecholamines may be increased by the stress of venipuncture.[22,27,28]

Physical Activity

Exercise has a number of effects on blood analytes. Mild exercise causes an increase in blood glucose, which is often followed by increases in cortisol and insulin.[3]

The results of two studies that have examined blood analytes after very severe exercise are summarized in Table 3-2. The most dramatic changes occur in enzymes, especially those associated with muscle, such as creatine kinase, lactate dehydrogenase, and aspartate aminotransferase. King and Statland[32] studied the time course of enzyme elevation following an hour of moderate exercise. Creatine kinase more than doubled its baseline values, peaking approximately 11 hours later. Lesser increases were noted for aspartate aminotransferase, lactate dehydrogenase, and alkaline phosphatase. Apparently, well-trained athletes have much smaller exercise-induced enzyme elevations than untrained ones.[33]

TABLE 3-2
CHANGES IN BLOOD ANALYTES FOLLOWING SEVERE EXERCISE

	Study	
Analyte	Refsum* et al.[29,30]	Riley† et al.[31]
Creatine	+ 40%	+45%
Urea	+ 46%	+31%
Hemoglobin	− 33%	—
β-Hydroxybutyrate	+203%	—
Calcium	− 5.7%	—
Magnesium	− 10%	—
Bicarbonate	− 12%	−17%
Lactate	+113%	—
Potassium	—	+23%
Uric acid	—	+37%
Phosphate	—	+65%

*Change from baseline immediately after finishing 90-km cross-country ski race.
†Change from baseline immediately after completing 40-km foot race.

Other constituents are affected by exertion. Mild exercise increases the creatinine clearance, whereas vigorous exercise lowers it.[34] Short periods of exercise cause a lymphocytosis, although neutrophilia is seen following more prolonged exercise.[35] During and following exercise, angiotensin, renin, and aldosterone levels are increased, but cortisol levels are variable.[3] Thyroxine, growth hormone, and prolactin are elevated during exercise.[36,37] Urinary levels of catecholamines are not increased by exercise unless emotional changes are present; plasma catecholamines (norepinephrine, epinephrine and dopamine), however, are increased by severe exercise.[3,24,38]

Caffeine

Caffeine is present in coffee, tea, many colas, and over-the-counter medications. It is a mild stimulant and mild diuretic that undergoes complicated metabolism. Like theophylline, to which it is chemically related, caffeine is a phosphodiesterase inhibitor. Within hours after ingestion, caffeine elevates plasma levels of triglycerides, free fatty acids, cortisol, and total lipids, but it decreases serum cholesterol.[39,40] Urinary catecholamines are increased as well.[41] Glucose and insulin show little change, even though glucose tolerance may be mildly impaired.[3]

Ethanol

Ethanol ingestion has both acute and long-term effects. Alcohol has a diabetogenic effect, causing an elevation in blood glucose shortly after ingestion, but because it also interferes with glycogenolysis, alcohol produces a delayed hypoglycemic effect.[3] Alcohol in moderate doses has been shown to cause ultrastructural injury to skeletal muscle in healthy volunteers, hence it is not surprising that alcoholics often have elevated levels of creatine kinase.[42,43] Table 3-3 shows the blood analytes that may be altered in healthy individuals following ethanol ingestion. Because chronic alcoholism is a disease, its effects on various laboratory tests fall outside the scope of this chapter; for interested readers, an excellent summary is available.[3]

Tobacco

Smoking tobacco causes elevation of blood nicotine, cadmium, carbon monoxide, and cyanide. Smokers also show secondary physiological effects in response to these substances. Although pCO_2 values are not affected by smoking, carboxyhemoglobin levels are greatly increased.[48] Values of arterial blood pO_2 are only very slightly lower in smokers, probably because reactive erythrocytosis increases the oxygen-carrying capacity of the blood.[3] In addition to erythrocytosis and elevated hemoglobin values, smoking causes leukocytosis.[44] Through release of catecholamines from the adrenal medulla, nicotine causes elevation of plasma and urine catecholamine levels.[3] Glucose

TABLE 3-3
EFFECT OF ETHANOL INGESTION ON VARIOUS ANALYTES IN NONALCOHOLICS

Blood analyte	Effect
Glucose	Increase*
Insulin	Decrease
Growth hormone	Increase
Calcitonin	Increase
Renin	No effect or increase
Antidiuretic hormone	Decrease
Creatine kinase	Increase
Alanine aminotransferase	Decrease
Gamma-glutamyl transferase	Increase
Lactate dehydrogenase	Increase
Triglycerides	Increase
Free fatty acids	Increase
Potassium	Decrease†
Magnesium	Decrease†
Phosphorus	Decrease†
Lactate	Increase
Uric acid	Increase

*Hypoglycemia may be a late effect of alcohol ingestion.
†Large doses of alcohol required to produce effect.

and insulin levels as well as cholesterol and triglyceride values are elevated by smoking.[45-47] Cortisol levels are higher in smokers than in nonsmokers, whereas vitamin C levels are reduced in smokers.[49,50]

Miscellaneous Effects

Travel over long distances ("jet lag") disrupts diurnal variations in hormone secretion, most notably cortisol, until sleep-wake patterns are reestablished. Urinary catecholamine levels are elevated.[3]

Acute transition to higher altitudes causes a number of biochemical alterations, most of which revert upon adaptation. Plasma glucose, iron, and CO_2 are reduced. Hemoglobin and 2,3-DPG increase, causing a decreased hemoglobin affinity for oxygen (hemoglobin disassociation curve is moved to the right).[51] Urine output is decreased transiently at high altitudes.[52]

Changes may occur from psychological stress, as might occur before an examination, or physical stress, for example, as a result of pain or injury. In a study of a group of students suffering the psychological trauma of awaiting a school examination,

TABLE 3-4
ANALYTE CHANGE IN RESPONSE TO STRESS

Blood analyte	Change
Corticotropin	Increase
Cortisol	Increase
Glucose	Variable
Cholesterol	Increase
Phosphorus	Decrease
Zinc	Decrease
Uric acid	Increase
Renin-angiotensin	Increase
Aldosterone	Decrease
Growth hormone	Increase
Catecholamines	Increase

Thomas and Murphy found that serum cholesterol increased.[53] More severe stress may cause other variations, which are summarized in Table 3-4. Drug influences are discussed in Chapter 4.

SPECIMEN COLLECTION

Early in this century, blood was collected in a glass syringe for laboratory determinations. The blood was then expelled into a glass test tube, capped with a cork, and taken to the laboratory. If plasma or whole blood was required, an anticoagulant such as heparin or oxalate was used. Often the anticoagulant was placed directly into the test tube or syringe just prior to adding the blood. This procedure, although crude, is still satisfactory for many analytes.

Vacuum Blood Collection Tubes

For collection of serum or plasma specimens, vacuum blood collection tubes represent a great improvement over earlier systems. They are suitable for almost every chemical, hematologic, and serologic test performed on blood, with blood gases the only principal exception. Proper procedures for routine blood collection are outlined in Table 3-5.

It is mandatory that the phlebotomist introduce himself or herself to the patient and explain the blood collection procedure. Correlation of the name and identification number on the requisition and tubes with the patient's hospital identification band is essential. Some phlebotomists prefer to use a syringe to collect blood and then transfer the specimen into various vacuum collection tubes. This procedure, even though often producing acceptable results, is inferior to using a vacuum tube holder. When multiple

TABLE 3-5
PROPER PROCEDURE FOR VENIPUNCTURE USING VACUUM BLOOD COLLECTION TUBES

1. Verify that patient identification band matches information on requisition.
2. Select venipuncture site (generally antecubital fossa). The site should be free of intravenous infusions, skin lesions, etc.
3. Place patient's arm in downward position. Observe vein.
4. Select tubes and examine for defects. Additive tubes should be tapped to dislodge clumped powder.
5. Insert first tube into holder. Push onto needle as far as guide mark.
6. Cleanse area with gauze soaked in 70% ethanol or isopropanol. (If it is desirable to ensure sterility, as for microbiological studies, the procedure discussed under "Blood Cultures" should be followed.) Allow to dry. Do not palpate vein after preparation.
7. Apply tourniquet, as required.
8. Perform venipuncture. Push tube to end of holder, puncturing diaphragm.
9. Remove tourniquet as blood enters tube.
10. When blood has filled tube, remove and insert next tube (see text for proper order of tubes).
11. After blood is collected, remove needle holder and cover wound with cotton gauze or bandage.
12. Gently invert additive tubes 10–12 times.

TABLE 3-6
RECOMMENDED ORDER OF DRAW FOR VACUUM BLOOD COLLECTION TUBES

1. Tubes for which sterility is mandatory (blood culture tubes, etc.)
2. Tubes with no additives
3. Tubes for coagulation studies
4. Tubes containing additives

samples are desired from the same venipuncture, the tube order listed in Table 3-6 is recommended. Tubes should always be allowed to fill completely.

Tube Stoppers

Tube stoppers are specially designed to remain inert. The plasticizer tris-(butoxyethyl)phosphate (TBEP) formerly was used in many stoppers. When this substance leached into plasma, it competed with binding sites of highly protein-bound basic drugs, such as quinidine,[54] lidocaine,[55] propranolol,[56] and tricyclic antidepressants.[57] It should be ascertained from the manufacturer that TBEP is not present in the stoppers used for determinations of highly protein-bound, basic drugs.

Additives

Some tubes may contain silicone to coat the interior and prevent surface wetting, and except for coagulation, this component does not affect results. Tubes containing glycerol should not be used for triglyceride or alcohol determinations.

Serum Separators

Serum separators recently have become popular as additives to blood collection tubes. These substances are gels that stratify between clot and serum, forming an impenetrable barrier. The gels are chemically inert and retard deleterious changes that occur in serum that is not separated from the blood clot—for example, glycolysis or leakage of enzymes from cells. Serum separates tubes are not trouble-free, and have been shown to produce falsely low values for several drugs, including lidocaine, phenytoin, and pentobarbital.[58]

PROCESSING BLOOD SPECIMENS

Filled blood collection tubes should be allowed to stand upright after collection. Stoppers should be left in place to avoid loss of volatile substances such as CO_2. In tubes lacking anticoagulants or other additives, clotting should proceed for at least 30 min before centrifugation. Centrifugation should be carried out at 1000 to 1300 $\times$ G for 10 min.

Collection of Urine

For routine urinalysis, a clean (not sterile) container is satisfactory. Special techniques, required for collection of uncontaminated urine specimens for culture and for urine chemical determinations such as trace metals, porphyrins, or catecholamines, will be discussed under "Microbiology" and "Chemistry," respectively.

Collection of Feces

Feces is collected for culture, for determination of fat content, or for parasite studies. It should be placed in a clean, nonsterile, leakproof container, but a bedpan may be used if contamination with urine can be avoided.

IN VITRO VARIABLES

Hemolysis

Hemolysis may occur as a result of disease or may occur in vivo as a result of traumatic venipuncture. Because erythrocytes are richer than serum or plasma in a number of analytes, hemolysis leads to elevation of these analytes in serum of plasma (Table 3-7).[59] In contrast, analytes such as insulin that have lower levels in erythrocytes decrease in serum or plasma when hemolysis occurs.

Hemolysis may cause direct interference with colorimetric determinations; for example, bilirubin and albumin may be falsely decreased. Hemolysis of any significance can usually be detected visually, but if doubt exists, a plasma (or serum) hemoglobin assay can be performed (see Chapter 4).

TABLE 3-7
CHANGES IN THE SERUM CONCENTRATIONS (OR ACTIVITIES) OF SELECTED CONSTITUTES DUE TO LYSIS OF ERYTHROCYTES (RBC)

Constituent	Ratio of concentration (or activity) in RBC to concentration (or activity) in serum	Change of concentration (or activity) in serum after lysis of 1% RBC, assuming a hematocrit of 50%
Lactate dehydrogenase	160 : 1	+272.0%
Aspartate aminotransferase (AST or GOT)	40 : 1	+220.0%
Potassium	23 : 1	+ 24.4%
Alanine aminotransferase (ALT or GPT)	6.7 : 1	+ 55.0%
Glucose	0.82 : 1	− 5.0%
Phosphorus	0.78 : 1	+ 9.1%
Sodium	0.11 : 1	− 1.0%
Calcium	0.10 : 1	+ 2.9%

Source: Statland BE, Winkel P: Pre-instrumental sources of variation, in Henry JB (ed): *Clinical Diagnosis and Management by Laboratory Methods,* ed 17. Philadelphia, WB Saunders, 1984, pp 61–73. Reproduced by permission of W. B. Saunders Co.

Lipemia

Lipemia can occur following fatty meals, but also is found as a pathologic condition in patients with primary or secondary dyslipoproteinemias. When found in a fasting patient, lipemia is always indicative of a pathologic process. Elevated triglyceride levels in healthy individuals cause turbidity in serum or plasma; elevated cholesterol levels cause no visual change; and chylomicrons form a creamy layer that floats on the surface. Turbidity produced by lipemia causes light-scattering during optimal measurements. Systems employing blanks and bichromatic measurements may compensate for mild lipemia, but severely lipemic specimens must be cleared, usually by ultracentrifugation, before analysis can be attempted (see Chapter 4).

CHEMISTRY

In general, serum is the preferred specimen because fibrin clots in plasma specimens can clog automatic instrumentation.

Electrolytes

The "electrolyte panel" usually consists of sodium, potassium, chloride, and CO_2. Serum is generally used, but this presents several problems. Before the specimen can be processed and analyzed, clotting, requiring up to 30 min, must be allowed to occur, thus delaying "stat" determinations. For this reason, heparinized plasma is preferable to serum for electrolyte analysis. To decrease processing time, a gel-type separator blood collection tube is recommended if serum is used. Plasma specimens should be processed immediately, and serum specimens should be processed as soon as clotting is complete.

The specimens should fill the collection tube, which must be kept tightly stoppered. Under these conditions, electrolytes are stable in separated serum or plasma for 1 week. Because of sodium leakage into cells, sodium values tend to decrease in unseparated blood or plasma or serum exposed to erythrocytes. Removal from the cells allows sodium to remain stable. Pseudohyponatremia and pseudohypochloremia result if large amounts of lipid or protein are present in the specimen. This problem may be avoided by the "direct" measurement of sodium using ion-selective electrodes. Because of the volatility of CO_2, tubes should be filled nearly to the top and kept tightly stoppered. Fluids placed in analyzer cups for CO_2 analysis should be kept covered unless processed at once.

Potassium is the electrolyte that presents the greatest challenge to the clinical laboratory. Erythrocytes are rich in potassium, and hemolysis of only 0.5 percent of the erythrocytes in a specimen increases plasma potassium by 0.5 mmol/liter.[2] Although the CO_2 and chloride levels in serum and plasma are essentially equal, potassium is significantly higher in serum because of release from platelets and leukocytes during clotting.[60,61] Storage conditions have a great influence on potassium as well: Potassium leakage from erythrocyte is accelerated by low temperatures, whereas storage at room temperature retards this process.[62]

Glucose

Proper interpretation of glucose levels requires knowledge of the time of the patient's last meal. For the glucose tolerance test, proper patient preparation is mandatory.[63] Glucose is most commonly measured in serum, but plasma and, rarely, whole blood are also used. Although others are suitable, oxalate is the most frequently used anticoagulant. Whole blood glucose values are 10 to 15 percent lower than in serum or plasma.[2] The major specimen-handling problem for glucose is preventing its artefactual decrease due to catabolism. Glucose levels in unseparated blood decrease at the rate of 7 percent per hour at room temperature,[64] but in specimens with leukocytosis or erythrocytosis, this process is accelerated.[65-67] Refrigeration of blood at 4°C for 24 hours reduces glycolysis from approximately 80 percent to approximately 20 percent. The use of an enzymatic inhibitor such as sodium fluoride renders glucose stable for 8 hours at 25°C and up to 3 days at 4°C.[68] Stability also can be obtained by the use of an impermeable gel separator blood collection tube. In sterile cell-free serum or plasma, glucose is quite stable.[69]

Enzymes

Serum is the specimen of choice for enzyme assays. If plasma is used, heparin is the preferred anticoagulant. Other anticoagulants may or may not be suitable; for example, citrate and oxalate may inhibit gamma-glutamyl transferase,[70] and chelating agents such as EDTA may bind metals that function as cofactors for certain enzymes. Detailed information is available regarding the suitability of different anticoagulants for assay of various enzymes.[70] For collection of enzyme assay specimens, the patient should be fasting because lipemia may interfere with colorimetric determinations. Also, as discussed above, recent meals may cause significant changes in enzyme activities. Because erythrocytes are rich sources of certain enzymes (see Table 3-6), hemolysis should be carefully avoided.

There are conflicting data on the stability of serum lactic dehydrogenase (LD) but it appears best to hold specimens at room temperature and assay as soon as possible. The LD-5 is the least stable isoenzyme.[69] Amylase is one of the most stable enzymes; it is stable for 1 week at 25°C and 1 month at 4°C.[69] Aspartate aminotransferase is stable in serum or plasma for 3 to 7 days at refrigerator temperature and for months at $-20°C$, whereas alanine aminotransferase is stable for 3 days at 25°C and 1 to 2 weeks at 4°C.[1,70] Creatine kinase (CK) is one of the most labile of the commonly measured enzymes, with activity rapidly lost after 2 to 4 hours at room temperature. Refrigeration will confer stability for 12 to 24 hours; but freezing at $-20°C$ or colder is suggested for longer storage. The least stable CK isoenzyme is that from brain (CK-1 or CK BB). Specimens for CK should be protected from light.[69] Some investigators find that alkaline phosphatase is quite stable at room or refrigerator temperature for 1 week,[71] but others disagree, reporting spurious alkaline phosphatase elevations after specimen storage in the refrigerator for 12 to 24 hours. Acid phosphatase is probably the most labile enzyme that the laboratory analyzes routinely. Activity is rapidly lost in serum at room temperature, but acidification to pH 6 with acetic or citric acid confers stability of up to 1 week when the specimen is stored at room or refrigerator temperature.[72,73] The specimen also can be collected as plasma directly into a tube containing an acid-citrate dextrose (ACD) solution or serum, which can be frozen at 20°C. Gamma-glutamyl transferase (GGT) is stable at room or refrigerator temperature for 1 week and at least 2 months at $-20°C$.[70]

Lipids

Specimens for lipid analysis must invariably be collected after a 12-hour fast. The patient should be allowed only water during this time, and all nonessential medications should be withheld. Either serum or plasma is suitable for cholesterol measurements. After collection, free cholesterol undergoes slow esterification, but this will not affect total cholesterol measurements. Total cholesterol levels are stable for several days at 4 to 25°C and indefinitely at $-20°C$.[69,74] Stability for triglycerides is similar to that for cholesterol, but plasma specimens tend to yield slightly higher levels than serum.[69]

Unlike measurements of cholesterol and triglycerides, lipoprotein analysis entails some problems in specimen selection and storage. Either serum or plasma may be used, but EDTA binds divalent cations, which catalyze lipoprotein degradation.[69] The effect of freezing on lipoproteins is controversial. Some studies have described decreased values owing to aggregation that occurs during thawing,[2,75] whereas others have found no change after freezing for several months.[76,77] It has been recommended

TABLE 3-8
STABILITY OF DRUGS IN SEPARATED SERUM OR PLASMA AT VARIOUS TEMPERATURES

Drug	25°C	4°C	−20°C
Acetaminophen	14 d	14 d	45 d
Barbiturates	3 m	3 m	3 m
Benzodiazepines	7 d	7 d	60 d
Lidocaine	7 d	7 d	30 d
Phenytoin	4 d	4 d	1–2 m
Quinidine	8 h	1 d	1 m
Salicylate	7 d	7 d	6 m
Tricyclic antidepressants	5 d	14 d	6 m

Source: Fody EP, Duby MM, Nadel MS, et al: Fascicle IV: Therapeutic drug monitoring and toxicology, in *Clinical Laboratory Handbook in Patient Preparation and Specimen Handling.* Skokie, IL, College of American Pathologists, 1985.

that the specimen be collected into an EDTA tube, the plasma stored in the refrigerator, and the lipoprotein analysis performed within 3 days.[1]

Drugs

Generally, specimens for therapeutic drug monitoring should be collected just prior to the next dose, preferably after at least 4 to 5 elimination half-lives to allow the attainment of steady state. For certain drugs, especially aminoglycosides, collection of specimens for "peak" levels must be carefully timed in relation to dose. Time of collection is more critical for drugs with shorter half-lives than for those with long half-lives.

The plasticizer tris-(butoxyethyl)phosphate (TBEP), now largely removed from rubber stoppers, has caused falsely low values for highly protein-bound basic drugs. Also, gel serum separators have caused decreased levels of lidocaine, pentobarbital, and phenytoin. With these exceptions, vacuum blood collection tubes are suited to therapeutic drug monitoring. Most common drugs are stable in separated serum for several days. Table 3-8 summarizes storage data for a number of drugs. A comprehensive review of preanalytical variables in therapeutic drug monitoring is available.[78] A few important problem areas deserve emphasis. To prevent inactivation of aminoglycosides, specimens containing beta lactam antibiotics (penicillins and cephalosporins) should be stored at −20°C for not more than 24 hours.[79] Certain drugs, such as ethosuximide, are volatile, so containers must be tightly capped. Because cyclosporin is the drug that presents the greatest challenge to the laboratory in terms of preanalytical variables, particular caution must be exercised in obtaining specimens for measurements of this drug.[78]

Trace Metals

Trace metals represent a considerable problem for the laboratory. Because of their ultra-low serum levels, contamination from extrinsic sources is a serious consideration. Proper quality control requires that frequent background checks be run on reagents, instruments, and specimen collection devices. The usual blood collection tubes are absolutely unsuitable for trace metal analysis. Special vacuum collection tubes may be suitable, but the preferred devices are commercially available plastic syringes designed especially for trace metal work. Ultrapure reagents, including water, must be used in trace metal analysis.

For determination of urine metal levels, contamination of the specimen from clothing should be avoided. Specimens should never be collected in the workplace. Polyethylene containers should be used after they have been soaked overnight in 1:1 ultrapure hydrochloric acid, rinsed with ultrapure water, again soaked in 1:1 ultrapure nitric acid, rinsed again several times, and dried. The preferred method of specimen preservation is acidification of urine to below pH 2 with ultrapure hydrochloric acid.[78]

Toxicology

Most drugs of abuse are quite stable in urine stored at room or refrigerator temperature. The most labile include flurazepam and secobarbital (stable for 2 to 3 weeks) and methaqualone (stable for 6 weeks). Freezing or the addition of fluoride confers indefinite stability to specimens for these drugs.[78,80]

Endocrinology

Extensive patient preparation is required for many endocrine tests.[81,82] Because protein hormones, such as insulin, ACTH, and renin, are unstable, plasma specimens should be used, placed on ice after collection, immediately transported to the laboratory, processed in a refrigerated centrifuge, and the plasma frozen at as low a temperature as possible. Steroid hormones in the blood are usually more stable than protein hormones. For example, serum cortisol is stable at refrigerator temperature for 2 days,[70] but aldosterone, which is more labile, should be frozen.

Most urinary hormones, such as 17-hydroxysteroids, 17-ketosteroids, 17-ketogenic steroids, 5-hydroxyindoleacetic acid, and estrogens, are stable up to several weeks at 4°C if acidified with boric or acetic acid. Catecholamines (including metanephrines, vanillylmandelic acid, and homovanillic acid) should be acidified to below pH 2 and stored in the dark.[1]

Blood Gases

Blood gases are the only frequently measured analytes for which specimens are not routinely collected in a vacuum tube. Instead, blood is usually drawn into a plastic syringe that has been prewetted with heparin. The needle is capped to prevent gas exchange and the specimen placed in crushed ice. Blood gases are stable under these circumstances for 1 hour. Exposure to air will result in a decrease in pCO_2 and an increase in pO_2.[2,69]

Miscellaneous

Both creatinine and urea are stable in serum, plasma, or urine for up to 1 week at 4°C. Acidification helps preserve these analytes in urine.[70] Specimens for bilirubin analysis should be stored in the dark, because even short exposure to ultraviolet radiation will cause degradation. In darkness, bilirubin is stable for 2 days at room temperature, 4 to 7 days at refrigerator temperatures, and 3 months when frozen.[2] Specimens for total protein, albumin, and immunoglobulins are stable several weeks refrigerated. Uric acid is reasonably stable, showing little change for up to 3 to 5 days at 4°C and up to 6 months at -20°C.[2] Ammonia is the most difficult nonprotein nitrogenous compound to analyze accurately, because values increase rapidly upon standing. Vacuum blood collection tubes are recommended and should be filled completely. Plasma should be used with lithium heparin, the preferred anticoagulant. Plasma should be separated immediately and, if analysis cannot be performed at once, the plasma frozen at -20°C or below. Such a specimen is stable 1 day.[70]

Total calcium is stable in serum or heparinized plasma for several days. Ionized calcium mandates special handling: Serum is preferred to plasma and should be collected without venous stasis. The specimen should be maintained anaerobically on ice until analysis, but correction for exposure to the air may be possible.[83,84] Because meals may increase or decrease phosphorus levels, a fasting specimen is preferred. Phosphorus is quite stable at room or refrigerator temperatures. Magnesium, which is unaffected by eating, is stable in refrigerated serum specimens for several days.[70]

HEMATOLOGY

Careful attention to patient preparation and specimen handling is mandatory for hematologic studies, especially coagulation. Because of interference with hemalotogic optical particle counters, lipemia is undesirable in hematologic specimens, whereas icterus and hemolysis have little effect.

The Complete Blood Count

The complete blood count, or its various components [leukocyte, erythrocyte and platelet counts, hemoglobin, hematocrit, mean corpuscular volume (MCV), mean corpuscular hemoglobin (MCH), and mean corpuscular hemoglobin content (MCHC), often accompanied by a differential leukocyte count] comprise the bulk of the work load for most hematology laboratories. Specimens for these studies are collected in vacuum blood collection tubes containing EDTA, usually as a 15 percent solution of the tripotassium salt.

The components of the complete blood count are stable for at least 24 hours at 4 to 8°C. At room temperature, the erythrocyte and leukocyte counts are also stable, but the erythrocyte MCV tends to increase and the MCHC to decrease.[85] The platelet count is stable at 25°C for 5 hours and at 4 to 8°C for 24 hours. Generally, the platelet count is the hematologic determination most subject to preanalytical variables.[1]

Coagulation

In no other area of the laboratory is careful attention to specimen collection as important as in coagulation. When collecting coagulation specimens, it is necessary to avoid trauma because release of tissue thromboplastin alters results. A butterfly infusion device may be helpful in patients from whom it is otherwise difficult to collect specimens. For coagulation studies, the first portion of blood collected should be discarded or used for other tests. Sodium citrate, in a concentration of 0.105 to 0.129 M, is usually used to collect plasma for coagulation studies. This anticoagulant is mixed with whole blood in a ratio of 1:9. If this ratio is not maintained, spurious results may occur, so it is mandatory that vacuum collection tubes be allowed to fill completely. Anticoagulant concentrations in commercial blood collection tubes are designed for hematocrits near the reference interval, and specimens with hematocrits below 20 percent[86] or above 60 percent[87] may cause discrepant coagulation results. The prothrombin time (PT) is stable for 2 to 4 hours at room temperature in filled, unopened tubes; exposure to air results in pH shifts that alter results.[88,89] The partial thromboplastin time (PPT) is stable for 4 to 6 hours at room temperature in unopened tubes.[88,90]

Proper procedure for collection of specimens for factor assays depends on the factor measured. Because Factors V and VIII are thermolabile, specimens for these assays should be collected into cold citrate tubes, processed in a refrigerated centrifuge at 4 to 8°C, maintained on ice, and assayed within 2 hours. If immediate assay is not possible, the plasma is stable at $-20°C$ for up to 1 week or at $-70°C$ for longer periods. Specimens for Factors IX, X, XII, and XIII may also be assayed using these procedures.[91] Factors VII and XI are stable at room temperature, and because aberrant results may occur if specimens for these assays are frozen, they should be refrigerated instead.[91]

Leukocyte Markers

Specimens of peripheral blood used for flow cytometry studies are usually collected into tubes with heparin, EDTA, or ACD. Although no definitive studies have appeared, the majority of workers favor heparin. At room temperature, unprocessed blood specimens maintain their leukocyte cell markers for at least 24 hours and possibly as long as 48 hours. If processing within this time is not possible, the whole blood may be mixed 1:1 with Roswell Park Memorial Institute (RPMI) solution to stabilize the specimen for up to 4 days at room temperature. Once the leukocytes have been tagged with monoclonal antibodies, they may be fixed (usually with paraformaldehyde) and remain stable indefinitely at refrigerator temperatures.

MICROBIOLOGY

In the area of microbiology, most preanalytical problems involve specimen handling.

Urine Cultures

Most specimens for urine culture are collected by the "clean-catch" technique, for which detailed instructions have been published.[92,93] The principal reason for this preparation is to avoid contamination from the flora of the external genitalia. There is no question that this is a problem in women; however, in men the need for "clean-catch midstream void" specimens has been questioned.[94] Other urine specimens submitted occasionally include suprapubic aspirates and those obtained from cystoscopy. Certain types of specimens are unacceptable, including indwelling catheter tips and urine from drainage bags.[93,95] Urine specimens from any source should be cultured within 2 hours, but if this is impossible, urine may be refrigerated for up to 24 hours.[92,93]

Blood Cultures

Careful preparation of the venipuncture site is essential to avoid contamination of blood culture specimens. Concentric swabbing of the site with 70 percent alcohol and an iodine compound is best. Multiple specimens should be collected from different sites.[92,96] Three blood cultures detect 99 percent of all bacteremias.[97] Reference to reviews is recommended for complete description of techniques.[92,96,97]

Lower Respiratory Tract Specimens

Sputum is the most frequently used specimen for delineation of lower respiratory tract infections. Other specimens likely to be submitted include those from open biopsies, needle biopsies, and bronchoscopies. Although they may generally be held overnight without loss of microbiologic integrity, prompt processing is recommended. All sputums should be Gram stained prior to culture to assure their origin from the lower respiratory tract.[98] Although sputum specimens may be refrigerated overnight, such storage is likely to make interpretation of Gram stains misleading.[99]

Upper Respiratory Tract Cultures

Specimens are usually taken from the upper respiratory tract for the diagnosis of streptococcal pharyngitis. Specimens for *Streptococcus pyogenes* do not require refrigeration[100]: The organism survives well up to 3 hours on an ordinary swab and up to 72 hours on a silica dry swab or in a transport system. With immunologic methods for the rapid identification of *S. pyogenes,* specimen storage prior to processing actually improves recovery, probably because of the relative hardiness of the organism compared to other upper pharyngeal flora.[101] Other pathogens, such as *Neisseria gonorrhoeae, Bordetella pertussis,* or *Corynebacterium diphtheriae,* require special handling procedures, which have been described in detail.[92]

Viral Cultures

Specimens for viral culture should be inoculated within 2 to 4 hours of collection. If this is not possible, they can be refrigerated for up to 48 hours. If longer storage is required, specimens should be frozen, preferably at −70°C. The only exception to this is general rule is cytomegalovirus, which is injured unless specimens are placed in 70 percent sorbitol solution prior to freezing.[92]

Stool Cultures

Organisms sought as pathogens in stool are most commonly *Salmonella, Shigella, Campylobacter, Yersinia,* and predominant staphylococcus or yeast. Although stool specimens should be cultured promptly, refrigeration may be used but is injurious to *Shigella.*[92] For ova and parasite examinations, a fresh specimen is ideal. If preservatives are used, several are available, with the choice depending on the type of parasite sought.[102]

Anaerobic Cultures

Because anaerobic organisms are very sensitive to oxygen and are destroyed by even brief exposure to air, it is preferable that material from the infection site (e.g., tissue, pus) be submitted in an appropriate anaerobic transport container. Anaerobes form part of the normal flora of the human body, and certain specimens, such as stool, throat swabs, skin biopsies, and sputum, should not be accepted for anaerobic culture.[1] Normally sterile body fluids other than blood are not generally cultured for anaerobes.

IMMUNOLOGY AND SEROLOGY

Only one comprehensive study of preanalytical variables in immunology has been published.[103] Most antibodies that are quantitated are quite stable at room or refrigerator temperatures for long periods of time, and even temperature extremes (−80°C to 58°C) have little effect.[104] In serology, the use of paired specimens (acute and convalescent) is recommended, as this may give more useful information than a single titer. These should preferably be analyzed together.

In blood banking, a cross-match specimen is used for up to 48 hours before a new one is required. A new specimen is required because of the possibility of the patient developing additional antibodies rather than because of in vitro antibody instability.

QUALITY CONTROL OF THE PREANALYTICAL PHASE OF LABORATORY TESTING

Knowledge of preanalytical factors is essential because they are so numerous and have such a profound effect on laboratory results.

Quality Control of Patient Preparation

The laboratory rarely has any direct control over patient preparation, but awareness of factors that can alter laboratory results is critical. Patients should be encouraged to fast prior to phlebotomy, and nonessential medications should be withheld. Most important, a comprehensive specimen collection manual should be available in every clinic and nurses' station.

Quality Control of Specimen Collection

Phlebotomists should be well trained before being "turned loose" in the wards or clinics. Periodic in-service training should be held and attendance documented. The laboratory should also offer phlebotomy training to nurses, physicians, and medical students. Patient identification must be rigorously established for every requisition and container. Mislabeled or unlabeled specimens should be discarded. The laboratory should establish a policy regarding unacceptable specimens and enforce it.

Quality Control of Specimen Handling and Storage

Specimens should be processed promptly and according to established guidelines. This chapter has provided much information regarding specimen storage and stability. References contained herein can provide considerable additional detail.

REFERENCES

1. Fody EP: Preanalytic variables: A management problem. Symposium on laboratory management. *Clin Lab Med* 1983, 3:525.
2. Tietz NW: *Fundamentals of Clinical Chemistry,* ed 2. Philadelphia, WB Saunders Co, 1976.
3. Young DS: Biological variability, in Brown SS, Mitchell FL, Young DS (eds): *Chemical Diagnosis of Disease*. New York, Elsevier North-Holland, 1979.
4. Statland BE, Winkel P: Effects of preanalytical factors on the intraindividual of analytes in the blood of the healthy subjects: Consideration of preparation of the subject and time of venipuncture. *CRC Crit Rev Clin Lab Sci* 1977, 8:105.
5. Bloomer JR, Barrett PV, Rodkey FL, et al: Studies on the mechanism of fasting hyperbilirubinemia. *Gastroenterology* 1971, 61:479.
6. Olusi SO, McFarlane H, Osunkoya BO, et al: Specific protein assays in protein-calorie malnutrition. *Clin Chim Acta* 1975, 62:107.
7. Weitzman ED: Circadian rhythms and episodic hormone secretion. *Ann Rev Med* 1976, 27:225.
8. Nokin J, Vekemans M, L'Hermite M, et al: Circadian periodicity of serum prolactin concentration in man. *Br Med J* 1972, 2:561.
9. Patel YC, Alford FP, Burger HG: The 24-hour plasma thyrotropin profile. *Clin Sci* 1972, 43:71.
10. Johns MV, Masterton JP, Paddle-Ledinek JE, et al: Variations in thyroid function and sleep in young men. *Clin Sci* 1975, 49:629.

11 De Costre P, Buhler U, De Groot LJ, et al: Diurnal rhythm in total serum thyroxine levels. *Metabolism* 1971, 20:782.
12 Tedeschi CG: Circadian challenges in "quality control." *Hum Pathol* 1973, 4:281.
13 Wiltink WF, Kruithof J, Mol C, et al: Diurnal and nocturnal variations of the serum iron in normal subjects. *Clin Chim Acta* 1973, 49:99.
14 Wesson LG Jr: Electrolyte excretion in relation to diurnal cycles of renal function. *Medicine* 1964, 43:547.
15 Stanbury SW, Thomson AE: Diurnal variations in electrolyte excretion. *Clin Sci* 1951, 10:267.
16 Maruhn D, Stroxyk K, Gielow L, et al: Diurnal variations of urinary enzyme excretion. *Clin Chim Acta* 1977, 75:427.
17 Halbreich U, Assael M, Ben-David M, et al: Serum prolactin in women with premenstrual syndrome. *Lancet* 1976, II:654.
18 Eisenberg S, Wolf PC: Plasma volume after posture change in hypertensive subjects. *Arch Intern Med* 1965, 115:17.
19 Eisenberg S: Postural changes in plasma volume in hypoalbuminemia. *Arch Intern Med* 1963, 112:544.
20 Widdowson EM, McCance RA: The effect of undernutrition and of posture on the volume and composition of the body fluids. Special Reports Series, Medical Research Council, London, 1951, no 275, p 165.
21 Statland BE, Bokelund H, Winkel P: Factors contributing to intra-individual variation of serum constituents: IV. Effects of posture and tourniquet application on variation of serum constituents in healthy subjects. *Clin Chem* 1974, 20:1513.
22 Pedersen KO: On the cause and degree of intra-individual serum calcium variability. *Scand J Clin Lab Invest* 1972, 30:191.
23 Husdan H, Rapoport A, Locke S, et al: Effect of venous occlusion of the arm on the concentration of calcium in serum, and methods for its compensation. *Clin Chem* 1974, 20:529.
24 Moerman EJ, Bogaert MG, de Schaepdryver AF: Estimation of plasma catecholamines in man. *Clin Chim Acta* 1976, 72:89.
25 Statland BE, Bokelund H, Winkel P: Factors contributing to intra-individual variation of serum constituents: 4. Effects of posture and tourniquet application on variation of serum constitutents in healthy subjects. *Clin Chem* 1974, 20:1513.
26 Skinner SL: A cause of erroneous potassium levels. *Lancet* 1961; I:478.
27 Helge H, Weber B, Quabbe HJ: Growth hormone release and venipuncture. *Lancet* 1969, I:204.
28 Davis J, Morrill R, Fawcett J, et al: Apprehension and elevated serum cortisol levels. *J Psychosom Res* 1962, 6:83.
29 Refsum HE, Treit B, Meen HD, et al: Serum electrolyte, fluid and acid-base balance after prolonged heavy exercise and low environmental temperature. *Scand J Clin Lab Invest* 1973, 32:111.
30 Refsum HE, Meen HD, Strommee SB: Whole blood, serum and erythrocyte magnesium concentrations after repeated heavy exercise of long duration. *Scand J Clin Lab Invest* 1973, 32:117.
31 Riley WJ, Pyke FS, Roberts AD, et al: The effect of long-distance running on some biochemical variables. *Clin Chim Acta* 1975, 65:83.
32 King S, Statland BE: The effects of a short burst of enzyme activity values in sera of healthy subjects. *Clin Chim Acta* 1976, 72:211.

33 Galteau MM, Siest G, Poortmans J: Continuous *in vivo* measurement of creatine kinase variation in man during an exercise. *Clin Chim Acta* 1975, 66:89.
34 Kachadorian WA, Johnson RE: The effect of exercise on some clinical measures of renal function. *Am Heart J* 1971, 82:278.
35 Sturgis CC, Bethell FH: Quantitative and Qualitative variations in normal leukocytes. *Physiol Rev* 1943, 23:279.
36 Terjung RL, Tipton CM: Plasma thyroxine and thyroid-stimulating hormone levels during submaximal exercise in humans. *Am J Physiol* 1971, 220:1840.
37 Noel GL, Suh HK, Stone JG, et al: Human prolactin and growth hormone release during surgery and other conditions of stress. *J Clin Endocrinol Metab* 1972, 35:840.
38 Christensen NJ, Mathias CJ, Frankel HL: Plasma and urinary dopamine; studies during fasting and exercise and in tetraplegic man. *Euro J Clin Invest* 1976, 6:403.
39 Avogaro P, Capri C, Pais M, et al: Plasma and urine cortisol behavior and fat mobilization in man after coffee ingestion. *Israel J Med Sci* 1973, 9:114.
40 Natsmith DJ, Akinyanju PA, Szanto S, et al: The effect in volunteers of coffee and decaffeinated coffee on blood glucose, insulin, plasma lipids and some factors involved in blood clotting. *Nutr Metab* 1970, 12:144.
41 Bellet S, Roman L, De Castro O, et al: Effect of coffee ingestion on catecholamine release. *Metab Clin Exper* 1969, 18:288.
42 Honma Y, Nimura T: Serum creatinine phosphokinase activity in chronic alcoholics. *Jpn J Stud Alcohol* 1969, 4:87.
43 Song SK, Rubin F: Ethanol produces muscle damage in human volunteers. *Science* 1972, 75:327.
44 Helman N, Rubenstein LS: The effect of age, sex, and smoking on erythrocytes and leukocytes. *Am J Clin Path* 1975, 63(1):35.
45 Sandberg H, Roman L, Zavodnick J, et al: The effect of smoking on serum somatotropin, immunoreactive insulin and blood glucose levels of young adult males. *J. Pharm Exper Thera* 1973, 184:787.
46 Boyle E Jr, Morales IB, Nichaman MZ, et al: Serum beta lipoproteins and cholesterol in adult men. *Geriatrics* 1968, 23:102.
47 Cryer PE, Haymond MW, Santiago JV, et al: Norepinephrine and epinephrine release and adrenergic mediation of smoking-associated hemodynamic and metabolic events. *N Engl J Med* 1976, 295:573.
48 Dawley HH Jr, Ellithorpe DB, Tretola R: Aversive smoking: carboxyhemoglobin levels before and after rapid smoking. *J Behav Thera Exper Psych* 1976, 7:13.
49 Wald N, Howard S: Variations in carboxyhaemoglobin levels in smokers. *Brit Med J* 1975, I:393.
50 Elwood PC, Hughes RE, Hurley RJ: Ascorbic acid and serum cholesterol. *Lancet* 1970, II:1197.
51 Eaton JW, Brewer GJ, Grover RF: Role of red cell 2,3-diphosphoglycerate in the adaptation of man to altitude. *J Lab Clin Med* 1969, 73:603.
52 Frayser R, Rennie ID, Gray GW, et al: Hormonal and electrolyte response to exposure to 17500 feet. *J Appl Physiol* 1975, 38:636.
53 Thomas CB, Murphy EA: Further studies on cholesterol levels in the Johns Hopkins medical students: The effect of stress at examination. *J Chronic Dis* 1958, 8:661.
54 Ooi DS, Poznanski WJ, Smith FM: Effects of contact with Vacutainer tube stoppers on the estimation of quinidine in serum and plasma. *Clin Biochem* 1980, 13:297.
55 Stargel WW, Roe CR, Routledge PA, et al: Importance of blood collection tubes in plasma lidocaine determinations. *Clin Chem* 1979, 25:617.

56. Cothan RH, Shand DG: Spuriously low plasma propranolol concentrations resulting from blood collection methods. *Clin Pharmacol Ther* 1975, 18:535.
57. Evans WE, Schentag JJ, Jusko WJ (eds): *Applied Pharmacokinetics*. San Francisco, Applied Therapeutics Inc, 1980, pp 561–566.
58. Quattrocchi F, Karnes HT, Robinson JD, et al: Effect of serum separator blood collection tubes on drug concentrations. *Ther Drug Monitoring* 1983, 5:359.
59. Statland BE, Winkel P: Pre-instrumental sources of variation, in Henry JB (ed): *Clinical Diagnosis and Management by Laboratory Methods*, ed 17. Philadelphia, WB Saunders, 1984, pp 61–73.
60. Bellevue R, Dosik H, Spergel G, et al: Pseudohyperkalemia and extreme leukocytosis. *J Lab Clin Med* 1975, 85:660.
61. Bronson WR, DeVita VT, Carbone PP, et al: Pseudohyperkalemia due to release of potassium from white blood cells during clotting. *N Engl J Med* 1966, 274:369.
62. Goodman JR, Vincent J, Rosen I, et al: Serum potassium changes in blood clots. *Am J Clin Pathol* 1954, 24:111.
63. National Diabetes Data Group: Classification and diagnosis of diabetes mellitus and other categories of glucose intolerance. *Diabetes* 1979, 28:1039.
64. Weissman M, Klein B: Evaluation of glucose determinations in untreated serum samples. *Clin Chem* 1958, 4:420.
65. Field JB, Williams HE: Artifactual hypoglycemia associated with leukemia. *N Engl J Med* 1961, 79:946.
66. Hanrahan JB, Sax SM, Cillo A: Factitious hypoglycemia associated with leukemia. *Am J Clin Pathol* 1963, 40:43.
67. Billington CJ, Casciato DA, Choquette DL, et al: Artifactual hypoglycemia associated with polycythemia vera. *JAMA* 1983, 249:774.
68. Tietz NW: *Clinical Guide to Laboratory Tests*, Philadelphia, WB Saunders, 1983.
69. Henry RJ, Cannon DC, Winkelman J: *Clinical Chemistry: Principles and Techniques*, ed 2. New York, Harper & Row Publishers, 1974.
70. Kaplan LA, Pesce AJ: *Clinical Chemistry: Theory, Analysis, and Correlation*, St. Louis, CV Mosby, 1984.
71. Bowers GN, McComb RB: A continuous spectrophotometric method for measuring the activity of serum alkaline phosphatase. *Clin Chem* 1966, 12:70.
72. Doe RP, Mellinger GT, Seal VA: Stabilization and preservation of serum prostatic acid phosphatase activity. *Clin Chem* 1965, 11:943.
73. Ellis G, Belfield A, Goldberg DM: Colorimetric determination of serum acid phosphatase activity using adenosine 3'-monophosphate as substrate. *J Clin Pathol* 1971, 24:493.
74. Grafnetter D, Fodor J, Teply V, et al: The effect of storage on levels of cholesterol in serum measured by a single direct method. *Clin Chem Acta* 1967, 16:33.
75. Frederickson DS, Levy RI, Lees, RS: Fat transport in lipoproteins: An integrated approach to mechanisms and disorders (continued). *N Engl J Med* 1957, 276:148.
76. Adlersberg D, Bossak ET, Sher IH, et al: Electrophoresis and monomolecular layer studies with serum lipoproteins. *Clin Chem* 1955, 1:18.
77. Winkleman JW, Wybenga DR, Ibbott FA: Quantitation of lipoprotein components in the phenotyping of hyperlipoproteinemias. *Clin Chim Acta* 1970, 27:181.
78. Fody EP, Duby MM, Nadel MS, et al: Fascicle IV: Therapeutic drug monitoring and toxicology, in *Clinical Laboratory Handbook in Patient Preparation and Specimen Handling*. Skokie, IL, College of American Pathologists, 1985.
79. Jones SM, Blazevic DJ, Balfour HH: Stability of gentamicin in serum. *Antimicrob Agents Chemother* 1976, 10:866.

80 Rockerbie RA, Campbell DJ: Effect of specimen storage and preservation on toxicological analyses or urine. *Clin Biochem* 1978, 11:77.
81 Wattts NB, Keffer JH: *Practical Endocrine Diagnosis,* ed 3. Philadelphia, Lea & Febiger, 1982.
82 Williams RH: *Textbook of Endocrinology,* ed 6. Philadelphia, WB Saunders, 1981.
83 Robertson WG, Marshall RW: Calcium measurements in serum and plasma—total and ionized. Medical Research Council Mineral Metabolism Unit, The General Infirmary, Leeds, United Kingdom. *CRC Crit Rev Clin Lab Sci* 1979, 11:271.
84 Wybenga DR, Ibbott FA, Cannon DC: Determination of ionized calcium in serum that has been exposed to air. *Clin Chem* 1976, 22:1009.
85 Britten GM, Brecher, G, Johnson C: Stability of blood in commonly used anticoagulants. *Am J Clin Pathol* 1969, 52:690.
86 Williams WJ, Beutler E, Erslev AJ, et al: *Hematology,* ed 2. New York, McGraw-Hill, 1977.
87 Joseph JI, Maenza R, Kaplan H, et al: Volume and hematocrit effect on prothrombin. *Am J Clin Pathol* 1966, 46:449.
88 Page E, Kavanaugh C, Hughes J: Plasma stability: Direct sampling from evacuated tubes for routine coagulation assays. Raitan, NY, Ortho Diagnostic Systems, 1983.
89 Schoen I, Prophai M, Weiss A: Storage, stability and quality control of prothrombin time by means of the Quick method. *Am J Clin Pathol* 1982, 37:374.
90 Koepke JA, Rodgers JL, Oliver MJ: Preinstrumental variables in coagulation testing. *Am J Clin Pathol* 1975, 64:591.
91 Fody EP, Tiersten D, Duby M, et al: Fascicle II: Hematology, in *Clinical Laboratory Handbook for Patient Preparation and Specimen Handling.* Skokie, IL, College of American Pathologists, 1982.
92 Fody EP, Tiersten D, Duby M, et al: Fascicle III: Microbiology, in *Clinical Laboratory Handbook for Patient Preparation and Specimen Handling.* Skokie, IL, College of American Pathologists, 1983.
93 Barry AL, Smith PB, Turch M: *Cumitech 2: Laboratory Diagnosis of Urinary Tract Infections,* Washington, DC, American Society for Microbiology, 1975.
94 Lipsky BA, Inui TS, Plorde JJ, et al: Is the clean-catch midstream void procedure necessary for obtaining urine culture specimens from men? *Am J Med* 1984, 76:257.
95 Gross PA, Harkavy LM, Barden GE, et al: Positive Foley catheter tip cultures: Fact or fancy? *JAMA* 1974, 228:72.
96 Reller LB, Murray PR, MacLowry JD: Blood cultures II, in *Cumitech 1A,* Washington JA (coord ed). Washington, DC, American Society for Microbiology, 1982.
97 Washington JA: Blood cultures: Principles and techniques. *Mayo Clin Proc* 1975, 50:91.
98 Bartlett JG, Brewer NS, Ryan KJ: Laboratory diagnosis of lower respiratory tract infection, in *Cumitech 7,* Washington JA (coord ed), Washington, DC, American Society for Microbiology, 1978.
99 Penn RL, Silberman, R: Effects of overnight refrigeration on the microscopic evaluation of sputum. *J Clin Microbiol* 1984, 19:161.
100 Redys JJ, Hibbard EW, Borman EE: Improved dry-swab transportation for streptococcal specimens. *Public Health Rep* 1968, 83:143.
101 Kjos PA, Anhalt JP: Abstract 13: Evaluation of direct or detection of group A streptococci in throat swabs. Program and Abstracts of the 24th Interscience Conference on Antimicrobial Agents and Chemotherapy, 1984, p 92.

102 Price DL: Comparison of three collection-preservation methods for detection of intestinal parasites. *J Clin Microbiol* 1981, 14:656.
103 Tiersten D, Duby M, Farrer S, et al: Fascicle I: Diagnostic immunology/serology, in *Clinical Laboratory Handbook for Patient Preparation and Specimen Handling*. Skokie, IL, College of American Pathologists, 1981.
104 Rippey JH, Hood P: Pretest temperature effects on CAP syphilis serology survey samples. *Arch Pathol Lab Med* 1985, 109:17.

CHAPTER 4

GENERAL ASPECTS OF LABORATORY QUALITY ASSURANCE

Steven J. Steindel, Ph.D.

Laboratory quality assurance starts at a preanalytical stage. Much of a laboratory quality assurance program involves control of measurable or verifiable quantities, such as control sera values or culture media adequacy, but all programs must begin with the ability to control those steps that enable the laboratory to produce a quality result. These factors include interferences, quality of reagents, quality of standards, tests of the measuring system, quality of personnel, and the ability to deliver the report to the requesting physician in a timely and usable fashion.

INTERFERENCES

An interferent is a substance inherent in the test system or sample that causes the determined result to be different from the true amount of material present. It may also be considered as a substance that prevents the identification of a chemical or an organism by masking the properties of the true substance. Many times an interferent is present, but the only revealing factor is a result that does not agree with clinical impressions.

Observable Interferents

Lipemia Lipemia, the visible cloudiness of sera due to chylomicrons or very low density lipoproteins, is a physical interferent. Fat particles cause volume displacement, increasing the apparent serum water concentration and falsely lowering the observed quantities of substances.[1-3] The most readily observable form of this effect is when direct-reading ion-specific electrode values are compared to those obtained following a dilution step.[4] In the latter case, the lipids aspirated by the dilution system are included as serum water, thereby falsely lowering electrolyte values. Lipemia also may block the light source and the observed absorbance then consists of two quantities: the actual reaction absorbance and that due to scatter from the fat particles. Measured absorbance is higher than that expected, and the calculated result is erroneous.

Lipemia can be corrected for by determining the serum water present and correcting the observed value for the constituent by the percent water present in the sample volume.[3] Methods for determining serum water are tedious. With the advent of inexpensive air-driven ultracentrifuges, physical separation of serum from fat particles has developed into the method of choice.[5] Optical correction for lipemia can be made by several automated instruments.[6] Usually this involves measurement of absorbance at high wavelengths where scatter is the greatest (about 630 nm). This absorbance then is used to correct the result obtained at the measuring wavelength for the degree of lipemia presumed present.

Although it is best to avoid analyzing lipemic specimens, many medical conditions cause sera to be lipemic and, in those cases, corrective measures should be taken. The final report should contain a note that lipemia was present, give an estimate as to the amount (slight, moderate, or gross), and comment on the possible effects it may have on the results (see Chapter 3).

Hemolysis Hemolysis is the release of cellular components from erythrocytes and may be due to hemolytic disease, but is usually caused by the phlebotomy process. Phlebotomists should be trained to use collection techniques that will avoid hemolysis. In difficult-to-collect patients, such as those with small veins or who have had repeated venipunctures, use of an alternate collection site or slightly smaller bore needle (20-, 22-, or 25-gauge needle) have been used successfully in avoiding hemolysis.[7] Other causes of hemolysis include too vigorous shaking of collected blood, pulling strongly on a syringe plunger, centrifugation prior to complete clotting, and transferring of blood through too small an opening.[8] In all cases, the collection equipment must be clean and dry because water may cause cells to rupture. After the specimen is collected, it should be handled gently and the sera harvested as soon as possible. When collecting specimens from neonates, hemolysis is difficult to avoid. A good heel stick should not be too deep, and blood should flow freely.[9] If the area was washed with alcohol, make sure it was evaporated before doing the heel stick, or hemolysis may occur.

If a specimen is hemolyzed, a judgment as to the amount of hemolysis empirically observed (slight, moderate, or gross) should be made. Specimens that show moderate to gross hemolysis should be recollected. If recollection is not possible, a decision as to whether the results will be clinically useful should be made prior to running the specimen.

Hemolysis causes two forms of interference. The first is optical. Hemoglobin has an intense absorbance at 431 and 555 nm and at 414, 531–543, and 577 nm.[10] Hemoglobin interferes with assays that use wavelength measurements in these regions. Most methods used today either avoid these wavelengths, use biochromatic correction techniques, or remove the heme. The second cause of interference with hemolyzed specimens is the release of cellular components other than heme. These cellular components falsely elevate the serum levels of many substances. Lactic dehydrogenase is most elevated, with lesser increases in potassium, creatine kinase, aspartate aminotransferase, alanine aminotransferase, and iron[11] (see Chapter 3).

Icterus Icterus is the observed orange-yellow color of serum caused by excessive bilirubin. It is strictly an in vivo phenomenon, and the laboratory can do nothing about preventing its presence, but should note it on a report.

Bilirubin is a product of heme metabolism and interferes with laboratory measurements in a fashion similar to heme. Bilirubin's absorbance maxima is at 460 nm for the protein-bound fraction and at 420 nm for free bilirubin.[12] Most methods compensate for bilirubin interference in a manor similar to hemoglobin.

Fibrin Fibrin is not a true chemical interferent, but is a physical interferent in instrument operation. As sample sizes get smaller and sampling devices become narrower, a small fibrin plug can effectively cause instrument shutdown. Waiting at least 20 to 30 min before centrifugation to allow for adequate clotting of the specimen prevents fibrin problems. In sera from patients receiving anticoagulant medication, such as hemodialysis patients, fibrin clots may continue to form after the usual 20 to 30 min allowed for in vitro coagulation. Addition of small amounts of thrombin may allow for more complete and rapid clotting with little impact on test results.[13] Barrier tubes contain small glass beads to accelerate the clotting process.[14] Specimens can be filtered to provide additional protection against fibrin interference.

Nonobservable interferents

Interferents that are nonobservable to the naked eye are the major cause of interference-related problems within the laboratory and are usually drug related. Unfortunately, the laboratory rarely knows what medication a patient is taking, though recent combined hospital databases may help provide this information.[15] Young, Pestaner, and Gibberman compiled a massive list of drug interferences on laboratory tests.[16] A book entitled *Drug Interference and Effects in Clinical Chemistry,* 1974, expands and updates this material.*

Drugs cause interference with laboratory results by their in vivo and in vitro effects. In vivo effects are produced when a drug changes the quantity of an analyte. A common example is drug induction of excessive amounts of liver enzymes released from the cells that are metabolizing the drug. Aspartate aminotranspeptidase and gamma-glutamyltransferase are commonly induced.[17,18] When a patient develops symptoms related to the drug, such as with corticosteroid administration, it is difficult to consider the drug as an interferent; the drug-related abnormal state simply is reflected by the laboratory results.

*Available from Apoteksbolaget, Forlagsavdelningen, S-105 14 Stockholm, Sweden.

The second form of drug-related interference is in vitro. It is usually caused by changing the reaction rate of the analyte, preventing determination of the correct level. Many nonspecific colorimetric methods are prone to this type of interference. Today, specific enzymatic methods are used in an attempt to avoid this type of interference. However, a drug may interfere with an enzyme reaction by inhibiting or accelerating enzymatic action, thus yielding false results. The effect of 5-fluorocytosine on creatinine anhydrase is an example.[19]

A common form of drug-related interference is the prevention of organism identification because antibiotic in the specimen interferes with organism growth. Another example of this type of interference is masking of physical properties (retention time, mass spectra fragmentation pattern) of a drug on a toxicology screen. In the latter case, the presence of metabolites contributes additional confusion to the attempted identification. When performing toxicology screens for sensitive cases, such as forensic or job related, results should be confirmed by at least one other nonrelated method.

Cross-Reactivity

Immunologic methods are gaining widespread use and present the laboratory with an interesting form of interference: cross-reactivity. Cross-reactivity is observed when the antibody shows significant binding to substances other than the desired analyte. Most suppliers try to minimize cross-reactivity to predicted compounds by antibody purification. However, even if the cross-reactivity is small, problems can develop if the concentration of the interfering substance is several orders of magnitude greater than the substance being measured. Examples include thyroxine in a triiodothyronine determination or human chorionic gonadotropin in a luteinizing hormone assay. Monoclonal antibodies are thought to be hapten specific, but may show cross-reactivity depending on the portion of the hapten to which they are antigenic. Highly specific monoclonal antibodies show very low sensitivity and yield assay systems with long incubation times.[20]

REAGENT QUALITY CONTROL

Reagents

Most laboratories do not prepare either their own reagents or media, but purchase ready-to-use products. In spite of this, the laboratory needs to be aware of reagent quality and establish checks of incoming reagents. Careful note should be made as to reagent arrival and proper storage conditions. Prior to use, the reagent should be checked against samples of known values to make sure the results are reproducible. If necessary, physical properties such as absorbance or pH should be verified.

Storage conditions determine the useful lifetime of the reagent. Cellular or biologic reagents are very sensitive and should be stored at either refrigerator or freezer temperatures. Sensitive material should not be stored for any length of time in compartments of frost-free freezer systems, because they defrost several times a day.

All reagents should have a realistic user-determined or -verified expiration date. A reagent date of "STABLE" is acceptable for those reagents that will not deteriorate with time, such as many bulk chemicals. For distribution within the United States, all manufacturers are required by the Food and Drug Administration to place an expiration date on their products.[21] It is rare that this date exceeds 2 years from the date of manufacture. If a reagent is performing adequately past the manufacturer's stated expiration date, then there is no reason to discontinue use provided that reagent adequacy can be documented.

Water is an important, sometimes forgotten, reagent in the laboratory. Acceptable purity of water depends greatly on the uses placed on it. For example, water for trace metal assays must be purer than water for media preparation. Standards for clinical laboratory water quality have been published (Table 4-1).[22,23]

The American Chemical Society has established a set of guidelines for varying grades of reagent quality.[24] When preparing reagents, use the grade that best suits the need. In many instances chemicals of the highest grade are not needed. Conversely, when performing analysis for trace quantities of metals, even the best grade may be inadequate without further purification. When using a lower grade of chemical, specifications should be checked for potential interferences, such as excess metal ions.

TABLE 4-1
SPECIFICATIONS FOR WATER QUALITY

Specification	Water grade		
	Type I	Type II	Type III
	NCCLS[23]		
Resistivity, megohm centimeter @ 25°C	10 (in-line)	2.0	0.1
Silicate (mg/liter SiO_2) (maximum)	0.05	0.1	1.0
pH	N.A.	N.A.	5.0–8.0
Microbiological content, colony-forming units per ml (CFU/ml) (maximum)	10	10^3	N.A.
Particulate matter	Will not pass a 0.2-μm filter	N.A.	N.A.
Organics	Passed through activated carbon	N.A.	N.A.
	CAP[22]		
Resistivity—specific resistance (megohms @ 25°C)			
In line	10		
Effluent (as used)		2.0	0.1
Silicate (mg/liter SiO_2)	0.05	0.10	1.00
pH	N.A.	N.A.	5.0–8.0
Microbiological content (CFU/ml) (maximum)	10	10^4	N.A.

History has shown that as certifying techniques become better, the purity of an organic or biologic compound is not as great as originally thought. Many enzymes determined as pure by paper electrophoresis were shown to be complex mixtures when isoelectric focusing methods were used. Many organic compounds pure by melting point are found to be mixtures when analyzed by thin-layer chromatography and determined to be even more complex when capillary gas chromatography or high-performance liquid chromatography methods are used. When in doubt, use organic-grade chemicals of at least 98 percent chromatographic purity or biologicals that show single bands or bands by isoelectric focusing only for isoenzymes.

Standards

Standards for the clinical laboratory fall into several categories, including those for procedures and guidelines, materials and preparations, device standards, building codes, and regulations (Table 4-2). Three types of "materials and preparations" standards have evolved for use in the clinical laboratory: primary, secondary, and reference. Validity of a laboratory measurement is only as good as the standard used to calibrate the measuring system. Listed in Table 4-3 are some selected standards available to chemistry laboratories. Standardization must be considered with respect to chemical quantification. Generally, it is assumed that all potentially measurable material is available for reaction; however, only at infinite dilution does that situation exist. The actual amount of material available for measurement is determined by interaction of the material with its environment or matrix. In complex analytical systems, we generally assume that deviation from an activity coefficient of 1 (100 percent availability for reaction) is a matrix effect.

TABLE 4-2
CLINICAL LABORATORY STANDARDS

1 *Procedures and guidelines* are written instructions for doing something and include:
   a Technical methods, definitive methods, reference methods, and bench methods
   b Written standards, which are procedures to be followed exactly
   c Guidelines, which are written procedures that may be modified to fit individual situations
2 *Materials and preparations* are things that have physical and chemical properties, one or more of which are known with sufficient certainty to be useful in the clinical laboratory. These include:
   a Physical standards
   b Chemical standards
   c Reference materials
   d Reagents
3 *Device standards* may be written documents or physical substances.
4 *Building codes* must be followed.
5 *Regulations* comprise written documents published by agencies having legal jurisdiction, enforceable by legal action, containing requirements for engaging in specified activities or providing specified services.

Source: McClatchey KD, Haupt CJ (eds): *Standards, Reference Materials, and Methods: A Practical Guide for the Medical Laboratory,* ed 2. Skokie, IL, College of American Pathologists, 1984, pp 1–2.

TABLE 4-3
EXAMPLES OF CLINICAL LABORATORY STANDARDS

Standard	Type of standard	Organization
Reference sera, blood anti-A	Materials and preparations	Bureau of Biologics
Bilirubin	Materials and preparations	National Bureau of Standards
Creatinine	Materials and preparations	College of American Pathologists
Digoxin	Materials and preparations	American Association for Clinical Chemistry
Erythropoietin	Materials and preparations	World Health Organization
Gases, compressed	Materials and preparations	American National Standards Institute
Microbiology specimen containers	Device standard	British Standards Institution
Radioiodine uptake	Procedures and guidelines	Institute of Electronic Engineers
Radiological protection	Procedures and guidelines	Finnish Standards Association
Electrical power requirements	Building code	National Committee of Clinical Laboratory Standards

Source: McClatchey KD, Haupt CJ (eds): *Standards, Reference Materials, and Methods: A Practical Guide for the Medical Laboratory*, ed 2. Skokie, IL, College of American Pathologists, 1984.

Primary Standards A primary standard can be thought of as a standard in which the material has an activity coefficient that is effectively 1 and the weighed-in amount of the standard can be used to determine concentration directly.[25] To prepare a primary standard, one takes a pure chemical, weighs an amount on a balance to sufficient accuracy that the weighing error is less than 1 percent (preferably less than 0.1 percent), adds a noninteracting solvent, and finally dilutes the solution to a known final volume. Primary standards are usually prepared in water, but organic solvents or protein-based solutions may also be used. When describing the concentration of a primary standard, its error should be stated.

Secondary Standards Secondary standards are those whose values are determined by comparison to a standard of known or assigned value. Implicit in the assignment of secondary standard values is the reference method system.[26,27] In the nineteenth century, scientists realized that measurements and methods must be transferable across international borders and established the International System of Units, based on the metric system. In 1901, the U.S. government formed the National Bureau of Standards (NBS) as its means of communicating with the international community and for developing an internal system of standardization. Until the middle of the 1950s, efforts to standardize the clinical laboratory were sporadic and loosely coordinated. The first major step was the acceptance of a hemoglobin standard based on cyanohemoglobin.[28,29] Since 1973 the College of American Pathologists has provided prepared primary standards for several basic analytes.[30] The NBS has since 1969 provided Standard Reference Materials (SRM) for the clinical laboratory.[31]

In 1967, Radin discussed the state of standardization in the clinical laboratory and solidified thoughts concerning primary, secondary, and reference standards.[32] In 1977 a meeting on "A National Understanding for the Development of Reference Materials and Methods in Clinical Chemistry" was held. An outgrowth of this meeting was the formation of the Council for the National Reference System for the Clinical Laboratory. The National Committee for Clinical Laboratory Standards (NCCLS) has published procedures and guidelines for definitive methods, reference methods, and reference materials.[33,34]

A definitive method is defined as "an analytical method that has been subject to in-depth investigation and evaluation for sources of inaccuracy, including nonspecificity." Implied in this definition are minimal imprecision and bias. The value produced by a definitive method is taken to be the true value of the substance.

A reference method is "a thoroughly investigated method, in which exact and clear descriptions of necessary conditions and procedures are given for the accurate determination of one or more property values. . . ." Three classes of reference methods are defined: A Class A reference method has been directly compared to a definitive method; a Class B method has the quality of a Class A method but has not been evaluated against a definitive method; and a Class C method is one in which no definitive method is likely to become available. At the present time, there are several candidate reference methods available.

Biological primary standards are virtually nonexistent, and secondary standards, prepared in large quantities and stored under conditions where deterioration is slow, are used for calibration. A value is assigned to the secondary standard by the supplier, and is usually based on an activity determination made using an in vivo test system, receptor binding analysis, or immunologic purity. The major supplier of biological secondary standards is the World Health Organization (WHO), which lists about 200 biologic substances as either International Standards (IS) or International Reference Preparations (IRP).[35] WHO standards were originally calibrated using biologic systems. With the advent of immunoassay systems, it was found that many of the older standards had immunoreactive material present beyond that indicated by the biologic potency, probably due to protein fragments. Value assignments for the newer immunoassay standards bear only a casual relationship to past standards. Particular problems were noted with the thyroid-stimulating hormone and human chorionic gonadotropin standards.[36,37]

In the United States, the NBS has released SRM909 as a serum-based reference material.[38] By isotope dilution mass spectrometry, certified concentrations were established for calcium, chloride, glucose, lithium, potassium, uric acid, cholesterol, and magnesium. When corrections are made for the weight of the lyophilized plug, values fell within acceptable limits. When no correction is made for the weight of the matrix material, high uncertainties for many of the analytes, in the range of 5 to 7 percent, are found. In addition to the above analytes, suggested values are given for acid phosphatase, alkaline phosphatase, alanine aminotransferase, aspartate aminotransferase, creatine kinase, lactate dehydrogenase, and gamma-glutamyltransferase at gallium melting point (29.77°C).[39] The NBS does not certify the enzyme values.

Reference Material According to the National Reference System in Clinical Chemistry (NRSCC), a reference material is "a material substance one or more properties of which are sufficiently well established to be used for calibrating an apparatus, assessing a measurement method or for assigning values to materials." Reference material acts as a transfer media from one method or laboratory to another.[34] In many instances, reference material is used for routine calibration of methods.

Proficiency Testing and Standardization Many, if not most, clinical analytes will never have primary standards. Assignment of secondary standard values has inherent error. If the value of a secondary standard is assigned by reference methodology of Class A caliber, then the value assumes the error of the reference method. If the secondary standard value is assigned by a Class B or C reference method, the error of the reference method and any bias that may exist from lack of comparison to a definitive method are both assumed. Secondary standard value assignment by definitive methodology might prove satisfactory, but definitive methods are not and probably will not be available for many analytes. An attempt to use definitive methodology for secondary standard value assignment through SRM909 was only moderately successful. Biologic secondary standards are only as good as the present means of assessing them. From all these inherent problems has evolved the ongoing testing of standardization by consensus through external quality control or proficiency testing programs.

Belk and Sunderman introduced the concept of using a standard sample sent to multiple laboratories as a means of gauging laboratory performance.[40] Laboratories achieving the same value, statistically, have some assurance of accuracy control, whereas those that are different need to assess their methodology. The proficiency testing system has undergone many changes both in form and use since those early days; however, not much has been written about its potential role in standardization.

In the United States, two major proficiency testing programs are in use. The College of American Pathologists (CAP)[41] program compares laboratories by analyte and method. For many analytes, material assayed by the CAP program has a well-determined mean value within a method. The CAP provides an all-methods analyte mean value but, besides scientific studies, makes no internal use of it. A second program is maintained by the Centers for Disease Control.[42] Reference laboratories determine analyte values, which are used to compare all methods used in the survey. In addition, a consensus analyte mean is calculated, which should verify the reference laboratories' means. Both programs provide, on a limited basis, vials of excess survey material. This material can be viewed as a secondary standard whose analyte value represents a consensus value indicative of the current state of the art in determining the true value of that analyte in a clinical matrix.

Recently, a Swedish study was reported in which 21 laboratories in the Stockholm area were mailed human sera with definitive method (isotope dilution mass spectrometry) values for creatinine, cholesterol, glucose, urea, and uric acid.[43] For all analytes except creatinine, the difference between the consensus value and the definitive method value was statistically insignificant. It was the authors' conclusion that a laboratory could participate in less external quality control if it used sera calibrated by definitive methods. Another conclusion may be drawn: Consensus values are equivalent to definitive method values and could serve as a substitute when these methods are not available.

In Germany, external proficiency testing is used as the standard for accuracy, where target values are determined by a small number of reference laboratories.[44,45] German laboratories must meet these target values, leading to mandated standardization by consensus. The German system would lead to constantly biased results if the reference laboratories do not use methodology that will produce an unbiased result.

In Great Britain, the external quality control program uses consensus results to determine analyte target values.[46] For analytes where the between-method bias is small, the system is quite capable of producing a standard value by consensus. If the intermethod bias is large, which is usually an indication of the lack of a transportable standard, lack of a good reference or consensus method, unsolved matrix effects, or varying antibody specificity or sensitivity, the consensus value has less meaning when used as a standard value.

A major problem in using standardization by consensus is the wide variance encountered in the mean value for many analytes. Laessig has recently proposed the use of a trimming method to help determine the true value of an analyte from an external quality control pool.[47] In his report, the analytes studied were pH, pCO_2, and pO_2, all of which can be measured with small variance and have good primary standards.

PREVENTIVE MAINTENANCE

Despite the regulatory requirement incorporated into all voluntary and governmental programs, hospitals and laboratories still pay only passing attention to the need for preventive maintenance. Preventive maintenance consists of an orderly program of *essential* steps to measure and maintain the quality of instrumentation and equipment. It also consists of the investigation of the adequacy of vital safety features. Ultimately, the goal of a preventive maintenance system is assurance that a measuring device or piece of equipment will be available in a usable and safe fashion when required.

When establishing a preventive maintenance program, the first step is to identify what needs maintaining. Manufacturers' literature indicates those checks and procedures that should be done and the frequency with which to do them. Checklists are available in *Medical Equipment Management in Hospitals,* American Society for Hospital Engineering Clinical Engineering Section, American Hospital Association, 840 N. Lake Shore Drive, Chicago, Il 60611. However, a preventive maintenance mentality seems to have developed in the United States that leads one to believe that sometimes maintenance is included solely for the sake of including it. Recently, an analyzer was introduced to the United States from overseas and the American operating manual had not yet been printed. The manufacturer was asked what was the daily maintenance and informed the laboratory that there was none, but they could do some minor house-cleaning if they desired. About a year later, the American version of the operator's manual appeared, detailing those and other apparently unnecessary steps as daily maintenance. Unfortunately, now that they are written, all inspection agencies will be looking for compliance.

Preventive maintenance should be confined to *necessary* steps and done at a frequency required by need and not to meet an arbitrary requirement of daily, weekly, monthly, and so on. It is probably the introduction of tedious, unnecessary steps that has given preventive maintenance its unwanted image.

Most manufacturers recommend some form of cosmetic cleaning on a regular basis. Many laboratories maintain a policy of instrument cleanliness for reasons of pride. However, instrument cleanliness goes beyond pride, neatness, and tedium, and should be the cornerstone of a preventive maintenance program. Safety in part dictates cleanliness, as spills of serum or other bodily products are biohazards. Chemical spills are potentially dangerous because of their corrosive effect on both machines and people. In solution, a chemical may be relatively safe; but dry, as either a powder or a potential aerosol, it may be quite dangerous. Cleanliness also allows regular inspection of all parts for unusual wear patterns, dry lubrication, or clogged filters. All of these conditions warrant corrective action to prevent instrument or equipment breakdown.

Periodic lubrication, filter changes, membrane replacement, tubing changes, and so forth, are recommended, when appropriate, by most manufacturers. In many instances, these recommendations are set arbitrarily at the time of the instrument's introduction. A conscientious vendor will modify a maintenance program regularly as service information is obtained. It is also good practice to recommend deletions of procedures no longer found valid.

Preventive maintenance should not be geared to a rigid time schedule, but performed based on an instrument check. It is not necessary to change operational parts until the need is indicated by this check. Life expectancies of membranes, electrodes, light sources, or measuring devices are variable and may fluctuate greatly from one time to the next. It is hoped that future instruments all will have some type of overall instrument function check for all or most stages of instrument operation. A valid instrument check may eliminate the need for some other daily quality control check.[48]

Today's microprocessor-controlled instrumentation requires little in the way of user maintenance. Preventive maintenance still needs to be done on a regular basis to adjust voltages and timing cycles for component degradation or wear. Most of this maintenance cannot be done by the casual laboratorian, but requires trained personnel with electronic test instrumentation suited for voltage monitoring.

PERSONNEL QUALIFICATIONS

At the heart of any laboratory quality assurance program are the people who monitor and do the tests. All aspects of quality laboratory work are difficult if not impossible to monitor objectively, and subjective judgment can be properly executed only by individuals who can be relied upon to realize when a test result may be compromised.

History of Personnel Qualifications

Clinical laboratory tests have been associated with medicine since humans first realized that they could change the natural course of an illness. Throughout most of history, laboratory tests have been simplistic, empirical, and sometimes outlandish.[49] It wasn't until the nineteenth century, when chemistry and microbiology developed, that clinical laboratory tests found reliability. However, the modern laboratory is a creation of the twentieth century. Nineteenth-century physicians, even knowing the actual organism or blood chemistry level, could do little with this knowledge to aid the patient. Anatomic diagnosis of surgical cases was not routinely needed, as surgery was still primitive and rare. Both situations changed about 1900 with the introduction of the first bactericidal agents[50] and the implementation of safe anesthesia.[51]

Clinical laboratories moved slowly out of physicians' offices, starting in 1889 at Johns Hopkins Hospital, and later in 1896 at both Massachusetts General Hospital and Boston City Hospital.[52] New York City and Massachusetts started public health laboratories in 1892 and 1894, respectively. Still, by 1914 only 48 percent of American hospitals had laboratories. Two significant changes occurred that advanced the introduction of clinical laboratories to hospitals. First was the realization that a hospital could sell laboratory tests to a patient at a profit, which then could be used to subsidize other areas.[52] Second was the growing use of surgery as a safe, accepted medical procedure. In order to assure the public of safe practices, the American College of Surgeons (ACS) was founded in 1918.[53] In 1920, the ASC required that the services of a pathologist, or a physician interested in pathology, be obtained and a laboratory be available for bacteriology, serology, and histology.[54] By 1926, the ACS required histologic examination of all tissue surgically removed and added chemistry and hematology to the list of required laboratory services.[55]

As laboratories and laboratory test volumes grew, it became obvious that all work could not be performed directly by the laboratory director, and technicians were hired. With the start of formal training programs and the loss of services of many physicians in World War I, acceptance and use of technicians became commonplace.[52]

Solidification of the technician's role started with the formation of the American Society for Clinical Pathology (ASCP) in 1921. By 1925, the ASCP started studying certification of technician qualifications, and a registry for certified medical technologists and laboratory technicians was started in 1929.[56] Technologists had a college degree, with at least 1 year of clinical training and 1 year of science. Technicians had a high school degree and 6 months experience. An exam was required at both levels. Success of the program was based on the willingness of an individual to be certified and the corresponding willingness of the pathologist to hire certified people.

A second cornerstone of the ASCP program was the certification of schools and training programs. No commercial schools were certified and, in 1950, most schools had an average of seven students. Most were hospital based, which had the obvious advantage in training replacement personnel.

Paralleling private-sector developments in personnel standards were developments in the public sector. Several states and New York City had personnel licensure programs before the enactment of the federal Medicare Act in 1965.[57] That act, and the Clinical Laboratory Improvement Act of 1967,[58] introduced governmental standards for laboratory personnel. As these standards were meant to encompass all laboratories, they allowed more personnel to be qualified at the director, supervisor, technologist, and technician levels than the private system. Due to tremendous inertia developed since the 1920s by the private system, there are no statistically valid studies that can be used to determine whether qualification differences impact on patient care or quality of test results. Several limited recent reports have shown that they do not.[52,59,60] A recent survey of instrument manufacturers shows that they expect the laboratory of 1995 to be staffed mostly with high school graduates, implying a lessening of personnel standards.[61]

How does this history affect quality assurance? First, it is evident that early decisions creating the clinical laboratory were based not on quality, but on both fiscal need and the requirement for monitoring quality of the then-emerging surgical programs. Pathologists, who were made directors of these early laboratories, structured them so that they could utilize a pool of highly trained technologists. In turn, this pool produced the fiscal resources need to operate the entire laboratory, and other parts of the hospital, but was not allowed to participate fully either in establishing qualifications or fiscal gains. Today, we see much discussion revolving around the qualifications for laboratory director, but have lost sight of changes revolving around the bench worker. Maintaining the present certifying systems has led to job dissatisfaction,[62] rating medical technology as one of the most stressful professions,[63] and rapid turnover of personnel, none of which is conducive to producing a quality laboratory result.[64]

Laboratory Director

The laboratory director's role is intuitively obvious. A modern laboratory has three separate and distinct roles: It is a technical organization performing complex scientific studies; it is a consulting service to its users, the physicians; and it is a business. In days past, it was felt that the laboratory director should be responsible for all aspects of laboratory operation. Today, this role is seen as multifaceted and perhaps best shared.

In a teaching and research institution, the role of the laboratory director is compounded by the need to support the sometimes unusual demands placed on the laboratory by the complex patient mix and specialized staff being served. Further adding to the complexity is the need to service the teaching of medical students, residents, and future laboratory workers.[65] Usually, these institutions are served by both a clinical and anatomic laboratory, each with its own director. Within each laboratory are subsections, each directed by a person with an M.D., M.D./Ph.D., Ph.D., or M.S. degree who specializes in that area of the laboratory. Daily personnel and budget matters often are handled either by a chief technologist or a fiscal officer. Although this system tends to be expensive, it does meet the research, service, and training demands placed on it.

Large urban hospitals have many of the problems of a teaching institution without the luxury of support income from tuition, grants, or endowments. Most of these hospitals have laboratories organized as one entity with an overall director who is, in most instances, a pathologist. Again, this person has help in the daily laboratory operation through a chief technologist. A business officer is also becoming more common and necessary as operational budgets easily exceed $1 million a year, with $3 million to $5 million budgets not uncommon. Today, fiscal pressures have turned the pathologist director in these laboratories away from providing technical leadership in the clinical laboratory and could lead to a decline in quality over the next several years.[66]

Smaller urban hospitals work very well under the system established in the 1920s. A pathologist director can truly oversee all aspects of laboratory operation and can provide meaningful guidance in most areas. Need for surgical review dictates the decision reached almost 70 years ago for the choice of laboratory director, and in most cases, the choice leads to quality for this type of laboratory.

Rural medicine is a problem throughout the world. It is a problem compounded in America by the desire of smaller communities to want nearby, first-class medical care. Despite the growing sophistication of rural hospitals, most still serve as stabilization centers for difficult cases, which are then transferred to a larger institution. One of the most perplexing problems for laboratorians today is the qualifications of the person chosen to head the laboratory in a small rural hospital. The amount of surgical pathology is not enough to support the on-site availability of a pathologist, so their time is divided among many laboratories. In order to meet regulatory demands, a staff physician is sometimes named as director of the laboratory. If that person has no knowledge of the needs of a modern laboratory, quality will suffer. In actuality, many believe that the director of such a laboratory is the senior technologist, who gets no recognition, either fiscal or otherwise, for filling this role. Many times this de facto head is ill prepared for the job.

Lack of an organizational career ladder admits many people to one rung with no chance of movement, no matter how high or low that rung may be. Lack of job satisfaction at all levels quickly sets in, and quality suffers.[62]

Staffing Levels

Adequate performance from laboratory personnel can be realized only when the number of workers is able to do the incoming work comfortably. As it is difficult to predicate staffing levels from billed test volume due to varying test complexity, application of industry-proven time-motion studies[67] was introduced into the clinical laboratory in Canada[68] and was soon adopted by the United States.[69]

As now implemented, the present work-load recording system uses time studies based on a standard format recorded at several volunteer laboratories for each procedure.[69] The studies record time segments for initial specimen handling, specimen testing, recording and reporting, daily performance, maintenance and repair, solution preparation, glassware washup, and direct technical supervision. From these studies an average unit value, in minutes, is derived. To use the system, the laboratory counts each unit performed, multiplies by the unit value, and then has a derived time proportional to the time spent by laboratory personnel on that test (Table 4-4). Summation of

TABLE 4-4
MONTHLY COMPARATIVE WORK-LOAD ANALYSIS REPORT

Statistic	Definitions	Laboratory section	Entire laboratory
A Total			
1 Raw counts	Total number of procedures, including QC, standards, and repeats	+	+
2 Unit value	Total raw count × unit values	+	+
B Worked			
1 Hours	Technical, clerical, and aide time minus vacations and sick time	+	+
2 Productivity*	Total unit value divided by worked man hours	+	+
C Paid hours	Technical, clerical, and aide time including vacation and sick time	+	+
D Paid hours productivity*	Total unit value divided by paid hours		
1 Last 6 months	Sum of last 6 months' productivities divided by 6	+	+
2 Last 12 months	Sum of last 12 months' productivities divided by 12	+	+
3 Current month		+	+
4 Peer size	Number of similar-sized labs	+	+
5 Peer type	Number of similar-sized labs	+	+
6 All labs	All participants	+	+

*Productivity in minutes per hour.

derived times for all tests gives an estimate for the amount of time spent performing laboratory work load.

Correct interpretation of the derived time is needed to ensure adequate laboratory staffing levels. Work-load factors are the same for large and small laboratories; they do not take into account levels of computerization; many new tests or instruments, which could encompass a large portion of a laboratory's work load, are not given factors for 1 or 2 years; supervisor time, other than direct technical supervision, is not counted, nor is pathologist or clinical laboratory scientist time; and time spent by the laboratory in needed development of new methods, tests, or procedures is not accounted for. From these factors one realizes that the work-load recording system should be viewed only as an estimate of actual time spent.

When converting estimates of derived time from work-load recording into personnel needs, corrections should be made for individual site differences. Staffing needs are based on hours actually needed to do the work versus working hours available/paid.[70] In addition, staffing needs vary by time of day and hospital case mix.[71] Intensive-care patients require large numbers of laboratory tests. Staffing at less than adequate levels will lead to compromises in quality[72] from either time constraints placed on the workers or turnover of workers from job dissatisfaction.

RESULT REPORTING

A test result is the quality product that a laboratory produces. That result must be produced in a timely fashion and reported in a form usable by physicians. As with most areas of quality assurance, no simple solution to either problem has evolved.

A laboratory report must provide all the information needed to identify the patient correctly; information about the particular test result itself, including units; and reference interval. Tests ordered for therapeutic drug monitoring should state the time of last dose.[73] Recently, most laboratories throughout the world have converted to SI (International System of Units), which uses meter, kilogram, second, ampere, kelvin, candela, and mole as base units.[74] Numeric values for many constituents change greatly when expressed in SI units versus traditional units, making the need for the unit description on the report even greater.[75] Such subtle changes as reporting in mass per liter instead of mass per milliliter can cause great confusion if not expressed properly.

Results must be accompanied by a reference range. Usually this range will refer to the values found in a statistically significant number of disease-free people.[76,77] Reference ranges, when necessary, should be characterized by age and sex and, if statistical differences appear, ranges should be given for differing age/sex combinations.[78-80] Reference ranges may also be established for other patient populations—for instance, healthy runners; pregnant females, first trimester; etc.[81] Harris has derived some useful transforms that help in the statistical analysis of reference-range data.[82]

Studies have shown that physicians appear to ignore unexpected laboratory test results (see Chapter 1).[83-86] To help make reports more useful, manual reporting systems are being replaced by computer-generated reports (see Chapter 16). Even computer-generated cumulative reports do not solve the presentation problem, as some physicians object to the format and tend to lose information in the mass of data presented.

To prevent results from being overlooked, the interpretative report apparently is the most successful way of presenting laboratory data.[87] Many examples of interpretative reports exist,[88-92] but they all have a common theme in that an abnormal result is highlighted either graphically or by locating it in a separate portion of the report. All have some type of explanation as to why the result may be abnormal. A positive quality assurance aspect of the report is the knowledge that the physician will see the odd results.[93] Because the interpretation is based solely on laboratory data and in many cases a single laboratory datum, it may either give no additional information or may be wrong.[93]

A second reporting responsibility of the laboratory is the need to get results to the physician within a period of time that is medically useful. Several studies have been done to determine acceptable turnaround time for tests.[87,94-97] Gambino has published a thoughtful set of criteria that describe four classes of tests based on turnaround time: immediate feedback; 15 min to 1 hour; same shift; and several days.[95] Immediate-feedback tests include those whose values have an immediate impact on the management of the patient and include blood gases, electrolytes, and coagulation studies. Intermediate emergency tests would include tests such as glucose, hematology studies, spinal fluid studies, electrolytes, and coagulation studies. Same-shift tests include enzyme studies, profiles, hematology studies, microbiology when possible, and drug levels. Other tests needed for diagnostic evaluation, such as hormone levels, may take several days. Barnett has surveyed 38 hospital laboratories and reported on the emergency turnaround time for many analytes and found most to be under 1 hour.[96]

Today the need for rapid test turnaround may deviate from the medical need criteria established in the 1970s for fiscal reasons.[98] Medical needs also change. Growing numbers of ectopic pregnancy cases and treatment modalities based on serum chorionic gonadotropin levels require faster turnaround time for this analyte.[99] When used for diagnostic purposes, fertility hormone values do not need rapid turnaround; but when used to monitor ovulation in a patient undergoing therapy, they do. Laboratory quality, as viewed by the users, the physicians, suffers when these needs are not met.

SUMMARY

Two recent articles[100,101] have tried to describe what constitutes a quality laboratory. It is interesting to note that both stress subjective items using terms such as credibility, reputation, leadership, and knowledge as key factors. When discussing quality control programs, Reece mentions four items that should be found in a quality laboratory: selection of the proper standards, internal and external control of the analytical process, reporting results in a form physicians can use, and aiding the physician in understanding the results.[100]

In this chapter, we have described how understanding interference phenomena can aid in test selection, the problems with and types of standards, the maintenance of equipment, the impact of personnel standards on laboratory testing and direction, and the impact of result reporting. Many aspects of these factors are subjective. Most literature cited deals with the small amount of objective data that can be obtained. Study needs to be given to those parts of a laboratory's quality that are not as easily quantifiable. We could then define more objective criteria, which then would allow us to monitor the impact of change on laboratory quality.

REFERENCES

1. Albrink MJ, Man EB, Peters JP: The relation of neutral fat to lactescence of serum. *J Clin Invest* 1955, 34:147.
2. Albrink MJ, Hald PM, Man EB, et al: The displacement of serum water by the lipids of hyperlipemic serum: A rapid determination of serum water. *J Clin Invest* 1955, 34:1483.
3. Steffes MW, Freier E: A simple and precise method of determining true sodium, potassium and chloride concentrations in hyperlipemia. *J Lab Clin Med* 1976, 88:683.
4. Ladenson JH, Apple FS, Koch D: Misleading hyponatremia due to hyperlipemia: A method-dependent error. *Ann Int Med* 1981, 95:707.
5. Haythorn P, Sheehan M: Ultracentrifugation does not affect results of analyses for digoxin, cortisol, and calcium in lipemic sera. *Clin Chem* 1981, 27:634.
6. Cowles JC: Theory of dual-wavelength spectrometry for turbid samples. *J Opt Soc Am* 1969, 55:690.

7. Moss G, Staunton C: Blood flow, needle size and hemolysis—Examining an old wives' tale. *N Engl J Med* 1970, 282:967.
8. Koebke J, McFarland E, Mein M, et al: Venipuncture procedures, in Slockbower JM, Blumenfeld TA (eds): *Collection and Handling of Laboratory Specimens: A Practical Guide,* Philadelphia, JB Lippincott, 1983, pp 3–45.
9. Meites S, Levitt MJ: Skin puncture and blood collection techniques for infants. *Clin Chem* 1979, 25:183.
10. Van Kampen EJ, Zijlstra WG: Determination of hemoglobin and its derivatives, in Sobotka H, Stewart CP (eds): *Advances in Clinical Chemistry,* vol 8. New York, Academic Press, 1965, pp 141–187.
11. Laessig RH, Hassemer DJ, Paskey TA, et al: The effects of 0.1 and 1.0 percent erythrocytes and hemolysis on serum chemistry values. *Am J Clin Pathol* 1976, 66:639.
12. Lauff JJ, Kasper ME, Wu TW, et al: Isolation and preliminary characterization of a fraction of bilirubin in serum that is firmly bound to protein. *Clin Chem* 1982, 28:629.
13. Steindel SJ: Evaluation of a thrombin-containing blood-collection tube. *Clin Chem* 1980, 26:173.
14. Laessig RH, Westgard JO, Habig RL, et al: Evaluation of an improved serum separator tube for clinical chemistry determinations. *Clin Chem* 1978, 24:1019.
15. Young DS: Interpretation of clinical chemical data with the aid of automatic data processing. *Clin Chem* 1976, 22:1555.
16. Young DS, Pestaner LC, Gibberman V: Effects of drugs on clinical laboratory tests. *Clin Chem* 1975, 21:1D.
17. Christian DG: Drug interference with clinical interpretations. *Am J Clin Pathol* 1970, 54:1.
18. Rosalki SB: Plasma gamma-glutamyl transpeptidase elevation in patients receiving enzyme inducing drugs. *Lancet* 1971, ii:376.
19. Sundberg MW, Becker RW, Esders TW, et al: An enzymatic creatinine assay and a direct ammonia assay in coated thin films. *Clin Chem* 1983, 29:645.
20. Nakamura RM, Maggio ET: Biomolecular 2. Monoclonal antibodies—Methods of production and applications. *Ligand Rev* 1981, 3:6.
21. FDA-DHEW: Regulations for the enforcement of the federal Food, Drug and Cosmetic Act and the Fair Packaging and Labeling Act: Part 1—*In vitro* diagnostic products for human use. *Fed Reg* 1973, 38:7096.
22. Commission on Laboratory Inspection and Accreditation: *Reagent Water Specifications.* Skokie, IL, College of American Pathologists, 1978.
23. NCCLS Approved Standard ASC-3: *Specifications for Reagent Water Used in the Clinical Laboratory.* Villanova, PA, National Committee for Clinical Laboratory Standards, 1980.
24. ACS Committee on Analytical Reagents: *Reagent Chemicals: American Chemical Society Specifications,* ed 6. Washington, DC, American Chemical Society, 1981.
25. Kolthoff IM, Sandell EB: *Textbook of Quantitative Inorganic Analysis,* ed 3. New York, Macmillan, 1952, pp 423–426.
26. Hason DJ: Suggested definitions of clinical laboratory standards and reference materials. *Am J Clin Pathol* 1970, 54(suppl):451.
27. Stamm D: Reference materials and methods in clinical chemistry. *J Clin Chem Clin Biochem* 1979, 17:283.
28. Cannan RK: Proposal for a certified standard for use in hemoglobinometry. *Am J Clin Pathol* 1958, 30:211.
29. International Committee for Standardization in Haematology: Recommendations for haemoglobinometry in human blood. *Br J Haemat* 1967, 13(suppl.):71.

30 Kambli V, Barnett RN: Control of accuracy of CAP clinical standard solutions. *Am J Clin Pathol* 1974, 61:912.
31 Cali JP: The NBS standard reference materials program: An update. *Anal Chem* 1976, 48:802A.
32 Radin N: What is a standard? *Clin Chem* 1967, 13:55.
33 NCCLS Tentative Guideline NRSCC2-T: *Development of Reference Methods in Clinical Chemistry for the National Reference System for the Clinical Laboratory.* Villanova, PA, National Committee for Clinical Laboratory Standards, 1984.
34 NCCLS Tentative Guideline NRSCC3-T: *Development of Certified Reference Materials for the National Reference System for the Clinical Laboratory.* Villanova, PA, National Committee for Clinical Laboratory Standards, 1984.
35 Zanelli JM: Reference materials: Standards and samples. *J Nucl Med Allied Sci* 1982, 26:227.
36 Cotes PM, Gaines-das RE, Kirkwood TBL, et al: The stability of standards for radioimmunoassay of human TSH: Research Standard A and the International Reference Preparation, initially 68/38. *Acta Endocrinol* 1978, 88:291.
37 Bangham DR, Storring PL: Standardisation of human chorionic gonadotropin, HCG subunits, and pregnancy tests. *Lancet* 1983, i:390.
38 NBS Certificate: Standard Reference Material 909: Human Serum. Washington, DC, National Bureau of Standards, 1981.
39 Thornton DD: The gallium melting point standard: A determination of the liquid-solid equilibrium temperature of pure gallium on the International Practical Temperature Scale of 1968. *Clin Chem* 1977, 23:719.
40 Belk WP, Sunderman FW: A survey of the accuracy of chemical analyses in clinical laboratories. *Am J Clin Pathol* 1947, 17:853.
41 Skendzel LP: Guidelines for the design of laboratory surveys. *Am J Clin Pathol* 1970, 54:437.
42 Radin R, Mehaffey MA, Wylie RL: Proficiency testing experiences, NCDC FY 1968. *Clin Chem* 1968, 14:833.
43 Bjorkem I, Blomstrand R, Eriksson S, et al: Use of isotope dilution-mass spectrometry for accuracy control of different routine methods used in clinical chemistry. *Scand J Clin Lab Invest* 1980, 40:529.
44 Hansert E, Stamm D: Determination of assigned values in control specimens for internal accuracy control for interlaboratory surveys. *J Clin Chem Clin Biochem* 1980, 18:461.
45 Laue D: Efforts to verify laboratory quality through standardization. *Clin Chem* 1984, 30:927.
46 Whitehead TP, Woodford FP: External quality assessment of clinical laboratories in the United Kingdom. *J Clin Pathol* 1981, 34:947.
47 Ehrmeyer SS, Laessig RH: Alternative statistical approach to evaluating interlaboratory performance. *Clin Chem* 1985, 31:106.
48 Steindel SJ: Process control systems—A question waiting to be answered. *Pathologist* 1984, 38:465.
49 Foster WD: *A Short History of Clinical Pathology.* London, E&S Livingstone, 1961.
50 Hedgecock LW: *Antimicrobial Agents.* Philadelphia, Lea & Febiger, 1967.
51 Garrison FM: *An Introduction to the History of Medicine,* ed 4. Philadelphia, WB Saunders, 1929.
52 White WD: *Public Health and Private Gain: The Economics of Licensing Clinical Laboratory Personnel.* Chicago, Maarouf Press, 1979, pp 47–77.

53 Standard of efficiency for the first hospital survey of the college. *Bull Am Coll Surg* 1918, 3:1.
54 Bowman JG: Hospital standardization series: General hospitals of 100 or more beds, report for 1920. *Bull Am Coll Surg* 1921, 5:3.
55 Besley FA, Walker JB, Sommer EA, et al: Standardization of clinical laboratories. *Bull Am Coll Surg* 1927, 11:11.
56 Montgomery LG: A short history of the registry of medical technologists of the American Association of Clinical Pathologists. *Am J Clin Pathol* 1970, 53:433.
57 Schenken JR: Laboratory accreditation, licensure, and regulation, in Snyder JR, Larsen AL (eds): *Administration and Supervision in Laboratory Medicine.* Philadelphia, Harper & Row, 1983, pp 360–385.
58 Clinical Laboratories Improvement Act of 1967 Part F of Title III of the Public Health Service Act, Atlanta, Centers for Disease Control, 1967.
59 Healey K: *The Effect of Licensure on Clinical Laboratory Effectiveness.* D.Ph. thesis, University of California, Los Angeles, 1973.
60 Kenney ML: *Laboratory Quality and Director Qualifications: An Empirical Assessment of the Medicare Requirement That Directors of Independent Clinical Laboratories Possess Earned Doctorates.* D.Ph. thesis, University of California, Berkeley, 1984.
61 Sullivan RH: How 1995's instrumentation will impact the lab. *Med Lab Obs* 1985, 17:55.
62 Benezra N: Lab salaries and benefits: The tight squeeze. *Med Lab Obs* 1982, 14:33.
63 Haber SL, Inhorn MC: Beating burnout in the laboratory. *Med Lab Obs* 1981, 13:44.
64 Benezra N: Lab salaries and benefits: Will a talent drain help. *Med Lab Obs* 1982, 14:43.
65 Garber AH, Fuchs VR, Silverman JF: Case mix, cost and outcomes: Differences between faculty and community services in a university hospital. *N Engl J Med* 1984, 310:1231.
66 DHHS-HFCA 42 CFR Part 405: Medicare program: payment for physician services furnished in hospitals, skilled nursing facilities and comprehensive outpatient rehabilitation facilities. *Fed Reg* 1983, 48:8902.
67 Smalley HE, Freeman JR: *Hospital Industrial Engineering: A Guide to the Improvement of Hospital Management Systems.* New York, Reinhold, 1966.
68 *Canadian Schedule of Unit Values for Clinical Laboratory Procedures.* Statistics Canada, Health and Welfare Division, Institutions Section, 1969.
69 Workload Recording Committee: *Manual for Laboratory Workload Recording Method,* ed 1985, Skokie, IL, College of American Pathologists, 1984.
70 Rubenstein NM: Realistic staffing via workload recording. *Med Lab Obs* 1984, 16:58.
71 Harper SS: The key to predicting laboratory workload. *Med Lab Obs* 1984, 16:65.
72 Whitlow KJ, Campbell DJ: Assessment of technologist workload as a factor in quality laboratory performance. *Am J Clin Pathol* 1983, 79:609.
73 NCCLS Proposed Standard PST/DM-1: *Standard for the Development of Requisition Forms for Therapeutic Drug Monitoring and/or Overdose Toxicology.* Villanova, PA, National Committee for Clinical Laboratory Standards, 1979.
74 International Standards Organization: SI units and recommendations for the use of multiples and of certain other units. International Standards IS 1000, 1972.
75 Lehmann HP: Metrication of clinical laboratory data in SI units. *Am J Clin Pathol* 1976, 65:2.
76 Schneider AJ: Some thoughts on normal, or standard, values in clinical medicine. *Pediatrics* 1960, 26:973.
77 Sunderman FW Jr: Current concepts of "normal values," "reference values," and "discrimination values" in clinical chemistry. *Clin Chem* 1975, 21:1873.

78 Boyd JC, Lacher DA: The multivariate reference range: An alternative interpretation of multitest profiles. *Clin Chem* 1982, 28:259.
79 Johnson TR: How growing up can alter lab values. *Diag Med* 1982, 5:12.
80 Munan L, Kelly A, Carrier G: Population-based pediatric reference intervals. *Diag Med* 1982, 5:21.
81 Brown GW: What makes a reference range? *Diag Med* 1984, 7:61.
82 Harris EK, DeMets DL: Estimation of normal ranges and cumulative proportions by transforming observed distributions to gaussian form. *Clin Chem* 1972, 18:605.
83 Schneiderman LJ, DeSalvo L, Baylor S, et al: The "abnormal" screening laboratory results. *Arch Intern Med* 1972, 129:88.
84 Bates B, Yellin JA: The yield of multiphasic screening. *JAMA* 1972, 222:74.
85 Korvin CC, Pearce RH, Stanley J: Admission screening: Clinical benefits. *Ann Intern Med* 1975, 83:197.
86 Fletcher SW, Sourkes M, Rabzel M, et al: Multiphasic screening: Case-forming tool in a teaching hospital and medical clinic. *JAMA* 1977, 237:887.
87 Speicher CE, Smith JW Jr: *Choosing Effective Laboratory Tests*. Philadelphia, WB Saunders, 1983.
88 Altshuler CH: The usefulness of laboratory information in medical monitoring, in Young DS, Uddin D, Nipper H, et al (eds): *Clinician and Chemist: The Relationship of the Laboratory to the Physician*. Washington, DC, American Association for Clinical Chemistry, 1979, pp 284–296.
89 Reece RL, Hobbie RK: Computer evaluation of chemistry values: A reporting and diagnostic aid. *Am J Clin Pathol* 1972, 57:664.
90 Henry JB: Introduction to organ panels, in Henry JB, Giegel JL (eds): *Quality Control in Laboratory Medicine*. New York, Masson Publishers, 1976, pp 1–13.
91 Galen RS, Gambino SR: *Beyond Normality: The Predicative Value and Efficiency of Medical Diagnoses*. New York, John Wiley & Sons, 1975.
92 Albert A: On the computation of likelihood ratios in clinical chemistry. *Clin Chem* 1982, 28:1113.
93 Reece RL, Hobbie RK: Use of a computer to issue interpretive reports: Do clinicians find this form of reporting useful? in Young DS, Uddin D, Nipper H, et al (eds): *Clinician and Chemist: The Relationship of the Laboratory to the Physician*. Washington, DC, American Association for Clinical Chemistry, 1979, pp 322–333.
94 Lundberg GD: *Managing the Patient-Focused Laboratory*. Oradell, NJ, Medical Economics Co, 1975.
95 Gambino SR: Laboratory services for intensive care units, in Kinney JM, Bendixen HH, Powers SR (eds): *Manual of Surgical Intensive Care*. Philadelphia, WB Saunders, 1977, pp 143–149.
96 Barnett RN, McIver DD, Gorton WL: The medical usefulness of stat tests. *Am J Clin Pathol* 1978, 69:520.
97 Chu RC, Williams WV, Eisenburg JM: The characteristics of stat laboratory tests. *Arch Pathol Lab Med* 1982, 106:662.
98 DHHS-HCFA: Medicare program; schedule of target rate percentages for limits on the rate of hospital cost increases and updating factors for transition prospective payment rates. *Fed Reg* 1983, 48:39746.
99 Kadar N, Caldwell BV, Romero R: A method of screening for ectopic pregnancy and its indications. *Obstet Gynecol* 1981, 58:162.
100 Reece RL: What to look for in a quality lab. *Pathologist* 1981, 35:203.
101 Gilmer PR Jr: The quality laboratory—Another view. *Pathologist* 1982, 36:25.

CHAPTER 5

MANUFACTURE OF QUALITY CONTROL MATERIALS

Richard S. Thuma
Joseph L. Giegel, Ph.D.
Alan H. Posner, Ph.D.

HISTORICAL PERSPECTIVE

Levey and Jennings[1] are credited with the introduction of a major tool for effecting laboratory improvement in 1950: the application and adaptation of industrial statistical quality control (QC) techniques to the clinical laboratory. Their application required a frozen plasma pool to be utilized in daily clinical chemical analysis in duplicate determinations. The statistical treatment of the daily values determined limits of acceptable day-to-day performance.

This approach used within-day variation as the basis for evaluation of day-to-day variations. Both within-day differences of duplicates and mean values of the pair of daily results were plotted on charts for interpretation. They observed that laboratory errors could be detected and attributed to personnel, instruments, reagents, standards, and laboratory environment. Changing results due to control material deterioration were also observed. A fundamental assumption of this method is that within-day laboratory variability is equivalent to long-term laboratory variability. Furthermore, application of the method assumes Gaussian distribution of the laboratory data variability. Another proposal includes limits of three standard deviations around the mean, as applied by Henry and Segalove,[2] even though they stated that the analytic results were not Gaussian in distribution.

Shortly thereafter, regional groups of laboratories contracted with commercial manufacturers for large pools of chemistry quality control materials for use in daily quality control programs. The controls were used daily, and the laboratories returned data to a central computer facility for calculation of standard statistical parameters and comparison with each other. This expanded approach allowed laboratories to compare their relative precision and relative accuracy (bias) to that obtained by peer laboratories on a daily basis.

Copeland and Rosenbaum soon followed in Massachusetts, contracting for both quality control products and computerized data reduction services.[3] In the United States, regional QC programs have since evolved into a major form of internal quality control.

UTILITY OF CONTROL MATERIALS

The assumption that quality of patient results can be assured by repetitive testing of control products is one that has sparked unresolved debate. The assumption can be true only if the control product is identical in all respects to patient specimens.

A number of factors, other than disease, affect analyte levels in patient sera. These include age, sex, and race, which are often recognized by the establishment of reference (normal) ranges. In addition, however, results are affected by controllable factors such as type of diet, duration of fasting, posture, time of day, and drug ingestion, the latter having potential in vivo effects on analyte levels as well as causing, in some cases, in vitro chemical interference. The entire process of patient specimen collection, preparation, and storage prior to analysis also uniquely affects patient specimen analyses, potentially causing greater errors than the analytic process itself. Thus, laboratories must pay increasing attention to these preanalytic factors in the future.

Control materials remain the tools by which compliance to medical precision performance standards is measured. The comparability of precision estimates using general chemistry control sera to fresh human sera has been established.[4] It is possible, generally, to draw reliable conclusions regarding medical usefulness from internal quality control precision data.

MANUFACTURE OF CONTROL MATERIALS

Manufacturers have kept pace with the increasingly sophisticated and quality-conscious laboratory professional in making improvements to commercially produced control materials. That is not to say that poorly produced control materials cannot be purchased in today's market, for they may be readily obtained. However, improved manufacturing techniques have resulted in control materials of considerably higher quality.

Some laboratorians feel that two analyte levels for control sera are sufficient for assuring quality of analysis; others prefer three analyte levels. Manufacturers generally provide at least two and sometimes three in order to cover adequately the normal and abnormal patient result levels routinely encountered in a clinical setting. Of course, manufacturers have added new constituents to existing products as well as adjusting levels of existing constituents such that they now generally reflect important clinical levels. Commercial control materials are available not only for the chemistry and special chemistry laboratory but also for the blood gas, coagulation, and hematology laboratories.

There are several performance characteristics of control materials of primary importance to both the manufacturer and the user, as shown in Table 5-1. The first two factors, stability and vial-to-vial variability, are of critical importance in the use of

TABLE 5-1
PERFORMANCE CHARACTERISTICS OF CONTROL MATERIALS

Stability
Vial-to-vial variability
Accuracy of assigned values
Number of constituents
Constituent levels

control products. Both these factors are carefully evaluated and controlled during the manufacturing procedure. The third factor, accuracy of assigned values, is important for assayed control products. The accuracy depends on how each method is performed and on the testing protocol followed to assign the values.

Knowledge of the stability characteristics of analytes in quality control materials assists in identifying shifts and/or trends in quality control data caused by changes in the control material itself. Commercially prepared controls are tested to establish their stability by applying several protocols. Results from these studies provide the data to support long-term stability claims for these products as described in their package literature. Both lyophilized and liquid controls have stability claims of up to 3 years in length when proper storage conditions are observed.

Manufacturers of quality control materials generally apply stability testing protocols modeled partially after those used by the pharmaceutical industry. An important part of the protocol includes differentially stressing the material, usually by heat, and testing at intervals to determine the effect on the analytes. Although stress testing yields valuable information, the ideal method for establishing stability is real-time testing over the entire shelf life of the product.

Control serums are many times more complex than relatively pure drug products, and so the effect of the stress on the material is much less predictable and more difficult to interpret. Environmental stress to the multicomponent control material can result in many reactions initiated because of the minimal but measurable residual water present in the dried product. The increased temperature that is used during such stress testing can impart enough energy to the analytes to result in analyte interactions.

Chemistry Control Materials

Commercially prepared chemistry control materials are of two basic types: lyophilized and liquid. A further division may be made by characterizing the storage conditions for liquid controls as either frozen or nonfrozen. Table 5-2 summarizes some of the relative merits of commercially prepared quality control material versus laboratory-prepared controls.[5]

Lyophilized Controls Lyophilized (freeze-dried) control materials have extensive shelf lives—up to 3 years for some controls. The lyophilized material is usually stored at 4°C, whereas liquid material must be stored in a freezer. Since they can usually be

TABLE 5-2

ADVANTAGES OF COMMERCIALLY FORMULATED CONTROL MATERIALS

1 Convenience
2 Uniformity
3 Reliability
4 Storage
5 Transportability
6 Capital outlay
7 Facilities requirements
8 Personnel
9 Service
10 Quality control

exposed to room temperatures for several days without demonstrating any adverse effects, freeze-dried controls are usually less expensive to ship. The dried control materials must be reconstituted with water or a special buffer. Rehydrated control material has stability that varies from a few hours to several days.

Liquid Controls Substitution of glycol for approximately one-third of the water in control samples imparts certain specific characteristics to these reagents. Bacterial growth is inhibited by the high osmotic pressure (however, this very advantage prohibits the control's application in osmometry). The high osmotic pressure can also lead to unique problems in instrument systems that employ dialysis membranes as well as in the DuPont aca.[6] The wetting and spreading characteristics of this control do not make it the material of choice for use in systems employing dry film technology.

Although enzymes are very stable in this matrix, the high glycol (or glycerol) content make the control valueless in monitoring triglyceride analysis because the hydrolytic portion of the enzymatic triglyceride reaction is not monitored. The physical appearance and clarity of the material is excellent, although the viscosity is not the same as that of serum. Liquid controls must be stored in the freezer and carefully mixed before being used in an analytical system.

Manufacturing Considerations A generalized process flow for preparation of commercial chemistry controls is represented in Fig. 5-1. The major steps are outlined in Table 5-3. This model, with the exception of the assay stage, is applicable to the preparation of nearly all control materials, including those for coagulation, hematology, and blood gases.

Base Pool Stage The first manufacturing step is the preparation of the base pool, which is analyzed and the constituents adjusted to the required target levels. After adjustment, the pool is filtered to remove particulate matter. Immediately after filtration, it is accurately dispensed into vials under carefully controlled conditions and lyophilized. Lyophilization is followed by rather extensive product testing to ensure that constituent levels are in the desired range and the product meets specific quality standards.

To prepare the base pool, serum or plasma is collected and pooled. If plasma is

FIGURE 5-1
Generalized process flow for preparation of commercial chemistry controls.

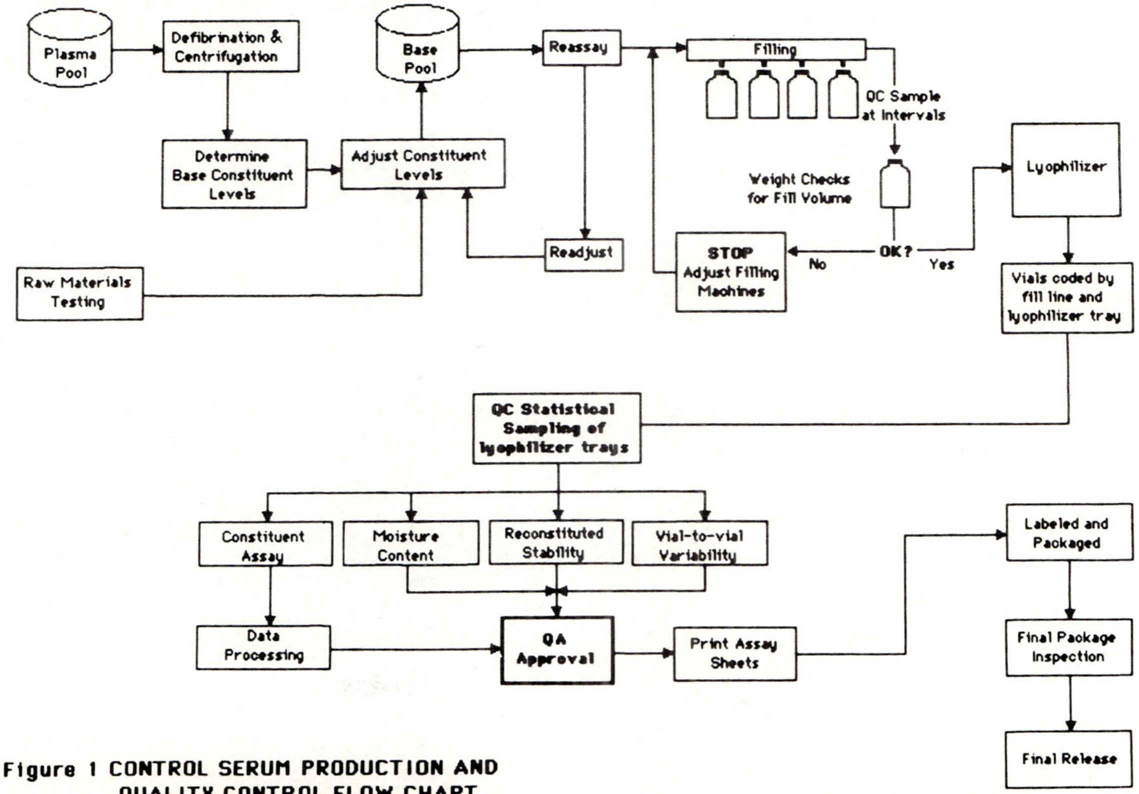

Figure 1 CONTROL SERUM PRODUCTION AND QUALITY CONTROL FLOW CHART

TABLE 5-3
MANUFACTURE OF QUALITY CONTROL POOLS

1. Preparation of base pool
2. Adjustment of constituent levels
3. Final filtration and filling
4. Lyophilization
5. Finished product testing
6. Assay

FIGURE 5-2
Mixing tank in which plasma is defibrinated. (Courtesy American Dade)

used, it is usually defibrinated (Fig. 5-2). Chemical tests are performed to ensure the integrity of the raw material serum/plasma pools. These "subpools" are stored frozen until used for production of a base pool. The base pool consists of about 1500 liters of the serum or defibrinated plasma placed in a refrigerated tank and mixed (Fig. 5-3). After mixing, samples are removed and assayed for key constituents. The results of the testing determine the adjustments required to bring the analytes into their predetermined target ranges.

FIGURE 5-3
Refrigerated tanks used for preparation of base pools. The middle tank is being cleaned following use. To prevent contamination, sterile precautions are used in this work area during pool preparation. (Courtesy American Dade)

Adjustments of Constituent Levels After each adjustment to the base pool, the effects of addition of one constituent on others is carefully evaluated. Additional testing is carried out and adjustments are made until the required level for each analyte is achieved. The levels in "normal" controls will vary considerably from those in "abnormal" controls. Often, specialized lots of material for large-volume users or survey materials are prepared to meet special analyte-level requirements. Manufacturing technology has been developed to allow adjustment of lipid, electrolyte, and enzyme levels to almost any specifically requested levels.

Final Filtration After adjustment, the pool is extensively filtered to remove particulate matter. Initially filtration is through a series of pads to clarify the pool, then through membranes capable of removing particles as small as 0.45 μm. A final membrane filtration of the pool through 0.22-μm filters is carried out as it is dispensed into vials. To protect sensitive constituents during filtration, the temperature of the pool is maintained between 2°C and 8°C, and exposure to light is eliminated.

The Filling Process The filling operation is the next major step in the production process. Delivery of a precise volume throughout the run is, of course, a critical part of the filling process. Maximum limits are set for the variablity of the volume of liquid delivered to each vial to assure low interval variability in the final product. Fill-volume checks are performed frequently in order to achieve minimal vial-to-vial variation. Pool homogeneity is also enhanced during this process by keeping the material at a low temperature and protected from light. After filling, the vials are loosely plugged with special stoppers. Each stopper is partly inserted into the neck of each vial. This allows sublimation to occur freely during lyophilization.

Lyophilization When filling is complete, the lyophilization process is initiated on all vials at the same time. By removing water to a very low level, this process produces the long-term stability required of a quality control material. Lyophilization is usually designed to achieve a residual moisture of less than 1 percent, although the cycle may be adjusted to achieve other residual moisture levels. The length of the lyophilization cycle is dependent on the volume of the liquid in a vial and may take as long as 3 days. After the cycle is completed, the lyophilizer shelves move to compress the stoppers, pushing them fully into the vials and thus sealing the bottles under vacuum (see Figs. 5-4 and 5-5).

Although an alternative process is sometimes used in which, prior to sealing, the vacuum is broken with an inert, dry gas, such as nitrogen, plugging under vacuum is preferable. During the manufacture of millions of vials, an occasional vial will fail to stopper properly and air may enter the vial. This improper stoppering leads to deterioration of some constituents. If the material is packed under nitrogen, leakage is not obvious when the vial is opened. If a vial plugged under vacuum has leaked, the absence of the characteristic sound of rushing air upon opening the vial tells the user immediately that the vial is defective.

Although lyophilization stabilizes the control, it also results in certain other changes in the control sample. One of these changes is the loss of carbon dioxide. This loss of CO_2 can result in an increase in pH when the material is reconstituted with water. Manufacturers may offer bicarbonate diluents as a means for restoring the CO_2 levels and for pH control of the product.

Another major change due to lyophilization is denaturation of lipoprotein. Lyophilization results in the loss of resolution of the pre-beta and beta lipoprotein bands detected during lipoprotein electrophoresis. This loss of resolution is the result of denaturation of pre-beta lipoprotein. This denaturation is also the principal cause of the increased turbidity seen with serum after it is lyophilized. This is not unexpected, because the pre-beta fraction contains the highest lipid-to-protein ratio of any lipoprotein class.

High-density lipoprotein (HDL), however, is relatively stable during lyophilization, because it has the lowest lipid-to-protein ratio of the lipoprotein fractions. Owing to this, it is possible to elevate the cholesterol levels in controls by adding bovine HDL. Bovine HDL is available in large quantities, is rich in cholesterol and cholesterol esters, and is comparable to the alpha lipoprotein fraction of human serum.

Raw Material Source and Costs Choice of starting materials is the starting point for manufacture of controls. Ideally, the control should be as qualitatively and quantitatively similar to the unknown as possible, but without the known instability problems of patient specimens. The cost of human plasma and serum has risen dramatically

FIGURE 5-4
External view of two lyophilizers (*left*). A worker is adjusting the control panel of one unit. (Courtesy American Dade)

as the competition for this material has increased. The increased demand is due largely to increased demand by therapeutic plasma fractionators and by increased control usage.

Because of the rapidly escalating prices, manufacturers are constantly exploring methods of reducing costs. One of the most popular methods is substitution of alternative plasma sources for the human materials; these alternatives include bovine, equine, and porcine sources. Some commercial control materials are blends of these and human source materials. Controls prepared from nonhuman sources do have certain benefits other than cost. One of the most important is that the material need not be screened for hepatitis or human T-lymphotropic virus, type III (HTLV-III).

Constituent Interaction Adjustments of analytic levels of base pools may appear to be relatively simple. For instance, in order to elevate the carbon dioxide level of a control, bicarbonate anion usually is employed in the diluent. Problems may arise if ammonium bicarbonate is used: Elevated urea and creatinine values may be recovered by certain enzymatic methods. Additionally, some ion-selective electrodes for measuring sodium or potassium may be desensitized by excess ammonium ions.[7]

The major difficulty presented to the manufacturer lies in choosing the source for

FIGURE 5-5
Interior of a lyophilizer showing shelves that compress, thereby sealing vials. (Courtesy American Dade)

biologically active components for addition to the control matrix. Naturally, these decisions are constantly undergoing reevaluation in light of current research.

Ideally, human sources should be used for biologically active constituents in control materials. In the case of enzymes, however, other choices must be made, because human tissue is difficult for the commercial manufacturer to obtain. For example, although human liver would be an excellent source of aspartate aminotransferase (AST), its relative unavailability requires sources such as porcine hearts. Other types of problems are encountered with alkaline phosphatase (ALP). That ALP in human specimens and control products differ in their response to changes in assay conditions is well documented.[7-10] This is not surprising because of the differences in ALP isoenzymes that occur among specimens and the difficulty mimicking isoenzyme composition of specimens using animal sources. The complexity of the problem is illustrated by some studies that report porcine kidney ALP has biochemical activity similar to that of human liver and serum ALP, whereas others have shown the porcine preparation differs in activity from human liver, kidney, and placental ALP.[8,10,11]

Amylase controls may contain amylase from many different sources, including human saliva, human pancreas, porcine pancreas, and bovine pancreas. It has been shown that pancreatic and salivary amylase isoenzymes have different affinity coefficients and activities depending on the substrate used.[12] Robyt and French[13] reported that porcine amylase activity is lower when maltotetrose is used as the substrate than when maltopentose is used. Older methods for determination of amylase were based on the enzyme's activity on saccharogenic, amyloclastic, and starch-dye substrates.[14]

When different substrate combinations are used, there is evidence that variable control results are obtained depending on the enzyme's source.

Numbers of Constituents   The number of constituents is a consideration in some comprehensive chemistry, immunochemistry, and therapeutic drug control materials. For purposes of convenience, most users prefer all the constituents of interest to their laboratory in a single vial. Although this has some practical limitations, chemistry control materials with more than 40 constituents assayed by several hundred instrument/reagent combinations are commonplace.

Almost all constituents of interest can be adjusted in some manner in the manufacturing procedure; they are generally adjusted to levels that are at critical decision points to the clinician. However, special problems that affect the usefulness of the control may arise by elevating some constituents. For example, elevation of lipids may increase the turbidity of the control material. Compromises are sometimes necessary in setting constituent levels so that values close to the desired level are achieved without detrimental effect on others. Table 5-4 contains a tabular representation of the constituents most commonly included in comprehensive chemistry control materials.

Lot-to-Lot Variation   The manufacturers of control materials maintain what may be called target ranges of concentration for every analyte contained in the final control material. These targets are more than just guides; they assist in the manufacture of lots that are quite similar to each other on a consistent basis. Although it is impossible to manufacture two consecutive lots of control materials that are identical, the application of these target ranges assures at least relatively small shifts in control values when a new lot is implemented.

Maintaining minimal lot-to-lot variability is an extremely difficult task and begins with the base pool: The matrix must have an albumin/total protein ratio close to that of previous lots. As adjustments for each analyte are made, some difficulties usually are found. The formulation of electrolytes, glucose, urea, uric acid, creatinine, inorganic phophorus, lipids, and even bilirubin presents no great problem. It is the biologically active components, mainly enzymes, that offer the most difficult challenge, because different lots vary considerably in their stability, activity loss upon lyophilization, and level of contaminating enzymes.

Assignment of Assay Values   Assay procedures for comprehensive control materials are labor and time intensive. For a chemistry control material such as Moni-Trol®, there are approximately 40 constituents in each level; more than 400 different methods are used for assigning values to those constituents using a combination of internal and reference laboratory generated data. The assay protocols are set up in such a way that vial-to-vial variability can be evaluated within a given run. The assay protocol is designed to obtain a reliable estimate of mean values. Information commonly furnished to users by manufacturers is summarized in Table 5-5.

The actual standard deviation and expected range may differ considerably. The expected range indicates the performance of the method in most laboratories. It is the range of acceptable mean values that may be expected when measured under different conditions. The standard deviation provides an estimate of how well the method may

TABLE 5-4
COMMON CONSTITUENTS OF CHEMISTRY CONTROLS

Electrolytes
  Calcium
  Chloride
  Copper
  Lithium
  Magnesium
  Phosphate
  Potassium
  Sodium
  Zinc
Lipids
  Cholesterol
  Total lipids
  Triglycerides
  HDL cholesterol
General
  Total bilirubin
  Direct bilirubin
  Blood urea nitrogen
  Creatinine
  Glucose
  Iron-binding capacity
  Iron
  Uric acid
Thyroid
  T-3 uptake
  Compensated T-4
  Thyroxine
  TSH

Enzymes
  Amylase
  Creatine phosphokinase
  Gamma glutamyltranspeptidase
  Hydroxybutyric dehydrogenase
  Lactate dehydrogenase
  Lipase
  Alkaline phosphatase
  Acid phosphatase
  Transaminase-AST
  Transaminase-ALT
Proteins
  Albumin
  Total protein
Therapeutic drugs
  Acetaminophen
  Digoxin
  Phenobarbital
  Phenytoin
  Salicylate
Radioassay
  Cortisol
  Folic acid
  Insulin
  Vitamin B_{12}

TABLE 5-5
ASSAY INFORMATION PROVIDED TO USERS

Mean values

Standard deviation of assay

Expected range

Method description

Reference intervals (normal ranges)

perform in a well-controlled laboratory. Each laboratory should establish its own mean and standard deviation.

Many manufacturers supply a brief method description, because many reagent manufacturers provide different methods for the same constituent. Also included is an estimate of the reference interval (normal range) for a reagent kit or instrument. This can be an aid in comparing results from differing methodologies.

TABLE 5-6
DESIRABLE CHARACTERISTICS OF BLOOD GAS CONTROLS

Matrix similar to the sample
Available in quantity
Long-term stability
Immediate availability for use
Convenient volume
No significant vial-to-vial variation
Target levels covering the expected range of results

Blood Gas Controls

Like controls in other clinical laboratory disciplines, blood gas analysis controls should have the same characteristics as those employed in the rest of the laboratory.[15] These include, but are not limited to, those tabulated in Table 5-6.

The characteristics listed in Table 5-6 are generally available for chemistry quality control materials, but are not completely available in the area of blood gas controls. Many commercially available blood gas controls require a temperature equilibration prior to measurement and generally have a shorter shelf life than chemistry controls. Also, blood gas controls are labile and easily contaminated by exposure to the atmosphere.

Although tonometry of whole blood may be the ideal method for control of blood gas analysis, many of the commercial materials offer advantages in terms of instrument control.[16] One of the principal problems with tonometry is its inappropriateness for determination of pH.[17] Other problems with application of tonometered blood for control purposes include the following:

1 The tonometered samples must be freshly prepared for each use. A source of whole blood, uncontaminated with hepatitis and HTLV-III, is required.
2 All technical staff must be trained in the use of the tonometer. This includes temperature monitoring, proper gas mixture and humidification, and adequate precautions to avoid air and bacterial contamination.
3 A tonometer represents additional capital expense.
4 pH controls still must be run.
5 Tonometry preparation usually requires between 20 and 30 min.

Types of Control Materials Currently, commercially prepared control materials are available in a number of formulations.

Aqueous buffers, with and without dyes, are equilibrated with different gas blends. These materials have the advantage of relatively low manufacturing expense and long shelf life. Disadvantages include their lack of resemblance to whole blood and extreme sensitivity to changes in levels caused by exposure to air during sampling or within the instrument.

Fluorocarbon emulsions are pH adjusted and gas equilibrated; generally they have viscosity adjusted to be more "blood-like" than aqueous-based materials. They have a high oxygen solubility and are less sensitive to changes on exposure to air, but also less sensitive to temperature changes within the blood gas instrument (see below).

Buffered protein controls are aqueous-based materials that have protein added to the matrix in order to approximate physiological conditions more closely. Because of the protein matrix, they may be less sensitive than other controls to changes or exposure to air.

Hemoglobin-based buffer solutions are adjusted for pH and equilibrated with carbon dioxide (CO_2) and oxygen (O_2). These controls are more blood-like than aqueous-based materials, but are more expensive to produce and have considerably shorter shelf lives.

Whole blood controls consist of a buffered suspension of erythrocytes that are tonometered to preset values with carbon monoxide, carbon dioxide, and oxygen. These controls represent the closest approximation to whole blood but are the most expensive to manufacture and have relatively short shelf lives.

Control Sensitivity Controls that are used in the assessment of the pH and partial pressures of CO_2 and O_2 measurements must also be sensitive to changes in temperature within the instrument. Leary et al.[18] have shown that tonometered whole blood, ampuled aqueous buffered controls, and a red cell-based control can all detect changes in instrument operating temperature by their changes in pH and/or PCO_2 assay values. Likewise, substantial temperature-induced shifts in PO_2 were observed for both the blood-based and whole blood samples, but had little effect on the aqueous buffered controls.

A disadvantage of the fluorocarbon control materials is their apparent insensitivity to temperature changes over a 5°C range.[19,20] In this regard, these controls may not be the controls of choice when detection of instrument temperature-control problems is desirable.

An important quality control consideration is the requirement for monitoring the constantly changing measurement system. There are many characteristics that can contribute to analytical/instrument variation in these measurements, some of which are tabulated in Table 5-7.

If the laboratory protocol required control analysis both before and after sample analysis, it would still be impossible to ensure that an error had not occurred—for example, incomplete washing of sample chamber, or the formation of an air bubble on a membrane. To ensure the quality of blood gas analyses, a three-phase quality control program has been used for blood gas analysis.[15] Included in this program are daily analysis of commercial blood gas controls at three levels; tonometry, at three known gas mixtures, of whole blood; and duplicate analysis of all specimens using different instruments. Data for the duplicate analyses are analyzed using *t*-test calculations for paired samples.[15]

Assay Assignment Assay value assignment for blood gas controls is similar to the procedures for other control materials, although not nearly as labor intensive for

TABLE 5-7
FACTORS CONTRIBUTING TO INSTRUMENT VARIATION

Electrode aging	Membrane aging
Protein buildup	Electrode drift
Pump tube aging	Clots
Calibration drift	Bacterial contamination

the manufacturer because of the relatively few instrument systems available. Most manufacturers market three levels of control materials, with values assigned for each level and instrument combination.

Stability A major factor in the blood gas control manufacturing cycle is the assurance of product free of nearly all microorganisms. Stability of most controls is dramatically affected by bacteria or mold metabolizing the material. Not only can these microorganisms consume oxygen; if they are numerous enough, they can interfere with instrument operation.

In summary, there is no perfect control for blood gas analysis because of the criteria outlined above. The intelligent application of controls can assist in the assurance of precise and accurate pH, PCO_2, and PO_2 analyses. The advantage of commercial controls is their ready availability and their ability to monitor three measured parameters in the blood gas instrument. The use of commercial controls also allows the user to participate in a quality control program with peer comparison.

HEMATOLOGY CONTROL MATERIALS

Control materials in hematology have the same basic criteria as controls in other disciplines; ideally, the material should have a structure and composition as similar as possible to that of the material being tested. The fundamental challenge facing the manufacturer of hematology control materials is preparation of a stable cell suspension that retains properties comparable to human leukocytes, erythrocytes, and platelets. Because of the heavy dependence on electronic cell-counting methods, the control red cells must not only resemble human cells in size and shape, they must react in like manner to the chemical lysing reagent used in such counters for the release of hemoglobin. Unlike chemistry and coagulation controls, with substantial stability intervals, the stabilization of blood preparations is very difficult: Erythrocytes (RBC) do not remain viable after stabilization, and the leukocytes (WBC) and platelets cannot be stabilized for long periods.[21]

Although manual counting methods with calibrated counting chambers are still in use today, automated analytical systems are the predominant techniques employed for counting blood cells. Electronic measurement of cell physical characteristics has achieved a remarkable level of precision and speed with the cell counting equipment currently available. In today's hematology laboratory, method errors of less than 1 percent for red cell–related measurements, MCH, and MCV are a necessity for diagnostic purposes.[22]

In order to provide a usable control material with adequate stability characteristics, manufacturers generally attempt improvement of the stability of the base constituents by use of various fixatives and stabilizers. Although the more strongly the cells are fixed, the greater their stability, there is a trade-off because cells that have been strongly fixed exhibit characteristics quite different from those of normal human blood cells in electronic counters.

The most easily demonstrated example of the effect of such fixatives is the rather lower spun hematocrit obtained with fixed cells. The lower hematocrit results from cell shrinkage due to the hypertonic suspension fluid.

On the other hand, if the manufacturing process fails to stabilize the cells properly, swelling or lysing may occur during the time the cells are being used, increasing mean cell volume (MCV) and hematocrit values. Clearly, the manufacturer must trade off between stability and the simulation of human blood.

These fundamental stabilization problems have provided the manufacturer with a formidable challenge: providing a material of reasonable stability so that assigned or assay values may be provided and used in a quality control program. Today, the most popular formulations for control materials are prepared from human blood in which red cells and platelets are preserved but unfixed. The white cell component typically consists of fixed red cells of avian origin. The unfixed red cells are preferred because during the white cell counting phase, the preserved but unfixed red cells are lysed, leaving the fixed avian red cells to be counted as leukocytes.

Types of Controls

Most manufacturers offer both seven- and eight-parameter control materials. As an adjunct to providing the control material, an assay representing determination of mean values and two standard derivation ranges and expected ranges is provided. Although the materials are called seven- or eight-parameter, more than seven or eight measurements are reported, because results include a number of calculated measures as shown in Table 5-8.

Hematology control materials are no different in their application than any of the other chemistry and coagulation controls: For hematology controls, assigned values and expected ranges are provided by the manufacturer. Variability in the composition of the control and accuracy of determination of the assigned values are two potential variables inherent in cell control reagents that may interfere with this process.

It is common for the hematology laboratory to run three levels of control on a daily basis; normal, abnormal high, and abnormal low. Control materials may or may not have assigned values (or ranges). Materials preferably are similar in composition to and are analyzed along with patient samples. Such controls must satisfy both count and size criteria. The cells in the control material are diluted in a medium containing substances critical in preserving the cells and preventing their aggregation. The medium must contain reasonable buffering to maintain pH as the cells age. Acidification of the control materials alters the cell volume. The advent of the multiparameter ana-

TABLE 5-8
PARAMETERS COMMONLY REPORTED
FROM AUTOMATED CELL COUNTERS

White cell count	WBC
Red cell count	RBC
Hemoglobin	HGB
Hematocrit	HCT
Mean cell volume	MCV
Mean cell hemoglobin	MCH
Mean cell hemoglobin concentration	MCHC
Red cell distribution width	RDW
Platelet count	PLT
Platelet crit	PCT
Mean platelet volume	MPV
Platelet distribution width	PDW

lyzer for the blood count has compounded the problem by demanding reliable multi-parameter control materials.

Composition

Most manufacturers utilize either a fixed or unfixed human RBC, mammalian or human platelets, and avian erythrocytes to simulate human WBC, although use of stabilized but unfixed red cells is the most popular. Most of these controls can be used quite successfully on particle-counting instruments. Obviously, because the instruments only count particles of selected sizes, the source of the particles is relatively unimportant if they simulate the behavior of human cells.

The red blood cells found in most manufacturer's controls are of human origin. Manufacturers describe their red blood cells as modified, stabilized, fixed, or unfixed. Fresh blood cells deteriorate rapidly and therefore require preservative for reliability as a control material.

Cell Stabilization Methods

When cells are "fixed," they are treated with a fixative such as aldehyde, which irreversibly changes the cell membrane. In contrast, "stabilized" cells undergo a process in which the suspending medium such as glycerol strengthens but does not irreversibly alter the cell membrane. "Unfixed" cells retain many characteristics of fresh whole blood cells and can be more stable than fixed cells. Also, fixed cells tend to be more difficult to resuspend.

There are, of course, some obvious advantages of unfixed control cells to the user: (1) Cells behave more like fresh whole blood cells; (2) complete mixing is easier to achieve; (3) complete lysis is effected during the WBC counting stage; (4) it is easier to verify or check the instrument result manually.

Erythrocytes (RBC)

The methods used to preserve cells influence their behavior in various analytical methods. Measured results depend on usual semipermeability and deformability of the RBC cell membranes. Stabilizing the cells has little influence on the red blood cell count (RBC) but greatly affects the hematocrit and the MCV. The impulse amplitude of the counter is influenced not only by the cell volume but also by the shape and the deformability of the cells. Aging impairs the deformability of the RBC and directly affects the hematocrit because of cell shrinkage. A number of disadvantages to the use of aldehyde-fixed RBC[23,24] include a tendency to clump and to adhere to walls of containers, RBC rigidity resulting in erroneously high hematocrit, and the danger of incomplete hemolysis during the very short lysing period used in modern blood flow cytometers.[25] These factors may lead to loss of accuracy and precision. In fact, undiluted fixed cells are not suitable for use in fully automated counters.[23] Low-temperature preservation of RBC in glycerol leads to progressive lysis[24] and unphysiologically high and inconstant MCVs.

Some manufacturing processes allow for the use of outdated bank blood as a raw material. There are, however, some disadvantages to the use of outdated blood. First, expired blood is more labile to the high centrifugal forces during the hematocrit determination, causing considerable hemolysis and decreasing hematocrit values. Second, after some 3 weeks the MCV of the outdated red cells becomes progressively more sensitive to temperature influences and to mechanical stress during the mixing stage prior to assay. Third, in modern so-called eight-parameter flow cytometers (which measure platelets simultaneously with WBC and RBC parameters), outdated blood is less suitable as a quality control material due to interferences of red cell fragments in the platelet range.

Leukocytes (WBC)

Commercial control materials generally use white cell substitutes to simulate the short-lived human white cells. One of the primary substitutes is avian red blood cells, which are larger than human red cells and have a nucleus that simulates the human white cell. There also have been attempts to use latex and other particulates.

Although artificial spherical particles, such as pollens, mold spores, yeast, polystyrene latex, and other plastic polymers, have been tried as substitutes for red cells or white cells, none has proved suitable.[24] For flow cytometers, it is necessary that the red cells or red cell substitutes in multiparameter quality control materials can be lysed. Because the red cells are roughly the same size as white cells, it is impossible to perform a white count with these instruments if the red cells are not lysable. Furthermore, unlysable red cells interfere with hemoglobin determinations and do not monitor the proper functioning of the lysing process. The very high cost of the artificial particles needed in large quantities as well as danger of clumping and possibly clogging of the instruments' apertures also are disadvantages.

Platelets

Because platelets are easily damaged, platelet counting is the most difficult aspect of hematology quality control. Control sources include human, equine, porcine, and bovine platelets. Latex substitutes have been used,[24] but with poor results.

Stabilization of platelets is possible, but the platelets tend to grow smaller with this treatment. This causes a generally lower response in the electronic counters than would be obtained with native platelets. Also, the platelets may tend to aggregate, and consequently be counted as white blood cells, or stick to glass.[26]

Assay Value Assignment

Mean assay values are established for controls by replicate analyses. Generally, commercial control manufacturers employ several analysts and/or laboratories in the generation of data. As demonstrated in Table 5-9, the mean value is method dependent in most instances, although variations in technique, equipment, reagents, and so on may

TABLE 5-9
COMPARISON OF HEMATOLOGY CONTROL ASSAY STATISTICS BY METHOD

Constituent	Method	Mean	SD
WBC $\times 10^3$ (per μl)	Coulter S,S SR,S 790	15.0	0.1
	Coulter ZBI, FN, ZF, D_2	15.0	0.2
	TOA Sysmex CC-120	14.9	0.1
	TOA CC-720, CC-700	14.1	0.2
	Sequoia cell dyne 800	14.5	0.3
RBC $\times 10^6$ (per μl)	Coulter S,S SR,S 790	5.46	0.04
	Coulter ZBI, FN, ZF, D_2	5.42	0.03
	TOA Sysmex CC-120	5.44	0.05
	TOA CC-720, CC-700	5.43	0.05
	Sequoia cell dyne 800	5.55	0.05
Hb (g/dl)	Coulter S,S SR,S 790	17.5	0.1
	Coulter ZBI, FN, ZF, D_2	17.6	0.1
	TOA Sysmex CC-120	17.4	0.2
	TOA CC-720, CC-700	17.4	0.1
	Sequoia cell dyne 800	17.4	0.1
	Manual spectrophotometer	17.3	0.1
Hct (%)	Coulter S,S SR,S 790	54.2	0.4
	Coulter ZBI, FN, ZF, D_2	54.2	0.7
	TOA Sysmex CC-120	53.4	0.5
	TOA CC-720, CC-700	53.5	1.1
	Sequoia cell dyne 800	53.5	1.0
	Manual hematocrit	51.5	0.3
MCV (u^3)	Coulter S,S SR,S 790	100	1.2
	Coulter ZBI, FN, ZF, D_2	100	1.0
	TOA Sysmex CC-120	98	0.8
	TOA CC-720, CC-700	99	1.3
	Sequoia cell dyne 800	96	1.2

result in individual laboratories establishing means that are different than those listed by the manufacturer.

Expected ranges usually do not represent a simple two standard deviation (SD) interval. Generally the expected range represents a consensus or manufacturers' estimate of the variation from the mean that will occur between all laboratories employing the control material and is almost always greater than 2 SD. Most manufacturers emphasize the expected range as a guide to determining the acceptability of laboratory values until sufficient determinations have been accumulated to establish each laboratory's own mean and limits.

COAGULATION CONTROLS

Despite intensive study in this field for more than 40 years, there are still many aspects of blood coagulation that are not clearly understood. Yet control materials play a critical role in the coagulation laboratory.

The manufacturer's role in providing control materials in coagulation lies primarily in the measurement of clot formation and with various quantitative assays for clotting factors requiring standardized reference materials and a means for assessing new reagents.

Manufacturing Considerations

Manufacture of controls for clinical coagulation is difficult because of the very nature of some of the clotting factors themselves. Manufacturers tend to be secretive about their methods for preparation of these materials.

The coagulation factors, except for fibrinogen and prothrombin, occur in small quantities in human plasma. Also, the characteristics of these proteins are not well understood, and, to make manufacturing more difficult, most factors tend to be extremely labile. The assay of clotting factors requires construction of a reference dose-response curve, from which the levels of coagulation factors in patients' plasma are determined. For control purposes, it is assumed that a pool of normal platelet-poor plasma, collected from a relatively large number of apparently healthy donors, will result in a final product with 100 percent activity for each clotting factor.[27] The number of donors used must be of sufficient size to ensure that calibration is not biased by any individual donor.

Collection, screening, and processing of plasmas for use in the manufacture of coagulation control and reference materials must be under carefully controlled conditions. After pooling and testing, the plasma is stabilized using a variety of proprietary methods. A buffer is used to balance the pH, and the plasma is filled into siliconized glass vials and lyophilized. Siliconization of the vials is essential to prohibit activation of some components. After lyophilization, the product is tested extensively to assure reliability and then assayed.

TABLE 5-10
COAGULATION CONTROL MATERIALS

Application	Source
PT or PTT controls	
Normal coagulation control	Human plasma
Abnormal coagulation control	Human and rabbit plasma
Factor-deficient materials	
Factor II deficient	Human and bovine plasma
Factor V deficient	Human plasma
Factor VII deficient	Human plasma
Factor VIII deficient	Human hemophilia A plasma
Factor IX deficient	Human hemophilia B plasma
Factor X deficient	Human plasma
Factor XI deficient	Bovine plasma
Proteolytic enzyme controls	Human plasma
Antithrombin III	
Plasminogen	
Alpha-2 antiplasmin	
Fibrinogen	

Types of Controls

Many control materials are available commercially for use in the coagulation laboratory. Essentially, they may be grouped into three categories: controls for prothrombin and partial thromboplastin time, controls for clotting factor assays, and controls for proteolytic enzyme assays. Many of the most common are listed in Table 5-10.

The factor-deficient plasmas listed are not controls in the same sense that the term is used in chemistry. These materials are used to measure the ability of patient plasmas to correct test results of known factor-deficient plasmas. Sources for these deficient plasmas can be extremely difficult to find and expensive for the manufacturer. Most manufacturers maintain a roster of individuals who are paid to donate plasma periodically. The constant search for new donors is a considerable cost.

For the control of prothrombin time and partial thromboplastin time, typically at least two and sometimes three levels of control materials are used. Because of differences between lots of reagents observed with a given control material, most manufacturers recommend the control product that should be used with their reagent system.

The proteolytic enzyme controls are generally prepared from citrated human plasma and then stabilized. Their application is as controls in the measurement of plasminogen, antithrombin III, fibrinogen, and alpha-2 antiplasmin by a variety of methods.

Assay Value Assignment

Manufacturers use protocols similar to those used in assay of other controls: Replicate determinations are performed over 2 or 3 days and are used to calculate the mean, standard deviation, and expected range. As with other assayed controls, the expected range is usually wider than two standard deviations.

Stability

Lyophilized control materials are stable for up to 2 years when stored at 2 to 8°C, or as recommended by the manufacturer. For most of these materials, reconstituted stability is quite short, usually 6 to 8 hours when stored at 2 to 8°C.

CONCLUSION

A wide variety of quality control reagents are available for clinical laboratory use. These usually are produced in a matrix that approximates the analyte measured. Elaborate checks during the manufacturing process assure product homogeneity and quality. Whereas these are biologic reagents, shelf life is limited from a few months to no more than a few years for the most stable analytes. By using aliquots of the same lots of reagents, performance can be monitored within and between laboratories.

REFERENCES

1. Levey S, Jennings ER: The use of control charts in the clinical laboratory. *Am J Clin Pathol* 1950, 20:1059.
2. Henry RJ, Segalove M: The running of standards in clinical chemistry and the use of control charts. *J Clin Pathol* 1952, 5:305.
3. Copeland BE, Rosenbaum JM: Organization, planning and results of the Massachusetts Society of Pathologists Regional Quality Control Program. *Am J Clin Pathol* 1972, 57:676.
4. Ross JW: Control materials and calibration standards, in *Clinical Chemistry,* vol I. CRC Handbook Series in Clinical Laboratory Science, Section G. Boca Raton, FL, Chemical Rubber Co, 1982.
5. Fraser GC, Peake MJ: Problems associated with clinical chemistry control materials. *CRC Crit Rev Clin Lab Sci* 1980, 12:59.
6. Technical Services Field Letter Wilmington, DE, DuPont, 1985.
7. McComb R, Bowers GN, Posen S: *Alkaline Phosphatase.* New York, Plenum Press, 1979, pp 229–372.
8. Rej R, Jenny RW, Bretaudiere J-P: Quality control in clinical chemistry: Characterization of reference materials. *Talanta* 1984, 31:851.
9. O'Donnel NJ, Lott JA: Interlaboratory survey of alkaline phosphatase methods. *Am J Clin Pathol* 1981, 76:567.
10. Copeland WH, Nealon DA, Rej R: Effects of temperature on measurement of alkaline phosphatase activity. *Clin Chem* 1985, 31:185.
11. Bretaudiere J-P, Drake P, Rej R: Influence of the origin of alkaline phosphatase on the behavior of quality-control specimens for interlaboratory surveys, abstracted. *Clin Chem* 1980, 26:1014.
12. Lorentz K: Evaluation of alpha-amylase assays with 4-nitrophenyl-alpha-oligosaccharides as substrates. *J Clin Chem Clin Biochem* 1983, 21:463.
13. Robyt JF, French D: The action pattern of porcine pancreatic alpha-amylase in relationship to the substrate binding site of the enzyme. *J Biol Chem* 1970, 245:3917.

14 Lee VW, Willis C: Activity of human and nonhuman amylases on different substrates in enzymatic kinetic assay methods—A pitfall in interlaboratory quality control. *Am J Clin Pathol* 1982, 77:290.
15 Quam EF, Haessig LK, Koch MJ: A comprehensive statistical quality control program for blood gas analyzers. *J Med Technol* 1985, 2:27.
16 Leary TL, Graham G, Kenny MA: Commercial available blood-gas controls compared with tonometered blood. *Clin Chem* 1980, 26:1309.
17 Ong ST, David D, Snow M, et al: Effects of variations in room temperature on measured values of blood gas quality-control materials. *Clin Chem* 1983, 29:502.
18 Feil MC: More on nonaqueous controls for blood gas determinations. *Clin Chem* 1983, 29:1859.
19 Wilding P, Silva JF, Wilde CE: Transport of specimens for clinical chemistry analysis. *Ann Clin Biochem* 1977, 14:301.
20 Lawson NS, Haven GT, Williams GW: Analyte stability in clinical chemistry quality control materials. *CRC Crit Rev Clin Lab Sci* 1981, 17:1.
21 Spaethe R, Tenger F, Lampart A: Artificial control materials—Haematology, in Rosalki SB (ed): *New Approaches to Laboratory Medicine,* Transactions of the 2nd Merz + Dade Exploratory Seminar. Darmstadt, G.I.T. Verlag Ernst Giebler, 1981.
22 Thom R: Calibration in haematology, in Rosalki SB (ed): *New Approaches to Laboratory Medicine,* Transactions of the 2nd Merz + Dade Exploratory Seminar. Darmstadt, G.I.T. Verlag Ernst Giebler, 1981.
23 Cavill I (ed): *Methods in Hematology, vol 4, Quality Control.* Edinburgh, London, Melbourne, New York: Churchill Livingstone, 1982.
24 Lewis SM: Standards and reference preparations, in Lewis SM, Coster JF (eds): *Quality Control in Hematology,* Symposium of the ICSH. London, Academic Press, 1975, pp 79–101.
25 Koepke JA: The calibration of automated instruments for accuracy in hemoglobinometry. *Am J Clin Pathol* 1977, 68:180.
26 Lomparts AJPF, Leijnse B: Preparation and evaluation of a 7-parameter intralaboratory control blood of 4-month stability. *Ann Clin Biochem* 1983, 20:302–307.
27 Dombrose FA, Barnes CC, Gaynor MS, et al: A lyophilized human reference plasma for coagulation factors. *Am J Clin Pathol* 1982, 77:32.

CHAPTER 6

PERFORMANCE CHARACTERISTICS AND ANALYTIC GOALS

John W. Ross, M.D.
Noel S. Lawson, M.D.

Clinical laboratory quality assurance practices encompass a number of broad categories of activity, designed to maximize quality and utilization of laboratory information. These categories include control of design and resource materials, internal and external control of analytic processes, and output, applicability, and verification control. A substantial portion of the literature on clinical laboratory quality control refers in one way or another to external and/or internal process control.

The discussion presented here will review current practices, drawing heavily on information obtained through organized interlaboratory quality control programs, in particular those relating to internal and external process control. Professionally organized programs have created an environment facilitating organizational structure and uniformity to reporting, nomenclature, statistical handling of data, quality control practices, and documentation. Furthermore, organized quality control programs have developed a massive database, with information on performance characteristics. This information influences clinical laboratory method design and development, management, and licensing and accreditation. The discussion will cover internal quality control and extended (regional) quality control, including general information, probes of regional quality control program data, and problems and goals. External quality control will also be reviewed, focusing on the origin and development of these programs, control materials, participant grading systems, and the closely related topic of analytic goals and medical usefulness.

PROCESS CONTROL AND REGIONAL QUALITY CONTROL PROGRAMS

Process control may be broadly divided into internal and external types (Table 6-1). Internal process control uses predominantly stable control samples but may be supplemented by information derived from patient data. Internal quality control primarily establishes the appropriateness of laboratory data in real time. Internal process control by the control sample technique employs samples of known target value, which are analyzed along with the patient specimens. In external process control, laboratories periodically analyze samples of unknown concentration, yielding data on laboratory accuracy. External quality control both quantitates laboratory bias and satisfies regulatory requirements for laboratory proficiency. Internal quality control testing by control sample technique may be extended to multiple laboratories through the vehicle of regional quality control programs.

A regional quality control program comprises an activity wherein large groups of laboratories, usually within a cohesive geographic region, share both pools of quality control material and data. The data are derived from internal quality control testing of pool analytes by the control sample technique. The essential elements of regional programs are the sponsoring organization(s), a source of control materials, data processing services, and participating laboratories. Regional quality control programs are an extension of internal quality control by the control sample technique. The concept was first introduced by Preston, in Colorado, in 1967, and has subsequently expanded to multiple additional regions within the United States and Canada.[1,2]

The programs are coordinated by professional representative(s) of the sponsoring organization, designated the regional coordinator(s). The functions of the regional coordinator include data review, development of guidelines for control materials, selection of control material and data processing vendors, education, and overall coordination.

Regional quality control programs may be broadly grouped into those with formal organized professional coordination and those coordinated by vendors of control ma-

TABLE 6-1
DATA DERIVED FROM INTERLABORATORY QUALITY CONTROL PROGRAMS

	Regional quality control programs	Proficiency testing/ survey programs
Individual laboratory bias	X	X
Individual laboratory precision	X	
Laboratory population bias	X	X
Laboratory population precision (within and between laboratory)	X	X
Laboratory population precision (within laboratory)	X	

terials. Professionally coordinated programs are characteristically sponsored by state pathology societies operating alone or in combination. Between 1967 and 1975, there was increasing participation of laboratories in regional programs.[2] In 1975, in the United States, there were approximately 1600 clinical laboratories participating in professionally coordinated programs and 4100 enrolled in industry-coordinated programs in clinical chemistry. During the intervening decade, the number of laboratories participating in professionally directed regional quality control programs increased to approximately 2000. The number of manufacturers of multipurpose chemistry quality control serum who also provide an interlaboratory database has decreased. Consequently, there are now fewer manufacturer programs available with interlaboratory databases. Information on the number of laboratories currently participating in all of these programs is unavailable. Interlaboratory database comparisons are available in routine clinical chemistry, coagulation, hematology, ligand assay, therapeutic drug monitoring, and blood gas analysis. Professionally directed regional programs use the Quality Assurance Service (QAS) data processing function, provided by the College of American Pathologists, 5202 Old Orchard Road, Skokie, Illinois. Vendors of quality control materials that supply interlaboratory data comparison with these products may be contacted directly for program information.

Computer-generated output of regional programs consists of individual laboratory data summaries and tabulations of interlaboratory grouped data. Individual laboratory data summaries contain information on statistical parameters of quality control, grouped by data file. Files are maintained with quality control data for each analyte-pool-method combination for which information is being collected and maintained. In the College of American Pathologists (CAP) Quality Assurance Services program, comparative precision is evaluated by a statistical technique allowing between-pool comparison. The method employs a series of polynomial regression equations describing the relationship of the coefficient of variation (CV) to analyte concentration at the 25th, 50th, 75th, and 95th percentile rankings of performance.

Programs also provide tabulated pool-wide statistics for multiple methods. These program-specific group data summaries describe the state of the art for method-related within and between laboratory precision and bias for the tested analytes.

The materials used for interlaboratory distribution within regional programs must share the features of within-lot uniformity and stability. Uniformity is required in order to ensure vial-to-vial comparability of analyte concentration and matrix throughout the geographic area comprising the program. Analyte stability is necessary to ensure that measured levels and changes of analyte are appropriately attributed to laboratory bias and imprecision. Sufficient material must be available in single lots to allow large numbers of laboratories to have access to materials for relatively long periods of time.

Typically, regional quality control programs for chemistry, ligand assay, therapeutic drugs, and coagulation use pools of materials for a minimum of 12 months. These pools are stabilized, most commonly, by lyophilization or by chemical additive—for example, ethylene glycol. Because of less stable control materials, regional programs in hematology cycle control materials more frequently—often at intervals of 1 to 3 months.

The number of participants in a regional program is limited by the maximum size of the pool that can be manufactured. This, in turn, reflects such factors as plant lyophilization capacity, duration of manufacturing process, and intraprocessing stability. The maximum number of laboratories that can simultaneously use the same lot of chemistry control materials for a minimum of 1 year is approximately 200 to 600. This number is expected to increase in coming years because individual laboratories' usage of chemistry controls is currently decreasing. This is attributable both to newer instruments that consume less sample and have increased analytic stability and to cost containment pressures, which encourage less consumption of control materials.

Multiple educational functions are carried out by regional programs. Program procedure manuals contain educational materials concerning quality control practices and are integral to an operating regional program. These are supplemented by periodic communications in the form of newsletters and organized educational seminars featuring quality control topics. Research based on data input from participants generates information concerning both laboratory performance and control material characteristics. The return of this information to the clinical laboratory community through scientific publications constitutes a major component of the educational function of regional programs.

Regional quality control programs provide clinical laboratories with a vehicle for cost containment through group purchasing, use of unassayed controls, and educational efforts directed toward cost containment. Group purchasing of large lots of control materials gives the participant laboratories access to these materials at reduced costs. Regional programs use multipurpose controls at clinically appropriate levels. For example, analytes for routine chemistry, ligand assay, and therapeutic drugs are commonly available in the same lots of chemistry control serum. This allows the user to avoid or minimize expenses for specialty controls. Traditionally, regional programs use unassayed materials for clinical chemistry. Unassayed materials are substantially less costly than assayed controls. The regional database comprises the "assay sheet" for the laboratory. Information is returned on methodologic comparisons obtained from multiple participants using the same lots of materials. Such summary information together with individual laboratory data serve the purpose of simplifying retrospective review for both management and accreditation purposes.

Through the educational component of regional quality control programs, proper use of quality control rules is promoted. The correct application of these rules optimizes the combination of error detection and false rejection for analytic runs and is cost effective. A common cause of inappropriate run rejection is the use of a control rule wherein an analytic run is rejected if a single control in a two-control system is between two and three standard deviations from the mean (1-2S rule).[3] Because this occurrence is expected approximately 1 time in 20 on the basis of chance alone, its routine employment results in a high incidence of false run rejection.

Insufficient data exist to quantitate the cost impact of inappropriate selection of acceptance and rejection criteria phenomena. A theoretical basis for such estimates has recently been presented;[4,5] inappropriate run rejection increases costs because of wasting of resources and withholding of clinical data. Howanitz has estimated the cost of a single therapeutic drug analytic run to be approximately $14. The costs due to delayed reporting derive from prolongation of hospital length of stay, unnecessary repeat testing, and medical consequences of delayed result reporting. In a simple example, consider a situation where an average laboratory inappropriately rejects two runs per day due to following a 1-2S rejection rule at a conservative cost of $10 per run. Assume also that a single patient day is added per month due to delayed laboratory reporting in a hospital where the daily rate is $350. Using very conservative estimates, the costs of applying inappropriate rejection criteria for run acceptance are approximately $10,000 per year.

Attributes of clinical laboratory procedures that may be quantitated include bias, precision, turnaround time, and cost. The cost-versus-quality evaluation requires reliable data on a laboratory's own performance experience, by method, supplemented by global state-of-the-art information derived from multilaboratory sources. Interlaboratory comparison programs, such as regional quality control programs, offer objective quantitative data for bias and precision. This information permits the laboratory to compare its own bias and precision by analyte to levels required for both medical need and peer-related performance.

Regional Quality Control Program Database Probes

Professionally organized regional quality control programs develop a database which comprises the analytic results attained in the course of testing control specimens. Periodic examination of the database yields information concerning laboratory practice. This information serves the dual functions of operational and educational feedback to participants and description of achieved state of the art for the laboratory community.

Analytic Precision   In a series of studies, Ross and Fraser[6-10] used polynomial regression equations to study the relationship between analyte concentrations and achieved analytic precision for a large number of analytes. Their studies used data from more than 1000 clinical laboratories participating in the College of American Pathologists' QAS program. The information derived from these studies permits the assessment of individual and grouped laboratory precision performance. Ross-Fraser equations permit assessment of interprogram comparative precision for laboratories employing different pools of control material.

In the 1982 review by Ross and Fraser,[10] the state of the art in long-term intralaboratory analytic precision is quantitated for 31 analytes. Polynomial regression equations relating intralaboratory long-term precision and concentration are developed for 50th, 75th, 90th, and 95th percentile rankings. The authors developed a medical precision index and concluded that approximately 97 percent of overall results met medical usefulness goals as described by Barnett for 14 analytes. Slightly better performance was obtained by automated compared to manual methods. The authors documented a general overall improvement in analytic precision for the 14 analytes, followed over a 6-year period (Table 6-2).

Control Material Stability   The regional quality control program database is updated monthly by new control data from participating clinical laboratories. Changes in analyte concentration in quality control materials are reflected by changes in grouped

TABLE 6-2
TRENDS IN STATE OF THE ART FOR ANALYTIC PRECISION
Average %CV (manual/automated)

Analyte, units	Concentration	1975	1980
Albumin, g/dl	3.5	5.26/3.80	4.82/3.37
Bilirubin, mg/dl	1.0	13.82/8.83	11.80/9.12
Calcium, mg/dl	11.0	3.27/2.46	2.92/2.15
Chloride, mmol/L	90.0	2.20/1.83	2.14/1.80
	110.0	2.01/1.64	1.87/1.59
Cholesterol, mg/dl	250.0	4.59/4.14	4.74/3.84
Creatinine, mg/dl	1.5	8.38/6.08	7.62/5.61
	5.0	5.38/3.16	4.87/2.88
Glucose, mg/dl	100.0	3.85/3.67	3.45/3.00
	120.0	3.47/3.29	3.22/2.67
Phosphorus, mg/dl	4.5	5.32/3.17	4.74/3.00
Potassium, mmol/L	3.0	2.86/2.91	2.34/2.53
	6.0	1.94/1.84	1.75/1.73
Sodium, mmol/L	130.0	1.28/1.18	1.15/1.13
	150.0	1.28/1.18	1.08/1.07
Total protein, g/dl	7.0	2.44/2.29	2.09/2.16
Triglyceride, mg/dl	130.0	7.51/6.71	7.28/5.23
Urea nitrogen, mg/dl	27.0	7.08/3.54	6.50/3.47
	50.0	6.12/2.68	5.20/2.88
Uric acid, mg/dl	6.0	5.32/2.68	5.53/2.96
	9.0	4.97/2.37	4.89/2.58

Source: Ross JW, Fraser MD: Clinical laboratory precision: The state of the art and medical usefulness based internal quality control. *Am J Clin Pathol* 1982, 78:578.

monthly means during the life of the lots. QAS data have been used for several studies of analyte stability in lyophilized quality control serum.

Linear regression coefficients of monthly mean values were determined for the time period during which pools were in use. An instability signal occurred when the linear regression coefficient was unequal to zero, with .05 or less probability of error. With this method, a tendency for decrease in concentrations of glucose,[11,12] inorganic phosphorous, and creatine kinase activity,[13] and increase in sodium,[13,14] chloride, and alkaline phosphatase activity were found.[13] Changes in concentration for numerous other analytes were noted, most likely arising from calibrator or other method-related changes implemented during the period of time in which a pool was being analyzed. The observed changes were relatively small in comparison to analytic variation. Using cumulative lot-to-date statistics or "rolling values" for run evaluation minimizes false error signals from instability.[15]

Laboratory Bias Rosenbaum, using the Massachusetts Regional Quality Control Program data,[16] evaluated concentration differences between grouped means and definitive method values for selected analytes in lyophilized human control serum. For calcium, he concluded that there were insignificant differences between the all-method mean values and those obtained by the U.S. National Bureau of Standards (NBS) with isotope-dilution mass spectroscopy (IDMS). The all-methods calcium mean, therefore, served as a useful target value on which to base bias estimates for laboratories using the program's control serum.

In a subsequent work, Rosenbaum has expanded this study to include analytes in addition to calcium.[17] NBS definitive methods and/or U.S. Centers for Disease Control (CDC) clinical reference methods for cholesterol, glucose, potassium, and sodium provide substantial agreement between benchmark values and all-method means.

Matrix Effect   Howanitz et al.[18] studied bias estimates in the New York State Society of Pathologists (NYSPATH) Regional Quality Control Program and CAP Survey data to evaluate matrix effect. In their study, biases obtained utilizing liquid control containing ethylene glycol were compared to those obtained with lyophilized quality control serum used in the CAP survey. Bias estimates were obtained by comparing the grouped mean participant values from laboratories using the Technicon SMAC Analyzer to the mean of all laboratories. Biases generally were found to be proportional to concentration. Substantially greater biases were noted with liquid versus lyophilized material, with negative biases noted for sodium and potassium and positive biases for chloride and uric acid.

Loehff et al. studied analytic clinical laboratory precision for commonly assayed enzymes.[19] For alkaline phosphatase (AP), creatine kinase (CK), lactate dehydrogenase (LH), aspartate aminotransferase (AST), and alanine aminotransferase (ALT), automated procedures produced lower coefficients of variation than manual procedures. Additionally, precision improved with increasing enzyme activity. These results confirmed previous observations for AP, LH, CK, and AST with regional program data.[20]

A portion of this study involved analysis of average laboratory precision for a variety of method-enzyme combinations, comparing liquid and lyophilized human quality control serum. No systematic differences in average analytic precision were noted for most analyte-method combinations. With the DuPont aca procedures (kinetic, 340 nm, 37°C), generally lower coefficients of variation were obtained by laboratories using liquid control than by those employing the lyophilized materials. A tendency toward somewhat lower average coefficients of variation with the DuPont aca AST procedure (kinetic, 340 nm, 37°C) was noted within programs using the lyophilized controls versus programs employing liquid materials.

PROBLEMS IN QUALITY CONTROL

Licensed versus Unlicensed Laboratories

Professional quality control principles and practices are applied predominantly in licensed laboratories. Substantial numbers of outpatient clinical laboratory tests are performed in the environment of physicians' unlicensed office laboratories. Here, there are minimal regulatory requirements for such activities as internal quality control, external quality control, maintaining personnel standards, and laboratory inspection.

The extension of regional quality control program applications to include unlicensed laboratories would provide improved quality control. This would be accomplished as control pools, data, and educational materials are distributed beyond the present participant base. Baer and Belsey have suggested that pathologists act as consultants to physicians' office laboratories.[21] A multifaceted relationship with a central laboratory, such as in a hospital, would facilitate the pathologists' consultative functions. Sharing of regional pools and/or other controls between physicians' office laboratories would provide a tie-in between consultants and office laboratories.

Control materials are produced according to guidelines determined by professional coordination of regional programs. They contain common analytes at concentrations approximating clinical decision levels. Use of the regional control materials gives laboratories access to the group's database. The statistics for bias and precision comprise quality dimensions that permit objective evaluation of performance. Bias estimates can be used to quantitate differences between observed and expected values. These data, then, may be used to judge bias between patient results from physicians' offices and from other laboratories in the program. Data on precision would be used both to quantitate variation and to evaluate relative performance. Unacceptably large bias or imprecision for an analyte would be cause to reexamine, change, or discontinue a procedure.

Educational activities traditionally sponsored by regional programs would benefit unlicensed laboratories. These activities include newsletters, procedure manuals, publications, and educational seminars. Of particular value would be educational material concerning recommended quality control techniques, including information on control materials, statistical data, method troubleshooting, and cost effectiveness.

Cost of Quality Control

Within the current reimbursement environment in the United States, there are pressures on clinical laboratories to contain costs. These pressures are subject to being applied indiscriminately, at the expense of quality-of-care considerations. In the clinical laboratory environment, it is critical that professional input be applied on the benefit side of the cost-benefit evaluation. Across-the-board constriction on expenditures within clinical laboratories affects quality control activities. Paradoxically, there is a strong point to be made for expansion of quality control activities within an environment where cost cutting threatens quality of care.

The cost of quality control in the clinical laboratory comprises numerous components, as described by Diamond, who estimated the proportion of total laboratory cost attributable to quality control procedures as 7.7 percent.[22] A higher estimate was obtained by Tydeman et al., who reported that quality control costs were approximately 30 percent of total costs.[23] Different methodology, patient acuity, and overhead account for the substantially differing estimates. Nevertheless, it is clear that a significant percentage of laboratory costs are attributable to quality control procedures. In the study by Tydeman et al., a substantial component of savings attributable to large-sized runs of automated procedures was due to reduction in quality control costs. Pressure to decrease length of stay leads to smaller analytic runs, because efforts within hospital laboratories to improve turnaround time leads to more weekend and off-hours work, and other STAT, unbatched work. Quality control costs may then increase as run size decreases.

Discussions of laboratory quality control costs typically fail to include the costs of failure to control. The implications of failure to control in an industrial environment have been discussed by Feigenbaum.[24] The costs of failure to control include internal failure costs affecting the controlling entity and external failure costs pertaining to the impact outside that facility. In the clinical laboratory environment, internal failure costs reflect the laboratories' expenses associated with waste of resources applied in an inadequate testing environment, increased expenses associated with licensure and certification problems, the cost of investigating and following inappropriate error signals, and unnecessary repeat testing requested by clinicians because of reduced confidence in laboratory results.

External failure costs in the medical laboratory milieu affect consumers, physicians, and patients. They suffer the medical consequences of data from a poorly controlled laboratory. The patients and the public, additionally, share the financial consequences of internal control failure. If increased expenditures in the clinical laboratory for processing and quality control yield a benefit to the hospital in terms of length of patient stay and reduction in internal and external failure costs, then the pathologist must be prepared to defend allocation of departmental resources for this purpose.

Single-Purpose Instrument-Related Controls

In the regional quality control scheme, large lots of quality control material are distributed to large numbers of laboratories for their simultaneous testing, as a prerequisite for developing a large database. A major benefit of the activity is the development of a database containing information on a wide variety of analytic methods and measurement systems. A multipurpose control distributed under the sponsorship of a regional quality control program has the advantage that a relatively broad cross section of methods and instruments is customarily reflected in the bias and precision database.

Currently, many instrument manufacturers also supply, directly or through distributors, quality control materials. Indeed, these materials may be produced in large lots, distributed to large numbers of laboratories, and used for development of a database for interlaboratory comparison. Under various types of innovative leasing or purchasing arrangements, the cost of quality control materials may be obfuscated to the point where it appears to be included at minimal or no charge.

In this environment, databases associated with instrument-associated controls tend to be weighted heavily in the direction of the dominant instrument(s), minimizing the interlaboratory comparison features of the regional program. A second complication derives from the requirements of an instrument for certain types of quality control materials and the physiochemical properties of the supplied material. Thus, it is now apparent that a product such as the ethylene glycol-stabilized liquid quality control serum, which performs acceptably on many manufacturers' chemistry analyzers, cannot be used on instruments using film technology. Differences in performance by laboratories using different instrument groups with an instrument-associated control may generate a database that reflects both material-method incompatibility and quality of the participating laboratory. The descriptive statistics for such a program may be misleading, and the value of much of the program data to given participants is questionable.

Changing Quality Control Requirements in a Changing Analytic Environment

Traditional concepts of quality control are rooted in control charts and Gaussian statistics. The intervals encompassing the analytic series have been relatively easy to define for both manual and automated methods. Consequently, decisions regarding placement of controls in runs, as well as numbers and frequency of observations, have been related to generally acceptable concepts of run or batch size. In recent years, new instrumentation has become available with extreme analytic stability and with random access for multiple analytes. When analytic systems are predictably stable for long periods, there is less need for frequent control observations. With random access multianalyte automated analysis, there is blurring of the traditional concept of run or batch as it pertains to a specific analyte.

The National Committee for Clinical Laboratory Standards (NCCLS) Subcommittee on Quality Control is currently addressing these issues. The goal of this activity is to develop both definitions of analytic intervals and guidelines for internal quality control practices. Presently in the commentary phase, these guidelines cover number and concentration of controls, run evaluation criteria, frequency of observations, recommended control material matrices, and definitions of analytic intervals.[25] The document, when published, will be useful to the laboratory director in planning and managing quality control activities; to instrument, reagent, and control material manufacturers in designing control procedures for analytic systems; to the analyst at the bench in applying good quality control practices; and to inspecting entities such as the CAP, the Centers for Disease Control (CDC), and state health departments, which require usable, consistent criteria to evaluate the acceptability of quality control procedures in clinical laboratories.

Goals for the Future

For the future, regional quality control programs are obliged to address both self-improvement as well as their contribution to improvement of the state of clinical laboratory practice.[26]

There is a need for internal improvement by increasing the number of participants, both overall and within individual regional programs. Increasing the number of participants improves the validity of the databases created by the regional program for analytic precision and for bias. As numbers of laboratories in a given program increase, the numbers of contributors to various laboratory-analyte-method data cells increase, improving the quality of the statistical assumptions as well as the accessibility to users of data on various analytic methods.

A second area for potential improvement concerns the correlation of quality assurance data derived from programs of proficiency testing/survey programs with those for daily control. Preliminary work has indicated a correlation between precision estimates for calcium and sodium, as determined in the CAP survey and QAS programs.[27] Additional studies to assess the correlation between bias and precision estimates for a wider range of analytes and disciplines are needed.

Both CAP surveys and QAS offer bias estimates and forms of precision estimates. It is a desirable goal that laboratories receive comparable information on their analytic bias and precision from both sources. This requires coordination of statistical terminology, method taxonomy, and output format.

The CAP has progressed considerably with respect to the operational steps toward improved interprogram coordination. Statistical terminology, method grouping strategies, and nomenclature are essentially uniform between surveys and QAS for most disciplines and analytes.

The microcomputer has been used to perform numerous functions in the clinical laboratory.[28,29] This device offers powerful, relatively inexpensive data manipulation for a wide range of applications. Both the CAP and various control material vendors provide microcomputer-based software with features allowing both within-laboratory and between-laboratory data processing. The within-laboratory programs provide real-time run evaluation algorithms for the purpose of ascertaining the acceptability of patient data. This feature complements or substitutes for alternative procedures using manual review centered on Levey-Jennings charts. The methodology of run evaluation employs the analyte-method-pool specific variables of target value and standard deviation. A common decision algorithm used in microcomputer-based quality control programs is that of Westgard et al.[3]

The microcomputer, additionally, simplifies the collection and sharing of multilaboratory information comprising the bias and precision database.[10] Mail is the traditional method of exchanging information between laboratories participating in regional programs and the data processing facility. This method has the advantages of being simple and inexpensive and allowing multiple types of input. Mail has the disadvantage of delay in information transfer. Management decisions in clinical laboratories benefit from timely information. With the microcomputer, periodically updated data from participating laboratories is transmitted electronically to the centralized data processing facility. Following update of the global database, a return electronic transmission of information updates the laboratories' interlaboratory statistical information.

Improvements in the use of microcomputers for quality control should follow in several areas. Downloading of quality control data from laboratory information systems to microcomputers would simplify and streamline the handling of quality control information. When a substantial majority of regional program participants use microcomputers for data transmission to the central data processing facility at different times during a month, more frequent (e.g., weekly or daily) updates of the interlaboratory database will be possible.

A major goal is the extension of probes of the regional quality control database.[26] Analytical precision data for additional analytes should be developed beyond the present 31 in the Ross-Fraser review.[10] A comprehensive analysis is needed to compare analytic precision with lyophilized controls to that obtained with liquid materials. This would supplement the study of Lohff et al., which contains comparative information on enzyme precision.[19] The studies on analytic bias such as those by Rosenbaum and Howanitz et al.[17,18] should be expanded to include additional analytes and matrices. Stability studies should likewise be expanded to include analytes in liquid matrix.

The state of the art in microbiology sensitivity testing by the Kirby-Bauer technique[30–33] using QAS data requires updating with information derived from laboratories using minimum inhibitory concentration (MIC) methods.

Future goals relative to development and implementation of specific performance levels for the clinical laboratory are presented in the following discussion on quality control, medical usefulness, and analytic goals.

EXTERNAL QUALITY CONTROL

Definition

External quality control is a quality assurance activity that neither controls the quality of results nor determines if results are suitable for release. Rather these are the aims of internal quality control. However, both external and internal quality control programs measure quality in a complementary manner and must be properly correlated to yield their full benefits to individual laboratories and to the clinical laboratory community as a whole.

In the broadest sense, external quality control is a procedure for using the results of multiple laboratories that analyze aliquots of the same sample for quality control purposes.[34] Related terms, which emphasize specific aspects of external quality control, are "proficiency testing" and "external quality assessment." Proficiency testing may be defined as distribution of unknown samples to laboratories for the purpose of determining the ability of laboratory personnel to achieve the correct analysis.[35] According to Whitehead and Woodford,[36] external quality assessment refers to a system of objectively testing laboratory results by means of an external agency in order to establish between-laboratory comparability. The term "assessment" is preferred, because quality is evaluated rather than controlled. When organized as a survey (interlaboratory testing program), assessment includes distribution of samples for analysis and comparison of a laboratory's result with those of other laboratories. Objections to the survey method as a quality assurance procedure include problems with the matrix of control materials and the possibility of special handling of the control materials in the surveyed laboratory. Although generally impractical, external quality assessment can also take place as physical inspections or as a pattern analysis of all results.[36,37] Pattern analysis is being evaluated for histopathology laboratories in Europe.[36]

Objective

The main objective of external quality control is to establish comparability between laboratories.[36–40] The means by which interlaboratory testing programs may contribute to comparability include: providing a mechanism to compare results with nationally accepted reference points; generating data allowing comparison between actual laboratory performance and accepted norms based on patient care needs; and providing information on performance characteristics of the measuring system.

The specific aims of external quality control are measurement of the state of the art of clinical laboratory practice; measurement of the quality of performance of individual laboratories; supplementation of internal quality control programs; creation of reference materials; evaluation of features of laboratory analysis, which cannot be studied by internal quality control and which can affect laboratory performance; and service as an educational stimulus to laboratory improvement.[34] The importance of external quality control as an educational tool has been emphasized recently.[37] An educational purpose has been an integral part of the philosophy of major national surveys since their inceptions.

State of the Art

The ability of external quality control programs to document the state of the art and trends in the state of the art is well established. Some results of the National Survey of the College of American Pathologists (CAP) performed in 1949 are listed in column 1 of Table 6-3.[41] In 1969, the descendent CAP Chemistry Surveys produced the data listed in column 2. In 1983, the coefficients of variation (CVs) listed in column 3 were obtained. The trends in these CVs, including both interlaboratory and intralaboratory variation across all methods, illustrate the impressive advances made in the state of the art in laboratory analysis over 34 years.

Strides advancing the state of the art reach most laboratory disciplines: general chemistry;[42-44] enzymology;[45-47] ligand assay;[48] blood gases;[49] coagulation;[50] microbial antibiotic sensitivity testing;[51] bacteriology;[52,53] mycology;[54] mycobacteriology;[55] and virtually all other laboratory disciplines.[56] These conclusions are often confirmed and complemented by data from programs of internal quality control, which may estimate independently the same parameters of laboratory testing.[10,19,27,56-61]

TABLE 6-3
NATIONAL CAP SURVEYS
Average %CV

	1949	1969	1983
Glucose	16.3	8.0	5.3
Urea nitrogen	63.5	13.3	8.2
Chloride	16.4	5.2	2.7
Calcium	27.6	11.1	3.9
Cholesterol	23.7	18.5	6.4

Source: Data from Skendzel et al[41] and CAP Comprehensive Chemistry Survey Participant Summaries, 1983.

TABLE 6-4
CAP COMPREHENSIVE CHEMISTRY SURVEY
Average %CV

	Survey year					
	1980			1983		
Analyte	$\bar{x}$	%CV	N	$\bar{x}$	%CV	N
Albumin, g/dl	3.9	5.9	2329	4.1	4.9	3379
Calcium, mg/dl	9.7	5.0	5533	9.7	3.9	6088
Chloride, mmol/L	92	3.4	5638	96	2.7	6162
Creatinine, mg/dl	1.1	17.4	6082	1.1	10.8	6652
Glucose, mg/dl	98	6.5	7040	102	5.3	7379
Magnesium, mg/dl	1.9	13.0	1849	2.1	9.4	2740
Osmolality, mOsm/kgH$_2$O	260	2.6	1599	256	2.0	2166
Phosphorus, mg/dl	4.4	7.0	2363	4.3	5.2	3511
Total protein, g/dl	6.3	3.6	2399	6.4	3.7	3415
Urea nitrogen, mg/dl	15	12.3	6544	15	8.2	6951
Uric acid, mg/dl	4.2	12.7	6065	4.3	7.3	6351

Source: 1980 data from Data ReCap 1970–1980. 1983 data from CAP Comprehensive Chemistry Survey Participant Summaries, 1983.

These trends continue into the most recent years. Advances during the decade of the 1970s are superbly illustrated in Data ReCap 1970–1980,[56] a CAP publication, for over 125 analytes and categories of clinical laboratory testing. Improvement in laboratory comparability during this decade is documented in virtually all test categories. Table 6-4 lists trends in survey precision through 1983 for 11 chemistry analytes.

Measurement of Individual Laboratory Quality

For details of available external quality control programs, see Chapter 14. Although measurement of the state of the art assists in establishing laboratory comparability, the individual laboratorian is probably more concerned with the ability of survey programs to measure the quality of individual laboratory performance accurately. Important characteristics of a survey program are properly selected target values, meaningful criteria for evaluation of the inaccuracy, and reliable control materials that simulate the behavior of clinical specimens. Surveys can accomplish their purpose only if the inaccuracy of the individual laboratory result is measured reliably. Gilbert[40] believed that "the certainty with which 'the correct' response is validated represents the cornerstone of a proficiency testing service." Certainly, if the target values selected are not close approximations of the true values, or at least values well worth striving for, the survey will not command the interest or confidence of the participants. The program's effectiveness as an educational stimulus toward improvement and as an integral part of quality assurance supplementing internal quality control programs also will be destroyed.

Target Values

The processes by which target values may be established have been described.[34,36,37,62] Four methods are available: (1) documented composition of a sample established by the method of manufacture; (2) analysis of the sample by definitive methods or by methods correlated to definitive methods; (3) concensus peer-group statistics after appropriate outlier exclusions; and (4) reference laboratory statistics.

Materials with documented composition are essential for microbiology identification, certain qualitative analyses, toxicology, qualitatively abnormal proteins, and immunohematology. Establishment of target values by composition documentation by the manufacturer is of little use for quantitative analysis.

For a limited number of clinical chemistry analytes, the correlation of participant results with definitive method results has been established.[44,62,63] The participant values that best correlate with the definitive method may be the average value obtained by a selected reference method used by a large number of participants, the average of several selected participant methods, or the average of all participants. The particular grouping selected can be selected to minimize bias relative to the definitive method. The accuracy of the selected groupings is sustained for several years.[44,63] The definitive method approach may become more prevalent in the future as the national reference system (see below) for the clinical laboratory[39] is implemented.

The use of participant peer-group means as target values may be appropriate where large intermethod bias exists due to control material matrix problems, unresolved differences in principles of analytic measurement, or unresolved variations in test standardization. For example, thromboplastin and partial thromboplastin have demonstrated variation since the inception of proficiency surveys,[64-66] and the principles of standardization of prothrombin time testing have not yet been agreed upon.[67] Measurement of sodium by direct potentiometry differs in methodologic principle from indirect potentiometry and flame photometry,[68,69] and a consensus has not yet been reached regarding the most useful method of standardization and reporting of results. However, the true value of an analyte in external quality control materials cannot be determined from the submitted participant data alone. For further information on target values, including use of reference laboratory values, see below and Chapter 14.

The professional judgment of the organizers of survey programs usually, but not always, provides useful target values based on available knowledge of reference and definitive methods, the numbers of participants, available knowledge of control matrix effects, and knowledge of the analytic specificity of field methods. Because some compromises are inevitable in survey groupings formed to establish target values, there may be justification for disagreement with survey evaluation by individual laboratories in specific circumstances.

Matrix Effects on Target Values Unavoidable matrix alteration may occur during preparation of control material. Matrix effects of available chemistry control materials have been evaluated[60,70–75] and, in general, found to allow analytically useful estimates of bias[59] and clinically relevant estimates of imprecision.[60] However, to the extent that analytic errors with proficiency testing samples do not correspond with those found with clinical specimens, the purpose of survey programs is compromised. It has been possible to improve matrices for general chemistry,[76] enzymology,[45–47,71,77] and blood gas analysis,[49,78] but more improvement is needed. Glucose, for example, may become artificially protein bound during the lyophilization process of chemistry controls.[11] The altered availability of glucose for chemical interaction introduces a method-specific performance characteristic of no clinical relevance. Aberrant dual-wavelength blank corrections occur with some chemistry control materials in analytic systems that perform reliably for clinical specimens.[70] The performance of animal enzyme additives has been compared to that of human additives in survey sera. Porcine heart, CK, LD, AST, and ALT simulate human additives closely.[45–47] However, a practical additive that satisfactorily simulates human liver alkaline phosphatase is not available, and clinically irrelevant matrix effects may occur in surveys of this enzyme. Human erythrocyte AST and salivary alpha-amylase also have been recommended as additives to simulate behavior of these enzymes in at least some types of clinical specimens.[71,77] Hematology control materials vary in their response in the particular analytic system, depending on the sodium and glucose concentration of diluent used in the particular analytic system.[79] Substitution of fluorocarbon blood gas control materials for aqueous materials resulted in more realistic simulation of preanalytic variation.[49,78]

Bovine-based chemistry control materials introduce intermethod bias for albumin, iron, iron binding, triglyceride, bilirubin, and enzyme activity and are unsuitable for ligand assay.[70,80,81] The clinical simulation characteristics of equine sera have not been well evaluated.[70] It is of historical interest that lyophilized horse serum was used for the first international biochemical "analytic trial" in 1954.[82]

Not all matrix effects are clinically irrelevant. A number of characteristics of control matrices have been implicated in producing intermethod bias for creatinine measurement, particularly by kinetic methods.[83] Clinically relevant method interferences due to ketoacids, intermediate substrate exhaustion, bilirubin, and other factors have been identified in part through survey experience.[84–87] Similar effects may occur in AST analysis.[77]

Liquid Controls Liquid chemistry control materials have not received wide use in proficiency testing. Recent data regarding intermethod bias produced by this matrix, noted in internal quality control programs,[18,19] are presented in Table 6-5.

Nonhomogeneity of lyophilized chemistry materials has been estimated by manufacturers to be in the range of 0.34 to 0.56 percent CV.[70,72] Thus, an irreducible underlying source of variation may be present within the control material itself. Available liquid control materials,[88] however, do not reduce the observed analytic imprecision,[60,72,89] perhaps due to compensating effects of the liquid control matrix such as increased viscosity and increased absorbance. Additional data supporting this conclusion are noted in the CAP quality assurance statistics presented in Table 6-6. Both between-laboratory and within-laboratory imprecision are increased in programs using

TABLE 6-5
INTERMETHOD BIAS DUE TO CONTROL MATRIX
CAP Quality Assurance Service Regional Programs, 1983*

Matrix	Analyte	Bias†	Method
Bovine	Albumin	Negative, 1.5–2.5 g/dl	*aca* BCP vs BCG
Liquid	Creatinine	Negative, 0.1 mg/dl 1.0 mg/dl (elevated)	Dialysis methods
Liquid	Calcium	Negative, 0.2–0.4 mg/dl	Dialysis methods
Liquid	Phosphorus	Negative, 0.2–0.3 mg/dl	Dialysis methods
Liquid	Sodium	Negative, 9 mmol/L	Diluted ISE vs direct flame
Liquid	Sodium	Negative, 5 mmol/L	Diluted ISE vs dialysis flame
Liquid	Sodium	Negative, 2 mmol/L	Dialysis flame vs direct flame

BCP = bromcresol purple; BCG = bromcresol green; ISE = ion selective electrodes.
*The 10 analytes listed in Table 6-4 were evaluated.
†Bias in normal range unless otherwise specified.
Source: Data from CAP Quality Assurance Service Group Summary Reports, all regional groups in general chemistry, October and November 1983.

TABLE 6-6
CAP QUALITY ASSURANCE SERVICE
Average Long-Term %CV (1983)

Analyte	Average within-laboratory %CV		Average between-laboratory %CV	
	Liquid	Lyophilized	Liquid	Lyophilized
Albumin	3.8	3.7	4.2	4.0
Calcium	2.7	2.3	3.5	2.3
Chloride	1.6	1.7	2.2	1.9
Creatinine	4.6	4.2	6.3	5.7
Glucose	2.9	2.8	4.1	4.6
Magnesium	5.4	6.7	9.1	8.4
Phosphorus	4.1	3.3	7.2	5.7
Total protein	2.8	2.5	3.2	3.5
Urea nitrogen	4.1	3.8	4.5	4.3
Uric acid	4.5	3.3	9.4	7.9

Source: Data from CAP Quality Assurance Service Group Summary Reports, all regional groups in general chemistry, October and November 1983.

liquid control materials. The within-laboratory CVs relate to the control material homogeneity as a factor in estimates of intralaboratory variation. Lyophilized and liquid control matrices for enzyme analytes have also been evaluated.[19] A slight increase in observed imprecision occurs in some CK methods for some lots of lyophilized control materials. However, similar estimates of imprecision are obtained from lyophilized and liquid controls for other commonly tested enzymes. Another type of liquid control, frozen serum, also yields estimates of imprecision similar to those obtained with the lyophilized sera.[60,70,90] Thus, the specimen nonhomogeneity inherent in lyophilized control materials does not appear to be an important problem for the present purposes of external quality control. Of historical interest, the CAP Standards Committee reached the same conclusion after evaluation of the CAP Chemistry Survey sera used in the early 1960s.[91]

Survey Evaluation Criteria

Perhaps more important to individual laboratories than selection of target values is the selection of the criteria used to evaluate (grade) disagreement of participant results with the chosen target value. At this time, ranges of acceptable performance are chosen by the professional judgment of survey personnel based on their evaluation of the existing state of the art and their opinions of medical usefulness. Evaluation criteria have been discussed in general terms by providers of external quality control programs in many countries.[34,36,37,92] The ability of this type of evaluation criteria to predict clinical efficacy of laboratory testing has not been documented.

Quantative Tests In the early years of the CAP survey, from 1963 to 1966, evaluation criteria for quantitative tests were based on the range of values obtained by selected reference laboratories.[93] Good performance was defined by the mean of reference laboratory results plus or minus two standard deviations, and limits of acceptable performance were defined by the reference laboratory mean plus or minus three standard deviations. From 1967 to 1969, acceptable performance limits for quantitative tests were defined as the consensus peer-group mean plus or minus two standard deviations of participant values. This change was occasioned by the observation that the range defined by the reference mean plus or minus three standard deviations was roughly equal to the range defined by the participants' mean plus or minus two standard deviations. This relationship held true over many analytes and survey years.[93,94] Later, Kurtz et al.[95] noted a similar phenomenon of equivalency between the performance of large laboratories and that of the prevailing state of the art in internal quality control programs. Similar results have been obtained in other countries.[36,96,97] Limits for "good" performance were set in the CAP survey as the participants' mean plus or minus 1.5 standard deviations.

Qualitative Tests Qualitative tests in 1970 were evaluated using the range defined by 80 percent agreement by at least 10 reference laboratories.[93] For the most part, this concept has been abandoned in favor of evaluation based on participant statistics (coagulation testing evaluation and recently immunohematology[98]) or consideration of participant and reference laboratory statistics (toxicology and microbiology). The extent of services provided also is considered in microbiology evaluation. Special consideration has been given to syphilis serology evaluation, which is based on a scoring system designed to consider the degree of disagreement of each result with participant consensus results.[99] As a general rule, the use of reference laboratory statistics is appropriate only in the case of new survey analytes until the validity of concensus participant values is established, and, in some cases, when the participant peer-group sizes are too small to reduce statistical uncertainty to acceptable levels.

Hematology From 1967–1969, good performance of hemoglobin testing was defined as the participants' mean plus or minus 4 percent and for acceptable performance as the participants' mean plus or minus 7 percent. The fixed limits applied to hemoglobin were based on the opinions of the professional personnel responsible for evaluating the hemoglobin survey during the previous 5 years.[100] After 1970, limits for "good" performance were changed to plus or minus one standard deviation, and for "acceptable performance" to plus or minus two standard deviations of participant values.

Chemistry Enzyme results were not evaluated (graded) in 1970, although reference laboratory results were provided to the participants. Peer-group size in enzyme analysis is frequently small. A system that allows a broader base of accuracy and precision evaluation, validation of reference ranges, and analysis of both short-term and long-term precision was developed by using a series of samples with linearly related enzyme activities. By application of linear regression analysis after conversion of results into common "base pool"-relative units, the appropriate statistics are calculated.[101] Other alternative means of evaluation have been investigated. A cumulative percentile performance rating with peer concensus and medical usefulness criteria has been evaluated in a state proficiency testing program.[102]

The basic concept of statistical evaluation based on peer-group data was unchanged until 1978. At that time, "fixed criteria" for the range of acceptable performance were applied to evaluation of potassium and calcium results. The fixed limits were centered on a target value calculated as a concensus peer-group mean that had been correlated with NBS definitive method results.[44,63] The continued reduction of intralaboratory and interlaboratory imprecision served as the stimulus to expand the use of fixed criteria as evaluation limits. State-of-the-art statistical evaluation limits were increasingly narrow and of questionable clinical relevance. Subsequently, fixed criteria have been introduced for evaluation of sodium, chloride, cholesterol, uric acid, creatinine, PO_2, PCO_2, and pH. The target value for the former four analytes is a concensus participant method grouping believed to correlate closely with the true value, and for the latter four analytes is the appropriate peer-group mean.

In the case of some analytes, imprecision has decreased to the point where the interlaboratory standard deviation is so small that use of a minimum standard deviation is warranted. A minimum standard deviation is applied for urea nitrogen and lithium evaluation. A minimum standard deviation of (0.40 g/dl) for hemoglobin evaluation is based on current perceived medical usefulness needs. Of historical interest is Sunderman's use[103] of smaller limits for acceptability of hemoglobin testing (0.15 to 0.20 g/dl) in 1947.

Survey Evaluation Criteria and Medical Usefulness Although it is apparent that the professionals supervising interlaboratory testing programs must respond to diverse needs in determining ranges for acceptable performance, consideration of two factors, the state of the art and medical usefulness, have been consistent. Thus, the Standards Committee of the CAP in 1968[104] recommended that evaluation criteria selected should stimulate gradual improvement in the state of the art. The committee expressed a definite perception of medical "nonusefulness" by recommending abandonment of a method when the "variability observed in surveys is consistently greater than that of other well-established procedures." However, an objective definition of medical usefulness in survey evaluation criteria was not provided.

The available literature at the time regarding fixed criteria was scanty.[92,103,105–108] Although there was an apparent awareness of the importance of individual biologic variation by the early 1950s and that intraindividual variation was smaller than group biologic variation,[109] little scientific data were available.[92,110–112] Some of the major publications with "fixed" or "medical usefulness" criteria for error limits were arbitrary, for example: "Such values [which have] been arbitrarily selected by the referee as limits that should be maintained for a satisfactory laboratory practice";[103] "allowable limits of error [that] were calculated by means of an empirical formula which the author has found to be useful";[108] and "a number of hospital clinicians . . . would regard as acceptable."[92] Barnett[107] provided "a synthesis of opinions by clinicians and laboratory specialists," but gave no further documentation as to the source and origin of the information. A second report of Campbell and Owen[113] provided a broader-based physician survey, and the reports of Acland and Lipton[105,114] employed a quantitative statistical model, which presaged those applied later in the 1970s.

The germinal medical usefulness criteria suggested in the 1960s were often phrased as either a fraction of a group reference range,[108] or a fraction of a statistic,[106,107] or a ratio of analytic variation to group biologic variation.[105,114] Thus, proposed allowable error limits were designed to account for a fraction of observed group (interindividual plus intraindividual) variation. These criteria were recognized as unreliable in view of inadequate knowledge of reference intervals and of intraindividual variation. The rapid expansion of knowledge regarding biologic variation, especially that within individual subjects, has been summarized.[60] In addition, survey personnel began to recognize sources of error other than allowable analytic error, which limits of acceptable performance must accommodate, including uncertainty in the target value and variation due to the sample matrix and nonhomogeneity.[44,115]

Exploration of medical usefulness criteria was not limited to quantitative disciplines. A report investigating concepts of medical usefulness in microbiology was issued in 1970.[116] During a review of microbiology survey evaluation criteria, an interesting insight into the interaction between developing concepts of medical usefulness and expected technical expertise was provided.[52] After pointing out that acceptability of a clinical microbiology report depended on the extent of services routinely offered by the laboratory, the authors stated that "acceptable" in most instances was "clinically relevant and in itself not detrimental to the clinical diagnosis and subsequent therapy of a patient. If a sample contained *Shigella sonnei,* an identification of Shigella species would be considered acceptable, since basic diagnosis and therapy would be affected." However, an identification of *Shigella flexneri* "would not be considered acceptable. This decision would be made not so much from the point of view of clinical relevance, but from the point of view of technical proficiency since an attempt was obviously made to speciate the organism and this attempt proved incorrect."

Identification and Solution of Analytic Problems

External quality control programs have identified significant problems in analytic performance that could not have been identified by internal quality control programs or by other means. Through use of interrelated general chemistry survey samples prepared from common base pools, Gilbert[43,57,58] identified and quantitated the sources of analytic variability and inaccuracy for most of the common chemistry serum analytes. He was able to establish that what had long been regarded as "interlaboratory variation" was due primarily to long-term intralaboratory imprecision. Inaccuracy, in the sense of fixed or interlaboratory bias, was relatively small. Similar estimates of long-term imprecision were obtained by independent evaluation of intralaboratory quality control data.[60] Another study revealed that long-term intralaboratory imprecision is a major source of ligand assay variation.[117] These important studies directed attention to the problem of long-term intralaboratory imprecision (random inaccuracy).

Evaluation of the outlying results detected by application of fixed ranges of acceptable performance (fixed criteria) to calcium results in CAP surveys later confirmed that method imprecision was a more significant problem than method inaccuracy.[44] Imprecision accounted for the perceived lack of medical usefulness of calcium analysis noted at the time. A similar conclusion was reached independently by analysis of internal quality control data.[10] Proficiency testing design has permitted confirmation of the resolution of state-of-the-art analytic problems such as the chemical specificity of vitamin B_{12} analysis[118] and has facilitated comparison of performance characteristics of systems of yeast identification[119] and systems of bacterial identification.[53] Method performance for detection of beta lactamase-resistant *Hemophilus influenzae,* penicillin-resistant *Streptococcus pneumoniae,* and methicillin-resistant staphylococci has been evaluated.[120,121] Insight into possible effective methods of standardization of prothrombin time testing has accrued from coagulation surveys,[67] and the relationship of coagulation reagents and instrumentation to performance in heparin monitoring has been evaluated.[65] Mutually productive relationships between internal and external quality control programs in microbiology are illustrated by development of internal quality control procedure recommendations based on proficiency survey performance in antimicrobial susceptibility testing.[122,123] The use of external quality control statistics with programs of internal quality control has been outlined by Haven et al.[124]

Survey-Validated Reference Materials

Survey-validated referenced materials (SVRMs) have been made available through the CAP Chemistry Surveys and are available for general chemistry, cerebrospinal fluid chemistry, urine chemistry, therapeutic drugs, and ligand assay. This type of reference material is a valuable resource within internal quality control programs.[124,125] The lots of survey-validated reference materials have been exhaustively analyzed by consensus methods, which in many instances are connected directly to National Bureau of Standard (NBS) definitive methodology. Grannis[125] considered these relationships and materials the rudiments of a "national system of quality assurance." He later described[126] production of linearly related samples using survey-validated reference materials for use in method evaluation and in setting internal quality control material target values.

The development of a national comprehensive measurement system in clinical chemistry began in 1977.[39] The concept is to use reference methods to develop target values for control material that can be used in turn for target values for use in internal quality control and external quality control. At present, the precise position of survey-validated reference materials within this system is undefined.

ANALYTIC GOALS

Inevitably, programs that declare results or procedures "unacceptable" must face the task of defining "acceptability." The dramatic improvement in laboratory performance that occurred in the 1970s kept concepts of medical usefulness and analytical goals in the forefront. The concepts stemming from survey data were discussed eloquently by Gilbert[43] and later were elaborated in the 1976 CAP Aspen Conference.[127] More recently, the need for continued progress toward survey evaluation criteria based on medical usefulness has been repeated by Batsakis.[128] For many analytes, the traditional peer-group concept of evaluation seems unnecessarily restrictive and fails to address the problem of method-related bias. Accuracy, often defined in terms of definitive methods, has superseded simple interlaboratory agreement as the goal to be attained.[36,44,62,63]

The state of the art was accepted as the minimum goal for analytic performance by the 1976 CAP Aspen Conference, by a later report from the World Association of Societies of Pathology,[38] and for purposes of laboratory management and accreditation.[129] However, as aptly stated by Inhorn, "the real purpose of quality assurance activities [has become] to determine how correct or incorrect the results emanating from the laboratory are, and to allow those managing the laboratory to determine whether or not the laboratory is fulfilling its function satisfactorily. . . . Correctness of results implies that performance standards are maintained. The central question in this regard is to how to rationally determine what these standards should be."[130]

There is a "flat of the curve" in medicine, on which additional input produces no detectable output.[131] For the laboratory a consensus has been reached that accuracy should not be pursued beyond the point of diminishing return from the standpoint of cost effectiveness.[130] The World Association of Societies of Pathology Report[38] calls for statistical models that provide a basis for estimating tolerable limits of inaccuracy for quantitative analysis; some useful models have been published.[132-137] In qualitative analysis, such as microbiology, the pursuit of medical relevance now also uses elements of decision analysis.[138]

In addition to their use in external quality control, guidelines for acceptable analytic performance are necessary for proper method selection and evaluation, proper control of quality in internal quality control programs, and for other aspects of laboratory management. Such guidelines are referred to as "analytical goals." However, the meaning of this term is often vague and implicit, and its distinction from related terms such as medical usefulness criteria, patient care requirements, allowable analytic error, and quality specifications is not clear. Analytical goals have been referred to as analytic performance standards derived from medical care requirements;[139] specifications of the amount of analytic error that is allowable or tolerable in the medical application of the test results;[140] analytic performance standards that are proper and adequate in a given medical context;[60] the analytic error acceptable for purposes of medical utility;[128] and "the standards of [analytic] performance that must be reached to provide optimal patient care, preferably at least expense."[96]

Performance Standards

Goals should not be applied to performance characteristics of an analytic method without a clear notion of the clinical relevance of doing so. Performance characteristics of an analytic method have been defined as a set of quantitative and experimentally derived values of fundamental importance in assessing the suitability of the method for a given purpose (see Westgard[141]). They have been categorized into pragmatic characteristics such as cost, technical skill requirements, dependability and safety, and into reliability characteristics such as inaccuracy, imprecision, chemical specificity, and detection limits.[142]

According to Westgard,[141] the important characteristics of the analytic method fall into three groups: (1) application characteristics, which are those factors that determine suitability of a method for a particular laboratory environment (including sample size, turnaround time, batch size, rate of analysis, equipment and personnel requirements, and safety); (2) methodologic characteristics, which are principles that should determine best performance (such as chemical specificity and sensitivity, choice of chemical reaction and optimum conditions, and method of calibration); and (3) performance characteristics, which are those factors that demonstrate in practice the analytic quality of the method (including accuracy, precision, recovery, interference, and detection limit).

Total Error

The performance (or reliability) characteristics of a method are those that determine analytic quality and that are measured in daily routine practice. Of these characteristics, it is the magnitude of the total analytic error affecting the final result that determines the test's performance. It makes little difference to patient or clinician which components of inaccuracy cause the error, only that the result deviates from the true value. Analytic goals for medical tests thus are best defined as the total allowable error, regardless of source.[140,141,143]

The complex taxonomy of analytic error also has been reviewed by Westgard.[141] One model of analytic error categorizes error into constant bias and proportional bias. Random error is divided into imprecision and random bias. In this model, random bias refers to those systematic errors that vary from patient to patient depending on the degree of specimen matrix effect or level of interfering compound. This error component is measured by method evaluation protocols using paired analysis of clinical patient specimens by reference and trial methods.[142,144]

Analytic Goals and Statistical Controls

Statistical control is achieved by limiting imprecision within groupings of results (analytic runs) while eliminating, controlling, or correcting for assignable causes of significant error. A state of "simple" statistical control is said to exist when assignable causes of error that give rise to a between-run component of variation are eliminated and when within-run imprecision is appropriately limited. A state of "complex" statistical control is said to exist when between-run variation is present. Although it is generally accepted that a degree of within-run imprecision is unavoidable, there is less acceptance of between-run variation as a usual component of imprecision. Because a state of complex statistical control is the usual case in clinical laboratory analysis, between-run variation must be taken into account for development of analytic goals and fixed criteria.

In clinical analysis it is not possible experimentally to isolate systematic effects from random effects. Commentary on "random inaccuracy" as a component of long-term clinical laboratory imprecision has been summarized;[60] see also Refs. 43, 95, 105, 133, and 144. The term "random bias" also has been applied to this component of error.[115] In this context, random bias is defined as systematic error due to constant but temporally limited influences in the analytic environment. When these influences are not eliminated or corrected, they produce changes in systematic error that average zero over time. Random bias probably does not differ generically from between-run variation, that is, variation due to assignable causes that are important to eliminate, control, or correct.[145] However, it is useful to isolate the concept of random bias in order to clarify the inseparability of random from systematic error in clinical analytic practice. Random bias arises in the application of the method rather than from fixed inaccuracy of the method. Changes in bias may be in terms of many weeks,[144] a period longer than ordinarily measured in method evaluation protocols, but an important period in long-term and interlaboratory patient follow-up, and, thus, in formulation of analytic goals.[43]

Analytic Goals, Methods of Calculations

The considerable body of literature on analytic goals for the clinical chemistry laboratory has been reviewed.[96,146,147] Analytic goals have been formulated by several means: current state of the art; opinions of clinical and laboratory professional personnel; statistical models using data based on physician responses to simulated clinical situations; statistical models allowing sensitivity analysis of changes in analytic performance on the reference range or the patient misclassification rate; and statistical models that allow sensitivity analysis of the effect of changes in analytic performance on diagnostic accuracy.

State of the Art

Analytic goals based on the state of the art have dealt with imprecision for the most part.[96,127,133,139,148,149] These goals are connected to medical utility only by the assumption that prevalent laboratory service levels have medical use. However, the state of the art in the sense of the best practical methods has become an accepted minimum standard of performance,[127,129] and there is no doubt that continued improvement is achieved through selection of methods that meet this criterion.[43,44]

Professional Consensus

Analytic goals representing the consensus of clinical and laboratory professional opinion have been useful guidelines for the evaluation of intralaboratory imprecision.[43,107] However, consensus goals may be linked to perceptions of the state of the art existing at the time of their formulation and, thus, may become dated. Moreover, the origin and sources of variation included in acceptable test imprecision cannot be analyzed, and their use as goals for analytic method imprecision may not be appropriate.

Physician Action Models

Statistics describing the recorded responses of physicians to changes in analyte concentrations have been calculated from data gathered through questionnaires. These statistics fix the variable of simple univariate statistical models used to calculate CVs or standard deviations (SDs), which are to serve as analytic goals for imprecision.[93,113,150–152] In these surveys, a number of physician respondents has varied from 62 to 745. No criteria are provided by which the changes recorded as significant by the physician can be attributed to analytic variation, preanalytic variation, or biologic variation. Frequently, variation is not related to an appropriate time interval, an important variable in the evaluation of analytic imprecision.[60] The lack of definition of the origin and sources of variation included in the goals proposed by the physician response method limits their usefulness. However, it is probably safe to accept the generalization offered by Skendzel et al.[152] that it is not productive to reduce intralaboratory analytic variation to CVs severalfold less than those calculated using these criteria.

Clinical Statistical Models

Statistical models have been used to evaluate the effect of analytic variation on outcome variables without independently defining a medical usefulness criterion or establishing a relationship of the variable to diagnostic accuracy.[20,38,105,107,127,139,146,153] The outcome variables evaluated are widening of the reference range and patient misclassification rate. Goals have been suggested that limit the widening of the true biologic distributions owing to imprecision from 2 to 15 percent and which limit the rate of patient misclassification with respect to a given range of clinical interest to 2 or 5 percent. These goals are arbitrary, because they do not define a medical benefit. It is intuitively apparent that if the broadening of biologic populations and increases in misclassification rates are small, it may be safely assumed that analytic variation does not substantially impair the diagnostic process. However, the precise effect of analytic error on diagnostic accuracy cannot be predicted by the statistical models used. Although these models can assist in development of specifications for performance, they are incomplete and self-confirming models that, in effect, formulate and support the hypothesis with the same data.

Analytic goals can be derived using statistical models that predict the effect of analytic variation on the efficiency of the diagnostic process.[132–136] Biochemical (physiological) and clinical decision models permit sensitivity analysis that evaluates the effect of minimizing biologic variation, preanalytic variation, and analytic variation on cost. Cost is stated in various terms: diagnostic misclassification rates; morbidity or mortality; and dollars. The models do not require difficult assumptions for the purpose of estimating the improvement in diagnostic efficiency. Outcome variables that can be optimized include minimization of the false-positive rate at a fixed false-negative rate and maximization of overall diagnostic efficiency with a simple formula for the relative value of false-negative to false-positive costs.

Statistical models simulating clinical processes can produce analytic goals based on clinical criteria defined independently of laboratory concerns. Because, in a given diagnostic strategy, the effect of bias is the same as a change in the discriminant value, the goal may be calculated as a CV at a given discriminant value[136] or as a goal including the effect of bias as well as imprecision.[133,143]

Total Error Goals and Imprecision

The goal for analytic bias usually has been set at zero,[38,96,145,153] which is a reasonable goal for fixed bias due to the method. However, random bias due to application of the method can be eliminated only in theory. Although its elimination is important to the concept of statistical control, between-run variation is a fact of present-day methodology and is unlikely to disappear.[60,95,139,154] Thus the proposed goal of zero for random inaccuracy[145] is impractical. However, the effect of this component of variation on control system design is important, because most rules for run rejection in internal quality control are much less efficient if between-run variation accounts for a large portion of interlaboratory disagreement. The effects of between-run variation can be estimated by analytic statistical simulation models.[155,156]

Goals have been proposed for many additional characteristics of methods, including linearity, turnaround times, preanalytic variation, and other factors, which are practical, methodologic, or application characteristics rather than performance characteristics.[96,147] Skillful selection of methods with characteristics that are appropriate for the intended environment is necessary, or evaluation of analytic performance characteristics is useless.

RELATION OF MEDICAL USEFULNESS CRITERIA, GOALS FOR TOTAL ERROR, AND PERFORMANCE STANDARDS

The remaining discussion will focus on those performance characteristics that are of primary importance to the clinical acceptability of the results: total error, bias, and imprecision. This is not to deny the importance of the other analytic performance characteristics: interference, detection limit, and recovery. However, interference is included in a comprehensive concept of accuracy[141] and contributes to observed biologic variation.[60] Without adequate sensitivity, the test is useless for the intended purpose, and the question of accuracy does not arise. Goals for sensitivity have been proposed,[147] but more data are needed to develop a formal approach.

Clinical statistical simulation models have been developed that permit calculation of analytic goals, given medical usefulness criteria. In the laboratory domain, analytic statistical models that simulate analytic error conditions and error control processes have been developed.[140,141,143,155,157,158] Analytic statistical models require independently derived error goals in their application to new method evaluation[143,159,160] and in design of internal quality control programs.[140,155-158,161] Given the error goal, the models calculate quality specifications for the performance characteristics of a trial method. Without both reliable clinical statistical models and analytic statistical models, it is not possible to derive analytic goals from medical usefulness criteria, to derive quality specifications from analytic goals, and, finally, to verify the clinical quality of the results produced.

There is abundant evidence from regional internal quality control programs and from external quality control programs of substantial improvements in accuracy and precision over the last 39 years. Methods are available that can accurately record variations due to normal physiology, minor aliments, and slight physiologic disturbances, the measurement of which produces no medically useful information. Thus, the background noise due to influences of no medical significance, in which medically important signals of necessity reside, can now be visualized. A case can be made for the view that analytic imprecision should not increase apparent noise levels so that otherwise clinically important signals would be hidden. However, when resources are limited or expensive, they should not be allocated to promote methods sufficiently accurate and precise to measure noise due to irreducible biologic variation, preanalytic variation, and clinical error when no means exist to translate the analytic data produced into diagnostic information. Rather, resources should be allocated to application or practicality characteristics such as control of preanalytic variation, patient standardization, verification of reference ranges, extension of reference ranges to clinically relevant groups, and the prevention of gross errors. By defining analytic goals through medical usefulness criteria based on diagnostic accuracy, the point of diminishing return in improvement of analytic performance can be recognized.

Observed Variation

Unless the clinical efficacy of a test is perfect, there is irreducible overlap of results between the population in question and other populations. The intersection of the populations is due to biologic variation. The degree of overlapping with a given test can be reduced by strategies such as serial sampling and algebraic transformation of results.[132,162] However, the biologic variation of a given analyte and its intersections with adjacent populations at some point become resistant to further reduction. At this point, clinical performance of the test is ideal, although not perfect.

Several factors may cause the observed clinical efficacy of the test to be less than that ideal. These factors include "clinical imprecision," preanalytic variation, random inaccuracy, and inherent analytic variation. Clinical imprecision in relationship to goal setting has been discussed by Elion-Gerritzen[151] and Oxley.[163,164] It may be the result of error in clinical interpretation of outcome, of error in the use of the proper discriminant values in a given diagnostic strategy, or of error in pretest patient evaluation. For example, clinical assessment of breast tumor response to hormone therapy may differ between clinical observers.[165,166] The discriminant value for a test in a given diagnostic strategy may vary between clinicians in the diagnosis of hypertension, obesity, diabetes mellitus, hypercalcemia, and other common and uncommon medical conditions.[167-170] Errors in physical diagnosis have been reviewed and classified as those due to errors in technique, of omission, of detection, and of interpretation.[171]

Obviously, a physician's diagnosis does not establish the presence of disease. In the case of opposed clinical judgments, existence of test results falsely classified is guaranteed and cannot be reduced by perfect method accuracy. The effect is to increase the observed variation in the biologic populations.

Preanalytic variation may be due to lack of standardization of patient-related variables such as diet, posture, time, and relationship to chronobiologic rhythms, or to errors in sample collection and specimen preservation.[172] Its importance to evaluation of imprecision[60] and goal setting[38,96] has been reviewed. The effect of these sources of error is to increase the observed variation.

Inherent or within-run method imprecision is unavoidable and irreducible.[60,141] Its effect is to increase biologic variation or any sum of biologic variation with other described error sources including random bias and random inaccuracy.

Thus, there are at least four identifiable components to irreducible observed variation: biologic factors, clinical errors, preanalytic factors, and inherent method variation. Their sum is the irreducible noise above which clinically important signals must rise. The aim of laboratory internal quality control, external quality control, and method evaluation is to reduce the controllable component of analytic variation to an amount that does not contribute significantly to the sum of the other four. The formula most appropriate for calculation of this sum is the quadratic propagation of error method,[132,143,150,173] in which the observed variation is the sum-square-square-root of the error factors. In this formula, one variance can dominate the others, whose combined contribution to total error may become relatively insignificant.[174] There is no cost justification for reduction of error that does not contribute to the overall observed error. For example, if clinical imprecision due to poor technique in physical diagnosis increases reliance on laboratory tests, the entire importance and benefit of laboratory improvement can be destroyed. Thus, clinical skills must be maintained, patient preparation and standardization improved, and specimens well preserved if analytic improvement is to result in a clinical benefit.

The Goal-Setting Process

A general model for the goal-setting process is illustrated in Fig. 6-1. The observed population is a population of results for a given test obtained from subjects during testing for a clinical characteristic of diagnostic, prognostic, or therapeutic importance. Because of clinical imprecision, preanalytic variation, and analytic variation, the dispersion of results will be greater than that found in those subjects who actually have the characteristics sought. The overlap with results from similar subjects, who lack the characteristic sought, is thereby increased and diagnostic accuracy is decreased.

A medical usefulness criterion is a statement of the allowable departure of observed

FIGURE 6-1
General model for analytic goal setting.

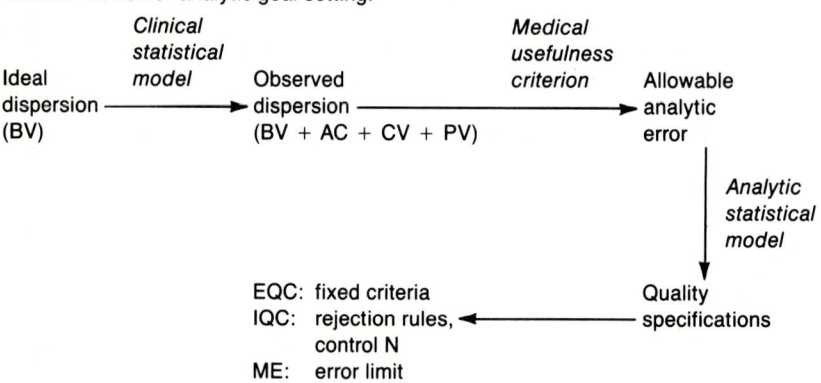

BV   = biologic variation
AV   = analytic variation
CV   = clinical variation
PV   = preanalytic variation
EQC = external quality control
IQC = internal quality control
ME   = method evaluation
N   = number

diagnostic accuracy from that ideally possible. The criterion allows calculation of tolerable analytic error in a clinical statistical model when the values of the other variables of the model associated with preanalytic, clinical, and inherent analytic errors are fixed. A value is then calculated for allowable analytic error. With the value of allowable error determined, analytic statistical models calculate specifications for performance characteristics at medical decision points. The specifications are then used in internal quality control program design, evaluation of new methods, and in developing fixed criteria performance in external quality control programs. The specifications calculated from a given analytic goal differ depending on whether the specification is applied in method evaluation, internal quality control, or external quality control.

For method evaluation, analytic statistical models in current use are linear regression models.[142,143,159,160] A total error model[156,161] and a predictive value model[157] are helpful in internal quality control program design. A model for external quality control quality specification prediction is described.[175] Clinical statistical models developed by Harris[133] and the Nordic Group[176] link the analytic goal-setting process to the important variables associated with the diagnostic process and express the calculated results in terms of diagnostic efficiency, health outcome, or economic cost.

The differences in quality specifications calculated from a particular analytic goal are illustrated in Fig. 6-2. Procedures for internal quality control and external quality control are similar. Certain variables are determined experimentally, the values entered into an appropriate model, and quality specifications for limits of the range of acceptable performance or for method bias in random error are calculated. In the case of external quality control, the direct application of the quality specification is for the purpose of quality evaluation. In contrast, the quality specifications for internal quality control are intended to define a level of quality to be maintained through process control. In each case, the quality specifications are the bias and imprecision allowable given the constraints of the analytical goal for total error and any applicable specific factors.

It is apparent that tests whose results are continuous variables are more amenable to the goal-setting process than discrete variables. However, all analyses, including those whose results are binary or discrete variables, have the method characteristics of detection limits, interferences, analytic sensitivity, analytic specificity, and accuracy. The clinical performance of all tests can be characterized in terms of clinical sensitivity, clinical specificity, and diagnostic accuracy. All tests are susceptible to errors of clinical interpretation, errors in preanalytic processing, and analytic error. Most tests, if not all, are subject to some form of biologic variation. Thus, there are no theoretical barriers to wider application to appropriate predictive statistical models.

The Goal-Setting Process in a Closed Information Loop

The entire goal-setting process presented as a closed information loop between the clinical domain and the laboratory domain is illustrated in Fig. 6-3. Types of health care costs should be specified into those of morbidity and/or mortality, and financial

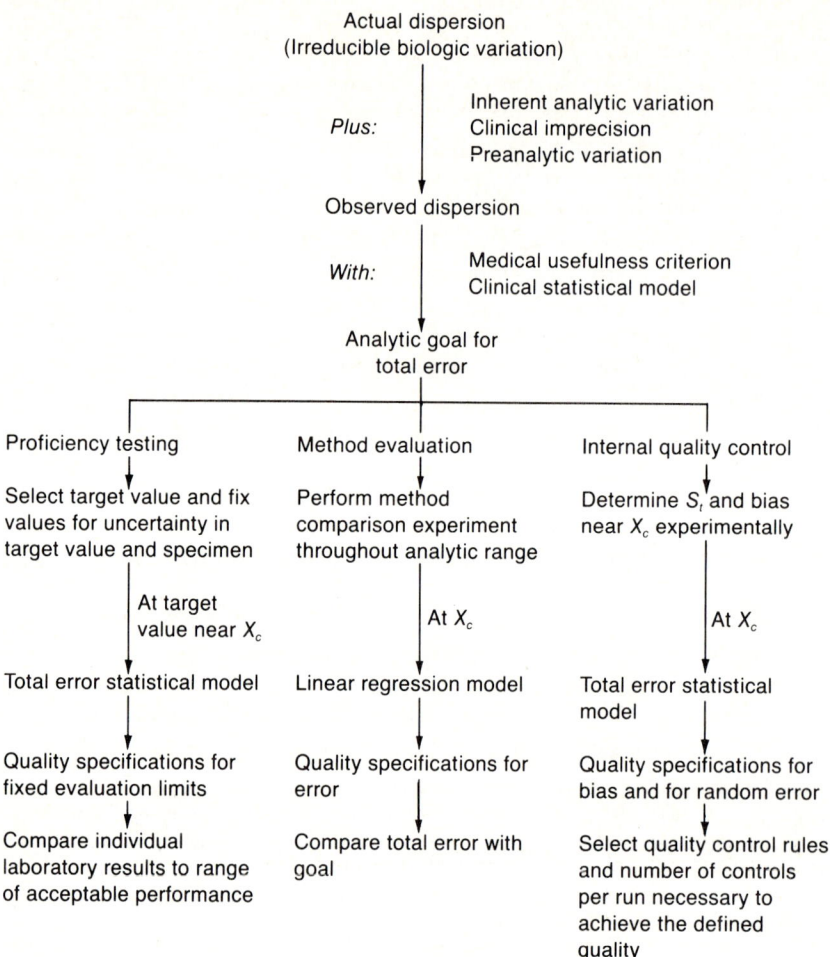

FIGURE 6-2
General model for derivation of quality specifications from analytic goals.

costs as medical and/or support costs. Obviously, the scheme provides for an analytic goal for each test/disease/diagnostic strategy combination. However, only those applications in prevalent use requiring the most accurate analytic performance need be evaluated. At the bottom of Fig. 6-3, transformation of analytic results is illustrated. Results may be reported directly, transformed algebraically, used to evaluate a statistical function, or used as a variable in a statistical model. Calculation of simple means and clearance rates, discriminant function analysis, and calculation of myocardial infarct sizes are examples of these transformations.[132] There are a variety of possible clinical methods of data transformation, including Bayesian probability analysis, categorical flowcharts, cluster analysis, and discriminant function analysis. However, the usual

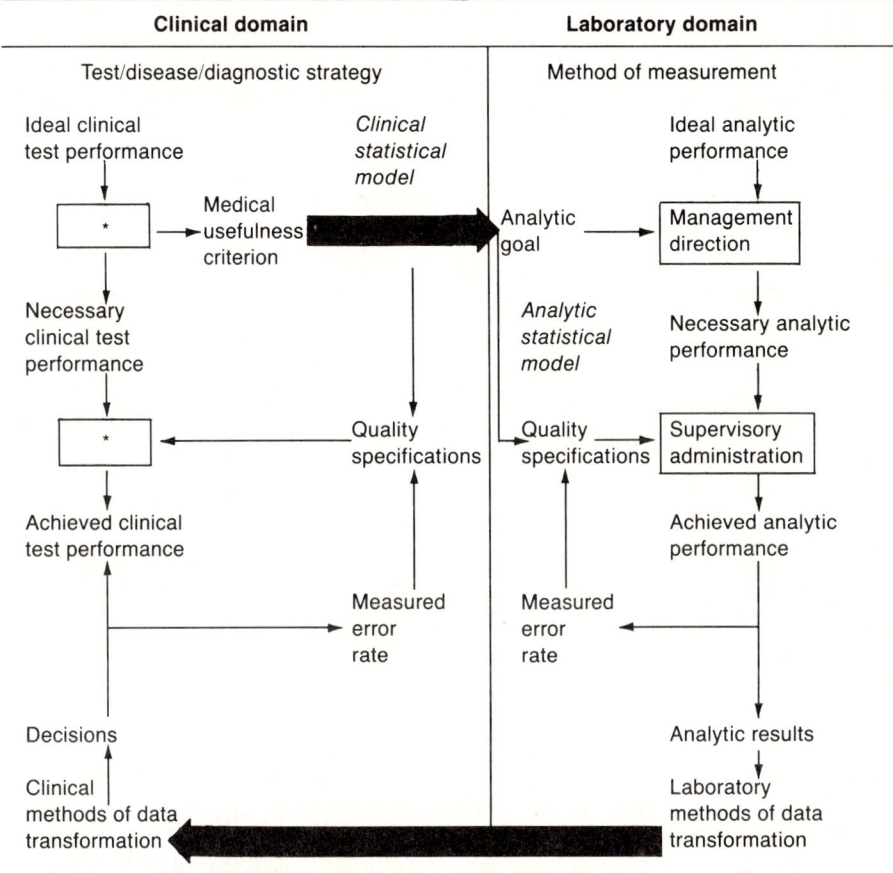

FIGURE 6-3
Information loop linking closed-efficacy analytical goals with clinical test.

method is simple comparison of the observed value to a population-based reference range or decision limit.

Groth[132] has observed that optimal analytic quality depends on accurate identification and description of the processes involved in the clinical transformation of laboratory data into useful information and medical decisions. These transformations determine the achieved level of clinical performance. When it is possible to measure achieved clinical performance, clinical efficacy of diagnostic tests can be measured, and the too-often open information loop between the clinical and laboratory domains can be closed.[115,137,177–184]

Once ideal clinical test performance has been expressed in terms of diagnostic efficacy, a number of choices exist for defining medical usefulness criteria. Diagnostic efficacy may be expressed in terms of a four-cell matrix, a nine-cell matrix,[180] a receiver operating characteristic curve,[137,181,182] or in statistical models simulating the clinical classification and decision processes.[132] The medical usefulness criterion is a statement of acceptable departure from ideals.

If the medical usefulness criterion is to lead to an analytic error goal worth striving for, it must be based on factors contained in the clinical domain. Acceptable costs of analytic error ideally should be specified in terms of available economic resources and social needs. A practical alternative is to evaluate the effect of analytic error on diagnostic efficiency, calculated with a widely accepted relative weighting of the cost of false-negative and false-positive results.[132,134,135,179]

ANALYTIC GOALS AND LABORATORY USAGE

In a discussion of clinical laboratory quality requirements from a public health point of view, Inhorn[129] describes public and government concern regarding the level of quality of medical care that can be provided by a system of balanced components including clinical laboratories, industry, professional organizations, and government. A dominant public concern is that of cost control, because 10 percent of the gross national product is devoted to health care, 10 percent of health care costs are attributed to clinical laboratory tests, and 25 percent of the expenses of laboratory operation are attributed to quality control costs. Application of analytic goals to external quality control and internal quality control provide a cost-effective approach to attain necessary quality.

Clinicians desire laboratory results that are reliable and cost effective. However, the clinician has a personalized perspective of the laboratory service. According to Young[185] the clinician expects the laborarian to have the following characteristics: of trustworthiness—as a partner in the enterprise in which the clinician is engaged; of an investigator—increasing the ways by which clinicians help their patients; of an educator—teaching clinicians to apply laboratory advances to their practice; and of a consultant—available and prepared to assist the clinician in the care of individual patients. Without attention to these qualities, the laboratory will not be successful, regardless of the analytic quality of the test performed.

REFERENCES

1 Copeland BE, Rosenbaum JM: Organization, planning and results of the Massachusetts Society of Pathologists Regional Quality Control Program. *Am J Clin Pathol* 1972, 57:676.
2 Lawson NS, Haven GT: The role of regional quality control programs in the practice of laboratory medicine in the United States. *Am J Clin Pathol* 1976, 66:268.
3 Westgard JO, Barry PL, Hunt MR: A multi-rule Shewhart chart for quality control in clinical chemistry. *Clin Chem* 1981, 27:493.
4 Westgard JO, Hyltoft Peterson P, Groth T: The quality-costs of an analytical process: 1. Development of quality-costs models based on predictive value theory. 2. A test yield formulation of the predictive value quality-costs model. *Scand J Clin Lab Invest* 1984, 44(suppl 172):221, 229.
5 Howanitz PJ: Old vs new quality control rules: Which rules are more cost effective? *Pathologist* 1985, 39:8.

6 Ross JW, Fraser MD: The effect of analyte and analyte concentration upon precision estimates in clinical chemistry. *Am J Clin Pathol* 1976, 66:193.
7 Ross JW, Fraser MD: Analytical clinical chemistry precision: State of the art for fourteen analytes. *Am J Clin Pathol* 1977, 68:130.
8 Ross JW, Fraser MD: Analytical clinical laboratory precision: State of the art for twenty-nine analytes. *Am J Clin Pathol* 1979, 72:265.
9 Ross JW, Fraser MD, Moore TD: Analytical clinical laboratory precision: State of the art for thirty-one analytes. *Am J Clin Pathol* 1980, 74:521.
10 Ross JW, Fraser MD: Clinical laboratory precision: The state of the art and medical usefulness based internal quality control. *Am J Clin Pathol* 1982, 78:578.
11 Lawson NS, Haven GT, Moore TD: Long-term stability of glucose in lyophilized quality control serum. A study utilizing data from the Quality Assurance Service (QAS) Program of the College of American Pathologists. *Am J Clin Pathol* 1978, 70:523.
12 Lawson NS, Haven GT, DiSilvio TV, Gilmore BF: Glucose stability in lyophilized chemistry quality control serum: A study of data from the Quality Assurance Service (QAS) Program of the College of American Pathologists. *Am J Clin Pathol* 1982, 78:597.
13 Lawson NS, Haven GT, Moore TD: Long-term stability of enzymes, total protein, and inorganic analytes in lyophilized quality control serum. *Am J Clin Pathol* 1977, 68:117.
14 Lawson NS, Haven GT, DiSilvio TV, Gilmore BF: Stability of sodium and potassium in lyophilized quality control serum: A study of data from the Quality Assurance Service Program of the College of American Pathologists. *Am J Clin Pathol* 1981, 76:581.
15 Lawson NS, Haven GT, Williams GM: Analyte stability in clinical chemistry control materials. *CRC Crit Rev Clin Lab Sci* 1982, 17:1.
16 Rosenbaum JM: Accuracy comparisons in Q.A.S. Programs. *Pathologist* 1978, 32:672.
17 Rosenbaum JM: Accuracy in clinical laboratories participating in Regional Quality Control Programs. *Arch Pathol* 1985, 109:485.
18 Howanitz PJ, Howanitz JH, Lamberson HV, et al: Analytical biases with liquid quality control material. *Am J Clin Pathol* 1983, 80:643.
19 Lohff MR, DiSilvio TV, Ross JW, et al: Analytic clinical laboratory precision: State of the art for selected enzymes. *Am J Clin Pathol* 1982, 78:634.
20 Lawson NS, Ross JW: Long-term precision for selected clinical chemistry analytes as determined by data from Regional Quality Control Programs, in Elevitch FR (ed): *Analytical Goals in Clinical Chemistry*, CAP Aspen Conference 1976. Skokie, IL, College of American Pathologists, 1977, pp 83–89.
21 Baer DM, Belsey R: *The Pathologist as a Consultant to the Physician's Office Lab*. Chicago, American Society of Clinical Pathologists, 1985.
22 Diamond I: The cost of quality control. *Pathologist* 1982, 36:192.
23 Tydeman J, Morrison JI, Hardwick DF, et al: The cost of quality control procedures in the clinical laboratory. *Am J Clin Pathol* 1982, 77:528.
24 Feigenbaum AV: What is total quality control?, in Rand RN, Eilers RJ, Lawson NS, et al (eds): *Quality Assurance in Health Care: A Critical Appraisal of Clinical Chemistry*. Washington, DC, American Association of Clinical Chemists, 1980, pp 3–12.
25 Barnett RN, Lawson NS, Ross, JW et al: Internal quality control testing: Principles and definitions, Manuscript in preparation.
26 Lawson NS, Haven GT, Ross JW: Regional Quality Assurance for the 1980's: Current status and future directions. *Am J Clin Pathol* 1980, 74:552.
27 Platt R, Batsakis JG: Intralaboratory analytic precision as estimated from two distinct programs from the College of American Pathologists. *Am J Clin Pathol* 1981, 76:578.
28 Hicks GP: Microcomputer applications in the clinical laboratory of the 1980's, in Hom-

berger HA, Batsakis, JG (eds): *Clinical Laboratory Annual: Nineteen Eighty-Two.* New York, Appleton-Century-Crofts, 1982, pp 51–72.
29. Lincoln TL, Aller RD: *Microcomputers in the Laboratory,* Special Topics, vol 22, number 5. Chicago, American Society of Clinical Pathologists, 1984.
30. Knowles RC, Moore TD: Quality control of agar diffusion susceptibility tests. *Am J Clin Pathol* 1979, 72:365.
31. Knowles RC, Moore TD: Quality control of agar diffusion susceptibility tests: Data from the Quality Assurance Service Microbiology Program of the College of American Pathologists. *Am J Clin Pathol* 1980, 74:581.
32. Knowles RC, Gilmore B: Quality control of agar diffusion susceptibility tests: Data from the Quality Assurance Service Microbiology Program of the College of American Pathologists. *Am J Clin Pathol* 1981, 76:590.
33. Knowles RC, Gilmore B: Quality control of agar diffusion susceptibility tests: Data from the Quality Assurance Service Microbiology Program of the College of American Pathologists. *Am J Clin Pathol* 1983, 80:603.
34. Buttner J, Borth R, Boutwell JH, et al: Quality control in clinical chemistry: Part 5. External quality control. International Federation of Clinical Chemistry, Committee on Standards. *Clin Chem Acta* 1978, 83:191F-202F.
35. Forney JE, Blumberg JM, Brooke MM, et al: Laboratory evaluation and certification, in Inhorn, SL (ed): *Quality Assurance Practices for Health Laboratories.* Washington, DC, American Public Health Association, 1978, pp 127–171.
36. Whitehead TP, Woodford FP: External quality assessment of clinical laboratories in the United Kingdom. *J Clin Pathol* 1981, 32:947–957.
37. World Health Organization: External quality assessment of health laboratories. *Med Lab Sci* 1983, 40:211–218.
38. World Association of Societies of Pathology, Ciba Foundation, London, England (U.K.): Analytical goals in clinical chemistry: Their relationship to medical care. Proceedings of the subcommittee on analytical goals in clinical chemistry. *Am J Clin Pathol* 1979, 71:624–630.
39. Tietz NW: A model for a comprehensive measurement system in clinical chemistry. *Clin Chem* 1979, 25:833–839.
40. Gilbert RK: Standards for an interlaboratory (proficiency) testing program. *Am J Clin Pathol* 1976, 66:276–278.
41. Skendzel LP, Hanson DJ, Givin JW: The 1949 College of American Pathologists Survey revisited. *Am J Clin Pathol* 1970, 54:493–495.
42. Gilbert RK: Analysis of results of the 1969 Comprehensive Chemistry Survey of the College of American Pathologists. *Am J Clin Pathol* 1970, 54:463–482.
43. Gilbert RK: Progress and analytic goals in clinical chemistry. *Am J Clin Pathol* 1975, 63:960–973.
44. Gilbert RK, Platt R: The measurement of calcium and potassium in clinical laboratories in the United States, 1971–1978. *Am J Clin Pathol* 1980, 74:508–520.
45. Lott JA, O'Donnell NJ, Grannis GF: Interlaboratory survey of enzyme analysis: III. Does College of American Pathologists survey serum mimic clinical specimens? *Am J Clin Pathol* 1981, 76:554–556.
46. Lott JA, Tholen DW, Massion CG: Survey of serum enzyme analyses: Human tissues as a source of enzymes. *Arch Pathol Lab Med* 1984, 108:949–953.
47. Lott JA, Wenger WC, Massion CG, et al: Interlaboratory survey of enzyme analyses: IV. Human versus porcine tissue as source of creatine kinase for survey serum. *Am J Clin Pathol* 1982, 78:626–633.

48 Hansell JR, Haven GT: Changes in level of precision of common ligand assays during a seven-year interval. *Am J Clin Pathol* 1979, 72:320–327.
49 Itano M: CAP blood gas survey—1981 and 1982. *Am J Clin Pathol* 1983, 80:554–562.
50 Christensen RL, Triplett DA: Factor assay (VIII and IX) results in the College of American Pathologists Survey Program (1980–1983). *Am J Clin Pathol* 1983, 80:633–642.
51 Jones RN, Edson DC, and the CAP Microbiology Resource Committee: Performance of disk agar diffusion and dilution antimicrobial susceptibility tests, 1979–1981. *Am J Clin Pathol* 1982, 78:651–658.
52 Gavan TL, King JW: An evaluation of the microbiology portions of the 1969 Basic, Comprehensive, and Special College of American Pathologists Proficiency Testing Surveys. *Am J Clin Pathol* 1970, 54:514–520.
53 Marymont JH III, Marymont JH Jr, Gavan TL: Performance of enterobacteriaceae identification systems: An analysis of College of American Pathologists survey data. *Am J Clin Pathol* 1978, 70:539–547.
54 Fuchs PC, Dolan CT: Summary and analysis of the mycology proficiency testing survey results of the College of American Pathologists: 1976–1979. *Am J Clin Pathol* 1981, 76:528–543.
55 Dreskin RB, Sommers HM, Edson D: A review of the CAP proficiency surveys for mycobacteriology, 1975–1981. *Am J Clin Pathol* 1982, 78:673–677.
56 Elevitch FR, Noce PS (eds): *Data reCap 1970–1980: A Compilation of Data from the College of American Pathologists Clinical Laboratory Improvement Programs*. Skokie, IL, College of American Pathologists, 1981.
57 Gilbert RK: The size and source of analytic error in clinical chemistry. *Am J Clin Pathol* 1974, 61:904–911.
58 Gilbert RK: *Survey Data 75—Chemistry*. Skokie, IL, College of American Pathologists, Skokie, IL, 1976.
59 Grannis CF, Lott JA: An interlaboratory comparison of analyses of clinical specimens. *Am J Clin Pathol* 1978, 70:567.
60 Ross JW: Evaluation of precision, in Werner M (ed): *CRC Handbook of Clinical Chemistry*, vol 1, Boca Raton, FL, CRC Press, 1982, pp 391–421.
61 Turcotte G, Bourget C, Talbot J, et al: Analytic clinical chemistry precision and medical needs: The Canadian Interlab Program (CIP). *Am J Clin Pathol* 1980, 74:336–339.
62 Gilbert RK, Rosenbaum JM: Accuracy in interlaboratory quality control programs. *Am J Clin Pathol* 1979, 72:260–264.
63 Gilbert RK: Accuracy of clinical laboratories measured by comparison with definitive methods. *Am J Clin Pathol* 1978, 70:450–467.
64 Koepke JA: The 1969 survey of prothrombin time. *Am J Clin Pathol* 1970, 54:502–507.
65 Triplett FA, Harms CS, Koepke JA: The effect of heparin on the activated partial thromboplastin time. *Am J Clin Pathol* 1978, 70:556–559.
66 Zucker S, Brosioius E, Cooper GR: One-stage prothrombin time survey. *Am J Clin Pathol* 1970, 53:340–347.
67 Van Den Besselaar AMHP, Evatt BL, Brogan DR, et al: Proficiency testing and standardization, of prothrombin time: Effect of thromboplastin, intrumentation, and plasma. *Am J Clin Pathol* 1984, 82:688–699.
68 Howanitz, JH, Okner J, Winkelman JW: Director potentiometric analysis of whole blood potassium using the NOVA 1. *J Clin Lab Automat* 1984, 4:125–128.
69 MacDonald NF, Williams PZ, Burton JI, et al: Sodium and potassium measurements: Director potentiometry and flame photometry. *Am J Clin Pathol* 1981, 76:575–577.
70 Fraser CG, Peake MJ: Problems associated with clinical chemistry quality control mate-

rials. *CRC Crit Rev Clin Lab Sci* 1980, 12:59–86.
71. Bretaudiere J, Rej R, Drake P, et al: M. Suitability of control materials for determination of alpha-amylase activity. *Clin Chem* 1981, 27:806–815.
72. Ross JW: Control materials and calibration standards, in *CRC Handbook of Clinical Chemistry,* vol 1 Werner M (ed.) Boca Raton, FL, CRC Press, 1982, pp 359–369.
73. Van Holden WCH, Visser RWJ, Van Den Bergh FAJ-TM, et al: Comparison of intermethod analytical variability of patient sera and commercial quality control sera. *Clin Chem Acta* 1979, 93:335–347.
74. Bretaudiere JT, Dumont G, Rej R, et al: Suitability of control materials: General principles and methods of investigation. *Clin Chem* 1985, 27:798–805.
75. Rej R, Jenny RW, Bretaudiere, JT: Quality control in clinical chemistry: Characterization of reference materials. *Talanta* 1984, 31:851–862.
76. Adams TH, Menson RC, Caputo MJ, et al: Comparison of inter-vial variations of Omega with four commercial control sera: Implications for improved quality control. Technical discussion 43, February 1979. Deerfield, IL, Hyhland Diagnostics, Division of Travenol Laboratories Inc, 1979.
77. Rej R, Fasee CG Jr, Vanderlinde RE: Interlaboratory proficiency, intermethod comparison, and calibrator suitability in assay of serum aspartate aminotransferase activity. *Clin Chem* 1975, 21:1141–1158.
78. Rej F, Schroder J: Emulsions of perfluorinated compounds for use in quality control of blood gas analyses. *Clin Chem* 1982, 28:1293–1296.
79. Savage RA, Hoffman GC: Clinical significance of osmotic matrix errors in automated hemotology: The frequency of hyperglycemic osmotic matrix errors producing spurious macrocytosis. *Am J Clin Pathol* 1983, 80:861–865.
80. Chu SY, Macleod J: Differences in reaction characteristics between human and bovine-based control materials for iron determination. *Clin Biochem* 1983, 16:287–290.
81. Ratcliffe WA, Logue FC, Ratcliffe, JG: Scottish immunoassay support service quality control scheme for thyrosine, tricodothyronine and digoxin assays: Analysis of first 18 months' experience. *Ann Clin Biochem* 1978, 15:203–207.
82. Wooten IDP: International biochemical trial 1954. *Clin Chem* 1956, 2:296–301.
83. Trainer TD: Creatinine-clearing of the chemistry: Summing up, Surveys Committee of the College of American Pathologists. 1982, 12:6–8.
84. Bowers LD: Kinetic serum creatinine assays: I. The role of various factors in determining specificity. *Clin Chem* 1980, 26:551–554.
85. Bowers LD, Wong ET: Kinetic serum creatinine assays: II. A critical evaluation and review. *Clin Chem* 1980, 555–561.
86. Chinn EK, Batsakis JG, Pelon H, et al: K. Serum creatinine: A CAP survey. *Am J Clin Pathol* 1978, 70:503–507.
87. Hearne CR, Fraser CG: Enzymatic vs Jaffee (continuous flow) assay of creatinine of serum. *Clin Chem* 1979, 25:1665–1666.
88. Pope WT, Caragher TE, Grannis GF: An evaluation of ethylene glycol-based liquid specimens for use in quality control. *Clin Chem* 1979, 25:413–418.
89. George H, Garrett PE, Kurtz SR: Two liquid and lyophilized control materials compared. *Clin Chem* 1983, 29:1999–2000.
90. Williams GZ, Harris EK, Widdowson CM: Comparison of estimates of long-term analytical variation derived from subject samples and control serum. *Clin Chem* 1977, 23:100–104.
91. Copeland BE, Blake WJ, Muelling RJ, et al: A report of the Standards Committee of the College of American Pathologists National Comprehensive Laboratory Survey 1965:

Chemistry Section. *Am J Clin Pathol* 1967, 48:104–126.
92 Campbell DG, Owen JA: Clinical laboratory error in perspective. *Clin Biochem* 1967, 1:3–11.
93 Skendzel LP: Guidelines for the design of laboratory surveys. *Am J Clin Pathol* 1970, 54:437–446.
94 Copeland BE, Skendzel LP, Barnett RN: Interlaboratory comparison of university hospital referee laboratories and community hospital laboratories, using results of the 1968 College of American Pathologists clinical chemistry survey. *Am J Clin Pathol* 1972, 58:281–296.
95 Kurtz SR, Copeland BE, Straumfjord JV: Guidelines for clinical chemistry quality control based on the long-term experience of sixty-one university and tertiary care referral hospitals: A reappraisal. *Am J Clin Pathol* 1977, 68:463–473.
96 Fraser CG: Desirable performance standards for clinical chemistry tests. *Adv Clin Chem* 1983, 23:299–339.
97 Saracci R: Factors affecting accuracy and precision in clinical chemistry: A survey of 404 Italian laboratories. *Am J Clin Pathol* 1969, 52:161–166.
98 Walker RH, Cooper S, Hoeltge GA, et al: Comprehensive blood bank survey. *Arch Pathol Lab Med* 1985, 109:215–220.
99 Williams CW, Bowman HE: Recent developments in the scoring for the CAP syphilis serology survey. *Pathologist* 1978, 32:177–180.
100 Skendzel LP, Copeland BE: Hemoglobin measurements in hospital laboratories: A report of 1962, 1963, and 1964 surveys conducted by Standards Committee, College of American Pathologists. *Am J Clin Pathol* 1965, 35:245–251.
101 Grannis GF: Interlaboratory survey of enzyme analysis: I. Preliminary studies. *Am J Clin Pathol* 1976, 66:206–222.
102 Ehrmeyer SS, Laessig RH: Alternative statistical approach to evaluating interlaboratory performance. *Clin Chem* 1985, 31:106–108.
103 Belk WP, Sunderman FW: Survey of the accuracy of clinical analysis in clinical laboratories. *Am J Clin Pathol* 1947, 17:853–861.
104 Standards Committee, College of American Pathologists: Guidelines for evaluating laboratory performance in survey and proficiency testing programs. *Am J Clin Pathol* 1970, 49:457–458.
105 Acland JD, Lipton S: Precision in a clinical chemistry laboratory. *J Clin Pathol* 1967, 20:780–785.
106 Barnett RN: Letter to editor. *Am J Clin Pathol* 1966, 45:329–330.
107 Barnett RN: Medical significance of laboratory tests. *Am J Clin Pathol* 1968, 50:671–676.
108 Tonks DB: A study of the accuracy and precision of clinical chemistry determinations in 170 Canadian laboratories. *Clin Chem* 1963, 9:217–233.
109 Inaccuracy in the laboratory, editorial. *Lancet* 1953, 1:476–477.
110 Acland JD, Gould AH: Normal variation in the count of circulating eosinophils in man. *J Physiol* (Lond) 1956, 133:456–466.
111 Fawcett JK, Wynn V: Variation of plasma electrolytes and total protein levels in the individual. *Br Med J* 1956, 2:582–585.
112 Zieve L: On interpreting variations in laboratory tests. *Postgrad Med* 1964, 35A:46–56.
113 Campbell DG, Owen JA: The physician's view of laboratory performance. *Aust Ann Med* 1969, 18:4–6.
114 Acland JD, Lipton S: Present day practice: Laboratory precision and diagnostic errors. *J Clin Pathol* 1971, 24:369–370.
115 Gilbert RK: Analytic error in clinical chemistry laboratories from the perspective of the

survey program of the College of American Pathologists in analytical goals in clinical chemistry, in Elevitch F (ed): *CAP Conference Aspen 1976*. Skokie, IL, College of American Pathologists, 1977, pp 63–82.

116 Barnett RN: Conference on the medical usefulness of microbiology: Report by the subcommittee on medical usefulness of the College of American Pathologists. *Am J Clin Pathol* 1970, 54:521–530.

117 Haven CT, Tholen DW, Oxley DK: Source of analytic variation in ligand assay: A study based on data from the 1976 and 1981 basic ligand assay surveys of the College of American Pathologists. *Am J Clin Pathol* 1983, 80:615–621.

118 Reynoso G, Mackenzie JR: Are ligand assay methods specific for cobalamin? *Am J Clin Pathol* 1982, 78:621–625.

119 Fuchs PC, Dolan CT: Performance of yeast identification systems: An analysis of the College of American Pathologists Special Mycology Survey. *Am J Clin Pathol* 1982, 78:664–667.

120 Jones RN, Edson DC, and the CAP Microbiology Resource Committee: Special topics in antimicrobial susceptibility testing: Test accuracy against methicillin-resistant *Staphylococcus aureus*, pneumococci, and the sensitivity of beta-lactamase methods. *Am J Clin Pathol* 1983, 80:609–614.

121 Oxley DK: Penicillin-resistant pneumococci. *Arch Pathol Lab Med* 1984, 108:106–107.

122 Jones RN, Edson DC, Marymont JV: Evaluations of antimicrobial susceptibility test proficiency by the College of American Pathologists survey program: A clarification of quality control recommendations. *Am J Clin Pathol* 1982, 78:168–172.

123 Jones RN, Edson DC, Gilmore BF, and the CAP Microbiology Resource Committee: Contemporary quality control practices for antimicrobial susceptibility tests: A report from the microbiology portion of the College of American Pathologists (CAP) surveys program. *Am J Clin Pathol* 1983, 80:622–625.

124 Haven GT, Lawson NS, Ross JW: Quality control in the 1980's. *Clin Lab Annu* 1982, 1:209–225.

125 Grannis GF, Caragher TE: Quality control programs in clinical chemistry. *CRC Crit Rev Clin Lab Sci* 1977, 7:327–364.

126 Grannis GF: Use of Survey-validated reference materials (Survey serum) to establish target values of quality control pools. *Am J Clin Pathol* 1978, 70:580–583.

127 Elevitch F (ed): *Analytical Goals in Clinical Chemistry: CAP Aspen Conference 1976*. Skokie, IL, College of American Pathologists, 1976.

128 Batsakis JG: Analytical goals and the College of American Pathologists. *Am J Clin Pathol* 1982, 78:678–680.

129 Wilcox KR Jr, Baynes TE Jr, Crable JV, et al: Laboratory management, in Inhorn SL (ed): *Quality Assurance Practices for Health Care Laboratories*. Washington, DC, American Public Health Association, 1978, pp 3–126.

130 Inhorn SL: What is expected from laboratory services in terms of quality: The public health point of view, in Rand RN, Eilers, RJ, Lawson NS, Broughton A (eds): *Quality Assurance in Health Care: A Critical Appraisal of Clinical Chemistry*. Washington, DC, American Association for Clinical Chemistry, 1980, pp 51–65.

131 Enthoven AC: Consumer-choice health plan. *N Engl J Med* 1978, 298(part 1):650–658; 298(part 2):709–720.

132 Groth T: Methods and approaches to determine "optimal" quality for clinical chemical data. *Scand J Clin Lab Invest* 1980, 40(suppl 155):47–63.

133 Harris EK: Statistical principles underlying analytic goal-setting in clinical chemistry. *Am J Clin Pathol* 1979, 72:374.

134 Horder M, Petersen PH, Groth T, et al: Influence of analytical quality on the diagnostic power of a single S-CK B test in patients with suspected acute myocardial infarction. *Scand J Clin Lab Invest* 1980, 40(suppl 155):95–100.
135 Jacobson G, Groth T, DeVerdier CH: Pancreatic iso-amylase in serum as a diagnostic test in different clinical situations: A simulation study. *Scand J Clin Lab Invest* 1980, 40(suppl 155):77–84.
136 Peterson PH, Rosloff F, Rasmussen J, et al: Studies on the required analytical quality of TSH measurements in screening for congenital hypothyroidism. *Scand J Clin Lab Invest* 1980. 40(suppl 155):85–93.
137 Robertson EA, Zweig MH: Use of received operating characteristic curves to evaluate the clinical performance of analytical systems. *Clin Chem* 1981, 27:1569–1574.
138 Bartlett RC: Medical microbiology: How far to go—How fast to go in 1982, in Lorian V (ed): *Significance of Medical Microbiology in the Care of Patients,* ed 2. Baltimore, Williams & Wilkins, 1982, pp 12–44.
139 Ross JW: Precision performance standards: Medical care and peer review criteria. *Pathologist* 1981, 35:193–198.
140 De Verdier CH, Groth T, Westgard JO: What is the quality of quality control procedures? *Scand J Clin Lab Invest* 1981, 41:1–14.
141 Westgard JO: Precision and accuracy: Concepts and assessment by method evaluation testing. *CRC Crit Rev Clin Lab Sci* 1981, 13:283–330.
142 Buttner J, Borth R, Boutwell JH, et al. International Federation of Clinical Chemistry, Committee on Standards: Quality control in clinical chemistry: Part 2. Assessment of analytical methods for routine use. *Clin Chim Acta* 1979, 98:145F–162F.
143 Westgard JO, Carey RN, Wold S: Criteria for judging precision and accuracy in method development and evaluation. *Clin Chem* 1974, 20:825–833.
144 Brauer GA, Rand RN: Techniques for defining and measuring quality in clinical chemistry, in Rand RN, Eilers RJ, Lawson NS, et al (eds): *Quality Assurance in Health Care: A Critical Appraisal of Clinical Chemistry.* Washington, DC, American Association for Clinical Chemistry, 1980, pp 207–223.
145 Westgard JO, Falk H, Groth T: Influence of a between-run component of variation, choice of control limits, and shape of error distribution on the performance characteristics for internal quality control. *Clin Chem* 1980, 26:394–400.
146 Fraser CG: Goals for clinical biochemistry analytical imprecision: A graphic approach. *Pathology* 1980, 12:209–218.
147 Fraser CG: Analytical goals in clinical biochemistry. *Prog Clin Pathol* 1981, 8:101–122.
148 Cresswell M: How useful is the clinical chemistry laboratory? *Lab-Lore* (Wellcome Reagents, Kent, UK) 1975, 6:353–356.
149 Duncan BM, Geary TD: A method for analyzing results of medical laboratory proficiency surveys. *J Roy Coll Pathol Aust* 1973, 5:91–98.
150 Barrett AE, Cameron SJ, Fraser CG, et al: A clinical view of analytical goals in clinical biochemistry. *J Clin Pathol* 1979, 32:893–896.
151 Elion-Gerritzin WE: Analytic precision in clinical chemistry and medical decisions. *Am J Clin Pathol* 1980, 73:183–195.
152 Skendzel LP, Barnett RN, Platt R: Medically useful criteria for analytic performance of laboratory tests. *Am J Clin Pathol* 1985, 83:200–205.
153 Glick JH: Expression of random analytical error as a percentage of the range of clinical interest. *Clin Chem* 1976, 22:475–483.
154 Haven GT, Hansel JR, Haven MC: Reproducibility of mean values of duplicate specimens in the basic ligand assay survey. *Am J Clin Pathol* 1978, 70:532–538.

155 Groth T, Falk H, Westgard JO: An interactive computer simulation program for the design of statistical control procedures in clinical chemistry. *Computer Programs in Biomedicine* 1981, 13:73–86.
156 Westgard JL, Groth T: Design of statistical control procedures utilizing quality specifications and power functions for control rules. In Quality control in clinical endocrinology: in Wilson DW, Gaskel SH, Kemp KW (eds): *Proceedings of the Eighth Tenovus Workshop*. Cardiff, Wales, Alpha Omega Publishing, 1981, pp 155–164.
157 Westgard JO, Groth T: A predictive value model for quality control: Effects of the prevalence of errors on the performance of control procedures. *Am J Clin Pathol* 1983, 80:49–56.
158 Westgard JO, Groth T, Aronsson T, et al: Performance characteristics of rules for internal quality control: Probabilities for false rejection and error detection. *Clin Chem* 1977, 23:1857–1867.
159 NCCLS Publication: Tentative guidelines for manufacturers for establishing performance claims for clinical chemical methods: Introduction and performance check experiment, vol 2, number 19, 1982.
160 NCCLS Publication: Tentative guidelines for manufacturers for establishing performance claims for clinical chemical methods: Comparison of methods experiment, vol. 2, number 21, 1982.
161 Westgard JO, Groth T: Design and evaluation of statistical control procedures: Application of a computer "quality control simulator" program. *Clin Chem* 1981, 27:1536–1545.
162 Kadar N, DeCherney AH, Romero R: Receiver operating characteristic (ROC) curve analysis of the relative efficiency of single and serial chorionic gonadotropin determinations in the early diagnosis of ectopic pregnancy. *Fertil Steril* 1982, 37:542–547.
163 Oxley DK: Hormone receptors in breast cancer: Analytic accuracy of contemporary assays. *Arch Pathol Lab Med* 1984, 108:20–23.
164 Oxley DK, Haven GT, Wittliff JR, et al: Precision in estrogen and progesterone receptor assays. *Am J Clin Pathol* 1982, 78:587–596.
165 Allegra JC, Barlock A, Huff KK, et al: Changes in multiple or sequential estrogen receptor determinations in breast cancer. *Cancer* 1980, 45:792–794.
166 Sears ME, Olson KB: Extramural review of clinical response of breast cancer to cytotoxic chemotherapy. *Cancer* 1980, 46:2928.
167 Clark TW, Schor SS, Elson KO, et al: The periodic health examination: Evaluation of routine tests and procedures. *Arch Int Med* 1961, 54:1209–1222.
168 Elsom KO, Ipsen J, Clark TW, et al: Physicians use of objective data in clinical diagnosis. *JAMA* 1967, 201:519–526.
169 Schneiderman LJ, DeSalvo L, Baylor S, et al: The "abnormal" screening laboratory result: Its effect on physician and patient. *Arch Int Med* 1972, 129:88–90.
170 Sisson JC, Schoomaker EB, Ross JC: Clinical decision analysis: The hazard of using additional data. *JAMA* 1976, 236:1259–1263.
171 Werner S, Nathanson M: Physical examination: Frequently observed errors. *JAMA* 1976, 236:852–855.
172 Statland BE, Winkel P: Physiologic variation of the concentration values of selected analytes as determined on healthy young adults, in Elevitch FR (ed): *Analytical Goals in Clinical Chemistry: CAP Conference, Aspen, 1976*. Skokie, IL, College of American Pathologists, 1977, pp 94–101.
173 Wilson DW, Nix ABJ, Rowlands RJ, et al: Analytical performance characteristics and chronobiological considerations in quality control, in Wilson DW, Gaskel J, Kemp KW

(eds): *Quality Control in Clinical Endocrinology.* Proceedings of the Eighth Tenovus Workshop. Cardiff, Wales, UK, Alpha Omega Publishing, 1981, pp 5–18.
174 Westgard JO, Carey RN, Wold S: Comments on the judgment of the acceptability of new clinical methods, response to letter. *Clin Chem* 1977, 23:776–777.
175 Ross JT, Tholen DW: Optimizing clinical laboratory analytical accuracy: A historical perspective, system analysis, and model of clinical utility in Howanitz PJ (ed): *Quality Assurance for the Physician's Office, Bedside, and Home Testing.* CAP Conference, Atlanta 1986, Skokie, IL, College of American Pathologists, 1986.
176 Hilden J: The concept of medical usefulness in clinical chemistry and the difficulty of applying it to questions of research policy. *Scand J Clin Lab Invest* 1980, 40(suppl 155):31–46.
177 Harris JM: The hazards of bedside Bayes. *JAMA* 1981, 246:2602–2605.
178 Robertson EA: Setting a diagnostic study's cutoff value by using its receiver operating characteristic curve, response to letter. *Clin Chem* 1983, 29:571–572.
179 Robertson EA, Zweig MH, Van Steirteghem AC: Evaluating the clinical efficacy of laboratory tests. *Am J Clin Pathol* 1981, 79:78–86.
180 Sappenfield RW, Beeler MF, Catrou PG, et al: Nine-cell diagnostic decision matrix: A model of the diagnostic process; a framework for evaluating diagnostic protocols. *Am J Clin Pathol* 1981, 75:769–762.
181 Hanley JA, McNeil BJ: The meaning and use of the area under a receiver operating characteristic (ROC) curve. *Radiology* 1982, 143:29–36.
182 Herman GA, Herrera N, Sugiura HT: Comparison of interlaboratory survey data in terms of receiver operating characteristic (ROC) indices. *J Nucl Med* 1982, 23:525–531.
183 Sappenfield RW, Beeler MF, Editorial Series: Disease, medical research and the American Journal of Clinical Pathology. IX. Experimental clinical operational research. *Am J Clin Pathol* 1984, 82:256–258.
184 Sheeps SB, Schechter MT: The assessment of diagnostic tests. A survey of current medical research. *JAMA* 1984, 252:2418.
185 Young DM: What do doctors expect from laboratory services in terms of quality? In Rand R, Eilers RJ, Lawson NS, Broughton A (eds): *Quality Assurance in Health Care: A Critical Appraisal of Clinical Chemistry,* Washington, DC, American Association for Clinical Chemistry, 1980, pp 51–65.

CHAPTER 7

COMPONENTS OF BIOLOGIC AND ANALYTIC VARIATION

Per Winkel, M.D., Doc. Med. Sci.
Adam Uldall, Ph.D.

Because clinical problems are often so involved and/or so loosely defined, in all likelihood it is impossible to define the demands that should be made on the performance of the clinical laboratory on a rational, scientific basis. Therefore it is difficult to be explicit about the quality one would like to assure. Even if the goals must be somewhat arbitrary, they are necessary because the alternative is anarchy. By analyzing the present quality of laboratory work and relating this performance to sources of bias, noise, and errors that for one reason or another are beyond the power of the laboratory to control, one may get a perspective of the relative importance of the various goals that one would like to define. The components of variation that are important to quantitate are (1) biologic components that appear unrelated to clinical problems, (2) random analytic variation, (3) variation caused by mistakes or malfunctioning, and (4) interlaboratory variation, which reflects a variation in quality as well as lack of standardization. As far as the definition of goals in quality assurance is concerned, the latter component of variation is of major interest only when data from many laboratories have to be pooled for some purpose, such as epidemiologic studies, the establishment of common reference values, or the monitoring of patients who are in contact with more than one laboratory. In this chapter, therefore, we shall review various components of analytic and biologic variation, discussing methods used to estimate and separate these components. In this context we shall focus on the problems involved in breaking the correlation between the analytic and biologic variation and between the analytic errors of different quantities.

BIOLOGIC AND RANDOM ANALYTIC VARIATION

Components of Analytic Variation

The analytic procedure begins when a biologic specimen is obtained and is completed when the results of the analysis of the material are written. As indicated in Fig. 7-1, it is convenient to divide the analytical variation into two major components, the preinstrumental and the instrumental component.[1] The preinstrumental analytic variation is the variation stemming from sources operating from the moment the collection of the biologic material (the specimen) begins and until the assay begins. From this time, the biologic material is referred to as a sample. The instrumental analytic variation is the variation resulting from the uncertainty of the assay itself. Examples of sample problems include variation in fluid dispensing of sample and reagents and variations in the electrooptical mechanisms.

The components of random analytic variation may be easily estimated experimentally. Figure 7-2 shows the results taken from a study of the components of the analytic variation of various assays of specific proteins.[2] These results, which reflect local analytic problems, illustrate the usefulness of examining the overall picture to locate the more important problems. For the majority of the quantities examined, the preinstrumental component predominates. Therefore, the first step should be to scrutinize the preinstrumental phase. A more detailed analysis of the various steps of a particular analytic procedure is of course possible, but rather elaborate experimental designs may be needed. For an instructive example the reader is referred to an analysis of the various steps of urine microscopy that was published some years ago.[3]

Components of Biologic Variation

Although it is generally recognized that analytic variability must be taken into account in the interpretation of laboratory data, it is often overlooked that there is also biologic variation.[4] This component of the test result variability is poorly understood. Therefore, as a rule, rather primitive models have been used to analyze this type of variation. Usually the so-called homeostatic model is used,[5,6] in which each subject is characterized by a set point around which the results fluctuate more or less at random. The variability among subjects (the interindividual variation) is then expressed as the variability among the individual set points.

Interindividual Variation In theory at least, the interindividual variability is difficult to estimate, because in the vast majority of cross-sectional surveys, there is no justification for making the assumption that the individuals selected represent a random sample from the category of individuals one wants to examine.[7] Judging from the studies available, it appears that for many quantities this component is a major component of the total biologic variation.[8] Furthermore, identifying the causes of this variability is difficult. Thus, attempts to reduce the interindividual variability by controlling easily recognized demographic factors such as sex, age, and race often lead to a surprisingly small reduction of the variability.[9,10] From a practical standpoint, it is

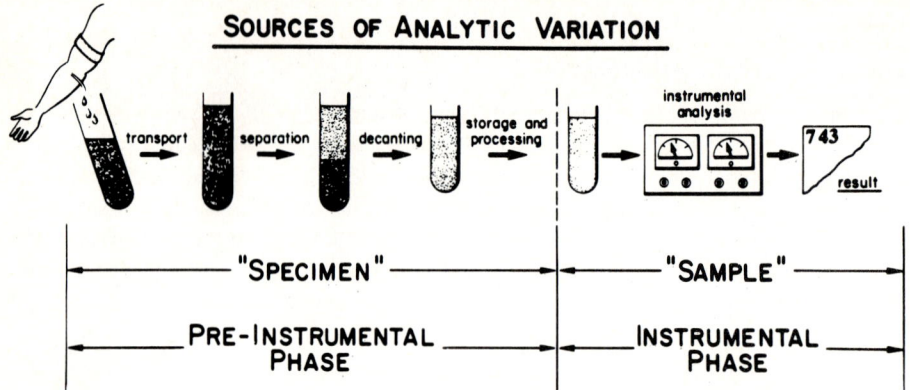

FIGURE 7-1
Partitioning of the analytic variation into preinstrumental and instrumental phases. [*Source:* Winkel P, Statland BE, Bokelund H, et al: Correlation of selected serum constituents: Interindividual variation and analytic error. *Clin Chem* 1975, 21:1952, by permission of the Nordic Clinical Chemistry Project (NORDKEM).]

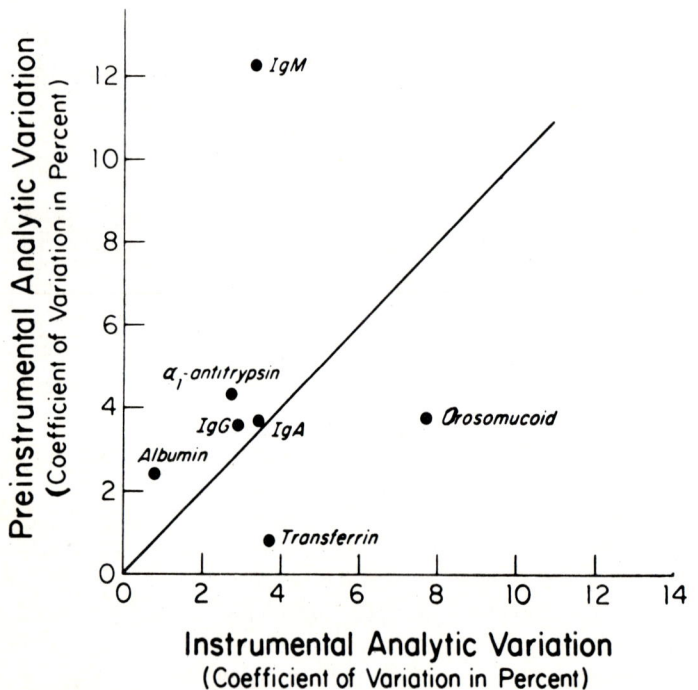

FIGURE 7-2
Comparison of preinstrumental analytic variation with instrumental analytic variation for each of seven serum proteins. (*Source:* Winkel P, Statland BE, Nielsen MK: Analytic variation and biologic within-day variation of specific serum protein concentration in a group of healthy young men. *Scand J Clin Lab Invest* 1976, 36:531, by permission of the *Scandinavian Journal of Clinical and Laboratory Investigation.*)

TABLE 7-1
RATIO VALUES (INTRAINDIVIDUAL OVER INTERINDIVIDUAL VARIATION) FOR SELECTED ANALYTES IN THE BLOOD OF HEALTHY SUBJECTS

Analyte	Ratio value	Analyte	Ratio value
Group I		Group III	
IgM	0.06	Lactate dehydrogenase	0.44
IgA	0.09	Alanine aminotransferase	0.45
Haptoglobin	0.12	Creatinine	0.47
Alkaline phosphatase	0.14	Total WBC	0.48
IgG	0.15	Cortisol	0.50
γ-Glutamyl transferase	0.16	Creatine kinase	0.56
Complement C3	0.17	Neutrophils	0.62
Complement C4	0.19	Thyroxine	0.63
α_1-Antitrypsin	0.19	Urea	0.73
α_2-Macroglobulin	0.19	Aspartate aminotransferase	0.90
		Uric acid	1.00
Group II			
Basophils	0.24	Group IV	
Cholesterol	0.25	Total protein	1.04
Transferrin	0.26	Chloride	1.05
Orosomucoid	0.26	Iron	1.15
Eosinophils	0.28	Potassium	1.19
Hemoglobin	0.29	Sodium	1.75
Hematocrit	0.29	Calcium	2.83
Platelets	0.30	Albumin	5.60
Lymphocytes	0.31		
Monocytes	0.34		
Triglycerides	0.36		

Source: Winkel P, Statland BE: Using the subject as his own reference in assessing day-to-day changes of laboratory test results, in Hercules DM, Hieftje GM, Snyder LR, et al (eds): *Contemporary Topics in Analytical and Clinical Chemistry,* vol 1. New York, Plenum Press, 1977, pp 287–317. Reprinted by permission of Plenum Press.

useful to characterize the interindividual variation in relation to the corresponding within-subject biologic variability. For this purpose, Harris introduced the so-called ratio value, which is defined as the intraindividual variation over the interindividual variation when both variations are in terms of standard deviations.[11] Table 7-1 shows the ratio values for a number of analytes found in serum or whole blood of healthy subjects. The smaller this ratio, the more important it becomes to compare a result to previous results from the individual when he or she was in a state of defined health rather than using the reference interval. This is because the reference interval will be relatively wide owing to interindividual variation.

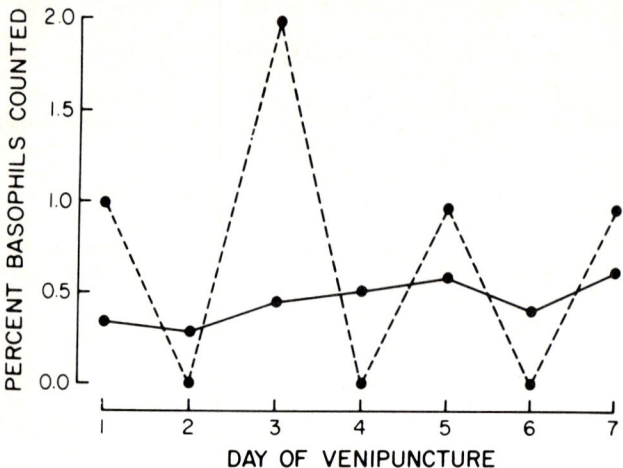

FIGURE 7-3
Percent eosinophils counted in blood specimens collected from same subject on each of seven days. Hemalog-D results versus manual eye count technique. (By permission of AutoAnalyzer Innovationen Band 1-section Medizin, Technicon GmbH.)

Intraindividual Variation   More than 70 years ago, Rietz pointed out that under apparently identical conditions, the quantitative measurement of physiological functions shows considerable variability within the same subject.[11] This variability may be assessed from results determined on multiple specimens obtained over time from the same subject. Using the homeostatic model, one could characterize the variation by the standard deviation of the results. The intraindividual variation we shall define as the biologic component of the total variation observed over time. This definition is convenient when one wants to identify relevant goals of quality assurance. In Fig. 7-3, the percentage of eosinophil leukocytes measured in peripheral blood from the same subject has been depicted as a function of time of venipuncture using manual differential count of 100 cells per specimen (dotted line) and an automated procedure based on the classification of 10,000 leukocytes per specimen. When the latter technique was used, the value was practically constant over time. This rather striking difference could have been predicted from a careful analysis of the nature of the analytic variation.[12] The impact of the sample size (i.e., number of leukocytes classified per specimen) on the analytic variation may be calculated and compared to the observed variation of the manual differential count of 100 cells. Such an analysis reveals that the number of leukocytes classified per specimen must be a major factor in determining the magnitude of the total variation. Once this is realized, it becomes obvious that the solution to the problem is to increase dramatically the number of leukocytes classified per specimen—that is, to automate the analytic procedure. Usually, however, it is necessary to estimate the analytic variation experimentally and then subtract it from the total variation observed to estimate the biologic component. Not until this has been done is it possible to assess whether it may be at all meaningful to try to improve the quality of the analytic procedure.

The clinician's ability to monitor patients on the basis of laboratory measurements will be improved if the biologic variation not related to the patient's clinical problems is minimized. For this reason, it is important to identify such factors. Sources of biologic variation include endogenous factors influencing the internal hormonal control, stress originating from outside environment, and activities undertaken by the subject prior to specimen collection. The magnitude of the observed intraindividual variation, therefore, will depend not only on the subject selected but also on control of preparation of the subject prior to specimen collection.[13,14] Times at which specimens are collected as well as the total period over which the specimens are obtained also may play an important role. Time-dependent, systematic variation, which presumably is governed by endogenous factors, is most pronounced for various hormones. Plasma cortisol, for example, displays a predictable circadian variation. Female gonadotropins show characteristic monthly variations.

It is convenient to divide the biologic variation into day-to-day variation and within-day variation. The latter may be divided into a systematic, predictable component and a random component. The systematic component may be further subdivided into the variation occurring because the same pattern is being repeated each day by all the subjects studied (group-specific diurnal variation) and the variation occurring because each subject repeats his or her unique daily pattern (subject-specific diurnal variation).

The random component comprises fluctuations relative to the systematic component. In addition to the within-day random biologic fluctuations, rather large random individual fluctuations of the daily mean level (day-to-day random variation) may be seen. If specimens are always collected at the same time of day, any systematic within-day variation that may occur could be eliminated. However, in many cases such a precaution may not be worth the effort. For the majority of the more commonly ordered serum constituents (hormones excluded), the systematic diurnal components of variation as measured in healthy subjects are unimportant from a quantitative point of view as compared with the random day-to-day and within-day fluctuations.[15] The case of serum potassium is the notable exception.[16] More than 70 percent of the total biologic variation for potassium is related to the subject's personal diurnal variation, which is consistent from day to day. Because the diurnal pattern is unique for each subject, it is furthermore unpredictable, unless of course the subject's diurnal pattern has been established previously. For certain leukocyte types, the systematic diurnal variation also comprises a considerable part of the total intraindividual variation.[17]

Most studies of intraindividual variation have been based on measurements obtained from healthy subjects. The relevance of such studies can be questioned, because it is implicitly assumed that intraindividual variation of patients is not strikingly different from that observed in healthy subjects.

For certain quantities, the intraindividual variation is expected to be larger in acutely ill patients than in healthy subjects simply because the quantities (e.g., certain enzymes in acute myocardial infarction) are changing due to the disease. This is neither very surprising nor very important. The situation is different when a patient is assumed to be stable and the clinician is monitoring some quantity to ensure that this is the case. Here it is of interest to know the magnitude of the intraindividual variation when the patient is stable, and it is tempting to use the large body of data that has been compiled on intraindividual variation in healthy subjects.[18] At least for the more commonly used quantities, there is some evidence that during stable conditions, the intraindividual variation observed in patients is of approximately the same order of magnitude as in healthy subjects.[19,20] For instance, the study by Raun et al.[21] showed that the intraindividual variation of plasma proteins and plasma lipids of patients with multiple sclerosis and chronic inactive pyelonephritis was similar to that observed in healthy subjects.

Design Considerations in Estimating Components of Analytic and Biologic Variation

Examples of Simple Designs The experimental design used to study the biologic variation depends on the purpose of the study. Figure 7-4 shows a rather complete design, where each subject is studied repeatedly within the day. Thus, individual diurnal patterns will be revealed by this design. The design in Fig. 7-5 is much simpler, but the within-day systematic variation will not be captured, because specimens are always collected at the same time of day. Thus, one should not expect the total intraindividual variation expressed to be the same if the studies compared employ different designs. The analytic components of variation as defined in this chapter may also be assessed using simple, straightforward designs (see Fig. 7-6).

Separation of Analytic Variation from Mistakes and Biologic Variation One of the weaknesses of the usual quality control schemes is that they have a rather low probability of revealing malfunctioning of equipment and/or operator errors that last for only a short time, such as a few seconds. Therefore, when an analytic technique is established, and perhaps as an occasional control procedure, it may be useful to use randomized duplicate specimens.[22] This design implies that two blood specimens are obtained by venipuncture (if the specimen of interest is venous blood). Each specimen is uniquely labeled and processed, and the technologist in charge of the resulting batch

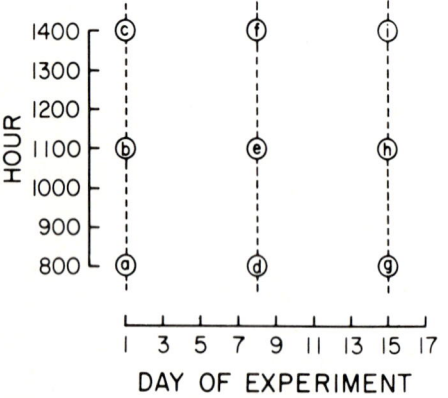

FIGURE 7-4
Protocol of hour-to-hour experimental study. (By permission of AutoAnalyzer Innovationen Band 1-section Medizin, Technicon GmbH.)

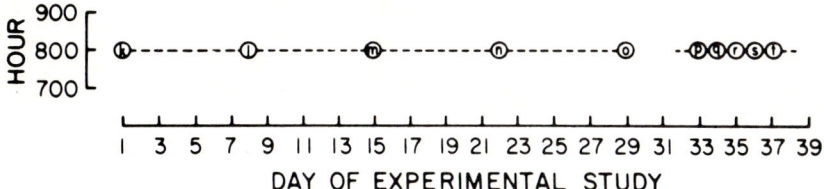

FIGURE 7-5
Protocol of day-to-day experimental study. (By permission of AutoAnalyzer Innovationen Band 1-section Medizin, Technicon GmbH.)

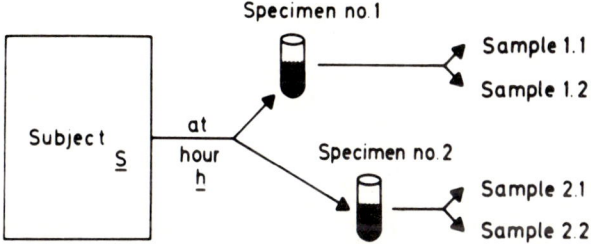

FIGURE 7-6
Experimental design used to estimate components of total analytic variation. Two specimens are obtained at each venipuncture, and the serum sample resulting from each specimen is analyzed in duplicate. (*Source:* Winkel P, Statland BE, Nielsen MK: Analytic variation and biologic within-day variation of specific serum protein concentration in a group of healthy young men. *Scand J Clin Lab Invest* 1976, 36:531, by permission of the *Scandinavian Journal of Clinical and Laboratory Investigation.*)

of specimens is not informed as to which two specimens are members of a duplicate pair. The specimens are placed in randomized order and assayed in that order. For each pair of duplicate values, the standard deviation estimates the total within-batch analytic variation. Once the relationship between mean and standard deviation of duplicate values has been established, intuition or some statistical technique may be used to identify "outliers."

By randomizing the sequence of specimens, any possible correlation between time of assay and the order of the specimen should be eliminated.[23] Thus, any general analytic drift during the time of assay will not be confounded with or mistaken as biologic variation. For instance, if specimens are assayed in the same order as they were obtained from a patient during a given day, a systematic within-day biologic increase (or decrease) of the value of the quantity examined cannot be distinguished from the effect of analytic drift taking place during the assaying of the batch. Duplicate specimens, one assayed immediately and the other stored, can be used to study other problems. If all specimens cannot be assayed in one batch unless they are first stored for some time, it may become very difficult to separate time-dependent biologic variation from analytic long-term drift. A change in concentration that depends on the time of storage can be confused with biologic variation if the first specimens have been stored for a longer time than the last specimens. For details the interested reader is referred to Ref. 16.

Separation of Analytic Correlation from Biologic Correlation Analytic errors of two or more quantities may be correlated within the same specimen and thus simulate a biologic correlation. For example, variations in the flow of gas may influence the simultaneous assay of two cations in a flame photometer in the same direction. The correlation between the analytic errors of two quantities may be eliminated using the so-called split samples technique.[24] With this technique, duplicate specimens are used to examine the biologic correlation between two quantities (quantity 1 and quantity 2). The duplicates are randomized and, for every other duplicate pair, the measurement of quantity 1 from duplicate number 1 and the measurement of quantity 2 from duplicate number 2 are used in the computations. For the remaining samples, the measurement of quantity 1 from duplicate number 2 and the measurement of quantity 2 from duplicate number 1 are used.

The term *same sample technique* refers to the procedure in which the two measurements are made in one and the same sample.

Figure 7-7 shows the intrasubject correlations of various combinations of serum constituents that were measured in specimens obtained over a number of days from 11 subjects.[24] In the figure, the results obtained using the same sample and the split samples techniques are compared. For two of the combinations, there is a definite and consistent change in the correlations. This indicates that to a large extent the correlation observed when using the same sample technique is assignable to a correlation between errors. To calculate if the within-sample errors of two quantities are correlated, the correlation is determined between two measurements obtained from duplicate samples. It may be shown that this correlation should be zero if the errors are independent.[24] Each measurement is a sum of two quantities, a biologic component and an analytic component. The assumption made is that the biologic component is the same for the two measurements obtained from duplicate samples.

INTERLABORATORY VARIATION

Components of Interlaboratory Variation

Interlaboratory variation consists of within- and between-laboratory variation. The latter is caused by differences among calibration techniques and the analytic techniques used. The difference among analytic techniques that depends on the composition of the test material is referred to as the matrix effect. Therefore, to achieve a realistic picture of the analytic performance, the test material should resemble patient specimens as much as possible; however, the matrices of different patient specimens may vary considerably. For instance, the matrix of specimens from orthopedic patients is very different from that of specimens from dialysis patients or patients suffering from liver disease. In addition, because of stability or because of lack of availability, the analyte in the test material may differ somewhat from that of the patient material (e.g., nonhuman enzymes in lyophilized test sera). Other technical properties of the test

CHAPTER 7: COMPONENTS OF BIOLOGIC AND ANALYTIC VARIATION   175

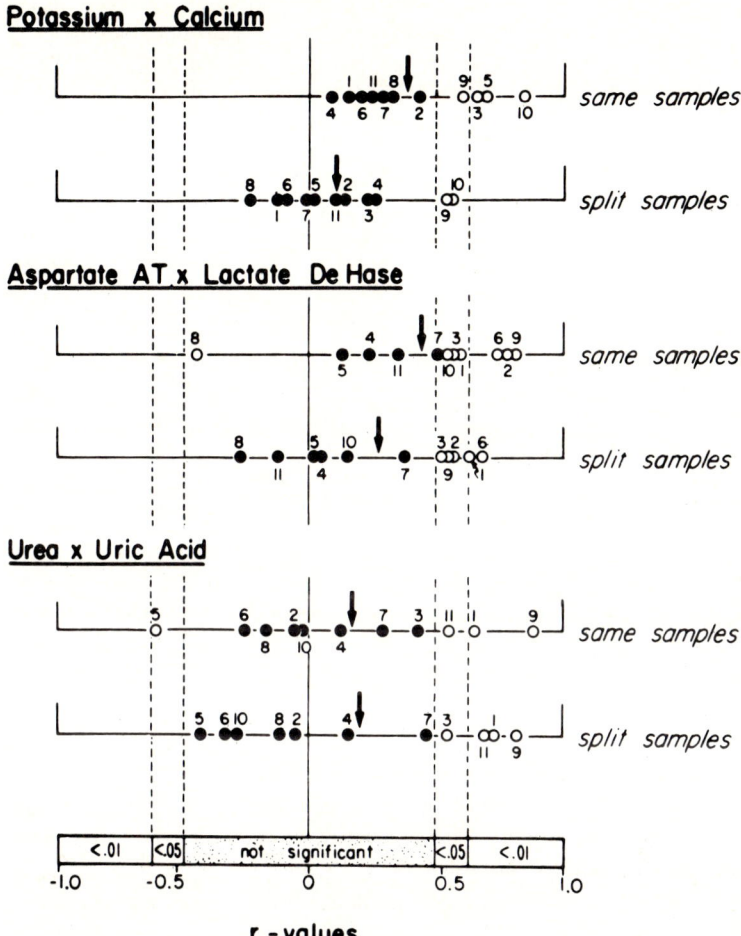

FIGURE 7-7
Eleven intrasubject correlation coefficients of three combinations of quantities before (same sample) and after (split sample) elimination of within-batch analytic error correlation. (*Source:* Winkel P, Statland BE, Bokelund H, et al: Correlation of selected serum constituents: Inter-individual variation and analytic error. *Clin Chem* 1975, 21:1952, by permission of *Clinical Chemistry*.)

material, such as concentration levels, vial-to-vial variation, stability, vulnerability to the handling, and so forth, may also influence the results.[25]

Choice of calibration material may affect the results for these same reasons. However, standardization of calibration materials does not necessarily solve the problems and may introduce new problems. Figure 7-8 presents various examples of the interaction between matrix and choice of calibration standard. The figure shows the responses obtained when a calibration standard and a patient specimen are assayed using a reference and three routine methods designed to measure the concentration of com-

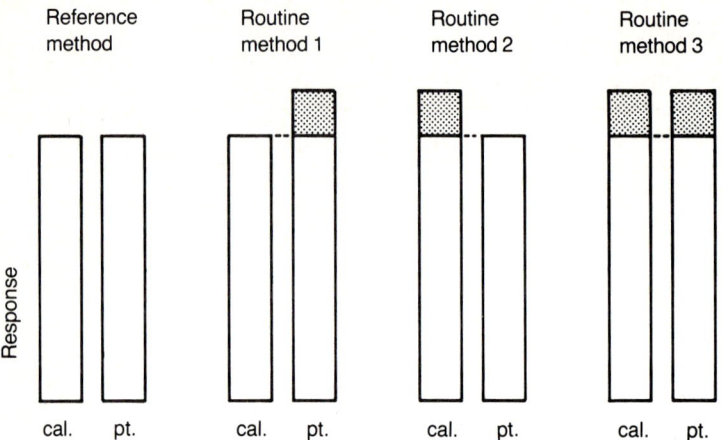

FIGURE 7-8
Constructed example showing the response by different methods when using a calibration standard and a patient specimen with the same concentration of analyte measured by the methods.

ponent X. It is assumed that the methods have not yet been calibrated and that the concentration of X is the same in the calibration standard as in the patient specimen. The instrumental response of a reference method is (or should be) independent of the matrix of the specimen. Therefore, when the reference method is used, the calibration standard and patient specimen show the same magnitude of response. Routine method 1 responds to a component that is different from component X and present in the patient specimen but not in the calibration standard. If this method is calibrated using the calibration standard with a nominal value as determined by the reference method, the concentration of X in the patient specimen will be overestimated. The value of the calibration standard can of course be adjusted so that the reading for the patient specimen will be correct (this adjustment, however, is valid only for this particular patient's specimen). In the case of routine method 2, a matrix effect takes place in the calibration standard but not in the patient specimen. If the calibration standard is used, the concentration of X in the patient specimen will be underestimated. An example of this situation is the calibration of a direct photometric method using a turbid calibration material. In the third example (routine method 3), there is a matrix effect in the calibration standard as well as in the patient specimen. Because both influence the result in the same direction, the effects are masked and the patient result will be correct but for the wrong reasons.

Because for a given method a manufacturer's choice of calibration material may be dictated by a need to compensate for matrix effects in patient specimens, it is quite unpredictable what effect standardization of calibration materials may have. Table 7-2 illustrates this point. Using the same material, ionized calcium was measured using five different instruments with calibration material supplied by the manufacturer. The material was reassayed using a single calibration standard, the set value of which was

TABLE 7-2
CALIBRATION OF ION-SELECTIVE ELECTRODES FOR MEASURING IONIZED CALCIUM IN SERUM USING CALIBRATION MATERIAL PROVIDED BY THE MANUFACTURER AND BY USING A MUTUAL CALIBRATION MATERIAL FOR ALL INSTRUMENTS*

Instruments	Overall mean values obtained on a CO_2-containing test serum (mmol/liter)	
	Individual calibration†	Mutual calibration**
AVL 980 electrolyte analyzer (AVL, Graz, Austria)	1.21	1.31
Nova 2 Ca^{2+} analyzer (Nova Biomedical, Newton, Mass.)	1.23	1.27
Orion SS-20 (Orion, Cambridge, Mass)	1.23	1.27
ICA 1 (Radiometer, Copenhagen, Denmark)	1.27	1.30
Microlyte (Kone, Espoo, Finland)	1.25	1.03

*Selected results obtained from 28 instruments in a survey in Northern Europe.
†Each laboratory calibrated with the calibration material provided by the manufacturer.
**The results from each instrument were adjusted with the corresponding findings on a protein-free calibration standard measured during the trial. The set value of this material originated from its preparation.

derived from its preparation.[26] For four (1–4 in Table 7-2) of the five instruments, the results are now more uniform, but instrument 5 now deviates considerably from the rest.

Regional Quality Control Programs and Proficiency Testing in Europe

Organizations and Regulations The philosophy of how to improve analytic performance in clinical laboratories varies somewhat among the individual countries in Northern Europe. The importance of individuals with high educational levels in the laboratory is widely accepted, and most laboratorians are free to choose the analytic methods.

In the Deutsche Demokratische Republik (DDR, East Germany),[27] however, the use of defined standard methods is as a rule mandatory, the external quality assessment programs are organized and controlled by the authorities, and participation in these programs is mandatory.

In the German Federal Republic (GFR, West Germany), participation in external quality assessment programs is also mandatory. Furthermore, the requirements for analytical performance are defined by regulations.[28] In general, these require within-laboratory day-to-day variation (CV) of 5 percent or less, and a bias relative to reference laboratory findings not exceeding 10 percent. Because results obtained by different methods are not compared, matrix effects are eliminated.[29] An office under the German Society of Clinical Chemistry administers most surveys.

In the United Kingdom (Great Britain) and in the Nordic countries, participation in external quality assessment programs (proficiency testing) is voluntary, and the programs are intended mainly as an aid for improving analytic quality and as an educational stimulus. These goals are facilitated by dividing each country into smaller regions, where the quality assessment data are discussed at informal regular meetings.[30] Although in the United Kingdom, external quality assessment programs are organized through the professional scientific societies,[31-34] a commercially available program is rather popular and more widely used than in the other countries. In Iceland, only commercially available programs are used.

Several noncommercial European multinational organizations have been established to improve analytic quality. In 1977 the Nordic Council of Ministers founded the Nordic Clinical Chemistry project (NORDKEM) to promote the quality of performance in hospital laboratories.[35] This organization, which is now supported by the national health authorities, has sponsored a number of surveys and publications[36] and has supplied financial support to the committees established by the Nordic Society of Clinical Chemistry. These committees include (1) the Nordic Committee of Quality Control, which recently initiated a publication on new developments within quality assessment;[37] (2) the Nordic Committee on Enzymes, which through the development of the standardized methods (SCE methods) has succeeded in decreasing the between-laboratory enzyme variation in the Nordic countries considerably (see Table 7-3[38]); and (3) the Nordic Committee on Reference Methods, which has concentrated on establishing reasonably easy reference methods for a number of components (e.g., cholesterol, creatinine, and glucose).[39] Each reference method is performed in one laboratory in each of the Nordic countries. These laboratories in turn are controlled by one lab-

TABLE 7-3
BETWEEN-LABORATORIES IMPRECISION (COEFFICIENTS OF VARIATION, %) OF DETERMINATION OF ENZYMES IN SERUM AS RECORDED IN NORDIC SURVEYS IN 1969, 1975, AND 1978*

Enzyme	1969		1975		1978†	
AST	30	(42)	6.3	(50)	7.3	(93)
ALT	49	(44)	7.5	(46)	6.8	(89)
LD	37	(58)	9.5	(46)	12	(84)
ALP	31	(107)	16	(31)	17	(76)
GT	—		—		13	(41)

*Figures in parentheses give the number of laboratories (i.e., results) included. Enzyme activities obtained in 1975 and 1978 by the SCE methods and in 1969 by the most frequently used methods at that time. CK has not been included in the surveys using recommended methods before 1979.

†The enzyme activities (U/liter) in the test serum used in 1978 were AST 147, ALT 166, LD 1052, ALP 439, and GT 84.

Source: Scandinavian Committee on Enzymes: Experiences with the Scandinavian recommended methods for determinations of enzymes in blood. *Scand J Clin Lab Invest* 1981, 41:107. Reprinted by permission of *Scandinavian Journal of Clinical and Laboratory Investigation.*

oratory where an elaborate reference method is used. The analytic principle of the reference method is close to a definitive method and is comparable to such definitive methods as those from the U.S. National Bureau of Standardization (NBS). The Common Market countries have formed the so-called Community Bureau of Reference (BRC). Its function is to establish reference materials[40] for hospital laboratories and similar institutions and, if needed, to supply these materials to the laboratories. The BRC is similar to the U.S. National Bureau of Standards but attempts to provide components that are not already available through the NBS. The European Committee of Clinical Laboratory Standardization (ECCLS)[41] corresponds to the National Committee for Clinical Laboratory Standards (NCCLS) in the United States. Some NCCLS standards have been adopted, but in general most standards are developed in Europe.

Types of Survey Design Differences of design philosophies may be illustrated by comparing some serum-based surveys. In Norwegian surveys, 12 vials of the original test serum are dispatched per concentration level (three in all) to each participating laboratory, where one vial is analyzed per day during the subsequent 12 days. To disguise the target value, unequal volumes of the test serum are placed into the vials before lyophilization, yielding 12 different vial types. Because the reconstitution volume is the same for all vials, the target values differ slightly. In surveys where this precaution is not taken, there may be a tendency to underestimate the within-laboratory variation because the target value is known. This is of minor importance if no legal regulations are involved and the main goal is to estimate the between-laboratory variation (or accuracy). The main program in Denmark and in some Swedish regions comprises daily analyses of vials obtained from the same batch of equine-bovine serum over an extended period (2 to 3 years).[31,34] In the Netherlands, internal and external programs are combined insofar as the same quality control material as is used for external programs is later supplied to the participating laboratories for internal quality control purposes.[42]

Evaluation of Survey Results At least four different approaches are being used for the evaluation of the results of external quality control programs. The simplest approach is to use the mean of all participating laboratories as a target value relative to which all laboratories are evaluated. It is, however, very difficult to know what such an overall mean value signifies. The overall mean is determined by differences among the technical qualities of the various laboratories, the methods, and the calibration standards used.

A better approach might be to use a target value for each method, namely, the overall mean of all laboratories using the same method. Because the number of laboratories participating in a given survey is much smaller than in the United States, only the more generally accepted methods can be included in such a survey. This approach also suffers unless the same calibration standard is used by all laboratories. Even if the same type of calibration material is used, different lots of the material usually will be used at different laboratories during any given time period. If the values of the various laboratories scatter at random relative to the mean, it does make sense to assume that the variation is caused by the within-laboratory variation plus hypothetical, laboratory-

TABLE 7-4
EXTERNAL QUALITY ASSESSMENT SURVEYS IN NORTHERN EUROPE

	Regular in all countries	Regular in one or more countries	Occasionally
Classical, 20–40 components in serum	+		
Specific protein in serum		+	+
Hormones in serum		+	+
TSH screening and bilirubin for newborns		+	+
Drugs and ethanol in serum		+	+
Coagulation		+	+
Blood gas		+	+
Hematology		+	+
Cerebrospinal fluid		+	+
Urine		+	+
Urinary/calculi		+	+
Spectrometer		+	+
Scintillation and gamma-counters			+

specific, random contributions reflecting local peculiarities. When the within-laboratory variation can be estimated, it should be possible to test the hypothesis that random laboratory-specific contributions are zero. Each laboratory's specific contributions then could be estimated and the laboratories ranked according to the absolute value of this deviation. This analysis-of-variance approach we feel is pragmatic without being silly. Of course, it is necessary to ensure the distribution; that is, outliers must not occur or rather should be recognized as such.

In some countries—for example, in the German Federal Republic—laboratories using a given method are compared to the mean obtained by a few reference laboratories using the same method. In Denmark and Sweden the problem of evaluating the participating laboratories is avoided, because laboratorians evaluate the data locally using whatever principles they consider appropriate. To evaluate the between-laboratory variation in the Netherlands, use of median, mode, or mean of the distribution of results has been proposed.[43]

Major Programs and State of the Art Considerable differences exist among the individual European countries, with only more routine types of components in serum controlled regularly (2 to 12 times a year);[31–34,42–50] the state of the art for serum enzymes for the Nordic surveys is shown in Table 7-3. Nearly all countries, however, conduct additional national programs (see Table 7-4) or participate in programs covering several countries. The latter type of program is becoming increasingly popular. For instance, recently a German and a Nordic program on urinary calculi were merged.[48] Large multinational programs may not be practical when the matrix effect

TABLE 7-5
RESULTS OF QUALITY CONTROL SURVEYS IN THE NORDIC COUNTRIES OBTAINED IN THE 1970s

	Imprecision, %CV			ASPEN conference requirement*
	Total	Intralab.	Interlab.	
S-sodium	1.5	1.0	1.0	0.4
S-potassium	3.0	2.0	1.5	2.8
				2.2
S-calcium	4.0	3.0	2.5	0.9
S-magnesium	8.5	4.5	7.0	
S-chloride	3.0	2.0	2.0	1.5
				1.0
S-phosphate	6.5	4.5	4.5	3.4
				2.9
S-iron	7.5	4.5	4.5	18.0
				13.0
S-bilirubin	8.5	5.0	7.0	
S-glucose	9.0	5.0	8.0	3.1
				2.2
S-urea	7.5	5.0	5.5	10.1
				6.2
S-urate	6.0	4.0	4.5	5.2
				3.7
S-creatinine	8.5	5.0	7.0	5.1
				2.2
S-cholesterol	8.0	4.0	7.0	10.0
				2.4
S-albumin	7.5	3.0	6.5	1.4
S-protein	3.5	2.5	2.5	2.0
				1.5
S-ALT	11	6.5	9.0	
S-AST	11	5.5	9.0	
S-phosphatase alk	12	5.5	11	13.0
				1.8
S-LD	9.0	4.5	7.5	
S-CK (2 surveys)	16–25	5–15	5–24	
S-amylase (2 surveys)	7–18	5–8	4–17	

*Upper figures are the required values for group screening, lower ones are for individual testing. If only one figure is given (e.g., for S-sodium), the requirement is the same for group screening and individual testing.
Source: Aronson T, Bjørnstad P, Leskinen E, et al: Present analytical quality in the Nordic clinical chemistry laboratories. Scand J Clin Lab Invest 1980, 40(suppl 155):11. Reprinted by permission of Scandinavian Journal of Clinical and Laboratory Investigation.

is a major problem. To eliminate undesired matrix effects, a program using frozen fresh serum from voluntary donors was started in Denmark. The capped glass vials with the material are forwarded using foam boxes and CO_2-ice.[31] A regional survey on blood gas using genuine patient specimens has been carried out.[46] Problems related to the determination of specific proteins and caused by lyophilization have been avoided by a regular program[31] based on serum from outdated bank blood.[51]

The present state of the art in the Northern Europe is illustrated by the data presented in Table 7-5. This table shows the within- and between-laboratory variation based on data recently compiled from all Nordic countries.[30]

REFERENCES

1 Statland BE, Winkel P: Pre-instrumental source of variation, in Henry TB (ed): *Clinical Diagnosis and Management by Laboratory Methods.* Philadelphia, WB Saunders, 1984, pp 61–73.
2 Winkel P, Statland BE, Nielsen MK: Analytic variation and biologic within-day variation of specific serum protein concentration in a group of healthy young men. *Scand J Clin Lab Invest* 1976, 36:531.
3 Winkel P, Statland BE, Jorgensen J: Urine microscopy, an ill-defined method examined by multifactorial technique. *Clin Chem* 1974, 20:436.
4 Cotlove E, Harris EK, Williams CZ: Biological and analytic components of variation in longterm studies of serum constituents in normal subjects: III. Physiological and medical implications. *Clin Chem* 1970, 16:1028.
5 Harris EK: Some theory of reference values: Stratified normal ranges and a method for following an individual's clinical laboratory values. *Clin Chem* 1975, 21:1457.
6 Harris EK: Some theory of reference values: II. Comparison of some statistical models of intra-individual variation in blood constituents. *Clin Chem* 1976, 22:1343.
7 Harris EK: Statistical aspects of reference values in clinical pathology, in Stefani M, Benson ES (eds): *Progress in Clinical Pathology,* vol VIII. New York, Grune & Stratton, 1981, pp 45–66.
8 Winkel P, Statland BE: Using the subject as his own reference in assessing day-to-day changes of laboratory test results, in Hercules DM, Hieftje GM, Snyder LR, et al (eds): *Contemporary Topics in Analytical and Clinical Chemistry,* vol 1. New York, Plenum Press, 1977, pp 287–317.
9 Williams GZ, Widdowson GM, Penton J: Individual character of variation in time-series studies of healthy people: II. Differences in values for clinical chemical analytes in serum among demographic groups by age and sex. *Clin Chem* 1978, 24:313.
10 Harris EK: Effects of intra- and inter-individual variation on the appropriate use of normal ranges. *Clin Chem* 1974, 20:1535.
11 Rietz HL, Mitchell HH: On the metabolism experiment as a statistical problem. *J Biol Chem* 1910, 8:297.
12 Winkel P, Statland BE, Burdsall MJ, et al: A study of variation of concentration values of leukocyte types: 2. Analytical considerations—manual versus automated cell counting, in *Advances in Automated Analysis, Technicon International Congress 1976,* vol 1, Tarrytown, NY, 1977, pp 317–324.
13 Statland BE, Winkel P: Effects of non-analytical factors on the intra-individual variation of analytes in the blood of healthy subjects: Consideration of preparation of the subjects and time of venipuncture. *CRC Crit Rev Lab Sci* 1977, 8:105.

14 Statland BE, Winkel P: Response of clinical chemistry quantity values to selected physical, dietary and smoking activities, in Stefani M, Benson ES (eds): *Progress in Clinical Pathology,* vol VIII. New York, Grune & Stratton, 1981, pp 25–44.
15 Winkel P, Statland BE: The theory of reference values, in Henry TB (ed): *Clinical Diagnosis and Management by Laboratory Methods.* Philadelphia, WB Saunders, 1984, pp 51–60.
16 Winkel P, Statland BE, Bokelund H: Effects of time of venipuncture on variation of serum constituents: Consideration of within-day and day-to-day changes in a group of healthy young men. *Am J Clin Pathol* 1975, 64:433.
17 Statland BE, Winkel P, Harris SC, et al: Evaluation of biological sources of variation of leukocyte counts and other hematological quantities using very precise automated analyzers. *Am J Clin Pathol* 1978, 69:48.
18 Ross JW: Evaluation of precision, in Werner M (ed): *CRC Handbook of Clinical Chemistry,* vol 1. Boca Raton, FL, CRC Press, 1982, pp 391–422.
19 Fraser CG, Williams P: Short-term biological variation of plasma analytes in renal disease. *Clin Chem* 1983, 29:508.
20 Fraser CG: Desirable performances for clinical chemistry tests, in Latner AL, Schwartz, MK (eds): *Advances in Clinical Chemistry,* vol 23. New York, Academic Press, 1983, pp 300–333.
21 Raun NE, Moller BB, Back U, et al: On individual reference intervals based on a longitudinal study of plasma proteins and lipids in healthy subjects, and their possible clinical application. *Clin Chem* 1982, 28:294.
22 Bokelund H, Winkel P, Statland BE: Factors contributing to intra-individual variation of serum constituents: 3. Use of randomized duplicate serum specimens to evaluate sources of analytical errors. *Clin Chem* 1974, 20:1507.
23 Winkel P: Experimental designs for the separation of analytical from biological variation. *Scand J Clin Lab Invest* 1980, 40(suppl 155):19.
24 Winkel P, Statland BE, Bokelund H, et al: Correlation of selected serum constituents: Interindividual variation and analytic error. *Clin Chem* 1975, 21:1952.
25 Uldall A: Apparent interlaboratory variation using different types of reference sera. *Scand J Clin Lab Invest* 1984, 44(suppl 172):163.
26 Uldall A, Fogh-Andersen N, Thode J, et al: Measurement of ionized calcium with five types of instruments: An external quality assessment. *Scand J Clin Lab Invest* 1985, 45:255.
27 Deutsche Demokratische Republik: *Deutches Arzneibuch: Diagnostische laboratoriumsmethoden,* DAB 8 (D.L.)-DDR, ed 8. Berlin, Akademie-Verlag, 1978.
28 Bundesarztekammer: Richtlinien der Bundesarztekammer zur durchfuhrung der statistischen qualitatskontrolle. . . . *Deutsches Arzteblatt* 1971, 68:2228; 1974, 71:959.
29 Stamm D: A new concept for quality control of clinical laboratory investigations in the light of clinical requirements and based on reference method value. *J Clin Chem Clin Biochem* 1982, 20:817.
30 Aronson T, Bjørnstad P, Leskinen E, et al: Present analytical quality in the Nordic clinical chemistry laboratories. *Scand J Clin Lab Invest* 1980, 40(suppl 155):11.
31 Blom M, Brock A, Christensen F, et al: External quality assessment programs in Denmark. *Scand J Clin Lab Invest* 1984, 44(suppl 172):175.
32 Gronroos P, Hohenthal U, Karjalainen E, et al: External quality assessment programs in Finland 1971–1983. *Scand J Clin Lab Invest* 1984, 44(suppl 172):179.
33 Theodorsen L, Bjørnstad P, Skrede S: External quality assessment programs in Norway 1976–1982. *Scand J Clin Lab Invest* 1984, 44(suppl 172):187.
34 Kallner A, Lindstedt S, De Verdier C-H: External quality assessment programs in Sweden on a coordinated regional basis. *Scand J Clin Lab Invest* 1984, 44(suppl 172):191.

35 Leskinen EA, Nyberg APW: NORDKEM—An organization to promote the collaboration between clinical laboratories in the Nordic countries. *Scand J Clin Lab Invest* 1984, 44:579.
36 Hørder M (ed): *Assessing Quality Requirements in Clinical Chemistry.* Helsinki, Finland, NORDKEM, 1980.
37 De Verdier C-H, Aronsson T, Nyberg APW (eds): *Quality Control in Clinical Chemistry—Efforts to Find an Efficient Strategy.* Helsinki, Finland, NORDKEM, 1984.
38 Scandinavian Committee on Enzymes (SCE): Experiences with the Scandinavian recommended methods for determinations of enzymes in blood. *Scand J Clin Lab Invest* 1981, 41:107.
39 Bjorkhem I, Elg P, Olesen H, et al: On accuracy in clinical chemistry. *Scand J Clin Lab Invest* 1982, 42:97–99.
40 Community Bureau of Reference: *Catalogue of BCR Reference Materials.* Brussels, BCR, 1983.
41 European Committee for Clinical Laboratory Standards: Revised by-laws 1982. *J Clin Chem Clin Biochem* 1983, 21:113.
42 Jansen RTP, Jansen ADP: A coupled external/internal quality control program for clinical laboratories in the Netherlands. *Clin Chim Acta* 1980, 107:185.
43 Jansen RTP: Comparison of routine analytical methods in the Netherlands for seven serum constituents using pattern recognition. *Ann Clin Biochem* 1983, 20:41.
44 Leskinen EA, Nyberg APW, Elfving S, et al: External quality assessment of serum drug determinations in the Nordic countries. *Scand J Clin Lab Invest* 1984, 44(suppl 172):135.
45 Ruokonen A, Leskinen EA, Nyberg APW, et al: External quality assessment of serum hormone determinations in the Nordic countries. *Scand J Clin Lab Invest* 1984, 44(suppl 172):125.
46 Bjaelager PAL, Jensen HA, Larsen E, et al: Inter-laboratory comparison of acidbase variables in human blood and in control materials. *Clin Chim Acta* 1981, 116:289.
47 Poller L, Thomson JM, Yee KF: Quality control trials of prothrombin time. *J Clin Pathol* 1979, 32:251.
48 Uldall A, Hesse A, Larsson L, et al: A joint Nordic and German external quality assessment scheme for the investigation of urinary calculi, in *NORDKEM Posters.* NORDKEM, Helsinki, Finland, 1984, p 47.
49 Whitehead TP: *Quality Control in Clinical Chemistry.* New York, John Wiley & Sons, 1977.
50 Deutsche Gesellschaft für Klinische Chemie: *Clinical Chemistry Surveys 1985.* Bonn, GFR, Deutsche Gesellschaft für Klinische Chemie e.v. External Quality Control, 1985.
51 Uldall A: Preparation of frozen reference sera and examples of applications. *Scand J Clin Lab Invest* 1984, 44:223.

CHAPTER 8

ASSESSMENT OF ANALYTIC VARIABILITY IN CLINICAL CHEMISTRY

John A. Lott, Ph.D.
Suman T. Patel, Ph.D.

Increasing sophistication of medicine has placed greater demands on clinical laboratories for reliable analyses. More sensitive and specific laboratory tests have simplified the diagnostic process and provided early indication of disease. Quality control programs provide a mechanism by which the analytic performance of clinical laboratories may be evaluated, documented, and improved.

THE REFERENCE SAMPLE METHOD OF QUALITY CONTROL

The reference sample method is the most efficient and widely used system of quality control in clinical chemistry laboratories. Controls that mimic patient specimens are analyzed repeatedly within-day and between-day. The reference sample method can be used to evaluate repeatability of results and proximity of results to correct values. When identical samples or sets of samples are sent to a group of laboratories, interlaboratory variability also can be monitored.

Concentrations of Analytes in Controls

Control samples should have concentrations or activities based on a number of considerations. Methods should be monitored at decision points; controls should be available with concentrations close to these decision values. Serum glucose, iron, protein, pCO_2, calcium, digoxin, cortisol, alkaline phosphatase, potassium, magnesium, and most drugs have more than one value where therapeutic, diagnostic, or management decisions are made. More controls are needed for these determinations than for other tests such as creatinine, aspartate aminotransferase (AST), and lactate dehydrogenase

(LD), which have only one decision region. Bilirubin has different decision points for newborns than for adults, and the quality control needs are more complex.

Most methods in clinical chemistry are designed to cover a wide dynamic range of concentrations. If possible, controls should be used to monitor the stability of the dynamic range or, if a loss in precision has occurred, at medically important analytical extremes of the method.

Interrelated Concentrations in Controls

Commercially prepared quality control materials that are distributed as sets of two or three should have the concentrations of analytes present in known interrelationships. If the concentrations of the common analytes are present in known ratios, then additional information is obtained by their analysis. For example, a set of controls could have glucose concentrations of 50, 100, 200, and 400 mg/dl. When the instrument response is graphed versus the expected concentration, an "operational line" for glucose can be constructed (see below). Much more quality control information is available from an operational line than from repetitive analyses of unrelated controls.[1]

MATERIALS

Commercially Available Controls

Purchased controls have the advantage of convenience. They cannot be used uncritically; criteria for selection must include qualitative characteristics, concentration, stability, and cost. Quality control materials must mimic patient specimens as closely as possible, be they plasma, serum, urine, body fluids, or other patient-derived materials. A basic assumption is that the repeatability and accuracy obtained with control materials is the same as that obtained with patient specimens. If this assumption is correct, the laboratory has an estimate of how well it is performing in the analysis of patient specimens. Often quality control materials from nonhuman sources must be used. For example, because of the difficulty of obtaining human tissue enzymes, animal-source enzymes are commonly used to fortify control sera. Porcine heart creatine kinase (CK) resembles human skeletal muscle CK;[2] however, calf intestinal alkaline phosphatase (ALP), a common source of ALP, is very different from ALP from human liver.[3]

Lyophilization tends to denature proteins; for example, albumin exhibits altered dye-binding characteristics following lyophilization. Liquid controls containing ethylene glycol are unsuitable for analytical systems employing dialysis.[4] However, they are very convenient and may be less costly than lyophilized controls, because there is less waste. Another advantage of liquid controls is better reproducibility of their target values, because the variable associated with reconstitution is absent (for further discussion of control materials, see Chapter 5).

Accuracy of Controls

The true concentration of an analyte in a control can only be estimated. A few analytes, such as calcium[5] and glucose,[6] have "reference methods" by which reliable values can

TABLE 8-1
SAMPLE OF INSERT VALUES FOR CONTROL SERA[a]

Manufacturer (control)	Calcium range (% range[b]) [no. methods]	Cholesterol range (% range) [no. methods]	Glucose range (% range) [no. methods]	Urea N range (% range) [no. methods]
Dade[c] (Mono-Trol I)	9.1–10.3 (12%) [15]	83–126 (52%) [18]	91–136 (50%) [20]	17.1–19.9 (16%) [16]
Fisher[d] (Normal)	9.5–10.8 (14%) [9]	160–206 (29%) [15]	69–84 (22%) [24]	13–18 (39%) [14]
Hyland[e] (Q-Pak-I)	9.1–10.1 (11%) [10]	73–106 (45%) [9]	87–111 (28%) [13]	18–21 (17%) [10]
Ortho[f] (QCS-Normal)	9.1–10.4 (14%) [26]	123–183 (49%) [37]	83–130 (57%) [47]	13–18 (39%) [37]

[a]Controls in current use. All units in mg/dl.
[b]Range as percent of lower value.
[c]Dade Division, American Hospital Supply, Miami, FL.
[d]Fisher Scientific, Orangeburg, NY.
[e]Hyland Diagnostics, Division Cooper Laboratories, Freehold, NJ.
[f]Ortho Diagnostic Systems, Raritan, NJ.

be determined. Reference methods have undergone extensive scrutiny; their bias, variability, sources of interference, and so on, are known. For chemistry, nearly all the common serum analytes have well-established methods of tested reliability.[7] Although control materials should have only *one* assayed result for most analytes, this is not always the case. For example, one manufacturer lists 47 glucose results for its "normal" control. For the same control, the listed glucose values range from 83 to 130 mg/dl, a spread of 47 mg or 57 percent of the lower value. Laboratories want to be "in control" for their method, yet they miss the much more serious problem of a substantial bias from the true value. Other examples like the above are listed in Table 8-1.

Use of Pooled Patient Sera as a Control

In spite of the cost of preparing and storing the pool, considerable cost savings can be effected using pooled patient sera. Supplementing solutions can be added to raise the concentration or activities of a particular analyte to the desired level. Because the supplementing material is of human origin, the common problems of nonhuman materials are avoided. Custom pools can be prepared of unusual analytes. For example, we prepare quality control pools of gastrin at two concentrations: 150 µg/l and 500 µg/l. Our gastrin pools from patient-derived sera are stable frozen for 12 to 18 months. Disadvantages of pooled serum as a control include loss of certain labile analytes such as LD-5, CO_2, and acid phosphatase. Also, it is very likely that the pool will be hepatitis B surface antigen positive[8] (HB_SAg) and human T lymphotropic virus, type III (HLTV-III) positive. Schultz and Gates[9] described the manufacture of HB_SAg-negative pools involving dialysis and preservation with phenylmercuric acetate. One group of workers has described preparation of controls with a high lipid content,[10] whereas others have described isoenzyme controls for CK.[11] Others have prepared an optically clear pool by precipitating pre-beta and beta lipoproteins with dextran sulfate and bivalent cations.[12] Directions for preparing controls are in the appendix to this chapter.[13]

FREQUENCY OF CONTROL SERA ANALYSIS

How often should patient specimens be interspersed with control materials? The frequency of analysis of controls is dictated by the variability of the test and what is acceptable "drift." The definition of acceptable drift is subjective, but it should include what is medically acceptable. *Acceptable drift* has been defined as the percent biological variation times the upper reference limit in the units of the test.[14] The calculated acceptable drift will be greater with tests that show large intraindividual variability, such as cholesterol and CK; the acceptable drift will be smaller for tests such as pH and calcium, where the interindividual variability is small.

The definition of drift in turn describes a "batch" of specimens. On a practical basis, a batch is 5 to 10 specimens for methods using an ion-specific electrode, flame photometry, or atomic absorption measurements; it is 15 to 20 specimens for spectrophotometry or for many multichannel instruments. Some instruments, such as the Du Pont aca III or IV, are very stable, and as few as one or two controls in an 8-hour day suffice for serum amylase, CK, phenobarbital, and urea nitrogen.[14] We found the Kodak Ektachem 400 to be particularly stable for serum amylase and lipase. Here, controls analyzed once in 24 hours probably suffice. For a very simple device such as a refractometer, a weekly or even monthly check with a control material is adequate. Regulatory requirements, however, often dictate more frequent use of controls, usually once per shift.

DETERMINATION OF LABORATORY VARIATION

The most widely used system of quality control employs the reference sample system.[15] Here, quality control specimens are analyzed repeatedly, and a mean and standard deviation (SD) are calculated. Two equations that can be used to calculate the SD are seen in Table 8-2. Equation b is more convenient to use with computers and is used with all hand calculators that have the SD function. With equation b, the individual points need not be stored by the computer. When new quality control materials are introduced, it is necessary to establish what is an acceptable SD. This can be done only if, during the period in which the data are gathered, the method is stable with few outliers as determined using the established control materials. Adequate data, at least 30 to 50 observations, must be collected, and the data must have a reasonably Gaussian distribution.

TABLE 8-2
ALTERNATE METHODS FOR CALCULATION OF STANDARD DEVIATION

a $\quad SD = \left[\dfrac{\text{sum of all (value } i - \text{mean})^2}{n - 1} \right]^{1/2}$

where (value i − mean) is the deviation of the ith value from the mean value and n is the number of values. The square root of the entire term equals the SD.

b $\quad SD = \left[\dfrac{(n(\text{sum value } i^2) - (\text{sum value } i)^2}{n(n-1)} \right]^{1/2}$

where (sum value i^2) is the sum of the squares of the values, (sum value i)^2 is the sum of the values squared, and n has the same meaning as above.

Use of Levey-Jennings Charts

A typical Levey-Jennings chart is shown in Fig. 8-1. Usually results outside ±2 SD are termed "warning limits," and those outside ±3 SD are designated as "action limits." If the mean and SD of the control were established during a period of stability, and if the procedure remains stable, new quality control data can be used to judge current performance. If the results follow a Gaussian pattern, 68.3 percent of the values will fall within ±1 SD, 95.5 percent will fall within ±2 SD, and 99.7 percent will fall within ±3 SD. One-in-twenty results should be expected to fall outside ±2 SD, and only 3 per 1000 should fall outside ±3 SD. Because they usually point to unacceptable analytical variability, values outside ±3 SD should always be questioned. If a small sample was used to establish the SD, more outliers should be expected. A small shift in values will result in more outliers if the variance is small.

Allen et al.[16] found that if the control was known to the analyst, the SDs were generally smaller than when the control was "blind," that is, disguised as a patient specimen. If generally true, the implication of this finding is that actual performance on patient specimens is worse than what is determined with quality control schemes.

Dispersion or Contraction A change in precision causes increased dispersion or contraction of the spread of the data. Increased dispersion is shown in Fig. 8-2; there is a host of reasons for worsening precision, which is usually apparent from a Levey-Jennings chart. Causes include more or new individuals performing the test, inattention to critical steps of the procedure, unstable line voltage, greater variability in pipetting specimens and/or reagents, and others.

Trend Trends in the data are shown in Fig. 8-2. Trends are commonly caused by a gradual change in standards, reagents, or instrument condition. A trend is always a signal for remedial action and is apparent when at least 10 consecutive values are above or below the mean.

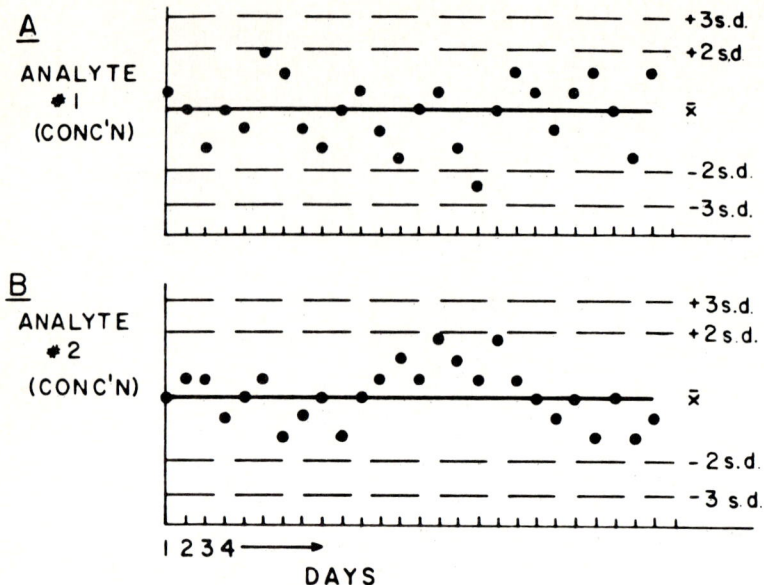

FIGURE 8-1
A Levey-Jennings chart showing characteristics of distributions of quality control data, using limits that include day-to-day variability. (A) The data are randomly distributed between the limits. (B) Over a short period of time, the data are clustered well within the designated limits; however, small shifts occur. (From Grannis GF, Caragher TE: Quality control programs in clinical chemistry. *CRC Crit Rev Clin Lab Sci* 1977, 7:327, with permission.)

Shift Shifts, as shown in Fig. 8-2, are commonly caused by the introduction of new standards, reagents, or methods. Shifts caused by a remedy of an unsatisfactory situation are unavoidable and at times desirable. Small trends or shifts within acceptable limits are not a problem.

Long-Term Data Records Levey-Jennings charts show long-term trends very well. Figure 8-3 shows monthly CVs for glucose data covering a period of 18 years. Each of the data points is a mean of 100 or more values at a concentration of 80 to 100 mg/dl. With improving technology, the CVs have become narrower. From 1967 to late 1974, the AutoAnalyzer ferricyanide method was used in our laboratory; monthly CVs usually were in the 5 to 6 percent range but occasionally close to 9 percent. Between late 1974 and late 1979, we analyzed glucose using a Technicon SMA-6 with a glucose oxidase method;[17] the precision improved, and the CVs were typically near 4 percent. In June 1981, we started using the Beckman Astra-8 with a glucose oxidase-oxygen electrode method and observed a further improvement in precision. Our CVs for glucose are now in the 2 percent region, that is, a fourfold improvement in the precision over the time period shown in Fig. 8-3.

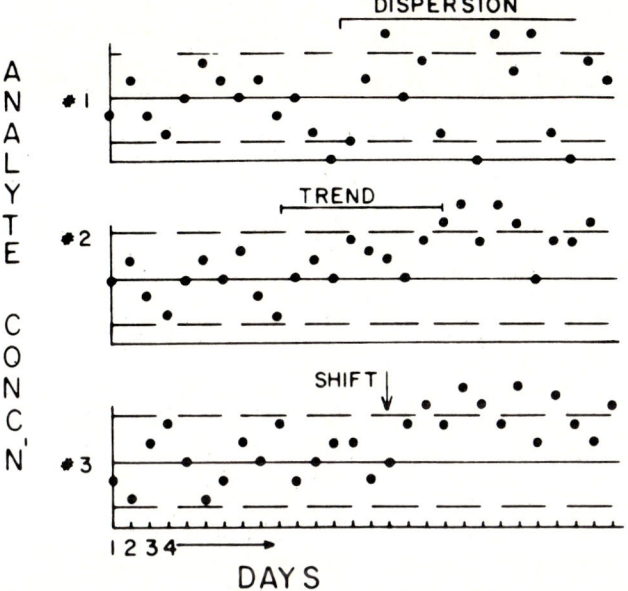

FIGURE 8-2
Examples of three type of changes in quality control data. Chart 1 illustrates dispersion of data characterized by an increased frequency of both high and low outliers. Chart 2 illustrates a trend in the data. Over a period of days the determined values drift progressively from the prior mean value. Chart 3 illustrates an abrupt shift in the data to a new mean value. (From Grannis GF, Caragher TE: Quality control programs in clinical chemistry. *CRC Crit Rev Clin Lab Sci* 1977, 7:327, with permission.)

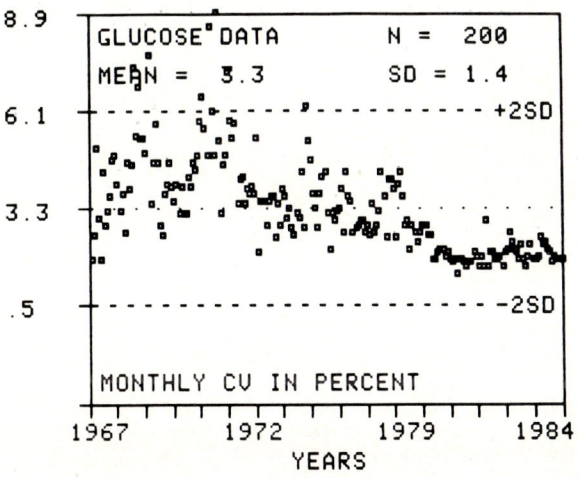

FIGURE 8-3
Long-term quality control for glucose. The monthly mean CVs are shown for controls with glucose concentration between 80 and 100 mg/dl. There is a clear trend toward better performance between 1967 and 1984.

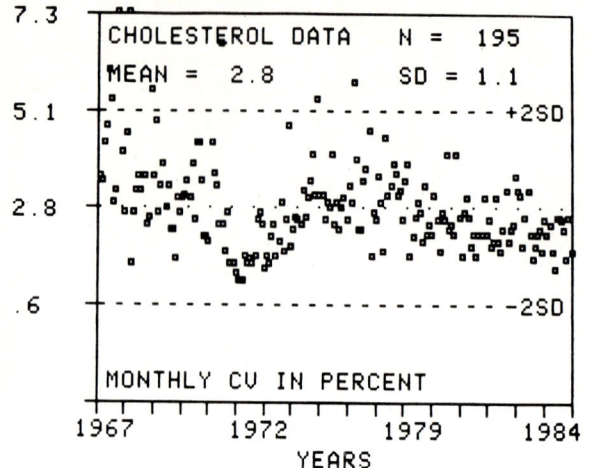

FIGURE 8-4
Long-term quality control data for cholesterol. The monthly mean CVs are shown for controls with cholesterol concentrations between 250 and 300 mg/dl. There is improvement in precision over the 17-year period.

Similar long-term data for cholesterol are shown in Fig. 8-4. Here, each point represents the mean of 25 to 30 values at a concentration of 250 to 300 mg/dl. A ferric chloride-H_2SO_4 method was in use from 1967 to late 1977. CVs averaged 4 to 5 percent; however, there were periods with considerably higher values. From late 1977 to 1984, a cholesterol oxidase method has been used on the Abbott ABA-100 Analyzer. The precision of the automated enzymatic method is clearly better than that of the manual procedure.

Application of Shewhart Control Rules

Westgard has described a series of control rules, called the Shewhart multirule system, for use in the clinical laboratory to identify unacceptable data.[18] Certain managerial decisions must be made before the system can be implemented, including how many controls are analyzed with each batch of specimens, what the desirable error detection rate is, and what the acceptable false rejection rate of otherwise acceptable data is.

Development of the Model The number of control samples analyzed per batch and the laboratory-defined acceptable SD determine the probability of detecting error (P_{ed}) and the probability of false rejection (P_{fr}) of acceptable data. P_{ed} and P_{fr} are defined as:

$$P_{ed} = \text{(proper rejection)}/\text{(proper rejection + false acceptance)}$$
$$P_{fr} = \text{(false rejection)}/\text{(false rejection + proper acceptance)}$$

Two extremes are easily imagined. If several controls are analyzed with every batch, and the acceptable SD limits are extremely narrow, the P_{ed} will be close to 1 but P_{fr}

TABLE 8-3
SHEWHART RULES

1_{2S} rule:	The run is accepted when both control results are within 2 SD limits from the mean value.
1_{3S} rule:	The run is considered out of control when one of the control results exceeds the mean ± 3 SD limits.
2_{2S} rule:	The run is rejected when both controls exceed their mean value $+2$ SD or the mean -2 SD limits.
R_{4S} rule:	The run is rejected when one control result exceeds a mean value $+2$ SD limit and the other exceeds the mean -2 SD limit, or when the range of a group of controls exceeds 4 SD.
4_{1S} rule:	The run is rejected when four *consecutive* control results exceed the mean $+1$ SD or the mean -1 SD.
10_x rule:	The run is rejected when the last 10 consecutive control results fall on the same side of the mean.

will be unacceptably large. Conversely, with very few controls and wide acceptable SD limits, P_{ed} and P_{fr} will be low, but many errors will be missed. Clearly a middle ground is needed. For information on the theoretical bases of the Shewhart multirule system and its performance characteristics, see references 19–23.

Application of the Model Two controls are analyzed with each batch of specimens, and the results are recorded on a Levey-Jennings chart. It is assumed that the SD limits are appropriate as described above. A decision for acceptance or rejection of a batch of results is based on the set of rules shown in Table 8-3. A flow diagram (Fig. 8-5) shows how the rules are applied; patient results are acceptable when none of the rules is violated. (For an explanation of how the rules are named, see Chapter 1.)

A violation of the 1_{3S} or R_{4S} control rules indicates a likely random error. Violations of the 2_{2S}, 4_{1S}, or 10_x rules are indicative of systematic error; however, violation of the 1_{3S} rule also points to a large systematic error. Although the multirule Shewhart procedure can be used with manual calculations, a computer makes the implementation more efficient. The mean and SD of the control must be well established before this procedure can be applied.

Test of the Model Figures 8-6 and 8-7 show the ability of the 1_{2S} rule to detect random and systematic errors, respectively. As the number of controls analyzed in a batch is increased, the sensitivity of the 1_{2S} rule is increased. With two controls, there is a 50 percent probability of detecting a 2-SD random error and a 73 percent probability of detecting a 2-SD systematic error.

The performance characteristics of several control rules are illustrated in Table 8-4. With the 1_{2S} rule, the probability for false rejection varies from 0.10 to 0.33

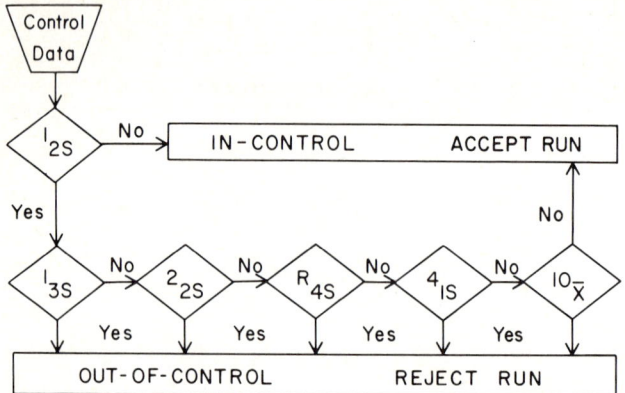

FIGURE 8-5
Logic diagram for applying a series of control rules in the multirule Shewhart procedure. (From Westgard JO, Barry PL, Hunt MR: A multi-rule Shewhart chart for quality control in clinical chemistry. *Clin Chem* 1981, 27:493, with permission.)

depending on the number of controls. The probability of detecting error, for example, a 2-SD shift, varies from 0.22 to 0.99 depending on the number of controls and the control rules. The third and fourth control rules in Table 8-4[22] have greater sensitivity in detecting 2-SD random or systematic errors than the multirule approach. With two control specimens, the P_{fr} values are 1 and 5 percent for the third and fourth control rules, respectively.

The efficiency of any combination of controls and control rules at a given precision can be obtained from power functions and the efficiency of the control procedure may be calculated. The control rules cannot be used uncritically; a small, unimportant shift could lead to control values occurring close to, but consistently on one side of, the mean. Used alone, the 10_x rule fails in this case, because it would lead to unnecessary rejection of a run. More rigorous quality control procedures should be used for monitoring quality during the start-up phase of any new analytical procedure.[22]

Criticism of the Levey-Jennings Methods

The ability of Levey-Jennings charts and/or the Shewhart multirule method to detect increasing dispersion, shifts, and trends depends on the SD of the method. If the procedure has a broad "acceptable" range, then small increases in imprecision, shifts, or trends likely will be lost in the overall scatter of the data. Amador showed that sudden new biases became obvious only when they were 1.5 times the SD.[24] Imprecise methods lull the analyst into a false sense of confidence; shifts and trends occur, but the method remains in control.

Levey-Jennings chart limits cannot be based solely on statistical criteria developed during periods of good performance. Grannis and Caragher recommend that allowable limits of error be based on ±2.2 SD developed during an "extended period of good performance."[25] They also recommend that the limits undergo periodic review and be

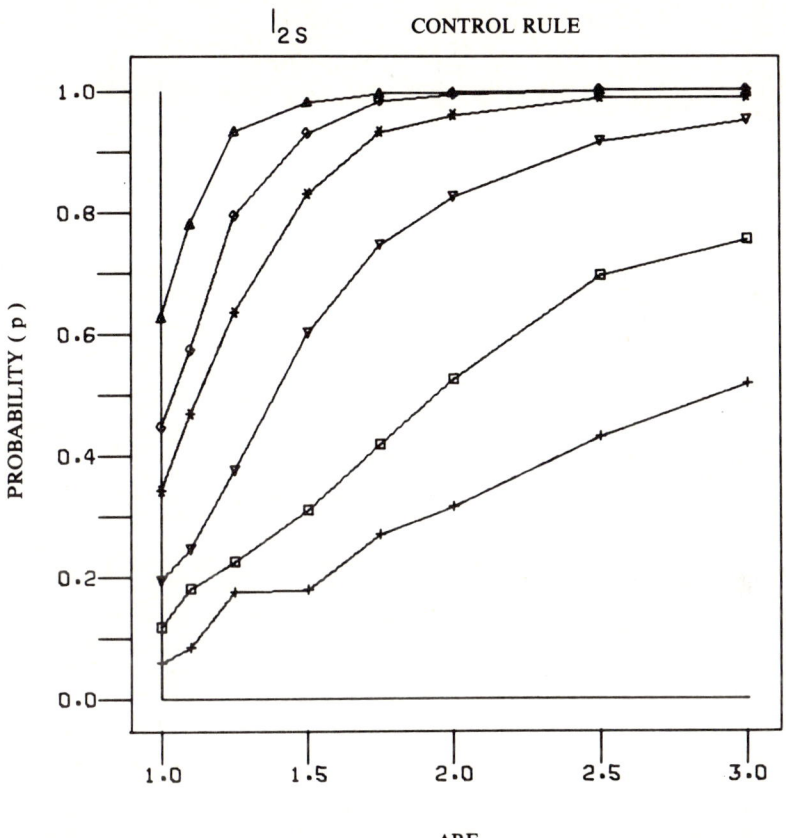

FIGURE 8-6
Power of the 1_{2s} control rule for detecting random error. The number of controls represented by the curves (top to bottom) are 20, 12, 8, 4, 2, 1. (From Westgard JO, Groth T: Power functions for statistical control rules. *Clin Chem* 1979, 25:863, with permission.)

"revised downwards whenever possible." When the laboratory is showing better performance, they recommend that the allowable limits (for example, ±2.2 SD) should be narrowed.

These recommendations must be revised in terms of current technology and medical needs. If only statistical criteria are used, such as ±2.2 SD, a preposterous situation can develop: Highly precise methods will, by definition, have small limits; medically unimportant outliers will create unnecessary concern and reanalysis. Less precise methods will have broader quality control limits; here, an outlier of the same magnitude as above will be inside the acceptable limits. In general, more frequent outliers occur with narrower ±SD limits.[26] The limits of acceptability must consider analytic reality, medical needs, and analytic goals. In light of this problem, the College of American Pathologists has chosen "fixed criteria" for selected chemistry survey results (see Chapter 1).

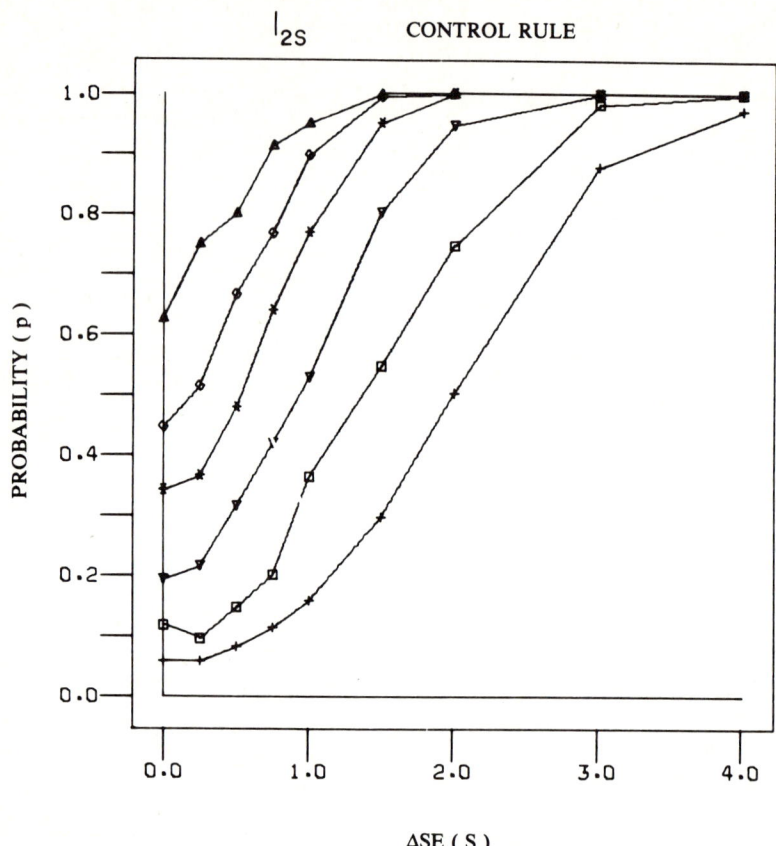

FIGURE 8-7
Power of the 1_{2s} control rule for detecting systematic error. The number of controls represented by the curves (top to bottom) are 20, 12, 8, 4, 2, 1. (From Westgard JO, Groth T: Power functions for statistical control rules. *Clin Chem* 1979, 25:863, with permission.)

ALLOWABLE ERROR IN MEDICAL NEEDS CONTEXT

Defining Allowable Error

Error can be defined as deviation of the measured value from the true value. Bias can be estimated by repetitive analysis of samples with known content of analyte. Error includes both bias and random analytic variation. Barnett used experts in the field and users of clinical laboratory data to define acceptable error.[27,28] These criteria are called *medically useful precision limits* and generally are broader than current state-of-the-art analytical precisions. Other criteria that have been suggested are Tonk's rule, or one-fourth of the reference range, or ±10 percent, whichever is less.[29] Cotlove et al. suggested the "tolerable analytic variability" is 50 percent of the total biologic variation;[30] the latter is defined as the combination of the inter- and intraindividual variability.[31]

TABLE 8-4
PERFORMANCE CHARACTERISTICS OF CONTROL RULES

Control rule	Rule definition	Number of controls	Probability of false rejection	Probability of detecting a 2-SD shift	Probability of detecting a doubling of SD
1_{2S}	Use of Shewhart-type control chart for single observations with control set as the mean ±2 SD	2 4 8	0.10 0.18 0.33	— — —	— — —
1_{3S}	Use of Shewhart-type control chart for single observation with control limits set as the mean ±3 SD	2 4 8	0.00 0.01 0.02	0.22 0.55 0.68	0.20 0.45 0.65
x:0.01/ R:0.01	Use of Shewhart-type control charts for both the mean and range of a group of N control observations, with control limits set so that the frequency of false rejections is 1%	2 4 8	0.01 0.01 0.01	0.62 0.92 0.99	0.30 0.53 0.65
x:0.05/ R:0.05	Use of Shewhart-type control charts for both the mean and range of a group of N control observations, with control limits set so that the frequency of false rejections is 5%	2 4 8	0.05 0.05 0.05	0.78 0.98 0.99	0.35 0.60 0.80
1_{3S} 2_{2S} 4_{1S} R_{4S} 10_x	Use of Shewhart-type control charts and following combinations of rules: One control observation exceeding 3 SD or Two consecutive control observations exceeding x + 2 SD or x − 2 SD or Four consecutive control observations exceeding x + 1 SD or x − 1 SD or Range of a group of N control observations exceeding 4 SD or Ten consecutive control observations on one side of x	2 4 8	0.00 0.01 0.02	0.38 0.80 0.95	0.25 0.47 0.70

Source: Westgard JO, Groth T, De Verdier C-H: Principles of developing improved quality control procedures. Scand J Clin Lab Invest 1984, 44(suppl 172):19.

Glick[32] recommended that random error be no greater than 20 percent of the population-based reference or therapeutic range, or no greater than 60 percent of the "medical decision range." For glucose, typical population limits are 65 to 115 mg/dl; 20 percent of this range is 10 mg/dl. At 120 mg/dl glucose, the medical decision range would be ±20 mg/dl, and 60 percent of the decision range would be 12 mg/dl. Lindberg and Watson[33] used a "loss to society" approach of a false diagnosis owing to laboratory error; improvements in laboratory precision result in less loss to society. They concluded that there is no simple answer to what is medically acceptable imprecision; the circumstances of test use dictate acceptability. For further discussion of control criteria, see Chapters 1 and 6.

Effect of Changing Precision on Predictive Value

Allowable error can be calculated for a specific test and purpose using one of three models described by Harris.[34] The first model is population screening to detect a biochemical abnormality. The effect of a change in precision on the predictive value of an abnormal test result can be calculated, but a subjective decision remains as to what loss in the predictive value is acceptable. The second model is the effect of increased (or decreased) precision on the ability to detect abnormal values in an individual. In the third model, Harris examines the effects of changes in precision on the ability to detect short-term or long-term trends of an analyte in an individual. Because intraindividual variation can be very significant, less precise measurements compared with those required in the second model appear to be adequate for detection of long-term trends.[34]

As described by Campbell and Owen,[35] Glick,[32] and Harris,[34] allowable error limit should be determined by the diagnostic application and certain other factors as described below. There is no single acceptable analytical error for any test.

Cost to Society of Missed Diagnoses

"Allowable error" will always have a subjective component. What costs to society are acceptable? With overlapping populations, false positive and false negative results are inevitable; the key issues are where the decision point or cutoff value is defined, and the allowance for analytical variability at this decision point.

Lindberg and Watson described the diagnosis of acute appendicitis as a test case.[33] It is desirable to have very few false negatives; a false negative carries greater weight than a false positive. Operating on a few patients with a normal appendix is acceptable, because the cost to society of a missed diagnosis leading to a ruptured appendix or peritonitis is much greater. The relative weights of a false positive and false negative error are subjective decisions. Where is the line to be drawn?

An example in which the laboratory plays a large role is the diagnosis of neonatal hypothyroidism. A false negative (missed) diagnosis carries a much greater cost than a false positive one; a large number of false positives are an acceptable cost. The decision point for the laboratory test used to identify "abnormal" newborns is set to allow for considerable analytical variation. The test must be as sensitive as possible at the cost of specificity. Assuming that thyroxine (T_4) is the primary screening test, hypothyroid and euthyroid neonates will have overlapping T_4 values. The cutoff point should be set to include all the hypothyroid cases (i.e., the highest T_4 found in any hypothyroid patient) plus 4 SD of the analytic variation. If a T_4 of 4 µg/dl includes all hypothyroid cases and the SD of the method is 0.5 µg/dl, then the decision point is 6 µg/dl. Thus, although there may be many false positives to ensure that analytic variation does not adversely affect the ability to identify all hypothyroid patients, any infant with a T_4 below 6 µg/dl should receive further testing to rule out hypothyroidism.

Variables Affecting Allowable Error

In instances where the overlap of well and sick populations is great, more laboratory imprecision is acceptable than in nonoverlapping groups. A change in test precision in the overlap region has much less effect on the predictive value of a positive test [PV(+)] compared with the same test for nonoverlapping populations with a value at a decision point.

In overlapping populations, disease prevalence is a major factor in determining PV(+) (see Table 8-5); the PV(+) may be such that the test is not worth doing regardless of the analytical variability. Watson and Tang showed the lack of value of serum acid phosphatase as a screening test for prostatic cancer;[36] the PV(+) was low owing to considerably overlapping values and low prevalence of the disease. Obviously a PV(+) of 50 percent or less is no better than an (educated) guess.

The data in Table 8-5 assume an overlap of 2.3 percent of the well and sick.[14] A decrease in precision has its greatest effect on PV(+) for tests that have a small interindividual biologic variability (C_B, Table 8-5). Calcium, which has a C_B of about 1 percent, shows the most rapid decline in PV(+) with decreasing prevalence. For glucose and urea nitrogen, which have much larger C_B values, the PV(+) at 10 percent disease prevalence is nearly twice that of calcium.

Medically acceptable error is a subjective value; however, certain circumstances

TABLE 8-5
EFFECT OF PREVALENCE AND CHANGE IN PRECISION ON PV(+)

Test	C_B[a]	C'_A/C_A[b]	PV(+)[c] 50%	PV(+)[c] 10%	PV(+)[c] 1%
Any	20%	1.0	97.7	82.5	30.0
Calcium	0.6%	1.9	87.1	42.9	6.4
Glucose	9.6%	1.5	97.6	81.9	29.1
Urea nitrogen	16.8%	2.3	97.1	78.8	25.3

[a]Percent interindividual biologic variability.
[b]Ratio of "poor" to "good" precision.
[c]Predictive value of a positive test at indicated prevalence.
Source: Adapted from Lott JA, Abbott LB, Koch DD: An evaluation of the Du Pont aca IV: Does it meet medical needs? *Clin Chem* 1985, 31:281.

require that highly precise laboratory values and/or a large number of false positives are acceptable. This is true when the overlap between the well and sick populations is small. An example is a borderline increase of serum gastrin in a patient with Zollinger-Ellison syndrome. A decision must be made regarding further testing: False positives are acceptable owing to the serious consequences of missing a treatable case. This also occurs when prevalence of disease is low and the within-individual biologic variability is small.[37]

INTERLABORATORY SURVEYS

Interlaboratory proficiency surveys, or better, "laboratory improvement programs," provide quality control and management information for participants. Because many laboratories analyze aliquots of the same material, group mean values can be determined that are excellent estimates of the true value if the cohort is large. From survey data, a participating laboratory can determine if its values are biased relative to peer laboratories using the same method, or if the laboratory's variability is generally larger than that of the peer group.

Most surveys report the methods used, statistical data, and how many participants are using a particular method. This provides management information; laboratories tend to abandon obsolete methods or those that give results consistently different from the consensus mean (see Chapter 1). Finally, surveys provide information on the state of the art of common analyses and can provide the basis for goal setting or improvements in methodology. Based on survey data, improved performance in the determination of serum calcium, creatinine, and thyroxine were recommended in a symposium on analytical goals.[38] Target values for improvement are shown in Fig. 8-8; calcium and creatinine are analytes that require further attention to improve precision.

Professional Organizations Providing Surveys

Three professional groups provide most of the external proficiency surveys in clinical chemistry in North America (further information is available in Chapter 14). The College of American Pathologists (CAP) survey is the largest and most comprehensive evaluation of the common and unusual tests performed in clinical chemistry laboratories. The American Association for Clinical Chemistry survey is limited mainly to therapeutic drugs; it has a continuing education component dealing with use of drugs, toxicity, methods, pharmacokinetics, and so on. The American Association of Bioanalysts provides surveys in clinical chemistry with a broad menu of tests.

Government Agencies Providing Surveys

The largest government survey is prepared by the Centers for Disease Control (CDC). Their menu is fairly comprehensive although smaller than that of the CAP. Many state health departments and regulatory agencies provide surveys. Prominent among these are the programs in New York, Georgia, and Wisconsin.

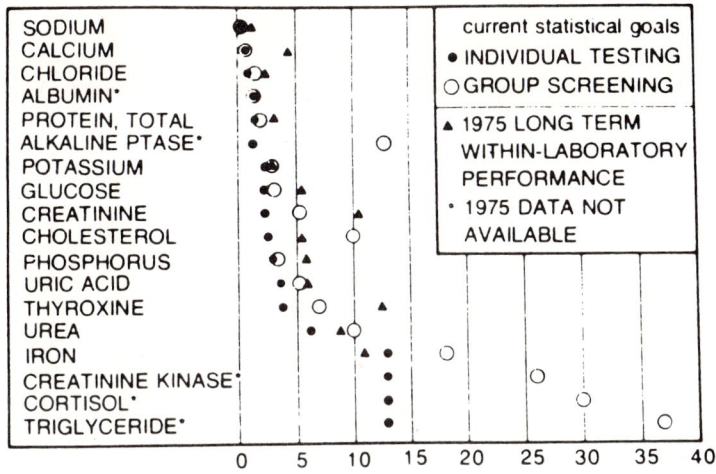

FIGURE 8-8
Analytical goals in clinical chemistry. (From *Aspen Conference on Analytical Goals.* Skokie, IL, College of American Pathologists, 1976, p 5, with permission.)

Other Surveys

Manufacturers of control materials and other groups provide surveys. Because the availability of these programs changes frequently, laboratories should discuss their needs with manufacturers' representatives. For example, the University of Pittsburgh offers a survey program for cyclosporine.*

SPECIMEN PROBLEMS: ENZYME ANALYSIS

CAP Enzyme Survey

Interlaboratory surveys of serum enzyme analyses present problems not encountered with common analytes such as cholesterol or glucose. Laboratories participating in the CAP Enzyme Survey showed marked heterogeneity in their methods, units of reporting, and temperature for the commonly performed serum enzyme tests: ALT, ALP, AST, CK, and LD.[39] Interlaboratory comparisons are difficult or impossible, because of diversity produced by these many small peer groups. Only the largest peer group, those using the Du Pont *aca*, had enough laboratories to permit calculation of meaningful statistics. To advance the state of quality control of enzyme analyses, a method was developed to permit merging data from all participants and to provide statistical evaluation to the smallest peer groups as well as to peer "groups" of one.

---

* For further information, see *Therapeutic Drug Monitoring* 1985, 7:129.

Relative Units

The first approach devised by Grannis et al. for merging the data was the calculation of "relative units" (RU), which are the laboratory's stated results converted to a common base.[40] From its inception in 1975 until 1983, the CAP Enzyme Survey consisted of four mailings per year of six samples each.[41] The six samples had graded enzyme activities; they differed in amount of enzyme supplement added to a base serum pool. The RU were approximately equal to the percent of enzyme supplement added to the base pool. Samples were all prepared and lyophilized at the same time, and extensive experience showed that they were stable at least 1 year.[41]

Theoretically, all participants should get the same RU for a given enzyme in a Survey. For any enzyme, the RU might be 5, 10, 20, 30, 50, 70 for the six samples in one mailing. Because slight changes in activities occurred during lyophilization, the RU were calculated after the results were received. The deviations between the actual percent supplementation and the "apparent" supplementation, however, were slight.[40] Most laboratories recovered the expected RU, so it was possible to identify laboratories reporting outliers.

Regression analysis of known RU (X) against a laboratory's reported values (Y) for any enzyme ideally gives a straight line with a correlation coefficient close to one. Scatter about the line was a measure of a laboratory's variability. A change in the slope of this line within-year and between mailings was a measure of analytical and calibration stability. Thus, despite divergency of methods, it was possible to estimate the short- and long-term variability of a laboratory's enzyme analyses.

Revised CAP Reporting Scheme

The reporting system was simplified somewhat in 1982, and now the Enzyme Survey provides more familiar statistics.[42] As before, multiple samples are analyzed for each enzyme; "the short-term CV" reflects the scatter about the regression line of expected versus actual results; and the "long-term CV" is a measure of within-year analytical stability, that is, a change in the slope of the line. A realistic goal is a short-term CV of 3 percent and a long-term goal of 6 percent; the majority of laboratories in the current CAP Enzyme Survey are able to meet these goals.[42]

Source of Tissue Enzymes for Supplementation

Although it would be preferable, cost and procurement difficulties have prevented the Enzyme Survey from using human sources for enzyme supplements. Early experience with ALP revealed that participants with more than one method showed good inter-method agreement for patient specimens, but a poor one for Enzyme Survey Serum. The problem was traced to the use of calf-intestine ALP, an enzyme unlike human liver or bone ALP.[3] A human-equivalent ALP source is under active study at this time. Porcine heart ALT, AST, CK, and LD have been shown to be satisfactory substitutes for the equivalent human-source enzymes.[39,43]

RESOLVING ANALYTIC ERROR

When an out-of-control situation arises in the laboratory, it is often difficult to identify if the problem arises from the instrumentation, reagents, or standardization. The use of interrelated samples in a constant, pooled human serum matrix can often resolve the problem. These materials have several advantages. Because these materials are prepared from pooled sera, they mimic patient specimens closely. Only the analytes of interest vary from specimen to specimen; the concentrations of protein, other analytes, and possible interferents are constant.

Reference-grade materials can be used as the supplement for some analytes; with careful weighing, the concentration added to the pool can be calculated. More than one analyte can be checked at a time. If an enzyme is being investigated, the supplement can contain, in addition to the enzyme, a simple analyte such as NaCl. If, upon analysis for sodium or chloride, the expected linear relationships are obtained, then the specimens were prepared correctly. If the enzyme results are unsatisfactory, the fault lies not with the specimens but with the method, instrument, or some other problem.

The supplementing material need not be highly purified; crude organ extracts can be used successfully for enzyme tests. For simple analytes such as sodium, chloride, glucose, and uric acid, pure materials should be used, because this permits calculation of the expected "delta" values (see below).

Example Case

Uric acid is the test analyte and creatinine has been added to permit checking if the samples have been prepared properly. Table 8-6 gives directions for preparation of interrelated specimens.

Analyze the specimens for uric acid and creatinine. If an independent method is available for uric acid, use it also for the six interrelated specimens. The values determined by analysis for samples 1 and 6 are used in the calculations. Incorrect values for uric acid as determined by analysis are unimportant; the data are still usable. Calculations are shown in Table 8-7.

If the deltas for the control analyte, creatinine, are very similar, and the found values are very close to the expected values, then the samples were properly prepared. If the deltas for the test analyte, uric acid, are highly variable, the method has poor precision. If values increase with increasing concentration of uric acid, the method has a positive proportional bias. If values decrease with increasing concentration of uric acid, the method has a negative proportional bias. If a plot of measured uric acid versus percent of pool A in the samples is not straight, then the response is nonlinear or there is a loss of linearity at higher concentrations.

Operational Lines

The analytic results for tests fall on an "operational line," which is a plot of found (Y) versus expected (X) analytic values.[44] Typical operational lines are shown in Fig. 8-9;

TABLE 8-6
PREPARATION OF INTERRELATED SPECIMENS WITH A URIC ACID SUPPLEMENT

1. Pool about 60 ml of fresh patient serum. Use only clean, nonturbid, nonhemolyzed, nonicteric sera. Strain through gauze to remove small fibrin clots. This is the "base pool."

2. Prepare the uric acid supplementing solution. Prepare on day of use. Do not add formaldehyde if a uricase method is being used.

Uric acid (reagent grade or equivalent)	100 mg (weight to nearest 0.1 mg)
Creatinine	100 mg (weight to nearest 0.1 mg)
Lithium carbonate	100 mg
Distilled H_2O, enough to make	100 ml of solution

3. Dissolve the Li_2CO_3 in 80 ml H_2O, add the uric acid and creatinine, dissolve, and bring to 100 ml in volumetric flask with distilled H_2O.

4. Prepare two pools as follows:

   Pool A: 25 ml base pool + 2 ml supplement (1 mg uric acid + 1 mg creatine/ml)
   Pool B: 25 ml base pool + 2 ml 154 mmol/liter NaCl (saline)

   (Note: The concentration of the uric acid in the supplement is about 10 to 20 times normal, and the volume of the supplement used is about 5 to 10% of the total volume of pool A. The volume of the supplement is kept low to prevent excessive dilution of the base-pool matrix.)

5. Prepare interrelated specimens as follows:

Specimen number	1	2	3	4	5	6
Pool A, ml	5	4	3	2	1	0
Pool B, ml	0	1	2	3	4	5
Total volume, ml	5	5	5	5	5	5

   - Note that the matrix of the interrelated specimens is constant.
   - The difference in uric acid and creatinine concentration, i.e., delta concentration, between adjacent specimens is constant if the specimens have been prepared properly.

---

they can be of great help in delineating analytic problems. Ideally, the operational line should have a slope of 1.00 and an intercept of zero.

Preparation of Operational Lines How are operational lines determined? A simple procedure is to analyze CAP Survey Serum or other serum-based material of known content and the calibrating materials being used by the laboratory. CAP Survey Serum has been analyzed by thousands of laboratories; the values can be assumed to be correct or an excellent estimate of the true values. Some examples of CAP data from the 1984 C-A Comprehensive Chemistry Survey are given in Table 8-8. Results for the well-accepted methods are shown together with the mean of all results; the means are extremely close, which supports the premise that extreme outliers become unimportant when the cohort is large.

TABLE 8-7
CALCULATIONS FOR EXAMPLE CASE

Calculate the expected values as:

$$\text{Pool A conc.} = \frac{25 \text{ (conc. base pool)} + 2 \text{ (conc. supplement)}}{27}$$

$$\text{Pool B conc.} = \frac{25 \text{ (conc. base pool)} + 0}{27}$$

Sample 1 = pool A

$$\text{Sample 2} = \frac{80 \text{ (pool A conc.)} + 20 \text{ (pool B conc.)}}{100}$$

$$\text{Sample 3} = \frac{60 \text{ (pool A conc.)} + 40 \text{ (pool B conc.)}}{100}$$

Etc.

The "delta" values are simply the difference in concentration of uric acid or creatinine of adjacent specimens; i.e.,

Delta 1, uric acid = uric acid$_1$ − uric acid$_2$
Delta 2, uric acid = uric acid$_2$ − uric acid$_3$, etc.

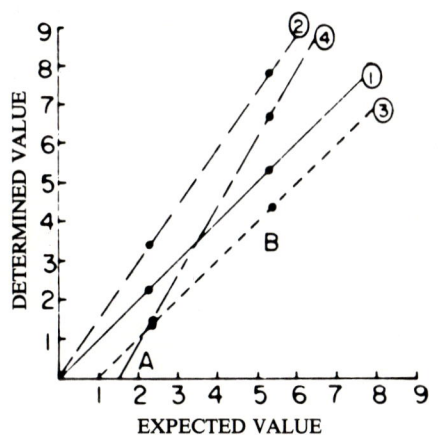

FIGURE 8-9
Illustration of some possible operational lines. When determined values are compared to expected values, the results should ideally correspond and fall along line 1. Actual results may fall along lines 2, 3, 4, depending on the standard curve used for the determination. The data illustrate typical "operational lines" for analytic procedures. The operational lines can indicate specific kinds of method misstandardization. (From Grannis GF, Gruemer H-D, Lott JA, et al: Proficiency evaluation of clinical chemistry laboratories. *Clin Chem* 1972, 18:222, with permission.)

TABLE 8-8
DATA FROM CAP C-A 1984 COMPREHENSIVE CHEMISTRY SURVEY[a]

Analyte	No. labs	Method	C-1		C-2		C-3	
			Mean	%CV	Mean	%CV	Mean	%CV
Albumin	2150	Bromocresol green	4.1	4.5	2.9	5.9	4.7	4.6
	3477	All	4.1	4.7	2.9	6.0	4.7	4.6
Bilirubin, total	2076	Jendrassik-Grof	5.0	7.0	1.0	14	3.2	6.3
	5729	All	5.1	7.7	1.1	17	3.2	7.2
Calcium	4907	Cresolphthalein complexone	12.6	3.8	9.7	3.6	8.0	3.6
	5724	All	12.6	4.1	9.7	3.9	8.1	3.9
Chloride	2017	Mercury-thiocyanate	114	3.0	97	2.5	113	2.4
	5734	All	115	2.7	97	2.5	114	2.2
Cortisol	1072	All	11.0	12.4	7.53	12	26.1	11
Creatinine	1889	Rate picrate	4.9	5.6	1.1	10	2.1	7.1
	6151	All	4.8	5.3	1.0	11	2.1	6.6
Glucose	3083	Hexokinase	285	4.4	103	5.3	50	8.2
	6823	All	283	4.7	102	5.5	49	7.5
Phosphorus	2194	UV molybdate	7.2	5.1	4.4	4.9	2.5	8.5
	3451	All	7.2	4.9	4.5	5.0	2.5	8.3
Potassium	2454	Flame	5.9	2.1	3.5	2.7	2.6	3.9
	6292	All	5.9	2.6	3.5	2.7	2.6	3.7

Analyte	No. labs	Method	C-4 Mean	C-4 %CV	C-4 Mean	C-4 %CV	C-5 Mean	C-5 %CV
Sodium	2428	Flame	147	1.6	125	1.7	145	1.4
	6243	All	148	1.9	125	1.6	146	1.9
Protein	3370	All: Biuret	6.5	3.2	4.6	3.6	7.4	3.2
Urea nitrogen	3324	Urease/GLDH	49	5.9	14	9.2	26	6.1
	6450	All	49	5.7	15	9.0	26	4.8
Uric acid	4497	Uricase	7.8	8.6	4.2	7.7	5.8	7.4
	5897	All	7.8	8.3	4.2	7.9	5.9	7.0

Analyte	No. labs	Method	C-4 Mean	C-4 %CV	C-5 Mean	C-5 %CV
Cholesterol	4636	Enzymatic	267	6.2	315	6.4
	5122	All	267	6.4	3.5	6.5
Triglycerides	1242	Enzymatic w/o blank	242	5.6	283	5.4
	2998	All	257	11	302	12

[a]In column 3, when a method is given, it is the most widely used procedure. In all cases, it is the automated version. Values expressed in common laboratory units. (Used with permission of College of American Pathologists, 5202 Old Orchard Road, Skokie, IL 60077.)

A plot of the results from the known material (Y) versus the calibrators (X) used in the laboratory produces the operational line. Grannis showed that laboratories produced the expected relationships of interrelated survey samples, suggesting that the mean values of all laboratories are excellent estimates of the true values.[45] For serum calcium, the mean survey results by atomic absorption agreed with the values determined by the National Bureau of Standards using an exacting method.[45] Assuming that the survey samples have not deteriorated, they are the most widely available materials that mimic patient specimens and for which an excellent estimate of the true value of the concentrations of the common analytes is available.

Analysis of Operational Lines The types of operational lines in Fig. 8-9 are summarized in Table 8-9. For line 2, the mirror image about line 1 could be imagined; that is, all values are too low by a proportional amount owing to standards that are more concentrated than believed. Line 4 occurs in an interesting way with instruments using single-point calibration if the baseline is set incorrectly.[46] Only results at the calibration point, or close to it, will be correct; if the baseline is, say, 0.05 rather than zero A, then all results below the standard will be too high, and all results above the standard will be too low. The error is not proportional to concentration, but is related to it in a complex way as calculated by the following equations:

$$\text{Percent error} = \left(\frac{(A_{observed} - A_{correct})}{A_{correct}} \right) \times 100$$

$$= Ab \left(\frac{1 - Cu/Cs}{As(Cu/Cs)} \right) \times 100$$

Ab is the absorbance setting of the baseline, As is the absorbance of the standard, Cs is the concentration of the standard, and Cu is the concentration of the unknown. The absorbance of the standard plays a role; the worst errors occur with specimens less concentrated than the standard and with standards having low absorbances.[46]

TABLE 8-9
ANALYSIS OF OPERATIONAL LINES IN FIG. 8-9

Line no.	Possible problem(s)	Constant bias	Proportional bias
1	None	No	No
2	Standards less concentrated than believed: incorrect preparation, dilution, decomposition, etc.	No	Yes
3	Inappropriate blank, all values too low by a fixed amount	Yes	No
4	Use of single-point calibration and inappropriate baseline; or combination of 2 and 3 above	?	?
5	Nonlinear response; loss of analytical sensitivity	No	?

LABORATORY MISTAKES

Defining Blunders

A mistake or blunder, as distinct from analytical error, can result in grossly incorrect results leaving the laboratory. Much attention has been given to improving precision; the worst culprit, mistakes, deserves more attention in the laboratory. Typically, physicians are more aware of laboratory mistakes than the laboratory staff.

Blunder Detection

Grannis et al. estimated the mistake rate in a clinical chemistry laboratory based on suspect values referred to the quality control section of the laboratory.[44] Laboratory mistakes, confirmed before they were counted, occurred at the rate of 3.5 percent. Northam estimated errors from a proficiency survey:[47] 13 percent of the outliers were more than 10 SD from the mean, 22 percent were between 5 and 10 SD, and 65 percent were between 3.2 and 5 SD from the mean. A 5-SD error for sodium was 11 mmol/liter. Some of the "worst" laboratories had a blunder rate of 10 percent.

In the CAP Enzyme Survey, specimen mix-ups are readily detected, because the results from a set of specimens within a mailing must be in a known sequence of increasing or decreasing values. Lott et al. estimated the blunder rate in the Enzyme Survey at 4.1 percent; the mistakes probably occurred because of specimen mix-ups.[39]

Types of Mistakes

Grannis et al. provided a rather complete list of typical blunders.[44] The most serious blunders were mislabeling errors and misplacing specimens in an analyzer tray. The latter error can affect all the specimens in the tray owing to an indexing error. Other types of mistakes were chart reading errors, calculation errors, inappropriate reagents or standards, neglect, unrecognized instrument problems, and mentally calculated results.

Reducing Laboratory Mistakes

Is a 3 to 4 percent mistake rate the irreducible minimum? For a clinical chemistry laboratory of our size, this means 60,000 mistakes per year or 164 per day! Based on our observations and those of Northam, we suggest that procedures like those listed in Table 8-10 be implemented to reduce blunders.[47]

CONCLUSIONS

Analytic variability of procedures in clinical chemistry can be determined with the reference sample method. The Levey-Jennings chart is an eminently useful tool; the use of the Shewart multirule system makes this tool even more useful.

Acceptable error must consider medical needs. For many analytes, such as glucose,

TABLE 8-10
PREVENTION OF MISTAKES

1 Label specimen at the bedside with a machine-readable label.
2 Sample labeled specimen (do not use transfer tubes, "pour-off" tubes, etc.).
3 Use as much automation with self-diagnostic steps and internal checks to detect malfunctions as possible.
4 Label reagents with machine-readable tags.
5 Do not perform manual calculations.
6 Check today's patient results against previous results.[48] Use multivariate computer checks of single results and sets of results to flag impossible values[49] (see Chapter 16).
7 Employ well-trained laboratory staff who can quickly identify unlikely results or unusual situations.[50]
8 Use computerized system for accessioning, interfacing equipment, reporting, log generation, inquiry, test requisitioning, calculations, identifying out-of-control results.
9 Keep the steps or procedures between specimen receipt (or collection) and the report delivery to an absolute minimum.[44]

the current level of analytic precision is better than what is required for medical needs. For other tests, greater precision is needed in certain medical contexts—for example, serum creatinine in the 1 to 2 mg/dl range for the renal transplant patient with possible rejection,[37] and calcium in the patient with "borderline" hypercalcemia. With increasing mechanization and computerization, it may be possible to reduce laboratory mistakes; the latter is an area that needs more attention.

APPENDIX: Preparation of Controls from Pooled Serum

Collection Pool leftover patient serum and reject any specimens that are visibly icteric, lipemic, turbid, or hemolyzed. Freeze sera in plastic bottles, and allow for expansion of the pool while freezing; that is, do not overfill bottles. Continue to collect pool and freeze until 3 to 4 liters are on hand.

Filtration Thaw sera by placing the plastic bottles in warm water, and combine sera into one container. Add 3 g of benzoic acid per liter of pool, and mix well. The benzoic acid is added to prevent loss of glucose. Strain through a plug of glass wool to remove fibrin clots. Analyze the pool, and supplement with the desired analytes.

Packaging Place a rubber hose into the pool, and fill the hose with pool. Pinch off one end. This hose will serve as a "vein," and plain 3-, 5-, 7-, or 10-ml labeled, evacuated tubes are used to collect pool from the "vein" and to store the finished product. Stir the pool with a magnetic stirrer while filling the evacuated tubes. Protect hands with plastic gloves.

Storage Store the prepared tubes at $-20°C$ in the dark until needed.

Stability Glucose, urea, phosphorus, cholesterol, total protein, albumin, globulin, chloride, Na^+, K^+, bilirubin, creatinine, and uric acid are stable for nine months. Low activities of amylase, AST, ALT, LD, and alkaline phosphatase also are stable for this time period, but high levels of enzymes and CO_2 are unstable even in frozen samples.[13]

REFERENCES

1. Caragher TE, Grannis GF: Performance evaluation of multi-channel analyzers by use of linearly-related survey specimens. *Clin Chem* 1978, 24:403.
2. Lott JA, Wenger WC, Massion CG, et al: Interlaboratory survey of enzyme analyses: IV. Human versus porcine tissue as source of creatine kinase for survey serum. *Am J Clin Pathol* 1982, 78:626.
3. O'Donnell NJ, Lott JA: Intralaboratory survey of alkaline phosphatase methods. *Am J Clin Pathol* 1981, 76:567.
4. Pope WT, Caragher TE, Grannis GF: An evaluation of ethylene glycol-based liquid specimens for use in quality control. *Clin Chem* 1979, 25:413.
5. Cali JP, Mandel J, Moore L, et al: *A Referee Method for the Determination of Calcium in Serum*. NBS Special Publication 260-36, US Dept of Commerce, National Bureau of Standards, catalog no C13.10:260. Washington, DC, US Government Printing Office, 1972.
6. Neese JW, Duncan P, Bayse D, et al: *Development and Evaluation of a Hexokinase/Glucose-6 Phosphate Dehydrogenase Procedure for Use as a National Glucose Reference Method*, US Dept of Health, Education and Welfare publication No. (CDC)778830. Atlanta, Centers for Disease Control, 1976.
7. Faulkner WR, Meites S (eds): *Selected Methods for the Small Clinical Chemistry Laboratory*. Washington, DC, American Association for Clinical Chemistry, 1982.
8. Ginsberg AL, Conrad ME: Australian antigen in laboratory control serum solutions: An unnecessary hazard. *N Engl J Med* 1972, 287:1097.
9. Schultz A, Gates L: Preparation of an HB_SAG negative serum standard for use with the SMA 6/60. *Lab Med* 1978, 9:19.
10. Williams JS, Taylor L, Kuchmak M, et al: Preparation of hypercholesterolemic and/or hypertriglyceridemic sera for lipid determinations. *Clin Chim Acta* 1970, 28:247.
11. Rosalki, SB: Preparation of stable creatine kinase isoenzyme controls (MM, MB, BB). *Clin Chem* 1976, 22:1753.
12. Proksch GJ, Bonderman DP: Preparation of optically clear lyophilized human serum for use in preparing control material. *Clin Chem* 1976, 22:456.
13. Barnett RN: Quality control, in *Clinical Laboratory Statistics*. Boston, Little, Brown, 1971, pp 72–89.
14. Lott JA, Abbott LB, Koch DD: An evaluation of the Du Pont aca IV: Does it meet medical needs? *Clin Chem* 1985, 31:281.
15. Levey S, Jennings EF: The use of control charts in the clinical laboratory. *Am J Clin Pathol* 1950, 20:1059.
16. Allen JR, Earp R, Farrell EC Jr, et al: Analytical bias in a quality control scheme. *Clin Chem* 1969, 15:1039.
17. Lott JA, Turner K: Evaluation of Trinder's glucose oxidase method for measuring glucose in serum and urine. *Clin Chem* 1975, 21:1754.
18. Westgard JO, Barry PL, Hunt MR: A multi-rule Shewhart chart for quality control in clinical chemistry. *Clin Chem* 1981, 27:493.
19. Westgard JO, Groth T, Aronsson T, et al: Performance characteristics of rules for internal quality control: Probabilities for false rejection and error detection. *Clin Chem* 1977, 23:1857.
20. Westgard JO, Falk H, Groth T: Influence of a between-run component of variation, choice of control limits, and shape of error distribution on the performance characteristics of rules for internal quality control. *Clin Chem* 1979, 25:394.
21. Westgard JO, Groth T: Power functions for statistical control rules. *Clin Chem* 1979, 25:863.

22. Westgard JO: An internal quality control system for the assessment of quality and the assurance of test rules. *Scand J Clin Lab Invest* 1984, 44:315.
23. Westgard JO, Groth T, De Verdier C-H: Principles of developing improved quality control procedures. *Scand J Clin Lab Invest* 1984, 44(suppl 172):19.
24. Amador E: Quality control by the reference sample method. *Am J Clin Pathol* 1968, 50:360.
25. Grannis GF, Caragher TE: Quality-control programs in clinical chemistry. *CRC Crit Rev Clin Lab Sci* 1977, 7:327.
26. Gooszen JAH: The use of control charts in the clinical laboratory. *Clin Chim Acta* 1960, 5:431.
27. Barnett RN: Medical significance of laboratory results. *Am J Clin Pathol* 1968, 50:671.
28. Skendzel LP, Barnett RN, Platt R: Medically useful criteria for analytic performance of laboratory tests. *Am J Clin Pathol* 1985, 83:200.
29. Tonks, DB. A study of the accuracy and precision of clinical chemistry determinations in 170 Canadian laboratories. *Clin Chem* 1963, 9:217.
30. Cotlove E, Harris EK, Williams GZ: Biological and analytic components of variation in long-term studies of serum constituents in normal subjects: III. Physiological and medical implications. *Clin Chem* 1970, 16:1028.
31. Harris EK, Kanofsky P, Shakarji G, et al: Biological and analytical components of variation in long-term studies of serum constituents in normal subjects: II. Estimating biological components of variation. *Clin Chem* 1970, 16:1022.
32. Glick JH: Expression of random analytical error as a percentage of the range of clinical interest. *Clin Chem* 1976, 22:475.
33. Lindberg DAB, Watson FR: Impression of laboratory determinations and diagnostic accuracy: Theoretical considerations. *Meth Inform Med* 1974, 13:151.
34. Harris EK: Statistical principles underlying analytic goal-setting in clinical chemistry. *Am J Clin Pathol* 1979, 72:374.
35. Campbell DG, Owen JA: Clinical laboratory error in perspective. *Clin Biochem* 1968, 1:3.
36. Watson RA, Tang DB: The predictive value of prostatic acid phosphatase as a screening test for prostatic cancer. *N Engl J Med* 1980, 303:497.
37. Lott, JA, Hebert LA, Baer SG: Use of computer graphics to assess trends in glomerular filtration rate (GFR) from sequential serum creatinine values. *J Med Tech* 1984, 1:361.
38. *Aspen Conference on Analytical Goals*. Skokie, IL, College of American Pathologists, 1976, p 5.
39. Lott JA, O'Donnell NJ, Grannis GF: Interlaboratory survey of enzyme analyses: III. Does College of American Pathologists' Survey Serum mimic clinical specimens? *Am J Clin Pathol* 1981, 76:554.
40. Grannis GF, Massion CG, Batsakis JG: The 1978 College of American Pathologists Survey of analyses of five serum enzymes by 450 laboratories. *Am J Clin Pathol* 1979, 72:285.
41. Lott JA, Massion CG: Interlaboratory quality control of enzyme analyses: The CAP experience, in Homburger HA (ed): *Clinical and Analytical Concepts in Enzymology*. Skokie, IL, College of American Pathologists, 1983, pp 233–265.
42. Lott JA, Gilmore BF, Massion CG: Interlaboratory survey of enzyme analyses: V. A simplified method of reporting participants' data. *Am J Clin Pathol* 1983, 80:577.
43. Lott JA, Tholen DW, Massion CG: Survey of serum enzyme analyses: Human tissues as a source of enzymes. *Arch Pathol Lab Med* 1984, 108:949.
44. Grannis GF, Gruemer H-D, Lott JA, et al: Proficiency evaluation of clinical chemistry laboratories. *Clin Chem* 1972, 18:222.
45. Grannis GF: Studies of the reliability of constituent target values established in a large interlaboratory survey. *Clin Chem* 1976, 22:1027.

46 Lott JA: Hazards of incorrect use of the calibration wheel and single-point calibration. *Lab Med* 1977, 8:25.
47 Northam BE: Whither automation? *Ann Clin Biochem* 1981, 18:189.
48 Ladenson JH: Patients as their own controls: Use of the computer to identify "laboratory error." *Clin Chem* 1975, 21:1648.
49 Lindberg DA, Van Peenen HS, Couch RD: Patterns in clinical chemistry. *Am J Clin Pathol* 1965, 44:315.
50 Lott, JA: Laboratory personnel: The most important aspect of quality control. *Med Instrument* 1974, 8:22.

CHAPTER 9

QUALITY ASSURANCE IN HEMATOLOGY

Paul Bachner, M.D.

Specific problems are inherent in analysis of anticoagulated specimens containing multiple cellular elements embedded within a complex fluid matrix. These concerns as well as those generic to the laboratory as a whole must be taken into account when developing a comprehensive quality assurance program for the hematology laboratory. Hematology specimens analyzed in previous decades by tedious manual methods, or more recently by relatively simple instruments susceptible to calibration and control of individual analytes, must now be analyzed by method-specific and complex multiparameter instruments. Calibration and control materials are usually sampled in an integral fashion, as is the patient specimen. The need to provide calibrator and control stability produces cell and matrix artifacts that have variable effects on the individual measured parameters. These effects are frequently instrument/reagent specific. Because the measured and calculated red cell parameters are related in a complex fashion, calibration and process control protocols are difficult to develop. The entire process is further complicated by the absence of a primary standard for any of the measured or derived analytes except hemoglobin.

The development of appropriate quality assurance strategies for the hematology laboratory must, therefore, accommodate these somewhat unusual impediments to calibration and process control. These strategies must also address sources of preanalytic (sampling), analytic, and postanalytic (reporting, communication, and interpretation) variation and error. Some sources of error are generic to all laboratory settings, but others inhere to the hematology lab and include sampling and anticoagulant artifacts, spurious analytic results arising from the interaction of pathophysiologic events with the complex biases of instrument detection systems, and the special problem of establishing reference ranges for hematologic parameters subject to diurnal, physiologic, environmental, age, and sex variation.

We will review problems of instrument selection, calibration, and process control for the common analytes and derived results currently subsumed under the broad clinical rubric of "CBC" as well as measurements that are becoming available coincident to development of new instrumentation. Candidate methods for quality control, utilizing control materials, patient specimens, and patient-derived data, will be presented in the expectation that they will assist the reader to select intelligently from the options offered to suit local circumstances and philosophy. For rigorous definitions specific to hematology, refer to the ICSH Proposed Definitions: 1980.[1] The term "quality assurance" is used in this chapter to denote the totality of procedures—cognitive and mechanical—designed to minimize or identify sources of preanalytic, analytic, and postanalytic variation that may affect the provision of high-quality patient care including patient preparation, specimen procurement and handling, test and method selection, reporting formats, and turnaround time, as well as the classical analytic safeguards customarily referred to as quality control or process control. Although much of this chapter will be devoted to the latter concept, it is our prejudice that events preceding and following introduction of a clinical specimen into an analytic system may have an impact on the patient that is equal to or greater than the specific "result" of the test. The cognitive process that occurs in the mind of the physician at the initiation and termination of the testing loop should not be ignored in attempting to define the boundaries of this quality assurance process.

INSTRUMENTATION

Selection of Instrumentation

Among the factors usually considered in selecting instrumentation are cost of acquisition and operation (labor and consumables); throughput; ease of operation and training; reliability (downtime); accuracy/linearity/sensitivity/precision data; and manufacturer support and reputation. Other factors considered in the selection are harder to define, but relate in a broad sense to how the proposed instrumentation "fits" with the existing mix of space, personnel, and instrument configurations. Thought also should be given to the hard-copy format produced by hematology analyzers in terms of adaptability to institutional charting requirements and ability to produce multiple copies for record-keeping, regulatory, or quality control (QC) needs. Most instruments now available have integral microprocessor capabilities that allow for some flexibility in formatting of reports and QC data. As clinical laboratories acquire minicomputer or networked microcomputer systems, reporting, archiving, and QC formats will become increasingly independent of instrumental constraints; however, prudent selection of analyzers and computer hardware/software should be made with the understanding that the process of "interfacing" may require more than the presence of an RS-232C port and may be considerably more complex than is suggested by the claims and promotional literature of either the instrument or computer system vendor.[2]

The astute purchaser of hematology instrumentation is usually cognizant of the above factors: it is less often recognized that selecting instrumentation on the basis of process control ease and the ability to utilize available QC materials, techniques, and programs may be a prudent and cost-effective strategy. Although the number and variety of automated and semiautomated hematology analyzers competing for a share of the market defy cataloging, most multiparameter systems use either electronic impedance or optical detection techniques coupled with various options for sample processing, hydraulics, and computation. As we shall discuss later in greater detail, sources of bias and analytic variation that are attributes of these systems may be identified not only by generic analytic system (i.e., electronic impedance) but also within the apparently homogeneous analytic line of a specific manufacturer.[3] Familiarity with these biases, best achieved by a review of the literature and College of American Pathologists (CAP) interlaboratory studies,[3-6] will allow for implementation of relatively simple and inexpensive QC protocols.

Instrument Function and Preventive Maintenance

Operating personnel and those responsible for implementation and approval of quality assurance programs must be familiar with the principles, methodology, and operating characteristics of their instrumentation as well as the manufacturer's claimed and field-validated data about performance, sensitivity, precision, and linearity. Meticulous preventive maintenance and protocols to ensure the reliability and integrity of replacement components, supplies, and reagents—particularly those susceptible to change during shipment and storage—should constitute the foundation of all programs of quality assurance and process control.[7]

Principles of Major Instrumentation

Operating principles of instrumentation currently available from major manufacturers differ considerably, and these differences will be alluded to in subsequent sections. The following summary in no way attempts to be complete, and the reader is referred to many excellent discussions about specific instrumentation.[8-12] This review concentrates on the instrumentation of only a few manufacturers, thus reflecting readily available literature and recognizing that the instrumentation discussed is dominant in American laboratories at present. Furthermore, many of the innovative and excellent analyzers that are now appearing utilize similar analytic principles.

Aperture-impedance cell counting is the basis of the instrumentation associated with the now-generic Coulter counter. Individual blood cells in suspension pass through a small aperture and induce an impedance change between two electrodes. The system counts these cells and sizes them based on the approximate proportionality between the amplitude of current displacement and cell volume. Cells that do not pass through the center of the aperture are perceived as larger, thus producing a "right-sided skew" to the cell-volume distribution curves. The newer generation of instruments made by Coulter and other manufacturers employ sheathed flow and electronic editing circuits to prevent this problem. These new instruments also incorporate advanced mechanical and electrical features to alleviate problems such as particle and debris accumulation as well as coincidence counting.[13]

A newer technique, exemplified by instruments made by Ortho Diagnostics Systems and other manufacturers, counts and sizes cells as they interrupt a narrowly focused beam of visible or laser-emitted light. The angle of light scatter is a function of cell size and other properties including shape, volume, and refractive index. These data are stored and used to report cell size and number. In contrast to impedance instrumentation, which calculates the packed cell volume (PCV) from the red blood count (RBC) and measured mean corpuscular volume of red cells (PCV = MCV × RBC), forward-angle light-scattering instruments measure the red count as well as the PCV directly. The PCV is determined by the area under the curve generated by the individual red cell pulses, and the MCV is then calculated from the other measurements. Sheathed-flow hydrodynamic focusing avoids the problem of protein buildup and minimizes coincidence counting.[14]

The Technicon flow-through cytochemical system (H6000) uses an electrooptical detection system in which red blood cells and platelets are isovolumetrically sphered by fixation and counted by light-scattering characteristics; hematocrit is measured by summing the signals from the red cell population. Hemoglobin is measured by a modified Van Kampen-Zijlstra cyanmethemoglobin method; whereas MCV, MCH, and MCHC are calculated mathematically. White cells are enumerated incidental to fixation and cytochemical staining preparatory to automated differential counting.[11,12]

CALIBRATION AND STANDARDIZATION

All discussions about quality control in the hematology laboratory must begin with a recognition of two central problems: (1) the absence of stable standard substances, and (2) the relative instability of most materials that are available for calibration and control. In the chemistry laboratory, the majority of commonly measured analytes (enzymes notably excepted) consist of elements or simple chemical compounds that exist in a pure and stable dry form. In contrast, the most frequently measured hematology parameters constitute a single multicompartment specimen, the components of which—with the sole exception of hemoglobin—are not available in a stable form that can serve as a primary or secondary standard. In this section we discuss some of the calibration and standardization strategies that have been employed to circumvent this deficiency.

Hemoglobin

The cyanmethemoglobin method as described by the International Committee for Standardization in Hematology (ICSH) is accepted as the reference method for hemoglobin determinations.[15] Certified standards are available (RIV-Dutch National Institute of Public Health or secondary national standards provided by the CAP) and specific instructions detailing methods of calibration are provided by manufacturers, the National Committee for Clinical Laboratory Standards, and in numerous publications.[16–20] The Van Kampen-Zijlstra reagent has been recommended over Drabkin's reagent, because of improved conversion of carboxyhemoglobin, better erythrocyte lysis, and decreased turbidity resulting from plasma globulin precipitation.[21] Because some manufacturers provide proprietary reagents the exact composition of which may not be disclosed, the laboratory does not always have the option of choice of specific methodology. The Hematology Resources Committee and the Commission on Laboratory Accreditation of the CAP have recently recommended ICSH calibration at the time of purchase and recalibration following a major change in an instrument component (flow cell, cuvette, photometer) or if control measurements demonstrate instrument drift.[22] Laboratories should be aware of the numerous methodological factors that may produce error in manual reference methods employed for calibration purposes or in patient sample testing. These may result from faulty specimen collection, sampling, mixing, diluting, reagents, measurements, and transcription.[23,24]

Hematocrit

The hematocrit, or packed cell volume, constitutes one of the oldest, and intuitively obvious, clinical laboratory measurements. In addition to the obvious variables of time and centrifugal force, the problems involved in calibrating and maintaining calibration of "manual" microhematocrit procedures appear relatively simple and involve methodology and equipment maintenance.[16] Most laboratories are aware of potential errors in accuracy attributable to inadequately maintained and calibrated centrifuges and non-calibrated or unclean glassware. Multiple determinations with faulty equipment or technique will only confirm the reproducibility of an inaccurate result.

Reference Methods

As discussed above, accurate and reproducible reference methods are available for hemoglobin determination. The situation for the hematocrit is considerably more complicated, particularly when the calibration and control of automated hematology analyzers is undertaken. However, ICSH and WHO selected and reference methods have been described for the Wintrobe and microhematocrit methods;[25,26] thus, standardization of the microhematocrit can be achieved in an operational sense with a high degree of precision even in the absence of a defined calibrator. Table 9-1 outlines important details. In contrast to both hemoglobin and hematocrit determination, hemocytometer-based reference methodology for cell enumeration suffers from very poor reproducibility as well as absence of defined, reliable, and stable calibrators.[27] The choice for most laboratorians who wish to use reference methodology for instrument calibration is between the tedious and poorly reproducible manual counting methods, which identify cells and only cells, and semiautomated counting instruments, which may produce erroneous counts due to particles, bubbles, or other electrical/optical interferences. Most will use the latter option, and results have proven to be acceptable if appropriate precautions are observed.

Calibration of Automated Hematology Instruments

Establishing and maintaining calibration of the current generation of seven- and eight-parameter automated hematology analyzers requires an understanding of the operating

TABLE 9-1
INTERNATIONAL COMMITTEE FOR STANDARDIZATION IN HAEMATOLOGY SELECTED METHODS FOR WINTROBE AND MICROHEMATOCRIT

	Wintrobe	Microhematocrit
Tube length (mm)	100	75
Tube bore (mm)	2.5–3.0	1.2
Acceleration (g)	2,000–2,300	10,000–15,000
Time (min)	30	5
Temperature (C)	< 45	< 45
Plasma trapping correction	None	None
Anticoagulant: K-EDTA	1.5 mg/ml of venous blood with container volume twice the volume of contained blood	

Source: England JM: Cell sizing, in Koepka JA (ed): *Laboratory Haematology.* New York, Churchill Livingstone, 1984.

principles of the specific instrumentation as well as an appreciation of the advantages and limitations of calibrating materials, reference methods, and process control systems. Some of these limitations have already been discussed but will now be considered in the context of automated multiparameter analyzers. The plethora of calibration and process control protocols that have been recommended suggests that none is completely satisfactory! However, a few broad alternative approaches can be identified and modified to the specific needs of the individual laboratory.[16,17] Calibration techniques for automated (as well as manual) analyzers either use fresh, whole blood specimens that are repetitively analyzed by reference methodology, or employ manufacturer-certified preparations of stabilized blood containing red cells, white cells (or substitutes), and platelets (or substitutes).

Whole Blood Calibration

Whole blood calibration consists of repetitive analysis of fresh whole blood specimens using "reference" or "definitive" or "selected" methods[1] performed in a careful manner by experienced technologists with well-maintained equipment. Some authorities recommend whole blood calibration as the most desirable strategy. The disadvantages of fresh whole blood calibration methods include the large amount of blood needed as well as the tedium and time requisite to perform the 10 to 20 replicate determinations on multiple specimens mandated by the inherent imprecision of manual reference methods. Compromise calibration methods have been described[17] that require fewer repetitive analyses but that use directly measurable quantities and volumes. The latter concept is of importance because the newer generation of analytic instruments (Coulter Model S and S Plus series; Technicon Hemalog D and H6000; Ortho ELT) are time-metered flow systems that measure the passage of cells per unit time. This type of instrument must be calibrated with instrumentation that is capable of recording cells or cellular contents in relation to volume. Representative examples would include semiautomated electronic particle gating analyzers such as the Coulter B-, F-, and Z-series analyzers.[28]

Stabilized Commercial Calibrators

For many labs, the problems associated with whole blood calibration preclude practical application. In addition to time and cost factors, many laboratorians will not wish to allocate space, personnel, and instrument-maintenance resources for analyzers used only for calibration purposes. Consequently, stabilized, commercially manufactured and assayed calibrators are used for purposes of initial calibration as well as periodic and sporadic recalibration of automated hematology analyzers. Materials of similar or identical formulation commonly are used for purposes of quality (process) control (confirmation of calibration stability during routine operation) but may be acceptable for calibration purposes if certain prerequisites are satisfied. The ICSH has defined a calibrator as "a substance . . . used to calibrate, graduate, or adjust a measurement" that is "traceable to a national or international reference preparation or reference material."[1] The manufacturer of the candidate calibrator should provide written documentation of analysis by reference methodology acceptable to the ICSH, CAP, or CDC.

The prime attribute of a stabilized calibrator is that the assigned value(s) is accurate and stable. Accuracy is customarily defined by multiple analyses with reference to definitive methods that are free of bias. As Bull has pointed out,[27] these methods may be considerably less precise than the automated methods in conventional clinical usage; this lack of reproducibility is circumvented by multiple analyses that are averaged to produce the final mean assay value(s). Stability, a property of almost equal importance, must be designed to withstand the rigors of the manufacturing process, storage, shipment, temperature variation, and other environmental events. Manufactured calibrators may vary considerably in stated stability, but as a general rule, they should be stable for at least one year or longer.[27] This will allow for interlaboratory evaluation and comparison and provide a usable time frame for the clinical laboratory.

Manufacturers of calibrating and control materials have addressed the stability problem either by fixation of cells with substances such as glutaraldehyde/formaldehyde or by changes in the suspending medium. In the former case, cell membranes undergo an irreversible change, and the resulting "embalmed" cells are small and nondeformable with stability in excess of one year. In contrast to patient blood specimens, there are substantial differences in how these cells are processed and "viewed" by the hydraulic, sensing and data-manipulating subsystems of aperture impedance and optical light-scattering instruments.[7] Glutaraldehyde-fixed red cells, selected from multiple animal species with varying MCVs to produce a mean MCV approximating unfixed human red cells, were the basis of the earliest commercial calibrator and control solutions. Because fixed red cells do not hemolyze readily, these preparations cannot be used in automated multiparameter analyzers.[29]

Stabilized controls, analogous to blood preserved with additives for transfusion purposes, have stability in the range of several months. Although these controls are less subject to interinstrument bias resulting from altered membrane deformability, the suspending medium may cause matrix effects, producing biases that vary from one instrument/reagent system to another.[3]

Calibrators and Controls: What Is the Difference?

The terms "calibrator" or "control" are used for products that may be of similar composition (type of cells and suspending medium) and even originate from the same primary pools of donor blood. Some manufacturers offer "cleaner" (less debris) pools for purposes of calibrator production; others market materials of identical composition and stability as calibrators and controls. In both cases, the material labeled as a "calibrator" must fulfill the previously stated ICSH criteria of traceability to a national or international reference material. As a matter of practice, the "calibrator" should have been subject to rigorous assay protocols using appropriate techniques; but assay values must be checked to ensure that no compromise occurred during shipment.

The Plasma Trapping Problem: Balloons and Bowling Balls

A recurring problem influencing both calibration and control protocols is that of plasma trapping. When red cells are packed as a result of the application of centrifugal force, a variable quantity of plasma is "trapped" in the interstices of the apposed cells. The amount trapped is related to the deformability of the red cell membranes. In an analogy used by Dr. Charles Arkin,[30] normal fresh red blood cells with intact membrane structure are highly deformable and when packed will behave as if they were biconcave discoid balloons allowing only small quantities of insinuated plasma between their tightly apposed membranes. Stabilized or fixed cells, on the other hand, may be likened to bowling balls—rigid spheres that when packed incorporate an inevitably large amount of trapped plasma between their nondeformable surfaces.

The loss of membrane flexibility producing the "stiff cell" is related to a generalized defect described as the red cell storage lesion, associated with ATP depletion and reversible by regenerating ATP or in vitro addition of adenosine. Loss of deformability can be measured by various techniques including filtration, pressure (required to produce deformation in micropipettes),[31] and ektacytometric analysis.[32] Centrifugation techniques also have been applied to confirm and quantitate decreased deformability in sickle cell disease, microcytosis, and hereditary spherocytosis.[33]

The majority of automated hematology analyzers use an electronic impedence technique that directly measures red cell size (MCV) and multiplies this result by the red cell count (RBC) to derive the hematocrit (PCV). Electronic impedance PCV values in the high range tend to be significantly lower than those obtained by spun microhematocrit. Three possible mechanisms for this phenomenon are (1) variation in MCV, (2) cell coincidence, and (3) plasma trapping, but the latter phenomenon is probably operative.[4] This discrepancy probably arises because the microhematocrit result includes a trapped plasma component not incorporated into the calculation producing the derived PCV. Many manufacturers and laboratorians have attempted to compensate for this by use of a plasma trapping correction. Plasma trapping with Wintrobe hematocrit methods is generally larger than with microhematocrit determinations.[34] Microhematocrit results demonstrate considerably greater variability but are in the range of 3 percent or approximately 1.5 hematocrit units.[35] A more recent study using isotope dilution techniques questions this customary value for plasma trapping and demonstrates a mean value of 1.53 percent for normals and from 1.41 to 1.82 percent for patients, including those with sickle cell disease, iron deficiency, and hereditary spherocytosis.[33] Based on data that suggest that other factors may be responsible for the reported discrepancies between reference method-determined and aperture impedance MCV, Coulter no longer recommends routine correction for plasma trapping in the calibration of their instruments. Their data suggest that characteristics of sampled subpopulations, such as differences in cell deformability, may be partially responsible for these discrepancies. This is consistent with the known tendency for aperture impedance instruments to "see" less deformable cells as larger than easily deformable cells of equal volume.[36] The reader is referred to several excellent discussions of this complex problem,[37,38] and is cautioned to be aware of potential discrepancies between manual and automated PCV, particularly if stabilized/fixed red cells are used for calibration of automated analyzers. In this circumstance, changes in shape and/or deformability may make the use of correction factors during calibration advisable.[39] To ensure that potential calibration, process control, or clinical discrepancies can be resolved, it is important to know whether or not a plasma trapping correction factor is in use.

PROCESS CONTROL AND QUALITY ASSURANCE OPTIONS

The Need for Process Control

After standardization of methodology and calibration of instrumentation, systems must be established to ensure that significant changes in calibration do not occur. Verification of calibration should be performed regularly and periodically. It is customary to perform these checks by analysis of control samples at the beginning of shifts and analytic "runs" and during the course of batched analytic runs of large numbers of specimens. In the latter situation, random rather than fixed placement of the specimen is preferable. When there is some instrumentation or maintenance change, control materials are frequently used to reconfirm calibration. Because of the need to reduce costs and the increasing availability of computer-based, on-line data acquisition and statistical manipulation, there has been an increasing interest in alternatives to the use of quality control materials. The following section will describe some of these options and suggest ways in which they could be integrated into a comprehensive program of process control and quality assurance.

Manufactured Quality Control Materials

Double, double, toil and trouble;
Fire burn, and cauldon bubble.
Fillet of a fenny snake,
In the cauldron boil and bake; Eye of newt, and
toe of frog, Wool of bat, and tongue of dog;

Adder's fork and blind-worm's sting,
Lizard's leg, and howlet's wing;
for a charm of pow'rful trouble,
Like a hell-broth boil and bubble.

Macbeth, Act IV, Scene 1

In previous sections we have emphasized that in some cases materials that are sold as "control" solutions differ little if at all from solutions offered as "calibrators." From a functional perspective, both types of material should demonstrate prolonged stability. In the case of calibrator substances, the accuracy of the methods used to assign assay values takes primacy. For control materials, stability in the user's laboratory becomes the single most important attribute. Using analyzers that have been previously calibrated by reference methods,[40] laboratory-derived point-of-assay values on commercial control materials can be established. The limitations of this approach are stability of the control material and the ability to perform the reference methods accurately.

In attempting to manufacture control substances of extended stability, vendors have used a varied menu of human and animal blood cells, particles of biologic and nonbiologic origin, and suspending/stabilizing media. Although calibrator materials may not necessarily share the attributes of the analytic specimen, it is intuitively obvious that control preparations should resemble the clinical specimen—fresh, whole human blood—in as many properties as possible (see Table 9-2). Unfortunately, extending the stability of the control product has often required considerable compromise in the degree to which the physicochemical properties reproduce those of fresh human blood.[23]

An impressive bestiary of human and animal sources is used in the preparation of multiparameter control products available for monitoring of erythrocyte, white cell and platelet counting and sizing, and related indices and hemoglobin measurement. For obvious logistical, economic, and ethical reasons, animal blood, particularly from large domestic animals, would be an ideal source.

Unfortunately, mammalian bloods do not conveniently center in the MCV range of human blood unless mixtures are used. For this and other reasons, stabilized human red cells are currently most commonly used, although donkey blood has been used with success.[29] Stabilized or partially fixed avian erythrocytes are most commonly used as leukocyte surrogates; these nucleated cells survive the hemolysis process, and the uniform, tubular nuclei are reproducibly counted by automated counters and are

TABLE 9-2
ATTRIBUTES OF IDEAL CONTROL SUBSTANCE

Prolonged stability
May be sampled directly
Suspends easily and does not agglutinate
Flow constants similar to blood
Optical and electrical properties similar to blood
Particle size and shape similar to blood
Assayable by independent methods

easily identified by manual methods.[29] A Noah's Ark of platelet surrogates has been prepared from human, porcine, bovine, equine, and artificial sources, although at present there appears to be a trend toward use of human platelets.[41,42]

Selection and Implementation of Control-Based Systems Multiple protocols for using commercial control materials in monitoring instrument/reagent/analytic system stability have been described.[16,17,43,44] Use of protocols recommended by the manufacturer is quite acceptable, particularly when instrumentation is new and performance and operating characteristics have not been fully defined. In some instances, there may be an obligation to use a particular source of reagents and/or controls because instrumentation has been acquired through nonequity funding. Manufacturers and vendor staff will often suggest that specific sources of control material will "work better" with their instrumentation and, not surprisingly, this source will often turn out to be the instrument vendor or one that is associated with the vendor in a co-marketing relationship. At times, this claim will have some validity. Attempts to reduce costs by competitive bidding, bulk or joint purchasing options, and participation in regional interlaboratory programs can be compromised because of real and imagined control "incompatibilities." For these reasons, the laboratory director, supervisor, or manager is well advised to inquire fully into compatibility of reagents, calibrators, and controls before deciding upon new instrumentation. A request for documentation about support-product compatibility should be honored by a reputable vendor.

Implementation of a QC program requires decisions about statistical techniques, charting, and control limits. Commonly, Levey-Jennings charts are used to document control determinations. Mean values may change from lot to lot, but the amplitude of "shifts and drifts" around the mean should be confined to a predetermined range. On-line and microcomputer-based software have revolutionized the ease and sophistication of data analysis; many alternative statistical options including cusum analysis and multirule analyses of the Shewhart type now can be readily implemented.

Process Control by Interlaboratory Comparison Commercial controls are used in a sporadic fashion to verify calibration at the beginning of or during a shift or run. However, a more complete program involves the use of a common lot of material by a group of laboratories.[7] These regional or interregional pools may be under the sponsorship of a vendor, a state or regional pathology society, or, as has recently evolved, a multiregional group composed of many regional quality control groups sharing a common control pool with extended stability and a common data base.[45] In the case of the vendor-supported pools, data processing is often supplied by the vendor; programs offered by professional groups process data through the Quality Assurance Service of the College of American Pathologists.[45] Depending on the size of the participant base, these programs attempt to establish method/instrument/reagent-based peer group comparisons, as well as to provide intralaboratory summary statistics and wall charts. The vendor-supplied programs appear to be less expensive because data processing costs are not specifically identified in the charges for the control material. However, professional supervision may be limited, and there may be only perfunctory attempts to preserve the integrity of the data base or evaluate the validity of the statistics. Both types of programs, however, can provide control materials at reduced cost as well as access to statistical resources and group comparisons. With the advent of microcomputers and telecommunications, an increasing potential for on-line and timely data acquisition and comparison is evident. Programs such as the CAP's QAS TODAY[46] have the capability to provide run rejection criteria and intralaboratory statistics in an interactive mode. Summated data are generated on a periodic basis, and comparative data are sent in a timely fashion. In evaluating changes in quality control programs—particularly if a change from written to keyboard entry is contemplated—consideration should be given to the time involved in data entry and to convenience of terminal entry. If location and usage patterns make terminal entry inconvenient, the transportability of paper may have some advantages.

Limitations of Control-Based Programs Specific limitations of interlaboratory programs relate to cost, limited stability of control materials, and difficulty in establishing meaningful data bases. This is due to small participant groups that are further segmented by numerous method/instrument/reagent biases. Generic limitations of all control-based programs inhere to the characteristics of manufactured control products and their interaction with specific instrumentation. Many studies and the Proficiency Surveys of the CAP have documented significant interinstrument bias resulting from hyperglycemic and hypertonic formulations of stabilized blood controls.[3,47] Stabilized red cells have altered deformability and tend to swell during storage, causing considerable impact on the measured result. Because clinical specimens do not have these characteristics, it is important to distinguish true analytic variation owing to loss of calibration from variation arising from peculiarities of the control material.

External Quality Control As in other laboratory sections, internal controls are used in attempts to detect loss of calibration and to identify sources of error and variation that may occur during the analytic process. Errors and trends must be detected in a timely fashion to allow for immediate corrective action and to prevent release of incorrect patient results. External quality control or proficiency survey testing is referred to by a number of alternative designations, including Interlaboratory Quality Control or Survey Program, Laboratory Improvement Program, Interlaboratory Comparison, and so on. The Hematology Survey Program of the College of American Pathologists is probably best known, but other programs are offered by the CDC, various state departments of health, and professional associations such as the American Association of Bioanalysts.[48] Participation in these programs is mandated for accreditation, regulatory, and reimbursement purposes. The design and implementation of these programs has been thoroughly discussed for those who are interested in the details.[48] Obviously, selection of analytes and target values, formulation and stability, distribution and data accumulation constitute formidable logistical problems for the organizers of these programs. The collection, categorization, and dissemination of the data determine how useful participation is to the individual facility. Because challenges are infrequent and results not immediately available, such programs are generally not useful for ongoing quality control. There is considerable educational value that can be derived from participation. Technical personnel may derive a great deal of satisfaction from the peer group comparison and external validation of their results; the latter is, in my opinion, an important and infrequently stated benefit. Proficiency testing programs lend themselves to incorporation into laboratory continuing education activities, and this function constitutes an inexpensive bonus even though participation may be required primarily for other reasons.

The relatively large data base provided by surveys such as the CAP proficiencies may be helpful in evaluating current methods against proposed alternatives. Interlaboratory trials have been very helpful in identifying problems areas and in defining the state of the art.[6] Certainly, one of the stated and implicit goals of these programs is to reduce interlaboratory variability. This increases the likelihood that patient results will be readily transportable from one clinical setting to another as well as over a period of time. Interlaboratory trials have clearly contributed to an overall improvement in laboratory performance and helped to decrease interlaboratory bias. The impact of these programs on precision is somewhat harder to separate from that owing to introduction of a new generation of automated analyzers.[49] Surveys contribute little, if anything, to defining and preventing postanalytic or preanalytic sources of variation, such as those due to specimen handling. Because controls specimens, despite the best of intentions, are impossible to disguise, they are almost always subject to special handling and analysis. This special treatment serves either to obscure procedural deficiencies, or, in some cases, to generate clerical error that is not inherent to routine laboratory operations. Some of the broader philosophic implications of monitoring analytic system performance with material other than fresh, whole blood have been well summarized by Bull.[49]

Process Control Using Patient Specimens or Data

Judicious use of patient specimens and data can supplement internal and external QC programs and in some cases fill gaps that control-material-based programs do not address. Patient specimens as well as data—numerical, clinical, or morphologic—can be used in a sporadic or systematic fashion to add a significant quality dimension to more routine process control protocols. Finally, patient data may, with computer assistance, constitute the foundation of an elegant and comprehensive program of quality control for red cell–related parameters.

Retained Patient Specimens Properly aliquoted patient blood specimens refrigerated at 4°C show no significant changes in major hematologic parameters for at least 24 hours.[50] In one study, anticoagulated blood that was refrigerated and mixed intermittently showed no significant change after three days for hemoglobin, hematocrit, RBC, red cell indices, leukocyte count, and platelets; whereas storage at room temperature produced significant increases in cell size within 24 hours.[51]

Once initial calibration has been achieved, the reliance on commercial controls for purposes of verification of calibration maintenance can be significantly decreased. Retained specimens may be used to verify calibration from run to run, during large batched runs, for sporadic or "stat" analyses during off-peak operation, and when shift changes occur.[7] A particularly attractive application is control "transferability" from major instrumentation to backup analyzers and to "satellite" lab facilities. The transferability function may be the most useful quality control application of retained patient specimens. If retained specimens are used systematically, a sufficient number of specimens—preferably with low, normal, and high analytic values—should be analyzed to ensure reliability. If retained samples are used sporadically and rerun results exceed tolerance limits, additional retained samples should be analyzed to distinguish between specimen deterioration and loss of instrument calibration.[16] Random duplicate assays of retained patient specimens may also be used to measure precision and to control within-run random errors.[52]

Morphologic Review and Clinical Correlation Minimum quality assurance procedures for morphologic observations should be correlation of findings with numerical data by someone with sufficient experience to make this comparison. Comprehensive systems of qualitative clinical and morphologic review have been described that stress ongoing educational effort, review of abnormal and random peripheral smears, as well as clinical correlation and consultation.[53] Unexpected results and pressures from clinical staff will force even the most reclusive pathologist to the bedside or at least to the chart. The pathologist who wishes to explore the full dimensions of the role of consultant and teacher will anticipate these exigencies and establish protocols for correlation of quantitative data with morphology, clinical investigation of aberrant results, and review of quantitative data for internal consistency. Tracking of linear data by sequential photocopying of laboratory master cards can be a useful monitor of lab operations[54] as well as an adjunct to patient care and teaching. The availability of computer-assisted delta checks and trend analysis will of course greatly facilitate such approaches.

"The Human Factor" Attention has been directed to the "human factor" and the impact of "fatigue, psychological pressures, illness, monotony, interruptions and distractions, time available to perform the task and motivation" upon the overall long-term quality of the analytic process.[53] These factors are very difficult to quantitate but are well worth considering.

Moving Averages of Red Cell Indices The modern history of the moving-averages approach to intralaboratory quality control began with a paper by Dorsey[55] reporting on use of daily averages of patient MCH to control the operation of an early model Coulter counter. This approach, which has been extensively studied, is the foundation of a novel and elegant system of quality control that is inexpensive and admirably suited to the control requirements of modern, multiparameter, automated hematology analyzers. The Hematology Resource Committee of the College of American Pathologists has approved, with stated reservations, use of weighted moving averages for longitudinal process control of seven- and eight-parameter analyzers.[56] Weighted moving averages has been accepted by the Commission on Laboratory Accreditation of the CAP, and questions pertaining to the system are now included in the current checklist for laboratory accreditation purposes.[57] Unless otherwise stated, the following discussion is based on Refs. 40, 49, 56, 58, and 59, which are recommended to the interested reader as eloquent and enthusiastic expositions; reservations and criticisms have been advanced and will also be presented.[60-62]

The weighted moving-averages method is based on the empirical observation that averaged red cell indices from patient populations in acute-care general hospitals show an approximately Gaussian distribution, are consistently stable, and are similar in all institutions studied. These properties reflect the physiologic consistency of red cell size and hemoglobin content in health, disease, and even many hematologic disorders. The dimensions of these properties are expressed by the Wintrobe indices (RBC size = MCV; hemoglobin content and concentration = MCH and MCHC, respectively). As ratios these values are independent of certain procedural errors (dilution, inadequate mixing) that may seriously compromise the measurements of hemoglobin, hematocrit, and red cell count. The weighted moving-averages system anchors the validity of the indices by referencing one primary measurement—hemoglobin—to a defined calibration event. It then proceeds, by use of a complex statistical algorithm, to evaluate and incorporate successive batches of patient specimen indices into a continually "updated" mean. These means are "trimmed and smoothed" (outliers eliminated and data from previous batches incorporated into the new mean), thereby diluting the effect of random error and abnormal results. Deviations of these means from specified limits indicate either loss of calibration or a shift in the characteristics of the population being tested. Specific patterns of change involving the monitored indices (MCV, MCH, and MCHC) are diagnostic of specific types of instrument malfunction.

Implementation requires verification that the mean cell indices of the patient population are identical to those that have been reported for hospital populations:

MCV: 88–91 fl
MCH: 30–31 pg
MCHC: 33.5–34.5 percent

This verification should be performed on a properly calibrated analyzer with 500 patient samples, confirming calibration after every 100 patient samples with commercial control materials. If the sampled population does not include large numbers of pediatric, chemotherapy, or iron-deficient patients, the above means, which were obtained from large international trials and calculated without plasma trapping corrections, should be reproduced.

Data entry and application of the Bull-Korpman algorithm may be done manually using programmable calculators, but the effort involved and the likelihood of data entry error make this option undesirable. The weighted moving-averages method is more applicable in larger laboratories where multiparameter hematology analyzers incorporating circuitry and software for on-line implementation are present. The algorithm is designed to minimize the effect of outliers (trimming function) and incorporate data from preceding runs into the estimation of the current mean (smoothing function), thus producing a more nearly Gaussian curve. These manipulations endow small batch sizes (20 samples) with the "robust" characteristics of larger samples; therefore, more frequent sampling and earlier detection of analyzer drift are made possible. The algorithm conversely minimizes the impact of abrupt data shifts and allows the operator to adopt a "wait-and-see" attitude before instituting corrective action. It must be stressed that because of the small sample sizes, random entry of raw data is mandatory, and each group of patients should be representative of the patient population as a whole. No more than one-third of a run should be composed of patients with deviations of MCV in the same direction (chemotherapy, pediatric, iron-deficient).

A large experience extending over 4 years has been reported by Koepke and Protextor during which the use of commercial controls was discontinued with considerable cost savings.[59] In this study, instrument malfunction was detected in 83 percent of instances by MCHC, 60 percent by MCH, and 36 percent by MCV. Bull and Korpman have reported a study validating the use of mean erythrocyte indices in an autocalibration loop and suggest that current technology could be readily adapted to such an approach.[63]

Several caveats should be repeated and noted before implementation of this type of approach. Because on-line data capture and processing is highly desirable, implementation should probably be limited to automated instrumentation designed or retrofitted with these capabilities. Careful attention should be directed to exclude nonrandom patient populations, and the method should not be used by laboratories performing fewer than 100 CBCs daily.[56]

Because of the large physiologic variability of the white cell and platelet counts, weighted moving averages cannot be used for longitudinal process control; commercial controls usually need be employed for these analytes. Many laboratorians will experience considerable discomfort in completely abandoning the use of commercial controls and will probably opt for periodic albeit reduced use of manufactured controls. The appropriate use of retained patient specimens may be useful in providing the bench worker with a "security blanket" as well as in meeting the objection that weighted moving averages do not allow for definition of analytic precision or provide adequate control of within-run random error.[64] In this regard, the use of the "random duplicates" method may be useful.[52]

Finally, weighted moving averages have been evaluated in comparison with conventional control-based protocols. These studies have identified deficiencies in weighted moving averages, showing that stabilized whole blood controls could better separate calibration change from patient variation.[61] The continued use of control preparations in conjunction with weighted moving averages therefore was recommended.[60] In a more recent study, Cembrowski and Westgard used computer simulations of multichannel hematology analyzers to evaluate the impact of outlier populations (neonates and oncology patients) on the utility of Bull's algorithm.[62] Using power function graphs, they concluded that "quality control by averaging patient red blood cell indices does not offer as good error detection as that available from conventional charting techniques using stable control materials . . . [and] . . . recommend caution in discontinuing the use of control materials."

REFERENCE RANGES AND SOURCES OF VARIATION

In the previous sections we have concentrated on a closeup view of the analytic process viewed from a narrow perspective. Calibration of instrumentation and methodology with subsequent maintenance of calibration represent necessary prerequisites for the generation of accurate and precise data. However, quality assurance requires control of sources of variation that occur before the specimen to be analyzed is presented to the work station or even before it arrives in the laboratory. Preanalytic variation is comprised of the manifold sources of patient-specific variation induced by physiologic, environmental, and pathologic causes as well as those produced by the process of obtaining and transporting the specimen to the analytic site. An evaluation of the quality assurance process should also include some consideration of how the value and integrity of the analytic loop is degraded by inappropriate, incorrect, and slow reporting formats and communication channels. A prerequisite for identification of significant sources of pre- and postanalytic variation and error is some understanding of analytic purposes and cognitive goals. Implicit in the latter requirement is the need to define normative standards and reference ranges for population groups and, ideally, the individual patient.

Analytic Goals

It is customary and not unreasonable to define analytic goals in terms of accuracy and precision; more recently, it has become popular and necessary to add cost. All three can be expressed in quantitative terms of bias, coefficient of variation, and dollars. Unfortunately, these dimensions do not answer the more subjective questions of how much accuracy and precision are needed and how much can be afforded. The advent of a new generation of increasingly automated hematology analyzers has improved the precision of most analytic methods by 10-fold, and both national and international surveys have demonstrated reduction in analytic bias.[6] For purposes of comparison with currently available analytic precision, Skendzel, Barnett, and Platt[65] have attempted to identify "medically useful criteria" by surveying a sample of physicians and submitting the responses to a questionnaire to statistical analysis. It was found that the "medically useful CV(%)" for hematocrit (5.4), hemoglobin (3.6), leukocyte count (16.4), MCV (3.2), as well as other commonly measured chemical analytes, was well above that customarily reported by most laboratories. It was suggested that medically useful CVs could serve as a guide in establishing analytic goals and that precision considerably in excess of the reported levels would not "increase diagnostic usefulness." It was further suggested that laboratory resources could be better directed to "the study and control of preanalytic factors affecting a test and to the development of more appropriate tests for diagnosis and treatment." It is, of course, mandatory for a laboratory to monitor analytic precision quantitatively; by doing so, the laboratory director may incorporate, if he or she so desires, medical usefulness criteria that are appropriate to the clinical setting. In this context, a potential objection to the uncritical acceptance of medical usefulness criteria is that they have been defined in terms of specific clinical situations that may not be universally applicable. Surely, different clinical decision limits for significant change in a hematocrit will apply for the clinician contemplating postoperative transfusion following bowel resection for an elderly patient with coronary insufficiency and the same physician evaluating the meaning of a drop in hematocrit upon annual examination of a young woman with menorrhagia.

Some perspective on these problems is provided by the predictive value and efficiency of hematologic data.[66] Reference to the predictive value model may be of some assistance in establishing analytic precision limits. The predictive value model forces a consideration not only of test sensitivity and specificity as well as disease prevalence but also the need to define analytic goals in terms of clinical problems.

Development of "Normal" (Reference) Ranges

Galen[66] has reviewed the many ambiguous usages by clinicians (as well as laboratory workers) of "normal" as applied to a specific analyte (hemoglobin), including "normal" as a code word for a Gaussian distribution, to describe the most representative values in a Gaussian or non-Gaussian population, or the commonest values in a Gaussian distribution from which outliers have been excluded (usual "normal" range). Alternatively, somewhat more vague normative standards related to optimum function or survival, "ideal," or consensus values may be implied. In an excellent brief review, Savage discusses sources of analytic, physiologic, and disease-related variation that must be considered in order to establish appropriate reference ranges for different population groups.[67]

Many alternative methods have been suggested[68] for derivation of normal or reference ranges, to use the currently favored terminology. Conventional wisdom suggests that reference ranges should be developed from local patient and nondiseased populations. Because this is not always practicable, laboratorians may turn to a growing literature that reports reference ranges for hematologic parameters based on sex, age, ethnic origins, pregnancy status, and oral contraceptive usage.[69-74] A problem of considerable practical significance is whether separate reference ranges need to be developed for the elderly and whether the so-called anemia of senescence represents an age-related decline of marrow function or a sign of occult treatable disease.[75-80] Other studies have reported the effects of exercise,[81] competitive swimming,[82] ultra-marathon training,[83] altitude,[84] hypobaric chambers,[85] and spaceflight[86] on hematologic analytes.

Sources of Variation

Variation in hematologic data may arise from the patient and as such is separable into physiologic variation related to diurnal or circadian cycles and changes produced by the environment or disease. Alternatively, variation or error may arise from preanalytic and analytic sources. In a landmark study, Statland and coworkers systematically evaluated hematologic variables using very precise automated analyzers while rigorously standardizing sources of analytic and preanalytic variation such as conditions and time of venipuncture. By partitioning biologic variation into components, they demonstrated that intraindividual variation was less than interindividual variation and that subject-specific diurnal variations occurred for leukocyte counts, individual cell counts, hemoglobin, and hematocrit. Diurnal variations were clearly identified as factors not to be confused with analytic or disease-induced sources of variation.[87] Kaplow and coworkers[88] evaluated accuracy and precision for common hematologic parameters in 20 VA laboratories using CAP survey and interlab-pool specimen results. Unexpectedly, within-day variation was greater than day-to-day variation, which, in turn, was more than interlaboratory variation.

Preanalytic Variation

Variables associated with specimen collection, including choice of needles, collection systems, containers, anticoagulants, and transport conditions, are summarized by Sackler.[89] Systematic variation has been associated with specimen source—earstick versus fingerstick, capillary versus venous—as well as specimen preparation.[90-92] Anticoagulant-produced artifacts, usually mediated by changes in tonicity or pH, affect quantitative parameters and morphologic features. Currently, the triple potassium salt of EDTA is used for most hematologic analyses. Macrocytosis, anisocytosis, and spherocytosis as well as increased platelet volume and leukocyte morphology alterations may occur if blood is in prolonged contact with excessive concentrations of EDTA secondary to insufficient filling of collection tubes.[89]

Spurious Causes of Macrocytosis

Considerable information has accumulated describing spurious macrocytosis manifested by increased MCV, hematocrit, and MCHC results with patient specimens, calibrators, and control materials. The best documented changes usually are attributable to matrix effects or are secondary to antibodies. The spurious results often are confined to specific instrument/reagent systems. The usual Coulter pattern of spurious MCV and MCHC elevation associated with cold agglutinins[93] is not always seen with Ortho ELT, possibly because of differences in the detection system and the determination of hematocrit directly from the area under the curve of red cell pulses.[94]

Spurious macrocytosis occurs when hyperglycemic red cells are suspended in the isotonic diluting fluids of electronic cell counters. The transient influx of fluid into the hyperosmolar erythrocyte produces cell swelling, the magnitude of which is partially determined by elapsed time between dilution and cell measurement; the shorter this interval, the greater the increase in cell size that will be recorded. Although there is considerable difference of opinion regarding mechanisms, the impact of this and related matrix phenomena produced by hypernatremia and increased urea concentrations on red cell sizing have been studied in clinical and experimental models.[95,96] Savage and Hoffman[47] have placed the problem in perspective by showing that spurious macrocytosis secondary to hyperglycemia is a rare event in a hospital population. In a study based on data from the CAP Hematology Survey program, Savage provided an elegant discussion of osmotic matrix effects and concluded that they are insufficient to explain all MCV variations described.[3] Data are presented to show that "instrument dependent analytic variation is present in addition to an osmotic matrix effect and appears intrinsic to the instrument systems studied." The interested reader is urged to read this paper and is referred to Table 9-3 for a comprehensive review of other reported causes of spurious results with automated hematology analyzers.[97]

TABLE 9-3
POTENTIAL CAUSES OF ERRONEOUS RESULTS WITH AUTOMATED CELL COUNTERS

Parameter	Causes of Spurious Increase	Causes of Spurious Decrease
WBC	Cryoglobulin, cryofibrinogen Heparin Monoclonal proteins Nucleated red cells Platelet clumping Unlysed red cells	Clotting Smudge cells Uremia plus immunosuppressants
RBC	Cryoglobulin, cryofibrinogen Giant platelets High WBC (>50,000/μL)	Autoagglutination Clotting Hemolysis (in vitro) Microcytic red cells
Hemoglobin	Carboxyhemoglobin (>10%) Cryoglobulin, cryofibrinogen Hemolysis (in vivo) Heparin High WBC (>50,000/μL) Hyperbilirubinemia Lipemia Monoclonal proteins	Clotting Sulfhemoglobin (?)
Hematocrit (Automated)	Cryoglobulin, cryofibrinogen Giant platelets High WBC (>50,000/μL) Hyperglycemia (>600 mg/dL)	Autoagglutination Clotting Hemolysis (in vitro) Microcytic red cells
Hematocrit (Microhematocrit)	Hyponatremia Plasma trapping	Excess EDTA Hemolysis (in vitro) Hypernatremia
MCV	Autoagglutination High WBC (>50,000/μL) Hyperglycemia Reduced red cell deformability	Cryoglobulin, cryofibrinogen Giant platelets Hemolysis (in vitro) Microcytic red cells Swollen red cells
MCH	High WBC (>50,000/μL) Spuriously high Hgb Spuriously low RBC	Spuriously low Hgb Spuriously high RBC
MCHC	Autoagglutination Clotting Hemolysis (in vitro) Hemolysis (in vivo) Spuriously high Hgb Spuriously low Hct	High WBC (>50,000/μL) Spuriously low Hgb Spuriously high Hct
Platelets	Cryoglobulin, cryofibrinogen Hemolysis (in vitro and in vivo) Microcytic red cells Red cell inclusions White cell fragments	Clotting Giant platelets Heparin Platelet clumping Platelet satellitosis

Source: Cornbleet J: Spurious results from automated hematology cell counters. *Lab Med* 1983, 14:509.

SPECIAL PROBLEMS OF WHITE BLOOD CELLS

White Blood Cell Counting

For white blood cells, as for erythrocytes and platelets, the changes in methodology over the past two decades have resulted in significant improvements in precision. In general, hemocytometric methods have CVs in the range of 10 percent, whereas semi-automated and fully automated particle counters exhibit CVs in the range of 1 to 2 percent.[98] For cell-counting instrumentation, leukocytes are operationally defined as particles of a stipulated size range that remain after lysis of far more numerous erythrocytes.[39] Therefore, most problems relate to erythrocyte lysis and the definition of the size thresholds of residual nucleated cells. Calibration, quality control, and patient specimen errors may occur due to poor mixing, incomplete lysis, protein buildup on apertures, red cell agglutinates, nucleated red cells, cryoproteins, and abnormal white cells in various disease states.[24]

As has been discussed, the very high physiologic variation of the normal individual's WBC (CV = 35 percent) precludes application of the moving average technique. However, in most multiparameter analyzers the WBC is sampled, diluted, and mixed in a manner analogous to hemoglobin. Taking advantage of these similarities, Bull has suggested redilution of a blood specimen with fixative (1:500). The fixed red cells are counted as white cells and the accuracy of the red cell count is transferred to the leukocyte count; calibration of the transducer is the final step.[49] The reader is referred to Ref. 49 for details as well as for a discussion of alternative options for monitoring the accuracy of WBC determination with multichannel hematology analyzers. These methods entail, respectively, the use of reference methods (digital particle counting) of fresh whole blood or the use of commercially assayed control materials.

The Differential Count

Quality assurance strategies for differential counting are essentially limited to the repetitive and tedious counting of large numbers of cells in order to compensate for the very large statistical, physiologic, and analytic variation that is present.[99] Sources of variation are attributable to sampling errors, cell distribution, and observer identification.[99] Recently, routine and repetitious performance of the standard 100-cell differential has been discouraged.[98-102] We advocate stringent limitation of routine differential counting, but as a matter of practicality believe that automated techniques such as optical image processing, flow-through cytochemistry, and the new, and in our opinion most promising, screening histogram instruments will prevail for a variety of technologic, economic, and scientific reasons.[99,103,104]

SPECIAL PROBLEMS OF PLATELETS

Manual methods using phase microscopy largely are being replaced by semiautomated or fully automated determinations, the latter methods demonstrating marked advantages in terms of precision as well as convenience. Because very serious clinical decisions—continuation of cytotoxic chemotherapy and platelet transfusions—are made on the basis of the platelet count, the quality control of this measurement, especially in the lower range, is of critical importance.

Calibration

Although hemocytometry is still recommended by some as a reference methodology,[24] the poor reproducibility of this method is leading to increasingly greater acceptance and use of electronic particle-counting instrumentation.[98] Significant problem areas in calibration of electronic particle counters have been described[24] and tend to be method-specific, relating to instrumentation, reagents, and sample (platelet-rich plasma or whole blood). Thus, a study of pertinent specific methods as well as of principles[49] of calibration and control of platelet counting instrumentation are commended to the reader.

Methodology

In an early paper, Wertz and Triplett compared interlaboratory performance in the 1979 CAP Platelet Survey and demonstrated considerable improvement in precision and accuracy compared with the 1976 Survey. This change was attributed to the advent of whole-blood counters that eliminated errors associated with platelet-rich plasma (PRP) and that used hydrodynamic focusing, high-resolution apertures, and computerized log-normal analysis techniques. At that time, they recommended phase-contrast calibration with fresh human blood and subsequent monitoring of instrument drift with stable suspensions of platelet controls.[41] Subsequent surveys demonstrated a further shift to the performance of platelet counts on eight-parameter hematology analyzers.[105]

There have been several comparative studies of phase, electronic impedance, and light-scattering instrumentation demonstrating good performance of available instrumentation as a whole but documenting some problem areas. In a group of 30 patients, Mielke and associates compared phase, Coulter ZBI, and Ortho ELT-8 results with counts in the low, normal, and high ranges. Phase and ZBI demonstrated similar results, and laser light scatter instrumentation showed better precision, particularly at low levels.[106] Studies from the M. D. Anderson Hospital[107] that evaluated the J. T. Baker Haema-Count MK-4/HC (impedance, PRP), Clay-Adams Ultra-Flo 100 (impedance, intact RBCs), Coulter S+ (impedance, intact RBCs), and Technicon Autocounter (optical, lysed RBCs) instruments showed all to be linear in ranges tested. With these instruments, precision was greater than with manual platelet counts, carryover was minimal, and "excellent" clinical correlations were obtained.

Recent concurrently reported studies evaluated the newer generation of eight-parameter impedance counters. Cornbleet and Kessinger[108] compared phase microscopy platelet counts in 400 samples with Coulter S+IV results; a small number of discrepant results were due to erratic phase microscopy. Falsely elevated results with the other instruments were due to counting of nonplatelet particles (microcytes, air bubbles, electrical noise, cytoplasmic fragments, and RBC stroma). The authors stressed the importance of inspecting the platelet histogram for return to baseline. In a study by Mayer and associates, Coulter S+IV values were precise and showed excellent linearity. They concluded that falsely high platelet counts in thrombocytopenic patients, a problem that occurred with earlier Coulter instruments, had been eliminated by the improved platelet flagging system.[10] Good performance characteristics and accurate platelet counts also were demonstrated by the same group in a study comparing automated multiparameter whole-blood cell (Coulter S+ and Ortho ELT-8) counters with single-parameter, semiautomated platelet counters. At times all instruments counted nonplatelet particles or debris as platelets with resulting spurious elevations of platelet count.[9]

Ross and associates addressed the problem of process control with light-scattering and aperture-impedance counters. They evaluated various commercial controls (preserved human and animal platelets; latex) and patient data-based QC systems. They concluded that either of these systems is acceptable if a program of instrument checks, internal control of the reference materials, and monitoring of results was followed.[42]

Mean Platelet Volume

A considerable body of information on platelet size and heterogeneity is based on sporadic clinical correlation of morphologic observations on stained peripheral blood films and on scholarly data of uncertain clinical relevance.[109] It is generally accepted that platelet volume distribution is sufficiently skewed to the right so that a log-normal distribution best describes both platelet volume and diameter.[37] Measurement of platelet volume is dependent on, among other variables, calibration method, anticoagulant, temperature, and the interval between venipuncture and analysis.[110,111] It is less well appreciated that platelet volume distribution varies considerably in healthy subjects.[112]

A series of papers by Bessman, Williams, and Gilmer[113] has demonstrated the inverse relation of platelet count and mean platelet volume (MPV) in healthy subjects. They also demonstrated the occurrence of spuriously elevated platelet counts secondary to erythrocytic and leukemic blast fragments. In a study that compared measurements of "reference controls" in light-scattering and electronic-impedance counters, MPV values were found to vary with the particular instrument used.[114] The validity of this observation is in question, because the reference materials were designed for precision control, not as a measurement of accuracy. Because reference material for platelet sizing is not available, it is suggested[115] that stabilized control materials are "species specific for a given manufacturer's cell counting apparatus." A subsequent report has confirmed the observation of an inverse relation between platelet count and MPV.[116]

Spurious Platelet Counts

A variety of preanalytic and pathophysiologic events have been reported to produce spurious platelet counts. Cytoplasmic fragments occurring during chemotherapy for the leukemic phase of lymphocytic lymphoma produced spuriously high platelet counts with an electrooptical (Hemalog 8) automated counter. This report[117] describes numerous other sources of falsely elevated counts, including Howell-Jolly bodies, nucleated red cells, white blood cells, malarial parasites, and erythrocyte stroma. With the same type of instrumentation, another study showed that cytoplasmic debris produced a spuriously high platelet count in a patient with hairy cell leukemia.[118] Falsely elevated platelet counts with an impedance automated instrument also have been reported in a burn patient with microspherocytosis.[119] These studies suggest the potential value of some form of quality control by parallel examination of peripheral smears, at least in patients with certain disease processes.

Pseudothrombocytopenia associated with platelet satellitism occurs in EDTA-anticoagulated blood. Savage confirmed significant pseudoleukocytosis and concomitant pseudothrombocytopenia secondary to time-dependent EDTA-induced platelet clumping, agglutination, neutrophile adherence, and satellitosis. He noted that the frequency of the problem was low with electronic-impedance instrumentation and avoidable by using fingerstick specimens or heparin as an anticoagulant.[120] EDTA-induced pseudoleukocytosis and pseudothrombocytopenia also were reported with laser-based instruments; however, heparin was shown to be an inappropriate anticoagulant for ELT instruments, apparently producing pseudoleukocytosis itself.[121] A review from the Mayo Clinic reported spuriously low platelet counts from many sources, including platelet satellitosis, cold agglutinins, giant platelets, improper withdrawal technique, or inadequate quantity of anticoagulant. EDTA-induced pseudothrombocytopenia was the most common cause, attributed to a reaction of platelet-specific antibodies (usually IgG) with platelets in the presence of EDTA. The phenomenon could usually be detected by examination of the peripheral smear or use of another anticoagulant. The histogram display of Coulter S+IV/V instruments or the peroxidase X-Y display of the Technicon H6000 alerts the operator to the phenomenon; Coulter S and S+ instruments did not detect platelet clumping.[122]

CONCLUSIONS

Space limitations preclude discussion of certain analytic procedures that are often performed in hematology laboratories. The interested reader is referred to papers that discuss some problems in quality control of the reticulocyte count.[123,124] We have chosen not to discuss some newer analytic parameters that are increasingly becoming available with automated multiparameter hematology analyzers. Perhaps the most interesting of these, the red cell distribution width (RDW), may prove of considerable value in the classification, differentiation, and early diagnosis of certain anemias, particularly certain forms of thalassemia, iron deficiency, and folate-depletion anemia.[125] Measurement of the CV of the red cell volume distribution (anisocytosis in morphologic terms) provides quantitation of red cell heterogeneity and, in conjunction with red cell histograms that identify red cell fragments and agglutinates, may prove useful in the control of the analytic process. Because many problems and limitations of this measurement have been described,[126,127] much additional work will have to be done before conclusions can be drawn.

Clearly, no single approach to quality assurance will be appropriate for all laboratories. Strategies should control sources of preanalytic and postanalytic variation as well as the more obvious and conventional problems such as calibration.

Because laboratories are under increasing pressure to reduce operating costs and expenditures, quality assurance will be an obvious target for cost containment. Quality control of hematology analyses provides multiple opportunities for innovative approaches that recognize regulatory constraints and fiscal reality. "Belt-and-suspenders" systems with excessive redundancy are intrinsically expensive and produce confusion as well as a tendency to ignore warning signs because of the excessive sensitivity of the system. Too spartan a system, encouraged by hasty and hysterical attempts to reduce budgets by fixed percentages, may fail to detect errors and compromise patient care. In any event, cost-effective quality assurance should rest on the premise that a systematic and comprehensive program to prevent error is ultimately far less expensive than responses to analytic mistakes. More than ever, the laboratory director must play a primary role in safeguarding the proper care of the patient by developing and maintaining quality assurance systems that will ensure the accuracy, precision, timeliness, and medical usefulness of hematologic data.

REFERENCES

1. Van Assendelft OW, England JM: Terms, quantities, and units, in van Assendelft OW, England JM (eds): *Advances in Hematological Methods: The Blood Count.* Boca Raton, La, CRC Press, 1982, pp 1–9.
2. Weilert M: Implementing an information system. *Clin. Lab Med* 1983, 3:223.
3. Savage RA: Evidence for hyperglycemic osmotic matrix effects on the Comprehensive Hematology Survey 1981–1982. *Am J Clin Pathol* 1983, 80:626.
4. Penn D, Williams PR, Dutcher TF, et al: Comparison of hematocrit determinations by microhematocrit and electronic particle counter. *Am J Clin Pathol* 1979, 72:71.
5. Fairbanks VF: Nonequivalence of automated and manual hematocrit and erythrocyte indices. *Am J Clin Pathol* 1980, 73:55.
6. Platt R, Tholen D, Couturier L, et al: Hematology, in Elevitch FR, Noce PS (eds): *Data Recap 1970–1980.* Skokie, Ill, College of American Pathologists, 1981, pp 203–221.
7. Bachner P: Candidate methods for hematology quality control. *Pathologist* 1983, 37:531.
8. Drewinko B, Bollinger P, Rountree M, et al: Eight parameter automated hematology analyzers: comparison of two flow cytometric systems. *Am J Clin Pathol* 1982, 78:738.
9. Mayer K, Chin B, Magnes J, et al: Automated platelet counters: A comparative evaluation of latest instrumentation. *Am J Clin Pathol* 1980, 74:135.
10. Mayer K, Chin B, Baisley A: Evaluation of the S-Plus IV. *Am J Clin Pathol* 1985, 83:40.
11. Kaplow L, Orlowski L, Vaznelis ME: Evaluation of the Technicon H6000 Hematology System. *J Clin Lab Automat* 1983, 3:167.
12. Hosty TA, Harris LG, Stonacek SM, et al: Evaluation of an automated continuous-flow hematology instrument: The Technicon H6000. *J Clin Lab Automat* 1982, 2:408.
13. England JM, Bain BJ, Chetty MC, et al: An assessment of the Coulter Counter Model S Plus II and III. *Clin Lab Haematol* 1983, 5:399.
14. England JM, Chetty MC, Chadwick R, et al: An assessment of the Ortho ELT-8. *Clin Lab Haematol* 1982, 4:187.
15. The International Committee for Standardization in Hematology: Recommendation for reference methods of haemoglobinometry in human blood (ICSH Stand. EP6/2:1977) and specifications for International Hemoglobin Cyanide Reference Preparation (ICSH Stand. EP6/3:1977). *J Clin Pathol* 1978, 61:139.
16. Gilmer PR, Williams LJ: The status of methods of calibration in hematology. *Am J Clin Pathol* 1980, 74:600.

17 Gilmer PR, Williams LJ, Koepke JA: Calibration methods for automated hematology instruments. *Am J Clin Pathol* 1977, 68:185.
18 Koepke JA: The calibration of automated instruments for accuracy in haemoglobinometry. *Am J Clin Pathol* 1977, 68:185.
19 National Committee for Clinical Laboratory Standards: Tentative standard: Reference procedure for the quantitative determination of hemoglobin in blood. Tentative standard H15-T. *NCCLS Publications* 1981, 2(112):337.
20 Goldberg ML: Certification of hemoglobin standards. *Pathologist* 36:293, 1982.
21 Zijlstra WG, van Kampen EJ: Spectrophotometry of haemoglobin: the standard of haemoglobin cyanide method and after. *J Clin Chem Clin Biochem* 1981, 19:521.
22 Hematology Resource Committee/Commission on Laboratory Accreditation: Hematology Quality Control, in Diamond I (ed): *Laboratory Accreditation Newsletter,* College of American Pathologists, Skokie, Ill, 1984, 11:8.
23 Lewis SM: Standards and reference preparations, in Lewis SM, Coster JF (eds): *Quality Control in Haematology.* London, Academic Press, 1975, pp 79–95.
24 Gibson FM: Standardization for routine blood counting, in Cavill I (ed): *Quality Control.* New York, Churchill Livingstone, 1982, pp 13–33.
25 Archer RK, Coster JF, Crosland-Taylor PJ, et al: Recommended methods for the determination of packed cell volume prepared on behalf of the World Health Organization by Expert Panel on Blood Cell Sizing of the International Committee for Standardization in Haematology. *Lab/80.4,* Geneva, World Health Organization, 1980.
26 Archer RK, Coster JF, Crosland-Taylor PJ, et al: International Committee for Standardization in Haematology selected methods for the determination of packed cell volume, in van Assendelft OW, England JM (eds): *Advances in Hematological Methods: The Blood Count.* Boca Raton, La, CRC Press, 1982, pp 93–98.
27 Bull BS: The use of patient values, calibrator, and control materials in the routine laboratory, in van Assendelft OW, England JM (eds): *Advances in Hematological Methods: The Blood Count.* Boca Raton, La, CRC Press, 1982, pp 217–227.
28 Mundschenk D: The calibration and control of automated, multi-parameter, whole blood analysis instrumentation: Problems. ICSH Blood Counting Symposium, Berlin, 1979.
29 Archer RK: Available animal bloods and their potential uses, in van Assendelft OW, England JM (eds): *Advances in Hematological Methods: The Blood Count.* Boca Raton, La, CRC Press, 1982, pp 207–216.
30 Arkin C: Personal communication.
31 England JM, Down MC: The effect of the red cell storage lesion on the pcv estimated by the ICSH Reference Method, the micromethod, and the Coulter Counter, Model S, in van Assendelft OW, England JM (eds): *Advances in Hematological Methods: The Blood Count.* Boca Raton, La, CRC Press, 1982, pp 29–35.
32 Ross DW, Wakins BS: The clinical utility of red blood cell deformability measurements with the Ektacytometer. *J Clin Lab Automat* 1982, 2:348.
33 Pearson TC, Guthrie DL: Trapped plasma in the microhematocrit. *Am J Clin Pathol* 1982, 78:770.
34 Chaplin H, Mollison PL: Correction for plasma trapped in the red cell column of the hematocrit. *Blood* 1952, 7:1227.
35 England JM, Walford DM, Waters DAW: Re-assessment of the reliability of the haematocrit. *Br J Haematol* 1972, 23:247.
36 Richardson-Jones A, Twedt DE, Anderson FC: Methodological factors in mean corpuscular volume measurement. Presented at ICSH Expert Panel on Haemocytometry, London, September 1983.

37. England JM: Cell sizing, in Koepke JA (ed): *Laboratory Hematology*. New York, Churchill Livingstone, 1984, pp 927–972.
38. Chanarin I: Critical appraisal of the PCV, in Lewis ML, Coster JF (eds): *Quality Control in Haemotology*. London, Academic Press, 1975, pp 103–110.
39. Jones AR: Counting and sizing of blood cells using aperture-impedance systems, in van Assendelft OW, England JM (eds): *Advances in Hematological Methods: The Blood Count*. Boca Raton, La, CRC Press, 1982, pp 49–72.
40. Bull BS, Korpman RA: Intralaboratory quality control using patients' data, in Cavill I (ed): *Quality Control*. New York, Churchill Livingstone, 1982, pp 121–150.
41. Wertz RK, Triplett, D: A review of platelet counting performance in the United States. *Am J Clin Pathol* 1980, 74:575.
42. Ross DW, Ayscue L, Gulley M: Automated platelet counts: Accuracy, precision and range. *Am J Clin Pathol* 1980, 74:151.
43. Rabinovitch A: Hematology quality control and the Ortho ELT-8. *Am J Med Technol* 1983, 49:649.
44. Ricketts C: Intralaboratory quality control using control samples, in Cavill I (ed): *Quality Control*. New York, Churchill Livingstone, 1982, pp 151–172.
45. *Quality Assurance Service*. College of American Pathologists, Skokie, Ill, 1985.
46. Kafka M, Howanitz PJ, Disilvio J, et al: Development and implementation of QAS today: A quality control system program. *Clin Chem* 1984, 30:959.
47. Savage RA, Hoffman GC: Clinical significance of osmotic matrix errors in automated hematology: The frequency of hyperglycemic osmotic matrix errors producing spurious macrocytosis. *Am J Clin Pathol* 1983, 80:861.
48. Ward PG, Wardle F, Lewis SM: Standardization for routine blood counting-The role of interlaboratory trials, in Cavill I (ed): *Quality Control*. New York, Churchill Livingstone, 1982, pp 102–120.
49. Bull BS: Quality assurance strategies, in Koepke JA (ed): *Laboratory Hematology*. New York, Churchill Livingstone, 1984, pp 999–1021.
50. Brittin GM, Brecher G, Johnson CA, et al: Stability of blood in commonly used anticoagulants. *Am J Clin Pathol* 1969, 52:690.
51. Cohle SD, Saleem A, Makkaoui DE: Effects of storage of blood on stability of hematologic parameters. *Am J Clin Pathol* 1981, 76:67.
52. Carstairs KC, Peters E, Kuzin EJ: Development and description of the "random duplicates" method of quality control in a hematology laboratory. *Am J Clin Pathol* 1977, 67:379.
53. Penner DW, Merry CC: Quality control of qualitative tests in haematology, in Lewis SM, Coster JF (eds): *Quality Control in Haemotology*. London, Academic Press, 1975, pp 137–142.
54. Pettit, JE: Inbuilt quality control, in Lewis SM, Coster JF (eds): *Quality Control in Haematology*. London, Academic Press, 1975, pp 123–135.
55. Dorsey DB: Quality control in hematology. *Am J Clin Pathol* 1963, 40:457.
56. Savage RA: Moving averages of red cell indices as a quality control routine for 7- and 8-parameter hematology analyzers. College of American Pathologists, Skokie, Ill, 1984.
57. Commission on Laboratory Accreditation: College of American Pathologists, Skokie, Ill, 1985.
58. Bull BS, Elashoff RM, Heilbron DC, et al: A study of various estimators for the derivation of quality control procedures from patient erythrocyte indices. *Am J Clin Pathol* 1974, 61:473.
59. Koepke JA, Protextor TJ: Quality assurance for multichannel hematology instruments: Four years' experience with patient mean erythrocyte indices. *Am J Clin Pathol* 1981, 75:28.

60 Lappin TRJ, Farrington CL, Nelson, MG, et al: Intralaboratory quality control for hematology: Comparison of two systems. *Am J Clin Pathol* 1979, 72:426.
61 Cavill I, Ricketts C, Fisher J, et al: An evaluation of two methods of laboratory quality control. *Am J Clin Pathol* 1979, 72:624.
62 Cembrowski GS, Westgard JO: Quality control of multichannel hematology analyzers: Evaluation of Bull's algorithm. *Am J Clin Pathol* 1985, 83:337.
63 Bull BS, Korpman R: Autocalibration of hematology analyzers. *J Clin Lab Automat* 1983, 3:111.
64 Ross JW: Internal quality control for automated hematology instrumentation based on monitoring average patient erythrocyte indices. *Am J Clin Pathol* 1981, 76:502.
65 Skendzel LP, Barnett RN, Platt R: Medically useful criteria for analytic performance of laboratory tests. *Am J Clin Pathol* 1985, 83:200.
66 Galen RS: Predictive value and efficiency of hematology data. *Blood Cells* 1980, 6:185.
67 Savage RA: Why "normal" varies in the normal complete blood count. *Pathologist* 1984, 38:424.
68 Koepke JA: An innovative method for the determination of normal values in hematology using peer group laboratories. *Am J Clin Pathol* 1978, 70:577.
69 Bain B, Seed M, Godsland I: Normal values for peripheral blood white cell counts in women of four different ethnic origins. *J Clin Pathol* 1984, 37:188.
70 Cauchi MN, Smith MB: Quantitative aspects of red cell size variation during pregnancy. *Clin Lab Haematol* 1982, 4:149.
71 Godsland IF, Seed M, Simpson R, et al: Comparison of haematological indices between women of four ethnic groups and the effect of oral contraceptives. *J Clin Pathol* 1983, 36:184.
72 Bjornsson OJ, Davidsson D, Filippusson H, et al: Distribution of haematological, serum and urine values in a general population of middle-aged men. *Scand J Soc Med & Suppl* 1984, 32:1.
73 Giorno R, Clifford JH, Beverly S, et al: Hematology reference values: Analysis by different statistical technics and variations with age and sex. *Am J Clin Pathol* 1980, 74:765.
74 Serjeant GR, Grandison Y, Mason K, et al: Haematology indices in normal Negro Children: a Jamaican cohort from birth to five years. *Clin Lab Haematol* 1980, 2:169.
75 Lipschitz DA, Mitchell CO, Thompson C: The anemia of senescence. *Am J Hematol* 1981, 11:47.
76 Freedman ML, Marcus DL: Anemia and the elderly: Is it physiology or pathology? *Am J Med Sci* 1980, 280:81.
77 Hale WE, Stewart RB, Marks RG: Haematological and biochemical laboratory values in an ambulatory elderly population: An analysis of the effects of age, sex and drugs. *Age Ageing* 1983, 12:275.
78 Jernigan JA, Gudat JC, Blake JL, et al: Reference values for blood findings in relatively fit elderly persons. *J Am Geriatr Soc* 1980, 28:308.
79 Htoo MS, Kofkoff RL, Freedman ML: Erythrocyte parameters in the elderly: An argument against new geriatric normal values. *J Am Geriatr Soc* 1979, 27:547.
80 Dybkaer R, Lauritzen M, Krakauer R: Relative reference values for clinical chemical and haematological quantities in 'healthy' elderly people. *Acta Med Scand* 1981, 209:1.
81 Lindemann R, Ekanger R, Opstad PK, et al: Hematological changes in normal men during prolonged severe exercise. *Am Correct Ther J* 1978, 3:107.
82 Willan PL, Bagnall KM, Mahon M, et al: Haematological characteristics of competitive swimmers. *Br J Sports Med* 1981, 15:238.
83 Dickson DN, Wilkinson RL, Noakes TD: Effects of ultra-marathon training and racing on

hematologic parameters and serum ferritin levels in well-trained athletes. *Int J Sports Med* 1982, 3:111.
84 Ruiz-Arguelles GJ, Sanchez-Medal L, Loria A, et al: Red cell indices in normal adults residing at altitudes from sea level to 2670 meters. *Am J Hematol* 1980, 8:265.
85 Sewchand LS, Lovlin RE, Kinnear G, et al: Red blood cell count (RBC) and volume (MCV) of three subjects in a hypobaric chamber. *Aviat Space Environ Med* 1980, 51:577.
86 Leach CS, Johnson PC: Influence of spaceflight on erythrokinetics in man. *Science* 1984, 225:216.
87 Statland BE, Winkel P, Harris SC, et al: Evaluation of biologic sources of variation of leukocyte counts and other hematologic quantities using very precise automated analyzers. *Am J Clin Pathol* 1977, 69:48.
88 Kaplow LS, Schauble MK, Becktel JM: Validity of hematologic data in Veterans Administration Hospital laboratories. *Am J Clin Pathol* 1979, 71:291.
89 Sacker LS: Specimen collection, in Lewis SM, Coster JF (eds): *Quality Control in Haematology.* London, Academic Press, 1975, pp 211–229.
90 Ross DG, Ross WB, Schreiner DE, et al: Rejection of prospective blood donors due to systematic errors in hematocrit measurement. *Transfusion* 1983, 23:75.
91 Peevy KJ, Grant PH, Hoff CJ: Capillary venous differences in neonatal neutrophil values. *Am J Dis Child* 1982, 136:357.
92 Green JE, Weintraub HA, Donnelly BS, et al: Sample preparation variation and its effects on automated blood cell differential analysis. *Anal Quant Cytol* 1979, 1:187.
93 Petrucci JV, Dunne PA, Chapman CC: Spurious erythrocyte indices as measured by the Model S Coulter Counter due to cold agglutinins. *Am J Clin Pathol* 1984, 56:500.
94 Solanki DL, Blackburn BC: Spurious red blood cell parameters due to serum cold agglutinins: Observations on Ortho ELT-8 cell counter. *Am J Clin Pathol* 1985, 83:218.
95 Beautyman W, Bills T: Osmotic error in erythrocyte volume determinations. *Am J Hematol* 1982, 12:383.
96 Holt JT, DeWandler MJ, Arvan DA: Spurious elevation of the electronically determined mean corpuscular volume and hematocrit caused by hyperglycemia. *Am J Clin Pathol* 1982, 77:561.
97 Cornbleet J: Spurious results from automated hematology cell counters. *Lab Med* 1983, 14:509.
98 Koepke JA: Instruments for quantitative hematology measurements, in Koepke JA (ed): *Laboratory Hematology.* New York, Churchill Livingstone, 1984, pp 903–925.
99 Pierre RV: Differential counting, in Koepke JA (ed): *Laboratory Hematology,* New York, Churchill Livingstone, 1984, pp 973–997.
100 Brecher G, Anderson RE, McMullin PD: When to do diffs: How often should differential counts be repeated? *Blood Cells* 1980, 6:431.
101 Connelly DP, McClain MP, Crowson TW, et al: The use of the differential leukocyte count for inpatient casefinding. *Hum Pathol* 1982, 13:294.
102 Korpman RA, Bull B: Whither the WBC differential? Some alternatives. *Blood Cells* 1980, 6:429.
103 Marchand A, van Lente F, Galen RS: Automated differential leukocyte counters: A comparison of three systems. *J Clin Lab Automat* 1983, 3:19.
104 Rock WA, Miale JB, Johnson WB: Detection of abnormal cells in white cell differentials: Comparison of the Hematrak Automated System with manual methods. *Am J Clin Pathol* 1984, 81:233.
105 Savage RA: Platelet rich plasma: Summing Up 1985, 14:5.

106 Mielke CH, Pritchard JA, Borgman B, et al: Comparative evaluation of phase, impedance, and laser platelet counting. *Lab Med* 1982, 13:363.
107 Dalton WT, Bollinger P, Drewinko B: A side-by-side evaluation of four platelet-counting instruments. *Am J Clin Pathol* 1980, 74:119.
108 Cornbleet PJ, Kessinger S: Accuracy of low platelet counts on the Coulter S-Plus IV. *Am J Clin Pathol* 1985, 83:78.
109 Rowan RM, Fraser C: Platelet size distribution analysis, in van Assendelft OW, England JM (eds): *Advances in Hematological Methods: The Blood Count.* Boca Raton, La, CRC Press, 1982, pp 125–141.
110 Threatte GA, Adrados C, Ebbe S, et al: Mean platelet volume: The need for a reference method. *Am J Clin Pathol* 1984, 81:769.
111 Thompson CB, Diaz DD, Quinn PG, et al: The role of anticoagulation in the measurement of platelet volumes. *Am J Clin Pathol* 1983, 80:327.
112 Paulus JM, Bury J, Grosdent JC: Control of platelet territory development in megakaryocytes. *Blood Cells* 1979, 5:59.
113 Bessman JD, Williams LJ, Gilmer PJ: Mean platelet volume: The inverse relation of platelet count in normal subjects, and an artifact of other particles. *Am J Clin Pathol* 1981, 76:289.
114 Lippi U, Cappelletti P: Quality control of mean platelet volume: A chimera? *Am J Clin Pathol* 1983, 79:648.
115 Bessman JD, Williams LJ, Gilmer PR: Letter to editor. *Am J Clin Pathol* 1983, 79:650.
116 Sassier P: The relation of platelet size and count: Its importance in diagnosing platelet disorders. *Am J Clin Pathol* 1985, 83:275.
117 Stass SA, Holloway ML, Peterson V, et al: Cytoplasmic fragments causing spurious platelet counts in the leukemic phase of poorly differentiated lymphoma. *Am J Clin Pathol* 1979, 71:125.
118 Stass SA, Holloway ML, Slease RB, et al: Spurious counts in hairy cell leukemia. *Am J Clin Pathol* 1977, 68:530.
119 Akwari AM, Ross DW, Stass SA: Spuriously elevated platelet counts due to microspherocytosis. *Am J Clin Pathol* 1982, 77:220.
120 Savage RA: Pseudoleukocytosis due to EDTA-induced platelet clumping. *Am J Clin Pathol* 1984, 81:317.
121 Rabinovitch A: Anticoagulants, platelets, and instrument problems. *Am J Clin Pathol* 1984, 82:132.
122 Payne BA, Pierre RV: Pseudothrombocytopenia: A laboratory artifact with potentially serious consequences. *Mayo Clin Proc* 1984, 59:123.
123 Gilmer PR, Koepke JA: The reticulocyte. *Am J Clin Pathol* 1976, 66:262.
124 Peebles DA, Hochberg A, Clarke TD: Analysis of manual reticulocyte counting. *Am J Clin Pathol* 1981, 76:713.
125 Bessman JD, Gilmer PR, Gardner FH: Improved classification of anemias by MCV and RDW. *Am J Clin Pathol* 1983, 80:322.
126 Roberts GT, el Badawi SB: Red blood cell distribution width index in some hematologic diseases. *Am J Clin Pathol* 1985, 83:222.
127 Cornbleet PJ, Buechel J: Red cell distribution width on the Coulter Model S-Plus. *Am J Med Technol* 1983, 49:865.

CHAPTER 10

QUALITY ASSURANCE IN MICROBIOLOGY

Ron B. Schifman, M.D.

A comprehensive quality control program is necessary to ensure reliability of microbiology results. Early recommendations for quality assurance in medical microbiology were proposed in the mid-1960s and quickly adopted by regulatory agencies. These quality control standards were similar to procedures employed in other laboratory sections and focused on monitoring the performance of equipment, media, reagents, and susceptibility tests. It was also recognized that the diagnostic value of a microbiology result is greatly influenced by clinical circumstances surrounding collection and transportation of a specimen. Proper specimen collection techniques, interpretive analysis and reporting of results, and ongoing educational activities were identified as key elements for creating an effective quality control program.[1]

Rapid progress has been made in standardizing clinical microbiology procedures, and excellent interlaboratory agreement has been achieved for routine bacterial identification and susceptibility testing methods.[2-4] However, the effectiveness of established quality control practices in monitoring reagent and media performance has been questioned.[5] It is likely that current recommendations will be modified as the efficiency of performing standard quality control procedures on certain materials is reevaluated.[6]

Perhaps the most challenging aspect of quality control for the medical microbiology laboratory is development of methods to evaluate specimen quality and accompanying information. This important activity requires ongoing education of laboratory personnel and effective communication with clinical colleagues.

QUALITY CONTROL OF THE MICROBIOLOGY SPECIMEN

Quality microbiology results can be achieved only by examining proper specimens. A poor-quality specimen or inappropriate request will produce information that is clinically useless and potentially misleading. This source of error is reduced by attention to proper guidelines for collecting and processing specimens submitted for microbiologic studies.

The Microbiology Requisition

The microbiology requisition should provide adequate information to evaluate a specimen's suitability for processing, including the following:

1. Patient identification
2. Requesting physician
3. Date and time of specimen collection
4. Type of examination requested
5. Specimen source
6. Specific comments and special requests

It is important to establish guidelines for rejecting a specimen or questioning its value when (1) incomplete information is provided (e.g., swab from unknown site), (2) an improper specimen is submitted (e.g., delayed specimen transport), or (3) an inappropriate test is requested (e.g., anaerobic urine culture).

It is also beneficial to know if a patient is receiving antibiotics, because this may influence culture procedures and affect the final result. For example, it is appropriate to extend the incubation period of a urine culture if a patient is receiving antibiotics, and blood culture sensitivity is improved when antibiotics are inactivated.[7] Finally, space should be provided on the requisition for specific comments and special requests.

Specimen Collection and Transportation

Adherence to standard collection and transportation procedures improves specimen quality and is necessary to achieve accurate and reproducible results. Quality control efforts in this area are difficult, because laboratory personnel generally do not perform these activities. Nevertheless, the laboratory is responsible for developing guidelines for proper specimen collection and transportation and ensuring that they are followed. This process requires ongoing education and frequent communication. It is beneficial to schedule regular meetings with medical and nursing staffs to review procedures and address problems. Written instructions must also be readily available in all clinical areas, and direct communication with the microbiology laboratory should be encouraged.[8,9]

It is helpful to structure specimen collection guidelines around general categories defined on the basis of anatomic site and pathogen. Indications for obtaining a specimen for culture should also be provided. Instructions for transporting specimens to the laboratory should include information about specimen stability, transport media, and proper containers. Materials for transporting patient specimens should be supplied or specified by the laboratory. Application of these procedures is facilitated when laboratory personnel gain the confidence of the medical and nursing staffs by demonstrating a concern for achieving valid results.

Specimen collection and transportation activities can also be monitored to a limited extent within the laboratory. Criteria for excessive cultures should be defined and employed to detect inappropriate laboratory utilization. The clinical relevance of examining a specimen must also be considered.[10,11] For example, material from a decubitus ulcer, periodontal lesion, nose, perirectal abscess, or Foley catheter tip rarely provides clinically useful information, and these specimens should not be cultured.

Communication is important when a poor-quality specimen is determined to be unsuitable for processing. The reasons for rejecting the specimen should be explained and, when possible, an alternative procedure or corrective action should be recommended. When disagreements about specimen quality occur, the rejected specimen should be held at 4°C until a final decision is made in conjunction with responsible medical staff. Processing a poor-quality specimen may be necessary when another specimen would be difficult or impossible to collect. However, a comment about the apparent problem should be included within the final report to avoid the possibility of a misinterpretation.

SPECIMEN PROCESSING

Gross Examination

The gross examination of a specimen will help determine its suitability for processing. Potential problems that may compromise a result include inadequate specimen volume, nonsterile container, or improper collection technique.[9] However, a sample should not be rejected on the basis of its gross appearance alone (e.g., a sputum specimen that macroscopically appears like saliva). In many cases (e.g., sputum, exudate), gross examination is necessary to select the most promising part of the specimen to evaluate. Areas containing mucus, pus, or blood should be selected for smear and culture. In addition, the specimen's gross description (or volume for blood cultures) should be indicated on the final report. This provides information about the nature of the specimen and may influence result interpretation.

Microscopic Examination

Examination of direct smears is beneficial for evaluating specimen quality, checking culture results, and establishing a preliminary diagnosis. This information should be quantitatively evaluated and reported. Quantitative results aid diagnostic interpretation and quality assessment of specimens. This is particularly important for those specimens that are contaminated with colonizing or commensal flora. For example, expectorated sputum containing excessive epithelial cells indicates a poor-quality specimen that is contaminated with oropharyngeal flora and will generally not provide valid results for diagnosing lower respiratory tract bacterial infections.[12–15]

Direct examination of urine specimens for leukocytes and bacteria is also beneficial for assessing quality. In some clinical situations, the presence of pyuria may be more diagnostically helpful than culture results.[16] Furthermore, positive direct smears from unspun urine samples should correlate with quantitative cultures, and comparisons can be used as an internal quality control method to check the accuracy of culture results.[17]

The quality of specimens from wounds and exudates should likewise be evaluated from direct smears. This information is useful for processing cultures and interpreting results obtained from these specimens.[18]

Preparation of the Primary Culture

It is important to establish guidelines for preparing primary cultures based on specimen source. Instructions should include requirements for media and incubation conditions. Culture techniques should also be standardized to achieve reproducible quantitative results. For example, instructions for streaking agar plates should specify the number of times the loop is struck back into the primary inoculum. The reproducibility of this technique can be checked by evaluating plates with standardized inoculum prepared by different technologists.

Errors may occur when preparing quantitative cultures by the calibrated loop method. The accuracy of this technique is influenced by the angle at which the loop is withdrawn from a specimen and the diameter of the container being sampled. Improper technique may cause dilution errors approaching 100%.[19] Therefore it is important that specimen containers and transfer techniques be standardized if this method is employed for quantitative cultures. The accuracy and reproducibility of the calibrated loop method can be determined by absorption spectroscopy or weight determination tests.[19]

Evaluation of Culture Results

A worksheet should be provided to document all observations made from reading culture plates. Documentation should include colonial descriptions and a flowchart describing all biochemical results, growth requirements, and susceptibility tests. The worksheet provides a permanent record of all observations and test results and can be employed to evaluate potential problems after culture plates are discarded. The worksheet also helps organize the evaluation of culture findings and ensures that all plates are examined. Furthermore, it aids those who must complete a culture already in progress. (See Fig. 10-1.)

It is occasionally necessary to reexamine culture plates after a final report is completed. This may occur when clinical or laboratory circumstances, previously unrecognized or absent, indicate that a result may be inaccurate or that additional information should be provided. Therefore, all positive culture plates should be retained for at least several days. Likewise, it is beneficial to save isolates encountered in high-quality specimens (e.g., CSF, blood), because it may be necessary to retrieve these organisms for epidemiologic study. Most commonly isolated pathogens can be stored for a prolonged period of time in bovine serum at $-40°C$.[20]

Quality Control of the Final Report

Decisions about reporting final results depend on specimen source, clinical relevance, direct smear results, quality and quantity of culture isolates, and communication with medical personnel.[21] The overall quality of a microbiology report is related directly to

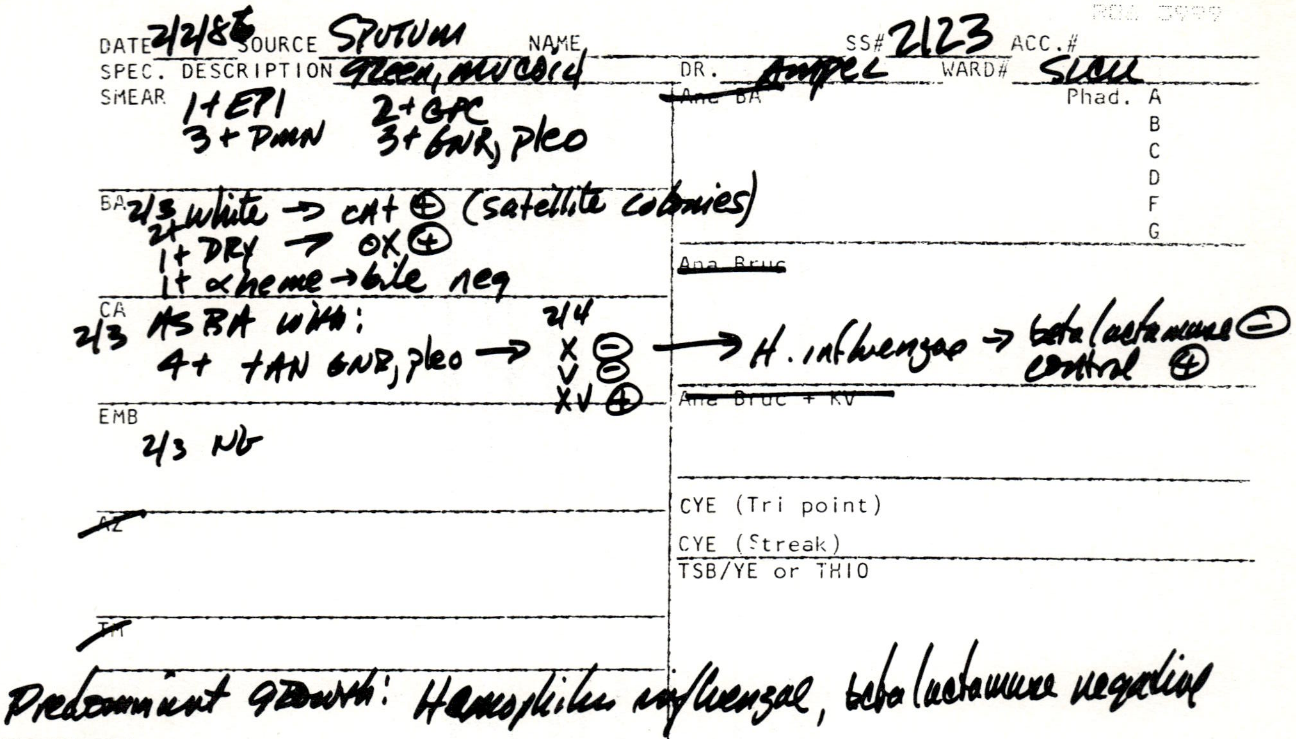

DATE 2/2/86 SOURCE SPUTUM NAME SS# 2123 ACC.#

SPEC. DESCRIPTION green, mucoid DR. Ampel WARD# Slall

SMEAR 1+ EPI 2+ GPC
3+ PMN 3+ GNR, pleo

~~Ana BA~~ Phad. A B C D F G

BA 2/3 white → cat ⊕ (satellite colonies)
1+ DRY → OX ⊕
1+ α heme → bile neg

~~Ana Bruc~~

CA 2/3 AS BA with:
4+ tan GNR, pleo → 2/4 X ⊖ V ⊖ XV ⊕ → H. influenzae → beta lactamase ⊖ control ⊕

~~Ana Bruc + KV~~

EMB 2/3 NG

CYE (Tri point)

CYE (Streak)

TSB/YE or THIO

~~AZ~~

~~TM~~

Predominant growth: Haemophilus influenzae, beta lactamase negative

FIGURE 10-1
Laboratory worksheet for documenting culture and smear findings.

its diagnostic validity. Final results from a culture that is accurately processed may be of poor quality because its significance is misunderstood. It is therefore necessary to ensure that appropriate information regarding the results is communicated adequately.

Specimens obtained from nonsterile sites that yield cultures of mixed bacterial flora of undetermined significance present a difficult reporting problem, because many of these specimens do not yield useful diagnostic information.[18] Complete identification and susceptibility testing of all isolates may be unnecessary, misleading, and require substantial resources. Therefore, guidelines based on the clinical relevance of reporting mixed flora results should be developed and followed consistently. For example, expectorated sputum samples are contaminated to some degree with upper respiratory flora. Thus, full identification and reporting of all organisms detected in these specimens is not required and in fact will be misleading.[13,15,18]

Decisions about performing susceptibility tests on isolates from mixed cultures should be given careful consideration. Inappropriate susceptibility testing and reporting increase the laboratory workload and may result in the patient receiving unnecessary antibiotic therapy. The direct smear and clinical circumstance are often helpful in making decisions about the significance of an isolate.[10,14,22]

Daily review of final reports is an important quality control procedure. Direct microscopic examinations should be qualitatively and quantitatively compared with culture results. Poor correlation between smear and culture results may occur as a result of inaccurate readings, poor technique, unsatisfactory media, inappropriate growth conditions, or the presence of dead organisms. The smear, culture, and worksheet should be reviewed if a discrepancy is detected. Results should also correlate with specimen source. For example, enterococcus is generally not recovered from sputum specimens, and *Streptococcus pneumoniae* is not an expected urinary tract pathogen. Finally, the susceptibility result should be consistent with the organism identification. For example, *Klebsiella* sp. is nearly always resistant to ampicillin and carbenicillin. A susceptible result may indicate an identification or susceptibility error and should be investigated before final results are reported. A list of common predictable organism susceptibility patterns is shown in Table 10-1.

QUALITY CONTROL OF MATERIALS AND PROCEDURES

The Procedure Manual

The procedure manual should contain all established laboratory methods and policies and should be employed as a reference guide to standardize the performance of all microbiology procedures. It is beneficial to maintain a consistent format within the manual for all methods. Guidelines for processing and reporting test results must be included. Appropriate scientific publications and written hospital policies may also be located in the procedure manual.

Reagents and Stains

All reagents should be dated when received and when first used. Expiration dates and storage requirements must be indicated on all reagent containers. A standardized label

TABLE 10-1
PREDICTABLE SUSCEPTIBILITY PATTERNS

Susceptibility result	Organism
Ampicillin susceptibility	*Proteus mirabilis* (tetracycline resistant) *E. coli* (tetracycline susceptible)
Ampicillin and carbenicillin resistance	*Klebsiella* sp. *Citrobacter diversus*
Ampicillin and cephalothin resistance	*Enterobacter* sp. *Citrobacter freundii* *Serratia* sp.
Ampicillin, cephalothin, and tetracycline resistance	*Providencia* sp. *Proteus vulgaris* *Morganella morganii*
Penicillin resistance	*Enterococcus*

helps ensure that all information is consistently provided.

The performance of reagents and stains is evaluated by demonstrating appropriate reactivity by stock control organisms.[20] There is generally a wide tolerance for analytic errors, because most reactions are interpreted as positive or negative. Furthermore, a single discrepancy will often not substantially affect the accuracy of a final result, because bacterial identifications are usually determined by multiple tests that have variable reactivities. Errors can be detected when a reagent does not show an expected reaction when compared with other test results. For example, multiple isolates of *Escherichia coli* that demonstrate negative indole reactions suggest a reagent deficiency (i.e., Kovac's or Ehrlich's reagent), because this organism almost always shows positive indole reactivity.

Current regulatory agency guidelines require that the performance of all reagents and stains be checked each day of use and do not consider the wide variability in performance between different reagents and stains. These recommendations have been challenged as excessive and inefficient.[5,6] Furthermore, these guidelines do not conform with published state-of-the-art consensus recommendations.[20] The appropriate frequency of reagent monitoring should depend on the stability and performance characteristics of materials, recommendations by manufacturers, and the frequency of use.

The performance of all reagents should be evaluated when first prepared or when a new lot is placed in service. The need for additional monitoring can be determined by assessing the frequency of deficiencies with each reagent or stain. Reagents that demonstrate a potential to fail or are seldom employed should be monitored with each use. Likewise, reagents that are demonstrated always to perform as expected can be evaluated at less frequent intervals. Ongoing evaluation of reagent and stain deficiencies should determine the frequency of monitoring these materials. Documentation of reagent performance provides a rationale for accepting or modifying current recommendations and helps demonstrate compliance with regulatory agency expectations (Table 10-2).[6,23]

TABLE 10-2
SURVEILLANCE OF MATERIALS

Item	Condition	Frequency
Stains	Expected staining characteristics	Each new lot or at least semiannually
Inorganic chemical reagents	Expected reactions	Each new lot
Organic chemical reagents	Expected reactions	Each new lot or at least semiannually
Antigens and antisera	Reactivity with homologous antigen or antisera	Each new lot or at least semiannually
Other biological reagents	Reactivity	Each new lot or at least semiannually
All items	Proper labeling, storage conditions, expiration dates	Monthly
User prepared media		
Additives after sterilization	Sterility, pH, inhibition and growth of selected control cultures	Each batch prepared
No additives after sterilization	pH, inhibition and growth of selected control cultures	Each new lot of dehydrated media
Commercially prepared media:		
Additives after sterilization (blood, hemoglobin, enrichment, etc.)	Sterility, pH, inhibition and growth of selected control cultures	New supplier: check first three lots shipped Change in composition stated by supplier: check affected lot Incomplete data from supplier: check each batch
No additives after sterilization	pH, inhibition and growth of selected control cultures	Incomplete data from supplier: check each lot

Source: Bartlett RC, Lennette EH (eds): *Manual of Clinical Microbiology,* ed 3. Washington, DC, American Society for Microbiology, 1980.

Media

Satisfactory performance of culture media is critical to achieve quality results. Media performance must, therefore, be carefully evaluated before it is placed into use. The constituents, characteristics, and performance of each new batch of media prepared within the laboratory must be carefully monitored. Likewise, it is worthwhile to know the extent and results of quality control procedures performed by manufacturers of commercially prepared media.

All media should be labeled with lot number, preparation date, expiration date, and constituents or media name. Media should also be marked with the date placed into service and stored according to the manufacturer's recommendations.

The evaluation of media includes visual inspection, sterility checks, and performance characteristics. Gross inspection is a simple and efficient procedure for assessing media quality. Proper clarity and color should be observed. Turbidity suggests the presence of a precipitate, and media should be used only if this finding disappears after incubation. A change in color between lots may indicate improper pH or constituents (e.g., concentration of red blood cells). The surface of plated media should be smooth and flat, and should not contain excessive moisture or cracks. Pitted or cracked media suggest improper preparation or storage conditions.

Gross examination may identify media contamination, although this may not be evident when media are stored at low temperatures. Contaminated media are a serious problem and have the potential to produce misleading results or invalidate culture findings. Before being placed into service, culture media must be monitored for contamination by incubating a proportion of each new lot overnight. It is recommended that 5 percent of small lots (<100) and 10 samples from large lots be tested.[23] Inhibitory media may not show contamination by this method. It is therefore recommended that a small amount of selective media from each new batch be incubated in sterile broth to detect contamination.[23] Finally, the performance characteristics of all new lots of media must be determined. Appropriate stock control organisms are employed to check for expected positive and negative reactions and growth requirements.[20] It is best to use a light, standardized inoculum for testing media performance. A recommended method suggests inoculating a 1:10 dilution of a McFarland 0.5 standard bacterial suspension with a 0.001 calibrated loop.[23] This approach provides semiquantitative results that can be employed to evaluate between-lot performance. A list of expected growth patterns and biochemical reactions for control organisms is shown in Tables 10-3, 10-4, and 10-5.

Culture media deficiencies may also be detected by observing apparent failures during routine processing. For example, sheep blood agar may support the growth and show expected hemolytic reactions for *Streptococcus pneumoniae* and *Streptococcus pyogenes* in control tests, but fail to produce an accurate CAMP test. This type of problem will be identified only if a high index of suspicion is maintained and media performance is continuously cross-checked with expected culture and identification findings.

The lot number, date, and results of all media evaluations should be recorded. In addition, quality control information should be obtained from the manufacturer. These records may be useful for determining the cause for a breakdown in media performance.

Most commercially available media consistently demonstrate satisfactory performance, because extensive quality control testing is performed before distribution. Reevaluation of all lots of commercially prepared media received in the clinical laboratory is expensive and labor intensive. For this reason, the practice of repeating identical quality control evaluations of commercial media has been questioned.[5,24] A subcommittee of the National Committee for Clinical Laboratory Standards (NCCLS) is preparing a report based on data from the College of American Pathologists' proficiency testing program and other studies that will propose recommendations for the frequency of monitoring commercially prepared media. It is expected that current guidelines will be modified as this area of quality control is reexamined. For example, three categories for media surveillance (extensive, limited, and no monitoring) may be developed based on expected frequency of deficiencies.[5]

Antisera and Antigens

Procedures for monitoring the performance of serologic tests with positive and negative controls are similar to quality control practices described for other reagents. However, these materials tend to be more labile and susceptible to contamination. Exposure to room temperature for prolonged periods should be avoided. Antisera should be grossly inspected before tests are performed and contamination suspected when a clear solution becomes turbid. It is generally necessary for antisera to be monitored each time a test is performed.[18] Controls not only ensure proper reactivity but also aid in the interpretation of agglutination and precipitation reactions that may be difficult to interpret.

QUALITY CONTROL OF ANTIMICROBIAL SUSCEPTIBILITY TESTS

Antibiotic susceptibility testing began in 1928, shortly after Alexander Fleming discovered penicillin. Fleming described the first diffusion susceptibility test (ditch plate assay) and the first broth dilution test, which were utilized primarily to study the inhibitory effects of penicillin on bacteria.[25] These original techniques, with substantial modifications, continue to be employed for routine susceptibility testing of rapidly growing bacteria. In the late 1960s, the Food and Drug Administration began to monitor and regulate the production of antibiotic-containing disks that were utilized for susceptibility testing.[26-28] In the early 1970s a great deal of progress was made in standardizing antimicrobial susceptibility test procedures, and since 1975, the NCCLS has published numerous recommendations for the performance, surveillance, and interpretation of broth dilution and agar diffusion susceptibility assays.[28-30] These standards have been widely adopted and provide a valuable framework for achieving reproducible interlaboratory susceptibility test results.[31-34]

The quality control of antimicrobial susceptibility tests consists of monitoring (1) the precision and accuracy of results, (2) the performance of materials, and (3) the execution of manual and automated procedures.[35] Susceptibility tests are monitored by testing genetically stable reference strains with materials and procedures that are used for routine susceptibility testing.[36] Although this practice eliminates the need to evaluate each component of the assay, it has the potential to fail if two deficiencies simultaneously offset each other, thus providing apparently accurate results (e.g., heavy inoculum tested against low-potency antibiotic disks).

Selection of Appropriate Organism and Method

An excellent quality control program for monitoring susceptibility methods is useless if valid results are inappropriately reported or the test is inappropriately applied. A

TABLE 10-3
CONTROLS FOR PLATED MEDIA

Medium	Atmosphere, length of incubation	Control organisms	Expected results	Comments
Blood agar	Aerobic, 24 h	Group A *Streptococcus* *Streptococcus pneumoniae* *Haemophilus influenzae* with *Staphylococcus* streak	Growth, beta-hemolysis Growth, alpha-hemolysis Satellitism	
Bismuth sulfite	Aerobic, 24 h	*Salmonella typhi* *Escherichia coli*	Black colonies, metallic sheen No colonies or inhibited (pale green)	
Bordet-Gengou	Moist jar, 6 days	*Bordetella pertussis*	Growth	Set up *B. pertussis* control each time patient specimen set up (use freshly prepared media)
Chocolate	CO₂, 24 h	*H. influenzae* *Neisseria gonorrhoeae*	Growth Growth	
Chlamydospore	Aerobic, 24 h, 25°C	*Candida albicans*	Chlamydospores	
Colistin-nalidixic acid	Aerobic, 24 h	Group A *Streptococcus* *Staphylococcus aureus* *Pseudomonas aeruginosa*	Growth, beta-hemolytic Growth No growth	
EMB	Aerobic, 24 h	*E. coli* *Shigella flexneri*	Growth, green metallic sheen Growth, lactose-negative	
Hektoen	Aerobic, 24 h	*Salmonella typhimurium* *S. flexneri* *E. coli*	Growth, green with black centers Growth, green Growth, orange (may be inhibited)	

Medium	Incubation	Organism	Expected Results	Comments
MacConkey	Aerobic, 24 h	E. coli	Growth, lactose-positive	
		Proteus mirabilis	Growth, lactose-negative, inhibition of spreading	
		Enterococcus	No growth	
Mueller-Hinton	Aerobic, 24 h with antibiotic disks	E. coli (ATCC 25922)	Acceptable zone sizes	150 by 15 mm for disk diffusion susceptibility testing, pH = 7.2–7.4 at 25°C, depth = 4–5 mm
		S. aureus (ATCC 25923)		
		P. aeruginosa (ATCC 27853)		
Phenylethyl alcohol	Aerobic, 24 h	Any Streptococcus	Growth	
		E. coli	Growth inhibited	
Sabouraud	Aerobic, 24 h, 25°C	C. albicans	Growth	
		E. coli	Growth inhibited	
Salmonella-Shigella	Aerobic, 24 h	S. typhimurium	Growth, lactose-negative	
		E. coli	No growth or inhibited	
Staphylococcus (mannitol salt, Staphylococcus 110, etc.)	Aerobic, 24 h	S. aureus	Growth, typical characteristics	
		E. coli	No growth	
Tellurite base agar (Tinsdale)	Aerobic, 24–48 h	Corynebacterium diphtheriae	Black colonies with brown halos	
		Corynebacterium pseudodiphtheriticum	Inhibited, no halo	
		S. aureus	Inhibited, or black without halo	
Thayer-Martin or modified Thayer-Martin	CO_2, 24 hr	N. gonorrhoeae	Growth	
		E. coli	No growth	
		S. epidermidis	No growth	
		Candida sp.	No growth	
XLD	Aerobic, 24 h	S. typhimurium	Growth, pink-red with black centers	May require full 24 h to show true colors
		S. flexneri	Growth, pink	
		E. coli	Yellow (may be inhibited)	

Source: Blazevic DJ, Hall CT, Wilson ME, Balows A (eds): *Practical Quality Control Procedures for the Clinical Microbiology Laboratory.* Washington, DC, American Society for Microbiology, 1976.

decision to perform susceptibility tests should be based on the clinical relevance of the culture findings as discussed above and elsewhere.[10,15,22] In addition, organisms that demonstrate predictable susceptibility patterns (e.g., *Streptococcus pyogenes* against penicillin G) should not be routinely tested.

The choice of antibiotics to test depends on the bacterial isolate and culture site.[31] In addition, some test results influence the interpretation and reporting of other reports. For example, methicillin-resistant *Staphylococcus* sp. often demonstrates false susceptibility to cephalothin. In these cases, it is appropriate to report resistance to cephalothin.[30]

Standardized susceptibility tests should be performed only on rapidly growing aerobic organisms. Susceptibility methods for testing most slow-growing, fastidious organisms are not standardized, and the utilization of methods designed for rapidly growing bacteria may yield invalid results.[30,31] In these cases, therapy should be guided by clinical experience and information derived from reference laboratories.

Control Strains

Standard reference strains are recommended for controlling susceptibility tests.[30,31] These organisms have been selected on the basis of genetic stability and reproducible performance in susceptibility assays.[36] It is essential that all of these organisms be available to assess the precision and accuracy of susceptibility tests. They may be stored for long periods at −40°C in 50 percent calf serum (Table 10-6).

Control tests should be performed from fresh subcultures that have been incubated for at least 18 hours. Subcultures should be checked for contamination and good growth before the reference strain is tested. Tests performed directly from stored stock cultures may produce unreliable results.[35]

Some recommended control strains are listed in Table 10-7.

Staphylococcus aureus ATCC 25923 is recommended for monitoring disk diffusion tests but is of less value for dilution procedures because of its susceptibility to very low minimum inhibitory concentrations of antibiotics.[30] *S. aureus* ATCC 29213, a weak beta lactamase producer, is recommended for broth dilution assays.[31] *P. aeruginosa* ATCC 27853, when repeatedly subcultured, may spontaneously develop resistance to carbenicillin. A new subculture should be prepared from stock culture when this occurs. With *S. faecalis* ATCC 29212 it is possible to detect inappropriately high levels of thymidine in Mueller-Hinton media that adversely affect trimethoprim-sulfamethoxazole susceptibility results. Because *E. coli* ATCC 35218 produces a beta lactamase enzyme, this organism has been selected to test the performance of disks with a combination of beta lactam antibiotic and beta lactamase inhibitor (e.g., augmentin).[30]

Additional control organisms may be selected by individual laboratories for specific purposes. For example, methicillin-resistant *Staphylococcus aureus* may be difficult to detect by standard and automated methods. Laboratories that encounter these stains should periodically test a well-characterized strain of methicillin-resistant *S. aureus* as part of routine quality control activities.[37]

TABLE 10-4
CONTROLS FOR BROTH MEDIA

Medium	Control organisms	Expected results	Comments
Blood culture	*Clostridium novyi*	Growth	Unvented bottle
	Group A *Streptococcus*	Growth	Unvented bottle Gram stain of uninoculated medium should show no bacteria
Cooked meat (with or without carbohydrate)	*Clostridium novyi*	Growth	Gram stain of uninoculated medium should show no (or few) bacteria
GN	*Salmonella typhimurium* *Shigella flexneri*	Growth on subculture to appropriate medium (e.g., MacConkey)	Subculture after 12-h incubation
Peptone-yeast-glucose	*Bacteroides fragilis*	Growth with pH < 5.7 after 48 h	Gas chromatographic analysis of each lot to determine levels of fatty acids in uninoculated medium
Thioglycolate or other routine enrichment broth	*B. fragilis* Group A *Streptococcus*	Growth Growth	
Selenite or tetrathionate	*S. typhimurium* *Escherichia coli*	Growth on subculture Inhibition of growth on subculture	Subculture to appropriate medium after 18 h

Source: Blazevic DJ, Hall CT, Wilson ME, Balows A (eds): *Practical Quality Control Procedures for the Clinical Microbiology Laboratory.* Washington DC, American Society for Microbiology, 1976.

Antibiotics

Proper activity of antibiotics utilized for susceptibility assays is critical for achieving consistent and accurate results. Substantial variability may occur from inactivation during transport and normal laboratory use. Beta-lactam antibiotics are especially labile in the presence of excess humidity and high temperatures.[10,38,39]

Prior to the standardization of antimicrobial susceptibility methods, commercially prepared antibiotic disks were not uniform, many had unsatisfactory potency, and in some cases disks had no activity.[10,26,29] This prompted the Food and Drug Administration (FDA) to require batch certification and standardization of all lots of disks and to specify control limits between 67 percent and 150 percent of labeled activity.[26-28,40] This improved the accuracy of diffusion susceptibility tests, but it did not ensure reliability under routine laboratory conditions. Furthermore, the FDA is no longer partic-

TABLE 10-5
CONTROLS FOR BIOCHEMICAL MEDIA AND TESTS

Medium[a]	Control organism[b]	Expected results
Acetate	*Escherichia coli*	Growth, blue color
	Shigella flexneri	No growth
Arginine dihydrolase	*Enterobacter cloacae*	Positive
	Proteus mirabilis	Negative
Bile-esculin	*Enterococcus*	Growth, black color
	alpha-*Streptococcus*, not Group D	No growth
Christensen urea	*P. mirabilis*	Pink throughout (positive)
	E. coli	No color change
Citrate, Simmons	*Klebsiella pneumoniae*	Growth, blue color
	E. coli	No growth
CTA sugars		
Dextrose	*Neisseria gonorrhoeae*	Positive
	Branhamella catarrhalis	Negative
Sucrose	*E. coli*	Positive
	N. gonorrhoeae	Negative
Maltose	*Salmonella*, or *Neisseria meningitidis*	Positive
	N. gonorrhoeae	Negative
Differential disks or strips:		
Bacitracin disks (A)	Group A *Streptococcus*	Zone of inhibited growth with heavy inoculum
	alpha-*Streptococcus* (viridans)	No inhibition of growth
Optochin disks (P)	*Streptococcus pneumoniae*	Zone of inhibited growth ($\geq$ 15 mm)
	alpha-*Streptococcus* (viridans)	No inhibition of growth
X and V disks (on BHI agar)	*Haemophilus influenzae*	Growth only between disks
Cytochrome oxidase	*Pseudomonas aeruginosa*	Blue color (positive)
	E. coli	No color change
DNA (toluidine blue)	*Serratia marcescens*	Pink
	Enterobacter	Blue
(1 N HCl)	*S. marcescens*	Zone of clearing
	Enterobacter	No clearing

Test	Organism	Expected result
Hippurate hydrolysis	Group B Streptococcus Group A Streptococcus	Positive Negative
Indole	E. coli K. pneumoniae	Positive Negative
Lysine decarboxylase	Salmonella typhimurium Shigella flexneri	Positive Negative
Lysine iron agar	S. typhimurium S. flexneri P. mirabilis	Purple butt and slant with H_2S Purple slant, yellow butt Red slant, yellow butt
Malonate	E. coli K. pneumoniae	No growth Growth, blue color
Motility	P. mirabilis K. pneumoniae	Positive Negative
Nitrate	E. coli Acinetobacter (var. lwoffi)	Positive Negative
Ornithine decarboxylase	S. marcescens K. pneumoniae	Positive Negative
OF dextrose	P. aeruginosa Acinetobacter (var. lwoffi)	Oxidizer No reaction
ONPG	S. marcescens S. typhimurium	Positive Negative
Phenylalanine deaminase	P. mirabilis E. coli	Positive Negative
Pigment media (Tech, Flo, P, F, etc.)	P. aeruginosa E. coli	Pyocyanin and pyoverdin produced No pigment
Triple sugar iron agar	Citrobacter freundii Shigella flexneri P. aeruginosa	A/A, H_2S K/A K/NR
Voges-Proskauer	K. pneumoniae E. coli	Positive Negative

[a]Abbreviations: BHI, Brain heart infusion; DNA, deoxyribonucleic acid; OF, oxidative-fermentative; ONPG, o-nitrophenyl-β-D-galactopyranoside; A/A, acid/acid; K/A, alkaline/acid; K/NR, alkaline/no reaction.
[b]Variability occurs within species. Choose strains to give the desired reaction.
Source: Blazevic DJ, Hall CT, Wilson ME, Balows A (eds): *Practical Quality Control Procedures for the Clinical Microbiology Laboratory*. Washington DC, American Society for Microbiology, 1976.

TABLE 10-6
METHODS OF MAINTENANCE FOR QUALITY CONTROL CULTURES

Organism	Maintenance[a]
Enterobacteriaceae, nonfermenters, staphylococci	TSA agar deeps at room temp CTA Cooked meat Quick-freezing; storage at < −40°C Lyophilization
Streptococci (including pneumococci), Listeria	Blood agar slants (4–8°C) Blood agar plates (subculture 2× weekly) CTA Cooked meat Quick-freezing; storage at < −40°C Lyophilization
Haemophilus influenzae	Chocolate slants (4–8°C) Chocolate plates (subculture 2× weekly) Quick-freezing; storage at < −40°C Lyophilization
Neisseria gonorrhoeae, N. meningitidis	Chocolate agar (subculture every other day) Quick-freezing; storage at < −40°C Lyophilization
Corynebacterium diphtheriae	Cooked meat Quick-freezing; storage at < −40°C Lyophilization
Bordetella pertussis	B-G agar (4–8°C) Quick-freezing; storage at < −40°C Lyophilization
Yeasts	Sterile distilled water (4–8°C or room temp)
Fungi	Sterile soil (4–8°C) Overlay with sterile mineral oil (4–8°C or room temp)
Mycobacterium spp.	Lowenstein-Jensen medium (25°C in dark) Freezing at −70°C

[a]Abbreviations: TSA, Trypticase soy agar; B-G, Bordet-Gengou.
Source: Blazevic DJ, Hall CT, Wilson ME, Balows A (eds): *Practical Quality Control Procedures for the Clinical Microbiology Laboratory*. Washington DC, American Society for Microbiology, 1976.

TABLE 10-7
RECOMMENDED CONTROL STRAINS FOR SUSCEPTIBILITY TESTING

Escherichia coli, ATCC 25922 and ATCC 35218
Staphylococcus aureus, ATCC 25923 and ATCC 29213
Pseudomonas aeruginosa, ATCC 27853
Streptococcus faecalis, ATCC 29212

ipating in batch certification of antibiotic disks.[41] Therefore, it is important that the activity of antibiotic disks be evaluated periodically by performing diffusion tests on susceptible control organisms. The measured zone diameters achieved with reference strains are indicative of antibiotic disk potency. Acceptable zone diameter control limits are established for reference strains.[30]

Repeat testing of control strains allows laboratories to determine a mean and standard deviation for each antibiotic tested. These values should fall within the accuracy control range established by the NCCLS.[30] A single value that significantly deviates below the laboratory's control range suggests deterioration of antibiotic, and this batch of disks should be discarded. Numerous mean values that are consistently above or below the NCCLS control means suggest a deficiency in inoculum preparation or inoculation technique. High mean values suggest an inoculum that is too light, and low mean values suggest a heavy inoculum. In addition, a deteriorating lot of antibiotic disks may be detected by a trend toward declining control mean zone diameters. When testing aminoglycosides and tetracycline, mean zone diameters that deviate in opposite directions suggest unsatisfactory media pH.

A study by Tardio and Westhoff demonstrated that 91 percent of disks with marginal potency (67 percent of labeled activity) would pass control limits established by the NCCLS and suggested that recommended tolerance ranges may be too broad and fail to detect low-potency antibiotic disks.[42] However, control limits for standardized disk diffusion methods were established as general guidelines from collaborative studies, and a relatively wide range is expected due to interlaboratory variability. Intralaboratory ranges should be tighter, which underscores the need for each laboratory to determine a working control mean and standard deviation for reference strains. Proficiency surveys have demonstrated that most laboratories can achieve acceptable results with standardized disk diffusion methods.[2,32–34,43]

Tolerance limits for minimum inhibitory concentration (MIC) endpoints are established for control reference strains to check potency and monitor the accuracy of broth dilution assays. It is important that broth dilution tests be configured to contain appropriate dilution schemes so that accuracy and precision can be properly evaluated. For example, the control range for piperacillin against *E. coli* ATCC 25922 is 1.0 to 4.0 $\mu g/dl$. The accuracy and precision of a broth dilution test cannot be satisfactorily determined for this antibiotic if the dilution begins off-scale at 8.0 $\mu g/dl$. This is a real limitation for many antibiotic dilution configurations present in commercially available broth dilution assays.[44,45]

A similar problem is encountered with automated methods (MS-2 and Autobac) that determine susceptibility as a function of bacterial growth in the presence of a single antibiotic concentration that is eluted from a disk into a broth solution. Susceptible reference strains produce scant turbidity that is quantitated at the far end of the instrument's interpretive scale. Therefore, significant deterioration of antibiotic may not be identified by routine monitoring with control organisms. However, antibiotic activity can be monitored by periodically testing disks using a standard agar diffusion method.[46] Control limits must be established within the laboratory, because the antibiotic content of disks employed for automated susceptibility testing is generally different than standard manual methods. Achievable precision with this quality control technique is about ±3 mm.

A precision control value for disk diffusion tests may be calculated from five previous susceptibility determinations on reference strains. A maximum range of zone diameter sizes is derived from these results and can be used to monitor intra-assay precision.[47] In addition, a cumulative mean zone diameter value can be determined. Suggested guidelines for acceptable precision control limits have been determined by the NCCLS.[30,31,47] These values are based on expected analytic variability of standardized diffusion susceptibility methods.

Acceptable precision limits may also be considered as the method of reproducibility that will yield the least tolerable interpretive error. That is, the consistency of disk diffusion results should be sufficient to minimize false susceptible and false resistant interpretations to 1 percent or less of all results. This theoretical precision limit can be determined for each antibiotic-organism combination by the formula[35]:

$$\text{standard deviation} = S_{min} - R_{max} / 2.33$$

where standard deviation = maximum allowable limit to minimize interpretive errors
S_{min} = smallest zone size interpreted as susceptible
R_{max} = largest zone size interpreted as resistant
2.33 = standard deviation that includes 98 percent of expected determinations.

Expected precision for broth dilution tests is plus or minus one twofold dilution from the modal MIC level. The precision of automated and commercially prepared broth dilution methods tends to be better than the reference broth dilution assay.[48] Furthermore, the control range of MICs may vary between methods. Therefore, some control ranges, determined from reference broth dilution methods, may not conform to commercial and automated dilution assays.[48]

Inoculum

The preparation of standardized inoculum is a critical component of susceptibility methods and must be precise. Inoculum is prepared by adjusting the turbidity of a bacterial suspension to a McFarland 0.5 standard, which is equal to about 2×10^8 CFU/ml. The turbidity standard is prepared by adding 0.5 ml of 0.048 M $BaCl_2$ to 99.5 ml of 0.18 N H_2SO_4. When tightly sealed and stored at room temperature in a dark container, this standard is generally stable for 6 months.[49] The $BaCl_2$ solution must be vigorously shaken before use.

Bacterial suspensions should be made with the aid of a light box or photometer,[50] whereas inoculum preparation without comparison to a turbidity standard should be discouraged. The accuracy of inoculum preparation techniques should be determined periodically by performing quantitative colony counts from standardized inocula. Accurate susceptibility results can be obtained with inoculum in either stationary or log-phase growth.[51,52]

Broth dilution tests must include a growth control (inoculation of broth media without antibiotics) to determine inoculum viability and as a control to interpret endpoints. The inoculum for broth dilution and automated susceptibility tests should also be tested for purity (single organism) by making a subculture from the bacterial suspension and observing for pure growth after overnight incubation.

Standardized suspensions of *E. coli* and *P. aeruginosa* reference strains apparently retain viability in sterile deionized water for up to 32 days and will yield acceptable quality control results when tested by the disk diffusion method.[53] The use of these inocula has the potential to decrease costs and eliminate variability associated with inoculum preparation.

Media

Mueller-Hinton agar or broth media are recommended for susceptibility testing. Alternative media should not be used, because control limits and interpretive criteria are valid only for tests performed with Mueller-Hinton media. Mueller-Hinton media are not uniform from batch to batch, and changes in media components have the potential to affect susceptibility results adversely. Three major constituents influence susceptibility tests and must be carefully monitored and controlled to obtain satisfactory results. These variables include cation concentration, pH, and thymidine concentration.

Mueller-Hinton media must have adequate levels of magnesium (25 mg/liter) and calcium (50 mg/liter) to detect reliably aminoglycoside resistance in *Pseudomonas aeruginosa*.[54-56] Deficient quantities of these cations most commonly occur with broth media. Cation deficiencies will not be identified by testing the control *P. aeruginosa* strain, because this organism is susceptible to aminoglycosides. The calcium and magnesium concentrations of each batch of Mueller-Hinton medium should be specified by the manufacturer or determined in the laboratory. Alternatively, a control strain of *P. aeruginosa* with a moderately resistant MIC (8 to 16 µg/ml) may be tested with each new lot of medium. A cation deficiency should be suspected if this organism fails to demonstrate aminoglycoside resistance.

The pH of Mueller-Hinton media should range between 7.2 and 7.4. This should be documented by the manufacturer or measured in the laboratory. Media pH can be determined with a surface pH electrode, or a standard pH electrode may be placed into mashed agar pieces. In laboratories that prepare Mueller-Hinton agar media, pH can be measured by allowing media to solidify around a pH electrode.

The activity of antibiotics is affected by media pH. The activity of penicillin, aminoglycosides, and erythromicin is decreased and that of tetracycline is increased when tested with low-pH media. Unsatisfactory pH may be suspected when mean zone diameters of control organisms tested against tetracycline and gentamicin deviate in opposite directions.

Another variable constituent in Mueller-Hinton media is thymidine concentration. This component affects susceptibility tests with sulfa antibiotics and trimethoprim.[30] Excess thymidine and thymine levels have the potential to cause falsely resistant results. A decreased zone diameter and inner colonies, or increased MIC observed when testing *Streptococcus faecalis* ATCC 29212 against trimethoprim-sulfamethoxazole, suggests an inappropriately high level of thymidine.[30]

Performance and Interpretation

Unsatisfactory technical performance is the most common source of error associated with susceptibility testing. A study reported by Bartlett[6] found that 3.9 percent of diffusion susceptibility results performed with control strains were inaccurate. In nearly all cases, errors were linked with performance failures. Material deficiencies were detected in only 0.06 percent of all control tests. Technical problems included unsatisfactory inoculum (most common), improperly placed disks, and, rarely, misreading of zone diameters.

Surveillance for this important source of errors has not been emphasized, and guidelines for monitoring technical performance are not available. One monitoring technique involves several technologists simultaneously performing identical susceptibility tests on reference strains.[57] An error that is demonstrated within all tests suggests a material deficiency, whereas an isolated error is consistent with a technical problem.

Errors may also occur when tests are performed correctly but results are misinterpreted or inaccurately reported. This problem is well illustrated by an interlaboratory proficiency survey conducted to assess the accuracy of detecting a strain of penicillin-resistant *Streptococcus pneumoniae*.[58] Nearly all participants accurately performed the test, but fewer than 15 percent reported a correct result because proper criteria for interpreting the oxacillin zone diameter were not applied.

Finally, critical errors may occur when methods are not standardized or controlled. For example, in vitro susceptibility testing has demonstrated that some strains of *Staphylococcus aureus* are killed only with penicillin or methicillin concentrations that are significantly higher than inhibitory levels of these antibiotics.[59,60] This phenomenon, referrred to as tolerance, has been implicated as a cause for treatment failures in patients with serious staphylococcal infections. However, the significance of this finding has been seriously questioned because the performance and interpretation of bactericidal assays is not standardized and results can be markedly affected by uncontrolled variables such as growth phase, mode of inoculation, and antibiotic carryover.[61,62]

Frequency of Quality Control Testing

Standard performance guidelines for diffusion susceptibility testing include daily quality control with reference strains. However, it is apparent that many laboratories can achieve acceptable results with less frequent quality control testing.[2,34] Revised NCCLS standards contain tentative recommendations for weekly quality control testing if a laboratory can document adequate daily performance for 30 days.[30] This is accomplished by observing at least 27 of 30 zone diameter test results within control limits for each antibiotic-organism combination tested. Daily quality control testing must resume when weekly surveillance demonstrates a potential problem and must continue until the problem is identified and corrected. In addition, reference strains should always be tested with all new lots of media and antibiotics. Daily quality control with reference strains is recommended for broth dilution and automated methods.[31]

REFERENCE LABORATORY

A commercial, state, or university referral clinical laboratory is a valuable resource for checking the accuracy of results and is essential for providing assistance when difficult culture, identification, susceptibility, or serologic problems are encountered. This is particularly important if an unusual result is obtained or a test is infrequently performed. Confirmation of results provides confidence in the laboratory's procedures and materials. New findings or discrepancies serve to resolve potential problems and enhance the education and experience of laboratory personnel.

PROFICIENCY TESTING

An important component of quality control in the microbiology laboratory is the processing of unknown specimens with defined constituents. Results obtained from these specimens are compared with expected results to evaluate the quality of laboratory performance.[63]

Internal proficiency testing is conducted by processing test specimens that are disguised as routine samples. This exercise has the advantage of evaluating all procedures and materials that are routinely employed to process specimens (transport, smear, culture, timeliness of reporting, etc.).

External proficiency testing is conducted by outside laboratories and agencies to evaluate interlaboratory performance. The largest clinical microbiology proficiency survey is conducted by the College of American Pathologists to evaluate identification and susceptibility procedures.[2] Important benefits of this program include (1) identification of individual laboratory deficiencies, (2) detection of inadequate or improved methods, (3) continuing education, and (4) standardization of methods and materials.[64] Proficiency testing in the clinical laboratory is discussed in Chapter 14.

QUALITY CONTROL OF EQUIPMENT AND THE ENVIRONMENT

The performance of laboratory equipment must be properly monitored to identify problems that will affect test results. This should include written instructions for preventive maintenance, performance checks, and calibration procedures. It is important to document all maintenance and performance activities, especially all equipment failures and repairs.

Temperature-sensitive equipment should be constantly monitored. A recording thermometer is recommended for identifying unacceptable drifts in temperatures. For critical temperature control, an alarm system can be employed that will indicate immediately when temperatures exceed tolerance limits. This is important because results can be severely affected by improper incubation temperatures.[65] Thermometers employed to monitor temperatures above freezing should be placed in water. Incubators with added CO_2 should be tested daily for CO_2 content with an indicator such as Fyrite.

Environmental chambers should be tested for proper atmospheric conditions with chemical indicators (e.g., methylene blue for anaerobic conditions) or control strains (e.g., *Campylobacter jejuni* for microaerophilic conditions).

The performance of autoclaves should be periodically checked with spore strips or spore solutions. Temperatures should be recorded with each use. Autoclave times should be established and adhered to in order to assure total decontamination of waste materials in a fully loaded chamber.

Centrifuges should be checked at least once a year for proper speed (with a tachometer), calibration, and braking. This check should also include inspection of brushes and bearings. Microscopes should be kept clean and periodically adjusted and lubricated. Dust covers should be used when microscopes are not in service.

Biologic safety cabinets should be inspected for proper air flow with an anemometer. Smoke sticks can be employed to determine the pattern of air flow. A schedule should be followed for replacing bacterial filters. Safety cabinets should be decontaminated before filters are removed. Ultraviolet (UV) lights should be periodically checked for light intensity with a UV light meter. It is recommended that a UV lamp be replaced when light intensity drops below 70 percent of initial readings.[66] Finally, the accuracy of calibrated loops and pipets should be periodically checked.

The laboratory environment must be kept clean and well ventilated. A minimum of at least 100 ft^2 should be available per FTE. Incandescent lighting should be used, when possible, for reading culture plates and tubes. Cultures should be processed in one area to avoid the hazard of transporting potentially harmful pathogens.

CONCLUSION

Accurate and reproducible results are obtained when tests are performed in a consistent manner with satisfactory materials. A final microbiology report generally requires numerous procedural steps and interpretation of many pieces of information. Although this creates a substantial challenge to ensure that all materials are in control, it also provides an opportunity to evaluate the consistency and interrelationships of method results. A single unexpected or inappropriate finding may suggest a specific quality control problem without producing an inaccurate result. Thus, each microbiologic study provides its own internal quality control checks to identify procedural errors and material defects.

REFERENCES

1. Dumoff M, Isenberg HD (eds): Quality control in the clinical microbiology laboratory (second round table). Morris Plains, NJ, General Diagnostics Division, Warner-Lambert Pharmaceutical Co, 1967.
2. Jones RN, Edson DC, Marymont JV: Evaluations of antimicrobial susceptibility test proficiency by the College of American Pathologists survey program. *Am J Clin Pathol* 1982, 78:168.
3. Gavan TL: A summary of the bacteriology portion of the 1972 basic, comprehensive and special College of American Pathologists (CAP) quality evaluation program. *Am J Clin Pathol* 1974, 61:971.

4 Marymont JH III, Marymont JH Jr, Gavan TL: Performance of Enterobacteriaceae identification systems: An analysis of College of American Pathologists survey data. *Am J Clin Pathol* 1978, 70:539.
5 Bartlett RC, Rutz CA, Knopacki N: Cost effectiveness of quality control in bacteriology. *Am J Clin Pathol* 1982, 77:184.
6 Bartlett RC: Cost effective quality control in microbiology. *Clin Microbiol Newsletter* 1985, 7:3.
7 Hansen SL, Hetmanski J, Stewart BJ: Resin-process methods for improved isolation of organisms from blood and other body fluids. *Am J Med* 1983, 75(1B):31.
8 Bartlett RC: Making optimal use of the microbiology laboratory. I. Use of the laboratory. *JAMA* 1982, 247:857.
9 Isenberg HD, Schoenknecht FD, VonGravenitz A: Collection and Processing of Bacteriological Specimens, Cumitech 9, Rubin SJ (ed). Washington, DC, American Society for Microbiology, 1979.
10 Heineman HS, DiAntonio RR. Bacteriology of sputum—purpose, significance, problems and role in diagnosis, in Lorian V (ed): *Significance of Medical Microbiology in the Care of Patients,* ed 3. Baltimore, MD, Williams & Wilkins, 1982, pp 169–196.
11 Clinical Relevance in Microbiology, CAP Aspen Conference 1979, College of American Pathologists, Skokie, IL, 1981.
12 Bartlett RC, Rutz CA: Processing control and cost in bacteriology. *Am J Clin Pathol* 1980, 74:287.
13 Bartlett JG, Brewer NS, Ryan KJ: *Laboratory Diagnosis of Lower Respiratory Tract Infections,* Cumitech 7, Washington JA (ed). Washington DC, American Society for Microbiology, 1978.
14 Murry PR: Macroscopic and microscopic evaluation of respiratory specimens, in Winn WC (ed): *Symposium on Respiratory Infections: Clinics in Laboratory Medicine,* Philadelphia, WB Saunders, 1982, vol 2, pp 259–267.
15 Sodeman TM, Colmer J: Microbiology of the respiratory tract. *Lab Med* 1983, 14:96.
16 Stamm WE: Measurement of pyuria and its relation to bacteriuria. *Am J Med* 1983, 75(1B):53.
17 Washington JA, White CM, Laganiere M, et al: Detection of significant bacteriuria by microscopic examination of the urine. *Lab Med* 1981, 12:294.
18 Barlett RC: Making optimal use of the microbiology laboratory II. Urine, respiratory, wound and cervicovaginal exudate. *JAMA* 1982, 247:1336.
19 Albers AC, Fletcher RD: Accuracy of calibrated loop transfer. *J Clin Microbiol* 1983, 18:40.
20 Blazevic DJ, Hall CT, Wilson ME, Balows A (eds): *Practical Quality Control Procedures for the Clinical Microbiology Laboratory.* Washington DC, American Society for Microbiology, 1976.
21 Lee A, Gooden H: Improving communication of microbiology test results. *Am J Clin Pathol* 1982, 77:443.
22 Bartlett RC: Making optimal use of the microbiology laboratory III. Aids of antimicrobial therapy. *JAMA* 1982, 247:857.
23 Bartlett, RC: Quality control in clinical microbiology, in Lennett EH (ed): *Manual of Clinical Microbiology,* ed 3. Washington, DC, American Society for Microbiology, 1980, pp 16–24.
24 Nagel JG, Kunz LJ: Needless retesting of quality assured commercially prepared culture media. *Appl Microbiol* 1973, 26:31.
25 Fleming A: On the antibacterial action of cultures of a penicillium with special reference to their use in the isolation of *B. influenzae. Br J Exp Pathol* 1929, 10:226.

26 Antibiotics intended for use in the laboratory diagnosis of disease. (21 CFR, 147). *Federal Register* 1961, 26:127.
27 Antibiotic susceptibility disc. (21 CFR 147). *Federal Register* 1971, 37:6899.
28 Antibiotic susceptibility disc. (21 CFR, 147). *Federal Register* 1972, 37:20525.
29 Thornsberry C: NCCLS standards for antimicrobial susceptibility tests. *Lab Med* 1983, 14:549.
30 National Committee for Clinical Laboratory Standards: Performance standards for antimicrobial disk susceptibility tests. Tentative standard M2-T3. Villanova, PA, NCCLS, 1983.
31 National Committee for Clinical Laboratory Standards: Methods for dilution antimicrobial susceptibility tests for bacteria that grow aerobically. Tentative standard M7-T. Villanova, PA, NCCLS, 1983.
32 Knowles RC, Moore TD: Quality control of agar diffusion susceptibility tests. *Am J Clin Pathol* 1980, 74(suppl):581.
33 Jones RN, Edson DC: Interlaboratory performance of disk agar diffusion and dilution antimicrobial susceptibility tests 1979–1981. *Am J Clin Pathol* 1982, 78(suppl):651.
34 Jones RN: Antimicrobial susceptibility testing (AST): A review of changing trends, quality control guidelines, test accuracy and recommendations for the testing of beta-lactam drugs. *Diagn Microbiol Infect Dis* 1983, 1:1.
35 Balows A, Gavan TL: Quality control methods for *in vitro* antibiotic susceptibility testing, in Lorian V (ed): *Antibiotics in Laboratory Medicine*. Baltimore, MD, Williams & Wilkins, 1980.
36 Coyle MB, Lampe MF, Aitkin CL, et al: Reproducibility of control strains for antibiotic susceptibility testing. *Antimicrob Agents Chemother* 1976, 10:436.
37 Hansen SL, Freedy PK: Variation in the abilities of automated, commercial and reference methods to detect methicillin-resistant (heteroresistant) *Staphylococcus aureus*. *J Clin Microbiol* 1984, 20:494.
38 Nickolai DJ, Lammel CJ, Byford BA, et al. Effects of storage temperature and pH on the stability of eleven beta-lactam antibiotics in MIC trays. *J Clin Microbiol* 1985, 21:366.
39 Barry AL, Effinger LJ, Badal RE: Short-term storage of six penicillins and cephalothin in microdilution trays for antimicrobial susceptibility tests. *Antimicrob Agents Chemother* 1976, 10:83.
40 Kirshbaum A, Kramer J, Arret B: The assay and control of antibiotic discs. *Antibiot Chemother* 1960, 10:249.
41 Final rule. Exemption of antibiotic drugs and antibiotic susceptibility medical devices from certification. *Federal Register* 1982, 47:39155.
42 Tardio JL, Westhoff D: Suitability of the ASM-2 standard test of the National Committee for Clinical Laboratory Standards for evaluation of antimicrobial disk potency. *J Clin Microbiol* 1984, 19:783.
43 Gavan TL, Jones RN, Barry AL, et al: Quality control limits for ampicillin, carbenicillin, mezlocillin and piperacillin disk diffusion susceptibility tests: a collaborative study. *J Clin Microbiol* 1981, 14:67.
44 Kellogg JA: Inability to control selected drugs on commercially obtained microdilution MIC panels. *Am J Clin Pathol* 1984, 82:455.
45 Kellogg JA: Inability to adequately control antibiotic agents on AutoMicrobic system gram-positive and gram-negative susceptibility card. *J Clin Microbiol* 1985, 21:454.
46 Boshard R, Matsen JM: Alternative quality control parameters for Autobac susceptibility testing disks: Use of agar diffusion zone size results. *J Clin Microbiol* 1981, 13:814.
47 Barry AL, Thornsberry C: Susceptibility testing: Diffusion test procedures, in Lennette EH

(ed): *Manual of Clinical Microbiology,* ed 3. Washington, DC, American Society for Microbiology, 1980, pp 463–474.
48 Hansen SL, Freedy PK: Concurrent comparability of automated systems and commercially prepared microdilution trays for susceptibility testing. *J Clin Microbiol* 1983, 17:878.
49 Washington JA, Warren E, Karlson AG: Stability of barium sulfate tubidity standards. *Appl Microbiol* 1972, 24:1013.
50 Stemper JE, Matsen JM: Device for turbidity standardization of cultures for antimicrobial susceptibility testing. *Appl Microbiol* 1970, 19:1015.
51 Barry AL, Badal RE, Hawkinson RW: Influence of inoculum growth phase on microdilution susceptibility tests. *J Clin Microbiol* 1983, 18:645.
52 Baker CN, Thornsberry C, Hawkinson RW: Inoculum standardization in antimicrobial susceptibility tests: Evaluation of the use of overnight agar cultures and the rapid inoculum standardization system. *J Clin Microbiol* 1983, 17:450.
53 Flournoy DJ: Facilitating quality control of the antimicrobial susceptibility test. *J Clin Microbiol* 1981, 13:231.
54 Reller LB, Schoenknecht FD, Kenny MA, et al: Antibiotic susceptibility testing of *Pseudomonas aeruginosa:* Selection of a control strain and criteria for magnesium and calcium content in media. *J Infect Dis* 1974, 130:454.
55 Pollack HM, Minshew BM, Kenny MA, et al: Effect of different lots of Mueller-Hinton agar on the interpretation of the gentamicin susceptibility of *Pseudomonas aeruginosa. Antimicrob Agents Chemother* 1978, 19:360.
56 Washington JA, Snyder RJ, Kohner PC, et al: Effect of cation content of agar on the activity of gentamicin, tobramycin and amikacin against *Pseudomonas aeruginosa. J Infect Dis* 1978, 137:103.
57 Barry AL, Braun LE: Reader error in minimum inhibitory concentrations with microdilution susceptibility test panels. *J Clin Microbiol* 1981, 13:228.
58 Jones RN, Edson DC: The ability of participant laboratories to detect penicillin resistant pneumococci. *Am J Clin Pathol* 1982, 78(suppl):659.
59 Sabath LD: Mechanisms of resistance to beta-lactam antibiotics in strains of *Staphylococcus aureus. Ann Intern Med* 1982, 97:339.
60 Sabath LD, Laverdiere N, Wheeler D, et al: A new type of penicillin resistance of *Staphylococcus aureus. Lancet* 1977, 1:443.
61 Taylor PC, Schoenknecht FD, Sherris JC, et al: Determination of minimum bacteriocidal concentrations of oxacillin for *Staphylococcus aureus:* Influence and significance of technical factors. *Antimicrob Agents Chemother* 1983, 23:142.
62 Murry PR, Jorgensen JH: Quantitative susceptibility test methods in major United States medical centers. *Antimicrob Agents Chemother* 1981, 20:66.
63 Fuchs PC: Microbiology proficiency testing in the care of patients, in Lorian V (ed): *Significance of Medical Microbiology in the Care of Patients,* ed 2. Baltimore, MD, Williams & Wilkins, 1982, pp 394–409.
64 Griffin CW, Mechaffey MA, Cook E: Five years experience with a national external quality control program for the culture and identification of *Neisseria gonorrhoeae. J Clin Microbiol* 1983, 18:1150.
65 Thornsberry C, Caruthers JQ, Baker CN: Effect of temperature on the *in vitro* susceptibility of *Staphylococcus aureus* to penicillin-resistant penicillin. *Antimicrob Agents Chemother* 1973, 4:263.
66 Strong BE, Kubica GP: *Isolation and Identification of Mycobacterium Tuberculosis.* US Dept of Health and Human Services publication No. (CDC) 81-8390, 1981.

CHAPTER 11

QUALITY CONTROL IN THE BLOOD CENTER AND TRANSFUSION SERVICE: CURRENT PRACTICES

Herbert F. Polesky, M.D.

Providing patients with safe and therapeutically effective units of blood and components is the goal of transfusion therapy. In establishing a quality control (QC) program for a blood center or transfusion service, one must be cognizant of the way various methods enhance this purpose. In addition, it is necessary to ensure that requirements of governmental and voluntary accreditation agencies are fulfilled. The American Association of Blood Banks (AABB) requires that "all blood banks and transfusion services shall utilize a program of quality control that is sufficiently comprehensive to ensure that reagents, equipment, and methods function as expected, and that there is compliance with the Standards."[1] Ideally, whatever approach is used, simplicity and relevance should be considered as important criteria in accepting or rejecting a particular procedure. If one uses these as guidelines, the QC program will be cost effective and helpful to the blood bank staff in carrying out its tasks.

Quality control in the blood bank usually consists of two parts, an internal program designed to monitor routine methods and an external program that is used to evaluate some aspect of the routine procedures and allows comparison with others using similar methods. Both types of programs are essential to a well-run blood bank. Included in the latter category are the periodic inspections by voluntary groups such as the Inspection and Accreditation program of the AABB, the College of American Pathologists (CAP), and the Joint Commission of Accreditation of Hospitals (JCAH) and subscriptions to proficiency testing surveys. For each step, from the selection of the donor through the evaluation and follow-up of the recipient, we will look at what should be done to assure the quality of the testing or the effectiveness and safety of other procedures used.

PROCEDURE MANUALS AND DOCUMENTATION

The cornerstone of a good quality assurance program is a current procedures manual containing directions for all methods in use, including techniques for determining that equipment and reagents are functioning as expected. Personnel should be familiar with appropriate sections of the manual and changes that have been made in its contents. Forms and records should be designed to make it easy to document quality control steps done either concurrently with patient or donor tests or as specific procedures. Not only should documentation indicate expected results, it should also include corrective action taken when unexpected results are observed.

The procedures manual should include schedules for the routine maintenance of equipment. The frequency and type of functional evaluation and/or calibration required must be described (see Table 11-1). Steps to be taken prior to introducing new equipment and those to assure instruments that have been repaired are acceptable need to be documented. It is not necessary to include detailed methods if these can be incorporated by reference to standard texts (an NCCLS standard, the Technical Manual[2]) or are part of the manual provided by the manufacturer.

DONOR RECRUITMENT AND SELECTION

Quality control of the recruitment and selection of blood donors is difficult. To evaluate recruitment, one needs to monitor the frequency with which blood or components are unavailable and contrast the shortages with the amount of outdating that occurs. Part of the difficulty of assessing these processes is that occasionally, despite careful planning, one is suddenly faced with unusual and excessive patient needs. In general, long-term review is necessary to evaluate whether the blood supply is maintained at adequate levels. Ascertaining the safety of the blood supply also is problematic, because of the long delay between the transfusion event and the onset of disease in the recipient. In the case of transfusion-associated HTLV-III/LAV infection, the mean incubation period in adults is about 20 months.[3] The director of the blood center needs to have a mechanism for recognizing donor characteristics associated with a higher incidence of transfusion complications. This type of monitoring detected the correlation between higher incidences of transfusion-associated hepatitis and paid donors.

The screening process for donors is designed to protect both the potential donor and the recipient. One way to assure that appropriate criteria are used in evaluating donors is periodically to review the reasons for donor rejection. This type of review is facilitated by computer-maintained donor records; however, a daily log can provide similar data. Several published studies[4,5] have shown that low hemoglobin and hepatitis exposure account for 15 and 30 percent of donor rejections, respectively, and that overall rates of rejection are between 7 and 10 percent of those attempting to donate. If a donor population has a rejection rate of 20 percent and the most common cause for deferment is small veins, the staff is probably not evaluating the donors properly. Another measure of this process is the incidence of reactions occurring during or fol-

TABLE 11-1
QUALITY CONTROL OF BLOOD BANK EQUIPMENT

Equipment	Performance check	Frequency	Calibration	Frequency
Centrifuges				
General lab	—	—	Tachometer	q 6 months
Hematocrit	—	—	Timer	q 3 months
			Standardize before initial use, after repairs	Yearly
Serologic	Observe cell buttons	Each use	Tachometer	Periodically
			Timer	At specified intervals (q 6 months)
			Function	If problem occurs
Automated	Observe controls	Each use	Tachometer	Same as above
			Timer	
			Washing	
			Reagent addition	
Refrigerated	Observe speed and temperature	Each day of use	Tachometer	Same as above
			Timer	
			Temperature	
			Component yield	
Autoclave	Temperature	Daily	Effectiveness in killing bacteria	Steam autoclave weekly spore strip
				Dry heat monthly swab

Waterbath Incubator Heat block Rh Viewbox	Observe and record temperature	Daily	Compare with calibrated thermometer	As necessary
Temperature recorder	Compare against thermometer	Daily	—	As necessary
Alarm system	Temperature of activation	At specified intervals	High and low temperatures	Monthly (NCCLS)
Laboratory thermometers	—	—	Compare with calibrated thermometer	Before initial use
Electronic thermometers	—	—	Thermometer tester supplied by manufacturer	Monthly
Serologic rotator	Observe controls	Daily	Speed	As needed
ELISA reader	Observe controls	Each run	Wavelength absorbance	As needed
Blood container scale	Known weight	Daily	Standard weights	As needed
Vacuum blood agitator	Weight of first container filled	Daily	Standardizing with container of known mass or volume	Before initial use After repairs or adjustment

lowing donation. If the donor phlebotomy staff is properly trained, then donor reactions should be infrequent (<1 percent), and incomplete or unsuccessful drawings should be rare.

The specific measurements performed prior to donation include donor temperature, pulse, blood pressure, and hemoglobin level. If, as is common, an electronic device is used to measure temperature, periodic checks on function as directed by the manufacturer should be done. Each newly purchased or repaired instrument should be calibrated before it is placed in use. To determine whether a donor has adequate hemoglobin (no lower than 12.5 g/dl or 38 percent PCV for females and 13.5 g/dl or 41 percent for males), screening may be done by using the copper sulfate method, a microhematocrit centrifuge, or a quantitative measure of hemoglobin. Quality control for the copper sulfate method should include evaluation of the specific gravity of each new bottle of the compound with a calibrated hydrometer. Periodic evaluation can be accomplished by comparing hemoglobin values obtained by another method on donors rejected by copper sulfate screening (values should be below the cutoffs for acceptable donors by the second method.[6] In addition, a sample of donors passing the copper sulfate screen should also be tested by the "reference" method to be sure they have acceptable values.

COLLECTION OF BLOOD AND COMPONENTS

Quality control of the blood collection requires evaluation of three areas: equipment, components obtained, and personnel.

In the United States, the majority of blood is collected into plastic bags with an attached needle and various configurations of satellite containers. Although this equipment is generally free of problems, we have found it useful to document the defects encountered (Fig. 11-1). The problems we have detected can at times be associated with a specific lot of bags, and ongoing monitoring makes the decision to stop using a specific lot easier. The most common problems with bags are bad needles, leaks of anticoagulant into the satellite bags, and pinhole leaks.

Donor blood must be collected in a manner that maintains sterility, provides for adequate mixing with the anticoagulant, and assures that the volume drawn is appropriate for the container used. Until recently, periodic cultures of a small sample of blood and component units were required. This is no longer the case, because contamination is rare when the current systems for blood collection are used properly. However, cultures and examination of stained smears for bacteria are recommended in the evaluation of patients with transfusion reactions thought to be caused by contaminated blood.[1] Whether mixing of blood during collection changes the yield of various components is controversial.[7,8] Without some mixing, the unit may clot. Accurate estimation of the volume of blood drawn is important because survival of the red cells depends on the ratio of whole blood to anticoagulant. It is also important for donor safety to limit the total volume collected, particularly in individuals in apheresis programs. Determining the volume of blood or plasma collected is usually done by weighing the unit. The accuracy of the scale used while drawing the donor should be checked by weighing on another type of scale. Similarly, devices used to stop the collection

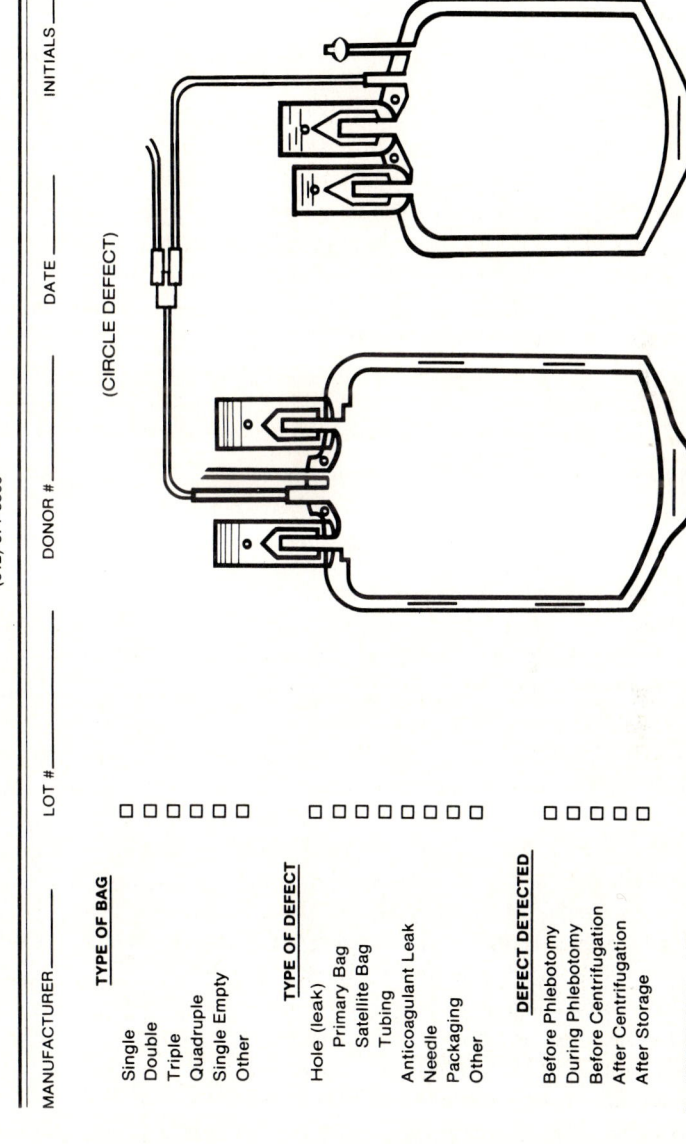

FIGURE 11-1
Form for use during blood collection and component preparation to record problems with blood bags.

automatically at a predetermined volume (vacuum-assist devices, trip scales) need to be calibrated periodically.[9]

Maintaining a log of errors and incidents is a useful method to monitor the performance of donor room personnel. An example is the report by a donor that a hematoma developed at the site of venipuncture. The individual who did the phlebotomy is asked to review the report and indicate any problem associated with the donor, equipment, and so forth. These records make it possible to detect whether any individual is having more problems than expected and needs special training. Other items to monitor are the number of incomplete or unsatisfactory draws, labeling errors, or excessive donor reactions attributable to one phlebotomist. As a periodic check on the technique of preparing the venipuncture site, we have taken cultures from the donor arm. Even though not all cultures are sterile, this exercise serves a useful educational function in reminding personnel that the goal of the arm prep is a sterile venipuncture site.[10]

BLOOD AND COMPONENT PREPARATION

The quality control procedures associated with blood and component preparation should detect errors in the testing of the donor samples [ABO and Rh grouping, antibody screening, hepatitis B surface antigen test (HBsAg), anti-HTLV-III screening], assure appropriate labeling of the units, and evaluate the content and characteristics of the components.

Blood Grouping and Antibody Screening

Testing of both donor and patient specimens requires antisera and reagent red cells that must be shown to react as expected on each day of use. Because most reagents used in the blood bank are licensed by the Office of Biologics Research and Review (OBRR) of the Food and Drug Administration (FDA), it unnecessary for the individual user to establish the specificity and potency of each lot.[9] It is important to document that the antibody does react with cells known to be positive for a given antigen and not with cells that are negative. If other than licensed reagents are used or the method of use differs from the manufacturer's recommendation, more extensive testing should be done. Reagent red cells should be shown to be reactive with examples of antibodies likely to react in the specific test system. Ideally, the test will include an antibody reactive only by the antiglobulin test (AGT). Thus one may be able to demonstrate the reactivity of antiglobulin reagent while assuring the function of the reagent red cells. The antibodies chosen for QC of the reagent red cells used in the antibody detection test should be weakly reactive (1 to 2+) so that minimal loss of reactivity of the test cells will become apparent (Fig. 11-2). There are no specific requirements for the testing of cells used in antibody identification (panel cells); however, careful observation of reaction patterns and use of supplemental test cells can provide clues to problems with one or more of the panel cells.

A unique feature of the testing in the blood bank is that most of the tests are of characteristics that are constant. ABO and Rh do not change with each new specimen from the patient or donor. Thus an important aspect of QC is comparison of current

MEMORIAL BLOOD CENTER OF MINNEAPOLIS DAILY QUALITY CONTROL RECORD
ANTI-SERUM AND REAGENT CELLS

Date_____ Tech_____

DONOR LABORATORY

Slide Reagent Man. & Lot No. | Test Cells | Grade Rx | ✓ if satis | A Cells / B Cells > Source

Slide Reagent Man.& Lot No.	Test Cells	Grade Rx	✓ if satis	
Anti-A	A1	ML		
	B	ML		
Anti-B	A1	ML		
	B	ML		
Anti-D	Rh+			
	Rh-			
Anti-CD	CD+	AH		
	CD-			

Pooled Lot No._____
A₁ Cells   B Cells

Microplate Reagent Man.& Lot No.	Test Cells	Grade Rx	✓ if satis
Anti-A	B	ML	
	A1	ML	
	A4		
Anti-B	B	ML	
	A1	ML	
	A4		
Anti-A,B	A4		
	O	ML	
Anti-D	Rh+		
	Rh-		
Anti-C	C+	AH	
	C-	H	
Anti-c	c+	H	
	c-	AH	
Anti-E	E+	H	
	E-	AH	

Date Drawn_____
Date Pooled_____
By _____

	Anti A	Anti B
pooled A cells		
pooled B cells		

Reagents — ✓ if satis
Pooled Scr Cells #
Anti-Human Ser #
30% Bovine Alb. #
Check Cells #

Control Test Serum
37°
	PAP	Alb-AHG
Anti-D dil		
Anti-Fyᵃ dil		

Tech:_____   Tech:_____

7/85
SH/mac

CELL WASHER #	BRAND & LOT #	TEST CELL	RX	✓ if OK
68	AHG	+ ✓ CELL		
	Donor Serum	- Pool O		
69	AHG	+ ✓ CELL		
	Donor Serum	- Pool O		

CHECK (✓) CELL SOURCE: ML   OTHER _____

EQUIPMENT TEMPERATURES	
Waterbath # 7	Waterbath #17
Viewbox #11	Waterbath #8
Viewbox #13	Waterbath #9
Refrigerator - Top	
Refrigerator - Bottom	
FREEZER:	

FIGURE 11-2
Example of a form for recording daily quality control results. This form includes information on the method, source of reagent, observed test result and whether it is as expected. Each piece of equipment is identified by number.

results with previous tests. This step helps to determine that each new specimen is from the same person and is an additional means of confirming that the reagents and methods are in control.

Monitoring of Equipment

Much of the routine quality control in the blood bank can be accomplished concurrently with the testing. The washing and centrifugation steps common to many procedures can be evaluated continually. If after centrifugation a well-packed button of cells is not obtained, or if the button fails to resuspend easily, then one should suspect that the equipment is not functioning correctly. To assure appropriate speed, centrifuges used for serologic tests should be checked with a tachometer upon receipt, after repair, and periodically. A stopwatch should be used to monitor timing devices. Because each centrifuge may vary slightly, it is important to do a functional calibration to determine the optimal settings for a given method.[11] If the washing procedure is incorrect, there may be too few cells left at the final stage of the test; or the antiglobulin reagent will be neutralized by remaining serum and the check cells (IgG antibody-coated reagent cells) will fail to agglutinate.

Typing of donor and patient cells and screening of sera for the presence of unexpected antibodies are always carried out at specified temperatures. Part of the blood bank quality control is to ensure that 37°C incubators are at the correct temperature. Thermometers used to measure water bath temperatures should be calibrated by comparison with a National Bureau of Standards reference thermometer. If dry heat blocks are used, every well should be evaluated periodically. If Rh viewboxes are used for slide typing, it is important they be between 40° and 50°C. Daily quality control sheets should include documentation of temperature readings.

Testing for Transfusion-Transmitted Disease

Currently, all donor units must be negative for HBsAg, anti-HTLV-III, and by a serologic test for syphilis prior to use. The quality control appropriate for these tests is method dependent. Thus, if one is using radioimmunoassay screening for HBsAg, one needs methods for assuring that the isotope counter used is calilbrated and functioning as expected. Similarly, if an enzyme-labeled immunosorbent assay is used, the spectrophotometer or other reading device must be functioning correctly. The other equipment used in these tests, such as pipetters, washing devices, and incubators, should be evaluated as part of the quality control program. It is usually necessary to run a series of negative controls and a strong positive with each batch to set cutoff values and assure that the reagents are working properly. In addition, we have found the inclusion of a borderline positive with all runs very useful.[12] To assure detection of all weakly positive specimens, we lower the cutoff point for positivity if the absorbance of the borderline positive control is less than the usual value. Large batches of the low and intermediate level controls are prepared to monitor variation between reagent lots as well as daily variation. Because positive findings in tests for HBsAg and/or anti-HTLV-III have many implications for the "healthy" donor, another important part of the quality control for these tests is that reactive specimens are confirmed as positive with a more specific test.[13,14] Donor specimens reactive in a screening test for HBsAg should be retested, tested in a neutralization test, or be shown to have identity with a known positive in an immunoprecipitin system. To test for antibody specificity for HTLV-III, a Western blot should be used for identifying antibodies to specific proteins associated with the virus. To assure the safety of the blood supply, all repeatedly reactive units identified by the screening methods for HTLV-III must be discarded. Quality control for the serologic test for syphilis should be done in accordance with the manufacturer's directions. In addition, a laboratory doing any of these tests must participate in an external proficiency testing program.

BLOOD COMPONENTS

Almost all donor blood is converted into two or more component parts before it is used for transfusion. Most of the methods for preparing components require a properly functioning centrifuge. For the centrifuge, appropriate quality control procedures include periodic testing of the rotational speed, the timer, and the temperature. However, for a refrigerated centrifuge,[15] the most important aspect of quality control is evaluation of the component prepared.

It is important to inspect each unit as it is processed. If there are problems in the centrifugation step, excessive red cells in the plasma or difficulty in resuspending the platelet button may occur. It is also important to be sure that the bags and seals are intact.

Red Blood Cells

Methods used to prepare other components (removal of plasma, platelets, etc.) should result in a unit of red cells with a hematocrit that does not exceed 80 percent.[1] This value may be less if additive solutions are used or more if the resultant cells are to be used shortly after preparation. The method of preparation and storage should ensure that 75 percent of the cells will survive for at least 24 h when transferred into a recipient. It is not expected that each institution preparing red cells will do survival studies; however, the method used "shall be known to produce" such results.[1] If red cells are modified to remove leukocytes (inverted spin, filtration, washing, etc.), the method for removal should reduce the total white count by 70 percent without losing more than 30 percent of the red cell volume. In some clinical situations, the absolute number of granulocytes may be more important than the total white count. Determining the red cell recovery is best accomplished by using the weight of the unit to calculate the volume. If frozen, thawed deglycerolized red cells are prepared, the amount of cryoprotective agent remaining should be minimal (less than 1 percent glycerol). This can be determined by measuring the osmolarity (<500 mOsm) or estimating it by refractometry.[16] All units should be inspected to be sure that the amount of supernatant hemoglobin is less than 200 mg/dl. A color comparator can be used to make this measurement. To determine red cell recovery (at least 80 percent), hemoglobin and/or hematocrits on an aliquot of the unit are needed along with an estimate of the unit's red cell mass prior to and following processing. In some institutions, washing of stored red cells with compatible solutions is done routinely. The method used for washing should be one that does not damage the red cells and that removes most of the plasma.[1] If this method is used as a means of producing leukocyte-poor blood, then quality control should include periodic evaluation of the amount of residual white cells.

Platelet Concentrates

At the time of maximum storage, platelet concentrates must have a minimum number of platelets in a volume of plasma adequate to maintain the pH at 6.0 or greater. If platelets are prepared from whole blood units, 75 percent of the tested units shall contain at least 5.5×10^{10} platelets.[1] Cytapheresis units should contain 3×10^{11} platelets.[1] If the method of preparation and storage is adequate, there should be no grossly visible platelet aggregates. In general, platelet concentrates should have minimal red and white cell contamination. When the method of preparation is modified, changes to new storage containers or anticoagulants are made when a new or repaired centrifuge is used; evaluation of platelet yields also should be done.[16] The ideal measurement of platelet preparation methods is patient response to transfusion. Unfortunately the many variables in the clinical status of patients needing platelets makes this almost impossible.[17] Feedback on poor patient response, increased numbers of reactions during platelet transfusions, and so on, can indicate problems in the method of collection, preparation, storage, pooling, or infusion of the component.

Granulocyte Concentrate

Granulocyte concentrate, which is generally prepared by cytapheresis, must contain a minimum of 1×10^{10} granulocytes in 75 percent of the units tested.[1]

Plasma and Plasma Components

The functional quality of the plasma and plasma components depends on the rapidity with which they are separated from the whole blood. Quality control should be designed to monitor the separation times and the freezing step. When single-donor cryoprecipitate (cryo) is made from fresh frozen plasma, the amount of Factor VIII in 75 percent of the units tested shall exceed 80 international units.[18] Because in our experience cryo also is used as a source of fibrinogen, we monitor the fibrinogen levels (target values 0.17 to 0.35 g/unit) on units tested for Factor VIII (see Fig. 11-3). Although the ideal way to monitor components transfused to replace coagulation factors is to follow patient response, this approach is not practical in other than a research setting.

Labeling of Blood and Components

It is essential that all blood and components be correctly labeled as to content, blood group, and time of expiration. It is also important that tests for transmissible agents

```
                    MEMORIAL BLOOD CENTER OF MINNEAPOLIS
              2304 PARK AVE., MPLS., MN 55404  TEL. (612) 871-3300

BLOOD COMPONENT QUALITY CONTROL    REVIEWED by _____ / _____ /
          JULY 1985                             Supervisor  Med Director
----------------------------------------------------------------------
                         PLATELETS   COMPONENT    RBC       WBC
PLATELET        pH       X 10(10)    VOLUME       PER       X 10(7)
CONCENTRATE              PER UNIT    (ML)         CU.MM     PER UNIT

7 DAY          6.36      10.1        45           3,950     3.5
7 DAY          6.83       9.2        43          21,050    10.4
7 DAY          6.98       7.0        44           6,050     7.3
7 DAY          7.12       8.0        43          12,200     4.3

TARGET         6 OR      5.5 X 10(10)
VALUES         GREATER   OR GREATER
----------------------------------------------------------------------
               FACTOR                COMPONENT
CRYO-          VIII      FIBRINOGEN  VOLUME
PRECIPITATE    (UNITS)   (GM/UNIT)   (ML)
----------------------------------------------------------------------
                82        .31        20
               115        .23        20
               145        .22        20
             *  75        .25        24

TARGET         80 UNITS  .17 - .35
VALUES         OR GREATER GM/UNIT
----------------------------------------------------------------------
FROZEN         PER CENT  PER CENT    SUPERNATANT
DEGLYCED       RESIDUAL  RED CELL    HGB          WBC PER
RED CELLS      GLYCEROL  RECOVERY    (MG%)        UNIT
----------------------------------------------------------------------
                <1        87         70           0
                <1        86         40           0
                <1        84         40           0
                <1        82         30           2x10(7)
TARGET                    80 OR      200 MG%
VALUES         LESS THAN 1 GREATER   OR LESS
----------------------------------------------------------------------
LEUKOCYTE      WBC       PER CENT    PER CENT
POOR           PER       WBC         RBC
RED CELLS      CU. MM    REMOVAL     RECOVERY     METHOD
----------------------------------------------------------------------
               1,870      81         88           SOFT
               2,750      83         87           SPIN


TARGET                   70 OR       70 OR
VALUES                   GREATER     GREATER
----------------------------------------------------------------------
REVIEWED by: _____ / _____ / _____
             Lab Supervisor Medical Director  Date
* Values outside target range
```

FIGURE 11-3
Monthly report of component quality control sent to each hospital served by the blood center.

be completed and nonreactive before the unit is transfused. Quality control of the labeling is important to prevent potentially serious reactions to the unit. To assure appropriate ABO and Rh labeling, one approach is to require that the transfusion service doing the compatibility test verify the ABO type of all units and the Rh of negative units on a sample from an attached segment.[1] If discrepancies are observed, this must be reported to the drawing facility. The use of machine-/eye-readable labels and a computer system can greatly facilitate detecting label errors.[19,20] In our institution, after the final label is affixed to the bag, the unique unit number, ABO and Rh type, and component name are read by a laser wand. The computer compares this information to the unit record. If a discrepancy is detected, the label check cannot proceed until the problem is resolved. Another approach to detecting labeling or other clerical errors is to introduce purposefully an error into your system and see if it is noted.[21] It has been documented that this technique can reduce the rate of errors and has an educational benefit as well.

Storage of Blood and Components

Storage conditions for blood and its components are rigidly defined. In general, the temperatures chosen are designed to help maintain sterility, maximize the survival of the cells, and ensure that the component has its intended therapeutic function. Monitoring of the temperature must be continuous, with a recording made at least every 4 hours.[1] To assure prompt corrective action if the refrigerator or freezer is not maintaining the appropriate temperature, audible alarms are required, activated at upper and lower limits. Temperature-sensing devices should be checked periodically to see that they are properly calibrated and will activate the alarm system at the intended levels.[22] It is also important to check that recording devices are functional. In the event of a power or equipment failure, a procedure to maintain blood and components at the proper temperature must be available.[1]

PATIENT TESTING

A hemolytic transfusion reaction due to ABO incompatibility following blood transfusion is the most common cause of fatality reported to the Office of the Director, Bureau of Biologics of the Food and Drug Administration (FDA) as required by the Code of Federal Regulations (CFR), Title 21 part 606.[23] Careful evaluation of these cases indicates that identification errors are usually at fault.[24] Thus one of the most important aspects of quality control in the blood bank is to be sure that patient and donor specimens are correctly identified. If collection of specimens from patients is not under the control of the blood bank, there must be strict rules about how specimens are labeled if they are to be accepted for testing. Similar care also must be used in releasing blood units for transfusion. One way to minimize clerical errors is to establish procedures that include only the essential tests. The testing should be conducted in a setting where the work can be done without interruption or distraction.

Quality control of the reagents and equipment is the same for patient testing as described for donor testing. Some additional controls are necessary when dealing with patient specimens. To prevent incorrect designation of an Rh-negative recipient as Rh positive, a control system appropriate to the reagent in use is required.[1] Testing for the D^u factor is not necessary on patient specimens.[1] When testing for unexpected antibodies, an IgG-sensitized cell must be added to each tube with a negative reaction in the antiglobulin test to detect false negatives.[1] The "check cells" should be evaluated to ensure that they are appropriately sensitized. When testing patient specimens, an autologous control (the patient's cells suspended in patient serum) or direct antiglobulin test is frequently included. Generally this type of control is necessary only if the recipient has been recently transfused or as part of a procedure to identify antibody(ies).[25] Quality control of the antiglobulin reagent used to screen for or identify patient antibodies can be limited to assuring the reactivity with cells coated with an IgG antibody.[2] These cells should react weakly (1 to 2+). Checking polyspecific antiglobulin reagents for anticomplement is not necessary. Monospecific antiglobulin reagents used for diagnostic purposes should be shown to function as expected.

In hospitals with obstetric services, the blood bank is usually responsible for identifying patients that should receive Rh immune globulin (RhIgG). A method should be available to monitor the administration of this material. It is important that all Rh-negative patients who deliver an Rh-positive infant be given RhIgG unless they are actively immunized to D.[26] All potential candidates for this treatment should be screened for the presence of a fetal-maternal hemorrhage requiring more than a standard dose of RhIgG.[27] Quality control of the screening test used can be done by preparing artificial mixtures with Rh-positive cells as a minor population. These should simulate a bleed of 20 to 30 ml of whole blood. If a quantitative method is used to confirm the presence and volume of fetal Rh-positive cells, mixtures of cord and adult cells should be used to be sure the test is working. A control should be run with each test.

TRANSFUSION PRACTICES

The most important quality control function of the blood bank is the monitoring of usage of blood and components.[28] The blood bank staff, working with the hospital transfusion committee, has the opportunity to assure that appropriate indications are used in selecting and administering components.[29] Part of the function of the blood bank is to provide consultation as to the best way to meet the specific needs of a patient. Guidelines should be available for the clinical parameters that justify the use of blood or a specific component. When the patient's condition does not appear to meet the established criteria, or the medical record lacks adequate documentation as to why blood was given, a detailed review by the transfusion committee is indicated. If misuse continues, the committee should attempt to improve the practices by educational programs.[30] In some cases, one-on-one confrontation may be the only way to make changes.

Transfusion Reactions

The blood bank usually is notified if a patient receiving blood or a component has an adverse reaction to the transfusion. If the transfusion is uneventful, it is unlikely that the blood bank will learn if the patient had the expected therapeutic result. With widespread use of computers, a program to monitor selected laboratory values (hemoglobin, platelet count, coagulation studies) in patients undergoing transfusion has the potential to provide a mechanism for quality control of the in vivo response to various components. Using this approach, one might be able to detect when patients are alloimmunized to platelets, or otherwise fail to respond to the components being used. If patients have symptomatic reactions to transfusion, these must be investigated. In my view, the workup of a transfusion reaction is a form of quality control. Although testing should be limited to that which is clinically relevant, the repeat testing on the donor and patient specimens and clerical checks are a periodic evaluation of the routines in use. Because most transfusion services depend on a blood center for their blood supply, a mechanism for central reporting of transfusion reactions could lead to early recognition of a problem common to several institutions. Ideally, the reports of the deliberations of the transfusion committee also should be shared with the blood center. Review of the reports from several institutions can provide the basis for active educational efforts to improve transfusion practices in the entire region.

In addition to the follow-up of symptomatic reactions, it is important that each transfusion service monitor the delayed infectious complications associated with blood.[31] The reporting of suspected transfusion-associated hepatitis, AIDS, and other infections to the facility supplying the donor units is an important part of assuring the safety of the blood supply. Good communication between the blood center and the transfusion services can facilitate the quality of the services provided to patients.

In the best of all worlds, the transfusion service is responsible for the collection of patient specimens, compatibility testing, and the infusion of blood and components. Under these circumstances, the quality control of the ancillary equipment used during transfusion will automatically be done by the blood bank personnel. It is important that devices used to warm blood be checked periodically to be sure the temperature does not exceed 37°C and that the alarms are functional.[1] If infusion pumps are used to administer blood, one needs to be sure they are not causing damage to the cells.[32] The transfusion service also should be involved in assuring that methods used for intraoperative salvage of blood are safe. If it is not reinfused in the operating room, it is essential that blood collected by these procedures is correctly labeled and stored.

SUMMARY

The quality and safety of transfusion depend on having good methods that function as intended. Appropriate and careful documentation of each step is an essential part of providing the patient with a therapeutically effective transfusion. Communication and consultations between the blood center, the transfusion service, and the clinical services are key elements in assuring quality.

REFERENCES

1 Schmidt PJ (ed): *Standards for Blood Banks and Transfusion Services,* ed 11. Arlington, VA, American Association of Blood Banks, 1984.

2 Widmann FK (ed): *Technical Manual*, ed 9. Arlington, VA, American Association of Blood Banks, 1985.
3 Feorino PM, Jaffe HW, Palmer E, et al: Transfusion-associated acquired immunodeficiency: Evidence for persistent infection in blood donors. *N Engl J Med* 1985, 312:1293.
4 Tomasulo PA, Anderson AJ, Paluso MB: A study of criteria for blood donor deferral. *Transfusion* 1980, 20:511.
5 Ferrales FB, Stevenson AR, Bayer WL: Causes of disqualification in a volunteer blood donor population. *Transfusion* 1977, 17:598.
6 Myhre BA: *Quality Control in Blood Banking*. New York, John Wiley & Sons, 1974.
7 Kasper CK, Myhre BA, McDonald JD, et al: Determinants of factor VIII recovery in cryoprecipitate. *Transfusion* 1975, 15:312.
8 Slichter SJ, Counts RB, Henderson R, et al: Preparation of cryoprecipitated factor VIII concentrates. *Transfusion* 1976, 16:616.
9 Widmann FK (ed): *Technical Manual*, ed 9. Arlington, VA, American Association of Blood Banks, 1985, pp 369–388, 477–478.
10 Polesky HF, Grindon AJ, Miller W, et al: Blood banking, in Inhorn SL (ed): *Quality Assurance Practices for Health Laboratories*. Washington, DC, American Public Health Association, 1978, pp 441–450.
11 Harris, GE, Boline JE, McClure DK: Equipment, in Taswell HF, Saeed SM (eds): *Principles and Practices of Quality Control in the Blood Bank*. Washington, DC, American Association of Blood Banks, 1980, pp 1–29.
12 Polesky HF, Hanson M: Improving the sensitivity of RIA for detecting HBsAg positives, abstract. *Amer J Clin Pathol* 1977, 68:102.
13 Alter HJ, Holland PV, Purcell RH, et al: The Ausria test: Critical evaluation of sensitivity and specificity. *Blood* 1973, 42:947.
14 Osterholm MT, Bowman RJ, Chopek MW, et al: Screening donated blood and plasma for HTLV-III antibody: Facing more than one crisis? *N Engl J Med* 1985, 312:1185.
15 Klein RE: Quality control of equipment, in Smit Sibinga C Th, Dos PC, Taswell HF (eds): *Quality Assurance in Blood Banking: Its Clinical Impact*. Boston, Martinus Nijhoff, 1984, pp 77–82.
16 Holley PW, Polesky HF, Saeed SM: Components, in Taswell HF, Saeed SM (eds): *Principles and Practices of Quality Control in the Blood Bank*. Washington, DC, American Association of Blood Banks, 1980, pp 63–97.
17 Menitove JE, Aster RH: Transfusion of platelets and plasma products. *Clinics in Haematol* 1983, 12:239.
18 *Code of Federal Regulations*, title 21, parts 640.1-640.57, 1984.
19 Polesky HF, Britt C: Advantages of bar code labels in blood preparation, abstract. *Transfusion* 1984, 24:451.
20 Chambers RW, Allen JW: Positive patient identification, in Polesky HF, Walker RH (eds): *Safety in Transfusion Practices*. Skokie, IL, College of American Pathologists, 1981, pp 227–238.
21 Taswell HF, Smith AM, Sweatt MA: Quality control in the blood bank—A new approach. *Am J Clin Pathol* 1974, 62:491.
22 Klein RE, Conley JE, Donahue D: Temperature monitoring and recording in blood banks. Proposed NCCLS Guidelines, 1984, vol 4, no 1.
23 Honig CL, Bove JR: Transfusion-associated fatalities: Review of Bureau of Biologics reports 1976–1978. *Transfusion* 1980, 20:653.
24 Myhre BA: Fatalities from blood transfusion. *JAMA* 1980, 244:1333.
25 Judd WJ, Butch SH: Streamlining serologic testing: Scientific considerations, in Smith D,

Judd WJ (eds): *Blood Banking in a Changing Environment.* Arlington, VA, American Association of Blood Banks, 1984, pp 15–40.
26 Polesky HF: Diagnosis, prevention, and therapy in hemolytic disease of the newborn. *Clin Lab Med* 1982, 2:107.
27 Sebring ES: Fetomaternal hemorrhage—Incidence and methods of detection and quantitation, in Garratty G (ed): *Hemolytic Disease of the Newborn.* Arlington VA, American Association of Blood Banks, 1984, pp 87–117.
28 *Accreditation Manual for Hospitals.* Chicago, IL, Joint Commission on Accreditation of Hospitals, 1985, pp 86–87.
29 Grindon AJ, Tomasulo PS, Bergin JJ, et al: The hospital transfusion committee: Guidelines for improving practice. *JAMA* 1985, 253:540.
30 Handler S: Does continuing medical education affect medical care: A study of improved transfusion practices. *Minn Med* 1983, 66:167.
31 Polesky HF, Hanson M: Transfusion-associated hepatitis: A dilemma. *Lab Med* 1983, 14:717.
32 Thompson HW, Lasky LC, Polesky HF: Evaluation of the suitability of a volumetric intravenous fluid infusion pump for transfusion of erythrocyte-containing blood components. *Transfusion,* 1986, 26:290.

CHAPTER **12**

QUALITATIVE AND SEMIQUANTITATIVE TESTS: CLINICAL MICROSCOPY, PHYSICIAN'S OFFICE, BEDSIDE, AND SELF-PERFORMED

Carl E. Speicher, M.D.
Thomas D. Stevenson, M.D.

Quality assurance of qualitative and semiquantitative tests is performed in a number of different settings (Fig. 12-1). *Quality control* can be defined as a system instituted to minimize laboratory errors by monitoring, recognizing, and correcting any deviations from what has been established as acceptable laboratory output.[1] In contrast, *quality assurance* is a system that addresses not only the quality of performance or the output of the technical operation, but also the effectiveness and efficiency with which the output is used in patient care.[2]

The data resulting from laboratory tests can be of several types: qualitative, semiquantitative, or quantitative. A qualitative measurement of urinary glucose, for example, identifies the presence or absence of glucose. Results of semiquantitative measurement of glucose indicate not only whether glucose is present or absent, but also the approximate amount of glucose present. Quantitative urinary glucose measurements denote how much glucose is present; for example, the urinary glucose concentration is 100 mg/dl.

Test results are variates, that is, variables that can take on a limited set of values. There are two types of variates, continuous and discrete. Quantitative test results, such as values of serum glucose concentration, constitute continuous variates because the possible values of glucose are theoretically endless. Qualitative test results, such as measurement of urinary glucose stating whether glucose is present or absent, constitute binary discrete variates because there are only two possible values. Semiquantitative tests are those in which the degree of positivity or negativity is roughly estimated, usually by visual observation; for example, urinary ketones are reported as trace, small, moderate, or large in amount.

As binary discrete variates, qualitative test results have intrinsic difficulties. The

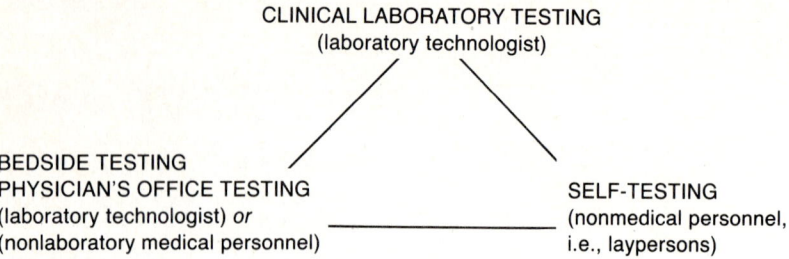

FIGURE 12-1
The triangle of testing for qualitative and semiquantitative tests. There are four different settings in which these tests can be performed. A key difference in settings is the training of the individuals performing the tests, as given in parentheses.

results of such tests are not by nature "yes" or "no," but we impose a "positive" or "negative" decision on the test result according to the level of the sensitivity of the test. A woman is either pregnant or not pregnant, but we impose on the pregnancy test an answer, which is either "positive" or "negative." The pregnancy test is not really a test for pregnancy, but a test for serum or urine human chorionic gonadotropin (hCG). Serum and urine chorionic gonadotropin levels are continuous variables that we turn into binary discrete variables, that is, "positive or negative pregnancy test." The challenge is to adjust the sensitivity and specificity of the test so that false positive and false negative results are minimized. Because it is impossible to design a test with 100 percent sensitivity and 100 percent specificity, the pregnancy test will always have false positive and false negative results. The matter is further complicated by the effect of the prevalence of pregnancy in the population being tested on the predictive value (see Table 12-1).[3]

With the test for pregnancy, and with any other qualitative test, it is important to distinguish analytical sensitivity and specificity, diagnostic sensitivity and specificity, and clinical utility.[4] For example, with the test for pregnancy, analytical sensitivity refers to the concentration of human chorionic gonadotropin that the test can detect, whereas analytical specificity refers to the ability of the test to distinguish chorionic gonadotropin from luteinizing hormone, follicle-stimulating hormone, and thyroid-stimulating hormone. Diagnostic sensitivity refers to the earliest time at which the test can detect pregnancy, in contrast to diagnostic specificity, which refers to the ability of the test to be negative in the absence of pregnancy. Clinical utility of the pregnancy test refers to how useful the test is in certain medical decision-making situations, such as the diagnosis of ectopic pregnancy. We should appreciate that for qualitative tests the manufacturer usually "locks us in" to certain analytical and diagnostic sensitivities and specificities according to the specifications against which the tests are manufactured. For example, using a reagent strip test for urinary hemoglobin that has "too high" an analytical sensitivity can cause significant anxiety and costs looking for urinary tract disease that does not exist—that is, false positive test results.

TABLE 12-1
PREVALENCE OF PREGNANCY, SENSITIVITY OF PREGNANCY TEST, AND SPECIFICITY OF PREGNANCY TEST PLUS PREDICTIVE VALUE OF A POSITIVE PREGNANCY TEST RESULT

	Number with positive result	Number with negative result	Total
Number pregnant	90	10	100
Number not pregnant	180	720	900
Total	270	730	1000
Prevalence:	10%		
Sensitivity:	90%		
Specificity:	80%		
Predictive value of a positive:	33%		

Note that although the sensitivity and specificity of the test are reasonably high, the predictive value of a positive test result is low because of the low prevalence of pregnancy.

TABLE 12-2
CLINICAL MICROSCOPY TESTS

Urinalysis[a]
Urinary protein electrophoresis
Fluid analysis: cerebrospinal and other body fluids
Fecal analysis: occult blood[a]
Pregnancy tests[a]
Evaluation of placental function
Evaluation of fetal condition
Evaluation of exocrine pancreatic function
Examination of gastric and duodenal contents
Evaluation of diarrhea and malabsorption

[a]Physicians' office tests.

KINDS OF QUALITATIVE AND SEMIQUANTITATIVE TESTS

Qualitative and semiquantitative tests performed in clinical laboratories frequently include microscopic examination and, for this reason, are referred to as clinical microscopy tests. Some of these same tests are often done in the physician's office (Table 12-2). The number of tests performed in physicians' offices is growing rapidly.[5]

Qualitative and semiquantitative tests that can be performed as self-tests are given in Table 12-3.[6,7] Some of these tests, as indicated, are often done at the bedside. We anticipate that the number of tests available for bedside and self-testing will rapidly increase. Already, several manufacturers have announced therapeutic drug monitoring

TABLE 12-3
SELF-TESTS

Urine:	Feces:
Glucose[a]	Occult blood
Ketone bodies[a]	pH and glucose
Nitrite	Blood:
Protein	ABO
Occult blood	Glucose[a]
Chorionic gonadotropin	Ketones[a]
Specific gravity	Urea
pH	Hemoglobin
Phenylpyruvic acid	Streptococcal antibodies
Salt	Hemoglobin S
Leukocytes	Throat:
Uric acid	Group A *Streptococci*
Urea	Vagina:
Calcium	*Candidiasis*
Bilirubin	Urethral fluid:
Breath:	*Gonococci*
Alcohol	
Carbon monoxide	

[a]Bedside tests.

(TDM) instruments that can be mounted on carts and rolled to the bedside.[8] Of course, all tests available for bedside and self-testing can also be used in clinical laboratories and physicians' offices. Usually they are not used because better but more technically difficult tests are preferable.

Clinical microscopy tests consist of qualitative or quantitative tests that are usually performed on nonblood specimens; microscopic examination is often, though not always, included. These tests do not fit neatly into traditional laboratory divisions such as blood bank, chemistry, hematology, or microbiology divisions, and are occasionally laboratory orphans, lacking a separate and distinct home. They are most commonly found in hematology division laboratories because of the microscopic and morphologic nature of some of the studies. There are few practitioners who claim a special interest in them; therefore, they are sometimes neglected. Many of these tests are relatively inexpensive, and this can contribute to an attitude that they are not worth as much as other tests and techniques. They are at once the oldest and the newest of tests. Testing of urine for the diagnosis of diabetes mellitus was one of the first clinical laboratory tests. Now these tests are resurfacing in the mantle of emerging technology to be performed not only in the clinical laboratory but at the bedside, in the physician's office, and in the patient's home—for example, reagent-strip monitoring of blood glucose at the bedside and self-administered pregnancy tests.

These tests can provide useful clinical information, and they deserve our careful attention. But which of them have real clinical relevance? How are they to be quality controlled and quality assured? What are their diagnostic sensitivities, specificities, and efficiencies in certain medical decision situations? What is their cost effectiveness compared to other tests? These are some of the issues that confront the user of this group of tests.[9]

CLINICAL MICROSCOPY TESTS AND PHYSICIAN'S OFFICE TESTS

Clinical microscopy tests, physician's office tests, and bedside tests have in common that they are usually performed by individuals with medical training, either laboratory personnel or nonlaboratory medical personnel. In this regard the level of training of the individual performing the test is higher than for self-tests, which are usually performed by laypersons.

Urinalysis and examination of feces for occult blood are examples of tests that are commonly done in both the clinical microscopy laboratory and the physician's office; whereas urinary protein electrophoresis and fluid analysis, such as analysis of cerebrospinal fluid and other body fluids, are examples of tests that are usually confined to the clinical microscopy laboratory. We use urinalysis, examination of feces for occult blood, and fluid analysis as examples to illustrate the quality control and quality assurance of clinical microscopy tests and physician's office tests.

A qualitative or quantitative radioimmunoassay for serum human chorionic gonadotropin can be performed as a pregnancy test. It has theoretical advantages over the assay for urinary human chorionic gonadotropin discussed later, under bedside and self-tests, because the procedure incorporates positive and negative controls and is usually performed by a trained technologist. Regardless of how the assay for human chorionic gonadotropin is performed, the specificity will be greater using an antibody raised against the beta subunit of human chorionic gonadotropin. This minimizes cross-reactions with luteinizing hormone, follicle-stimulating hormone, and thyroid-stimulating hormone.

Urinalysis[10,11]

Chemical testing and microscopic evaluation of a urine specimen provide valuable information. Properly evaluated routine urinalysis will aid in the diagnosis and management of renal or urinary tract disease and the detection of metabolic or systemic disease not related directly to the kidneys.

Either a morning urine or a random urine specimen can be collected in a clean, dry container. However, a first morning urine specimen is advantageous when evaluating renal concentrating ability and when looking for urinary-formed elements. When testing for urinary glucose in a diabetic patient, the bladder should first be emptied and the urine discarded. A short time later the bladder should again be emptied, and the second specimen should then be tested. The specimen should be examined fresh, within 1 hour after voiding, or it may be refrigerated for up to 6 hours.

Obviously, qualitative and semiquantitative determinations are subject to preanalytical variation and interferences. For example, a first morning specimen is usually the most concentrated and, therefore, best suited for determination of protein and sediment analysis. To avoid deterioration of the sediment or a change in the chemical and physical composition, urine specimens should be refrigerated at temperatures between 2° and 8° C if processing cannot be completed within 1 hour. False positive protein results may be found during therapy with phenazopyridine hydrochloride, or with infusions of polyvinylpyrrolidone, a blood substitute. Large amounts of ascorbic acid (vitamin C) in the urine (following ingestion of vitamin tablets or fruit juices) can produce glucose readings that are too low or falsely negative, lower the sensitivity of the bilirubin test, or give false negative readings for the blood test. Phenylketone or phenolphthalein compounds give red-orange to red color shades in the ketone test. False positive readings in the bilirubin test may be produced by medications that color the urine red.

Intralaboratory Quality Control of Urinalysis Quality control of urinalysis includes use of daily quality control material as well as surveys. Controls are run at the start of each shift. Lyophilized, tablet, liquid, or reagent-strip control preparations are available with varying concentrations of the constituents sought in routine urinalysis. Control solutions can be formulated by the laboratory staff at considerably less cost.[11]

Known ranges are defined by the manufacturer. Values outside the established limits should be recorded, marked as abnormal, and the corrective action noted on the laboratory work sheet. Participation in an extralaboratory proficiency testing program is strongly recommended and is required for accreditation. Such a program, available from the College of American Pathologists (CAP), checks chemical proficiency by wet specimens and urinary sediment proficiency by transparencies with case histories.[12]

Stool Occult Blood[13]

Detection of blood in the stool is usually performed using a simplified variation of the guaiac test for occult blood. Upon application of a stool specimen to a specially prepared guaiac-impregnated paper, the peroxidase in any hemoglobin present in the specimen comes in contact with the guaiac reagent. Application of a developing solution, which is a stabilized dilute mixture of hydrogen peroxide and denatured alcohol, creates a reaction between peroxidase and guaiac that turns the test paper a blue to blue-green color. In order for the reaction among occult blood, guaiac, and hydrogen peroxide to occur, the blood cells must be hemolyzed to release peroxidase. When blood is present in the stool, substances in the stool, primarily water and salts, hemolyze the blood cells, thereby releasing peroxidase, permitting the guaiac reaction to occur. Patient preparation should include instruction to include liberal amounts of high-residue foods, such as prunes, bran, raw vegetables, corn, and peanuts, in their diet. It also may be necessary to exclude meat from the diet before and during the test period to eliminate false positive test results.

The myoglobin and hemoglobin of ingested meat and fish have peroxidase activity that may falsely indicate the presence of occult blood. In general, the guaiac-type tests (less sensitive for occult blood) are least affected by meat in the diet. Bacteria in the bowel, as well as ingested vegetables, such as horseradish, turnips, and bananas, contain peroxidase and can falsely elevate fecal peroxidase activity.

Errors may result from inaccurate measurement of reagents, inaccurate ti[...] the reaction, and variable interpretation of the color developed. In routine testi[ng for] occult blood, an aliquot from the center of the formed stool should be used. Fi[lter] paper techniques are limited in reproducibility by the tendency for liquid stools to be absorbed into the substance of the paper. Reagents should be checked daily by testing a sample known to contain blood.

Fluid Analysis[14]

Determination of abnormal volume and/or composition of a body fluid can provide information relating to the diagnosis and management of a patient. The analysis may consist of appearance before and after centrifugation, erythrocyte and leukocyte counts, a differential leukocyte count, specific gravity, and examination for crystals (on synovial fluid).

Fluids should be processed within 30 minutes, because cells may begin to lyse after this time. Cerebrospinal fluid specimens have priority over all other tests in the laboratory. Glucose measurements on fluids are easier to interpret if the patient has been fasting for at least 6 hours.

All procedures used to quantify analytes in fluids should be carefully controlled according to recommended procedures for quantitative procedures. All morphologic interpretations (cells, crystals, etc.) should be monitored concerning their accuracy. An intralaboratory program and an extralaboratory program are recommended. The CAP proficiency testing programs offers transparencies of fluids with case histories.[12]

BEDSIDE TESTS AND SELF-TESTS

Bedside tests and self-tests (Table 12-3) have in common the fact that they are performed outside the clinical laboratory and the physician's office and do not necessarily require the use of an analytic instrument. They differ from one another in that bedside tests are performed by laboratory or other medical personnel, whereas self-tests are usually performed by nonmedical personnel, i.e., laypersons (Fig. 12-1). Quality assurance principles are applicable to all semiquantitative bedside tests and self-tests. The pregnancy test is a qualitative test that is often used as a self-test. Self-tests where the sample is sent to a laboratory for reading—for instance, feces for occult blood—have theoretical advantages over self-tests where the individuals themselves read the test results—for example, the pregnancy test. Blood glucose estimation is a good example of a common test that is both a bedside test and a self-test.

Self-testing has a very important caveat. Self-test results should not be interpreted and acted on without consulting the individual's physician because interpretation of self-test results by laypersons can lead to potentially disastrous results. For example, a diabetic patient interprets a negative urinary test for glucose as evidence that less insulin is required. In reality, the serum glucose is rising and the diabetes is getting worse—the negative urinary test for glucose is due to renal failure with decreased urinary clearance of glucose.

Although self-tests can be accurate and reproducible, they are prone to errors relat-

...he individuals performing the tests and vested interests of ...the tests. In this regard, a recent study from the Albert ...ine is of interest.[15] This study disclosed that the majority of ...r-than-actual blood glucose values in their log books. Fibs in-...er values than those indicated by reflectance meters, selectively ...ce meter readings, and entering phantom results from nonexistent ...ications were detected by using specially modified reflectance meters that contained memory chips capable of storing the actual value with the time and date of the reading.

Proper education of the person performing the test is extremely important in achieving accurate and precise test results. Values for blood glucose using split samples should be obtained comparing self-test results with clinical laboratory results. Common pitfalls should be emphasized, such as the following[16]:

1 Failing to cover the strip with enough blood gives a falsely low reading, particularly when read with a meter.
2 Rubbing the strip too hard with a cotton ball can also cause a falsely low reading. Similarly, wiping it with an alcohol swab appears to inhibit the reaction and results in less color change.

Pregnancy test kits suitable for physician's offices and for self-testing are available. Urinary human chorionic gonadotropin is detected by using red blood cells or some other indicator in conjunction with antibody against human chorionic gonadotropin. Proper education of the person performing the test is extremely important in achieving accurate and reproducible results. Usually, the layperson performing the test has no opportunity for expert instruction, so it is especially important that the directions are written in a clear and simple manner. In this regard, pictures or photographs of positive and negative test results are preferable to descriptions of positive and negative test results. Common pitfalls such as the following should be emphasized in the directions:

1 True negative test results can occur in the first weeks of pregnancy.
2 Failing to use a first morning specimen can cause a false negative test result.
3 Proteinuria and hemoglobinuria may interfere with test results. Perhaps it would be useful if reagent-strip tests for protein, hemoglobin, and specific gravity were included with the pregnancy test kit. This would alert the individual performing the test of a possible erroneous test result.

No standards are used during the performance of the test. The tests are precalibrated by the manufacturers. No controls are used to detect a malfunctioning test system. Therefore, it is particularly important to follow the manufacturer's directions carefully, including storage of reagents, outdating of reagents, appearance of positive and negative test results, and so on.

The number of determinations that have been modified for use in the physician's office and for self-testing is growing rapidly. Urine specific gravity can now be estimated by dipstick, stool guiac testing has been simplified, and a device now makes it possible to estimate total white blood count, platelet count, and packed red cell volume from what is essentially a microhematocrit tube. The American Association for Clinical Chemistry has initiated a publication entitled *SPOT* (Satellite and Physician Office Testing) *News,* and the College of Pathologists is planning an Aspen Conference on the topic. The question of how the quality of these tests is being or will be controlled is not yet answered. The hope is that they will permit good medical care, but this is dependent on how well these tests are performed.

REFERENCES

1 Statland BE, Westgard JO: Quality control: Theory and practice, in Henry JB (ed): *Clinical Diagnosis and Management by Laboratory Methods,* ed 17. Philadelphia, WB Saunders, 1984, pp 74–93.
2 *AMH/85 Accreditation Manual for Hospitals.* Chicago, Joint Commission on Accreditation of Hospitals, 1984.
3 Speicher CE, Smith JW: *Choosing Effective Laboratory Tests.* Philadelphia, WB Saunders, 1983.
4 Burke MD: Assessing the clinical utility of laboratory methods. *Clin Lab Med* 1981, 1:21.
5 Trends in clinical testing: High growth for M.D. office diagnostics. *Biomed Business Int* 1984, 15:138.
6 Free AH, Free HM: Self testing, an emerging component of clinical chemistry. *Clin Chem* 1984, 30:829.
7 Fuerst ML: The home test movement shifts into high gear. *Med World News,* February 11, 1985, p 94.
8 Pippenger CE, Galen RS: Drug dipsticks: What do they do? How do they work? *Diagnostic Med* 1985, 8:38.
9 Speicher CE, Brandt JT: Committee responds to charge to improve clinical microscopy. *Pathologist* 1985, 39:7.
10 Bradley M, Schumann GB: Examination of urine, in Henry JB (ed): *Clinical Diagnosis and Management by Laboratory Methods,* ed 17. Philadelphia, WB Saunders, 1984, pp 380–458.
11 Urinalysis, in *Hematology Procedure Manual.* Columbus, The Ohio State University Hospitals, 1984.
12 College of American Pathologists Computer Center, P.O. Box 1234, Traverse City, MI 49684.
13 Kao YS, Scheer WD: Malabsorption, diarrhea, and examination of feces, in Henry JB (ed): *Clinical Diagnosis and Management by Laboratory Methods,* ed 17. Philadelphia, WB Saunders, 1984, pp 562–575.
14 Kjieldsberg CR, Krieg AF: Cerebrospinal fluid and other body fluids, in Henry JB (ed): *Clinical Diagnosis and Management by Laboratory Methods,* ed 17. Philadelphia, WB Saunders, 1984, pp 459–492.
15 Mazze RS, Shamoun H, Pasmantier R, et al: Reliability of blood glucose monitoring by patients with diabetes mellitus. *Am J Med* 1984, 77:211.
16 Moldovanyi C, Wilcox W, Redmond GP: Helping patients get accurate blood glucose results. *Diagnostic Med* 1985, 8:46.

CHAPTER 13

QUALITY ASSURANCE IN ANATOMIC PATHOLOGY

Donald W. Penner, M.D.

The present state of the art and science of diagnostic pathology and cytopathology has achieved a level of excellence that almost certainly would not have been considered possible a life span ago. Although autopsies were conducted in ancient times, it was not until 1632 that the first textbook on pathology was written by Steverino.[1] In the eighteenth century, Morgagni published a number of books and Hunter made a number of significant contributions to surgical pathology. By this time, advances in the development of the microscope began to make possible a better understanding of cellular histopathology. A major contribution to this understanding was the classical publication on cellular pathology by Virchow in 1858. During the first half of the twentieth century, a number of important contributions in North America marked the beginnings of the modern era of surgical pathology and cytopathology. In cytopathology, the contributions by Papanicolaou and Traut to the early cytologic diagnosis of cervical carcinoma are well recognized; with the publication of their atlas in 1941, the new era of cytologic diagnosis began.

To progress from a emerging era of surgical pathology and cytopathology in the 1930s and 1940s to the present general level of performance in less than half a century is no small accomplishment. Although much has been achieved, much remains to be done. Recognition and then acceptance of this self-evident truth also has been evolving, as have a variety of activities to help improve diagnostic performance.

In 1973, the status of the then-emerging concepts and application of quality assurance in surgical pathology and cytopathology was reviewed and the findings were published.[2] Much progress has been made in the intervening decade. Perhaps the most important factors in making progress in quality assurance possible are the rapidly evolving awareness of the need for quality assurance and the changing attitude of pathologists. In a relatively short time, pathologists have progressed through a phase of unquestioning acceptance of diagnostic performance, to recognition of imperfections without openly addressing the issues, and, finally, to a recognition that only through a process of evaluation and appropriate educational programs can real and effective progress be made in performance improvement. Although not all pathologists embrace the latter with equal enthusiasm, almost all would agree that, if evaluation and educational programs are to be used, they should be designed and directed by pathologists.

TABLE 13-1
ANATOMIC PATHOLOGY QUALITY ASSURANCE

I Internal components
  A Personnel
    1 Staff qualifications
    2 Continuing education
  B Specimens
    1 Acquisition
    2 Handling and preparation
  C Reports
  D Performance Evaluation
II External components
  A Procedures
    1 Source and type of material
    2 Standards for evaluation of diagnosis
  B Types of programs
    1 Educational
    2 Evaluational

QUALITY ASSURANCE IN ANATOMIC PATHOLOGY

What does quality assurance in pathology mean? "It means what I want it to mean." This Alice in Wonderland definition may not be far from the truth, because definitions of quality assurance vary considerably. For the purpose of this chapter, quality assurance is a total program that has many components, internal and external, in which the final goal is improved diagnostic performance in the specified areas of anatomic pathology. The term "quality assurance" is preferable to the term "quality control," which in the past has been used interchangeably with quality assurance. Conceptually, it it perhaps difficult, if not impossible, to "control" the quality of value judgments. A total quality assurance program for diagnostic surgical pathology and cytopathology includes a number of critical elements for internal and external quality assurance (Table 13-1).

INTERNAL COMPONENTS OF QUALITY ASSURANCE

Personnel

All staff, not only pathologists, should have appropriate qualifications that meet standards set by recognized professional or peer groups. Not only should qualifications be documented, there should also be mechanisms for providing continuing education to improve qualifications where appropriate. The mechanisms by which ongoing continuing education is achieved for the pathologists and technologists include reading, audiovisual educational programs, slide sets, slide seminars, lectures, and short courses.

The nature and extent of the educational efforts should be documented with periodic review to evaluate the appropriateness and effectiveness of the educational efforts.

Specimens

The time and effort spent in achieving a good technical product can be very cost-effective. Poor-quality technical preparations are a major factor in diagnostic problems and can be very wasteful of professional time, resulting in unnecessary additional sections and delay. Even though poor technical material may give rise to diagnostic errors, it cannot be used as a justification for errors.

To best serve the needs of patients, education, and/or research at the institution, standards for handling tissue and cytologic material should be developed in conjunction with the appropriate medical staff. Standards should include those for the following procedures: prebiopsy or surgical excision consultations, the handling of tissue from excision to interpretation, and requirements for special procedures. Standards for specimen documentation (gross descriptions) and specimen sampling should be developed, or standards set by appropriate professional organizations should be followed. Monitoring systems for the technical aspects of tissue handling should be used and documented, with special evaluation of the various technical procedures for detection of changes in quality that indicate need for corrective action. These monitoring systems work best when they are the responsibility of an appropriate individual, use a simple, standard form, and are signed. For further details on technical standards for tissue handling, sections, and monitoring, see Chapter 7 in *Quality Assurance Practices for Health Laboratories*.[3]

Reports

The consultation report (the pathologist's diagnostic report) should be appropriate to meet the defined needs. Consultations should be timely, with verbal discussions with attending staff as indicated. Filing systems should allow rapid retrieval and correlation with previous reports on individual patients. All operating room consultations should be documented and then correlated with the final diagnosis.[4] Slides made in the operating room should be kept, because on occasion they may be the only diagnostic evidence available. It becomes increasingly important to save all material, as portions of biopsies are needed for special procedures such as receptor assays of breast biopsies. Discrepancies in diagnoses should be periodically reviewed, as should the definition of what constitutes a discrepancy.

Performance Evaluation

In 1973, Penner[2] suggested that an annual review of the numbers and types of diagnoses made (patterns of diagnoses) might provide useful data on diagnostic performance. To help provide quality assurance in anatomic pathology, Macartney, Henson, and Codling[5] have further expanded the statistical approach to the analysis of diagnostic patterns generated in various geographic areas. This approach warrants further investigation to determine the role it might eventually play.

Internal peer review or evaluation of performance by random samples or specified groups of diseases or types of tissues also is useful.[6] Obviously, because performance cannot be improved unless the areas in need of improvement are demonstrated, the results of these internal reviews should be periodically evaluated. Professionals also need assurance that what they do is good.[3] Another valuable peer review mechanism, often essential for providing information on patient management, is to review, whenever possible, all previous material from the patient. This provides a good learning experience on the progress of the disease and on its response to treatment. Surgeons should be encouraged to provide dates, accession numbers, and sources of previous material.

Consultations provide opportunities to improve specific patient care, to educate, and to be more sensitive in identifying those cases in which consultations should be obtained. Groups of pathologists, to their collective advantage, from time to time identify certain diagnostic situations in which they agree to obtain a second opinion in surgical pathology. Internal consultation should be recognized as a valuable educational tool and, as a by-product, protection against legal challenges. Internal consultation patterns should be documented.

In cytology, the internal diagnostic performance evaluation should include, where possible, correlation of surgical biopsies and cytology. Rescreening of positive, negative, or false positive or false negative cervical smears has also been used as a quality assurance procedure. Rescreening by technologists of 10 percent of negative smears is a controversial procedure. It is generally agreed that such rescreening is not likely to produce a very high yield of missed abnormal cases. However, many cytopathologists use some, perhaps periodic, rescreening of certain classes of slides. Appropriately selected and rescreened cases provide useful information on performance of the technical staff. There is generally wide agreement on the use of rescreening of previous negative smears when patients present with positive cervical smears. Some cytopathologists review negative smears if an untreated patient has had a positive smear at any time in the past.

Every autopsy provides an opportunity to evaluate previous diagnosis made in surgical pathology or cytology. State, province, or local tumor registries or other records also provide an opportunity for follow-up. Many years ago, most of the diagnoses made at Memorial Hospital (now Memorial Sloan Kettering Cancer Center), New York, were reviewed at 5-year intervals (or other periods of time). Neither the original diagnosis nor the patient outcome was known to the reviewer. Because this hospital had its own follow-up registry, this review provided a unique performance evaluation in terms of biologic outcome.

The group practice of pathology in large hospitals, with or without association with a medical school, provides a setting in which it is generally easier to initiate and maintain internal quality assurance programs. Solo-practicing pathologists, or several pathologists providing services to multiple hospitals, can achieve many of the desirable goals by cooperative efforts with pathologists located within a geographic area in which it is practical to operate collectively. All internal quality assurance programs should be periodically reviewed to evaluate their effectiveness.

EXTERNAL COMPONENTS OF QUALITY ASSURANCE

Procedures

If groups of pathologists have diversified expertise, many resources, and sufficient volume of diagnostic material to provide an excellent internal quality assurance program, is an external component necessary?

The simple answer is yes. External reviews are used to evaluate the overall performance of hospitals, medical schools, and clinical pathology, as well as anatomic pathology, because they are deemed desirable and indeed necessary to provide "assurance," not only to the professionals or the institution, but to the public at large, that performance is being evaluated by independent reviewers and identified deficiencies are corrected.

Important characteristics of an evaluation mechanism for diagnostic surgical pathology and cytopathology are (1) the source and type of material to be evaluated and (2) the standard by which diagnoses are measured. If performance is to be assessed in a manner simulating how pathology is practiced on a day-to-day basis, the evaluation material should be slides and diagnostic reports from the patient files. Would slide sets with expert diagnoses sent to the pathologist for diagnoses achieve the same purpose? To date, it has not been demonstrated that diagnostic performance on such external slide sets is identical to day-to-day performance. The traditional "best" standard for the correct diagnosis has been expert opinion and/or biologic outcome. Another standard that is becoming generally accepted is the peer consensus diagnosis. The peer group must be large enough to be statistically valid, and all reviewers must see the same slide on which the evaluation diagnosis was made.

Any evaluation program instituted must be logistically practical and economically feasible. If peer group performance is to be compared, all participants must evaluate the same material. A standard nomenclature must be used in order to analyze and compare data. Performance evaluation and educational mechanisms that are closely integrated are most likely to be cost-effective and logistically practical. To stratify cases in terms of degree of consensus, patient file cases are measured against a peer consensus standard. Cases in which there is great interobserver variation represent the areas in which there is most need of education, and those cases with a very high level of interobserver concordance identify the areas in which there is least need of education. Slides from the problem cases can be used to create a "lending library" of educational material. Experts can be used to confirm (or dispute) the peer consensus diagnosis, write appropriate critiques describing how the diagnosis was established, and provide references. Photographs can be taken to illustrate problems and/or the diagnosis. Ongoing seminars using the lending library would illustrate the major areas of interobserver variation and allow for contact between program participants and experts.

To provide ongoing monitoring of patient-related diagnostic performance, participants could be requested to contribute cases from their patient files with designated diagnoses. These cases could then be evaluated by experts and/or peers; critiques, references, and photographs could be prepared and put into the lending library for recycling as described above. Using cases from patient files would ensure that the diagnostic material used for the educational component actually represents the problems in the real world of practice. Cases used for education also could be specifically tailored to meet the needs of the individual pathologists.

Types of Programs

Educational Program Continuing medical education (CME) programs have evolved gradually over the past several decades, with a vast increase in number during the 1960s and 1970s. Not only do these programs provide many opportunities for ongoing education, but participation in CME has become a requirement in order to maintain specialist status for some specialty groups, or to be able to continue to practice medicine. Although the trend toward compulsory participation appears to have peaked, participation in CME still is mandated by some professional organizations and institutions. Many organizations and educational institutions are appropriately involved in providing ongoing educational programs in histopathology and cytopathology. In the area of tumor pathology, excellent study slide sets are available from the Armed Forces Institute of Pathology in the United States and in Canada from the Canadian Tumor Reference Center (National Cancer Institute of Canada).

The final desired objective of any performance improvement program is demonstrated improvement. Ongoing evaluation as outlined above would make it possible to document performance trends of pathologists who participate in the program for varying periods of time. Overall trends of performance in relation to specific problems over a period of time also can be documented. The concept of structured quality assurance programs, especially as outlined above, is of fairly recent origin. However, many pathologists routinely use many elements of a good total quality assurance program, although these activities may not be well defined or documented.

Evaluation Programs There are a few programs with an element of limited evaluation where the primary thrust is education. These programs generally fall within the categories of microscopic slides or case seminar programs. Many medical organizations, institutions, and even individuals are involved in this type of education. This important tool is widely used and plays a very important educational role. Some of these programs have become "institutions" in themselves and remain very popular after many years; the annual slide seminars of the American Society of Clinical Pathology, of the Canadian Association of Pathology, and of many state pathology societies are but a few.

In addition to the above, there are other programs that provide a structured evaluation using slides that are obtained from sources other than the files of the participating pathologists. The cases used are compiled and diagnosed by experts. The Quality Assurance Program in Anatomical Pathology of the Royal College of Pathology in

Australia[7] was started in 1968 and distributes slides and clinical data from four cases every fourth month. The cases are chosen by experts from the entire field of anatomic pathology; included are both rather rare and more common problem cases. These are evaluated by the participants, who then receive the correct diagnoses with a summary of the performance of the group and critiques with references for each case. This program is voluntary, and approximately 150 pathologists participate. Short questionnaires that relate to customary practices in the pathologists' laboratories are included for completion.

Another model is the Laboratory Proficiency Testing Program (LPTP) of the Ontario Medical Association,[8] which evaluates performance in all areas of clinical pathology and also includes a program designed for proficiency evaluation in diagnostic cytopathology of the cervix. One batch of six microscopic slides, generally consisting of selected lesions of the cervix with an occasional negative smear, is sent to all government-licensed cytology laboratories in Ontario, Canada. For the approximately 160 licensed laboratories, participation is compulsory by provincial law. The program is operated by the Cytology Committee of the Pathology Section of the Ontario Medical Association. The nomenclature used is that recommended by the Walton Report on Cervical Cytology.[9] Variances from the expert Committee diagnoses are categorized as plus or minus 1, 2, or 3 degrees of deviation in the diagnostic classification of no abnormal cells, benign atypia, mild dysplasia, moderate dysplasia, severe dysplasia, and malignant. For example, benign atypia, one diagnostic class from the expert diagnosis of mild dysplasia, was classified as -1 degree of deviation. Although it is recognized that six cases are inadequate for a statistically valid evaluation of performance, the accumulated data do provide information on group performance and identify problem areas.

By the use of questionnaires, data are collected on the number and types of cytology examinations performed in each laboratory and the number of professional, technical, and clerical staff used. This program is compulsory, and although the major objective is to detect problems and provide assistance in improving diagnostic skills, there is an implied punitive element.

Problems exist with proficiency testing programs used to evaluate competence. The Wisconsin model was started in 1967 under supervision of the Wisconsin Laboratory of Hygiene, University of Wisconsin.[10] Sixteen cases of cytology were mailed in batches of 4 cases every 3 months to 15 independent laboratories. The slides were obtained from patient files (not from those being tested), and the correct diagnoses provided by four reference laboratories. Although it was recognized that program performance might not reflect daily practice, arbitrary standards were set. Ten of the 15 laboratories met the standard. A second major state program was sponsored by the New York State Department of Health[11] to evaluate performance of cytotechnologists. Again concern was raised that performance in such a program would not actually reflect day-to-day practices. One reason for varying performance was that even though matched sets of cytology slides were used, the test material evaluated by each participant was not identical.

In 1956, the Canadian Association of Pathologists, in conjunction with the Advisory Committee on Records and Statistics of the National Cancer Institute of Canada, organized an as-yet-unpublished study on the diagnosis of breast lesions. Fifty consecutive cases were taken from a university hospital's patient files; duplicate slides were cut and sent to 34 pathologists at university and nonteaching hospitals. All pathologists actively practiced surgical pathology, and all except one were certified by the Royal College of Physicians and Surgeons of Canada as specialists in anatomic pathology. Thirty-three cases had complete agreement, one case did not reach a consensus, and 16 had disagreements which varied from 1 to 8 per case as measured by the consensus diagnosis for the presence or absence of cancer. There was 97.3 percent agreement for "cancer is present" and 97.7 percent for "cancer is not present."

THE COLLEGE OF AMERICAN PATHOLOGISTS ANATOMIC PATHOLOGY PROJECT

In 1970, the College of American Pathologists (CAP) appointed a histopathology/cytopathology committee to develop and test a performance evaluation program for diagnostic surgical pathology and cytopathology. The long-term objective was to help improve diagnostic performance. The basic concept underlying this objective was that to achieve improvement, it is essential to know the frequency and the nature of diagnostic problems.

The pilot project has been previously described in 1973 by Penner.[2] A summary of the histopathology and cytopathology programs initiated before the introduction of the Performance Improvement Program (PIP) (see p. 311) is shown on Table 13-2. The model project (Histopathology Project 1) was designed and tested based on the principles shown in Table 13-3. Groups of volunteer pathologists were established, and each pathologist was required to select from his or her files the first breast lesion, lymph node biopsy, epithelial skin tumor, abnormal liver biopsy, and endometrial le-

TABLE 13-2
SUMMARY OF COLLEGE OF AMERICAN PATHOLOGISTS PILOT PROJECTS

Program	Number of enrolled laboratories	Number of cases	Number of participant diagnoses per case
Histopathology I* (pilot project)	50	250	10
Histopathology II, Olympians (breast)	20	200	10
Histopathology II, peers (breast)	100	1000	10
Histopathology III (breast)	290	4275	15
Histopathology IV (prostate)	165	2025	15
Effusion cytology	180	1800	20
Cervical cytology I	160	1575	20
Cervical cytology II	310	4600 (new) 1000 (old)	10–15

*Breast, skin, lymph node, endometrium, liver.

TABLE 13-3
PRINCIPLES FOR PERFORMANCE EVALUATION PROGRAMS

1. Evaluation must be based on slides and reports from participant's own files.
2. The standard of performance is measured by peer consensus. Where practical the expert diagnoses could be used.
3. In order to achieve a peer consensus, all participants examine the same material.
4. Uniform terminology is used.
5. The program is acceptable to the participants.
6. The program is logistically practical and economically feasible.

sion occurring antecedent to an identified date. Each pathologist was requested to provide duplicate hemotoxylin and eosin (H&E) stained slides from each block, all of which had to show the same diagnostic features of the lesion as the original slide. The cases from each group were sent to group coordinators, who removed all identification and renumbered the slides to make a slide set. Each slide set, consisting of 50 slides (10 slides from each of the five selected sites), was sent to each participating pathologist. Each participant was requested to use the then newly introduced systematized nomenclature of pathology (SNOP) system in reporting the diagnosis.

In this model, each pathologist in turn was a "submitting pathologist" who submitted five cases from his or her patient files and a "participating pathologist" when examining other slides. These cases were evaluated against the consensus diagnosis created by each participating pathologist diagnosing all the 10 submitted cases. Included in these 50 slides were 45 cases originating from the other nine pathologists as well as the five from the tenth pathologist's now examined as unknowns. Thus it was possible to measure submitting pathologists' performance on cases from their own patient files and participating pathologists' performance similar to that of diagnosing cases in the "slide seminar mode." The performance of each individual was measured against the group peer consensus standard that was created. However, performance as a participant may or may not reflect performance on a day-to-day basis. When 51 percent or more of the peer group diagnoses were in agreement, peer consensus was said to occur. The degree of consensus or concordance thus could vary from 51 to 100 percent, and not all cases necessarily reached a peer consensus agreement.

Although a great deal of other information was obtained from this pilot project, it clearly demonstrated that such a model was logistically, practically, and economically feasible. There were some problems in data collection, including some unfamiliarity with the nomenclature and clerical errors in assigning code numbers. Although participant performance was based on the evaluation of 10 cases per tissue site, each participant received only one of his or her own cases for each site. Because each of the groups of pathologists diagnosed different cases, the performance between groups could not be compared. For the type of data produced, see Fig. 13-1. The total cases in which consensus occurred was 193 (77 percent).

Following the pilot project, a series of diagnostic peer review or evaluation programs using source material from patient files specified body sites were conducted. The study model remained essentially the same as in the pilot project but with the

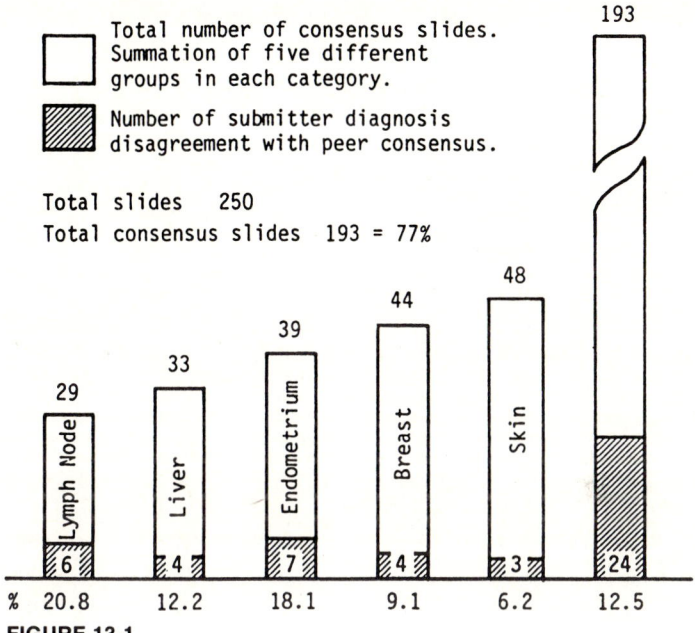
FIGURE 13-1

following changes. The number of cases from the patient files requested from each pathologist (submitting pathologists) varied from 10 to 20, as did the number of pathologists in each peer group. In most groups, each participating pathologist reviewed 200 cases. For the cytopathology programs, the same slide for each participant was used with each member of the peer group diagnosing the slide sequentially.

Prior to establishing the CAP Performance Improvement Program in Diagnostic Surgical Pathology and Cytopathology (see below), four programs in Histopathology (II–V) as well as effusion cytology and two cervical cytology projects were completed.

HISTOPATHOLOGY PROGRAMS

Lesions of Breast: Histopathology Program III
Performance Data

For this program, 380 pathologists contributed almost 4300 cases, making over 60,000 diagnoses. By consensus, the lesions were diagnosed as benign in roughly two-thirds of the cases and as malignant in the other one-third. Consensus agreement in the benign consensus cases ranged from 97.9 to 99.2 percent and performance for the malignant consensus cases was equally good, varying from 98.3 to 99.2 percent.

Table 13-4 shows the interobserver variations for various consensus diagnoses, in-

TABLE 13-4
HISTOPATHOLOGY III DATA COMPARISON*
Interobserver Variation When the Peer Consensus Diagnoses Were Infiltrating Ductal, Infiltrating Lobular, Intraductal, and in Situ Lobular Carcinoma

Peer consensus diagnosis infiltrating ductal carcinoma						Peer consensus diagnosis infiltrating lobular carcinoma				
Diagnosis	No. participating pathologists	Percent	No. submitting pathologists	Percent		Diagnosis	No. participating pathologists	Percent	No. submitting pathologists	Percent
Infiltrating ductal	12,175	80.4	938	86.5		Infiltrating lobular	954	64.0	43	40.1
Infiltrating lobular	1,086	7.1	51	4.7		Infiltrating ductal	402	26.9	55	51.4
Medullary	427	2.8	22	2.0		CIS lobular	23	1.5	6	5.6
Intraductal	265	1.7	26	2.3		Malignant NOS	31	2.0	1	0.9
Other	1,185	8.0	47	4.5		Other	80	5.6	2	2.0
Total	15,138	100.0	1,084	100.0		Total	1,490	100.0	107	100.0

Peer consensus diagnosis intraductal carcinoma						Peer consensus diagnosis in situ lobular carcinoma				
Diagnosis	No. participating pathologists	Percent	No. submitting pathologists	Percent		Diagnosis	No. participating pathologists	Percent	No. submitting pathologists	Percent
Intraductal	499	61.9	38	64.4		CIS lobular	85	59.0	4	36.3
Infiltrating ductal	120	14.8	10	16.9		CIS ductal	11	7.6	1	9.0
Papillomatosis	35	4.3	4	6.7		Infiltrating lobular	10	6.9	0	0
In situ papillary	32	3.9	2	3.3		Fibrocystic disease	9	6.2	2	18.1
Other	120	15.1	5	8.7		Other	29	20.3	4	36.6
Total	806	100.0	59	100.0		Total	144	100.0	11	100.0

*Up to 20 different diagnoses were made for some of the peer consensus diagnoses. The above tables record the most common diagnoses made. Totals include all diagnoses made in each group.

cluding infiltrating ductal and infiltrating lobular carcinoma; medullary carcinoma; malignant, not otherwise specific (NOS); and lobular and ductal carcinoma in situ (CIS). The interobserver variations for other consensus diagnoses (not shown in the table) for the program were as follows:

1 Benign papilloma or papillomotosis (123 cases): 92.3 percent of participants and 94.4 percent of submitter pathologists agreed that the lesions were benign.

2 Benign lesions (not otherwise specified) 174 cases: 98.7 percent of participants and 93.4 percent of submitter pathologists agreed that the lesions were benign.

3 Sclerosing adenosis (61 cases): 98.7 percent of participants and 93.4 percent of submitter pathologists agreed that the lesions were benign.

4 Fibrocystic disease of the breast (1640 cases): 99.1 percent of the participants and 98.7 percent of the submitter pathologists agreed that the legions were benign.

5 Papillary in situ (7 cases) and infiltrating papillary carcinomas (18 cases) constituted 1.7 percent of all malignant tumors in this program. These cases showed a rather high level of interobserver variation.

6 With medullary (67 cases) and colloid carcinomas (56 cases), 68.2 percent of the participants and 49.2 percent of the submitter pathologists agreed on the definitive classification of medullary carcinoma, whereas 87.4 percent of the participants and 82.1 percent of the submitters agreed on the classification of colloid carcinomas. In both of the above tumors 99 percent of the pathologists agreed with the consensus diagnosis of malignant tumor.

Lesions of the Prostate: Histopathology Project IV Performance Data

The most frequently made diagnosis was benign hyperplasia of the prostate. In 1123 cases, 97 percent of the pathologists agreed with the benign consensus diagnosis, and 88 percent agreed on the specific diagnosis of benign prostatic hyperplasia (BPH).

Of the 342 malignant lesions, 325 were acinar adenocarcinomas. The consensus diagnosis of very well-differentiated small acinar adenocarcinoma was made in 117 cases; 87 percent agreed that the lesion was malignant, and 64 percent agreed on the specific diagnosis. In the remaining 208 cases, which were "all other types of acinar adenocarcinomas," there was 97 percent agreement that the lesions were malignant and 77 percent agreement with the specific diagnosis. Small foci of very well-differentiated small acinar adenocarcinoma can be difficult to recognize as carcinoma; in some cases a difficult value judgment must be made between BPH and cancer.

Intraobserver Variations in Lesions of Breast and Prostate

The model used in the CAP programs made it possible to examine intraobserver variations in approximately 25 percent of the breast and prostate cases. It is not possible to be certain that the same pathologist made "submitter" diagnoses and "participant" diagnoses (see Table 13-5) in all the cases. It is certain, however, that all the submitter and participant diagnoses were made by pathologists from the same department.

TABLE 13-5
INTRAOBSERVER VARIATIONS IN LESIONS OF BREAST AND PROSTATE

	Histopathology Project III, breast	Histopathology Project V, prostate
Number of all cases in program	4,275	2,025
Total number of diagnoses made to date	62,600	29,800
Number of identical diagnoses made twice by the same pathologist	823	434
Cases submitted as benign, diagnosed later as benign but different specific diagnoses	133	62
Cases submitted as malignant, diagnosed later as malignant but different specific diagnoses	86	30
Submitted as in situ, later as infiltrating	6	
Submitted as infiltrating, later as in situ	5	
Cases submitted as benign, diagnosed later as malignant	9	6
Cases submitted as malignant, diagnosed later as benign	15	14
Cases submitted as benign, diagnosed later as "inadequate for diagnosis"	4	0
Total number of cases diagnosed twice by same pathologist*	1,070	546

*These cases were entered into the program with a specific diagnosis made by the original submitting pathologist. These cases were then sent back to these pathologists as unknowns over a two-year period. Initial instructions to the pathologists participating in the program were to make the diagnosis on the same basis as was the practice in the department. Two assumptions were made in compiling the intraobserver data: (1) that the submitter pathologist made the initial diagnosis with or without consultation; (2) that the same submitter pathologist, now acting as a participant pathologist, made the second diagnosis on the same slide with or without consultation.
Breast
25% (1070/4275) of all cases were sent back to submitters as unknowns.
2.2% (24/1070) changed their diagnosis from malignant to benign or benign to malignant.
77% (823/1070) made identical diagnoses.
Prostate
27% (546/2025) of all cases were sent back to submitters as unknowns.
3.7% (20/546) changed their diagnosis from malignant to benign or benign to malignant.
80% (434/546) made identical diagnoses.

Breast The same submitter and participant diagnosis was made in a total of 823 cases (77 percent). This group of cases included 521 benign and 302 malignant lesions, which is a higher ratio of malignant tumors than for the entire rest of the program. Of the 388 malignant cases diagnosed twice, 86 had their definitive classification changed, and of these, 2.6 percent were changed between infiltrating and in situ. In the 24 cases where discordance occurred between the two diagnoses, 10 cases went from consensus agreement to disagreement and 10 the converse. Initial analysis of the data does not indicate a difference in performance between submitter and participant pathologists.

Prostate The two diagnoses made by the same observer were in agreement in 434 cases (80 percent) of the total cases seen twice by the same observer. In these cases, 362 were diagnosed as benign and 72 as malignant. Thirty of the malignant cases (29.4 percent) were rediagnosed as malignant, but the histologic type was changed. Almost all these cases were very well-differentiated or less well-differentiated acinar adenocarcinoma, and all differences in the two diagnoses were shifts between these two types. As in the breast cases, the data presently available from these two programs do not provide sufficient information to distinguish between submitter performance and participant diagnostic performance.

Cytology Programs

Because of difficulties in providing duplicate cytology slides, each pathologist saw the same original slide in rotation. Prior to the beginning of the study, it was recognized that a rotation of the slides to groups of 10 to 20 pathologists would require a considerable period of time and, indeed, time schedules were rarely achieved. Because the standard used to measure performance was a peer consensus, it often required many months before a diagnostic consensus was achieved (51 percent or more agreement) and hence before participants could be informed of their performance. The long interval was perceived by many as much too long to achieve any teaching benefit from the program, because by the time the results were received many of the participants could not remember the slides examined. The question of teaching benefit was raised even though participants were informed that the programs were designed to evaluate, not to educate. There also were complaints about the technical quality of some of the slides, especially those used for the cytology effusion program. Significant slide breakage no longer occurred after a suitable form of shipment was devised. Occasionally slides were broken when returned in inadequate containers, but only a few slide sets were "lost" in the participants' department. The eight cytology programs provided a vast amount of information on diagnostic performance including specific areas of inter- and intraobserver variation.

Cytology Performance Data: Cervical Cytopathology I Table 13-6 shows the diagnostic terms used in this project. The project resulted in over 30,000 diagnoses; data have been published in part.[12] Of the 1575 cases in the project, 78 percent were classified as negative, 9 percent as suspicious, 7 percent as positive, and 5 percent did not achieve a consensus diagnosis. Where consensus was achieved, there was 100 percent agreement in greater than 50 percent of negative cases and 13 percent of positive cases. Comparison of submitter and participant diagnoses with the consensus diagnosis is shown on Table 13-7.

Effusion Cytopathology Data Of the 1800 cases in this project, the consensus diagnosis was as follows: "cancer is not present," 74 percent; "cancer is present," 22 percent; "unable to make a definitive diagnosis, 0 percent; and "inadequate (technical) for diagnosis," 4 percent. A consensus diagnosis was achieved in 89 percent of the cases. Overall, participant pathologist agreement with the consensus diagnosis was 80

TABLE 13-6
DIAGNOSTIC TERMS USED IN CYTOLOGY PROGRAMS

	No action required		Action required			Recommendation
Descriptive diagnosis	Inflammatory atypia	Mild dysplasia	Moderate dysplasia	Severe dysplasia or Ca in situ	Invasive carcinoma	Colposcopy
CIN* classification		I	II	III		
Papanicolaou classification	I II	III	IV		V	
CAP program classification	Negative	Suspicious		Positive		Yes No

*Cervical intraepithelial neoplasm.

TABLE 13-7
CERVICAL CYTOPATHOLOGY I DATA

Consensus diagnosis	Percent making diagnosis	Negative	Suspicious	Positive	Inadequate for diagnosis
Negative	Submitters	93.7	5.9	0.4	
	Participants	93.2	3.5	0.3	3.0
Suspicious	Submitters	6.2	84.2	9.6	
	Participants	19.4	65.9	14.2	0.5
Positive	Submitters	1	40	59	
	Participants	2.8	16	80	1.2

percent compared with 85 percent for the submitter pathologists. When the consensus diagnosis was "cancer is present," discordance with the consensus diagnosis occurred with 7.6 percent of the submitter and 8 percent of the participant interpretations. When the diagnosis was "cancer is not present," discordance occurred with 4.3 percent of the submitter and 5.4 percent of the participant diagnoses. Figure 13-2 shows the distribution of diagnostic agreement for the 1800 effusion cases.

Summary

These data define the present state of the art of diagnoses (the current standard of diagnostic performance) in the areas studied. Perhaps more important, the data provide a huge resource that, if used appropriately, could provide the diagnostic material for an educational program. Each slide is characterized as to the level of consensus (if achieved), and those with the most interobserver variation represent the areas most in need of improvement. Equally or perhaps more important is the identification of areas in which there was a high level of agreement. This occurred in the majority of cases and provides the assurance that there is little need for educational efforts in these areas.

PERFORMANCE IMPROVEMENT PROGRAM (PIP)

In 1982, the CAP committee responsible for developing the performance evaluation program undertook a critical review of their activities to date. It became evident that it was possible and practical to evaluate the performance of day-to-day diagnosis in surgical pathology and cytopathology and to assess pathologists' performance when making diagnosis under "slide seminar" conditions with no patient implication. In keeping with the perceived needs of accrediting and funding agencies, considerable time and effort were spent exploring ways and means of setting standards of performance in diagnostic anatomic pathology. The issues addressed did not relate to the need of good performance standards for patient care, but rather to who should set and monitor these criteria and by what means. Important characteristics for performance standards include: (1) accepted scientific validity; (2) capability of being fairly and uniformly applied; (3) relation to patient care.

The problems related to evaluation of value judgments have been documented in many clinical areas, as summarized and discussed by Koran.[13,14] The 58 articles cited in Koran's two-part paper attest to the considerable available literature up to 1975. Some pertinent observations on "the art of clinical decision making" by Gorry[15] also provide interesting reading on the complexity and difficulty of making value judgments in medicine. It is now generally accepted that considerable interobserver and intraobserver variation occurs when making certain value judgments and that these are related to a number of variables, many of which can be identified. Silverberg,[16] for example, recorded the difficulty of achieving reproducibility of the mitotic count in the histologic diagnosis of the smooth muscle tumors of the uterus. Similarly, Graem[17] published data on the variation of histological grading of malignant tumors.

Training and experiences are important in value judgments, as is the development of reproducible diagnostic criteria and their consistent application to the vast variations

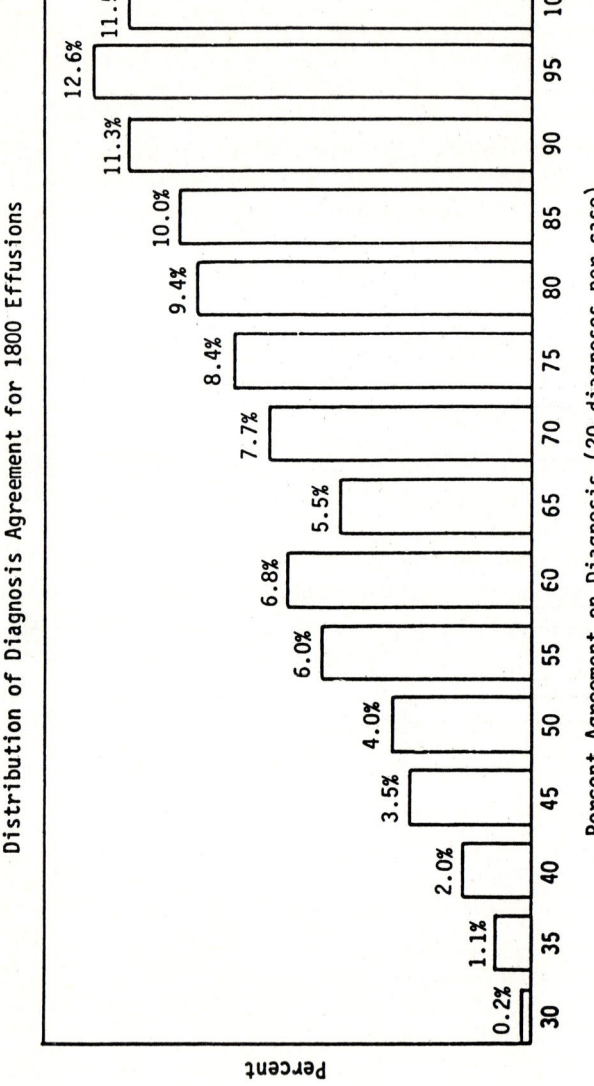

FIGURE 13-2

of biologic reactions in health and disease. A better understanding of making value judgments and the teaching of their application to medicine during early medical training might enhance their application during the practice of medicine.

Although the CAP peer-review evaluation programs demonstrate the nature and frequency of inter- and intraobserver variability, there still are difficult problems in setting standards. Ranking performance on the basis of the number of variations from the peer consensus diagnosis can be done readily. Some of the differences in agreement relate to diagnoses that will have no consequences for patient management, whereas others are very significant. Lack of concordance with a 51 percent consensus is a different magnitude than that with a 100 percent consensus. Modifiers are often used to better equate variations of interpretation in relation to patient care, but they add yet another level of value judgment.

After much study and effort, no fair, scientifically justifiable, consistently applicable performance standards in relation to patient care could be devised. Failure to develop a suitable performance standard does not negate the need for performance standards, but knowingly to recommend or use inappropriate performance standards is counterproductive to the goal of improving diagnostic performance. However, the pilot projects had in fact provided data on current performance standards by which professionals are generally judged, that is, performance as compared with their peer group.

The CAP Performance Improvement Program for Surgical Pathology and Cytopathology, an evaluation program that also provides expert assistance to improve diagnostic performance, was made operational in April 1984. It closely follows the peer review model used in the previous peer review-evaluation program, and the diagnostic improvement model developed is almost identical to the external educational program outlined previously. To monitor (evaluate) diagnosis as it is actually practiced and, equally important, to provide unique teaching material that reflects the needs of those participating, slides from patient files are used.

For the first annual program (cycle 1), problem cases (cases with a 35 percent or greater interobserver variation) that were already available to the CAP that had been used in the previous peer review programs were circulated. These were "processed" by experts who made their diagnosis, wrote critiques with references for the diagnosis, and took photomicrographs to illustrate the diagnosis or problems. Cases from each program were sorted into sets of 15 slides, each of which was representative of the various problems and their frequency. Participants could request any mix of sets up to a total of four sets per cycle, which represents a total of 60 different cases.

To join the PIP, the participants were required to provide four cases from their patient files for each designated lesion type for a total of 16 cases. This was later reduced to three per tissue site for a total of 12 cases. Lesions of the cervix, endometrial lesions, pigmented skin lesions, and spindle-cell mesenchymal lesions were "processed" by experts and used in the next cycle. As soon as the patient file cases were received, they were sent to 40 peer experts who had volunteered to participate in the program. These experts "processed" the cases as described above. Participants received batches of 15 slides of their choice at 3-month intervals, and returned these slides with their diagnosis within a month. As soon as their diagnosis and slides were returned, participants were sent the expert diagnoses and diagnostic critiques with references and photomicrographs that could be kept for future consultation and educational purposes. In addition to the 60 cases received each cycle, pathologists also received expert evaluation of 12 cases from their patient files.

As data are accumulated on peer group performance, expert diagnoses and eventually peer consensus diagnosis data will be shared with participants. Thus each annual cycle has two phases, an operational phase using existing "processed" cases and a phase for preparation of material for the next cycle. Each annual cycle will have new tissue sites or disease processes added.

In 1985–1986 participants can choose from nine programs, lesions of breast, prostate, cervix, endometrium, pigmented skin, spindle-cell mesenchymal tumors, cervical effusion, and fine-needle aspiration cytology. The following year, lesions of ovary, thyroid, urinary bladder, and gastrointestinal tract (large bowel) will be added. Following receipt of the second sets of slides, participants in cycle one were requested to evaluate the overall program and the various components such as photomicrographs and critiques. This preliminary evaluation indicated that almost all participants rated the program "as good as or better than expected." There were some delays in receiving the patient file case and some delays in completing the reviews on schedule. Most of the material was of adequate or excellent technical quality; however, some slides were technically poor, and a few could not be used. This program is very heavily pathologist-dependent and imposes a very heavy work load on members of the committee, who are responsible for inviting experts to participate and for coordination and monitoring of the "processing" of the new material. The very important and significant contribution by the many experts is most gratifying to those responsible for the program. Without the ongoing volunteer contributions of the many participating experts, there would be no program. The organization and operation of this program is an excellent example of pathologists helping pathologists improve their contribution to patient care.

THE AUTOPSY AS A QUALITY ASSURANCE MECHANISM IN MEDICINE

As stated elsewhere in this chapter, the characteristics of quality assurance programs as they apply to professional performance should include:

1 The ability to provide evaluation of performance;
2 The ability to provide a mechanism to help improve performance;
3 The ability to provide the assurance, equally essential to professionals, that performance is good.

For professionals to know that their performance is acceptable is equally as important as identifying areas in need of improvement.

It is obvious that the autopsy has played and can continue to play an important role in all quality assurance programs. Today the above statement of opinion is perhaps not the issue. The question to be asked and answered is whether the autopsy is an essential component of quality assurance programs, or whether there are alternatives equally as cost-effective or even better.

Two conferences on the autopsy[18,19] were held to examine critically the role of the autopsy. Both conferences concluded that the autopsy has been and should continue to be used to provide quality assurance in many aspects of the practice of medicine. The autopsy has made and continues to make valuable contributions to society as a whole in the areas of law and justice, public health, advancement of medical knowledge, improvement in medical education, and assisting in the economic planning for future health care programs. This includes the identification of and coping with health hazards. Perhaps most importantly, "the autopsy provides the ultimate control over the assurance of quality in the practice of medicine."[19] This is equally important to those providing medical care as it is to those receiving and funding this care.

Why, then, did the number of autopsies drop from regional averages (in Chicago) of over 50 percent in 1962 to less than 20 percent in 1982, with a number of hospitals having rates below 5 percent? The reasons for this decline are considered to relate to funding and the belief that the autopsy no longer is a priority. However, the lack of leadership, enthusiasm, and interest in the autopsy by the pathologist were considered of greatest importance. Further, to be an effective quality assurance tool, autopsies themselves must be of good quality and performed on sufficient numbers of the appropriate types of cases. The information obtained must be communicated in a timely and effective manner to all concerned, with appropriate follow-up mechanisms to assure that the lessons learned are translated into appropriate improved patient care. Only then will the autopsy serve its ultimate usefulness.

Programs for evaluating and improving the quality of all aspects of the autopsy, especially those aspects relating to maximizing the effectiveness of ultimate patient and social benefits, can be designed and implemented. Such programs might help to revitalize professional pride in the autopsy.

Few would argue the need for quality assurance programs in all aspects of medicine. Most patients don't die while under medical care, but evaluation of their medical management is being done on a regular basis in many institutions. Cannot the same mechanisms be used to evaluate those who die? Survival in itself is not proof of good patient management, nor is death proof of bad management. The autopsy can provide evidence for or against the quality of care provided. Although we tend to focus on what we do wrong, the autopsy can, and often does, focus on what we do well. This type of assurance is of tremendous importance to the medical profession and the society it serves. There is no quality assurance substitute for a well-performed autopsy.

REFERENCES

1. Hazard JB: An introduction to the history of surgical pathology. *Am J Clin Pathol* 1981, 75(suppl):444.
2. Penner DW: Quality control and quality evaluation in histopathology and cytology, in Sommers SC (ed): *Pathology Annual*. New York, Appleton-Century-Crofts, 1973, pp 1–19.

3 Derman H, Chandler FW, Hicklin MD, Penner DW: Quality assurance practices in anatomic pathology, in Inhorn S (ed): *Quality Assurance Practices for Health Laboratories.* Washington, DC, American Public Health Association, 1978, pp 381–409.
4 Nakazawa H, Rosen P, Lane N, et al: Frozen section experience in 3000 cases. *Am J Clin Pathol* 1968, 49:41.
5 Macartney JC, Henson, DE, Codling BW: Quality assurance in anatomic pathology. *Am J Clin Pathol* 1981, 75:467.
6 Owen D, Tighe J: Quality evaluation in histopathology. *Br Med J* 1975, 1:149.
7 Royal College of Pathologists of Australia, Board of Education, Sydney: *Reports of Quality Assurance Programs in Anatomical Pathology: 1969–1983.* Sydney, The College, 1969–1983.
8 LPTP Cytology Committee: Proficiency testing of cytology labs. *Ont Med Rev,* February 1981.
9 Cervical Cancer Screening Programs: The Walton report. *Can Med Assoc J* 1976, 114: 2–32.
10 Inhorn, SL, Clarke EA: A state-wide proficiency testing program in cytology. *Acta Cytol* 1971, 15:562.
11 Collins DN, Kaufman W: New York State computerized proficiency testing program in exfoliative cytology development and evaluation. *Acta Cytol* 1971, 15:562.
12 Derman H, Koss LG, Hyman MP, et al: Cervical cytopathology: I. Peers compare performance. *Pathologist* 1981, 35:317–325.
13 Koran LM: The reliability of clinical methods, data and judgements (first of two parts). *N Engl J Med* 1975, 293:642.
14 Koran LM: The reliability of clinical methods, data and judgements (second of two parts). *N Engl J Med* 1975, 293:695.
15 Gorry GA: New perspective on the art of clinical decision making. *Am J Clin Pathol* 1981, 75(suppl):483.
16 Silverberg SG: Reproducibility of the mitosis count in the histologic diagnosis of smooth muscle tumors of the uterus. *Hum Pathol* 1976, 7:451.
17 Graem N, Helweg-Larsen K, Keiding N: Precision of histological grading of malignancy. *Acta Path Microbiol Scand Sect A* 1980, 88:307.
18 A symposium of the autopsy. *Am J Clin Pathol* 1978, 69(suppl):215–265.
19 College of American Pathologists Foundation Conference on the Autopsy, Snowmass, Colo, July 20–23, 1983. *Arch Pathol Lab Med* 1984, 108:437–512.

CHAPTER 14

PROFICIENCY TESTING

John H. Rippey, M.D.

DESCRIPTION AND DEFINITIONS

Interlaboratory comparisons, external quality control, proficiency testing, and surveys are essentially synonymous terms. The term used depends on whether emphasis is placed on accuracy, regulatory requirements, or state-of-the-art monitoring. Regardless of emphasis, results from different laboratories are compared for common specimens. Usually the samples for analysis are sent to the participant laboratories on a quarterly basis, and subsequently results are tabulated from each participant's worksheet. Summaries comparing results from all the participating laboratories are then distributed to the individual laboratories.

Programs of this type are of distinct value to both participants and monitoring agencies, but there are definite limitations. Proficiency testing, in itself, does not function as the singular indicator that a given laboratory performs adequately or inadequately.[1-3] Also, proficiency testing is not a replacement for daily, internal quality control formats. To some degree, proficiency testing as an external quality control mechanism reflects the laboratory's performance regarding accuracy, whereas internal quality control represents the laboratory's performance regarding precision.[4]

HISTORY

The first interlaboratory comparison program was a syphillis serology program launched by the U.S. Public Health Service in 1935.[5] This was the predecessor of the current Centers for Disease Control program, which was developed in the mid-1940s and further expanded in 1968. Under the auspices of the Philadelphia County Medical Society, Dr. F. William Sunderland developed a chemistry survey program in 1945.[6]

The College of American Pathologists' (CAP) first survey efforts began in 1948, but these efforts did not result in a sustained program until 1963. Similarly, the American Association of Bioanalysts initiated their first proficiency testing in 1949 with subsequent program enlargement occurring in the late 1960s. Some states—for example, New York—also developed proficiency test programs during this time. The American Association for Clinical Chemistry began sponsoring programs in 1979.

Most of the early interest in interlaboratory comparisons centered on determining the state of the art. The first efforts of the Centers for Disease Control were aimed primarily at infectious diseases and public health laboratories. However, the marked growth of these programs during the past 15 years has been due predominantly to mandatory state and national requirements. The initial focus of the College of American Pathologists was directed toward voluntary self-assessment. The American Association for Clinical Chemistry bundled their programs with a heavy educational component. Currently, most proficiency testing programs are further enhancing their benefits to participants by incorporating additional educational components, narrative analyses, and specific reagent method tabulations. Table 14-1 lists some of the current control programs, their size, and comparison statistics available from professional organizations, government agencies, and industry.

SURVEY DESIGN AND ADMINISTRATION

Survey program design involves analyte selection, number of challenges per analyte, number of mailings per year, sample preparation, and result tabulations. Survey challenges are generally available for most routine tests performed in the laboratory subsections of clinical chemistry, diagnostic immunology, hematology, immunohematology, and microbiology. Survey challenges are also available for less routine testing such as histocompatibility tests, cytogenetic testing, nuclear imaging, and receptor assays. Flow cytometry and immunologic cell marker challenges, although needed, are not yet available.

Proficiency testing challenges are usually offered in sets of related tests or related test procedures sometimes referred to as modules. The ideal situation would make it possible for each individual laboratory to purchase analyte challenges for only those tests it performs regularly. This ideal has been more closely approximated with the introduction of surveys for small test groups (minimodules), but true single-test ordering has not yet been perfected.

The number of challenges per analyte and the number of mailings per year are dictated largely by regulatory requirements. In order to meet federal requirements, proficiency testing programs must be equivalent with corresponding programs sponsored by the Centers for Disease Control. Consequently, this currently requires at least four mailings per year, with each clinical chemistry mailing containing two or three challenges per analyte, each hematology mailing containing two challenges per analyte, each microbiology mailing containing five challenges, each immunohematology mailing containing three challenges, and each diagnostic immunology mailing containing one challenge per analyte plus two syphilis serology challenges and two rubella antibody challenges.

TABLE 14-1
SOME EXTERNAL QUALITY CONTROL PROGRAMS

Program	Number of participants (1985)	Basis of comparison	Acceptability criteria
American Association of Bioanalysts	4,853	SD	±2SD
American Association for Clinical Chemistry	948	SD/Z score	Undefined
American Society of Internal Medicine	1,600	SD	±2SD
Ames Division, Miles Laboratory	150*	SD	±2SD
College of American Pathologists	12,000	SD/SDI	±2SD
California Thoracic Society	715*	Z score	Points based on Z scores of 3 samples
Centers for Disease Control	1,600	Weighted reference range	Cumulative grade based on range calculated using reference laboratory results

*Number of instruments.

In the area of public health, the tendency is to require a larger number of challenges. Only recently was the syphilis serology requirement decreased from 40 to 8 challenges per year and, indeed, some states still require the larger number of challenges. Forty challenges per year are still required for hepatitis testing. It has been proposed that a relatively high number of challenges should be required for alpha fetoprotein testing.

Due to ever-changing instrumentation and methodology, sample preparation continually represents a potential problem for surveys. Stabilized liquid serum, mixtures of sera, or spiked sera are the preferred samples for diagnostic immunology except for complement challenges. Such samples also would be ideal for clinical chemistry, but some equipment performs suboptimally on liquid serum samples such as those stabilized with ethylene glycol. Consequently, many chemistry survey programs use lyophilized samples. Fluorocarbon-based samples rather than whole blood are usually used for blood gas challenges (see Chapter 5). Because lyophilization sometimes compromises antibody integrity, other types of products have been used for diagnostic immunology. Simulated samples of antibody plus albumin or antibody plus serum have been tried, but results with these preparations are less than ideal.[7]

Stabilized red cell suspensions and simulated whole-blood samples give a reasonably satisfactory product for immunohematology and hematology proficiency testing. However, matrix effects in these samples give distinct differences in hematology results depending on equipment used, making reagent-instrument-method tabulation an absolute necessity. Simulated microbiology samples must be prepared in a manner that allows for appropriate mixed cultures, production of which can be a trial-and-error process.

Because of this type of problem, it is mandatory that survey program sponsors retain knowledgeable laboratory consultants. The consultants, who must understand both the capabilities of the working laboratory world and the medical utility of laboratory test results, should be ready to work with equally able and motivated vendors and manufacturers. In this manner, the preparation of suitable, stable, and relevant samples is optimized. Such consultants also should be used to select the most appropriate mix of positive and negative challenges for qualitative tests and to select the most appropriate mix of low, normal, and high values for quantitative challenges.

Worksheets, directions for data entry, and the resulting tabulation are important parts of proficiency test programs. Complicated result worksheets and imprecise instructions reduce a survey to an evaluation of formsmanship rather than laboratory proficiency. Because laboratorians usually receive survey worksheets only four times a year, their accuracy in using these forms is in no way analogous to their accuracy in using routine laboratory forms every day at work.

The peer group to which a laboratory's results are compared depends on the analyte in question. In general, tabulations for routine clinical chemistry challenges can be appropriately listed in a single all-participant grouping, because most of these tests are relatively highly standardized and most reagent-instrument methods give comparable results. In contrast, for coagulation and diagnostic immunology challenges, it is preferable for the tabulation format to list analyte results by groupings that specify method, commercial reagent, and instrument. This is because there is a relative unavailability of widely accepted reference standards for many of these tests and procedures. Consequently, different reagent-instrument methods often do not yield comparable results. By employing reagent-instrument-method groupings for survey result tabulations, individual laboratory evaluations are more meaningful, and useful reagent-instrument-method performance data are provided to the survey participants. Hematology challenges also require tabulation by reagent-instrument-method groupings, because on stabilized, simulated samples different instruments produce incomparable results, predominantly because of matrix effects.

EVALUATION FORMATS

Results can be evaluated by a number of approaches; four major ones are (1) target values, (2) referee results, (3) participant consensus, and (4) fixed criteria. Target value methods involve precisely measuring in, or spiking, the analyte to be challenged and requiring the participant to obtain a result within some set degree of the calculated target value. In general, the state of the art in sample preparation is not sufficiently precise to justify such a format.

Participant evaluations based on referee laboratory results are used in many survey programs. The referee group may be composed of highly recognized, established laboratories, or it may be composed of a certain percentage of the best performers on a stated number of the most recent mailings. Some programs construct result means plus or minus two standard deviations from referee results for evaluation purposes. Other programs transfer referee results to geometric data and construct fairly intricate formulas, indices, and ratios with subsequently derived grades for evaluation purposes. Although there are definite arguments for instituting such numerical manipulations instead of means and standard deviations,[8] they tend to be difficult to understand, decrease useful informational feedback to participants, and could feasibly reduce surveys to solely a regulatory vehicle.

If the referee group predominantly uses a single reagent-instrument method, users of an alternative reagent-instrument method could be unfairly penalized because of incomparable results. Unacceptable evaluations based on such referee-group method bias have been observed to occur. This type of evaluation situation, if fully backed with regulatory impact, could feasibly stifle the development of superior emerging methodology.

Most survey programs use referee laboratory evaluation of microbiology challenges. A given percentage of referees must achieve a certain result for evaluation to be effected. Some microbiology programs have developed a graduated program, often referred to as an "extant" format, whereby more complex and sophisticated laboratories are expected to achieve a higher level of identification.

Evaluation by participant consensus, or peer evaluation, can be utilized for both qualitative and quantitative challenges. As usually instituted, participant qualitative challenge results are tabulated and the result achieved by greater than a stated percentage of participants, usually 80, is designated the acceptable result.[7] Similarly, participant quantitative challenge results are tabulated, the participant mean is calculated, and participants achieving results within plus or minus two standard deviations from the mean are evaluated as acceptable. All-participant means and standard deviations can be used for highly standardized test procedures. Individual reagent-instrument-method means and standard deviations can be calculated for less standardized test procedures. In the CAP surveys, peer groups are defined in various ways depending on the constituent. Most commonly the peer group is defined by method (or method principle) and by system (or instrument). When the peer group consists of more than 20 laboratories, the results obtained are evaluated against results obtained by the group. When fewer than 20 laboratories submit results for a particular method, the participant's results are placed into a similar group or are evaluated by the comparative method. For further information on definition of comparative methods, see *1985 CAP Surveys* manual.[9] Peer group performance limits are determined by calculating the mean and standard deviation of all data and then performing outlier exclusion. This is done by excluding results beyond three standard deviations from the mean calculated for all data and then repeating the process.[9] Results then are compared to the resultant mean and standard deviation. The CAP reports these values as well as the participant's value and standard deviation interval (SDI). The SDI is obtained by subtracting the group mean from the participant result and then dividing by the group standard deviation.

$$SDI = \frac{\text{participant value} - \text{group mean for method}}{\text{group SD for method}}$$

When a comparative method has been designated, the report also includes statistics comparing the participant's results with the comparative method. The main disadvantage of this type of format is that 5 percent of the participant results are always "unacceptable" because acceptable limits are defined by the mean plus and minus two standard deviations. Also, participant consensus formats have been criticized[10] as systems that perpetuate the status quo.[11]

Evaluation by fixed criteria based on analytical goals and medical utility[12,13] is a newly emerging evaluation format. It lends itself best to test procedures that are highly standardized and have well-accepted and readily available reference standards. Interest in fixed criteria has developed for situations in which the interlaboratory precision is so tight that it far exceeds the requirements for clinical interpretation. To date, two different approaches have been taken for the development of fixed criteria. One is a mathematical model based on biologic[14] and analytic[15-17] variability; the other is based on clinicians' perceptions regarding the degree of change in a result value that is considered significant.[18,19] The CAP, for example, uses the following fixed criteria to evaluate their blood gas survey:

pH target value ± 0.04
pO_2 target value ± 10% or ± 6 mm Hg (whichever is greater)
pCO_2 target value ± 10% ± 3 mm Hg (whichever is greater)

Target values are the mean of each instrument group (when used by 20 or more participants), or the mean of results from all instruments from the same manufacturer regardless of model (for fewer than 20 participants), or the mean of all participant results (for fewer than 20 instruments from the same manufacturer).

REGULATORY REQUIREMENTS

The great majority of regulatory requirements regarding proficiency testing stem from the Social Security Act of 1965, that is, the Medicare Act; and the Clinical Laboratories Improvement Act of 1967, that is, CLIA 1967. The Medicare Act requires hospital laboratories and independent laboratories not involved in interstate commerce to participate in proficiency testing covering the laboratory procedures offered. The laboratory can use any proficiency testing program approved by the U.S. Department of Health and Human Services, a program approved by an appropriate state agency, or the Centers for Disease Control program. For hospital laboratories and independent laboratories that solicit or accept interstate specimens, the CLIA 1967 requires participation in proficiency testing covering the laboratory procedures performed. The laboratory must use the Centers for Disease Control proficiency testing program, or a program that is equivalent, such as an approved state accrediting body's, for example, New York's, or an approved national accrediting body's, for example, the College of American Pathologists'. To date, the CLIA requirements have been somewhat more stringent than the Medicare requirements; for example, the CLIA requires three routine chemistry challenges per quarter for each analyte, whereas Medicare requires only two. Currently, no federal proficiency testing requirements exist for physicians' office laboratories.

Many states also have requirements regarding proficiency testing. One tabulation of state requirements[20] showed that 18 states required at least some proficiency testing by hospital and independent laboratories, 9 of which required participation in their own state program. Some states, such as New York, require essentially complete proficiency testing for all tests performed, but others require only a narrow range of coverage, such as syphilis serology. Due to this diversity and constantly changing requirements, individual state health departments should be contacted for specific current requirements. One city, New York City, has a proficiency testing program, which is required for laboratories under its jurisdiction. At least one state, California, now requires state proficiency testing for physicians' office laboratories.

The regulatory requirements have been developed in an attempt to assure adequate performance by clinical laboratories. In general, regulatory agencies monitoring proficiency testing results require evidence of corrective actions taken if a laboratory obtains three consecutive, unacceptable results on a given analyte challenge. Although proficiency testing is only one of many facets for determining the adequacy or inadequacy of laboratory performance, it probably has been one of the more useful vehicles in achieving such monitoring.

AVAILABILITY

An array of proficiency test programs is available in the standard laboratory disciplines of clinical chemistry, diagnostic immunology, hematology, immunohematology, and microbiology, including bacteriology and parasitology. Selection is more limited in the areas of blood gas analysis, coagulation, chromatography, cytogenetics, electrophoresis, enzymology, immunology of viral and fungal diseases, hepatitis testing, lead levels, mycology, virology, and specific immunologic antibody testing. There are four sponsors of nationwide programs from which a variety of different modules can be ordered (Table 14-2). Because of variation in the number and type of analyte challenges offered, precise comparisons of the areas covered and costs is extremely diffi-

TABLE 14-2
PROFICIENCY TEST SERVICES

Service	Number of modules	Number of mailings per year	Result receipt cutoff time	Approved Medicare	CLIA-interstate
AAB	18	4	2 weeks	Yes	No
AACC	8	12	6 weeks	Yes	No
CDC*	22	4	4 weeks (usually)	Yes	Yes
CAP	38	4	2–6 weeks (depending on module)	Yes	Yes

*Currently limited to city, county, and state public health laboratories.

cult. Also, because these programs are frequently modified, the sponsors should be contacted directly for current specific information.

The American Association of Bioanalysts (AAB) Proficiency Testing Service [205 West Levee, Brownsville, Texas 78520, (512) 546-5315], offers a program of 18 different modules. In general, the module configurations provide basic analyte coverage and appear to be aimed primarily at relatively small hospital and independent laboratories with a relatively modest breadth of procedures performed. Many of the modules also would be suitable for physician office laboratories and, indeed, this organization currently packages a physicians' office program for the American Society of Internal Medicine. Instructions, worksheet forms, and summaries are clearly understandable. Informational feedback might be considered somewhat limited, but the programs are bundled with a modest educational component. The program is Medicare approved, but not CLIA-interstate approved. Depending on the module, evaluations are based on either a participant consensus or a referee format. Challenges in coagulation are limited to prothrombin times, and challenges in immunology are limited to antistreptolysin-O, infectious mononucleosis, rheumatoid factor, rubella antibody, and syphilis serology. There are no immunoglobulin, no complement, and no mycology challenges. For most small laboratories the estimated cost for relatively complete program would be approximately $600 to $800. Most observers would conclude that the breadth of analyte challenges offered is too narrow for some medium-sized laboratories and all large laboratories.

The American Association of Clinical Chemistry (AACC) [1725 K Street, N.W., Washington, D.C. 20006, (202) 857-0717] offers a program of eight different modules that are limited to the areas of therapeutic drug monitoring, toxicology, endocrinology, and protein testing. In general, these module configurations are relatively extensive in analyte coverage and appear to be aimed primarily at medium-sized to large hospital and independent laboratories with a broad range of tests performed in these particular laboratory disciplines. Instructions, worksheet forms, and summaries are very understandable, and informational feedback is good. The programs are bundled with an extensive, excellent educational component. Although result receipt cutoff date to evaluation mailing date is 6 weeks, a tabulation of intended targets is mailed shortly after the cutoff date. Evaluations are based on a participant consensus format. The programs are Medicare approved but not CLIA-interstate approved. Depending on the size of modules selected, it would cost from approximately $1500 to $2100 for proficiency testing coverage in the areas of therapeutic drug monitoring, endocrinology, toxicology, and protein testing. This initially seems relatively high, but becomes more reasonable when considerations include the broad spectrum of analyte challenges, the monthly mailings, and the extensive educational component. An example of participant phenobarbitol results for the therapeutic drug monitoring module is seen in Fig. 14-1.

The Centers for Disease Control, Performance Evaluation Branch [1600 Clifton Road, N.E., Atlanta, Georgia 30333, (404) 329-3877], maintains a program of 22 modules that include routine proficiency testing coverage as well as many relatively unusual areas of coverage. Some of the modules are aimed primarily at public health

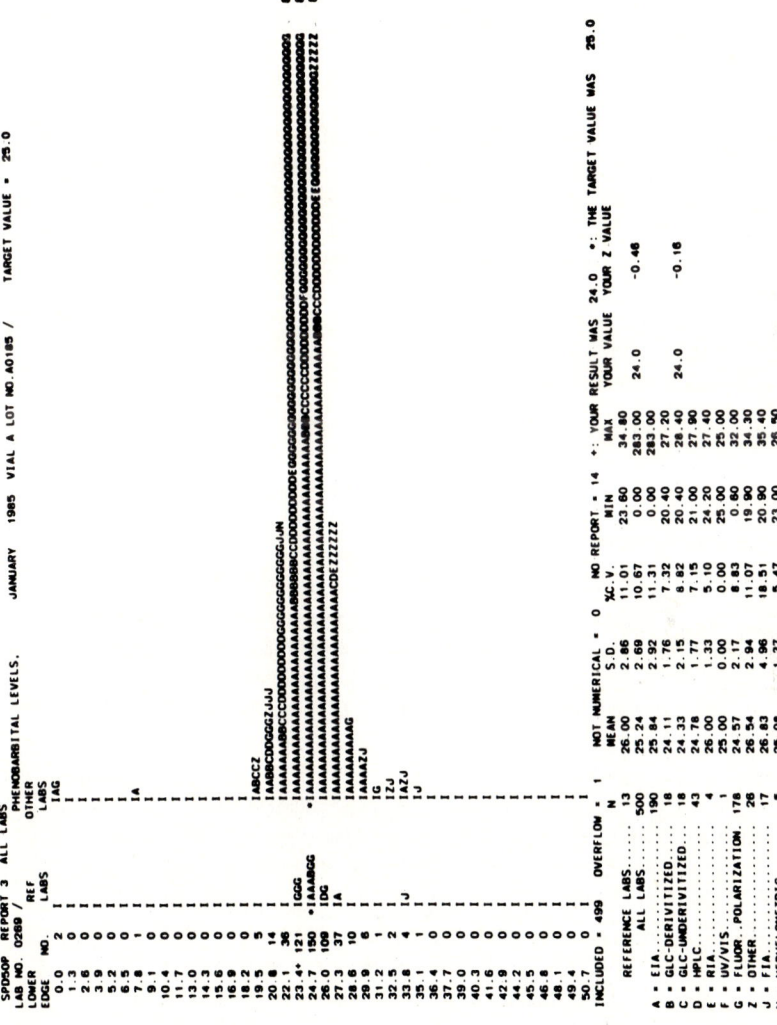

FIGURE 14-1

Histogram of results of phenobarbital levels from a therapeutic drug monitoring (tdm) module sponsored by the American Association of Clinical Chemistry (AACC). For this analyte, the target value is 25 μg/ml was established by weighing in a known amount of drug. In this example, the 499 participating laboratories' values are divided in intervals of 1.3 μg/ml, the number of laboratories reporting each result, and the method used as a frequency histogram. Laboratory performance is evaluated by a Z value.

laboratories. These programs are the programs to which other proficiency testing services must be compared regarding analyte coverage, number of challenges, and frequency of challenges in order to obtain regulatory equivalence. Instructions, worksheet forms, and summaries are complex and therefore may be difficult to understand. Similarly, informational feedback is sometimes difficult to understand. In general, there is a moderate educational component. Result receipt cutoff date to evaluation mailing date is usually 4 weeks. Evaluations are based on referee formats. The programs that are the standards for regulatory equivalency are both Medicare and CLIA-interstate approved. Relatively unusual areas of coverage include mycology, hepatitis testing, neonatal screening, blood lead levels, and genetic abnormalities. Challenges are offered in antibody testing for *Herpes, Cytomegalovirus, Toxoplasma, Coccidioides, Histoplasma, Brucella, Salmonella,* and specific immunologic antigens. The only coagulation challenges offered are prothrombin times and partial thromboplastin times. There is no charge for these programs, but there is currently pending legislation to require user's fees. At this time subscriptions are limited to city, county, and state public health laboratories. Examples of data presentation of Reference Laboratory Results and Distribution of Participant Grades are seen in Tables 14-3 and 14-4, respectively.

The College of American Pathologists [5202 Old Orchard Road, Skokie, Illinois 60077, (312) 677-3500] offers a program of 38 different modules and additionally has an Excel program designed for physicians' office laboratories. Module configurations vary in scope from basic to very extensive; consequently, they can provide appropriate analyte challenge coverage for essentially any laboratory. Instructions, worksheet forms, and summaries are clear. Informational feedback is excellent, with many modules providing comprehensive reagent-method-instrument tabulations. Some of the modules are bundled with only a minimal educational component, whereas others provide an extensive educational component, especially for the microbiology and toxicology modules. Some modules are evaluated by referee format, some by participant consensus, and some by fixed criteria. The programs are approved for both Medicare and CLIA-interstate. In addition to varying-sized routine modules, relatively unusual modules are offered in advanced diagnostic immunology, blood gas analysis, comprehensive coagulation, cytogenetics, electrophoresis and chromatography, enzyme chemistry, mycology, nuclear imaging, receptor assays, and virology. Challenges are provided for antibodies to specific immunologic antigens, some coagulations factor assays, high-density lipoproteins, reticulocyte counts, viral cultures, and viral antigen detection. It is estimated that a relatively complete program for most small laboratories would cost approximately $800 to $1100, although a comprehensive complete program for many large laboratories could cost $4000 to $5000. An example of data presentation for an analyte evaluated by participant consensus is seen in Fig. 14-2 and 14-3.

Formats for data presentations, data reduction and grading for the many state proficiency programs, industrial proficiency programs, and medical society proficiency programs are diverse. An example of the printout from one of these is seen in Fig. 14-4.

TABLE 14-3
DISTRIBUTION OF PARTICIPANT GRADES, CDC PROFICIENCY TESTING, PUBLIC HEALTH IMMUNOLOGY, 1984 II*

Analyte	NP	100	99–95	94–90	89–85	84–80	79–70	69–60	59–50	49–25	24–0	Number of labs	Average
Rubella	55	431	0	1	2	4	8	23	6	1	2	481	96
Cytomegalovirus	36	97	0	2	0	8	1	21	8	3	10	151	84
Herpes virus	88	69	0	0	0	5	0	13	4	0	1	93	91
Rheumatoid factor	48	369	0	0	0	13	1	24	41	1	1	451	93
C-P factive protein	53	224	0	0	1	12	3	23	85	1	7	356	83
Infectious mononucleosis	52	403	0	3	8	6	4	32	29	1	5	492	93
Toxoplasma	39	177	0	1	2	10	1	38	11	4	2	247	90
Histoplasmosis	28	90	0	0	1	1	1	0	2	4	5	105	91
Syphilis serology	51	532	0	2	10	7	20	33	5	0	3	613	96
Coccidioidomycosis	24	93	0	0	2	0	1	3	9	0	2	111	93
Rubella (IGM)	62	39	0	0	0	0	0	0	0	1	11	52	77
Herpes simplex virus type 1	13	65	0	0	0	5	0	14	6	1	0	92	90
Herpes simplex virus type 2	52	52	0	0	0	4	0	22	6	2	2	89	84

*Reference laboratories established acceptable ranges for results. Target values for qualitative results are based on consensus (greater than 80%) report of the reference laboratories. To determine accuracy for each quantitative result, the geometric mean of the reference laboratory result is multiplied and divided by a factor which may be different for different analytes) to obtain the acceptable range. Precision grades are calculated on pairs of samples as a ratio of the higher result to the lower result. The ratio of results for reference labs is multiplied and divided by a factor (different for each analyte) to determine acceptable ranges. NP = nonparticipant.

TABLE 14-4
REFERENCE LABORATORY RESULTS, CDC PROFICIENCY TESTING, GENERAL IMMUNOLOGY, 1984 I*

Analyte Procedure Sample number	Number of qualitative reports	Number of quantitative reports	Number of reports	Percent positive	Geometric mean	Geometric standard deviation	Acceptable range
Anti-streptolysin O							
Anti-streptolysin O							
Accuracy (titer)							
BG4-A07	34	34	34	100.0	335	1.390	186–602
BG4-A08	34	34	34	100.0	339	1.318	188–610
Precision							
BG4-A08/BG4-A07		34	34		1.012	1.267	0.666–1.500
Anti-dnase B							
Anti-dnase B							
Accuracy (titer)							
BG4-A07	32	32	32	46.8	88	1.397	48–157
BG4-A08	32	32	32	43.7	88	1.380	48–157
Precision							
BG4-A08/BG4-A07		33	33		1.000	1.091	0.666–1.500
Multiple streptococcal antibodies							
Accuracy (titer)							
BG4-A07	35	34	35	97.1	263	1.776	145–472
BG4-A08	35	34	35	97.1	287	1.763	159–517
Precision							
BG4-A08/BG4-A07		34	34		1.094	1.421	0.666–1.500
Rheumatoid factor							
Accuracy (IU/ml)							
BG4-A05	44	24	44	61.3	32.5	2.068	8.5–123.5
BG4-A06	47	30	47	100.0	201.4	2.044	53.0–765.5
Precision							
BG4-A06/BG4-A05		28	28		6.714	1.932	4.000–16.000

*Acceptable performance is a cumulative grade of 75% or greater for the last three shipments, on an analyte-by-analyte basis.

CONSTITUENT UNIT OF MEASURE YOUR LABORATORY'S METHOD/SYSTEM COMPARATIVE METHOD	EVALUATION STATISTICS					
	COMPARATIVE STATISTICS					
	SPECIMEN NUMBER	CODE	YOUR RESULT	MEAN	S.D.	NO. OF LABS.	YOUR SDI
GLUCOSE-SERUM MG/DL HEXOKINASE, UV TECHNICON SMAC	C-19	11	53	50.6	2.6	208	+.9
	C-20	11	299	302.3	8.0	209	-.4
	C-21	11	288	289.5	6.9	197	-.2
HEXOKINASE, UV ALL INSTRUMENTS	C-19			50.3	4.8	2991	+.6
	C-20			295.0	12.3	2965	+.3
	C-21			284.4	11.6	1565	+.3

FIGURE 14-2
Summary results for glucose from the College of American Pathologists' (CAP) comprehensive chemistry survey. Survey lists analyte (glucose), units of measure, laboratories' method, and the reference method (hexokinase, all methods). Results of the laboratories' analysis of these samples (C-19, C-20, C-21) are compared to group means and the reference group.

PARTICIPANT BENEFITS

Surveys with adequate specimen integrity, accurate result tabulations, and understandable informational feedback to participants provide an excellent vehicle for voluntary self-assessment with regard to interlaboratory result comparison, methodology comparison, instrument comparison, and reagent comparison. This is particularly true for relatively inexact test procedures that are not highly standardized. The fairly recent emergence of survey-associated educational enhancements further accentuates this positive benefit. Whether these mechanisms have actually succeeded in educating laboratorians and improving laboratory performance has been both affirmed[3] and questioned.[21]

Surveys also provide participants with at least some feedback regarding accuracy. For some standardized routine chemistry challenges, it has been strongly suggested that the all-participant mean very closely approximates the true value.[22] Others criticize this concept,[10,11] taking the stance that reference method results are more accurate. The concept of accuracy based on all-participant means is clearly untenable for less standardized test procedures with relatively large variations in reagent-instrument-method results.

It is possible that survey tabulations have had a beneficial effect in stimulating commercial manufacturers to develop products that provide less variation in interlaboratory results, that is, enhance product standardization. As a postulated example, comparison of survey reagent-method tabulations for digoxin levels between 1975 and 1980 demonstrates a marked tightening of interlaboratory result variation. Whether surveys played a role in this improvement is not documented, but there is no question that commercial manufacturers, from a marketing standpoint, are deeply interested in survey performances.

OBJECTIVES AND RATIONALE

Although the initial objective of surveys to monitor the state of laboratory art still exists, additional objectives have developed with time. These include contributing to

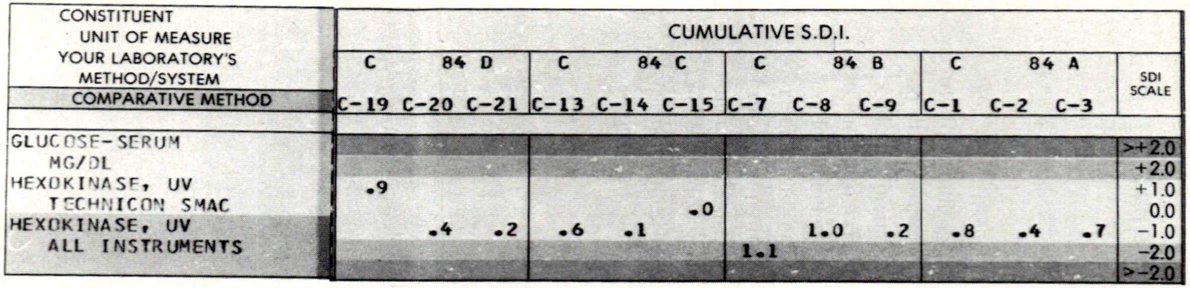

CONSTITUENT UNIT OF MEASURE YOUR LABORATORY'S METHOD/SYSTEM	CUMULATIVE S.D.I.								SDI SCALE
COMPARATIVE METHOD	C C-19	84 D C-20	C C-21	C C-13	84 C C-14	C C-15	C C-7	84 B C-8	C C-9	C C-1	84 A C-2	C-3	
GLUCOSE–SERUM MG/DL										>+2.0 +2.0 +1.0 0.0 −1.0 −2.0 >−2.0
HEXOKINASE, UV	.9	.4	.2	.6	.1	.0				
TECHNICON SMAC										
HEXOKINASE, UV ALL INSTRUMENTS							1.1	1.0	.2	.8	.4	.7	

FIGURE 14-3
Retrospective analysis for one of the CAP survey glucose results. Results are plotted as standard deviation intervals from average values of other participants using the reporting laboratory's method.

					INSTRUMENT REGISTRATION
					99175
			MODEL	UNIT	DATE
			I1303	01	3/23/85

VIAL CODE NUMBER	ALL INSTRUMENTS			SUMMARY BY MODEL MODEL- I1303-01			YOUR INSTRUMENT			
	MEAN	S.D.	N	MEAN	S.D.	N	VALUE	Z-SCORE*	EVALUATION**	REMARKS
*PH										
G211	7.237	.012	709	7.227	.011	34	7.230	.3	2	
G708	7.345	.013	708	7.341	.015	34	7.337	.3-	2	
G749	7.624	.016	711	7.511	.013	34	7.614	.2	2	
									6 TOTAL SATISFACTORY	
*PCO2										
G211	62.0	2.8	712	61.1	1.6	34	61.0	.1-	2	
G708	85.3	4.3	713	85.0	2.2	34	84.2	.4-	2	
G749	43.9	1.7	713	43.6	1.2	34	42.5	.9-	2	
									6 TOTAL SATISFACTORY	
*PO2										
G211	36.8	4.7	710	34.2	1.5	34	35.6	.9	2	
G708	202.0	11.1	703	200.2	4.0	34	201.8	.4	2	
G749	133.7	5.2	713	133.6	2.2	34	134.6	.4	2	
									6 TOTAL SATISFACTORY	

* Z-SCORE BASED ON MEAN AND S.D. OF YOUR MODEL UNLESS N<20; IN THIS EVENT "ALL INSTRUMENTS" MEAN AND S.D. USED.
**EVALUATION

IF Z SCORE ≤ 2, EVALUATION = 2
IF Z SCORE ≤ 3 BUT > 2, EVALUATION =1
IF Z SCORE > 3, EVALUATION = 0

IF TOTAL IS 5 OR 6, SATISFACTORY
IF TOTAL IS 3 OR 4, MARGINAL
IF TOTAL IS < 3, UNSATISFACTORY

FIGURE 14-4
California Thoracic Society, Blood Gases Proficiency Report. Comparisons of all instruments and specific instrument groups by analyte. Laboratory evaluation is in terms of Z score.

the maintenance of quality results, providing a mechanism of voluntary self-assessment, functioning as a vehicle for tabulation of continuously updated reagent-instrument-method performance, supplying at least some input regarding accuracy, developing as another vehicle for continuing education, and, in addition, fulfilling regulatory requirements.

For many reasons,[11,23] proficiency testing cannot be used as the sole determiner of adequate laboratory performance. Sample integrity and stability, as well as exposure of the sample to temperature extremes during shipment, are potential sources of error that undoubtedly are sometimes real, and, on relatively rare occasions, documented as real. It has been anecdotally observed that proficiency testing samples receive particularly careful attention in some laboratories and consequently the results do not adequately reflect day-to-day performance. To date, a realistic format for blind proficiency testing[24,25] has not been developed. On-site proficiency testing[24] of samples carried in by inspection examiners logistically can be done only very infrequently; this approach is generally limited to regulatory follow-ups on laboratories that have been experiencing difficulty obtaining acceptable results.

The relative infrequency of proficiency testing, usually quarterly, is still another reason that proficiency testing should not be the sole determiner of adequacy. Challenges could easily be provided more frequently, but at a corresponding increase in cost. A potential compromise is automatically to follow up unacceptable results with an additional mailing. At some point in the future, perhaps, appropriate mathematical formats can be applied to daily internal quality control data,[26] in essence replacing proficiency testing. Finally, it is possible that the frequency of some proficiency testing, such as sodium levels, could be realistically decreased, whereas for other procedures, such as alpha fetoprotein testing, the frequency of proficiency testing could be increased. Hopefully, the data that currently exist can be developed to either document, or refute, the efficacy of such potential innovations.

For the reasons just described, such things as daily internal quality control formats, utilization of accepted available reference standards, periodic accreditational inspections, capable and informed laboratory personnel, satisfactory equipment maintenance, and suitable clerical functions are all equally important as proficiency testing in producing quality laboratory results. Laboratorians, survey sponsors, accreditational bodies, and regulatory agencies all need to maintain an awareness of the appropriate balances between these interrelated features of laboratory quality assurance.

REFERENCES

1 Batsakis JG: *Response to Report of the Office of Inspector General to Assistant Secretary of Health on Proficiency Testing.* Skokie, IL, College of American Pathologists, 1982.
2 Boutwell JH: The perspective of center for disease control, in Davis M (eds): *Proceedings of Second National Conference on Proficiency Testing.* Bethesda, MD, Informational Services, 1975, p 17.
3 LaMotte LC: The perspective of center for disease control, in Davis M (ed): *Proceedings of Second National Conference on Proficiency Testing.* Bethesda, MD, Informational Services, 1975, pp 33–35.
4 Rippey, JH: Quality control in the diagnostic immunology laboratory. *Pathologist* 1983, 37:252.
5 Cumming HS, Hazen HH, Sanford FE, et al: Evaluation of serodiagnostic tests for syphilis in the United States: Report of results. *Vener Dis Informat* 1935, 16:189.
6 Belk WP, Sunderman FW: A survey of the accuracy of chemical analyses in clinical laboratories. *Am J Clin Pathol* 1947, 17:853.
7 Rippey JH: The CAP surveys program and problems of quality assurance, in Rippey JH, Nakamura RM (eds): *Diagnostic Immunology: Technology Assessment and Quality Assurance.* Skokie, IL, College of American Pathologists, 1983, pp 111–114.
8 Taylor RN, Huong KM, Fulford VA, et al: *Quality Control for Immunologic Tests* HHS Publication No. (CDC) 82-8376. Atlanta, Centers for Disease Control, 1979.
9 *1985 Manual CAP Surveys* Interlaboratory Comparison Program. Skokie, IL, College of American Pathologists, 1984.
10 Hansert E, Stamm D: Determination of assigned values in control specimens for internal accuracy control and for interlaboratory surveys. *J Clin Chem Clin Biochem* 1980, 18:461.
11 Tonks, DB: Some faults with external and internal quality control programs. *Clin Biochem* 1982, 15:67.

12 Batsakis, JG: Analytical goals and the College of American Pathologists. *Am J Clin Pathol* 1982, 78(suppl):678.
13 Elion-Gerritzen WE: Analytical precision in clinical chemistry and medical decisions. *Am J Clin Pathol* 1980, 73:183.
14 Statland BE, Winkel M: Physiologic variation of the concentration values of selected analytes as determined in healthy young adults, in Elevitch FR (ed): *Proceedings of the 1976 Aspen Conference on Analytical Goals in Clinical Chemistry.* Skokie, IL, College of American Pathologists, 1977, pp 94–101.
15 Lawson NS, Ross JW: Long term precision for selected clinical chemistry analytes as determined by data from regional quality control programs, in Elevitch FR (ed): *Proceedings of the 1976 Aspen Conference on Analytical Goals in Clinical Chemistry.* Skokie, IL, College of American Pathologists, 1977, pp 83–89.
16 Ross JW, Fraser MD: The effect of analyte and analyte concentration upon precision estimates in clinical chemistry. *Am J Clin Pathol* 1976, 66:193.
17 Westgard JO: The development of performance standards and criteria for testing the precision and accuracy of laboratory methods, in Elevitch FR (ed): *Proceedings of the 1976 Aspen Conference on Analytical Goals in Clinical Chemistry.* Skokie, IL, College of American Pathologists, 1977, pp 105–114.
18 Barnett RN: Medical significance of laboratory results. *Am J Clin Pathol* 1968, 50:671.
19 Skendzel LP, Barnett RN, Platt R: Medically useful criteria for analytical performance of laboratory tests. *Am J Clin Pathol* 1985, 83:200.
20 Kaufman W: State and federal regulations governing the licensure of laboratories, in Rose NR, Friedman H (eds): *Manual of Clinical Immunology,* ed 2. Washington, DC, American Society for Microbiology, 1980, pp 1073–1077.
21 Taylor RN: Standards and quality assurance for immunologic tests: Centers for Disease Control survey program and problems of quality assurance, in Rippey JH, Nakamura RM (eds): *Diagnostic Immunology: Technology Assessment and Quality Assurance.* Skokie, IL, College of American Pathologists, 1983, pp 115–123.
22 Gilbert RK: CAP interlaboratory survey data and analytic goals, in Elevitch FR (ed): *Proceedings of the 1976 Aspen Conference on Analytical Goals in Clinical Chemistry,* Skokie, IL, College of American Pathologists, 1977, pp 63–82.
23 Jeffcoat SL: Who shall control the controllers? *Ann Clin Biochem* 1981, 18:1.
24 Boone DJ, Hansen HJ, Hearn TL, et al: Laboratory evaluation and assistance efforts: Mailed, on-site, and blind proficiency testing surveys conducted by the Centers for Disease Control. *Am J Public Health* 1982, 72:1364.
25 Glenn GC, Hathaway TK: Quality control by blind sample analysis. *Am J Clin Pathol* 1979, 72:156.
26 Stamm D: New concept for quality control of clinical laboratory investigations in the light of clinical requirements and based on reference method values. *J Clin Chem Clin Biochem* 1982, 20:817.

CHAPTER **15**

LABORATORY LICENSURE AND ACCREDITATION

John K. Duckworth, M.D.

Since World War II, a variety of regulatory and voluntary programs designed to establish and maintain minimum standards for clinical laboratories have developed. Such programs were inevitable considering the explosion of technological and medical knowledge during the last 40 years relating to clinical laboratories, the increasing percentage of the health care funds spent for laboratory services, and the increased reliance of physicians on the laboratory.

GENERAL PRINCIPLES OF LABORATORY LICENSURE AND ACCREDITATION

Whether clinical laboratory standards are mandated by law or voluntarily accepted, the general principles on which they are based follow the same guidelines. The common theme is *minimum* standards defined for each general area, and laboratorians are expected to comply with these standards. Laboratory standards are designed to ensure continuous, high-quality service to patients. Compliance thus is expected throughout the whole day each day of the year, including nights, holidays, and weekends. The principle of continuous compliance to minimal standards is violated if standards are met only during feverish periods of preparation for a laboratory inspection. In the case of laboratory safety, the same principle is self-evident: The environment must be safe at all times, not just during efforts to achieve compliance with standards. The topic areas described in this chapter are adapted from the current standards and checklists of the College of American Pathologists (CAP). Other programs (either governmental or voluntary) treat key areas (Table 15-1) in a similar but perhaps not identical manner. Pertinent definitions are shown in Table 15-2.

TABLE 15-1
KEY AREAS

A Administrative
 1 Director qualifications and responsibilities
 2 Qualifications of personnel
 3 Safe working environment
 4 Computers
 5 Records
 6 Physical facilities
 7 Space
 8 Supplies and inventory
 9 Continuing education
 10 Communications
 11 Reference laboratories

B Analytical
 1 Quality control
 2 Equipment maintenance (preventive maintenance/function)
 3 Proficiency testing (surveys)
 4 Reagents, stains, and media
 5 Controls and standards
 6 Procedure manuals
 7 Validation of methods and instruments

VOLUNTARY ACCREDITATION PROGRAMS (TABLE 15-3)

College of American Pathologists' Laboratory Accreditation Program

In 1961, the College of American Pathologists Assembly (now the House of Delegates) passed a resolution that led to development of the laboratory accreditation program. The CAP Board of Governors approved the concept of the program and formed a commission to develop standards and operate the program. By 1962, the CAP Inspection and Accreditation Program (later renamed the Laboratory Accreditation Program) became operational. Participant growth for the first 16 years was steady, with approximately 100 new laboratories accredited each year. Beginning in 1979, participant growth accelerated, partly because of recognition of the CAP program by the Joint Commission on Accreditation of Hospitals and partly because of federal insistence that laboratories performing special functions such as blood gas analysis be either licensed or accredited. By 1986, approximately 3600 laboratories were accredited. The CAP-accredited laboratories include hospital, independent, and outpatient facilities in the private sector, the military, the Veterans Administration, the Indian Health Service, and university settings. The accredited laboratories are located in all 50 states, Central America, Europe, the Middle East, and the Far East. Once accredited, laboratories are reaccredited with a program that requires on-site inspection every two years, successful participation in a self-evaluation in the interim year, and a laboratory proficiency testing comparison system.

TABLE 15-2
DEFINITIONS

Accreditation: Approval for meeting certain standards, which is conferred upon a facility by a nationally recognized agency or association such as the American Association of Blood Banks, College of American Pathologists, or Joint Commission on Accreditation of Hospitals.

Deficiency: Lacking in some essential; incomplete.[1]

Function verification: Those activities that usually involve the checking of system operations (electronic/mechanical functions) of an instrument daily or before using the instrument.[2]

In vitro: Within a glass; observable in a test tube; in an artificial environment.[3]

In vivo: Within the living body.[3]

License: A right or permission granted in accordance with law by a competent authority to engage in some business or occupation which but for such license would be unlawful.[1]

Preventive maintenance: Those activities that prolong the life of an instrument and minimize breakdowns, for example, mechanical malfunctions.[2]

Proficiency testing: A program in which specimens of quality control material are periodically sent to members of a group of laboratories for analysis and comparison of their results with those of other laboratories in the group through some central organization.[4]

Quality control: A surveillance process in which actions of people and performance of equipment and materials are observed in some periodic, systematic way to provide a record of consistency of performance and action taken when performance does not conform to standards that have been established in the laboratory.[5]

Quality control—external or interlaboratory: Evaluation and monitoring of the accuracy and precision of any analytical process in one laboratory by comparison with the same parameters of the same process performed in other laboratories. The process takes two common forms, proficiency testing and regional quality control.[4]

Quality control—internal or intralaboratory: An organized system for continuously studying the variability of the analytical processes performed in the laboratory. This involves all aspects of the process, including collection and treatment of the specimens, quality control of the analytical process, reporting of the results, and others.[4]

Special-function laboratory: Separately administered laboratory, within the same institution but not under the direct jurisdiction of the main laboratory, which provides services that fall within the general definition of clinical laboratory services.[6]

Standard: A consensus description of the attributes of a defined entity with which similar entities may be compared for quantitative measurement or qualitative comparability.[7]

TABLE 15-3
VOLUNTARY ACCREDITATION PROGRAMS

1. CAP: Laboratory Accreditation Program, College of American Pathologists, 5202 Old Orchard Road, Skokie, IL 60077
2. JCAH: Hospital Accreditation Program, Joint Commission of Accreditation of Hospitals, 875 North Michigan Avenue, Chicago, IL 60611
3. AABB: Inspection and Accreditation Program, American Association of Blood Banks National Office, 1117 North 19th Street, Arlington, VA 22209
4. AABB (Parentage Testing): American Association of Blood Banks National Office, 1117 North 19th Street, Suite 600, Arlington, VA 22209
5. ASC: Laboratory Accreditation Program, American Society of Cytology, 130 South 9th Street, Suite 810, Philadelphia, PA 19107.

The Commission on Laboratory Accreditation, composed of the chairman, vice chairman, and 10 regional commissioners, operates the program under the auspices of the CAP Board of Governors. Each of the 10 regions is divided into smaller areas led by state or deputy commissioners. Educational programs are offered to train laboratory inspectors and periodically to update experienced inspectors. The usual inspection team is led by a pathologist, usually supplemented by other pathologists, doctoral scientists, and/or medical technologists. Size, type of team, and duration of inspection visit is predicated upon requirements and complexities of the subject laboratory.

Once the inspector assignment is made, the inspector reviews the laboratory's application and pertinent material. A mutually satisfactory date is arranged; then, on the day of the inspection, the team usually meets the laboratory staff and tours the laboratory. The inspectors use a checklist that is organized by laboratory section, answering each numbered question with N/A (for nonapplicable), yes, or no.* The questions are divided into phase 0, phase I, and phase II. Phase 0 questions are for information only. Phase I questions represent items that are considered important in the management of an outstanding laboratory service; any phase I deficiencies should be corrected.

Phase II questions are of major importance, representing those items that are essential for management of a laboratory. Because phase II deficiencies are major defects, they must be corrected before accreditation can be granted. At the conclusion of the inspection, a summation conference is convened to review the findings and settle any misunderstandings. Following the on-site visit, the inspection team's report is processed and deficiencies identified are transmitted to the laboratory director for response. Most laboratory directors correct deficiencies in a timely fashion, resulting in their laboratory's accreditation.

Laboratories must participate successfully in an interlaboratory comparison (survey) program appropriate to the laboratory's size and scope. For information on available survey programs and interpretation of results, see Chapter 14. The inspector reviews the laboratory's performance in proficiency testing, and the regional commissioner reviews the performance on a regular basis. Any problem areas are brought to the attention of the laboratory director, who then is asked for documentation of corrective action in the category specified, for example, mycology, or parasitology. If the laboratory does not improve performance, the laboratory director may be instructed to cease accepting specimens in that particular category (e.g., mycology or parasitology).

Accreditation by the CAP is voluntary; however, laboratories found noncompliant with the CAP Standards (i.e., denied accreditation) are reported to the Joint Commission on Accreditation of Hospitals (JCAH) (if a JCAH-accredited hospital) or to the Health Care Financing Administration (HCFA) (if an interstate laboratory).

The CAP's laboratory program is constantly changing in response to input changes from pathologists, clinical scientists, and medical technologists. Technical expertise to the Commission on Laboratory Accreditation is provided by approximately 15 CAP technical resource committees.

Although the program has grown in complexity and effectiveness, its goal remains

---

* Checklists are available from the College of American Pathologists, 5202 Old Orchard Road Skokie, IL 60077.

one of laboratory improvement through peer review and education. The CAP Laboratory Accreditation Program examines all aspects of quality control in the laboratory, including methodology, reagents, control media, equipment, specimen handling, procedure manuals, reports, and proficiency testing, as well as personnel, safety, and the overall management principles that distinguish a quality laboratory. The program is accepted in lieu of part or all of the requirements of the Joint Commission on Accreditation of Hospitals, the Health Care Financing Administration, and the Centers for Disease Control, as well as 24 states. In addition, the Veterans Administration, the Indian Health Service, and the Navy contract with the CAP to have many of their laboratories inspected.[8,9]

Joint Commission on Accreditation of Hospitals (JCAH)

In 1918, the American College of Surgeons (ACS) began a Hospital Standardization Program to develop standards. In 1950, the ACS sought support from other health care organizations, including the American College of Physicians (ACP), the American Hospital Association (AHA), the American Medical Association (AMA), and the Canadian Medical Association (CMA), and together established the Joint Commission on Accreditation of Hospitals (JCAH). Later, the CMA withdrew from the Joint Commission and the American Dental Association joined.

The JCAH, a private, not-for-profit organization, began their accreditation program for hospitals in 1951. The JCAH program encompasses the following:

1. General acute care hospitals
2. Adult psychiatric facilities
3. Children's and adolescents' psychiatric facilities
4. Drug abuse treatment and rehabilitation programs
5. Alcoholism treatment programs
6. Community mental health services
7. Long-term care facilities
8. Services for developmentally disabled persons
9. Ambulatory health care organizations

The standards that apply to laboratories are included in the *Accreditation Manual for Hospitals* in the section entitled "Pathology and Medical Laboratory Services."[10] In 1985, approximately 5000 acute care and general hospitals held JCAH accreditation.

The JCAH is governed by a 21-member Board of Commissioners appointed by five member organizations. The commissioners provide leadership and direction in the development of standards, survey procedures, and granting of accreditation.[10-12] A hospital inspection visit is conducted by a physician, a registered nurse, a hospital administrator, and, when appropriate, a laboratory technologist. The laboratory standards are similar to those of the CAP Laboratory Accreditation Program.

In 1978, the JCAH began formal recognition of CAP accreditation of laboratories. This led to the present arrangement whereby laboratories that are accredited by the

CAP do not require additional survey or review by the JCAH as relates to the "Pathology and Medical Laboratory Services" Standard.

American Association of Blood Banks (AABB)

Blood Banks and Transfusion Services   Discussions concerning the development of an accreditation program for blood banks and transfusion services were held in 1956 by the American Association of Blood Banks (AABB) Board of Directors. To improve blood banks and transfusion services to donors and patients, the AABB began its Inspection and Accreditation Program in 1958. The National Committee on Inspection and Accreditation, composed of the chairman, vice chairman, several area chairmen, and various liaisons, administers the program. The AABB *Standards for Blood Banks and Transfusion Services,* the basic document for the AABB Inspection and Accreditation Program, provides minimum performance guidelines, whereas the AABB Inspection Report Form is the inspector's checklist.

The AABB inspection satisfies state requirements in several states, including Arizona, Connecticut, Georgia, Illinois, Maryland, Massachusetts, New Jersey, Tennessee, and Wisconsin. By 1985, approximately 1200 blood banks had been accredited.[13,14]

Parentage Testing Laboratories   In 1984, the AABB Committee on Parentage Testing conducted a study on international laboratory practices involved in establishing paternity. The findings indicated that several different approaches are used and courtroom decisions based on erroneous information occurred. Because universal standards for testing and accreditation procedures were needed, the AABB developed an accreditation program for laboratories involved in parentage testing. The requirements include the following areas: personnel, equipment, proficiency testing, identification and specimen identification, records, reports, red blood cell surface antigen testing, HLA testing, red cell enzyme testing, and serum protein testing.[15,16]

American Society of Cytology (ASC)

In 1971, the American Society of Cytology (ASC) undertook the development of an accreditation program for cytopathology laboratories. In 1972, details of standards, accreditation criteria, and the mechanism for inspection, accreditation, and renewal were finalized. The Laboratory Accreditation Committee, composed of a pathologist chairman, three pathologists, and three cytotechnologists, administers the program. The program, which was organized in 1973, approved eight laboratories during its first year of operation. By 1985, approximately 50 laboratories were accredited.

Diagnostic cytopathology laboratories are eligible to apply for accreditation if they meet one of the following criteria: (1) receive at least 10,000 gynecologic specimens annually; (2) receive at least 300 nongynecologic specimens annually; (3) maintain a staff of at least one cytopathologist and one full-time cytopathologist.

Areas inspected are: the physical facilities (space, safety, equipment); the laboratory operation (procedures, management practices, record retention); personnel records; quality control (specimen preparation, microscopy, clinical correlation, proficiency testing, personnel performance); compliance with state, federal, and local laws; and ethics.[17]

U.S. GOVERNMENTAL AGENCIES RESPONSIBLE FOR LABORATORY LICENSURE OR SPECIFIC AREAS OF LABORATORY ACTIVITY (TABLE 15-4)

Health Care Financing Administration/Centers for Disease Control (HCFA/CDC)

Two major federal programs currently are involved in laboratory regulation. The Medicare/Medicaid certification program enacted in 1965 to regulate laboratories receiving Medicare/Medicaid funds was followed by the Clinical Laboratories Improvement Act of 1967 (CLIA-1967) to regulate laboratories involved in interstate commerce.

The Social Security Act of 1965 (Public Law 89-97) established payment benefits for medical care through Medicare (Title XVIII) and Medicaid (Title XIX) programs. The Medicare program is designed primarily for the elderly, whereas the Medicaid program provides funds for a number of groups, such as the blind or disabled, whose resources are insufficient to meet the cost of medical assistance. The Medicaid program is a state responsibility, with the federal government providing matching funds to support the program. The total number of beneficiaries under both programs is around 50 million people.[18] The Department of Health and Human Services (HHS), through its agency the Health Care Financing Administration (HCFA), has responsibility for promulgating, implementing, and enforcing applicable regulations. Usually HCFA contracts with state Medicare agencies to survey or inspect laboratories.

The 1965 Medicare act recognized two voluntary programs, the Joint Commission on Accreditation of Hospitals (JCAH) and the American Osteopathic Association (AOA), that could substitute for on-site surveys by the HCFA. Because these programs can act as substitutes, they are considered equivalent and are said to have "deemed

TABLE 15-4
GOVERNMENTAL AGENCIES

1 HCFA
   a National
      Ambulatory Services, Health Care Financing Administration, 6325 Security Boulevard, Area 202, Baltimore MD 21207
   b Regional Offices
      Located in Boston, New York, Philadelphia, Atlanta, Chicago, Dallas, Kansas City, Denver, San Francisco, and Seattle
2 FDA
   Division of Blood and Blood Products, Bureau of Biologics, Food and Drug Administration, Bethesda, MD 20205
3 NRC
   The individual state agency, usually the Laboratory Licensure Division of the state's Department of Public Health

status." To date, approximately 5000 hospitals are accredited by these two organizations. Although the Medicare provision diminishes the number of inspections or survey visits experienced by laboratories, the HCFA retains a monitoring role and is responsible for assuring that these two programs continue to meet federal criteria. Occasionally, the HCFA may elect to conduct survey visits for validation purposes and for investigation of complaints.

The 1965 Medicare law forbade the federal government from establishing standards higher than those set by the JCAH and AOA, but in 1972 an amendment was passed that deleted this provision. This later amendment provided that voluntary programs should have standards "equivalent to" but not necessarily identical on a "one-on-one" basis to those of the federal agency.

The Clinical Laboratories Improvement Act of 1967 (CLIA-1967) is an interstate licensure program enacted in 1967 following congressional motivation to assure the quality of testing performed on specimens crossing state lines. This law affects all specimens in interstate commerce and is not restricted to Medicare/Medicaid patients. Proficiency testing is a major portion of the regulatory provisions of this act, with the Centers for Disease Control (CDC) in Atlanta, Georgia, an arm of the Public Health Service, designated as the responsible agency.

This law provided the CDC certain latitude in the enforcement provisions:

1 It recognized the CAP Laboratory Accreditation Program as an acceptable alternative to federal licensure so long as an "equivalency arrangement" was maintained. (Thus, laboratories accredited by the CAP need not undergo another inspection so long as appropriate notification is provided to the HCFA by the CAP and the laboratory.)

2 The Department of Health and Human Services could recognize licensure by a state agency if found equivalent to federal requirements in specialty areas. To date, the only state program recognized is that of New York.

3 Laboratories receiving fewer than 100 specimens in interstate commerce in specific categories were exempt on the basis of a "low-volume exemption" in that specific category.

Under this law, approximately 1100 interstate laboratories became regulated by the CDC; approximately 200 were provided exemption because they were CAP accredited; and 60 were exempt because of New York State accreditation.

By 1984, there were approximately 12,000 laboratories across the United States subject to federal regulation. These include hospital, independent, and group practice clinical laboratories. Federal agencies became involved in the affairs of these laboratories from two different, significant tacks: quality assurance and cost control. The federal agencies must use careful discretion so that the former is not compromised in attempting to achieve the latter. Unfortunately, hospital laboratories accredited by the JCAH and AOA were not "deemed equivalent" for CLIA interstate licensure purposes.[18]

To carry out the Clinical Laboratories Improvement Act of 1967 and Medicare regulations, the HCFA and CDC operate under an interagency agreement signed in 1978. According to this agreement, the HCFA is mainly responsible for the administrative and procedural aspects, whereas the CDC covers the scientific and technical aspects (Table 15-5). For the appropriate agency to contact for information on licensure, certification, or exemption, see Table 15-6.

Food and Drug Administration (FDA)

Because blood and blood product transfusions are one of the most dangerous therapeutic measures in medicine, it is not surprising that there are both federal and voluntary quality assurance programs. For many years and until recently, the FDA had direct authority for scrutinizing and regulating facilities engaged in testing and preparation of blood and blood products. In 1980, the HCFA adopted existing FDA standards obviating the need for visits by the FDA unless the facility was engaged in collection, processing, and transmission of blood and blood products. This arrangement led to a major reduction in the number of redundant federal surveys. Currently, the HCFA investigates fatal transfusion reaction reports received by the FDA. The FDA retains a technical assistance role in the area of blood banking and continues its regulatory role for approximately 1000 facilities.[18] The FDA also operates programs that approve medical devices including equipment, reagents test units, and instruments used by clinical laboratories. Like the CDC, the FDA is a branch of the Public Health Service (PHS).

Nuclear Regulatory Commission (NRC)

The Nuclear Regulatory Commission requires a general license for physicians, veterinarians, clinical laboratories, and hospitals using radioactive materials. Licensure is required even for small quantities of radioactive materials used only for in vitro clinical tests. In most instances, one license is issued to cover an institution's entire radioisotope program.[19]

States and Cities

Approximately one-half of the states in the United States have laws regulating clinical laboratories, with most of these states requiring an on-site survey or visit (usually annually) and proficiency testing. Applicable state laboratory licensure laws are enforced by the same personnel who perform the state Medicare inspections. For those states without licensure laws, agreements to accept voluntary programs such as those of the JCAH, AABB, and CAP in lieu of a state program are common. New York City is the only city with its own regulatory program for clinical laboratories.

STANDARDS (TABLE 15-7)

Voluntary Standards

    National Committee on Clinical Laboratory Standards (NCCLS)   Probably the standards that are most widely accepted by professional organizations, governmental agencies, and industry are those of the National Committee on Clinical Laboratory Standards (NCCLS). These standards and guidelines are developed by a consensus

TABLE 15-5
COMPARISON OF THE REQUIREMENTS FOR CLINICAL LABORATORIES UNDER THE MEDICARE AND CLIA-1967 PROGRAMS

	Medicare	CLIA-1967
Approval process	The laboratory is subject to yearly inspections. Independent laboratories are certified by specialty and subspecialty to participate in the program if they are in substantial compliance with all the requirements. Laboratories will only be certified and paid for tests which meet the program's requirements of being reasonable and necessary. Hospital laboratories are approved as part of the overall hospital certification and are not given a separate approval as is done for independent laboratories. All facilities must be in compliance with state and local laws to receive Medicare reimbursement.	The laboratory is subject to yearly inspections. Licensure is by specific test procedures (but can be given in an entire specialty or subspecialty) if the facility is in compliance with all the standards. Licensure of a procedure or test is not related to the test being eligible for reimbursement under Medicare or Medicaid. Tests do not have to be ordered by a physician as in Medicare. There is no regulatory distinction between hospital and independent laboratories as in Medicare. There is no requirement that the facility meet state and local laws (including licensure) as in Medicare.
Personnel standards	INDEPENDENT LABORATORIES—Education, training, and experience requirements for directors, supervisors (general and technical), technologists, and technicians. Grandfather clauses based on training, experience, and/or examination requirements for individuals already employed in facilities when the regulations were made more stringent. HOSPITAL LABORATORIES—Specific requirements only for the director. Also a requirement for an adequate number of trained (training and education not specified) technologists.	CLIA cross-referenced the Medicare independent laboratory requirements for personnel with the exception that CLIA does not regulate technicians. CLIA also does not require the presence of a general supervisor on the premises unless interstate testing is being performed. There is no requirement that the personnel be licensed in accordance with state and local laws as in the Medicare program. CLIA has the same requirements for personnel in hospital and independent laboratories, unlike Medicare which has separate sets of requirements.
Quality control	Medicare cross-referenced the CLIA regulations with the exception that Medicare also adopted the FDA requirements for blood banking and transfusion services. Medicare also has specific requirements for histocompatability testing.	There are general requirements for procedure manuals, preventive maintenance, reagents, equipment calibration, system and procedural checks, normal ranges, error detection and correction, and the review and reporting of results. There are also requirements specific to each specialty and subspecialty reflective of their unique nature.
Management	Requirements of laboratory safety; adequacy of space, facilities and equipment; specimen collection; receipt and referral of specimens; test ordering and test reporting. All tests must be	CLIA has requirements similar to Medicare to assure that good laboratory management, recordkeeping, safety and organizational practices are followed to assure the quality, accuracy and

Source: Edinger SE: Evolution and future directions of federal regulation of clinical laboratories. *J Med Tech* 1984; 10:776–785, with permission.

TABLE 15-5
(Continued)

	Medicare	CLIA-1967
	ordered by a physician. Referrals are only made to another Medicare approved laboratory. Records are retained for two years or longer if required by state or local law. Some of the recordkeeping requirements are reflective of Medicare being a payment program.	timeliness of the results and their reporting. CLIA does not have a specific requirement that a physician must order a test but does not require referral to a Medicare approved laboratory. There is also no requirement that records be maintained in accordance with state and local laws.
Proficiency testing	Medicare requires successful participation in a proficiency testing program approved by the Secretary of DHHS for each specialty and subspecialty in which the laboratory is approved and for which a program is available. The currently approved programs include the CDC program, state programs, and private sector (accreditation organizations such as CAP, AAB, ASIM, and commercial) programs.	CLIA requires laboratories to successfully perform in the CDC program unless they are exempt on the basis of being in the CAP Inspection and Accreditation Program or licensed by New York State. No stand alone (i.e., not part of a total inspection and accreditation program) PT program is approved for CLIA. Passage or failure is on an individual test basis. Action against a facility is taken on a test basis rather than by specialty or subspecialty as in Medicare. Grading scheme is defined in the regulations unlike in the Medicare program.
Adverse action process	INDEPENDENT LABORATORIES—Payment in Medicare and Medicaid can be stopped to a laboratory in a specialty or subspecialty or to the entire facility if it is found out of compliance with the conditions of coverage (or found guilty of fraud or abuse). The facility has the right to appeal the decision and receive a hearing before an administrative law judge (DHHS-employed lawyers who are independent of the Department). There are additional hearing and appeal processes for both the Department and the laboratory. DHHS cannot prevent a facility from testing but can only deny payment for Medicare and Medicaid services. HOSPITAL LABORATORIES—Hospital laboratories can only be decertified or not paid if the entire hospital is decertified. There are various criminal and civil monetary penalties for fraud and abuse.	The laboratory can only have its license denied, revoked, or amended after it has had the opportunity for a hearing before an administrative law judge. Unlike Medicare, the laboratory can have its license limited for a specific test—the limitation or revocation does not have to be by specialty or subspecialty (but it can include a specialty or the entire laboratory). The Department can obtain an injunction (in U.S. District Court) to prevent a laboratory from further testing in interstate (but not intrastate) commerce. If the DHHS can show that the facility poses a hazard to public health and safety. There are misdemeanor (criminal) penalties of $1000 per test for operating in violation of the statute or regulations.

Source: Edinger SE: Evolution and future directions of federal regulation of clinical laboratories. *J Med Tech* 1984; 10:776–785, with permission.

TABLE 15-6
INTERSTATE LICENSURE, CERTIFICATION, OR EXEMPTION

1 Licensure (CLIA)	HCFA Regional Offices
2 Low-volume exemption (CLIA)	HCFA Regional Offices
3 Certification (Medicare)	State of HCFA Regional Offices
4 Exemption based on CAP accreditation (CLIA)	HCFA National Office
5 Exemption based on New York State licensure	New York HCFA Regional Office

TABLE 15-7
STANDARDS: AGENCIES AND ASSOCIATIONS

A Voluntary
   1 NCCLS: National Committee for Clinical Laboratory Standards, 771 E. Lancaster Avenue, Villanova, PA 19085
   2 NFPA: National Fire Protection Association, Batterymarch Park, Quincy, MA 02269
B Regulatory
   1 OSHA: U.S. Department of Labor, Occupational Safety and Health Administration, Washington D.C. 20210. Regional offices are located in Boston, New York, Philadelphia, Atlanta, Chicago, Dallas, Kansas City, Denver, San Francisco, and Seattle.
C Other
   1 Association for the Advancement of Medical Instrumentation, 1901 N. Fort Meyer Drive, Suite 602, Arlington, VA 22209
   2 American National Standards Institute, 1430 Broadway, New York, NY 10018
   3 Bureau of Biologics, 8800 Rockville Pike, Bethesda, MD 20205
   4 Centers for Disease Control, Atlanta, GA 30333
   5 European Committee for Clinical Laboratory Standards, % Wellcome Research Laboratories, Langley Court, Beckenham, Kent BR3 3BA UK
   6 Food and Drug Administration, Bethesda, MD 20205
   7 International Committee on Thrombosis and Haemostatis, Riks Hospitalet, Oslo 1, Norway
   8 World Health Organization, Geneva 27, 1211 Switzerland

process and are for voluntary compliance, not for accreditation or licensure requirements. Individuals appointed to committees directed to develop standards include representative members from clinical laboratories, industry, professional organizations, and government. The approval process includes solicitation of comments from the entire NCCLS membership.

National Fire Protection Association (NFPA) The NFPA is a nonprofit organization developed to encourage fire safety in the home and at work. Similar to the NCCLS, a representative committee develops the standard or code and public comment is solicited. Several NFPA published standards and codes touch on aspects of clinical laboratory fire safety; however, NFPA 99, *Standard for Health Care Facilities*, is the primary document containing operational safety criteria for laboratories.

Compliance with these standards and codes is voluntary, but due to their acceptability and their development by a consensus process, they are widely utilized.[20]

Other Voluntary Standards In addition to the standards developed by the CAP, JCAH, AABB, and ASC for their individual accreditation programs, additional documents have been developed that are widely used (see Table 15-8).

Regulatory Standards

Occupational Safety and Health Administration (OSHA) The Occupational Safety and Health Act, enacted by Congress in 1970, was written to protect the safety and health of employees in their workplace. The enforcement agency is the Department of Labor. The standards developed cover such specific occupations as construction work, ship building, commercial diving, and sawmills, but also areas such as fire safety, and toxic or hazardous substances. The document *Emergency Response in the Workplace* outlines handling of health and safety emergencies in the workplace.[21,22]

Environmental Protection Agency (EPA) As relates to laboratories, the Environmental Protection Agency (EPA) is the agency responsible for implementing regulations pertaining to hazardous waste management and toxic substances control. The EPA's goal is a "cradle-to-grave" management system for hazardous solid wastes. The policy of the EPA on infectious waste is included in the 1982 document entitled *Draft Manual for Infectious Waste Management*.[23]

Other Standards

Some national, international, or voluntary agencies that have standards of interest to laboratories are listed in Table 15-7. Two documents are references that provide additional information on standards-setting groups.[24,25]

TABLE 15-8
HELPFUL DOCUMENTS

1 AABB Technical Manual, 1984
2 AABB Selection of Procedures for Problem Solving, 1983
3 AABB Guidelines to Transfusion Practices, 1980
4 CAP Systematized Nomenclature of Medicine, 1980
5 CAP Laboratory Workload Recording Manual (updated annually)
6 CAP Clinical Laboratory Handbook for Patient Preparation and Specimen Handling—Fascicles 1–4
7 NCCLS Library of Standards
8 NFPA 99, Standard for Health Care Facilities, 1984 (also NFPA 10, 30, 77, 80, 101, 220)
9 American Society of Microbiology Cumitechs (approximately 20)

AREAS OF RESPONSIBILITY

Table 15-9 illustrates the variety of voluntary and federal organizations or agencies described in the text, and the areas of responsibility usually assigned. The list is not intended to be all-inclusive. Even though there is no indication that an agency has primary responsibility in a given area, it doesn't necessarily mean that the agency has no authority in that area; for example, many have requirements in the fire safety area. Because of areas of overlapping responsibility, it is little wonder that the inexperienced laboratorian can easily become confused as to which agency controls what sector or discipline within the laboratory!

REDUCTION IN DUPLICATE SURVEYS/INSPECTIONS

One of the most frequent complaints by laboratory directors in the late 1960s and early 1970s was the large number of redundant, annoying, and seemingly unnecessary visits by agents of the federal or state government, or individuals representing the various voluntary accreditation programs. At that time, it was not unusual for a hospital laboratory to be visited within a 12-month period by a state official; representatives from the JCAH; the CAP; and, if blood banking facilities were present, the AABB and the FDA. Many facilities experienced unannounced visits by sometimes overzealous officials of the newly created Occupational Safety and Health Administration (OSHA). The exasperation of the director of laboratories in those situations was understandable, and by the early 1980s led to policy changes. Table 15-10 summarizes the current responsibilities and functions of the various Department of Health and Human Service agencies in clinical laboratory regulation.

QUALIFICATIONS OR SURVEYORS/INSPECTORS

In our experience, genuine progress has been made during the last two decades regarding the competence and experience of the various individuals representing both voluntary and regulatory programs. Government surveyors are now usually medical technologists; in a few instances, they may be doctoral-level scientists who are either federal or state employees. The JCAH now provides for a medical technologist to be included on the hospital survey team when the laboratory is not accredited by the CAP. The head of a CAP inspection team should be (1) a qualified pathologist, (2) a fellow of the CAP, and (3) associated with an accredited laboratory.

RESPONDING TO CHANGE

By statutory necessity, proposed changes in federal regulations must undergo a rather rigorous course before adoption. Because the U.S. government is founded upon full disclosure and debate, it is not surprising that even the most innocent technological refinement must undergo definition, debate, rumination, and rebuttal. Consequently, change in extant regulation is slow and arduous.

In contrast, voluntary agencies are bound by only the "equivalency" requirement,

TABLE 15-9
PRIMARY AREAS OF RESPONSIBILITY

Organization or agency	Accreditation/Licensure						Standards				Proficiency test (surveys)
	Laboratories										
	Hospitals	Hospitals	Interstate	Blood banks	Cytology	Laboratory	Fire safety	Nuclear safety	Environmental	Safety	
JCAH	X									X	
CAP	X	X	X	X	X	X	X			X	X
AABB				X		X					
ASC					X						
NCCLS						X					
NFPA							X			X	
ASM						X					
CDC			X			X					X
HCFA		X		X	X						
EPA									X		
OSHA							X			X	
FDA				X		X					
NRC								X			
BOB						X					
State agencies		X		X	X						

that is, equal but not identical. The net result is that voluntary agencies are able to modify, refine, and improve their survey and inspection requirements so as to adapt more closely to the rapidly changing technological milieu within the clinical laboratory. The CAP uses computer technology to retain and rapidly modify their inspection checklist (a multipart document encompassing approximately 2000 questions or requirements). Approximately 15 scientific committees composed of experts are available as a resource.

Efforts are currently underway to coordinate federal standards with those of voluntary standard-setting groups, such as the National Committee on Clinical Laboratory Standards (NCCLS), with the goal of achieving uniform laboratory standards.[18] Progress is being made in this area, but because of the sheer bulk and magnitude of the task, several years will be required before this job is accomplished.

NONCOMPLIANCE WITH STANDARDS

With regard to consequences owing to noncompliance with standards, the difference between the voluntary and regulatory sectors becomes boldly apparent. The voluntary agencies can only deny accreditation; no legal sanctions or restrictions are available to these voluntary groups. Significantly, however, loss of accreditation by any of these agencies is likely to be associated with embarrassment, loss of morale, damage of ego, and cause for concern. With voluntary programs, no laboratory is required to participate unless forced by institutional or medical influence. In contrast, state and federal agencies possess major "clout" in reserve, should a laboratory fail to meet accepted standards. The most obvious consequence of noncompliance is loss of certification for payment under the Medicare/Medicaid programs, and few laboratories or institutions can survive such financial sanctions. Moreover, if warranted by the situation, criminal prosecution is a possibility. Thus, there are adequate enforcement provisions suitable for the charlatan or ne'er-do-well who elects to dabble in this arena.

INSPECTION DAY—OR THE DAY OF RECKONING!

What should one expect? Are the inspectors "sticklers" for detail? What will they look for? Can we "pass"? Are we ready? What did we forget? These are the most frequent concerns of the laboratory personnel about to undergo inspection. Unfortunately, when dealing with such a variety of agencies and entities, the recipient is held accountable for a multitude of standards, regulations, and questions that frequently change. Furthermore, the personality, experience, background, and fluctuating temperament of the visiting official introduces another set of variables. Add to this personnel turnover, requiring constant in-service and procedure review, and it is small wonder that most laboratories find that the average inspection visit always turns up a few discrepancies—no matter how intense the advance effort to achieve compliance.

Fortunately, both regulatory and voluntary agencies have provided for the realities of the above situation. Most agencies have procedures for delaying final accreditation or licensure decision until the laboratory has had an opportunity to clarify misunderstandings or correct minor deficiencies. In my experience, although occasional over-

TABLE 15-10
RESPONSIBILITIES AND FUNCTIONS OF THE DHHS AGENCIES FOR THE CLINICAL LABORATORY REGULATORY PROGRAMS—1984

Health Care Financing Administration (HCFA)	Public Health Service (PHS)		
	Centers for Disease Control (CDC)	Food and Drug Administration (FDA)	

Health Care Financing Administration (HCFA)	Centers for Disease Control (CDC)	Food and Drug Administration (FDA)
Publish regulations for Medicare	Publish regulations for CLIA laboratories	Publish regulations for licensed and registered blood banks and transfusion services and for medical devices
Publish administrative requirements for Medicare and CLIA laboratories	Develop technical regulations for Medicare and CLIA programs	Inspection by FDA surveyors of licensed and registered facilities and manufacturers of medical devices
Publish technical standards for Medicare laboratories with advice of PHS/CDC and FDA	Develop technical guidelines for Medicare and CLIA	Licensure and registration decisions for blood banks and transfusion services and approval of medical devices
Make final decision on certification and CLIA licensure status or exemption status of laboratories	Manage CLIA PT program	
	Evaluate PT programs and requests for deemed status approval and make recommendation to HCFA	Issue forms, regulations, survey documents and survey guidelines
Issue forms and survey and certification instructions and documents for Medicare and CLIA (including technical guidelines)	Provide technical advice to HCFA	Investigate fatal transfusion reactions
Approval of proficiency testing programs for Medicare (with advice of PHS/CDC)	Perform special direct federal surveys	Provide technical advice to HCFA in the area of blood banking and transfusion services
	Monitor the CLIA and Medicare clinical laboratory programs	Assist in training HCFA laboratory surveyors
Approval of deemed status for organizations for Medicare (with advice of PHS/CDC)	Assist in training HCFA laboratory surveyors	Assist HCFA personnel in conducting complaint surveys involving blood banks and transfusion services, including fatal transfusion reactions
Sole responsibility for the survey of blood banks and transfusion services not routinely processing, collecting and shipping blood and blood products and for all CLIA (interstate) laboratories	Manage the proficiency examination program for clinical laboratory technologists	
	Provide training and technical assistance to state health departments	

Public Health Service (PHS)

Health Care Financing Administration (HCFA)	Centers for Disease Control (CDC)	Food and Drug Administration (FDA)
Investigate fatal transfusion reaction reports received from FDA	Perform research in the area of public health	Take adverse actions and other legal and regulatory actions under the Food, Drug and Cosmetics Act; Biologics Act; and the Medical Device Act
Perform validation surveys in JCAH and AOA facilities	Perform research in the area of the clinical laboratory sciences including proficiency testing	Perform research and studies in a variety of areas related to the agency's functions
Perform complaint investigations in facilities (utilizing either regional or state agency personnel or both)		
Take adverse actions under Medicare and CLIA		
Monitor the performance of carriers, intermediaries and state agencies		
Determine what is to be reimbursed and how much to reimburse—Medicare		
Approve state survey agency budgets		
Conduct research and demonstration projects		

Source: Edinger SE: Evolution and future directions of federal regulation of clinical laboratories. *J Med Tech* 1984; 10:776–785, with permission.

zealous officials may create a lot of unrest and apprehension, it is seldom that official adverse action (whether it be accreditation denial or revocation of licensure) is taken without an opportunity for appeal and rectification of problems. Although such situations are rare, the laboratory director who ignores suggestions and recommendations of the visiting official jeopardizes his or her laboratory's accreditation.

REFERENCES

1. *Webster's New World Dictionary.* New York, Wm Collins Publishers, 1979.
2. Koenig AS III, Day JC, Sodeman TM et al: *Laboratory Instrument Verification and Maintenance Manual,* ed 3. Skokie, IL, College of American Pathologists, 1982.
3. *Dorland's Illustrated Medical Dictionary,* ed 26. Philadelphia, W B Saunders, 1981.
4. *Nomenclature and Definitions for Use in the National Reference System for the Clinical Laboratory,* Villanova, PA, National Committee on Clinical Laboratory Standards, 1985.
5. Bartlett RC, Carrington GO, Mailert C: *Quality Control in Clinical Microbiology.* Chicago, American Society of Clinical Pathologists, 1968.
6. *Commission on Laboratory Accreditation Policies and Procedures Manual.* Skokie, IL, College of American Pathologists, 1986.
7. *Definitions of standard, guidelines, and quality. CAP Policy and Guidelines,* app J. Skokie, IL, College of American Pathologists, 1985.
8. *Standards for Laboratory Accreditation.* Skokie, IL, College of American Pathologists, 1982.
9. Duckworth JK, Gregg DP: How and when the accreditation program began, and where it is today. *Pathologist* 1984, 38:1.
10. *Accreditation Manual for Hospitals/86.* Chicago, Joint Commission on Accreditation of Hospitals, 1985.
11. Affeldt JE: A Message from the President, Chicago, Joint Commission on Accreditation of Hospitals, 1981.
12. *Facts about Evaluation and Accreditation.* Chicago, Joint Commission on Accreditation of Hospitals.
13. *The Inspection and Accreditation Program.* Arlington, VA, American Association of Blood Banks, 1982.
14. Klein RE: Inspection and accreditation: Elevating and maintaining blood bank policies and procedures. *Lab World* 1981, 32(10):42–47.
15. *Standards for Parentage Testing Laboratories.* Arlington, VA, American Association of Blood Banks, 1984.
16. First accreditation program for parentage testing laboratories. *Lab Medicine* 1984, 15(8):557.
17. *Criteria for Cytopathology Laboratory Accreditation.* Philadelphia, American Society of Cytology, 1984.
18. Edinger SE: Evolution and future directions of federal regulation of clinical laboratories. *J Med Tech* 1984, 10:776–786.
19. *Regulatory Guide.* Washington, DC, U.S. Government Printing Office, 1980.
20. *Codes and Standards.* Quincy, MA, National Fire Protection Association, 1984.
21. *Emergency Response in the Workplace.* Washington, DC, Occupational Safety and Health Administration publication 3088, 1984.
22. *General Industry.* Washington, DC, Occupational Safety and Health Administration publication 2206, 1983.

23 *Draft Manual for Infectious Waste Management.* Washington, DC, Environmental Protection Agency Publication SW-957, 1982.
24 *Standards, Reference Materials, and Methods—A Practical Guide for the Medical Laboratory.* Skokie, IL, College of American Pathologists, 1983.
25 Bayless WC, Pacela AF, *The Guide to Biomedical Standards,* ed 11. Brea, CA, Quest Publishing, 1984–1985.

CHAPTER 16

QUALITY ASSURANCE AND LABORATORY INFORMATION FLOW

David Chou, M.D.
Donald P. Connelly, M.D., Ph.D.
James S. Fine, M.D.

A laboratory result is a product of a complex information processing cycle to which many individuals contribute and from which many errors may result.[1] Because the information cycle is largely a serial process, quality assurance efforts directed toward only one step in the process are not adequate. Careful attention to precision and accuracy of the analytical phase of laboratory operation can be meaningless if the specimen is mislabeled, a specimen is misplaced, or a laboratory value is miscopied onto a report.

Although all phases of the information processing cycle may give rise to errors and deserve attention, there are practical limits to the energy, time, and cost that can be expended in the pursuit of quality. Perfection in information handling, although a worthy goal, may not be achievable or affordable. Priorities must be established that take into account the costs of reducing errors as well as the benefits. But it is usually difficult to quantitate error rates, weigh their consequences, assess the benefits of error reduction, or arrive at a cost for such a reduction. There is little existing theory on which to base information processing decisions. Setting priorities under such conditions will necessarily involve subjective values. In many situations, there may be more than one way to solve a problem. In other cases, no solution is practical. Experience, judgment, and common sense are critical elements for decision making. Thus, information flow quality assurance will be an ongoing process involving uncertainty, personal values, good judgment, and experience.

The modern notion of quality assurance—people working together to identify, understand, and resolve problems[2,3]—is especially appropriate when considering quality assurance of the clinical laboratory information processing cycle. The general patient-care quality assurance guidelines of the Joint Commission on Accreditation of Hospitals (JCAH) that particularly fit laboratory information processing activities include: (1) maintaining flexibility in approaches to problem definition, assessment and resolution; (2) focusing quality assurance activity on problems whose resolution will have a significant impact on patient care and outcomes; (3) focusing quality assurance activity on areas where demonstrable problems exist; and (4) using multiple data sources to identify problems. With such a problem-oriented approach, valid priorities are established, effective and affordable solutions are identified, and united resolutions are obtained.

Although personal commitment and dedication to careful laboratory practices is vital to maintaining the quality of the laboratory information processing cycle, this is not enough. People, no matter how well motivated or supported, make errors at a significant and seemingly irreducible rate.[4] The computer is one of the most important tools available to laboratory professionals working together to improve information processing quality. Computer-based systems, per se, do not guarantee high levels of quality. In fact, quality assurance in data processing is a relatively new and seldom touched upon topic.[5] Computer programmers make errors, but programming errors, if detected and corrected, can be reduced over time. Computers, too, make errors, but these occur rarely relative to human performance and are usually detectable. If a laboratory is to optimize quality, a well-functioning computer-based information system in both the laboratory and hospital are necessary. Of course, computer-based information systems are not practical for all laboratories. In such settings the quality assurance goals should realistically reflect this resource limitation.

Most quality assurance activities address problems that fall within the domain of operational management.[6] The focus at this level is on the detail of day-to-day laboratory processes and resources associated with the work of the laboratory in obtaining specimens and measuring and reporting analyte values. Of import here are the patient, the specimen, the request form, the laboratory personnel, the laboratory process, the resources used, and the final product—the reported result. Quality assurance is also needed at the management control level. Management control is oriented toward planning for resources and coordinating their use so that operations are efficient and effective. Quality standards are established, resources are allocated, conformance to practice standards is appraised, necessary action is taken, and plans for improvements are developed.[7] Management control activities are more difficult to define in quality assurance. Anthony points out that "the absence of quality measures in management control systems may lead to detrimental emphasis on quantity. . . . Thus every effort should be made to find some acceptable quality measure, even though it is crude."[6]

In this chapter, approaches to assuring quality of each of the major phases of the information processing cycle are first considered. Although the presentation presumes the existence of a functioning computer-based laboratory information system, some of the quality assurance activities can be effectively pursued in the noncomputerized environment as well. Next, quality assurance of the information processing resource is discussed, with consideration given to operational and management control. With computer systems come special problems, which are discussed, including the issues of error management, system integrity and security, and patient privacy.

QUALITY ASSURANCE AND THE INFORMATION PROCESSING CYCLE

General Issues

The information processing cycle in the clinical laboratory requires detailed record keeping. Although the process is quite complex, a number of functional elements recur and can be addressed as general topics. The information system must record the time of completion of significant events throughout the cycle. It must also record the identity of those individuals who make any modification to the database. Functionality should be optimized at each interaction with the system. To maintain data integrity, all manual entries should be compared to expected inputs stored in computer system tables.

Laboratory procedures assess human biological processes. These processes are subject to time considerations such as circadian rhythms, menstrual cycles, time of medication, and fasting. Therefore, it is essential that the laboratory management system track the time of specimen collection. The time the specimen is received in the laboratory must be recorded. This will allow for determination of transportation time, a critical factor in the evaluation of microbiological cultures as well as assessment of specimen constituent degradation. The completion time of the assay, associated control specimens, result entry, and the time of report printing should also be recorded. The laboratory information cycle can then be divided into time periods and critical points. With these time references established, each laboratory process, including transportation, specimen processing, specimen testing, and result reporting, can be monitored.

In addition to time records, the laboratory must keep track of individuals responsible for the performance of each activity. To accomplish this, the laboratory information system must note by some mechanism, usually the individual's initials or identification code, who performed which process in the cycle. This includes phlebotomy, specimen login, test performance, result entry, result verification, and, if necessary, result correction. The system must also store the identifier of the physician ordering the procedure. Other records reflect on the overall performance of the laboratory. Therefore, the logs of ordinary functions such as print schedules and reagent preparation should carry the initials of the person completing the task. Completed worklists should be initialed. Procedure descriptions, as well as changes to such procedures, must also be logged in a similar fashion by the appropriate individuals.

The security password system can be used to facilitate the recording of individuals responsible for each laboratory task. If every person is required to use a private password, the computer can verify authority to enter a particular function and, if permission is granted, attach the user's initials to the particular piece of data being entered or updated.

The most tenuous link in the entire data processing chain is the communication between the fingertips and the keyboard. A computerized laboratory information system can facilitate specimen and data management best if it is easy to understand and use. Prompts must be clear and concise. To minimize errors and promote employee efficiency, responses should be as short as possible. Where possible, default answers, such as "blood" for specimen type, should be employed to assist the person interacting with the system. The need for repeated information entry should be kept to a minimum. Mnemonics for test names, and so on, should be brief but effective reminders and are generally preferable to numeric codes.

A laboratory information system is built on a series of files or tables. Some of these are established and modified by the computer programming or maintenance staff (e.g., the files containing the specimen descriptions, worklist layouts, or location lists). Other files actively change as the system is in operation, such as the master file containing patient demographic information. Each of these files can be used to check for appropriate data entry (i.e., edit checks). For example, the location file can be used to certify that a ward and room number input into the system is a valid location in the laboratory's service area. Test code definition files serve to define all parameters pertaining to a given test. Thus, when the test is ordered, this file is reviewed by the computer to assure that a valid test mnemonic has been entered and that the correct specimen type has been obtained. This same file is again used to screen entered results for the appropriate number and type of characters and, for numeric results, a check against reference limits and laboratory critical values is made. Proper maintenance of these tables is absolutely critical to the functioning of the laboratory information system.

Requisition Processing

The requisition is an essential link between the ordering location and the laboratory. It identifies the patient, provides demographic information, specifies the requested tests, and indicates the priority of the request. The requisition often contains information that may be necessary in performing the test and interpreting the result. The requisition form must indicate the clinical information needed by the laboratory. The forms should be organized so that they are easy to understand and complete. In addition, the requisitions should include most of the procedures available from the laboratory to minimize the need for handwritten entries.

The patient's name, patient identification number (PIN), age, and sex should appear on the requisition. The patient's name without an identification number is inadequate. Patients change their names through marriage, use aliases, or share a common name with others. Misspellings can result in multiple system admissions for a given individual, resulting in several disassociated lab reports. Age and sex are essential for proper reference limit checking and can be useful to the phlebotomist in verifying patient identity.

Because the PIN is so central to the identification of the patient and his or her specimens, additional care must be taken to ensure that the correct number is employed. This is usually accomplished by means of a check digit. A check digit is usually a single appended digit that is related mathematically to the remaining digits of the PIN (Table 16-1). It is ideally suited to computerized systems, which can recalculate and verify the integrity of the identification number each time it is entered. The check digit should be used whenever a test request or patient demographic information is entered or modified.

TABLE 16-1
IBM MODULUS 2 CHECK DIGIT ROUTINE

	Example
Patient number	1-4-1-2-3-8-3
Step 1: Starting on left, multiply first digit of number by 1, second by 2.	1, 8, . . .
Step 2: Continue multiplying alternately by 1 and by 2.	1, 8, 1, 4, 3, 16, 3
Step 3: Add results of multiplication (consider each digit separately).	1 + 8 + 1 + 4 + 3 + 1 + 6 + 3 or 27
Step 4: To obtain check digit, subtract this result from next highest decade.	30 − 27 = 3
Step 5: Append *check digit* to number to obtain patient identification number (PIN).	1-4-1-2-3-8-3-3 original # check digit

In processing the requisition, information regarding the requested tests must be transferred from the order form to the laboratory information system. To minimize keystrokes, test codes are usually employed. Each code must be unique and associated with a specific specimen type. The linking of the test to the specimen type is important, because this combination is used to define potential reference ranges, critical values, and worklists. The test codes should be screened for duplication and appropriateness. Duplication may occur when tests are ordered both individually and by laboratory-defined groups or batteries. Test orders should also be screened for appropriateness. Can the test be performed on the specimen provided? (For example, both a blood and a urine specimen should accompany a creatinine clearance request.) The system should also check, where possible, whether a combination of tests is logical.

Additional laboratory-specific information must be included in the requisition processing. As mentioned earlier, the time the specimen was obtained and time of requisition login must be noted. The specimen status (e.g., stat, routine) is necessary for properly scheduling the analysis. This status assignment should follow the specimen throughout its sojourn in the laboratory, appearing on specimen labels and worklists. The requisition must contain the name of the ordering doctor and the patient location to facilitate result reporting. In some environments, billing information must also be supplied. Some institutions have multiple potential laboratory locations that can perform a specific test. It is therefore incumbent on the laboratory system to assign the location for performance of the test in concert with the request.

Information on work requisition forms should be legible, complete, and accurate. Consistent policies should be in place for dealing with improperly completed forms. Once requisitioning information has been entered, the computer system can serve to track all subsequent processing stages. This tracking capability can be of great utility in preventing "lost" samples and in the identification of operational bottlenecks and error sources.

Specimen Procurement and Preanalytic Processing

Work requests may come to the laboratory accompanied by the specimen or require subsequent specimen procurement by laboratory personnel. For requests involving specimen procurement, laboratory systems can provide the phlebotomist with collection lists and specimen labels. Such labels include patient identification information (e.g., name, PIN, and location) as well as phlebotomy information (e.g., ordered tests, tube types, handling requirements, and precautions) and should be placed on specimens at the time of collection. Only constant alertness and care by the phlebotomist can ensure that the specimen is matched to the correct label. Accurate identification of patients and positive association of a patient with a specimen remains an elusive problem. Although it is possible to identify patients with portable automated devices and automatically associate them with a specific phlebotomy request, the cost of such technology has limited its use.

Specimens delivered to the laboratory with a requisition form should be carefully inspected for identification accuracy. Ordering information can then be entered in the requisitioning process and a label produced. Before this label is placed on the specimen, it should be carefully cross-checked against the requisition. Various methods are used for specimen labeling. Some systems provide a master label with all relevant information as well as multiple tube and aliquot labels, eliminating the need for handwritten labels and consequent transcription errors. Labeled tubes and aliquot cups are then delivered to laboratory sections for analysis. Labels may also be applied to specimens that are to be stored for subsequent repeat testing or "reflex" testing.

Machine-generated labels will not eliminate mislabeling of specimens, even though they do reduce the tedium and transcription errors that otherwise come with handwritten labels.[4] Numerous errors can still occur in specimen identification throughout the processing cycle. The ultimate reliability of any computerized data still depends greatly on the personal commitment of laboratory staff.

Specimen Analysis

Once the specimen is delivered to a laboratory work station for analysis, its label serves to identify the patient and the tests requested. The specimen is followed throughout the laboratory by means of the specimen identification number (SID), which is usually assigned by the computer. If the specimen is to be run in a batch process, the computer can automatically generate the worklist, including placement of the standards and controls. In situations where specimens do not arrive at the work station at the same time, it may be desirable to create a worklist manually by entering a series of SIDs into the computer. SID entry at this stage is a potential source of error. Technologists can match the patient names on the worklists and specimens as a check, but oversights can still occur. An important computer check at this stage is that ordered tests awaiting results must match the test being performed by the technologist. Otherwise, a clear error message should be generated. Some systems also provide for a check digit in the SID.

Batched, automated instruments, especially high-volume instruments, may provide for entry of the number of each specimen placed in the analyzer. Analytic results with a specimen identifier then pass directly without transcription into the computer system, matching patients with results automatically. On-line, batch-oriented analyzers not providing for specimen identification can be loaded in the order specified by a worklist and results transferred without transcription. A single test result entry mode may be more appropriate for instruments such as Coulter S series analyzers and low-volume manual procedures. In such cases, worklists are not appropriate. Specimen numbers are entered into the computer immediately before result entry. The computer then waits for the result from the instrument or technologist.

Quality control (QC), typically, is a part of most routine specimen processing, and QC samples are usually identified as such by the laboratory computer. For batched procedures, the QC samples are typically specified automatically. The control results are checked against laboratory-defined limits in real time (e.g., as the control results are generated). Daily, weekly, or monthly QC reports are subsequently printed. Systematic acceptance or rejection of the worklist batch based on QC values can be tied to Westgard rules by the computer system.[8] For unbatched laboratory processing, the Bull algorithm is one example of a real-time QC technique.[9] In this approach a running average of hematology indices for quality control is maintained and checked for variance.

Result Verification

In most computer-based laboratory information systems, entered results are initially maintained in a restricted status, available within the laboratory but not for external reporting. These restricted results can be printed on an internal report (the verification report) or displayed on a video display terminal (cathode ray tube or CRT), allowing comparison with a workbook or analyzer printout to assure correctness of the entered data. Patient values on the verification report should be clearly labeled with patient name, PIN, and specimen number. If the data are judged to be correct, the result is then "verified" or "certified" and becomes reportable outside of the laboratory.

If the verification is batch oriented (i.e., worklists are used), the computer should allow for selective verification of results. Questionable entries requiring further study are deferred until further analysis. Without this feature, reporting of the large majority of readily verifiable results will be unnecessarily delayed.

To facilitate the verification process, the verification report format should be consistent with that of the printed worksheet if one is used. Quality control results outside the acceptable range should be highlighted. In some systems, patient values associated with an aberrant control value cannot be verified unless a proper authority code is entered. Patient values that exceed predefined technical limits or the reference range may be automatically highlighted to alert the technologist to results having a higher probability of error.

In a computerized laboratory, delta checking is useful for detecting specimen identification errors. Delta checking is the process of comparing a new result to the last analyzed result for a specific test on a patient where the time duration between specimens is not beyond a prespecified limit.[10] In many current systems, delta limits can be defined as an absolute or a percentage change (Table 16-2). In most instances, delta criteria are established on the basis of local experience. If a delta criterion is exceeded, the result is held by the system until properly verified by a technologist. Too narrow a delta range will lead to many false positive alerts, whereas an overly wide range will decrease the sensitivity of the delta check process. The effectiveness of delta checking has been reviewed by Sheiner et al.[11] and Wheeler and Sheiner.[12]

Where applicable, logical checks for internal consistency can be made automatically. (Do the individual components of a leukocyte differential add to the proper total?) However, many contemporary computer systems lack the capability to associate related analyte values (e.g., the platelet count derived from an electronic counter and the platelet estimate arising from a manual leukocyte differential count).

Result verification should be a responsibility clearly delegated and restricted to a certain level of laboratory personnel. Personnel with verification authority should have a clear understanding and appreciation of the rapid and wide dissemination of results secondary to their action. Most systems routinely capture the verifier's identification number, check the individual for appropriate authority, and log the identification number and time with the completed result. Occasionally a verified result is incorrect. Because the verified result may already have been used for a clinical decision, the correction process should follow a strict and well-defined policy. Changes must be clearly identified, with both the incorrect and correct values displayed on reports.

Internal Reporting

A number of mechanisms are provided by the laboratory information system that assist the technologist directly. The worklist is central to the technologist's activity. It is the worklist that defines what work is to be done and where it is to be done, and acts as the internal record of tests performed. The worklist must include enough information to identify the specimen being assayed. When the procedures have been performed and results entered, a completed worklist can be generated that serves as a feedback mechanism to the technologist and will remain as an archival record of laboratory activity.

TABLE 16-2
EXAMPLE OF DELTA CHECK FOR MEAN CORPUSCULAR VOLUME (MCV)

Threshold value	90
High %[a]	5
Low %[b]	10

Calculation: $(|value\ 2 - value\ 1|/value\ 1) \times 100 = \%\ change$

Example of value that would be flagged:

MCV day 1 = 85 (initial value)
MCV day 2 = 68 (current value)
$(|68 - 85|/85) \times 100 = 20\%$ (i.e., $> 10\%$[b])

[a]Change allowed if current value $>$ threshold value.
[b]Change allowed if current value $<$ threshold value.

Closely associated with worklist recording is quality control recording. Quality control is a mandatory activity in the clinical laboratory. The raw QC data are of little value if they are not kept up to date. Controls can be monitored using a number of techniques, including Levey-Jennings graphs, cumulative sum plots, and so on. The Westgard multirule technique has been employed by some to systematize performance control rules.[8] Whatever methods are used, the results must be tabulated, analyzed, corrective action taken if required, and decisions documented. Monthly reports should list the calculated mean, standard deviation, and coefficient of variation (CV) for each control along with the expected statistical parameters.

Laboratory information systems can also monitor laboratory trends through the use of population statistics. Moving averages of patient values, such as the Bull algorithm,[9] can be used as an adjunct to quality control. They may also provide the only way to detect trends in derived values, such as the ion gap. Population monitoring is especially important in microbiology, where trends in antibiotic susceptibility may indicate a change in the antibiogram of an organism. This information becomes essential to clinicians in the early treatment of infections.

Pending and overdue test reports serve to ensure that all work is completed in a timely fashion. The pending report lists all tests that have not been completed. This report can be generated for any specified time period and can include tests just ordered but not yet performed. The overdue test report is a modified pending report in that it notes only results not entered that have exceeded a laboratory-defined reasonable time period since order entry.

The computer can further support the professional staff by tabulating work load statistics. The system should automatically capture work load for patient results and quality control results. However, additional work load resulting from standards, repeats, and dilutions must be entered separately. Work load data must be associated by test, method, and shift. College of American Pathologists (CAP) work load units can then be used to calculate the weighted work load. This information then serves to assist in the evaluation of and adjustment to work load pressures.

External Reporting

Once a laboratory result is verified, it becomes available for reporting outside the laboratory in many forms and for many purposes. The primary purpose of external reporting is to communicate laboratory results to a physician who has requested the analysis. Other reporting tasks include documentation and production of a semipermanent record of patient results. Whether the report's purpose relates to clinical communication, documentation, or archival storage, the report must be legible, timely, accurate, usable, and comprehensible. What makes a report complete and usable for one reporting purpose may not be appropriate for another purpose. For instance, the name of a reference laboratory clutters the report and impairs its readability by clinicians, even though it is required for documentation purposes. Thus when designing or assessing the effectiveness of a report, its purpose should be clearly stated. If the report is multifunctional, the objectives and means of achieving them should be compatible and complementary.

Even if a report is meant primarily for clinical communication, its form may be quite different depending on its intended use. In terms of reporting immediacy, three levels can be identified. An immediate report (i.e., a "stat" report) usually relates to a single laboratory procedure and is often printed automatically in certain patient care areas (e.g., a blood gas result in an intensive care unit). An interim report summarizes all the results so far derived within a particular time period (e.g., since the last cumulative chart report) for each patient associated with a particular nursing unit, subspecialty clinic, or other location. Delivery of the interim report should be dependable and on a schedule that is consistent with clinical needs. Finally, a cumulative chart report may be generated on a daily or less frequent schedule. This report serves to combine results from many days in a format suitable for insertion in the permanent medical record. Clearly, the reporting format will be different if each level of reporting immediacy is to be met in a most effective manner.

The optimal report format also depends on the decision task being supported. The reporting format related to clinical monitoring and follow-up may be quite different from that used for diagnostic decision making. For instance, tests used for monitoring may be more effectively reported using graphic time-trend representations[13] rather than a conventional tabular format. Tests being used primarily for diagnosis may be conveyed more effectively with an interpretation.[14,15] Interpretive reports communicate the test result and its meaning. If the interpretation is appropriate, quality assurance is promoted through better use of the laboratory. Although interpretive reporting remains controversial,[14] there is a growing acceptance among clinicians in primary care.[16]

The nature of some results poses special reporting challenges if the information is to be communicated effectively. Lupovitch has dealt with the many unique issues related to microbiology reporting.[17] Similarly, Salway has presented the communication of drug interference information.[18]

In spite of the importance of the clinical laboratory report, few studies relate to what constitutes a good and effective report.[19] A report issued more than a decade ago by the Standards Subcommittee on Medical Usefulness Criteria Task Force on Reporting Laboratory Data spoke to the principles of effective clinical communication. These principles are still very pertinent to today's practice:

1 Compactness
2 Consistency of terminology, format, and usage of symbols and abbreviations
3 Clear understandability
4 Logical and accessible location in medical chart
5 Statement of date and time of collection
6 Gross description and source of specimen where pertinent
7 Sharp differentiation of normal and abnormal values
8 Sequential order of multiple results on single specimen
9 Identification of patient, patient location and physician
10 Assurance of accuracy of transcription of request
11 Ease of preparation
12 Administrative and record-keeping value

The subcommittee report concluded that there is no one "best method" for communicating laboratory test results, but reporting effectiveness may be improved by following a few general principles. Wilding also acknowledged that there is little likelihood for a uniform approach to reporting in the clinical laboratory in the near future.[21] He found that much of the variability of reporting techniques was influenced by the nature of the laboratory, the population served, and the data processing resources available. Table 16-3 indicates Wilding's prescription for essential information. Ten years later this list is still relevant. Wilding's inclusion of laboratory accession number in a physician's report might be questioned, because it is not of interest to the clinician in making decisions. In this case the multiple purposes of the report may be in conflict. Although the accession number may be needed for documentation purposes within the laboratory, such information on the clinician's report can be unnecessary clutter. The physician rarely needs such information, and the laboratory should have alternative ways of obtaining it (e.g., the laboratory-oriented summary report of all work done on a particular day).

Bold strongly stressed the "urgent need for standardization of report formats" and called for reports that included guidance on abnormal values, a cumulative format that better integrated the time course relationship of tests, and a realistic statement regarding analytical variability.[22] Grams also called for reports that better conveyed analytic variability and reference ranges and, where appropriate, employed multivariate analysis.[23] However, a sample report indicated the challenges in designing a report of this complexity that retains characteristics of clarity and readability. Korpman has discussed some of the weaknesses of conventional cumulative reporting techniques and how they may work against achieving clinically relevant goals of reporting timeliness.[24]

Supplementing the printed media as a means of result reporting are the CRT and the telephone. Even though increasing attention is being given to the design of CRT screens that promote communication, most current guidelines are rooted in common sense and experience rather than theory.[25] Reporting via CRT raises special problems regarding patient privacy (see next section).

The telephone represents another medium for laboratory reporting rarely dealt with in a formal fashion. Verbal reports often greatly facilitate rapid reporting, especially in emergency situations. At the same time, they represent a major potential source of errors.[26] The laboratory staff answering telephone requests must be well trained and recognize the importance of potential sources of errors. Callers should state their name

TABLE 16-3
ESSENTIAL INFORMATION FOR LABORATORY REPORTING

1. Name and address of laboratory
2. Patient identification: name with middle initial; date of birth; address, clinic, or nursing unit
3. Specimen identification: date and time of collection; laboratory accession number
4. Doctor identification: name; address (if a referred specimen)
5. Test information: test name or meaningful abbreviation; units; reference values; date of analysis
6. Relevant clinical details

and role, then provide the patient's name, identification number, and location, along with the test results of interest. The encounter very well might be logged by laboratory personnel to help identify potential problem areas.

Complaints regarding external reporting should be documented when they arise and sufficient information collected to allow investigation and classification of problems. Such a list may be useful in focusing quality assurance activities. Management control systems directed at decreasing missing reports have been described by Bloch[27] and Friedman.[28] Automatic monitoring of specimen receipt to report time (i.e., turnaround time) can provide a convenient metric for monitoring the timeliness of laboratory processing.[29]

Aside from the general principles and guidelines described earlier, there is little explicit information today that specifically defines effective laboratory-to-physician communication.[26] Recognizing the diversity in laboratory settings, clinicians, hospitals, and patient populations, this lack of standardization may be appropriate and even beneficial. This diversity of reporting and lack of specific standards should not stymie those interested in promoting quality assurance in results reporting. Site-specific problems should still be identified, and these problems should determine changes needed rather than misdirecting efforts toward the pursuit of standards. With external forces now encouraging more homogeneity across laboratories and a growing understanding of the medical problem-solving process, standardization of laboratory reporting may increase in the future.

QUALITY ASSURANCE AND THE INFORMATION PROCESSING RESOURCE

Key elements to the operation of any information system are the personnel and the associated computer resources. It is, therefore, essential that quality assurance controls are implemented for the administration of these two resources. These controls should include those designed to prevent errors, detect problems, report this activity, document corrective actions, and recover from the errors. Careful attention to system integrity and security issues will improve the overall quality of the laboratory's information processing effort. But with this enhanced performance, the computer also brings about special challenges, one of these being assuring the privacy of patient information.

Error Management

Errors will occur in the entry of data into any computer system. In fact, the unrealistic assumption that errors will not occur may lead to major operational difficulties. Recognizing that errors will occur means that error management methods should be developed and put in place to promote quality assurance of laboratory information flow. Four components of error management are considered here: (1) minimizing human data entry errors; (2) detecting systematic errors resulting from programming and other computer errors; (3) developing monitoring systems for errors of any type; and (4) forming policies designed to reduce and detect errors.

Data Entry Errors In a stress-free environment, it is estimated that the raw error rate for data transcriptions is 3 percent.[4] Grannis reported an error rate of 3.5 percent of all specimens processed in a clinical chemistry laboratory.[1] The first premise in reducing the error rate is early detection of errors, because the correction of an error becomes more involved the further it is propagated in the information cycle. Most computer systems provide edit or validity checks on data at entry time. For example, result values for a laboratory test might have both credibility checks and abnormal checks (see previous section).

A second method of reducing error is simply to reduce or eliminate the need for some data entry. Instrument interfaces to a laboratory computer greatly reduce manual data entry. Similarly, computer-computer interlinks also reduce the possibility of entry error, especially in areas such as the exchange of demographic data.

Once the data have been entered into the computer, certain monitoring of reports may help in the detection of errors. Delta check reports of patient results may identify mislabeled specimens. The examination of randomly selected patient reports frequently uncovers inconsistencies suggesting problems. Although these secondary methods of identifying errors are less effective than the first two techniques, they still may uncover a significant number of errors.

Computer Errors The entry of data may not be the only source of invalid data. Programming errors may corrupt correctly entered data. Quality assurance in data processing has only recently been recognized as an important area.[5,30] Traditionally program and system testing have been informal activities. Conventionally, programs undergo alpha testing (in the developer's environment) followed by beta testing (by an early user). Frequently, some errors escape both levels and fall into the general user community. It is not unusual for errors to be so extensive that packages require complete rewriting at this stage. Fortunately, most programming errors do not affect the integrity of the stored data. However, it is most important for the user to maintain a high index of suspicion when using new or recently modified software.

The single most difficult problem in eliminating programming errors involves problems that are a consequence of the interaction of multiple events. Usually such errors occur with such low frequency that the specific problem is difficult to identify. Such errors may actually remain characteristic of computer systems for many years. Systematic search and elimination of such chance errors may be so expensive or difficult that it is prohibitive.

Although less likely, hardware problems can also corrupt data in a manner that is difficult to detect and correct. Some hardware failures mimic software errors. Periodic hardware integrity checks during preventive maintenance may identify some problems.

Preventive Monitoring No single technique will detect all of the errors just mentioned. The two most important factors in maintaining reliable and valid data remain a high index of suspicion by computer users and thorough understanding of the data collection and storage process, including potential problem areas. One method is to examine the data for consistency. For example, by sorting and printing the patient name file, duplicated patient names are readily found. Data associated with erroneous patient numbers can then either be deleted from the system or merged with the data stored under the correct patient number.

Other techniques for verifying computer data integrity include a periodic sampling of patient specimens, observing their progress through the system with a manual audit trail. Similar techniques may be used with controls using dummy patients. Simple examinations of patient reports can also uncover errors. Review of cumulative reports may uncover missing results, inappropriate comments, and results incompatible with physiological variation. Appropriately established delta checking can provide similar information.

Error Policies Most error policies are directed toward reducing the incidence of errors or detecting and correcting errors. Unfortunately, the two goals may have opposing effects. An excessively punitive policy for errors may result in the reluctance of technologists to detect and correct errors. Error prevention, detection, and correction policies should be problem oriented. The emphasis should be placed on resolving the nature of the problem rather than on assigning blame.

System Integrity and Security

The design of the computer room is important to the integrity of the system. All electrical power serving the computer and data communication equipment should be protected from fluctuating electrical loads by using isolation devices. For automatic fire suppression, a system using a dry contact halogenated agent should be considered. If overhead water sprinklers are required by the building code, they should be a dry waterpipe type, charged by the first activation of a fire alarm and released by the fire itself. Adequate air conditioning is essential for the maintenance of temperature and humidity. If possible, it is best to have two air conditioning units sharing the load, allowing at least limited operation if one should fail. Temperature and humidity charts should be maintained, reviewed, and, with any corrective action taken, recorded. Smoking and eating should be prohibited in computer access areas to prevent potential damage to equipment.

Disaster planning is an absolute necessity. Over the course of time the laboratory will come to be dependent on the operation of the computer system. Short lapses in system support, such as those associated with preventive maintenance, can usually be tolerated with a minimum of inconvenience. However, prolonged, unscheduled computer failures will result in excessive stress for the laboratory, patient care areas, and administration (e.g., billing). It is essential that the laboratory have a well-organized manual backup system that will allow laboratory operations to continue during computer failure. Once the computer is again functional, it should facilitate entry of work received or completed during the failure.

Safeguards are necessary to ensure the adequate recovery and restart of the computer system after failures that may have corrupted programs or data stored on disks. Backup copies of all programs and static files should be maintained either on magnetic tape or disks. Daily, all active files should be copied to disk or tape. Weekly, a set of these backup copies should be stored in a location removed from the computer room.

Some computer systems maintain a transaction log containing all data inputs and modifications. This transaction log allows for recovery of all activities that occur between backup procedures.

Just as laboratory technologists keep worklists and other records to track work, computer operators should be required to maintain a log of their activity on the system. Examples include system backup information, report print times, system errors, and associated remedial actions. System logs must be reviewed on a periodic basis to evaluate conformance to schedules, errors and actions taken, security violations, and so on.

For laboratories that do local program development, there should be standing policies that specify software support responsibility and processes. Such policies are important for a growing number of laboratories as software support of microcomputers becomes an important issue. Frequently, locally developed software is written without adequate consideration to long-term support. Programming policies should address issues such as (1) documentation (both user and program), (2) program testing and verification, (3) software and hardware maintenance, (4) backup of data, and (5) security of data. Documentation should cover basic information about the program purpose and its overall use. Program documentation should be available for future program support, either in the form of extensive comments in the program or separate flowcharts and outlines. The need to test programs is obvious. Extensive work has been made in this area for systematic checking of programs. At the very least, testing must be sufficient to make errors unlikely. Program maintenance should be directed to correcting errors as needed. Programs should be sufficiently protected as to prevent inadvertent changes in the program during use. Backup of patient data and programs should be sufficient to make recovery of data and programs possible. This might be as simple as maintaining printed listings for short programs. Usually duplicate disks of programs and data should be maintained.

Computer security involves technological and procedural safeguards for computer hardware, software, and data. Privacy relates to the protection of data from unauthorized access or alteration.[31] Employee cooperation and commitment are vital to the success of any security plan. Clearly stated policies can promote supportive employee attitudes and actions. Basic system security usually involves the use of passwords for personnel and lockwords for files to protect unauthorized access and modification. The system should limit each user to the type of transactions that are authorized for that individual. Only a limited number of illegal password entry attempts should be allowed before the terminal is disabled.

The most vulnerable part of many computer systems lies in the dial-in telephone access ports. Although complex and expensive, security devices are available to limit such access to authorized personnel. These devices can fail if they are shared by many users. The convenience and flexibility of using telephone access must be balanced by the resulting increased vulnerability to unauthorized use.

Privacy of Patient Information

Those involved in medical care have traditionally sought to protect the patient's right to privacy. This need for confidentiality mandates that the laboratory information system is constructed with safeguards limiting access to the patient's laboratory results. The accessibility of the patient chart cannot be used as a model for computer-based records. In particular, placing a terminal in a nursing station without other safeguards is generally considered insufficient even though that may be the level of security currently provided the patient chart. In this setting the greatest benefit associated with computers, the rapid and widespread dissemination of information, becomes its largest liability. For example, the results of a pregnancy test may be known widely by hospital employees long before they are known by family members. The potential publicity of computer-based information for celebrities poses an even more serious privacy problem. Some institutions handle VIP data outside of computers; others use pseudonyms. Today's computer system's are insufficient to discourage inappropriate use of patient data because of the difficulty in defining appropriate use and the complexity of implementing such security systems.

Computer security and information privacy are issues of growing concern because of rapid technologic advances that have enabled large masses of data to be economically obtained and stored and readily transferred. The development of large databases by health insurance companies is one such example and poses difficult choices in balancing the benefits of data availability against the right to personal information privacy. To deter inappropriate data aggregations, the Privacy Act of 1974 discouraged the use of the Social Security number in personal databases. Overviews of current approaches to security and privacy issues in the health-care setting can be found in Korpman,[32] Waters and Murphy,[33] Worthley,[34] Covvey et al.,[35] and Thompson and Handelman.[36]

REFERENCES

1 Grannis GF, Grumer H-D, Lott JA, et al: Proficiency evaluation of clinical chemistry laboratories. *Clin Chem* 1972, 18:222.
2 Kaplan KO, Hopkins JM: *QA Guide: A Resource for Hospital Quality Assurance.* Chicago, Joint Commission on Accreditation of Hospitals, 1980.
3 Roberts JS, Walczak RM: Toward effective quality assurance: The evolution and current status of the JCAH QA standard. *QRB* 1984, 10:11.
4 Lincoln TL, Korpman RA: Computers, health care, and medical information science. *Science* 1980, 210:257.
5 Keller AE: Quality assurance in DP. *Infosystems* 1985, 3:28.
6 Anthony RN, Herzlinger RE: *Management Control in Nonprofit Organizations.* Homewood, IL, Richard D. Irwin, 1980.
7 Eilers RJ: Quality assurance in health care: Missions, goals, activities. *Clin Chem* 1975, 21:1357.
8 Westgard JO, Barry PL, Hunt M, Groth T: A multi-rule Shewhart chart for quality control in clinical chemistry. *Clin Chem* 1981, 27:493.
9 Bull BS, Korpman RA: Autocalibration of hematology analyzers. *J Clin Lab Auto* 1983, 3:111.
10 Nosanchuk JS, Gottman AW: CMS and delta checks: A systematic approach to quality control. *Am J Clin Pathol* 1975, 62:701.
11 Sheiner LB, Wheeler LA, Moore JK: The performance of delta check methods. *Clin Chem* 1979, 25:2034.

12. Wheeler LA, Sheiner LB: A clinical evaluation of various delta check methods. *Clin Chem* 1981, 27:5.
13. Connelly DP, Lasky LC, Keller RMI, et al: A system for graphical display of clinical laboratory data. *Am J Clin Pathol* 1982, 78:729.
14. Speicher CE, Smith JW: Interpretive reporting. *Clin Lab Med* 1984, 4:41.
15. Aller RD: Interpretive reporting. *Clin Lab Med* 1983, 3:205.
16. Speicher CE, Smith JW: Interpretive reporting in clinical pathology. *JAMA* 1980, 243:1556.
17. Lupovitch A, Menninger JJ, Corr RM: Manual and computerized cumulative reporting systems for the clinical microbiology laboratory. *Am J Clin Pathol* 1979, 72:841.
18. Salway JG: Drug interference causing misinterpretation of laboratory results. *Ann Clin Biochem* 1978, 15:44.
19. Gabrieli ER (ed): *Clinically Oriented Documentation of Laboratory Data.* New York, Academic Press, 1972.
20. Burns EL, Hanson DJ, Schoen I, et al: Communication of laboratory data to the clinician. *Am J Clin Pathol* 1974, 61:900.
21. Wilding P: Presentation of results. *Ann Biol Clin* 1975, 33:182.
22. Bold AM: Clinical chemistry reporting. Problems and proposals. *Lancet* 1976, 1:951.
23. Grams RR: A proposal for laboratory data reporting. *J Med Sys* 1979, 3:193.
24. Korpman RA: Laboratory computerization. A new analysis of work flow and reporting. *Clin Lab Med* 1983, 3:79.
25. Shneiderman B: Human factors experiments in designing interactive systems. *Computer* 1979, 12:9–10.
26. Chou D, McLendon WW: Information management, in Henry JB (ed): *Clinical Diagnosis and Management by Laboratory Methods,* ed 17. Philadelphia, WB Saunders, 1984.
27. Bloch DM: The laboratory computer as a management tool. *Clin Lab Med* 1983, 3:149.
28. Friedman BA: A technique for monitoring the placement of computer-generated laboratory reports in patients' medical records, in *Seventh Annual Symposium on Computer Applications in Medical Care,* New York, IEEE, 1983, p 241.
29. Bloch DM: Computer-generated management tools for the clinical pathology laboratory. 1. Throughput report. *J Med Sys* 1980, 4:367.
30. Basili VR, Perricone BT: Software errors and complexity: An empirical investigation. *Commun ACM* 1984, 27:42.
31. Dalal JR: Security, in Hannan J (ed): *Data Processing Management.* Pennsauken, NJ, Auerbach, 1982.
32. Korpman RA: System reliability—Assurance of quality and security. *Clin Lab Med* 1983, 3:165.
33. Waters KA, Murphy GF: *Systems Analysis and Computer Applications in Health Information Management.* Rockville, MD, Aspen Systems Corporation, 1983.
34. Worthley JA: *Managing Computers in Health Care.* Ann Arbor, MI, AUPHA Press, 1982.
35. Covvey HD, Craven NH, McAlister NH: *Concepts and Issues in Health Care Computing,* vol 1. St. Louis, CV Mosby, 1985.
36. Thompson G, Handelman I: *Health Data and Information Management.* Boston, Butterworths, 1978.

CHAPTER 17

FUTURE TRENDS IN LABORATORY QUALITY ASSURANCE

Peter J. Howanitz, M.D.
Joan H. Howanitz, M.D.

The practice of pathology has changed remarkably in the past 5 years. Recent major reforms in Medicare regulations have introduced fundamental changes in incentives for patients, physicians, hospitals, and laboratories. These changes continue to evolve. Currently, it appears that many more changes will occur, at least in payment for physicians' and laboratories' services and to hospitals. What is certain is payment will not be as open-ended as it was in the past, because the public is demanding restraint in government spending and third-party payers are seeking to reduce costs.

What will be the impact of the new Medicare physician payment system and other cost-saving measures on the price and quality of patient care, patient access to services, and finally on laboratory quality and usage? What will be the regulatory role of the government in the future, when federal programs are eliminated or curtailed by fiscal cutbacks? For laboratories, pressures to contain costs will probably continue as the major impetus to change. In this atmosphere of fiscal constraint, the predicament laboratorians face is whether or not quality can be maintained.

Approximately 6,200,000 million laboratory tests are performed each year, amounting to $11 billion in payments. Laboratory testing has continued to grow by 10–15 percent per year since the early 1950s.[1] This increase in testing is due to the greater number of patients, the increased use of laboratory tests per patient, and the introduction of new tests. Tests are now performed at three sites: hospital laboratories, independent (reference or commercial) laboratories, and physician office laboratories. At least at the present time, it is the physician responsible for the patient's care who determines which and how many tests will be performed. Whether financial considerations will eventually erode this well-established practice remains to be seen. This could occur because the tests may be ordered, not because of the patient's needs, but simply for such reasons as the physician's convenience, curiosity, or benefit.

The majority of tests are still performed in hospital laboratories, but 30 percent are performed in independent laboratories, and approximately 15 percent are performed in the physician's office. It is the percentage of tests performed in the physician's office that is increasing most rapidly today. Recently manufacturers have aimed their technology at a new market, the home, and are producing simple instruments and convenient test kits for the patient to use. (These tests are usually ordered by physician's prescription.) Costs of the first and most widely used instrument with accompanying reagents, the home glucose reflectance meter, are reimbursed under current Medicare legislation. In the past, responsibility for quality assurance has been shared among government, the health profession, manufacturers of instruments and reagents, and other professionals. With the changes that have occurred, the role of manufacturers in quality assurance is expanding—especially in the physician's office, where manufacturers have a major role, and in home testing, where they have the dominant role.

The next few years appear filled with challenges. The application of quality assurance practices developed over the past 30 years will become even more important as we try to preserve quality and lower costs. With the introduction of laboratory procedures into settings where they have not previously been performed, and the increased range of procedures in other areas where laboratory professionals are found in relatively low numbers, the need for monitoring achievement of analytic goals, ascertaining acceptability of patient data, identifying unsatisfactorily analytic performance, and allowing for interlaboratory comparison of bias and imprecision will become even more important. The future will require redefinition and reassignment of the responsibilities for quality assurance among government, the professional medical community, and the health care product manufacturers.

PREANALYTIC VARIABLES

Some of the most important influences on laboratory results are changes which occur in specimen values prior to analyte quantitation. Information on intra- and interindividual variability, effect of specimen source, and changes in analyte values during specimen collection, transport, and processing is meager. Studies to obtain meaningful information have been arduous in design and implementation. Especially difficult is measurement of preanalytic change and assessment of laboratory performance in minimizing preanalytic variability by using methods similar to standard practices of laboratory quality control. With increases in physician office testing and immediate quantitation of analyte values in whole blood, changes owing to specimen processing, storage, and transport will be reduced.

Based on convenience and ease of use, the ideal specimen will no longer be serum obtained from a venipuncture in the antecubital fossa, but whole blood obtained from a skin puncture (finger prick). From extensive comparative data it is common knowledge that serum values are approximately 10–15 percent higher than whole blood values, but this approximation is influenced by hematocrit. Very little information is available comparing whole-blood skin puncture (finger-prick) specimens with whole-blood venous specimens. Such studies as those of Larsson-Cohn indicate that finger-prick whole-blood glucose values are higher than those of venous whole-blood glucose specimens, and that the magnitude of this difference may be up to twofold.[2] Limited information is available describing differences in analyte concentrations between venous specimen and specimens obtained from finger pricks, except in newborns.[3] Studies such as these indicate that the differences in sources and types of specimens will probably result in large differences between analyte values measured in clinical laboratories and physician office laboratories.

QUALITY CONTROL

Materials and Programs

Earlier, materials used for quality control procedures were derived from fresh human sera. After requested measurements were performed, excess specimen was pooled, aliquoted, and stored frozen until used for quality control.[4] Analyte performance was assessed by measuring an aliquot of these specimens in each assay and comparing results. With the development of regional (interlaboratory) quality control programs in the 1960s and the need for large amounts of control sera, the use of commercial lyophilized reagents for daily quality control became standard practice. Data indicating analyte instability in human serum matrix led to development of reagents with extended stability using a matrix of ethylene glycol.[5] Although more convenient because reconstitution is not necessary, these reagents are extremely viscous. Viscosity higher than that of human sera precluded use for instruments with narrow-bore pipetting tips, for instruments using dry reagent strips, and for those with organic liquid in the pipette apparatus. Recent instrument developments have emphasized smaller sample requirements and increased use of dry chemistry strip reagents; both these trends make current liquid control materials less desirable. A "second generation" liquid quality control material, offering advantages not currently available, should be introduced in the next few years.

The first materials used for quality control by Levey and Jennings were of human origin.[4] During the past 30 years, other matrices from bovine, equine, and porcine sources also have been used because of inexpensiveness when compared with human material. Routinely, human-based reagents are supplemented with materials from animal and plant sources. For example, supplementation of enzymes is usually from a variety of nonhuman sources. Because most commonly measured human serum enzymes have isoenzymes which change in proportion with health and disease, it is difficult, if not impossible, to simulate patient specimens exactly. In practice, only a few instances of differing reactivity between human and nonhuman enzymes and other serum constituents have been reported. (See Chapters 5 and 8.) These differences are not great, or can be minimized by method improvement or by prudent selection of the supplementing source. Although purists continue to support use of control material in a human matrix, measured differences between human and nonhuman material appear to be as great as the variables introduced by material used for analyte supplementation. It is now common practice to test sera used for quality control pools for hepatitis B surface antigen; if positive donor units are found, they are excluded. Recently, quality control reagents in use by laboratories have been tested for antibody to HTLV-III, and a large percentage of pools were antibody-reactive.[6] In the future, all human donor sera units will be tested prior to pooling by the manufacturers and, if reactive, will be discarded, thereby increasing quality control reagent cost. The prohibitive cost of human-based control materials is responsible for widespread continuing increase in use of nonhuman material.

The size of lyophylizers has limited production of larger quality control pools for interlaboratory comparisons. In addition, the investment necessary for producing these pools is a factor: the larger the pool, the more capital is tied up during the life of the pool, and the greater the risk of financial loss if a problem arises with the pool. If a large pool is produced, advantages to the user include a larger database and a more useful interlaboratory comparison. With introduction of instruments requiring smaller specimen and reagent volumes, thereby requiring smaller quality control samples, manufacturers will be able to increase the number of participants without increasing the size of the pool and, hence, their financial risk. As the volumes of quality control materials needed by laboratories decrease, no longer will current economies of scale continue. Hence, resulting price increases may occur, causing quality control reagent costs, expressed in terms of cost per milliliter of reagent, to increase. Because less reagent will be used, overall laboratory reagent costs probably will continue to decrease as they have for the past 5 years.[7]

Criteria for Assessing Control Results

Participant data from interlaboratory quality control programs indicate a small yearly increase in participation. This increase, expressed as an increased number of files (analytes), has occurred because many laboratories continue to increase services, especially in areas of hormone assay and therapeutic drug monitoring. In contrast, a small number of laboratories have withdrawn participation from interlaboratory comparisons, so that fewer laboratories now participate in these programs. This decrease occurred, in part, because laboratories have consolidated testing due to changes in prospective payment; some laboratories have computerized and now perform their own intermethod comparisons; and, finally, some laboratories simply can no longer afford the cost of interlaboratory comparisons. For the next few years, small increases of data in interlaboratory databases will probably continue.

New technologies, mainly in remote locations, require use of whole-blood measurements. Examples of such instruments include whole-blood glucose analyzers, whole-blood electrolyte analyzers, and instruments with a wide test mix, such as the Boehinger-Mannheim Reflotron and the Abbott Vision. Currently there are no widely available commercial whole-blood controls for whole-blood chemistry analyzers. Quality control practices make it imperative that use of materials which mimic human whole-blood specimens be developed and used.

Changes in criteria for run rejection and acceptance have been the most important development in quality control during the past 10 years. Whereas most laboratories currently use criteria which are ± 2 standard deviations (SD) about the mean for acceptability of results, alternatives shown in Table 17-1 have been advocated. Limits derived from a population of patient specimens measured in the course of a day (av-

TABLE 17-1
PROPOSED QUALITY CONTROL RUN REJECTION PROCEDURES

Criteria	Use	Comment
A Control sample		
Statistical		
1 ± 3SD	Rarely	First limits recommended
2 ± 2SD	Most labs	Easy to implement
3 ± 2.5SD	Recently recommended	Easy to implement
4 Shewhart Multirule	Common	Requires computer
5 CUSUM	Rarely	Trend analysis
6 Triggs' technique	Rarely	Trend analysis
7 Other multirule schemes	Rarely	Requires computer
B Patient specimen		
1 Bull's algorithm	Widely	Used in hematology only
2 Koepke's algorithm	Rarely	Modified Bull's algorithm
3 Average of normals	Not used in chemistry	Impractical
C Other		
1 CAP modified	Widely	Easy to implement
2 Medical usefulness	Rarely	Requires computer

erage of normals) have received attention for chemistry quality control mainly because of inexpensiveness and apparent ease of implementation; they are widely used and of proven value in hematology. When studied for chemistry, these limits have proven impractical, because the number of specimens needed for statistically significant data is exceedingly large; these techniques have limited power for error detection based on population demographics; or the specimens that hospital laboratories have been sent reflect widely changing daily ambulatory populations, most of which are seriously ill with a variety of diseases.[8] In the future, more complex algorithms will be introduced with improved power of error detection and decreased false run rejections than those currently used.[9-11]

General laboratory practice has been to use quality control rules which express run acceptance and rejection statistically, or about a mean. This approach was useful initially when laboratory performance was relatively poor; however, with improvement in precision, data were accumulated that indicated laboratory analytic[1] performance, for most analytes measured, far outstripped medical need. To provide for laboratory results which fulfill medical need, medical usefulness criteria were suggested and implemented for run acceptance and rejection. If the data indicated that laboratory analytical performance was suboptimal for patient care, then tight statistical limits were recommended. If laboratory performance exceeded medical needs, then limits for medical use were recommended, and laboratory results withheld only if quality control values exceeded these limits. If quality control results exceeded statistical limits but were within medical usefulness limits, a warning signal occurred.[12] Such an approach—using limits in terms of patient needs—holds great promise for the future, but data documenting these limits are sparse and will take years to develop.

COMPUTERIZATION OF LABORATORY PROCEDURES AND RESULTS

Large mainframe computers have been used in clinical laboratories for many years, but quality control applications on these instruments, for the most part, have been rudimentary. In contrast, the use of microcomputers has become widespread, and, beginning in 1982, microcomputer-based quality control programs were implemented in clinical laboratories, usually to apply Shewhart Multirule schemes. Initially, Apple II Plus, Tandy Model 3, and Commodore PET hardware was used; recently, almost all more advanced versions use IBM PC hardware (see Table 17-2). Table 17-3 shows features of the most widely used systems.[13] In addition to the Shewhart rules, software enhancements including CUSUM statistics, Trigg's Trend Analysis, preventive maintenance, and telecommunications have been added in successive releases. A detailed list of features and characteristics has recently been developed.[14] Future developments appear clear: software is being introduced for large mainframe computers identical to that available on microcomputers, including run rejection criteria such as Shewhart Multirules, Trigg's Trend Analysis, and CUSUM techniques. One major problem with a stand-alone microcomputer-based quality control system is that access for data entry and manipulation is limited by competition with laboratory technologists from other work stations for the dedicated instrument. With networking of microcomputers, complex statistical quality control applications will become more available to technologists and thereby will be more useful for laboratories.

Laboratory analyzers continue to become more heavily computerized, and this trend will require addition of quality control software, either as part of the instrument or in the form of an attached microcomputer. Signaling the operator of acceptability of the result to preprogrammed limits will allow quality control decisions to be made at the time of the measurement. The incorporation of an analyte- as well as level-dependent run acceptance or rejection will be automated and individualized for each analyte throughout laboratories by this method.

Computerization will make intralaboratory statistical data manipulation instantaneously available for interlaboratory comparisons. Data manipulation for interlaboratory programs will be done more frequently than monthly, offering laboratories use of data from a new pool at the time of initiation, or for troubleshooting.

Perhaps the most widely used computerized patient value control system is the delta check. Selection of appropriate preset limits is critical: too small a value may yield too many false positive results for technologists to validate, while too wide a value will miss many errors. As yet, there is no extensive recommendation; the largest includes only 12 analytes.[15] A comprehensive list of recommendations should be forthcoming shortly.

TABLE 17-2
QUALITY CONTROL MICROCOMPUTER PROGRAMS

Program	Supplier	Computer system	Data storage
ACLAIM-QAP	American Dade Division of American Hospital Supply Corporation	Apple IIe IBM PC-XT IBM PC	Floppy disk Hard disk Floppy disk
LabTrak QC-2	Fisher Scientific	Commodore 8032 IBM PC-XT	Floppy disk Hard disk
QAS Today	College of American Pathologists	IBM PC-XT IBM PC Apple IIe Kaypro Televideo	Hard disk Floppy disk Floppy disk Floppy disk Floppy disk
RealTime	Beckman Instruments	AT&T Tandy 3 or 4	Floppy disk
STAT/SCAN	Hyland-Worthington Diagnostics Cooper Biomedical Group	Apple IIe	Floppy disk

TABLE 17-3
MICROCOMPUTER PROGRAM FEATURES

Feature	ACLAIM-QAP	LabTrak QC-2	QAS Today	RealTime	STAT/SCAN
Data volume					
Number of control levels	3	6	4	3	3
Data entry					
Single point entry	Yes	Yes	Yes	Yes	Yes
Batch entry	Yes	Yes	Yes	Yes	No
Panel definition	No	Yes	Yes	Yes	No
Statistics					
Levey-Jennings charts	Yes	Yes	Yes	Yes	Yes
Mean, SD (month-to-date)	Yes	Yes	Yes	Yes	Yes
Mean, SD (lot-to-date)	Yes	Yes	Yes	Yes	No*
Shewhart Multirules	Yes	Yes	Yes	Yes	Yes
CUSUM	No	Yes	No	No	Yes
Trigg's trend analysis	No	Yes	No	Yes	Yes
Calibration check	No	No	No	Yes	No
Mean check across	No	No	Yes	No	No
Change of lot number routine	Yes	No	Yes	Yes	No
Telecommunications (Use of modem)	Yes	No	Yes	No	No
Training and assistance					
Complete user's manual	Yes	Yes	Yes	Yes	Yes
Training sessions	Yes	Yes	No	Yes	No
Program help screens	Yes	Yes	No	Yes	No
1-800-assistance number	Yes	Yes	Yes	Yes	Yes

*Modified from Stewart and Oxford, 1985.

PROFICIENCY TESTING

The past 20 years have seen the growth of proficiency programs operated by professional societies (for additional details, see Chapter 14). In contrast, federal government programs have not expanded as dramatically, but in the current era of cost containment, we will continue to see federal government involvement in daily workings of proficiency testing programs. The character of this involvement will probably change; the federal government will no longer directly operate such programs, but will develop mechanisms to track and statistically evaluate laboratory performance based on data from the proficiency programs of professional societies and other groups. Such monitoring will probably be performed by the Centers for Disease Control (CDC), following installation, programming, and implementation of their large mainframe computer. This Clinical Laboratory Information, Profile, and Reporting System (CLIPARS) will establish the CDC as the monitor of performance in areas not only of proficiency testing but also personnel evaluation, daily quality control, and demographic laboratory data. The former CDC role in operating a variety of proficiency surveys will be absorbed by other groups with similar programs. In 1985, only a few states sponsor proficiency programs for clinical laboratories; cost containment measures will restrict more states from developing such programs.

The relative importance of five variables on proficiency test performance in six specialty areas has been examined.[16] Previous history of adverse regulatory actions, length of participating in the CLIA program, and quality control deficiencies documented on inspections were all unrelated to proficiency performance. These authors also caution drawing conclusions pertinent to current laboratory proficiency performance from their work because their study data were generated 7 years prior to publication and were derived from modes, policies, and standards no longer in use. Great interest in defining determinants of proficiency testing performance has been expressed by many groups. In the next few years, data on current performance will be forthcoming.

Currently, there is no minimum standard as to the number of analytes included in a survey sample (or so-called challenge). Although programs which fulfill CLIA requirements are generally more rigorous than those of Medicare, the number and type (below, at, or above the reference interval) of challenges is not controlled, at least for most analytes. This situation has generated much interest in defining the number of challenges needed for proficiency testing in expectation of lowering overall laboratory costs for survey programs. Certainly, more frequent challenges are more likely to detect unsatisfactory laboratory performance, but there are little data comparing effectiveness of less frequent challenges. Rippey and Tholen have developed a mathematical model which estimates the influence of the number of challenges in measuring adequacy of laboratory performance.[17] In the future, their model or others similar to it will be used to evaluate challenge frequency.

Some grading schemes do not use comparison statistics to quantitate error magnitude, in part because their participant base is small. Those proficiency grading schemes which do not quantitate error magnitude are less efficient for performance evaluation than those which rate performance statistically among participants. Other models will be developed and implemented to more frequently monitor analytes where accurate measurement is critical or performance assessment has indicated need for improvement. In contrast, for less critical measurements or for measurements that already have low medical importance, error rates will be monitored less frequently. Table 17-4 lists some criteria on which challenge frequency could be based.

Programs for the physician's office laboratory have been available since the early 1970s. One of the programs was the College of American Pathologists' Performance Evaluation Program (PEP), which later evolved into EXCEL (External Comparative Evaluation for Laboratories). EXCEL includes challenges in

1. Hematology
2. Coagulation
3. Urinalysis
4. Chemistry
5. Microbiology
6. Blood Bank
7. Immunology

The American Society of Internal Medicine (ASIM) also sponsors a program for

1. Hematology
2. Chemistry
3. Enzymes
4. Microbiologic Culture

TABLE 17-4
PROPOSED CRITERIA FOR CHALLENGE FREQUENCY

Practical considerations	Example
1 Survey logistics	HTLV-III viral isolation difficult
2 Availability of material	Whole-blood sodium sample unavailable
3 Method expensive	Estrogen receptor assay
4 Method grouping by instrument	Sodium, potassium measured simultaneously
5 Adequacy of challenge material	Blood gas human sample unavailable
6 Volume of use	Glucose frequently measured
Theoretical considerations	**Example**
1 Criticality for patient care	Theophylline
2 New analyte	HTLV-III antibody
3 Only laboratory disease marker	Acid phosphatase (prostatic carcinoma)
4 Degree of agreement on standard method	Cyclosporin values discrepant
5 Adequacy of current lab performance	Calcium performance inadequate
6 Indicator of lab proficiency	?
7 Indicator of analyte proficiency	?

5 Parasitology
6 Antibiotic/Drug Susceptibility
7 Diagnostic Immunology
8 Urinalysis

Generally, EXCEL has more participants than the ASIM program, but the scope of both these programs is rapidly increasing, as are the number of participants. Hematology, Diagnostic Immunology, and Urinalysis comparisons of participant results are by instrument in both programs; in Chemistry, the ASIM participant comparisons are by method, rather than subdivided further by instrument as in EXCEL. As the use and scope of these programs rapidly increase, the level of participant comparisons for each will extend from method to the instrument. There is logic for consolidation of both programs into one, operated jointly by the professional societies involved.

Major drawbacks for extending programs used in the United States to other parts of the world have been differences in units of measurement, language, standard methods, and conditions of assay. Worldwide similarities of instrumentation and reagents already exist between clinical laboratories. With widespread conversion by United States clinical laboratories to molar SI (Système International) units by 1988, one drawback to worldwide proficiency testing will be eliminated. Electronic communication has made data transmission so rapid that geographic location will not be a problem. During the last 2 years, over 100 laboratories in Japan have begun to use the CAP's proficiency program. Undoubtedly the trend toward international participation will continue.

For most surveys, limits of $\pm$ 2 SDI from the peer group mean are used to evaluate adequacy of laboratory performance. Generally, performance data within these limits are judged acceptable. Recently, fixed criteria have been introduced for performance assessment in some CAP chemistry surveys and in the American Thoracic Society's blood gas surveys. When $\pm$ 2 SDI limits are used and one peer group is much less precise than another peer group, some participants in the more precise peer group will be judged unacceptable although their performance surpasses many whose performance is acceptable in the other peer group. As methods continue to improve, more survey results will be expressed as fixed limits.

Laboratory proficiency samples are identified as such in most laboratories, and, because of the implications of poor performance, are given special attention by technologists. Therefore, laboratory performance on these specimens is considered the best laboratories can provide. In many respects, daily quality control is a better indicator of true laboratory performance than proficiency testing. In the future, attempts will be made to incorporate daily quality control results as part of a protocol for laboratory proficiency testing.

ANATOMIC PATHOLOGY

In contrast to quality assurance practices in clinical pathology, application of quality assurance to anatomic pathology has not been extensive. Literature on anatomic pathology quality assessment has not generally included nomenclature used by clinical laboratories, such as internal quality control, external quality control, interlaboratory comparisons, and quality assurance. Because anatomic pathology deals with concepts rather than analytic results, there is a widespread notion that it is not amenable to the quality assurance methods now so well entrenched in clinical pathology. The quality assurance demands made of various branches of clinical pathology by accrediting agencies are not yet required in surgical pathology. In addition, the unquestioning acceptance by clinicians of a pathologist's diagnosis has reinforced opinions that quality assurance techniques are adequate as currently practiced.

Macartney, Hensen, and Codling have identified some variables in pathologists' performance.[18] One of these is the preparation of materials for expert examination. Although little effort has been directed at standardizing histological preparative techniques, one can hypothesize that poor technique is associated with inferior diagnostic results. Barr's small study of 17 departments in Wales offers proof that interlaboratory technical performance comparisons are feasible and reasonable.[19] The most important variable is the pathologist's diagnostic performance, and one of the factors that directly affects performance evaluation is how familiar the individual pathologist is with the particular diagnostic problems represented by the survey specimens. Because supporting data have repeatedly shown that specialized pathologists are more consistent diagnosticians than nonspecialists, it can be argued that two standards are necessary. In addition, consensus is also important in achieving accuracy, and in small hospitals or in solo practices, less opportunity for consensus among pathologists exists than in large hospitals. Others have suggested, though without evidence, that professional standards of pathologists in small hospitals may not be equivalent to those in large teaching institutions.[18] Another variable is the surgical pathology report. When reports have been studied, extensive variation has been found in descriptions and interpretations. Even for the relatively straightforward cases, studies have indicated that content of information in routine pathologic reports varies considerably.

One form of external audit is onsite laboratory inspection for accreditation purposes. Recently, more questions relating to anatomic pathology have appeared on laboratory accreditation surveys. Although interlaboratory comparisons for anatomic pathology are not practiced extensively, it is reasonable to envision requirements for such comparisons in the near future. Although administrative costs are high and difficulties are great in mounting external schemes based on circulation of histologic material for review on a regular basis, great benefits can be obtained from a well-organized program with an educational component.

Much has been written about the autopsy and its role in quality assurance. Over the past 40 years, the percentage of all deaths for which postmortem examination is performed has continued to decline and currently is estimated at less than 14 percent nationally.[20] An autopsy performed by a knowledgeable, experienced pathologist using all available information—clinical, radiological, laboratory, and postmortem—is one of the best available measures of quality of medical practice. Unfortunately, information from autopsies often is not provided to clinicians in a timely manner and thereby decreases in usefulness. Unless the timeliness of information from autopsies is improved, or autopsies are required by law, autopsy rates will continue at their current low rate.

ACCREDITATIONS AND REGULATION FOR CLINICAL LABORATORIES

Laboratory standards and accreditation originated in 1918 with a program developed by the American College of Surgeons. As professional accreditation programs grew, their influence resulted in two important federal programs for laboratory regulation, the Medicare-Medicaid Program of 1965, and the Clinical Laboratory Improvement Act (CLIA) of 1967. Currently, independent and hospital laboratories are subject to quality regulation by the Health Care Financing Administration (HCFA). Federal regulations are directed at proficiency testing, quality control, and laboratory personnel. Laboratories under regulation must participate in externally administered proficiency programs and meet accuracy standards. They must perform surveillance of equipment, instruments, methods, reagents, and results; provide adequate facilities and a safe environment; maintain standard operations procedure manuals; keep operational records; and adequately control results. They must also fulfill educational experience requirements for their personnel.

Unfortunately, government regulations for quality control were formulated more than 20 years ago. In the intervening period, regulatory changes have not kept pace with the rapid advances in instrument and reagent technology. Reasons for many laboratory practices are ingrained in technologies that are no longer used, thereby resulting in inappropriate tracking and unnecessary work. An example of this is the following: In the 1960s, only manual chemistries were performed; laboratory quality control schemes were used for monitoring the raw materials, the preparation of reagents, and the instruments as well as the final laboratory procedure. With development of instruments that use prepackaged reagents, vendors have already performed quality control on raw materials, on the formulation steps, and on the final product; therefore, laboratories need monitor only instrument performance and the final results. Experience has shown that quality of vendor prepared prepackaged reagents far exceeds that prepared by individual laboratories. Schifreen has charted yearly instrument failure for over 4000 DuPont *aca*s, instruments that use prepackaged reagents (Table 17-5).[21] On this analyzer, most failures are complete instrument failures detected by self-contained sensors. An exception is the optical system, where failure is gradual. Here, error detection is performed by a special procedure, similar to the control sample format. Despite infrequent instrument failures (detected by sensors) and high-quality reagent preparation (monitored by elaborate manufacturing quality control schemes), laboratories are still required to use those same quality control methods, which for the DuPont *aca* are unsophisticated, insensitive, and unnecessary for error detection. Review of current regulations must occur soon, and revised quality control standards must be implemented.

During the past 50 years, there has been much discussion of quality of laboratory performance. Analytic laboratory improvements have been well documented; part of this improvement resulted from improved reagents, methods, and instrumentation and is described in detail in Chapter 6. However, another major reason for improved laboratory quality has been the influence of accreditation programs. Recent data have indicated continual marked improvement with reinspection in the CAP voluntary accreditation program.[22] In this program, laboratories are graded based on answers to

TABLE 17-5
DUPONT aca COMPONENT REPLACEMENT RATES

Module	Number replaced yearly	Type of failure
Photometer	55	Catastrophic
Pump	120	Catastrophic
Electronics	200	Catastrophic
Breaker mixers	230	Catastrophic
Filter #1	400	Gradual

questions relating to operational guidelines and performance. More important criteria are called "phase II," whereas those of less influence on patient care are "phase I." Failure to fulfill criteria results in a deficiency. Data presented in Table 17-6 indicate a most impressive decrease in percentage of phase II deficiencies with reinspection. Duckworth believes that the greatest decreases occur between the first and second inspection, with more modest changes occurring in subsequent years. During the time of this study, refinements in accreditation criteria have also extended the scope of these requirements. Current trends indicate laboratory deficiencies will occur less frequently, and, because of the overall excellence of some laboratories, a program frequency of onsite inspections will be developed based on laboratory performance. In this way, laboratories with poor performance will be subject to more frequent challenges and have more opportunities for onsite help than laboratories with excellent performance.

With rapid improvements of technology and miniaturization of laboratory analyzers, increased ancillary or ward testing has occurred. In many circumstances, these procedures are performed by individuals who may not have adequate training in operation or use of these devices and reagents. Additionally, quality control measures frequently are not appropriately utilized. Until recently, manufacturers did not provide quality assurance aids to those who perform these procedures. The development of extensive high-quality educational tools and standards of performance by Ames and Boehringer Mannheim Diagnostics, two manufacturers who provide instrumentation and reagents for these locations, indicates a willingness of manufacturers to share responsibilities for procedures performed in these areas.[23,24] With rapid expansion of these activities, it is increasingly important that accreditation groups monitor laboratory services at patient care locations and develop mechanisms to ensure quality of performed services. We feel confident this will occur.

With the development of physician testing in locations other than clinical laboratories, debate has raged over the likelihood of regulating these testing locations. Data such as those in Table 17-7 indicate that physician office laboratories may perform analyses less reliably than clinical laboratories.[25] Some have argued that the analytical test performance should be tied to the site at which it is performed, thereby endorsing at least two levels of performance. Because the use of the analytic result is for diagnosis, treatment, or monitoring of patients with identical diagnoses in both locations, it is essential that equivalent levels of reliable test performance exist. Even though the

TABLE 17-6
DEFICIENCY RATE (%) IN CAP PROGRAMS BY YEAR

Type of question	1977	1978	1979	1980	1981	1982	1983
All	4.2	2.7	2.3	1.5	1.1	1.2	1.4
Quality control (QC)	4.6	3.2	2.6	1.7	1.1	1.4	1.5
Microbiology QC	2.7	2.6	1.3	1.5	0.6	1.5	1.5
Hematology QC	4.6	4.2	2.6	2.1	1.9	2.1	1.9
Chemistry QC	12.6	5.6	5.5	3.1	3.3	3.1	2.3

TABLE 17-7
PERFORMANCE COMPARISONS OF LABORATORIES

	Laboratory type					
	Physician's office			Hospital		
Analyte, unit	Number	Mean	CV (%)	Number	Mean	CV (%)
Bilirubin, mg/dl	1187	53	16.9	3236	5.5	5.6
Cholesterol, mg/dl	1185	324	9.2	4645	316	5.9
Glucose, mg/dl	1727	274	7.2	3485	283	3.7
Urea, mg/dl	1360	46	8.6	3431	49.6	4.4
RBC $\times 10^9$	1628	4.05	3.7	2820	3.2	1.8
Hemoglobin, gm/dl	1837	12.7	3.1	2910	11.7	1.5
Hematocrit, %	1917	34.4	9.0	2870	29.6	3.2
WBC, $\times 10^6$	1855	7.6	6.5	2872	5.8	6.4

performance of clinical laboratories is better than that of physician office laboratories and the cost of performing laboratory measurements in physician laboratories is greater than in hospital laboratories, patient convenience may outweigh these factors, at least for some tests.

There are many arguments for and against regulation of physician office laboratories; however, it is our feeling that some form of regulation will be instituted. The general legal opinion is that discretionary power needs congressional supplementation before regulation of physician office laboratories can occur. However, general trends indicate that HCFA's main priority is cost containment and that quality assurance is secondary. If this perception is correct, it will be for cost containment reasons that physican office laboratories will be regulated.

Already, professional organizations, such as ASIM (American Society for Internal Medicine), CAP (College of American Pathologists), and AAFP (American Academy of Family Physicians), have developed the professional group COLA (Committee on Laboratory Accreditation) to begin the program of laboratory self-evaluation. These

TABLE 17-8
LABORATORY LICENSURE LAWS

	License clinical laboratories	Physician office regulation by		Hospital and clinical laboratories licensed separately	Deemed status	Clinical laboratory personnel license
		Number of physicians	Referral			
Alabama	X					
Alaska						
Arizona	X	1	X		CAP, JCAH, MC	
Arkansas						
California	X		X	X		All
Colorado			X			Director
Connecticut	X				JCAH	Director
Delaware	X					
D.C.	X					
Florida	X	5	X	X	AABB	All
Georgia	X		X	X		Director
Hawaii	X					All
Idaho						
Illinois	X		X	X	JCAH	
Indiana	X					
Iowa						
Kansas	X			X	MC	
Kentucky	X		X			
Louisiana						
Maine	X				CAP, JCAH	

TABLE 17-8
(Continued)

	License clinical laboratories	Physician office regulation by		Hospital and clinical laboratories licensed separately	Deemed status	Clinical laboratory personnel license
		Number of physicians	Referral			
Maryland	X	3 and	X		MC, CLIA, AABB	
Massachusetts	X	3		X	MC, CLIA, AABB	
Michigan	X	5 and	X	X	CAP	
Minnesota	X					
Mississippi	X					
Missouri						
Montana	X					
Nebraska	X					
Nevada	X			X		All
New Hampshire	X		X		JCAH	
New Jersey	X	4				Director
New Mexico						
New York	X	1	X	X		Director
North Carolina	X					
North Dakota						
Ohio						
Oklahoma						
Oregon	X	4 and	X	X	CAP, JCAH	

TABLE 17-8
(Continued)

	License clinical laboratories	Physician office regulation by		Hospital and clinical laboratories licensed separately	Deemed status	Clinical laboratory personnel license
		Number of physicians	Referral			
Pennsylvania	X			X	CAP, JCAH	
Rhode Island	X		X		CAP, JCAH	Director
South Carolina						
South Dakota	X					
Tennessee	X		X	X	CAP, AABB	All
Texas	X					
Utah						
Vermont						
Virginia						
Washington	X					
West Virginia						
Wisconsin	X	2			CAP, JCAH	
Wyoming	X	1	X	X	CAP, JCAH, MC	
Number	35	10	15	13	18	5/6 Director

AABB—American Association of Blood Bank
CAP—College of American Pathologists
JCAH—Joint Commission Accrediting Hospital
MC—Medicare
CLIA—Clinical Laboratories Improvement Act

groups hope that the COLA program or programs similar to COLA will be the major form of regulation for the physician office laboratories.

Another approach would be a requirement that all physician office laboratories participate in a proficiency testing programs operated by a state agency. Table 17-8 lists regulations that pertain to clinical laboratory and physician offices. At present, only a few states regulate tests performed in these locations, but there is a rapidly increasing trend toward inclusion of physician office laboratories in state regulatory programs. Massachusetts recently began enforcing a law that requires physician office laboratories serving more than two physicians to meet the same standards as independent laboratories. The Massachusetts action reflects a growing tendency to define the physician office laboratory in terms of the number of physicians participating.

CONCLUSION

Since 1950, when Levey and Jennings published their paper on quality control, the clinical laboratory has seen a burgeoning of technological advances that were unanticipated at that time. Not until recently, however, was there a realization that these technical advances directly effect the laboratory's quality assurance goals and needs. Changes are occurring, as addressed by this book, but more changes are to come.

Technological advances coupled with pressures to contain costs may influence quality assurance practices, but should never force laboratorians to loose sight of their role in providing precise, accurate, useful data to the patient's physician in a timely manner. As our sophistication in developing and using quality assurance procedures increases, it becomes important to refocus our attention on the laboratory's product, the result. Although, of course, it is important to maintain involvement with the quality of processes used in producing the result, it is the end product that ultimately affects patient care. The laboratory result must do what it is supposed to do—provide the physician with valuable information which can be used in diagnosing and monitoring the patient's disorder. To that end, laboratorians must continue in their efforts to provide the most reliable, cost-effective results possible and, to the best of their ability, ensure these results are used in ways that provide maximum benefit to the patient.

REFERENCES

1 Myers LP, Eisenberg JM, Pauly MV: The effects on clinical laboratory services of selected alternatives for paying physicians under the Medicare Program. Draft Report, Office of Technology Assessment, 1985.
2 Larsson-Cohn V: Differences between capillary and venous blood glucose during oral glucose tolerance tests. *Scand J Clin Lab* 1976, 36:805.
3 Blumenfeld TA, Hertelendy WG, Ford SH: Simultaneously obtained skin-puncture serum, skin-puncture plasma, and venous serum compared, and effects of warming the skin before puncture. *Clin Chem* 1977, 23:1705.
4 Levey S, Jennings ER: The use of control charts in the clinical laboratory. *Am J Clin Pathol* 1950, 20:1059.
5 Hartmann AE, Juel RD, Barnett, RN: The long-term stability of a stabilized liquid quality-control serum. *Clin Chem* 1981, 2:1448.

6 Howanitz PJ, McBride JH, Kliewer K, Rodgerson DO: Prevelance of antibodies to HTLV-III in quality assurance sera. *Clin Chem* 1986, 32:773.
7 Tydeman J, Morrison JI, Hardwick DF, et al: The cost of quality control procedures in the clinical laboratory. *Am J Clin Pathol* 1982, 77:528.
8 Cembrowski GS, Chandler EP, Westgard JO: Assessment of "average of normals" quality control procedures and guideline for implementation. *Am J Clin Pathol* 1984, 81:492.
9 Westgard JO, Barry PL, Hunt MR, et al: A multi-rule Shewhart chart for quality control in clinical chemistry. *Clin Chem* 1981, 27:493.
10 Eckert GH, Carey RN: Application of statistical control rules to quality control in radioimmunoassay. *J Clin Immunoassay* 1985, 8:107.
11 Blum AS: Computer evaluation of statistical procedures, and a new quality-control statistical procedure. *Clin Chem* 1985, 31:206.
12 Howantiz PJ, Kafka MT, Steindel SJ, et al.: Quality control of run acceptance and rejection using fixed and medically useful limits for QAS Today. *Clin Chem* 1985, 31:1016.
13 Stewart CE, Oxford BS: Quality assurance programs and quality control data management. *J Med Technol* 1985, 2:621.
14 Westgard JO: Software considerations in the selection of a microcomputer quality control system. *J Clin Automation* 1984, 4:402.
15 Steindel SJ: New directions in quality control. *Lab Med* 1986 (In Press).
16 Peddecord KM, Taylor RN: Evaluation of laboratory quality assurance activities. *NCHSR* 1984, 84–94.
17 Rippey JH, Tholen D: Personal communication.
18 Macartney JC, Kenson DE, Codling BW: Quality assurance and surgical pathology. *Pathologist* 1983, 37:788.
19 Barr WT: Technology quality control in histopathology. *J Clin Pathol* 1978, 31:996.
20 Carter JR: The problematic death certificate. *N Engl J Med* 1985, 313:1285.
21 Schifreen RS: Quality control: Challenge for the future, in Colvin HM, Schoenfeld E (eds): The impact of alternate reimbursement methods on laboratory practice. Proceedings of the 1984 Institute on Critical Factors in Health Laboratory Practice. Wilmington DE, DuPont, 1984, 143–151.
22 Duckworth JK: Effect of voluntary accreditation on performance in microbiology, in The role of microbiology in cost effective health care, Smith JW (ed): *Microbiology,* proceedings of 1984 College of American Pathologists Conference, Skokie IL College of American Pathologists, 1985, pp 561–565.
23 QA Resource Program. Multimedia educational tools for teaching quality assurance in blood glucose testing. Elkhart IN, Ames, Miles Laboratories, 1986.
24 Ancillary blood glucose testing: Standards of performance using chemstrip bG and Accu-Chek bG. Indianapolis, IN, Boehringer-Mannheim Diagnostics, 1984.
25 Kenney ML: *Laboratory Quality and Director Qualifications: An Empirical Assessment of the Medicare Requirement That Directors of Independent Clinical Laboratories Possess Earned Doctorates.* D.Ph. Thesis, University of California, Berkeley, 1984.
26 College of American Pathologists: *Chemistry Surveys, Set C, 1984.* Skokie, IL, College of American Pathologists, 1984.
27 College of American Pathologists. *Hematology Survey, 1984.* Skokie, IL, College of American Pathologists, 1984.

INDEX

Accreditation:
  defined, 336
  future trends in, 382–388
  programs of, 335–340
Accuracy:
  defined, 4, 9, 21
  loss of, 42
Acetaminophen, stability of, 68
Acid-citrate dextrose (ACD), 67
Acid phosphastase, 67
  posture and, 58
Additives for specimen collection, 63
Adrenal medulla, effect of tobacco on, 60
Alanine aminotransferase, 67
  effect of ethanol on, 61
  hemolysis and, 65
  posture and, 58
Albumin, 57
  effect of menstrual cycle on, 58
  hemolysis and, 64
  posture and, 58
  tourniquet application and, 59
Alcohol, effect of, on blood analytes, 60
Aldosterone:
  effect of exercise on, 60
  posture and, 58
  stress and, 62
Alkaline phosphatase, 58
  effect of recent meals on, 57
  tourniquet application and, 59
Allowable errors, 196, 197–200
  defined, 196, 198
  variables affecting, 199–200
Alpha error, 40
American Academy of Family Physicians (AAFP), 384

American Association of Bioanalysts (AAB), 200, 318
  Proficiency Testing Service of, 324
American Association of Blood Banks (AABB), 270
  inspection and accreditation program, 339
American Association for Clinical Chemistry (AACC), 10, 200, 318, 324
American Chemical Society, 84
American College of Physicians (ACP), 338
American College of Surgeons (ACS), 338, 382
American Dental Association, 338
American Hospital Association (AHA), 338
American Osteopathic Association (AOA), 340
American Society of Clinical Pathology, 301
American Society of Cytology (ASC), accreditation program, 339–340
American Society for Internal Medicine (ASIM), 324, 384
Amino acids, effect of recent meals on, 57
Aminoglycosides, 68
Amylase, 67
Anaerobic cultures, microbiology and, 73
Analytes:
  analytic precision and, 128
  concentrations of in controls, 185–186
  effect of menstrual cycle on, 58
Analytic correlation, separation from biologic correlation, 174

Analytic error resolution, 203–208
  operational lines and, 203–204
    analysis of, 208
    preparation of, 204, 208
Analytic goals, 145–150
  clinical statistical models, 149
  laboratory usage and, 156
  methods of calculations of, 147–148
  performance standards and, 146
  physician action models, 148
  professional consensus and, 148
  state of the art and, 148
  statistical controls and, 147
  total error and, 146
  goals and imprecision, 149
Analytic method, 11–13
  characteristics of, 146
Analytic precision, 128
  analytes and, 128
  trends in, 129
Analytic variable and variation, 167
  clinical chemistry and, 185–213
    allowable error and, 196–200
    analytic problem resolution, 203–208
    determining laboratory variation, 188–196
    enzyme analysis, 201–202
    frequency of control sera analysis and, 188
    interlaboratory surveys, 200–201
    laboratory mistakes, 209
    materials and, 186–188
    reference sample method of quality control and, 185–186
  estimating components and design considerations, 172
  partitioning of, 168
  preinstrumental comparison of, 168
  separation from mistakes and biologic variation, 172–174
Anatomic pathology:
  future trends in, 380–381
  quality assurance and, 296–316
    autopsy and, 314–315
    College of American Pathologists (CAP) project, 303–305
    external components of, 300–303
    histopathology programs, 305–311
    internal components of, 297–300
    performance improvement program (PIP), 311–314
Angiotensin:
  effect of exercise on, 60
  posture and, 58

Antibiotics, susceptibility testing and, 257
Antidiuretic hormone:
  effect of ethanol on, 61
  posture and, 58
Antigens, quality control for, 253
Antimicrobial susceptibility tests (see Susceptibility tests)
Antisera, quality control for, 253
Aqueous buffers, 113
Aspartate aminotransferase, 67
  hemolysis and, 65
  tourniquet application and, 59
Autopsy, quality assurance and, 314–315

B-Hydroxybutyrate, effect of exercise on, 59
B-Lipoprotein, effect of recent meals on, 57
Barbiturates, stability of, 68
Beta error, 40
Bias, defined, 21
Bicarbonate, effect of exercise on, 59
Bilirubin, 57
  effect of recent meals on, 57
  hemolysis and, 64
  icterus and, 82
  tourniquet application and, 59
Binomial distribution, 31–32
  curve, 27
  statistics of quality control and, 42
Biochemical media and tests, controls for, 258–259
Biologic variation:
  components of, 167–174
    interindividual, 167–170
    intraindividual, 170–172
  estimating components and design considerations, 172
  separation from mistakes and biologic variation, 172–174
Blind controls, 15
Blood:
  coagulation of, 71
  components of, 279–282
  control for whole, 114
  granulocyte concentrate, 280
  labeling of, 280, 282
  leukocyte markers and, 71
  occult stool, 292–293
  plasma, 280
  platelet concentrates, 280
  red cells, 279–280
  storage of, 282

Blood (*Cont.*):
  tonometry of whole, 113
  transfusion practices, 283–284
  white cells, 234
Blood analytes:
  effect of diurnal variation on, 56–58
  effect of ethanol on, 60
  effect of food on, 56, 57
  effect of menstrual cycle on, 58
  effect of physical activity on, 59–60
  effect of tobacco on, 60–61
  physical activity and, 59–60
  posture and, 58
  ratio values of, 169
  tourniquet application and, 58–59
Blood center:
  blood bag defects form, 275
  blood collection components, 274, 276
  blood and component preparation, 276–279
  donor recruitment and selection, 271, 274
  monitoring of equipment, 278
  patient testing, 282–283
  procedure manuals and documentation, 271
  quality control results form, 277
  transfusion practices, 283–284
  transfusion-transmitted disease, testing for, 278–279
Blood chemistry, 65–70
  blood gases and, 69–70
  drugs and, 68
  electrolytes and, 65–66
  endocrinology and, 69
  enzymes and, 66–67
  glucose and, 66
  lipids and, 67–68
  toxicology and, 69
  trace metals and, 69
Blood collection tubes, 62–63
  order of draw for, 63
  proper venipuncture procedure, 63
  serum separators, 64
Blood count, complete, 70–71
  coagulation, 70–71
  leukocyte markers, 71
Blood cultures, microbiology and, 72
Blood gas controls, 113–115
  assay valve assignment, 114–115
  control sensitivity and, 114
  material types of, 113–114
  stability of, 115
Blood gases, 69–70

Blood nicotine, effect of tobacco on, 60
Blood specimens, processing of, 64
Breast, 308
  lesions of, 305, 307–308
Broth media, 263
Buffered protein controls, 114

Cadmium, effect of tobacco on, 60
Caffeine, 60
Calcitonin, effect of ethanol on, 61
Calcium, 57
  effect of exercise on, 59
  hemolysis and, 65
  posture and, 58
  tourniquet application and, 59
Calibration and standardization, 217–222
  automated hematology instruments, 218–219
  hematocrit, 218
  hemoglobin, 217–218
  plasma tapping and, 221–222
  reference methods of, 218
  stabilized calibrators and, 220–221
  whole blood and, 219–220
Calibrators, stabilized commercial, 220
Canadian Association of Pathology, 301, 302
Canadian Medical Association (CMA), 338
Carbon dioxide, 65
  effect of altitude on, 61
Carbon monoxide, effect of tobacco on, 60
Carboxyhemoglobin, effect of tobacco on, 60
Catecholamines:
  posture and, 58
  stress and, 62
  tourniquet application and, 59
  uninary, caffeine and, 60
  urinary levels of, effect of exercise on, 60
Cell counters, automated, causes of erroneous results with, 233
Center for Disease Control (CDC), 5, 133, 200, 318
  Performance Evaluation Branch, 324
  proficiency testing program, 88, 322
Central limit theorem, defined, 21
Cephalosporins, 68
Chance agreement, 47
Chemical control materials, 103–113
  lyophilized controls and, 103–104

Chi-square:
  comparison of two differential counts, 33
  distribution, 32
  test of linearity, 36
Chloride, 65
  effect of menstrual cycle on, 58
Cholesterol:
  effect of recent meals on, 57
  levels: effect of foods on, 56
  posture and, 58
  serum: caffeine and, 60
  stress and, 62
  tourniquet application and, 59
CK isoenzymes, 67
Clinical chemistry laboratories, analytic variability and, 185–213
  allow error, 196–200
  analytical problem resolution, 203–208
  enzyme analysis, 201–202
  frequency of control sera analysis, 188
  interlaboratory surveys, 200–201
  laboratory mistakes, 209
  laboratory variation and, 188–196
  materials and, 186–188
  reference sample method, 185–186
Clinical Laboratories Improvement Act of 1967 (CLIA), 322, 340, 341, 343–344, 382
  compared with Medicare, 343–344
Coagulation:
  assay value assignment for, 121–122
    control materials, 120–122
      manufacturing considerations, 120
      stability of, 122
      types of controls for, 121
  blood, 71
Coefficient of determination, 36
Coefficient of variation (CV), 26
College of American Pathologists (CAP), 5, 10, 15, 87, 126, 200, 318
  Aspen Conference, 145
  Chemistry Surveys, 136, 137, 145, 195
  Commission on Laboratory Accreditation of the, 218, 227
  enzyme survey, 201, 202
  Hematology Resources Committee of the, 218, 227
  Hematology Survey Program of the, 225
  Laboratory Accreditation Programs, 335–338
  noncompliance with standards of, 337

College of American Pathologists (CAP) (*Cont.*):
  pathology project, 303–305
  Performance Improvement Program, 311, 313–314
  Platelet Survey, 235
  proficiency testing and, 88, 326
  Quality Assurance Service (QAS), 88, 126, 128, 134, 224
  Standards Committee, 143
  surveys: fixed criteria for, 12
College of Physicians and Surgeons of Canada, 303
Commission of Laboratory Accreditation, 337
Committee on Laboratory Accreditation (COLA), 384
Committee on Parentage Testing, 339
Community Bureau of Reference (BRC), 179
Computer errors, 366
Computers in laboratories, future trends in, 376–377
Confidence interval (CI):
  defined, 22
  of sigma, 26
Consensus value, 10–11
Control bases systems and programs, 224
  limitations of, 225
Control charts:
  dangers of, 3
  Levey-Jennings, 3, 134, 189, 190, 224
    criticism of, 194–195
  Shewhart, 3
Control materials:
  advantages of commercially formulated, 104
  bovine-based chemistry, 139
  chemical: manufacturing considerations, 105–108
  hematology, 139
  lyophilized, 4
  liquid, 4
    chemistry, 139, 141
  manufacturing of, 102–115
    blood gas, 113–115
    chemistry, 103–113
    coagulation, 120–122
    hematology, 115–120
    history of, 101–102
  performance characteristics of, 102–103
  stability control protocols and, 103

Control materials (*Cont.*):
    stability of, 128–129
    target value establishment, 138
        matrix effect on, 138–139, 140
    utility of, 102
Control results, 13
Control rules, performance characteristics of, 197
Control values, distribution of variation of, 4
Controls:
    accuracy of, 186–187
    attributes of ideal substances, 223
    biochemical media and tests and, 258–259
    broth media and, 257
    commercially available, 186
    concentrations of analytes in, 185–186
    evaluation of results, 6–8
    interrelated concentrations in, 186
    materials, 4
    plated media and, 254–255
    pooled patient sera as, 187–188
    strains for susceptibility testing, 256, 260
    unassayed, 5
    use of, 4–6
Correct value: defined, 10–11
Corticosteroids, 57
Corticotropin (ACTH), 57, 62
    stress and, 62
Cortisol:
    caffeine and, 60
    effect of exercise on, 60
    secretion, 57
    stress and, 62
    tourniquet application and, 59
Council for the National Reference System for the Clinical Laboratory, 87
Creatine, effect of exercise on, 59
Creatine kinase (CK), 67
    effect of ethanol on, 61
Creatinine:
    effect of exercise on, 60
    effect of menstrual cycle on, 58
Cultures:
    evaluation of culture results, 247
        worksheet for, 248
    primary culture preparation, 247
    quality control methods for maintenance of, 260
Cumulative summation (*see* Cusums)

Cusums, 37–40
    calculation of, 9
    F-Test and t-Test, 37
        on the variance, 37–38
    graph, 7
    one-tailed vs. two-tailed tests, 39
    paired t-Test, 38–39
        problems of, 39
    statistics of quality control applications and, 42
    student's t-Test, 38
    t-Test on the means, 38
    techniques, 7
    values: systematic errors and, 8
Cyanide, effect of tobacco on, 60
Cyanmethemoglobin method, 217
Cyclosporin, 68
Cytology programs, 309

Data, nonquantitative, 47
    chance agreement, 47
    nominal, 47
    ordinal, 47
    titers, 47
Data distribution, 27
    Gaussian, 27–29
Data entry errors, 366
Deficiency, defined, 336
Degrees of freedom (df), 22
Delta check, 14, 360
    example, 361
Department of Health and Human Services (HHS), 340
Diagnosis, missed, cost of to society, 198–199
Diagram rule of quality control, 8
Distribution:
    bionomial, 31–32
        curve, 27
    chi-square, 32
        comparison of two differential counts, 33
    Gaussian, 27–29
    Poisson, 29–31
        curve, 27
        probability of a given event formula, 30
        standard deviation of, 28
    random, 32–33
Diurnal variation effect on blood analytes, 56–58
Dopamine, effect of exercise on, 60

Drabkin's reagent, 217
Draft Manual for Infectious Waste Management, 346
Drug-related interference, 82–83
Drugs:
    blood chemistry and, 68
    stability of in serum or plasma, 68

Emergency Response in the Workplace, 346
Endocrine tests, patient preparation and, 69
Endocrinology, blood chemistry and, 69
Environmental Protection Agency (EPA), 346
Enzyme analysis, 201–202
Enzymes:
    blood chemistry and, 66–67
    urinary excretion of, 57
Epinephrine, effect of exercise on, 60
Error, defined, 21
Errors, 365–366
    computer, 366
    data entry, 366
    influence, 40
    management of, 365
    policies concerning, 367
    preventive monitoring, 366–367
Errors of inference, 40
    alpha error, 40
    beta error, 40
Erythrocytes (RBC):
    hematology control materials and, 118
    hemolysis and, 64–65
Escherichia coli, 256, 260
Estrogens, effect of menstrual cycle on, 58
Ethanol, effect on blood analytes, 60
Ethosuximide, 68
European Committee of Clinical Laboratory Standardization (ECCLS), 179
External quality control, 8–11, 135–145, 225–226
    defined, 135, 336
    measurement of laboratory quality and, 137–138
    objectives of, 135–136
    programs, 319
    purpose of, 9
    survey evaluation criteria, 141–145
        chemistry and, 142–143

External quality control, survey evaluation criteria (*Cont.*):
    hematology and, 142
    medical usefulness and, 143–144
    problem identification and solution, 144
    qualitative tests, 141–142
    quantative tests, 141
    validated reference materials, 145
    target values of, 138
        matrix effect on, 138–139, 140

F-test, 37, 45, 46
    on the variance, 37–38
Fasting, laboratory results and, 56
Fatty acids, free:
    caffeine and, 60
    effect of ethanol on, 61
Feces, collection of, 64
Fibrinogen, effect of menstrual cycle on, 58
Fluid analysis, 293
Fluorocarbon emulsions, 114
Flurazepam, 69
Food and Drug Administration (FDA), 257, 342
Free fatty acids:
    caffeine and, 60
    effect of ethanol on, 61
Free thyroxine, posture and, 58
Freeze-dried control materials, 103–104
Function verification, 13
    defined, 336

Gamma-glutamyl transferase (GGT), 67
    effect of ethanol on, 61
Gaussian distribution, 27–29
German Society of Clinical Chemistry, 178
Globulins, effect of menstrual cycle on, 58
Glucose:
    blood chemistry and, 66
    caffeine and, 60
    effect of ethanol on, 61
    effect of recent meals on, 57
    hemolysis and, 65
    plasma: effect of altitude on, 61
    stress and, 62
    tobacco and, 60
Goal setting, 152–153

Goal setting (*Cont.*):
    closed information loop and, 153–156
Gonadotropins, effect of menstrual cycle on, 58
Gosset, William S., 4
Granulocyte concentrate in blood, 280
Growth hormone:
    effect of ethanol on, 61
    effect of exercise on, 60
    stress and, 62
Guidelines for Service of Clinical Laboratory Instruments, 13

Health Care Financing Administration (HCFA), 5, 382
Health Care Financing Administration/ Centers for Disease Control (HCFA/CDC), 340–342
Hematology:
    analytic goals of, 230–231
    calibration and standardization of instruments and, 217–222
    control-based systems and programs, 224
        limitations and, 225
    external quality control and, 225–226
    internal quality control and:
        binomial theorem applied to, 45
        chi-square applied to, 45
    patient indices vs. commercial whole blood, 5–6
    patient preparation and:
        coagulation, 71
        complete blood count, 70–71
        leukocyte markers, 71
    platelet problems, 234–237
    preanalytic variation of, 232
    process control and, 222–229
        interlaboratory comparison and, 224
        need for, 222
        using patient specimens or data, 226–229
    quality assurance and, 214–243
        instrumentation, 215–217
    reference ranges and sources of variation in, 229–233
    spurious causes of macrocytosis, 232
    variation, sources of, 231–232
    white blood cell problems, 234
Hematology control materials, 115–120, 139
    assay value assignment and, 119–120

Hematology control materials (*Cont.*):
    cell stabilization methods of, 117–118
    composition of, 117
    control types for, 117
    erythrocytes (RBC) and, 118
    platelets and, 119
Hemoglobin:
    effect of altitude on, 61
    effect of exercise on, 59
Hemoglobin-based buffer solutions, 114
Hemolysis, 64–65, 81–82
    phlebotomy process and, 81
Histopathology programs, 305–311
    breast, 308
        lesions of, 305, 307–308
    cytology, 309
        cervical cytopathology, 309
        effusion cytopathology data, 309, 311
    prostate, 309
        lesions of, 307–308
Hyperprolactinemia, 58

Icterus, 82
Immunology, specimen handling and, 73
Imprecision interval, defined, 22
In vitro, defined, 336
In vitro variables, 64–65
    hemolysis, 64–65
    lipemia, 65
Indian Health Service, 335
Inspections of laboratories, 349, 352
Instrument maintenance, defined, 13
Instrumentation:
    preventive maintenance and, 216
    principles of, 216–217
    selection of, 215–217
    standardization and calibration of, 217–222
Instrumentation Verification and Maintenance Manual, 13
Insulin:
    caffeine and, 60
    effect of ethanol on, 61
    effect of recent meals on, 57
Interferent, defined, 80
Interindividual variation, 167–170
Internal quality control, 2–8
    binomial theorem applied to hematology, 45
    chi-square: applied to hematology, 45
    control materials, 4
    control use, 4–6

Internal quality control (*Cont.*):
    defined, 336
    evaluation of control results, 6–8
    rules: power to detect error and, 42
    use of rules, 42
Intraindividual variation, 170–172
Ionized calcium, posture and, 58
Iron:
    effect of altitude on, 61
    effect of menstrual cycle on, 58
    posture and, 58
    tourniquet application and, 59
Isoenzymes, 67

Jaffe reaction, 10
Joint Commission on Accreditation of
        Hospitals (JCAH), 5, 15, 16, 335,
        337, 340
    accreditation program, 338–339

Laboratories:
    clinical chemistry (*see* Clinical
        chemistry laboratories)
    information flow and, 354–369
    licensure and accreditation, 334–353
        government agencies and, 340–352
        principles of, 334–335
        voluntary programs, 335–340
    mistakes made by, 209
    special-function, defined, 336
Laboratory Accreditation Program, 335
Laboratory licensure:
    agencies responsible for, 340–346,
        350–351
    areas of responsibility, 347, 348
    inspections by, 349, 352
    noncompliance and, 349
    reducing duplication, 347
    surveyors' qualifications, 347
    laws, 385–387
Laboratory Proficiency Testing Program,
        302
Laboratory quality assurance (*see* Quality
        assurance)
Laboratory quality: measurement of, 137–
        138
Laboratory standards, 85
    examples of, 86
Laboratory testing:
    effect of food on results, 56, 57
    ordering and reporting cycle, 56

Laboratory testing (*Cont.*):
    phases of, 55
        preanalytical, 73–74
    reporting results of, 95–96
Lactate:
    effect of ethanol on, 61
    effect of exercise on, 59
    effect of recent meals on, 57
    hemolysis and, 65
    tourniquet application and, 59
Least squares analysis, 34, 36
Leukocyte markers, 71
Leukocytes (WBC), hematology control
        materials and, 118
Levey-Jennings charts, 3, 134, 189, 190,
        224
    criticism of, 194–195
License, defined, 336
Licensure (*see* Laboratory licensure)
Lidocaine, stability of, 68
Linear regression, 33–37
    coefficient of determination, 36
    least squares analysis and, 34, 35, 36
Lipemia, 55, 65, 80–81
Lipids:
    blood chemistry and, 67–68
    caffeine and, 60
    posture and, 58
Lymphocytosis, quality, 60
Lyophilized, control materials and, 103–
        104, 108

Macrocytosis, spurious causes of, 232
Magnesium:
    effect of ethanol on, 61
    effect of exercise on, 59
Maintenance, instruments and, 13
Manufacturing control materials, 102–115
    blood gas, 113–115
        assay value assignment, 114–115
        control sensitivity and, 114
        material types of, 113–114
        stability of, 115
    chemical, 103–113
        assay value assignment, 111–113
        considerations in, 104–108
        constitute interaction and, 109–111
        constitutes of, 112
        liquid, 104
        lot-to-lot variation, 111
        lyophilized controls and, 103–104
        raw materials in, 108–109

Manufacturing control materials (*Cont.*):
  coagulation, 120–122
    assay value assignment for, 121–122
    considerations for, 120
    stability for, 122
    types of controls for, 121
  hematology, 115–120
    assay value assignment of, 119–120
    cell stabilization methods of, 117–118
    composition of, 117
    control types for, 116–117
    erythrocytes (RBC) and, 118
    leukocytes, 118
    platelets and, 119
Massachusetts Regional Quality Control Program, 129
Mean, calculation of, 24
Mean deviation of control results, 13
Measures of central tendency, 24
Measures of dispersion of variability, 24–25
  standard deviation and, 24
Media:
  biochemical and test controls, 258–259
  broth, 263
  controls, 257
  for plated: controls for, 254–255
  quality control of, 251–253
  susceptibility testing and, 263–264
Medicaid Act, 340
Medical Equipment Management in Hospitals, 13, 89
Medicare Act, 322, 340, 341
  compared with CLIA-1967, 343–344
Menstrual cycle, effect on analytes, 58
Methaqualone, 69
Microbiology, 72–73
  anaerobic cultures and, 73
  blood cultures and, 72
  collection and transportation of specimens in, 245–246
  evaluation of culture results, 247
    worksheet for, 248
  preparation of primary cultures, 247
  processing specimens, 246–249
  quality assurance and, 244–269
  quality control: of equipment and environment, 265–266, 272–273
    of final report, 247–248
    of materials and procedures in, 249–253
  quality control of specimens, 244–245

Microbiology (*Cont.*):
  requisition, 245
  respiratory track and, 72
  stool cultures and, 73
  urine cultures and, 72
  viral cultures and, 73
Microcomputers, quality control programs and features, 134, 377
Microhematocrit:
  blood trapping and, 221–222
  method, 219
Mueller-Hinton agar, 263

National Bureau of Standards (NBS), 11, 87, 179
National Cancer Institute of Canada, 302
National Committee for Clinical Laboratory Standards (NCCLS), 5, 87, 179, 217, 252, 342, 345, 349
  Subcommittee on Quality Control, 133
National Committee on Inspection and Accreditation, 339
National Fire Protection Association (NFPA), 345–346
National Reference System in Clinical Chemistry (NRSCC), 88
National Survey of the College of American Pathologists (CAP), 136
Neutrophilia, effect of exercise on, 60
New York State Department of Health, 302
New York State Society of Pathologists (NYSPATH) Regional quality control Program, 130
Nominal data, 47
Nonquantitative data, 47
Nordic Clinical Chemistry project (NORDKEM), 178
Nordic Society of Clinical Chemistry, 178
Norepinephrine, effect of exercise on, 60
Nuclear Regulatory Agency (NRC), 342
Null hypothesis, defined, 23
Numbers, rounding off, figures, 23

Observed variation, 151–152
Occult blood, stool, 292–293
Occupational Safety and Health Administration (OSHA), 346
One-tailed vs. two-tailed tests, 39
Ontario Medical Association, 302

Operational lines:
  analysis of, 208
  preparation of, 204, 208
Ordinal data, 47
Outlying value, 37

Paired *t*-Test, 38–39
  problems of, 39
Parameter, defined, 21
Patient data:
  application of the central tendency and, 46
    average of normals (AON), 46
  privacy of, 368–369
  use of, 45
Patient preparation, 55–62
  caffeine and, 60
  effect of altitude on, 61
  effect of recent meals on, 56
  endocrine tests and, 69
  ethanol and, 60
  hematology and, 70–71
    coagulation, 71
    complete blood count, 70–71
    leukocyte markers, 71
  microbiology and, 72–73
  physical activity and, 59–60
  posture and, 58
  quality control of, 74
  tobacco and, 60–61
  tourniquet application and, 58–59
Penicillin, 68
Performance verification, 13
Personnel qualifications, quality assurance and, 90–94
  laboratory director, 92–93
  staffing levels, 93–94
pH, effect of recent meals on, 57
Phenytoin, stability of, 68
Philadelphia County Medical Society, 317
Phlebotomy, hemolysis and, 81
Phosphate:
  effect of exercise on, 59
  effect of menstrual cycles on, 58
  effect of recent meals on, 57
Phosphorus:
  effect of ethanol on, 61
  hemolysis and, 65
  stress and, 62
Photometric Quality Assurance Instrument Check Procedures, 13

Plasma:
  catecholamine: effect of exercise on, 60
    effect of tobacco on, 60
  components in blood, 280
  glucose: effect of altitude on, 61
  stability of, 68
  trapping, 221–222
Platelets:
  concentrates, 280
  hematology control materials and, 119
  problems with, 234–237
Poisson distribution, 29–31
  curve, 27
  probability of a given event formula, 30
  standard deviation of, 28
Population, defined, 21
Potassium, 65, 66
  effect of ethanol on, 61
  effect of exercise on, 59
  hemolysis and, 65
  tourniquet application and, 59
Power function curves, 7, 193–194, 195, 196
Preanalytic variation, 151
  future trends in, 372–373
Precision:
  changings effect on predictive value, 198
  defined, 4, 21–22
  limit formula, 262
  loss of, 42
Predictive value, changing precision and, 198
Premenstrual syndrome, 58
Preparation of Manuals for Installation, Operation and Repair of Laboratory Instruments, 13
Preventive maintenance:
  defined, 336
  programs, 89–90
Probability (p): defined, 22
Process control:
  control-based systems, 224
  external, 125
  interlaboratory comparison and, 224–225
  internal, 125
  quality control programs and, 125–130
  quality options and, 222–229
  regional quality control programs and, 125–135
  using patient specimens or data, 226–229

Process control, using patient specimens
   or data (*Cont.*):
  morphologic review and clinical
   correlation, 227
  moving averages of red cell indices,
   227–229
  retained, 226–227
Process quality, regional quality control
  programs and database probes,
  128–130
Proficiency, defined, 336
Proficiency surveys, 46
Proficiency testing, 88–89, 317–333
  availability of, 323–329
  evaluation formats, 320–322
   fixed criteria, 322
   participant consensus, 321–322
   referee results, 320–321
   target value, 320
  future trends in, 378–380
  history of, 317–318
  objectives and rationale of, 329, 331–332
  participant benefits of, 329
  regulatory requirements, 322–323
  services, 322
  survey design and administration of,
   318–320
Progesterone, effect of menstrual cycle
  on, 58
Prolactin, 57
  effect of exercise on, 60
  effect of menstrual cycle on, 58
Prostate, 309
  lesions of, 307–308
Protein:
  effect of menstrual cycle on, 58
  posture and, 58
Pseudohypochloremia, 66
Pseudohyponatremia, 66
Pseudomonas aeruginosa, 256, 260
Psychological stress, patient preparation
  and, 61
Public Health Service, syphillis serology
  program, 317

Qualitative tests (*see* Tests, qualitative
  and semiquantiative)
Quality:
  aspects of, 1
  defined, 1

Quality assurance:
  accreditation programs of, 15–16
  defined, 1, 215, 287
  external components of, 300–303
   educational programs, 301
   evaluation programs, 301–303
   procedures, 300–301
  future trends in, 371–389
   accreditations and regulations, 382–388
   anatomic pathology and, 380–381
   computers and, 376–377
   preanalytic variables and, 372–373
   proficiency testing and, 378–380
   quality control and, 373–376
  information processing cycle and, 356–365
   external reporting, 362–365
   initial reporting, 361–362
   requisition processing, 357–358
   specimen analysis, 359–360
   specimen procurement, 359
   verifying results, 360–361
  information processing resources and,
   365–369
   errors and error management, 365–367
   patient information, 368–369
   system security and integrity, 367–368
  interferences and, 80–83
   cross-reactivity, 83
   fibrin, 82
   hemolysis, 81–82
   icterus, 82
   lipemia, 80–81
   nonobservable, 82–83
   observable, 80–82
  internal components of, 297–300
   performance evaluation, 298–300
   personnel, 297–298
   reports, 298
   specimens, 298
  laboratory information flow and, 354–369
  microbiology and (*see* Microbiology:
   quality assurance and)
  personnel qualifications, 90–94
   laboratory director, 92–93
   staffing levels, 93–94
  process control and, 222–229
   controlled-based systems, 224
  reporting results and, 95–96

Quality assurance in hematology (*see* Hematology: quality assurance and)
Quality Assurance Practices for Health Laboratories, 298
Quality control:
  analytical goals of, 13–15
    blind controls, 15
    delta checks, 14
    identifying and preventing mistakes, 14
  application of statistics and, 40–47
    standard deviation, 41–42
  cost of, 131–132
  defined, 1, 287, 336
  external, 8–11, 135–145, 225–226
    defined, 135, 336
    measurement of laboratory quality and, 137–138
    objectives of, 135–136
    programs, 319
    target values of, 138–139
  future trends in, 373–376
  goals of, 133–135
  instrument programs of, 13
  internal, 2–8, 135
    control materials, 4
    control use, 4–6
    defined, 336
    evaluation of control results, 6–8
    standard deviation and, 41–42
  manufactured materials, 222–224
  materials, 186–188
    commercially available, 186
  Nordic surveys of, 181
  patient preparation and, 74
  preventive maintenance and, 89–90
  problems in, 130–135
    changing requirements, 133
    cost of, 131–132
    instrument associated controls, 132–133
  problems of, 130–131
  proposed rejection procedures, 375
  reagents and, 83–89
  reference sample method of, 185–186
  regional programs: process control and, 125–135
  reliability of results, 11–13
  rules: depending on number of controls used per run, 9
    diagram of, 8

Quality control, rules (*Cont.*):
    purpose of, 6
    random variation and, 6–7
    rejection limits, 6
    use of internal, 42
  specimen collection and, 74
  specimen handling and storage and, 74
  statistics of, 20–54
  (*see also* Statistics of quality control)
Quality control in anatomic pathology (*see* Anatomic pathology: quality assurance and)
Quality control materials (*see* Control materials)
Quality control programs:
  process control and, 125–130
  regional, 125–130
    database probes, 128–130
    testing in Europe and, 177–182
Quinidine, stability of, 68

Random, defined, 22
Random bias, defined, 147
Random distribution, 32–33
Random variation, 4
  quality control rules and, 6–7
Reagents:
  quality control and, 83–89
  quality control of, 249–251
  stains, quality control of, 249–251
  standards for, 85–88
  storage of, 83
  Van Kampen-Zijlstra, 217
  water: quality specifications for, 84
Red blood cells, 279–280
Red cell indices, 227–229
Reference material, defined, 88
Rejection limits, 6
Renin:
  angiotensin-aldosterone secretion, 57
  effect of ethanol on, 61
  effect of exercise on, 60
  posture and, 58
  stress and, 62
Respiratory tract:
  cultures: upper, 72
  specimens: lower, 72
Rounding off numbers, 23
Royal College of Pathology, Quality Assurance Program in Anatomical Pathology, 301

Salicylate, stability of, 68
Sample, defined, 21
Secobarbital, 69
Semiquantitative tests (*see* Tests:
    qualitative and semiquantitative)
Sera:
  frequency of analysis of, 188
  insert values for control, 187
  pooled patients as a control, 187–188
Serology, specimen handling and, 73
Serum:
  cholesterol: caffeine and, 60
  enzymes, 57
  iron, 57
  lactic dehydrogenase (LD): stability of, 67
  protein, 57
  separators, 64
  stability of, 68
Shewhart chart, 3
Shewhart control rules, 7
  application of, 192–194
Significance, defined, 22–23
Significant figures, 23
Social Security Act, 322, 340
Sodium, 65
  hemolysis and, 65
  effect of menstrual cycle on, 58
  effect of recent meals on, 57
Special-function laboratory, defined, 336
Specificity, defined, 12
Specimen collection, 62–64
  additives and, 63
  quality control of, 74
  serum separators, 64
  tube stoppers and, 63
  vacuum blood tubes, 62–63
Specimen handling:
  microbiology and, 72–73
    anaerobic cultures, 73
    blood cultures, 72
    respiratory tack, 72
    stool cultures, 73
    urine cultures, 72
    viral cultures, 73
  quality control of, 74
Specimens:
  analysis of, 359–360
  blood: processing of, 64
  external reporting on, 362–365
  initial reporting on, 361–362
  preanalytic processing of, 359

Specimens (*Cont.*):
  preparation of, interrelated with uric acid supplement, 204
  process control using patient, 226–229
    morphologic review and clinical correlation, 227
    moving averages of red cell indices, 227–229
    retained, 226–227
  procurement of, 359
  quality control of microbiology, 244–245
  verifying results of, 359–360
Sputum, 72
Standard, defined, 336
Standard deviation:
  calculation of, 189
  control results and, 13–14
  formula for, 321
  index, 12
  statistics of quality control applications and, 41–42
  variance and, 25
Standard error of the estimate, 35
Standard error of the mean (SEm), 26
Standard for Health Care Facilities, 345
Standard Reference Materials (SRM), 87
Standards:
  agencies and associations responsible for, 345
  agencies responsible for, 340–346, 350–351
  clinical laboratory, 85
  laboratory: examples of, 86
  noncompliance with, 349
  reagents and, 85–88
Standards for Blood Banks and Transfusion Services, 339
Staphylococcus aureus, 256, 260
Statistic, defined, 21
Statistics of quality control, 20–54
  applications of, 40–47
    external, 46–47
    standard deviation and, 41–42
  bionomial distribution, 31–32
  curve, 27
  coefficient of variation (CV), 26
  confidence interval of sigma, 26
  data distributions and, 27
  definitions of, 21–23
  measures of central tendency and, 24

Statistics of quality control (*Cont.*):
   measures of dispersion or variability and, 24–25
   Poisson distribution, 29–31
      curve, 27
      probability of a given event formula, 30
      standard deviation of, 30
   random distribution, 32–33
   rounding off numbers and significant figures, 23
   standard error of the mean (SEm), 26
   variance (*v*), 25
Statistics of quality control applications:
   cusums and, 42
   use of internal control control rules and, 42
Stool cultures, microbiology and, 73
Stool, occult blood, 292–293
Streptococcus faecalis, 256, 260
Stress:
   blood analytes and, 62
   psychological: patient preparation and, 61
Student's *t*-Test, 38
Sunderland, F. William, 317
Survey programs, 8–11
   purpose of, 9
Susceptibility tests, quality control of, 253–265
   antibiotics and, 257, 261–262
   control stains for, 256, 260
   inoculum, 262–263
   media, 263–264
   organism and method selection, 253–256
   performance and interpretation, 264
   testing, 264–265
Syphillis serology program, 317

t-Test, 37, 45
   on the means, 38
   paired (*t*-dependent), 38–39, 46
      problems of, 39
   student's (*t*-independent), 38
Target values:
   establishment of, 138
   matrix effects on, 138–139, 140
Testing, proficiency (*see* Proficiency testing)
Tests:
   bedside, 293–295

Tests (*Cont.*):
   clinical microscopy, 289, 291–293
   qualitative and semiquantitative, 287–295
   self, 290, 293–295
   urinalysis, 291–292
Thyroxine:
   effect of exercise on, 60
   free: posture and, 58
Thyrotropin, 57
Titers, 47
Tobacco, effects on blood analytes, 60–61
Tonometry of whole blood, 113
Tourniquet application, blood analytes and, 58–59
Toxicology, blood chemistry and, 69
Trace metals, blood chemistry and, 69
Transfusion service (*see* Blood center)
Tricyclic antidepressants, stability of, 68
Triglycerides:
   caffeine and, 60
   effect of ethanol on, 61
   effect of food on, 56–57
Tube stoppers, 63

Ulysses syndrome, 16–17
Urea, effect of exercise on, 59
Urea nitrogen, effect of recent meals on, 57
Uric acid:
   effect of ethanol on, 61
   effect of exercise on, 59
   effect of menstrual cycle on, 58
   effect of recent meals on, 57
   interrelated specimens preparation of, 204
   stress and, 62
Urinalysis, 291–292
Urinary catecholamines:
   caffeine and, 60
   tobacco and, 60
Urinary creatinine, 57
Urine, 57
   effect of altitude on output, 61
   collection of, 64
   drug abuse and, 69
Urine cultures, specimen handling of, 72

Vacuum blood collection tubes, 62–63
   order of draw for, 63
   proper venipuncture procedure, 63

Vacuum blood collection tubes (*Cont.*):
  serum separators, 64
Van Kampen-Zijlstra reagent, 217
Variation:
  analytic, 167
    estimating components and design considerations, 172
    partitioning of, 168
    preinstrumental comparison of, 168
    separation from mistakes and biologic variation, 172–174
  biologic:
    components of, 167–174
    estimating components and design considerations, 172
    interindividual, 167–170
    intraindividual, 170–172
    separation from mistakes and biologic variation, 172–174
  components of, 166
  interlaboratory, 174–182
    components of, 174–177
  observed, 151–152
  preanalytic, 151

Variation (*Cont.*):
  random, 4
Venipuncture, vacuum blood collection tubes and, 63
Verification, performance, 13
Veterans Administration, 335
Viral cultures, microbiology and, 73

Water, quality specifications for as a reagent, 84
White blood cells, problems with, 234
Wintrobe hematocrit, 219
  plasma trapping and, 221
Wisconsin Laboratory of Hygiene, 302
World Association of Societies of Pathology, 145
World Association of Societies of Pathology Report, 145
World Health Organization (WHO), 87

Zinc, 57
  stress and, 62